THE ASHGATE HANDBOOK OF LEGAL TRANSLATION

Law, Language and Communication

Series Editors
Anne Wagner, Lille University – Nord de France and
Vijay Kumar Bhatia, City University of Hong Kong

This series encourages innovative and integrated perspectives within and across the boundaries of law, language and communication, with particular emphasis on issues of communication in specialized socio-legal and professional contexts. It seeks to bring together a range of diverse yet cumulative research traditions related to these fields in order to identify and encourage interdisciplinary research.

The series welcomes proposals – both edited collections as well as single -authored monographs – emphasizing critical approaches to law, language and communication, identifying and discussing issues, proposing solutions to problems, offering analyses in areas such as legal construction, interpretation, translation and de-codification.

The Ashgate Handbook of Legal Translation

Edited by

LE CHENG

Zhejiang University, China

KING KUI SIN

Hang Seng Management College, Hong Kong

ANNE WAGNER

Lille University – Nord de France

Routledge
Taylor & Francis Group
LONDON AND NEW YORK

First published 2014 by Ashgate Publishing

Published 2016 by Routledge
2 Park Square, Milton Park, Abingdon, Oxfordshire OX14 4RN
711 Third Avenue, New York, NY 10017, USA

First issued in paperback 2016

Routledge is an imprint of the Taylor & Francis Group, an informa business

British Library Cataloguing in Publication Data
A catalogue record for this book is available from the British Library.

Library of Congress Cataloging-in-Publication Data
The Ashgate handbook of legal translation / by Le Cheng, King Kui Sin and Anne Wagner.
pages cm. -- (Law, language and communication)
Includes bibliographical references and index.
ISBN 978-1-4094-6966-7 (hardback) -- ISBN 978-1-4094-6967-4 (ebook) -- ISBN 978-1-4094-6968-1 (epub) 1. Law--Translating. I. Cheng, Le, editor. II. Sin, King Kui, 1947- editor. III. Wagner, Anne, 1968- editor.
K213.A744 2014
418'.0334--dc23

2014016422

ISBN 13: 978-1-138-70078-9 (pbk)

ISBN 13: 978-1-4094-6966-7 (hbk)

Contents

PART II LEGAL TRANSLATION IN PRACTICE

List of Figures

List of Tables

Notes on the Editors

Anne WAGNER is an Associate Professor at the Université Lille – Nord de France. She is a research member at the Centre de Recherche Droits et Perspectives du Droit, équipe René Demogue (http://crdp.univ-lille2.fr/equipe-rene-demogue). She is a Research and Adjunct Professor at China University of Political Science and Law (Beijing). She is the Editor-in-Chief of the *International Journal for the Semiotics of Law* (Springer) and the Series Editor of *Law, Language and Communication* (Ashgate). She is President of the *International Roundtable for the Semiotics of Law* and Vice President of the *Multicultural Association of Law and Language*. She serves as an international jury member of the *Mouton d'Or prize* for *Semiotica*. She has been granted the French National Award of Scientific Excellence. She has lectured in Asia, Australia, Europe and North America. She has extensively published research papers in the area of legal translation, law and semiotics, legal discourse analyses. She is guest editing several Special Issues on Legal Translation, focusing on legal translation theories and practices worldwide, with (1) the *International Journal for the Semiotics of Law* (with Jean-Claude Gémar – volume 26/4: *The Process of Translabiliting: Translating and Transferring Law, its Concepts, Notions and Language*); (2) *Semiotica* (with Jean-Claude Gémar – *Decision-Making in Legal Translation, Interpretation and Speech Act – Legal Semiotic Cultural Mediation Techniques*; to be published in 2014); and (3) the *International Journal for the Semiotics of Law* (with Jean-Claude Gémar – volume 27/4: *Legal Translation and Jurilinguistics: Globalizing Disciplines*; to be published in 2014).

King Kui SIN is currently Adjunct Professor and Special Consultant at the School of Translation, Hang Seng Management College, Hong Kong. From 1987 to 2013 he taught and designed undergraduate and postgraduate courses in interpretation, translation, language, and law at City University of Hong Kong. Before that he had been a court interpreter and certified translator in the Judiciary of Hong Kong and a training officer for translators and interpreters at a French petroleum corporation based in China. From 1990 to 1997 he served on the Bilingual Laws Advisory Committee, a statutory body responsible for advising the Hong Kong Government on the translation of the law into Chinese. He was later awarded MBE by the British Government for his contribution. Among his professional engagements, he is President of the *Multicultural Association of Law and Language*, which has organized eight international conferences since 2011.

Le CHENG, having completed his MPhil in Linguistics, MPhil in Law, PhD in Language and Law, and postdoc in Professional Communication in English, is now a full professor and a PhD supervisor, and Director of the Center for Legal Discourse and Translation at Zhejiang University. He has been a member of the Bar of the PRC since 2001 and holds concurrent professorship at China University of Political Science and Law. He is Chief Editor of the *International Journal of Law, Language & Discourse*, Chief Editor of *Translated Series on Law and Language*, Editorial Board member of *Semiotica, International Journal for the Semiotics of Law*, Deputy Director of Research Centre for Legal Translation, Vice President and Secretary General of the *Multicultural Association of Law and Language*, and Scientific Committee of *International Academy of Linguistic Law*. His interests are in the areas of law, legal translation, language and law, corpus linguistics, and discourse analysis.

Notes on Contributors

Janet AINSWORTH is the John D. Eshelman Professor of Law at Seattle University. A graduate of Harvard Law School with a master's degree from Yale University, her undergraduate degree was earned at Brandeis University. Before joining the Seattle University law faculty, she practiced criminal law at the Seattle-King County Public Defender Association. Her research interests include criminal law and procedure, comparative legal theory, and the intersection of law and linguistics. The author of more than 30 articles and book chapters, she has published in law reviews such as the *Yale Law Journal*, the *Cornell Law Review*, and the *Washington University Law Quarterly*, as well as in linguistics journals such as *Gender and Language*, *Multilingua*, and the *International Journal of Speech, Language and Law*. She currently serves on the editorial board of the Oxford University Press series, *Law and Language*.

Rafat Y. ALWAZNA works as an Assistant Professor of translation studies, TESOL, and legal translation at the Department of European Languages and Literature, Faculty of Arts and Humanities, King Abdulaziz University, Jeddah, Kingdom of Saudi Arabia. He has obtained two MAs and a PhD; his first MA was in Theory and Practice of Translation from SOAS, University of London in 2006, while his second MA was in TESOL from the IOE, University of London in 2010. In that same year, he finished his PhD in Legal Translation at SOAS, University of London. He has a number of publications in the field of translation studies and legal translation, some of which have been published in academic journals, while others have been published in conference proceedings. His PhD thesis on translating Hanbali Sharia Code has also been published in 2013 in Germany. He currently serves as an International Advisor for the *International Journal for the Semiotics of Law* (Springer).

Łucja **BIEL** is an Assistant Professor in the Department of Translation Studies, Institute of English Studies at the University of Gdańsk, Poland (since 2004), where she is a coordinator of specialized translator training and a teacher of legal and EU translation. She is also a visiting lecturer on MA in Legal Translation at City University London (UK, since 2009). She has been a practising English-Polish legal translator since 1997, a sworn translator certified by the Polish Ministry of Justice, and an expert member of the Polish Association of Sworn and Specialized Translators (TEPIS). She holds an MA in Translation Studies (Jagiellonian University of Kraków), PhD in Linguistics (University of Gdańsk), Diploma in English Law and the Law of the European Union (University of Cambridge), and Diploma of School of American Law (Chicago-Kent College of Law/UG). She is a deputy editor of the *Journal of Specialised Translation* and a member of the editorial board of *Comparative Legilinguistics and the International Journal for Legal Communication*. She has published nearly 30 papers on legal translation, communication, and translator training and has read many papers at international conferences. Her research interests include legal translation, terminology, phraseology, institutional discourse, corpus linguistics, and contrastive linguistics. Her current postdoctoral research project examines the textual fit of translated EU law to nontranslated Polish law by examining overrepresented and underrepresented lexicogrammatical patterns in the JRC Acquis corpus and the Polish Law Corpus.

Deborah CAO is a Professor at Griffith University, Australia. She is a linguist and a legal scholar, originally trained and qualified as a United Nations Chinese/English interpreter. She is a major writer on legal translation, contributing to many publications in the field. She has also published in other areas including legal theory, legal semiotics, pragmatics and court interpreting, and philosophical and linguistic analysis of Chinese law and legal culture. She also teaches and writes about animal law and is an advocate for the legal protection of animals in China. She is Editor of the *International Journal for the Semiotics of Law*. Her books include *Chinese Law: A Language Perspective* (2004, Ashgate), *Translation at the United Nations* (2006, co-authored with Zhao Xingmin, Beijing FTPC), *Translating Law* (2007, Multilingual Matters), *Animals are not Things* (2007, China Law Press), and *Animal Law in Australia and New Zealand* (2010, Thomson Reuters).

Marta CHROMÁ has been teaching legal English, legal linguistics, and legal translation at the Faculty of Law of Charles University in Prague, Czech Republic, for almost 25 years. In her research, she focuses on the semiotics of legal translation, in particular on issues of semantic and legal interpretation of legal concepts and texts for the purposes of translation between different systems of law (such as continental law and common law). Another direction of her research interests is analyzing the potential application of comparative conceptual analysis aimed at establishing relevant equivalents to be used in compiling legal dictionaries and in legal translation. Marta has authored several multifunctional textbooks of legal English aimed not only at law students, but also at legal translators. She has compiled English-Czech and Czech-English law dictionaries widely used by translators working with Czech and English.

Celina FRADE, PhD in Linguistics, is a Professor of Adjunct IV of English for Specific Purposes (ESP) in the Department of Technologies and Languages, Multidisciplinary Institute, Federal Rural University of Rio de Janeiro. Her main areas of interest and research include legal English and legal discourse across legal systems, genre analysis, semiotics, and the design and delivery English courses for academic, institutional, and professional purposes, particularly in business and law areas.

Mariusz Jerzy GOLECKI (PhD, LLM Cantab.) has been educated both in Civil Law (B.C.L. 1998 University of Warsaw) and the Common Law (LL.M. 2001, University of Cambridge, Trinity College). Since his 2004 appointment as an Associate Professor in the Department of Legal Theory and Philosophy of Law, University of Łódź, he has also been a Visiting Scholar in the Centre for European Legal Studies in the Faculty of Law, University of Cambridge (2008–2009) and Visiting Lecturer at International Christian University in Tokyo (2010). He specializes in Law and Economics, Jurisprudence, and Comparative Law. He is the author of two monographs and approximately 40 articles.

Víctor GONZÁLEZ-RUIZ is a lecturer in the field of legal translation at the Universidad de Las Palmas de Gran Canaria, Spain, where he obtained his PhD in translation in 2002. For the past 18 years, he has also worked as a part-time *traductor-intérprete jurado* (an official translator and interpreter in Spain). He is particularly committed to achieving clarity in legal translations, and has made it the focus of his teaching and study. He has reported the results of his research in several international conferences and publications.

Maurizio GOTTI is Professor of English Language and Translation, Head of the Department of Foreign Languages, Literatures and Communication, and Director of the Research Centre for LSP Research (CERLIS) at the University of Bergamo. His main research areas are the features and origins of specialized discourse (Robert Boyle and the Language of Science, 1996;

Specialized Discourse: Linguistic Features and Changing Conventions, 2003; Investigating Specialized Discourse, 2011). He is also interested in English syntax and English lexicology and lexicography, with particular regard to specialized terminology and canting. He is a member of the Editorial Board of national and international journals, and edits the Linguistic Insights series for Peter Lang.

Sandy LAMALLE is a researcher at the Research Centre in Public Law (CRDP) and the Centre for International Research and Studies (CÉRIUM), a lecturer at the Faculty of Law of the University of Montreal, and an associate researcher at the Institute for International and Strategic Studies (IRIS) in Paris. She has worked as a legal consultant in international and European affairs (CEIA) in London, and as a legal adviser in various international organizations and intergovernmental negotiating bodies. She has coordinated and conducted European and international studies, as well as legal translations from German, English, and Spanish to French. She holds a PhD in international law (Geneva), a PhD in European Union law (Strasbourg), and degrees and diplomas in international relations, political science, law, and philosophy. She has researched and published on legal critique and theory, international legal language, legal linguistics, and semiotics. She is a member of the Editorial Board of the *International Journal for the Semiotics of Law.*

Janny HC LEUNG is an Associate Professor in the School of English at the University of Hong Kong. She teaches in a double degree programme in Law and Literary Studies. She holds a BA (1st hons) in linguistics and translation from the University of Hong Kong, an MPhil and PhD in applied linguistics from the University of Cambridge, and an LLB from the University of London. Her current research interests cover interdisciplinary areas in law, linguistics, and psychology, especially legal discourse and legal bilingualism. Her project on the bilingual legal system of Hong Kong has attracted government funding. She was a Rotary Scholar, Sir Edward Youde Memorial Fellow, and a Harvard-Yenching Scholar. She has recently been appointed English Book Review Editor for the *International Journal for the Semiotics of Law.* For recent publications, please visit www.english.hku.hk/staff/leung.htm.

Jian LI is currently a PhD researcher at City University of Hong Kong and Research Associate Professor at China University of Political Science and Law. Her publications and interests are in the areas of forensic linguistics and phonetics and legal discourse.

Heikki Eero Sakari MATTILA is Professor *Emeritus* of Legal Linguistics (University of Lapland) and Docent of Comparative Law (University of Helsinki). He now works in the field of law and language studies, where he draws comparative research at national and international levels. He is one of the authors of the *Finnish Law Abbreviation Dictionary* (2004), and the Editor-in-Chief of a database of Finnish legal terms (2012–present). Prof. Mattila is a recognized expert in legal languages at the Translator Examination Board of Finland. He also holds other major responsibilities as a member of the Finnish language policy committee (Consultative State Committee for Language Matters), as a member of the Scientific Council of the *Revista de Llengua i dret* (Barcelona), and as a founding member of the *International Language and Law Association.* Prof. Mattila also published a general treatise in the field of comparative law and language studies, first in Finnish and later in English and French. An updated second English edition of his book, *Comparative Legal Linguistics: Language of Law, Latin, and Modern Lingua Francas,* was published in 2013, with a French edition, *Jurilinguistique comparée: langage du droit, latin et langues modernes,* published in 2012.

Fernando PRIETO RAMOS is Full Professor of Translation and Co-Director of the Centre for Legal and Institutional Translation Studies (Transius) at the University of Geneva's Faculty of Translation and Interpreting. His research interests include interdisciplinary methods in legal translation, international legal instruments, institutional translation and specialized terminology management. He studied Translation and Interpreting (with national academic distinction at graduation) and Law at the University of Granada, and completed a PhD in Applied Linguistics at Dublin City University, where he was a lecturer and a researcher at the Centre for Translation and Textual Studies for several years. He has published widely on legal translation and discourse analysis, and has received several research and teaching awards, including a European Label Award for Innovative Methods in Language Teaching from the European Commission and a "Ramón y Cajal" research award from the Spanish Department of Science and Technology. He also gained extensive experience as a sworn translator and as a freelance translator for several organizations before joining the World Trade Organization's dispute settlement translation team in 2003.

Colin ROBERTSON holds a Law Degree from Aberdeen University (1975) and is a member of the Law Society of Scotland. For 20 years until retiring in September 2013 he worked as legal-linguistic reviser ("lawyer-linguist") at the Council of the EU, checking and revising draft EU legislative texts in English. He has knowledge of several languages, including English, French, German, Italian, Czech, Slovak, Bulgarian, and some Chinese. After starting in private law practice, he worked from 1979 to 1991 as a lawyer in UK public service, which included two years in the Legal Service of the European Commission on detachment (1982–1983). He passed the EU lawyer-linguist competition in 1990 and worked in the Court of Justice of the EU before joining the Council in 1993. He is interested in EU multilingual legal language and terminology, and has a number of published articles, as well as publications in Scots dialect (Lallans). He is married with two children.

Yasuhiro SEKINE is a system engineer, researcher, and graduate student based in Tokyo. He has developed legal database systems, including the "Japanese Law Translation" run by the Japanese Ministry of Justice, a legal support system for Japanese local governments, and tools for processing legal documents. He is a researcher at the Japan Legal Information Institute, where he has designed a document type definition (DTD) system for Japanese law XML. He is also a student in the Graduate School of Intercultural Communication at Rikkyo University, focusing on translation studies. As a research project, he has been developing a memory system for translating Japanese laws.

Lijin SHA, a professor in China University of Political Science and Law (CUPL), where she teaches Legal English and Translation, and she taught Chinese law for the Summer Session of Dukeen University of the US and Montreal University of Canada (in Beijing) from 2001–2007. She has also been a visiting professor at Temple/Tsinghua Master of Laws legal English training program from 2005–2011 and a professor for Temple Law School's Judicial Training Program at the Supreme Judicial College in Beijing. In 2008, she lectured as a visiting professor in Akureyri University of Iceland, where she taught the course of Chinese Law. She is also the Vice President of China Association of Forensic Linguistics, Vice President of Multicultural Association of Law and Language, and Director of Research Center for Legal Translation in CUPL.

Kayoko TAKEDA is Professor of Translation and Interpreting Studies in the Graduate School of Intercultural Communication at Rikkyo University, Japan. Dr Takeda received an MA from Monterey Institute of International Studies and a PhD from Universitat Rovira i

Virgili. She has over 20 years of experience as a conference and legal interpreter and translator, with a court certification in California. Her research interests include sociocultural aspects of translating and interpreting, translator and interpreter education, translation and interpreting history, and translation technology. She is the author of *Interpreting the Tokyo War Crimes Trial* (University of Ottawa Press, 2010).

Svetlana V. VLASENKO has an MA in modern languages (1981, Maurice Thorez Moscow Foreign Languages Institute) and a PhD in Linguistics (1996, Institute of Linguistics, Russian Academy of Sciences, Moscow), thesis on translation theory in psycholinguistic perspective. From 1982–1984 she worked as a senior editor at the UNESCO Journals Editorial Board in the USSR Progress Publishers. In 1997, she was appointed as Associate Professor in the Moscow State Linguistic University Graduate School for Professional Translators. Since 2004 she has been engaged in postdoctoral research and university teaching in legal English, legal, financial, and economic translation. In 2009, she joined the Faculty of Law, National Research University Higher School of Economics, Moscow. Her main research interests comprise legal language and legal translation, pragmatics, psychosemantics and frame semantics, and intercultural professional communication. She has extensive and diversified experience in translating/interpreting for international institutions (IMF, IBRD, ISO, etc.), with current involvement in translation for the UN programmes. Svetlana is a translator and co-translator of books on financial management, investment policies, international business, and albums on arts and iconography. Her publications comprise a monograph, 60 scholarly articles, two textbooks, a translation dictionary, and an English-Russian dictionary on systems analysis.

Catherine WAY is Senior Lecturer in Translation at the University of Granada (AVANTI research group). She is author of numerous publications on legal translation and translator training, co-editor of books on directionality in translation and training, a member of the Editorial Board of the journal *Puentes* and of *The Interpreter and Translator Trainer*, which she previously edited. She is a member of the International Advisory Board of numerous translation and special language journals such as *Fachsprache* and the *International Journal of Law, Language and Discourse*. She has recently co-edited the Proceedings of the 6th EST Conference. She has participated as an expert legal translator training in the EU TRAFUT workshops. Her fields of research are Legal Translation, Translator Training, and Court Interpreting.

Foreword
New Challenges for Legal Translation

Heikki Eero Sakari Mattila

Major languages are used as legal lingua francas in various contexts. This usage is particularly visible in the field of international public law (treaties between States, law-related activities of international organizations, etc.). A second important context is cross-border business (contracts between companies, international arbitration, etc.). Furthermore, legal translations between small languages must often be done through a major language, a legal lingua franca.

The constellations of economic and political dominance dictate the choice of specific language(s) used in cross-border legal activities. Therefore, the lingua franca usage of legal languages has never been static. Historically, there has always been a more or less slow or rapid change: the position of one major language (or some languages) has (have) been strengthening, that of others weakening, and entirely new languages have entered into lingua franca usage.

During the past few centuries, Europe has been the leading continent, and the major European languages were spread to other continents. This also applies to legal contexts, in which the spreading was strengthened by the weight of European legal systems based on Roman law, technically superior as compared with other systems. From the end of the twentieth century, the economic and political centers of gravity of the globe started moving towards other continents, notably Asia. In the long term, this will certainly produce important changes in the interaction between cultures of law; there are likely to be more and more legal influences flowing from East to West. As a consequence, languages from the East will certainly gain more ground in the field of international legal activities too.

On the other hand, since the second half of the twentieth century, the dominance of English as a lingua franca has become overwhelming in all fields, legal activities included. Even if other major European languages also have an important role as legal lingua francas at the beginning of the third millennium (e.g., French in Africa and in the EU), the position of English is strengthening continuously. Lawyers of various countries use more and more English in all contexts of international communication, from conferences of legal scholars to contracts between businesses. International organizations provide a good example. French has been largely replaced by English as the first language in EU legal activities, except in the European Court of Justice. This means that more and more translations between legal English and other legal languages are being produced. This trend is especially visible in contexts where English is used as a bridge, a link language between two relatively minor languages when a direct translation between them is not possible.

In addition to changes in the lingua franca usage of legal languages, there are important changes in situations where documents in minor languages are used in cross-border legal contexts. A minor language often has an official position in a State or in a region of a State, which means that this language is used in all administrative and judicial documents produced by the civil servants and the law courts of this State or region (e.g., in the fields of labour and family law). In fact, the position of many such languages in the administration and judiciary of a State or a region of a State has been recently strengthened by the processes of democratization or independence (e.g., Catalan in Spain, Guaraní in Paraguay, Estonian in Estonia, several languages in the Republic of South Africa).

With globalization and internationalization in general, the mobility of citizens has increased. They travel and migrate for the purposes of employment and leisure. This creates more and more new language combinations in all professional contexts, including legal matters. For instance, tourism between Europe and southeast Asia produces relations in family law, which may require that various administrative and judicial decisions are applied for in Asian countries, followed by requests for their validation in Europe—or vice versa. For this purpose, these decisions must be translated. For instance, a divorce decree of a Thai court has to be translated from Thai to Finnish in order to permit its validation in Finland. Certainly, the existence of these kinds of language combinations is not entirely new. In colonial times, translations were frequently made between European languages on the one hand, and Asian languages on the other. However, the number of language combinations is much higher today, and they are often more complicated; moreover, translations involve not only two languages but several due, *inter alia*, to frequent movement between various countries.

The changes described above mean that there are growing numbers of cases where legal translation has to be performed between two legal languages that are conceptually divergent. To a substantial degree, the terms used in these languages are not equivalent. This means that the translator encounters a problem of "translatability".

In the context of lingua francas, this problem is compounded by the unprecedently widespread use of English in legal activities in international contexts. It is well-known that the concept structure of the common-law system differs considerably from that of the civil-law system. The terminology of common law often reflects the original concepts (divisions and institutions) of that law. Consequently, translation between legal texts in English and legal texts in continental languages involves the problem of translatability. The theory of legal translation has discussed this problem for decades. However, there is a good reason to continue the discussion, especially when we take into consideration that English as the lingua franca of legal practice makes it necessary to nuance the position of problem in this context.

In cases where texts written by genuine common-law lawyers (from England, US, Australia, etc.) are to be translated, there are no major changes at the level of principles. The problem of translatability between common and civil law still appears in its classical form. On the contrary, this is not the case in texts written by continental lawyers in English. These texts normally describe institutions and rules of civil law. Consequently, the conceptual system of the terms they use is not that of common law. The legal language written by continental lawyers is often a kind of conceptual hybrid: traditional common-law terms may be used in a civil-law sense. With its growth as a legal lingua franca, English is becoming increasingly detached from its common-law background (Mattila 2012: 454–459; Mattila 2013: 347–351). This phenomenon needs to be carefully analyzed from the point of view of legal translation.

In the long term, other important problems of translatability will arise, notably due to the growth of non-European legal languages. The cross-border usage of Asian languages, in particular Chinese, will give more weight to the basic problems attached to translation between legal Chinese and other legal languages. As generally known, Chinese is an exceptionally interesting study because of the original traditions of China in the field of law as well as due to the means of expression and the system of writing of this language.

As far as small languages are concerned, the growing number of new combinations of these languages in cross-border legal relations is also reflected in the field of translation. Even in continental Europe, the conceptual systems of legal orders are not entirely uniform. There are differences between them. This is the case in spite of the common tradition of Roman law and of the activities of legal harmonization in the framework of the EU. Quite naturally, these differences often are much bigger outside of Europe due to the influence of religious law (such as Islamic law or Hindu law) or due to the tradition of local customary law.

At the same time, it is not possible to train a significant number of translators who would be able to translate directly complicated legal texts from one minor language to another (unless the two languages are neighbours or otherwise close to each other). An expertly made legal translation from a minor source language to a minor target language via a major language (i.e., a translation via a link usage, also known as serial translation) allows for a more reliable result. However, the use of a third language tends to heighten the risk of change of meaning, and thus requires special attention, in particular in cases where the legal tradition underlying the link language is not the same as that of the source and target languages.

The increasing use of English as lingua franca in law implies that the link language used to translate from and to minor languages will mostly be English, which can be an important challenge. When a translation is made from a minor continental legal language into a second minor continental language through English, this means that a message created in the framework of a civil-law system and addressed to receivers in the framework of a second civil-law system passes via a language developed in the framework of the common-law system. Consequently, the danger of meaning distortion is particularly high and the translators need to exercise special caution.

The above considerations show that legal translation, notably the problem of translatability, today offers new research challenges of utmost importance. Taking this into account, the editors of the *Ashgate Handbook of Legal Translation* have designed a work, which clearly places itself at the leading edge of its field of study. They have brought together an important number of specialists who represent several cultures and linguistic zones and with varied professional experiences. The Handbook is therefore able to meet the new challenges of legal translation in a wider context. Previous publications in the field, notably comprehensive monographs, such as Susan Šarčević's *New Approach to Legal Translation*, have provided solid cornerstones for the theory of legal translation. This theory is now developed further in several articles of this Handbook. It is based on new and fresh experiences in the practice of legal translation, both from 'the biggest translation office in the world', the European Union, and from other contexts inside and outside of Europe, in Asia and in the Americas. Due to the indistinct line between theory and practice in the field of translation, there is all the more reason for the analysis of practical experiences, which ultimately will help to develop translation theory.

References

Mattila, H.E.S. 2013. *Comparative Legal Linguistics: Language of Law, Latin, Modern Lingua Francas.* 2nd edn. Aldershot: Ashgate.

Mattila, H.E.S. 2012. *Jurilinguistique comparée: Langages du droit, latin et langues modernes.* J.C. Gémar trans. Cowansville: Yvon Blais.

Acknowledgements

The Ashgate Handbook of Legal Translation is a collaborative work between the Editors and the contributors to this project. It is the outcome of several years of research whereby we have shared information and exchanged views to reach a common understanding in our field of expertise. The *Handbook* could not have been completed without the support of a number of institutions and well-established academics with whom we have had the pleasure of brainstorming and interacting.

As a prelude to this handbook, the Editors prepared and organized several international conferences worldwide in order to provide platforms for face-to-face discussions and to open up a series of promises, alternatives, and compromises. The International Roundtables for the Semiotics of Law in 2011 (School of Law of Fluminense Federal University – Rio de Janeiro, Brazil) and 2013 (Zhejiang Police College – Hangzhou, China) facilitated encounters between disciplines to set the main themes of this project. The Multicultural Association of Law and Language followed the same path, having organized several international conferences on Law, Translation and Culture in 2011 (China University of Political Science and Law – Beijing, China) and 2013 (Zhejiang Sci-Tech University, China and Shanghai Jiao Tong University, China) to invite disciplines to explore practical possibilities in the field of legal translation. *The Ashgate Handbook of Legal Translation* will thus provide an opportunity for a general discussion on legal translation issues as well as open discussions to enhance our understanding of the broader context of law, language and communication.

The Editors would like to express their gratitude to a number of people who have contributed to the preparation of this manuscript in various ways. First and foremost, we would like to convey our sincere appreciation to Prof. Mattila Heikki and Prof. Deborah Cao for their inspiring insights and deep reflections on Legal Translation. We are indebted to Prof. Vijay Bhatia, Dr Sarah Marusek, and Dr Sandy Lamalle for their generous help throughout the preparation and revisions of our manuscript. A special thanks goes to Alison Kirk (Ashgate Publishing) for her constant help and invisible presence throughout the various stages in the preparation of this *Handbook*.

Boulogne/Mer (France) and Hong Kong – 14 March 2014
Anne Wagner, King Kui Sin, Le Cheng

Introduction
Legal Translatability Process as the "Third Space" – Insights into Theory and Practice

Anne Wagner, King Kui Sin, and Le Cheng

> *[. . .] we should remember that it is the 'inter' – the cutting edge of translation and negotiation, the in-between, the space of the entre that Derrida has opened up in writing itself – that carries the burden of the meaning of culture. [. . .] It is in this space that we will find those words with which we can speak of Ourselves and Others. And by exploring this hybridity, this 'Third Space', we may elude the politics of polarity and merge as the others of our selves.*
>
> (Bhabha 1995: 209)

1. Introduction

Legal translatability is a space of possibilities, an autonomous realm of 'cross-cultural events' (Snell-Hornby 1988: 43) within which the 'system-bound' (Cao 2003: 23) of legal concepts and notions deeply rooted in language, history and societal evolution (Šarčević 2000; Wagner and Gémar 2013; 2014a) of one country are transformed and integrated into the language of another, and as a result, stratified over the course of time (Pozzo 2012: 186):

> *(A)ll legal systems are mixed – derived from imported structures, concepts and ideas but also emanating from different normative systems which are based on customs, religions and languages, habitat and natural resources, families, geography and climate, conceptions of morality, and other features. (Demleitner 1999: 749)*

Accordingly, the main complexity in legal translatability will be to gather terminology of multiple origins (Sherry 1996: 134) and to transfer it into another linguistic framework (Wagner and Gémar 2013). This linguistic framework is originally a binary code and comprises two semantic spaces: the source space and the target space. The legal translatability process would then constitute the "Third Space",[1] a space 'which enables other positions to emerge [. . . and where . . .] all forms of cultures are continually in a process of hybridity' (Rutherford 1990: 211) of evolution. This Third Space is undefined, vague, and fluid. It is a precondition for the negotiation, transformation and translation (Ikas and Wagner 2009: 120) between two cultures. Bhabha (1995: 208, emphasis added) posits:

1 'For me the importance of hybridity is not to be able to trace two original moments from which the third emerges, rather hybridity to me is the "Third Space", which enables other positions to emerge'(Rutherford 1990: 211).

> *It is that Third Space, though unrepresentable in itself, which constitutes the discursive conditions of enunciation that ensure that the meaning and symbols of culture have* **no primordial unity or fixity**; *that even the* **same signs can be appropriated, translated, rehistoricized, and read anew.**[2]

Indeed, this "Third Space" permits manipulation of the consciousness and unconsciousness of legal discourse when the translatability process is underway. It is a 'Third Space of enunciation between the poles of cultural identity, a space within which cultural identities themselves are transformed' (Ikas and Wagner 2009: 120). The Third Space acts as a multistage dynamics (Wagner 2005a), as an absent structure (Eco 1972) where mechanisms of transfer, of importation from one culture to another have to be fairly analyzed (Wagner and Gémar 2014a; Budick and Iser 1996). However,

> 1. *The passage brought effects of* **distortions and appropriation.**[3] *These effects inevitably accompany any important movement of ideas; the result from the diversity of interests and desires, which command the exchange, from the* **reformulation and renewals**[4] *demanded of the target language. (Sherry 1996: 11)*
>
> 2. *This* **struggle – between possession and dispossession, or between reinscription and obliteration**[5] *– is necessary perilous [. . .]. (Budick and Iser 1996)*
>
> 3. *Decision-making needs to elaborate multiple and viable solutions [. . .] and so to have "***cultural mediation***"*[6] *in the legal field. (Wagner and Gémar 2014b)*

This 'cultural mediation' (Wagner and Gémar 2014b) is an essential pillar within the "Third Space" as it opens up a series of promises, alternatives, and compromises to create encounters, crossroads (Sinclair 2005) between disciplines for practical possibilities in the legal translatability process:

> *Put differently, the likelihood of identical concepts possesses both an innate component (our cognitive design) and a cultural one (how culture structures experience and represents it in that culture's language). (Paunio 2013: 143)*

The Ashgate Handbook of Legal Translation seeks to offer broader and worldwide perspectives for understanding the roles of "translatability" and "Third Space" in the debate of legal translation, from theoretical to practical angles with professional and academic insights. The *Handbook* construes presentations of this "Third Space", orientates our vision of "legal translatability" and finds acceptable and readable transfers in the legal communicative space—a 'protean, moving and complex process' (Wagner and Gémar 2014c). Contributors to *The Ashgate Handbook of Legal Translation* offer us criticisms and innovative perspectives on legal translatability in this Third Space.

2 Our emphasis.
3 Our emphasis.
4 Our emphasis.
5 Our emphasis.
6 Our emphasis.

2. Legal Translation in Theory

The Ashgate Handbook of Legal Translation begins by the exploration of legal translatability on a theoretical angle. Theory is crucial in the study of law, language, and translation in society. It means that the way beliefs and values are socially constructed, and the way they reflect their images and disseminate their views provide potential and valuable keys for research in the field of legal translation theory. Challenging legal translation theories is an unavoidable aspect of social and legal interaction within the transfer and exchange of communication in the legal sphere. The roles of legal translators, jurilinguists and/or lawyer-linguists are then crucial to achieve a comprehensible and readable "Third Space" in the target language,

> *[. . .] of what is immediately presented as a* **spatio-temporal whole**[7] *that transcends what is immediately presented, is not only a means of experiential knowing, it is also a fundamental kind of practical knowledge –* **knowing how to orientate oneself in space and time, knowing how to construe presentations or appearance in terms of spatial and temporal 'reality'**. *(Heron 1989: 87)*

This 'spatio-temporal whole' leads to considerations of the aspects of 'foreignization' and/or 'domestication' of concepts, terms, notions in the target language (Yang 2010; Munday 2001; Venuti 1995; Nida 1964): 'The translator can either leave the writer in peace as much as possible and bring the reader to him, or he can leave the reader in peace as much as possible and bring the writer to him' (Wilss, 1982: 33).

In the translatability process, this "whole" cannot be evaluated in a mechanical way (Vermeer 1994). Tomášek (1990: 113) suggests 'a procedure based on both linguistic and legal comparative approaches; (see also Chroma 2008: 303–316). This process needs interpretation of the objective legal reality where translators, jurilinguists and/or lawyer-linguists will be educated with specific legal translation programs:

> *Translation always falls short of its goal of conveying the meaning and the style of a text in a new text that reads like an original composition in the second language. The law is always subject to interpretation; the idea that it is "carved in stone" is only an illusion. Nor is the meaning of words ever fixed: the kind of precision the law demands of language, and formal semantics attempts to represent, is again based on an illusion of human linguistic behaviour, which has evolved very efficiently for a large number of purposes, though pinning down precise meaning is not among them. This has implication for translation as well, for if indeterminacy is already the condition within languages, it holds a fortiori between languages. (Joseph 1995: 14)*

Part I of the *Handbook* permits eight of our contributors to expose their views on theories and training programmes for legal translation with philosophical, rhetorical, terminological and lexicographical perspectives.

Chapter 1, from Mariusz Jerzy Golecki, concentrates on two approaches towards the relationships between legal and economic concepts called translation and decoding. Whereas translation concerns the substitution of legal meanings and terms by economic assumptions and relations between some parameters, decoding is being developed and treated as a kind of linguistic game in Wittgensteinian sense. Both approaches refer to different theoretical models. Translation strategies concentrate on transforming legal meanings into economic models,

7 Our emphasis.

whereas decoding pertains to special features of communication and the difference between legal form and economic content. The point of departure for these observations consists in the existence of specific entanglement between the philosophical narration, the moral normative theory and its recognition within a framework of legal discourse. Eventually, the contributor exposes the dichotomy of power between free exchange and institutions with their hierarchy, stating that the most advisable strategy would be to embrace both of them. As such, the perspective of law and economics as an interdisciplinary project may provide important insights both in jurisprudence and in economic theory.

Chapter 2, from Anne Wagner, King-Kui Sin, and Le Cheng, expounds their views of cultural transfers and the way concepts, notions and language are conceptualized within the legal discourse. Their investigations start questioning the idea of "hybridization", which is being discussed among practitioners, experts and theoreticians in legal discourse analyzes (Bhatia 2004: 58). Legal discourse is being contaminated by morality and politics where its decoding and transfer in the target language will pertain not only to the legal sphere but also to other disciplines. Legal translation is across disciplines. This contamination results in a language being highly slippery, fluid, unpredictable, having hidden dimensions, which may need to be re-contextualized and decoded in the target language (see also Wagner 2005a; 2005b).

Chapter 3, from Janet Ainsworth, investigates legal translation and the challenges translators will have to face to ensure plain meaning in law. Translating legal texts 'comes to perform an act of comparative law, but coupled with a translation process' (Wagner and Gémar 2014b). It has long been recognized that legal translation—the creation of equivalent legal texts in different languages—poses a series of challenges to the translator, some grounded in the nature of language, some in the relationship of language to culture, and some inherent in the nature of language use within the domain of law. This chapter explores some of those challenges in the context of the developing norms of legal translation used within the European Union and Chinese legal systems. It also suggests that a careful examination of the processes through which legal transplants are assimilated into national legal cultures shows that the theoretical problems inherent in legal translation are also at play in the reception of legal transplants.

Chapter 4, from Janny H.C. Leung, analyzes the specific nature and significance of translation equivalences as legal fictions and the purposes they may serve. Although it is well known that translations are rarely perfect, the law insists on the unsafe assumption of translation equivalence, presumably because it has certain utility. Translation equivalence is, in short, a legal fiction. This chapter sets out to analyze the specific nature, motives and significance of this emerging legal fiction, and then to use it as a site to examine broader issues. The author follows Weston's stance when he states, 'the basic translation difficulty of overcoming conceptual differences between languages becomes particularly acute due to cultural and more specifically institutional reasons' (Weston 1991: 207). The main point is then to find the most adequate functional equivalence described by Newmark (2005: 83) as 'a procedure that occupies the middle, sometimes the universal, area between the SL and the TL'.

Chapter 5, from Víctor González-Ruiz, develops a plain approach to clear legal translation where vagueness, fuzziness, ambiguity and indeterminacy (Bhatia et al. 2005) are central issues for him. The literature on plain language has widely demonstrated that it is possible to be both legally precise and stylistically clear. By applying the principles of plain language to legal translation, translators could produce simple and plain texts, and still claim them to be professionally acceptable. The author engages and reflects the constituent elements of flaws in legal language (see also Wagner 2005b), then he examines and gives examples of how to constitute a framework which 'could use plain language, better comprehensibility, readability and access to legal texts' (Wagner et al. 2006: 22) to prepare the most adequate legal translation.

Chapter 6, from Svetlana V. Vlasenko, analyzes legal language from another angle. She follows Peter Newmark's arguments when he states the 'language of thought means that a word is missing in the source language, but you find an expression in the target language. All languages have gaps but our thoughts do not have these same gaps' (Shea 2005: 394). She finds proximity between legal translation and neurobiology of consciousness where she confronts minimal units in legal translation to minimal units of thought. The chapter attempts to detail some mechanisms behind the English-Russian translator's legal language switch through describing respective techniques and extrapolating them onto the legal translation theoretical framework at large.

Chapter 7, from Fernando Prieto Ramos, proposes and develops an integrated model with parameters to solve equivalences in legal translation. As a lexicographer, the author follows Oliver Holmes's point: 'a word is not a crystal, transparent and unchanging, it is the skin of a living thought and may vary greatly in colour and content according to the circumstances and time in which it is used' (cited in Mac Aodha 2014: Preface). Translation needs not only macrotextual and microtextual parameters but also the 'contextualization and coherent reasoning of decisions about this acceptability' (cited from his chapter) with specific scenarios (see also Šarčević 1989; 2009). He, then, investigates how legal terminology is being managed in international institutional settings.

Chapter 8, from Catherine Way, concludes this part by presenting a framework for decision-making in legal translators' training framework. The framework is based on Kelly's competence model (2005) and decision-making strategies adapted from business administration. Whilst initially appear a complex approach, the framework allows trainers to select texts for different stages of training and change the difficulty of the decision making required by simply adapting the translation brief to best fit the trainees' profile or stage of training. Furthermore, it allows trainers to select test texts and weight assessment according to the competence and/or decision-making, which they wish to evaluate at that particular point of training. Training professionals in this field is a challenging task, which requires dual skills—both linguistic and legal ones. Accordingly the decision-making aspect in legal translation is primordial and should be considered within the training process.

From these chapters it seems obvious that the challenge is important for accurate legal translations in practice:

> - *The translator of a legal text* **aims at introducing foreign legal worldviews into a different legal life-world**. *His task is to make the foreign legal text accessible for recipients with a different (legal) background. (Sieglinde 2012: 283)*
>
> - *In the area of intercultural communication, requiring not only language mediation but heightened cultural expertise, the (human) translator (and interpreter) plays an increasingly important role, whereby he/she will take the full responsibility for the final product.*[8] *(Snell-Hornby 2006: 133)*

8 Our emphasis.

3. Legal Translation in Practice

This "Third Space" in legal translatability entails analyzing the roles of actors involved in the translation process, the actions they take and the final product they constitute from their practices (see also Prieto Ramos and Borja Albi 2013). Given the power legal translation could imply, Part II of *The Ashgate Handbook of Legal Translation* advocates close analyzes of the discursive *modus operandi* in relation to their context, a 'cultural turn' (Snell-Hornby 2006: 50) which is necessary for describing, analyzing, and interpreting social relations reflected in the text, before delivering the final translation in the target language (Bhatia 2004: 123). We take "cultural turn" to mean that legal discourse reflects 'the organization of society and its institutions and the roles and power structures inherent therein' (Wodak et al. 1989: 155). By revealing practices in legal translation, our *Handbook* aims to encourage a better understanding of these practices to avoid a language/practice duality, to assume translation:

> *[. . .]* **an assumed translation**[9] *would be regarded as any target-culture text for which there are reasons to tentatively posit the existence of another text, in another culture and language, from which it was presumably derived by transfer operations and to which it is now tied by certain relationships [. . .] within that culture. (Toury 1995: 35)*

Therefore, the reconstruction of the meaning of the source language (SL) necessarily involves references to a meta-level parameter, as the SL text cannot be encapsulated within the limits of the SL legal system, but has to be "colonized" and/or "domesticated" in the target language (Sin and Roebuck 1996). Talmy states, 'language somehow mirrors thought, and thought in turn, some external reality' (cited in Jemielniak 2013: 41). Accordingly, legal language is culturally labelled (Toury 1995: 33). However, Nietzsche moderates the culture-bound system when he expresses his scepticism that 'the various languages, juxtaposed, show that words are never concerned with truth, never with adequate expression . . .' (1873: 248).

Legal translatability can thus be compared to a rhizome, an activity, which keeps growing and expanding in various directions:

> *The rhizome itself assumes very diverse forms, from ramified surface extension in all directions to concretion into bulbs and tubers . . . the rhizome includes the best and the worst. (Deleuze and Guattari 1987: 6–7)*

Part II of *The Ashgate Handbook of Legal Translation* permits nine of our contributors to expand our inquiry of the "Third Space" in legal translatability to show multiple and pluralistic perspectives and to make sense of legal translators' experiences.

Chapter 9, from Colin Robertson, with his experience as a lawyer-linguist at the Council of the European Union, explains how EU legal texts are drafted, construed, and then translated with different plausible scenarios (Robertson 2012; 2010). The role of lawyer-linguists is then crucial and the selection process is highly demanding to meet EU expectations in terms of translations, and follows Paunio's (2013: 17) stance:

> *This hybrid-like political process of creating EU legislation – comprising political negotiations, translation and interpretation – often requires that the final text adopted is fuzzy and vague so that it can cater for different political interests present in the law-making process.*

9 Our emphasis.

Chapter 10, from Łucja Biel, addresses a hitherto neglected area of legal translation: phraseology. Legal language is marked by formulaicity, which is partly due to high fixedness and conservatism of legal phraseology. The recent intertwining of theoretical literatures on phraseology and terminology along with practical legal applications based on a EU corpus provides new insights to the legal translation field (see also Kjaer 2007; 1990).

Chapter 11, from Maurizio Gotti, investigates legal translation in international arbitration settings. The contributor shows that globalization has led to a mixture of cultures and languages, that international arbitration identifies 'common elements in arbitration legislation as they are constructed and interpreted across multilingual and multicultural contexts' (Bhatia, Candlin and Engberg 2008: 7). Therefore, translation is even more complex and demanding in terms of topical, linguistic, textual, and cultural aspects (see also Šarčević 2008).

Chapter 12, from Celina Frade, draws a comparison on two official English versions of the Brazilian Law on arbitration of 1996. She bases her research first on legal translation theories and then compares with great details the differences that appear between these two official versions (see also Bhatia, Candlin and Gotti 2012; Frade 2014).

Chapter 13, from Kayoko Takeda and Yasuhiro Sekine, gives a detailed historical presentation of legal translation in Japan followed by a project to translate Japanese Law into English, to render Japanese law more accessible to foreigners. English translation of some Japanese laws had existed, but it was produced in a decentralized way, resulting in quality issues, and inconsistencies in the translation of legal terms and phrases, and difficulty in locating the translated texts. Therefore, in tandem with the actual work of translating laws, this project has been focusing on establishing a foundation for ongoing efforts to provide quality translation of Japanese laws in a centralized way with standard terminology lists in place, and for easy access to the translation for users. As a result, the website called 'Japanese Law Translation', with a database system, was launched in 2009. Despite the positive aspects of this system, such as the centralization of various data and the availability of a standard dictionary, there are some issues to be addressed.

Chapter 14, from Rafat Y. Alwazna, describes the methods and strategies proposed for legal translation before analyzing in details Hooper's translation of the *Ottoman Majalla* into English. He validates that the translation of Hooper consists of specific sets of translation strategies to achieve the communicative transmission within the translatability process.

Chapter 15, from Lijin Sha and Jian Li, deals with the Criminal Procedure Law of the PRC with an approach based on legal reality and societal evolution in Mainland China. Contributors show the various proposed translations and state they are just given as indicators and cannot influence the original document in Chinese. However, the comparative work of these former translations permits the identification of the linguistic and cultural obstacles, the inconsistencies, and the lack of clarity and plain approach (see also Cao 2012).

Chapter 16, from Marta Chromá, discusses the recently adopted new codification of private law, effective January 1, 2014. She argues that there is a necessity to draw extensive comparative research with a focus both on the conceptual analysis of terminology used in the existing Code and of the new one. The analyses provided in her chapter generate concepts and structures, which the existing Code does not contain.

Chapter 17, from Sandy Lamalle, concludes Part II with the analysis of the concept of legal personality and the process of "multileveled translation" worldwide. Taking into account legal pluralism and evolution, the chapter proposes a reflexion on the function, roles, and limits of such a key concept in the international legal language in constant interaction with different legal languages and systems. Studying the implications of the multileveled translation of the concept of legal personality sheds light on ontological and epistemological structures, limits issues of compatibility, as well as impacts on legal cultures, traditions, and systems (see also Cao 2005; Mattila 2012; Mattila 2013; Sacco 1992).

4. Conclusion

Legal translation issues have been extensively addressed over the last two decades,[10] and transferring concepts, and terms into other linguistic/legal systems has been a salient characteristic. *The Ashgate Handbook of Legal Translation* shows how language is powerful and active, conveying social experiences and shaping the reality of legal translation both in theory and in practice. It is noteworthy that practitioners and experts in this field are sensitive to an 'assumed translation' (Toury 1995: 35). Theories and practices are structured to understand this "Third Space", where legal translation could accommodate both the source and target languages.

For this reason, contributors to the *Handbook of Legal Translation* make decisions and choices that reflect common knowledge (see Šarčević 2000), but they still operate within the constraints set by the principle of cultural reality in the target language:

> *Semiotically speaking, it will be clear that it is the target or recipient culture, or certain section of it, which serves as the initiator of the decision to translate and of the translating process [. . .] Translators operate first and foremost in the interest of the culture into which they are translating, and not in the interest of the source text, let alone the source culture. (Gideon Toury, cited in Snell-Hornby 2006: 49)*

Finally, the "Third Space" in the translatability process leads to mitigating solutions. Indeed, various strategies in the *Handbook of Legal Translation* were employed invoking both tradition and "emancipation" from legal translation theories and practices:

> *Translation thus is not simply an act of faithful reproduction but, rather, a deliberate and conscious act of selection, assemblage, structuration, and fabrication [. . .] In these ways translators, as much as creative writers and politicians, participate in the powerful acts that create knowledge and shape culture. (Gentzler, Tymoczko 2002: xxi)*

References

Bhabha, H. 1995. 'Cultural Diversity and Cultural Differences'. In: B. Ashcroft, G. Griffiths and H. Tiffin eds. *The Post-Colonial Studies Reader*. London: Routledge, pp. 206–209.

Bhatia, V.K. 2004. *Worlds of Written Discourse. A Genre-Based View*. London: Continuum.

Bhatia, V.K., Candlin, C. and Engberg, J. 2008. *Legal Discourse Across Cultures and Systems*. Hong Kong: Hong Kong University Press.

Bhatia, V.K., Candlin, C. and Gotti, M. 2012. *Discourse and Practice in International Commercial Arbitration: Issues, Challenges and Prospects*. Law, Language and Communication Series. Aldershot: Ashgate.

Bhatia, V.K., Engberg, J., Gotti, M. and Heller, D. (eds). 2005. *Vagueness in Normative Texts*. Bern: Peter Lang.

Budick, S. and Iser, W. 1996. *The Translatability of Cultures – Figurations of the Space Between*. Stanford: Stanford University Press.

Cao, D. 2007. *Translating Law*. Clevedon, UK: Multilingual Matters.

10 See the works of Wagner and Gémar (2013; 2014a; 2014b; 2014c); Mattila (2012; 2013); Gémar and Kasirer (2005); Gémar (1982; 2000); Sacco (1992); Šarčević (2000); and Cao (2003).

———. 2012. 'Linguistic Uncertainty and Legal Transparency: Statutory Interpretation in China and Australia'. In: V.K. Bhatia, C. Hafner, L. Miller and A. Wagner eds. *Transparency, Power and Control: Perspectives on Legal Communication*. Law, Language and Communication Series. Aldershot: Ashgate: pp. 13–30.
Chroma, M. 2008. 'Semantic and Legal Interpretation: Two Approaches to Legal Translation'. In: V.K. Bhatia, C. Candlin and P. Evangelisti eds. *Language, Culture and the Law: The Formulation of Legal Concepts across Systems and Cultures*. Bern: Peter Lang.
Deleuze, G. and Guattari, F. 1987. *A Thousand Plateaus*. Minneapolis: University of Minnesota Press.
Demleitner, N.V. 1999. 'Combating Legal Ethnocentrism: Comparative Law Sets Boundaries', *Arizona State Law Journal*, vol. 31(37), pp. 748–749.
Eco, U. 1972. *La structure absente: introduction à la recherché sémiotique*. Paris: Mercure de France.
Frade, C. 2014. 'Legal Translation in Brazil: An Entextualization Approach'. In: A. Wagner and J.C. Gémar guest eds. *Legal Translation and Jurilinguistics: Globalizing Disciplines. Retrospects and Prospects, International Journal for the Semiotics of Law*, vol. 27(4).
Gémar, J.C. and Kasirer, N. (eds). 2005. *Jurilinguistics: Between Law and Language*. Montreal: Editions Thémis.
Gémar, J.C. 2000. *Traduire, ou, L'art d'interpréter*. Québec: Presses Universitaires du Québec.
———. (ed.). 1982. *Langage du droit et traduction, Essais de jurilinguistique*. Montreal: Linguatech.
Gentzler, E. and Tymoczko, M. 2002. 'Introduction'. In: M. Tymoczko and E. Gentzler eds. *Translation and Power*. Amherst: University of Massachusetts Press, pp. xi–xxviii.
Heron, J. 1989. *Philosophical Basis for a New Paradigm*. Paris: Edition du Seuil.
Ikas, K. and Wagner, G. (eds). 2009. *Communicating in The Third Space*. Routledge: London.
Jemielniak, J. 2013. *Legal Interpretation in International Commercial Arbitration*. In: Law, Language and Communication Series. Aldershot: Ashgate.
Joseph, J.E. 1995. Indeterminacy, Translation and the Law. In: M. Morris ed. *Translation and the Law*. Amsterdam/Philadelphia: John Benjamins Publishing Company.
Kelly, D. 2005. *A Handbook for Translation Trainers: A Guide to Reflective Practice*. Manchester: St. Jerome.
Kjær, A.L. 1990. 'Context-conditioned word combinations in legal language', *Journal of the International Institute for Terminology Research*, vol. 1(1–2), pp. 21–32.
———. 2007. 'Phrasemes in Legal Texts'. In: H. Burger, D. Dobrovol'skij, P. Kühn and N.R. Norrick eds. *Phraseology/Phraseologie: An International Handbook of Contemporary Research/Ein internationales Handbuch der zeitgenössischen Forschung*. Berlin/New York: Walter de Gruyter, pp. 506–516.
Mac Aodha, M. 2014. *Legal Lexicography*. In: Law, Language and Communication Series. Aldershot: Ashgate.
Mattila, H.E.S. 2012. *Jurilinguistique comparée: Langages du droit, latin et langues modernes*. J.C. Gémar trans. Cowansville: Yvon Blais.
———. 2013. *Comparative Legal Linguistics: Language of Law, Latin, Modern Lingua Francas*. 2nd edn. Aldershot: Ashgate.
Munday, J. 2001. *Introducing Translation Studies: Theories and Applications*. London and New York: Routledge.
Newmark, P. 2005. *A Textbook of Translation*. New York: Prentice Hall Longman.
Nida, E. 1964. *Toward a Science of Translation*. The Netherlands, Leiden: E.J. Brill.
Nietzsche, F. 1873. *On Truth and Lies in a Nonmoral Sense*. New York: CreateSpace Independent Publishing Platform.
Paunio, E. 2013. *Legal Certainty in Multilingual EU Law: Language, Discourse and Reasoning at the European Court of Justice*. In: Law, Language and Communication Series. Aldershot: Ashgate.

Pozzo, B. 2012. 'English as a Legal Lingua Franca in the EU Multilingual Context'. In: C.J.W. Baaij ed. *The Role of Legal Translation in Legal Harmonization*. The Netherlands: Wolters Kluwer.
Prieto Ramos, F. and Borja Albi, A. (eds). 2013. *Legal Translation in Context: Professional Issues and Prospects*. Vienna: Peter Lang.
Robertson, C. 2012. 'What EU Legislative Texts Reveal about Power, Control and Transparency'. In: V.K. Bhatia, C. Hafner, L. Miller and A. Wagner eds. *Transparency, Power and Control: Perspectives on Legal Communication*. Law, Language and Communication Series. Aldershot: Ashgate, pp. 109–124.
———. 2010. 'LSP and EU Legal Language'. In: Heine and Engberg eds. *Reconceptualizing LSP*. Online proceedings of the XVII European LSP Symposium 2009.
Rutherford, J. 1990. 'The Third Space: Interview with Homi Bhabha'. In: *Identity: Community, Culture and Difference*. London: Lawrence & Wishart.
Sacco, R. 1992. *La traduzione giuridica. Il linguaggio del diritto*. Milan: Scarpelli.
Šarčević, S. 1989. 'Conceptual Dictionaries for Translation in the Field of Law', *International Journal of Lexicography*, vol. 2(4), pp. 277–293.
———. 2000. *New Approach to Legal Translation*. The Hague: Kluwer Law International.
———. 2008. 'Translation in International Arbitration'. In: V.K. Bhatia, C. Candlin and J. Engberg eds. *Legal Discourse across Cultures and Systems*. Hong Kong: Hong Kong University Press, pp. 291–308.
———. (ed.). 2009. *Legal Language in Action: Translation, Terminology, Drafting and Procedural Issues*. Zagreb: Nakladni zavod Globus.
———. 2012. 'Coping with the Challenge of Legal Translation in Harmonization'. In: C.J.W. Baaij ed. *The Role of Legal Translation in Legal Harmonization*. The Hague: Wolters Kluwer.
Schleiermacher, F. von. [1838] 1982. 'Über die verschiedenen Methoden des Übersetzens'. In: W. Wilss ed. *The Science of Translation. Problems and Methods*. Tübingen: Günther Narr.
Shea, D. 2005. 'Interview with Peter Newmark, Pioneering Theoretician in Scientific Translation', *Semblanzas*, vol. VI(21–22), pp. 392–394.
Sherry, S. 1996. *Gender in Translation*. London: Routledge.
Sieglinde, E.P. 2012. 'The Hermeneutic Approach in Legal Translation'. In: Cercel and Stanley eds. *Unterwegs zu einer hermeneutischen* Übersetzungswissenschaft. *Radegundis Stolze zu ihrem 60. Geburtstag*. Tübingen: Narr, pp. 274–287.
Sin, K.K. and Roebuck, D. 1996. Language Engineering for Legal Transplantation, *Language and Communication*, vol. 16, pp. 235–254.
Sinclair, J. 2005. 'Trust the Text'. In: M. Coulthard ed. *Advances in Written Text Analysis*. London: Routledge, pp. 12–26.
Snell-Hornby, M. 1988. *Translation Studies: An Integrated Approach*. Amsterdam/Philadelphia: John Benjamins Publishing Company.
———. 2006. *The Turns of Translation Studies: New Paradigms or Shifting Viewpoints?* Amsterdam/Philadelphia: John Benjamins Publishing Company.
Tomášek, M. 1990 'On Selected Problems in Translation of the Legal Language'. In: *Translatologica Pragensia IV*. Acta Universitatis Carolinae Philologica 4(1994). Prague: Karolinum, pp. 113–120.
Toury, G. 1995. *Descriptive Translation Studies and Beyond*. Amsterdam/Philadelphia: Benjamins.
Venuti, L. 1995. *The Translator's Invisibility: A History of Translation*. London and New York: Routledge.
Vermeer, H.J. 1994. 'Hermeneutik und Übersetzung (swissenschaft)', *TextConText*, vol. 9(3), pp. 163–182.
Wagner, A. and Gémar, J.C. (eds). 2014a. 'Decision-Making in Legal Translation, Interpretation and Speech Act – Legal Semiotic Cultural Mediation Techniques', *Semiotica*.

———. 2014b. 'Communication and Cultural Mediation Techniques in Jurilinguistics'. In: A. Wagner and J.C. Gémar eds. *Decision-Making in Legal Translation, Interpretation and Speech Act – Legal Semiotic Cultural Mediation Techniques. Semiotica.*

———. 2014c. 'Jurilinguistique et Juritraductologie – A Collective and Societal Dimension: Multiplicity of Meaning Between Sciences and Society'. 'Legal Translation and Jurilinguistics: Globalizing Disciplines. Retrospects and Prospects', *International Journal for the Semiotics of Law,* vol. 27(4).

———. (eds). 2013. 'The Process of Translabiliting: Translating and Transferring Law, its Concepts, Notions and Language', *International Journal for the Semiotics of Law,* vol. 26(4).

Wagner, A. and Caccaguidi-Fahy, S. (eds). 2006. *Legal Language and the Search for Clarity.* Bern: Peter Lang.

Wagner, A. 2005a. 'Semiotic Analysis of the Multistage Dynamics at the core of Indeterminacy in Legal Language'. In: V.K. Bhatia, J. Engberg, M. Gotti and D. Heller eds. *Vagueness in Normative Texts.* New York: Peter Lang, pp. 173–199.

———. 2005b. 'Les apports de l'analyse linguistique dans la conception du flou et de la sécurité juridique', *La Semaine Juridique. Edition Générale,* vol. 51, pp. 2355–2359.

Weston, M. 1991. *An English Reader's Guide to the French Legal System.* Oxford: Berg.

Wilss, W. 1982. *The Science of Translation: Problems and Methods.* Tübingen: Günther Narr.

Wodak et al. 1989. *Language Power and Ideology: Studies in Political Discourse.* Amsterdam: Benjamins.

Yang, W. 2010. 'Brief Study on Domestication and Foreignization in Translation', *Journal of Language, Teaching and Research,* vol. 1(1), pp. 77–80.

PART I
LEGAL TRANSLATION IN THEORY

Chapter 1
Translation vs. Decoding Strategies in Law and Economics Scholarship[1]

Mariusz Jerzy Golecki

In this chapter I will claim that methodology of law and economics should be changed from adopting economic analysis of law, namely translating legal concepts into economic models implementing price theory (economization of law), to other, more interdisciplinary and balanced strategies.

The point of departure for these observations consists in the existence of specific entanglement between the philosophical narration, the moral normative theory, and its recognition within a framework of legal discourse. Thus it could be envisaged that legal discourse is heavily dependent on the overlapping between the legal and moral vocabulary (Hart 1994). The most characteristic feature of this kind of discourse is heavily dependent on the linguistics constrains commonly accepted among law and economics scholars. My main thesis thus pertains to the distinctive features of the law and economics models as compared to typical jurisprudential narratives.

The key distinction to be implemented in this respect concentrates on the difference between translation and decoding. Whereas translation concerns the substitution of legal meanings and terms by economic assumptions and relations between some parameters, decoding is being developed and treated as a kind of linguistic game in the Wittgensteinian sense (Wittgenstein 1953). The economic model is being treated as the simplified representative of the interrelations between the objects (Maki 1998). Decoding deploys some metaphors used by both F. Nietzsche and L. Wittgenstein, whereas the model can never be based on the metaphor, simply because that the model is supposed to contain the direct representation of the given aspect of the object and this representation of the modelled object must be univocal. Decoding is a mutual operation transforming a primary message produced by legal or economic systems. This narrative is supposed to be overwhelming and thus satisfies the need for the ultimate answer to the given set of questions such as that about the nature of law, the essence of rights, and the character of justice, whereas from the perspective of the law and economics discourse those questions are senseless in a strong, Wittgensteinian sense, i.e., they cannot be addressed and answered according to the adopted verification procedure. This comparison between the two competitive frameworks of the legal theory—the narrative based discourse and the model based discourse—lead to two preliminary remarks. First, the narrative based discourses are general and their legitimacy is based on their integrity whereas the model based discourses are partial, do not claim integrity, and their legitimacy is based on their utility. Second, the two different discourses are legitimized in different ways. The narrative-based discourse derives

1 Acknowledgment: The chapter has been prepared within a framework of the FOCUS programme sponsored by the Foundation for Polish Science.

its legitimacy from the completeness, coherence, and general plausibility of the narrative structure, be it philosophical or sociological. The model based discourses are founded on the coherence between the assumptions, the conclusions, and the control on a given object. In other words, models are based on coherence and legitimized by their usage and the effect of their predictive functions.

In this chapter, the term "economics of law" will be used in the same way as the majority of scholars use the term "law and economics". However, I would like to avoid the association of this term with the theory purported by Posner. Therefore, Posner's theory will be named economic analysis of law.[2] Economics of law as well as law and economics certainly have a broader meaning. The meaning is associated with a methodological approach: the economic analysis of law as well as the revision within economics itself. I prefer the name economics of law to law and economics because it seems more realistic at the moment; the insight of law in economics is either poor or redefined in economic terms. The impact of economics on law is enormous, and a realistic approach cannot neglect this fact.

1. Economic Analysis of Law as a Translation Strategy

Economics of law is most often associated with the so-called "Chicago school" of law and economics (Mercuro and Medema 1997: 3–24). According to R. Posner, the popularity of this approach results from two factors: the crisis of traditional legal doctrine, and the success of the economics of non-market behaviour (Posner 2001: 31–46). The starting point for economic analysis of law is the assumption that decisions may be based either on intuition and vague moral beliefs or on scientific data. If economics is just a theory of choice, it should *prima facie* be an excellent data provider for judges and legislators. Thus the rationale of the economic analysis of law is rather simple: to implement economics to legal decision-making process (Posner 1992: 10; Cooter and Ulen 1997: 41). The Chicago school implemented welfare economics with its theory of self-interest, price, and efficiency. The three major assumptions of this movement may be summarized in three parts. First, individuals act according to the theory of rational choice, which was presented by J. von Neumann and O. Morgenstern in the book of 1944 *Theory of Games and Rational Behaviour*.[3] The notion of rationality of players means that both of actors aim at maximization of their functions of utility. Moreover, the concept of rationality is based on the theory of revealed preferences based on subjective theory of values. Hence, moral norms are limited to hypothetical imperatives and should be linked to the actions of a player aimed at maximalization of satisfaction. Therefore, the notion of rationality is a purely instrumental concept. It is connected to effective realization of aims rather than to autonomous choice of those aims.

According to this theory, a given subject has permanent (invariable), ordered, and non-transferrable preferences in regards to all possible states of things or actions (Becker 1976). Such a subject may be termed *homo oeconomicus*. This notion is not connected to behaviour of particular individuals but rather is used as a convenient tool for predicting future actions. Therefore, the concept of *homo oeconomicus* is predicative rather than descriptive. The only criteria of rationality used within this notion are connected to the existence of a limited coherence of preferences. Nevertheless, the process of their formation is basically outside the scope of research of law and economics. According to R. Posner, the concept of *homo oeconomicus*

2 As suggested by Deakin (1999: 31).
3 The detailed analysis of the notions of rationality and utility within the theory of Neumann-Morgenstern may be found in Załuski (2006: 42–71).

should not serve as a basis for explaining the mechanism of decision-making process, hence it is not a psychological theory but rather a model for predicting decisions which are to be made in the future. The primary aim of this notion is to introduce some order in existing relations rather than to describe or to explain them.

The second assumption of the Chicago school is connected to the choice of a proper criterion for evaluation of actions aimed at creation and application of law. This criterion for the proper critique of norms should be economic efficiency. According to Posner (1990), the only useful criterion of allocative efficiency is the so-called 'Kaldor-Hicks efficiency' (Posner 1990: 374–387).

Third, in economics of law it is assumed that individuals react in the same way in market and extra market environments. Hence, sanctions that accompany legal norms are treated as a kind of cost that must be suffered in case of disobeying an obligation stemming from those norms. One may conclude that sanctions are treated in an analogous way to prices. The information contained in a legal norm is thus transformed by individuals in order to enable them to calculate rationally the possible costs and benefits connected to their prospective intentions or engagement in particular actions. The resulting preferences are stemming from the process of observation of the choices made by individuals.[4]

The three above-presented assumptions are mutually connected. Therefore, acceptance of the theory of rational choice – commonly used within neoclassical economics – implies the acceptance of a particular theory of instrumental rationality and specific conditions for this type of rationality to occur. Those conditions may be divided into two broad categories: external and internal.

External conditions are connected with the necessary information for various alternative actions. Assuming that subjects of law tend to maximize their satisfaction (maximization of the utility function), one may state that for a rational choice to be made, it is necessary to evaluate various options and put them into order from the most to least preferred. Within the context of law, such information, which enables one to make rational instrumental choices, is the category of sanction measured in regard to utility function or measured in monetary units as a cost in economic terms.

The internal condition may be described as an ability of acting subjects for the exact measurement of costs and losses, as well as ability for initializing actions which are effective from Kaldor-Hicks criterion, i.e., which benefits are more significant than costs. One may ask about the method for making rational decisions that maximize satisfaction, without the full access to information on the possible costs and benefits? According to Posner, rational action may be performed, and in reality most often is performed, within a state of uncertainty and ignorance, as the cost of access to full and excessive information is too high and, hence, ineffective.

The above assumption seems to be a paradox. The rational action should not be subordinated to the principle of knowledge, which is used as a basis for evaluating the consequences of actions, but rather should be performed according to the effectiveness criterion, within the cost-benefit analysis. This paradox is not real when one assumes that the principle of effectiveness (wealth maximization) is a normative principle. Hence, according to R. Posner, it is possible to accept the epistemic limits of a subject without abandoning the theory of economic rationality. The latter is only subject to certain modifications. Posner observes accordingly:

4 This assumption was later confirmed by the broadly accepted (within contemporary economics) theory of revealed preferences, first presented by Samuelson (1938; 1948). Nevertheless, the theory has met with the criticism of some scholars (Sen 1971).

> *(. . .) People are not omniscient, but incompletely informed decisions are rational when the cost of acquiring more information exceed the likely benefits in being able to make a better decision. A fully informed decision in such circumstances – the sort of thing a person makes who cannot prioritize his tasks – would be irrational. (Posner 1992: 19)*

The theory of rational choice does not aim at a precise description of the method of decision-making. R. Posner uses similar methodological assumptions as M. Friedman, according to whom the theory of rational choice serves as a convenient tool for predicting various actions or processes (Friedman 1994: 14). Thus, the theory is to serve prescriptive purposes rather than descriptive ones.

Whereas the programme of the Chicago school has been the fundament for further development of various detailed theories on law and economic efficiency, as well as the analysis of legal norms with the use of economic criteria like Kaldor-Hicks and wealth maximization, the legitimacy of law and economics scholarship is no longer based on its utilitarian origins. Moreover the majority of ideological and moral propositions could possibly be at the same time attacked and defended on the level of law and economics as it in fact happens. The most characteristic feature of this kind of discourse is heavily dependent on the linguistics constraints commonly accepted among law and economics scholars. My main thesis thus pertains to the distinctive features of the law and economics models as compared to typical jurisprudential narratives. The key distinction in this respect is the difference between the narrative and the model. The narrative is supposed to be overwhelming and thus satisfies the need for the ultimate answer to the given set of questions such as those about the nature of law, the essence of rights, and the character of justice, whereas from the perspective of the law and economics discourse, those questions are largely senseless; i.e., they cannot be addressed and answered according to the adopted verification procedure. Conversely, the model is supposed to contain the direct representation of the given aspect of the object. This representation of the modelled object must be univocal.

Additionally, the model-based discourse of law and economics will also be analyzed within the light of the distinction between three different types of discourses as proposed by Deleuze (1994). The French philosopher distinguished between three essentially different types of discourses, namely the philosophical discourse, the scientific discourse and the discourse of arts. The analysis of the legal discourse specifically pertains to the difference between philosophical and scientific discourses. The first one concentrates on concepts. Deleuze envisaged that the essence of philosophical discourse is always intimately related with the possibility of producing new concepts. Philosophical thinking is thus concept-oriented. This way of constructing discursive structures within the realm of philosophy (including legal philosophy) is substantially different from the scientific discourse. Science is function-oriented. Philosophy produces concepts and analyzes the relations between those concepts. Science does not concentrate on concepts. Different concepts could be applied, advanced and then immediately renounced depending on their utility, robustness, or explanatory power. Scientific discourse is thus not only function-oriented but also pragmatic.

The distinction between philosophy and science as established and explained by Deleuze can quite successfully be applied to the explanation between the traditional narration-based legal theory and the model-based law and economics. The former is built upon philosophical concepts as created by some philosophical systems and later on transformed into narrations. The later seems to be rather functional and purpose oriented. The question remains however about the relationship between the two. It is obvious that the philosophical concept-oriented discourse instructs different approaches and models within the law and economics mainstream. Thus some indirect interdependence between traditional jurisprudence and economic jurisprudence is undeniable. Moreover it seems that economic models borrow from traditional legal vocabulary. It is however not clear to what extent the content or substance of those philosophical-narration involved concepts, such as "distributional justice", "equity", "rights", "liberties", "entitlements", "fairness", etc., influence the outcome of the modeling procedure, accepted in law and economics. The prima facie observation is that those concepts at least to some extent shape the formulation of the basic assumptions accepted within a given model. Economic modeling is always "assumption sensitive". One may ask whether the basic assumptions of the economic analysis of law, like the economic rationality or efficiency, should be subject to critical examination stemming from postmodernist thought. It may be stated that the overall perception of the economic analysis of law places this theory within the typical modernist, rational, and utilitarian conceptions of law (Schlag 1989).

At the moment economic analysis of law might be regarded as one among equal trends of the contemporary jurisprudence.[5] The movement found strong opposition from many authors (Fried 1977: 180; Coleman 1980: 531; Weinrib 1995: 46–50). One of the strongest critics is Ronald Dworkin, who opposes the recognition of wealth as a basic value within society and the dependence of other values and allocation of rights upon wealth maximization (1998: 276–280). Dworkin points out that the initial allocation of rights cannot be instrumental, i.e., based on efficiency principle because the argument is deteriorated by its circularity (Dworkin 1980: 191–95). The other critics, such as Leff, debunked the pretended empirical and scientific character of Posner's analysis. According to Leff (1974: 457), there is nothing scientific in this approach, which turns out to be a purely normative and perfectly unverifiable project. The crucial issue, however, seems to be the scepticism among economists or economically oriented lawyers (Klevorick 1975: 237–243). Coase, in his polemics with Posner, refuted not only his economic imperialism, but rather the whole methodology attached to welfare economics.[6] For Coase, economics of law was to overcome narrow and artificial approach of the welfare economics, especially concentrated on the price theory and equilibrium model. He directly opposed the expansion of principles of traditional economy to non-market sectors.[7]

Another problem with economic analysis of law is firmly related to the notion of efficiency. For the Chicago school, the idea of efficiency is central and indisputable (Posner 1986: 12–13). According to Kaldor-Hicks criterion, the notion of efficiency is perceived as a static factor, whereas other concepts of efficiency are not attached to allocation of resources between economic agents. Summarising, it may be stated that economic analysis of law substitutes moral and legal concepts with their central notion of justice by economic theory with its central notion of efficiency (Kaplow and Shavell 2006: 52–81). The economic imperialism is however, not only a theoretical project. It rather reflects a wider social, political and historical phenomenon: the "economisation" of social life. In the last twenty years moral and ideological debates in politics as well as wider part of social discourse have been dominated by economic argumentation. Economy plays a more and more important role within the society, due to the long historical process of the collapse of traditional moral and political thinking, technical progress, civilization changes, globalization process and the bankruptcy of the centrally planned economies (Fukuyama 1989: 8). Social sciences, legal theory, and moral philosophy admit the omnipotence of economic relations within the contemporary society. In democratic and liberal pluralistic societies the only linkage among individuals seems to be economic exchange (Hayek 1976: 114). The contemporary society is no longer based on moral consensus but on free market and liberal democracy being values themselves (Morton 1998:16–18). In these circumstances, it is not surprising that traditional legal doctrine can hardly explain

5 Kronman (1993: 226) describes it as: 'the most powerful current in American teaching today. [It] now completely dominates some fields and is a significant presence in others'.
6 Coase-Posner debate (Posner 1993b: 200–209; Coase 1993b: 96–98).
7 Coase (1988: 3–5). His approach is influenced by A. Smith and J.R. Commons.

judicial decisions, and those modern theories explain little about the contemporary legal order in which a large part of regulations is based on economic reasoning (Deakin 1997: 288).[8] At the same time, modern economics of nonmarket behaviour is based on philosophical assumptions regarding human nature, ethics and political philosophy. These assumptions and other axioms of economic theory, especially its abstract character and repugnance of realism, are too rigid and narrow when applied to such complex social reality as law (Bell 1981). The processes of formalism and axiomatization of economics was purported principally by Marshall, who believed that economics had to limit its scope to processes that had a price measurement. According to this approach, the economic laws are simple generalizations about human behaviour measured in terms of money (Bell 1981: 56). Thus economics has been definitively founded on models based on axioms abstracting from the real world. Such models embrace the set of ideas such as the notion of equilibrium as stated by Marshall or the concept of the system of markets and general equilibrium endorsed by Walras. This evolution in one word lead from economics regarded as political economy studying historical society as it was understood by A. Smith, to formalized abstract study of interrelated variables applicable to any system of production or exchange, and after Becker's discovery of the economics of nonmarket behaviour, even to any social relations (Becker 1976). As a result the vast number of economic analysis remains a normative project derived from the translation strategy rather than a positive description or explanation.[9]

2. Decoding Strategy and Possibility of Law and Economics as an Interdisciplinary Project

In order to explain legal phenomena, a richer ontology and a broader scientific perspective enabling decoding legal concepts, rather than simply translating than into economic terms, seems to be required. Therefore, a new methodological approach is necessary in order to introduce a truly interdisciplinary research based on the assumption about the relative autonomy of legal discourse even if remaining strictly connected with economic context. It seems that the relations between law and the institutional context could have been successfully explained within a framework of the wider theory of society, referring both to legal and economic aspects. This could be achieved by different versions of system theory and institutional approaches. The system theory may be traced back to Talcot Parsons and his *structural-functionalism* (Parsons 1967). The paradigm shift from translation to decoding is however associated with the *functionalist-structuralism* and the theory of law as *autopoiesis* endorsed by Niklas Luhman (1985).[10] According to his theory law is characterized as operationally closed self-referential and self-replicating *autopoietic* social subsystem. Law may also be defined as congruently generalized normative behavioural expectation. Thus, for Luhman, the use of force in the form of physical enforcement has no separate meaning as it gives only necessary feedback spreading information about fulfilled expectations. The system theory of law does not refer exclusively to legal system. Social communication is common for all subsystems as a kind of inter-systemic interface. Law is 'the product of an emergent reality, the inner dynamics of legal communications' (Luhman 1985: 283). Law emerges in

8 According to Deakin (1997: 284), such a conception is Weinrib's concept of private law based on Kantian idea of right and Aristotelian concept of commutative justice (Weinrib 1995: 75–83).
9 Lawson (1997: 113–26) points out Carl Menger as the author of this approach.
10 This shift, and a radical novelty of Luhman's scientific project, have been recognized by some legal philosophers such as Bűllesbach (Kaufman et al. 1994: 381–393).

course of the communication process, which is not linear but circular. The same is to be said about economy, which is also a closed system. According to Teubner, law encodes information regarding *legality/illegality*, whereas economy concerns information about *payment/non-payment*. Both systems are totally autonomous, but intellectually some influence is possible while decoding and translating information (Teubner 1993: 92). The example of such process of translation of the legal information into economic language is sanction. Legal sanction is translated by economic environment as a mere cost or price. If such rationale is put into the circulation within legal system of communication some kind of "economisation" of legal system takes place. Teubner (1993: 57) mentions 'hand formula' and 'doctrine of efficient breach' as examples of this process. It does not mean that law depends on economics or vice versa. Both systems are operationally closed, and the possible interaction is possible only due to the process of communication and spread of information within the system of social communication (Teubner 1993: 88). At the same time law and economics evolve and the process of evolution is in fact a kind of co-evolution of the whole social system. Teubner criticized both Hayek's and Posner's theory of legal evolution. He refers to the fact that Hayek's theory of spontaneous order:

> *leads to a grotesque overvaluation of traditional customary law and similar "spontaneously" formed orders and to a devaluation of political law making as "constructivist". In the case of Posner's theorem, it leads to a systematic failure to note the capacity of the legal system to select economic input. If we are to find a way out of the impasse, we must adopt models of the co-evolution of economic and legal processes. (Teubner 1993: 57)*

On the other hand, Teubner observes that legal evolution is based on circularity. Circularity may seem inadmissible way of scientific explanation, but law is paradoxical so that the only way to deal with this problem is 'to shift the paradox from the world of thinking about law into the social reality of law' (1993: 8).

Thus law seems to be a kind of hyper-cycle defined by legal procedure, the notion of legal act, legal norm and legal doctrine, but perhaps the most important observation is that '[l]egal norms are thus defined by reference to legal acts; that is legal components are produced by legal components (Teubner 1993: 41).

The process of co-evolution of law and economics requires new regulatory attitude; instead of traditional "command-and-control" approach, law should adopt "option policy". Such regulation influences upon economic systems in very complex and more appropriate ways because it is based on the observation that

> *[L]egal acts 'stand up' to autopoiesis of both systems. Therein lays their regulatory success. (Teubner 1993: 80)*

Such regulatory success would be possible if only legal regulation respected the autonomy of economic system translating legal command into the language adequate to its institutional environment.

To summarize, it should be admitted that the social systems theory provides an interdisciplinary insight into law-economy relations. Subsystems are autonomous but at the same time the process of translation between them occurs. Why is it possible? The crucial issue seems to be the idea of law regarded as a process of communication. The enforcement of law is perceived as closed to reality. For Luhman, physical power and its use are the ultimate foundations of pre-modern law (Luhman 1985: 88). Due to the evolution, decision-making process has become proceduralized; dispersed legal information sufficient to enhance legal conformity does no longer need sanction. The last thread with reality has thus been broken. The circularity and *autopoiesis* is a next step on the road to the cognitive perspective on law. The social system is substantialized—it is a real ontological being (Kaufmann 1994: 19). The rest is just an element of the system.

To some extent the social systems theory remains an antithesis of Hayek's theory of *catalaxy*. The borders between private and public law does no longer exist. The process of fragmentation of private law and decomposition of the historical idea of justice is thus finally approved (Tamanaha 1997: 112–114; Weinrib 1995: 215).

The translation strategy and the decoding strategy applied in law and economics seem to contradict each other. This contradiction may be explained within the historical perspective. The problem is in reality closely connected with the controversy on historical justice in private law (Simmonds 1984: 25). The notion of historical justice is often derived from Aristotelian theory of justice. In my opinion there is no possibility of finding solid bases for interdisciplinary project combining law and economics without explaining the path-dependant co-evolution of both disciplines. One general remark may be added: both economists and lawyers trace back very often to Aristotelian tradition. Polanyi (1968: 81) called Aristotle the founder of economics, whereas Weinrib has even suggested that Aristotle, at least to some extent, invented the very idea of private law and analyzed the interconnection between legal form and economic content (Weinrib 1995: 56). Even if this opinion seems exaggerated, the fifth book of *Nicomachean Ethics* contains a detailed explanation of the concept of justice, which in fact seems to be an interdisciplinary reflection on both: economic exchange and the basis of legal relations and obligations. In this context, it may be stated that the fundamental difference between utility-value and exchange-value was itself discovered by Aristotle, who for the first time successfully applied the decoding strategy.[11] He referred commutative justice to what is now called market exchange. Accordingly, the price and exchange-value are usually defined by market forces. Only in case of collapse of voluntary exchange the judge determines the price. He represents not only state but a kind of justice no longer based on commutative but rather on distributive justice (Lewis 1978: 83; Meikle 1979: 163–169).

As Polanyi had pointed out, according to Aristotelian tradition there were three levels of social interaction: "gift", "exchange", and "threat". The "gift" operated on the level of friendship and morality, the "exchange" on the level of market transactions, and "threat" on the level of law and sanctions imposed by state. As Polanyi observed, perhaps the most dramatic process in the history of economic thought was its concentration solely on market exchange. This was not the case as far as Adam Smith and his *Lectures on Jurisprudence* or *Wealth of Nations* are concerned.[12] Such identification of all possible social interactions with market exchanges resulted with "economic imperialism". The true interdisciplinary decoding strategy should thus consider the existence of multiplicity and complexity of social relations. According to this one can differentiate among various levels of reality and different aspects of the same social relations.[13] It may be suggested that there are two basic aspects of law: First, law may be perceived as centralized information in form of cognitive resource maintaining expectation about behaviour of other agents (Hayek 1973: 101–109). Such nature of law as a cognitive resource is related to the legal norms and principles communicated in advance

11 The best exponent of the thesis is Soudek (1952).

12 In this respect, Smith continued Aristotelian tradition. Compare his notion of jurisprudence as a science on commutative and distributive justice in *Lectures on Jurisprudence* (Smith 1982: 397–401). Regarding the wider scope of Smith's analysis, not limited to the notion of 'economic man', but embracing morality, sympathy and generosity, see Sen (1995: 15).

13 Lawson (1997: 56–61), who finds the basis for social relations in 'human intentional agency', implementing the methodology he calls 'transcendental realism'.

and used as a kind of mechanism harmonising social co-operation. This is what Luhman and Teubner would call the essence of law.

Second, law is an institutionalized mechanism resolving conflicts and, as such, it seems to be regarded as a foundation of social order. The reality of enforcement is not virtual, as system theory suggests, but rather vicarious. Many legal rules are in fact self-imposing and may resemble conventions. This may happen if the certainty of "natural sanction" is an observable fact. The payoff is visible and obvious (Lewis 1969: 124). This is not the case with complex social interactions. As Cooter emphasises, the compliance with legal rules is a process composed out of self-imposing and externally enforced mechanisms (Cooter 1996: 1661–1690). The ultimate character of legal sanction gives rise to law as a unique normative system. The situation changes when the transaction encapsulated in legal form needs to be interpreted or if parties cease to co-operate out of self-interest, opportunistic behaviour or any other reason. Then the third party—namely, the arbiter—is needed in order to solve potential conflict. Thus, we shift from free market to the scope of internal relationship within institution. Such exemplary institution may be the firm—acting according to its procedure, e.g., company, but eventually it is a state as a "special type of firm" that provides with legal responses to the conflicts. Such an ultimate response is necessarily connected with court and judiciary process (Hayek 1973: 94–100).

3. Conclusion

One may suggest that the limits of the market are identical to the limits of the process of formation of exchange-value. The regular market exchange takes place without any direct intervention of legal institutions. Law is only a kind of information. But if there is a collapse within the process of exchange, if parties are unable to determine exchange-value in course of bargaining process, when the problem of interpretation of conditions of exchange or the problem of enforcement of freely made contract arises, law takes over. Thus judge is the ultimate value-determining institution. In accordance with legal rules and principles, a judge establishes new conditions and resolves the conflict between the parties. This solution is guaranteed by state enforcement.

Normative legal order operates only on the level of the legal system, which does not refer to reality in a direct way—the sanctions and "payoffs" have conventional and variable meaning (as in system theory). The artificiality of the system means that the translation strategy is based on the correspondence between the predictions and the axioms (Keynes 1921: 4; Hicks 1946: 5; Hahn 1984: 136–142). Lawson claims that the contemporary economic system is such a deductive system (1997: 91–126). According to the positivistic version embedding the translation strategy, the legal system is simply another kind of normative set of axioms and prediction creating rules.[14] The normative nature of the economic model is parallel to the notion of the legal one, but on the normative level both systems do not interfere.

The crisis of jurisprudence enabled economic analysis of law to penetrate legal practice, legal theory, and legal education. Legal theory is in crisis because the contemporary jurisprudential theories attacked by pragmatism provide very weak bases for legislation and adjudication. Economics seems more solid. However, economic theory is in a state of crisis, perhaps even deeper than jurisprudence. The model of the perfect market has been revised. Various theories of market imperfections attract attention. Economics as well as jurisprudence requires a broadened perspective, more realistic assumptions, and richer ontology. These propositions may be satisfied by an interdisciplinary approach addressing the question how law as well as

14 Such a model is also adopted by institutional theory of law as proposed by Morton (1995).

economy are possible, how they work within social reality—the reality of complex networks, patterns of exchange, and systems of communication.

Within the landscape of such a market society, we face dichotomy between free exchange on the market based on protection of property and freedom of contract and institutions with their hierarchy, power, and common purposes. What we really need is a theory on law and economics embracing both: market and institutions and explaining the interrelations between them. Such a theory would be interdisciplinary: social, legal, and economic. It would be based on the assumption that legal norms play a double role in society. On the one hand, they provide expectation about the behaviour of other agents and thus may form a kind of cognitive resources; on the other, law as an enforceable normative system protects rights and physically or conventionally enforces obligations. Meanwhile, the translation strategy adopted in law and economics scholarship leads to economization of law rather than widening the methodological perspective.

Acknowledgement

This research was supported in the framework of TÁMOP 4.2.4. A/2-11-1-2012-0001 National Excellence Program—Elaborating and operating an inland student and researcher personal support system.

Key project. The project was subsidized by the European Union, and co-financed by the European Social Fund.

References

Becker, G.S. 1957. *The Economics of Discrimination*. Chicago: University of Chicago Press.

———. 1976. *The Economic Approach to Human Behavior*. Chicago: University of Chicago Press.

Bell, D. 1981. 'Models and Reality in Economic Discourse'. In: D. Bell and I. Kristol eds. *The Crisis in Economic Theory*. New York: Basic Books Publishers, p. 46–56.

Blaug, M. 1991. *Aristotle: Pioneers in Economics*. vol. 2. London: An Elgar Reference Collection.

Coase, R.H. 1988. *The Firm, the Market and the Law*. Chicago and London: University of Chicago Press.

———. 1993a. 'Law and Economics at Chicago', *Journal of Law and Economics*, vol. 36, p. 239–259.

———. 1993b. 'Coase on Posner on Coase', *Journal of Institutional and Theoretical Economics*, vol, 149, p. 96–126.

Coleman, J. 1980. 'Efficiency, Utility, and Wealth Maximization', *Hofstra Law Review*, vol. 8, 509–518.

Cooter, R. 1982. 'Law and the Imperialism of Economics: An Introduction to the Economics Analysis of Law and a Review of the Major Books', *UCLA Law Review*, vol. 29, p. 1260–1279.

———. 1996. 'Decentralized Law for a Complex Economy: The Structural Approach to Adjudicating the New Law Merchant', *University of Pennsylvania Law Review*, vol. 144, 1643–1668.

Cooter, R. and Ulen, T. 1997. *Law and Economics*. Cambridge Massachusetts: Addison-Wesley.

Deakin, S. 1997. 'Private Law, Economic Rationality and the Regulatory State'. In: P. Birks ed. *The Classification of Obligations*. Oxford: Clarendon Press, p. 283–310.

———. 1999. 'Law *Versus* Economics? Reflections on the Normative Foundations of Economic Activity'. In: M. Richardson and G. Hadfield eds. *The Second Wave of Law and Economics.* Federation Press: Sydney, pp. 30–47.
Deleuze, G. and Guattari, F. 1994. *What is Philosophy?* London: Verso.
Demset, H. 1964. 'The Exchange and Enforcement of Property Rights', *Journal of Law and Economics*, vol. 7, p. 11.
Dworkin, R. 1977. *Taking Rights Seriously*. Cambridge Mass.: Harvard University Press.
———. 1980. 'Is Wealth a Value?', *Journal of Legal Studies*, vol. 9, p. 191.
———. 1998. *Law's Empire*. Oxford: Hart Publishing.
Freeman, M.D.A. 2001. *Lloyd's Introduction to Jurisprudence*. London: Sweet & Maxwell.
Fried, C. 1977. 'Difficulties in the Economic Analysis of Rights'. In: G. Dworkin et al. *Markets and Morals*. New York: Halsted Press, p. 175.
Friedman, M. 1994. 'The Methodology of Positive Economics'. In: *Essays in Positive Economics.* Chicago: University of Chicago Press, p. 3.
Hahn, F. 1984. *Equilibrium and Macroeconomics*. Cambridge Mass.: MIT Press.
Hart, H.L.A. 1994. *The Concept of Law*. Oxford: Oxford University Press.
Hicks, J.R. 1939. 'The Foundations of Welfare Economics', *Economic Journal*, vol. 49, p. 696.
Hovenkamp, H. 1986. 'Chicago and its Alternatives', *Duke Law Journal*, vol. 6, p. 1014.
Kaplow, L. and Shavell, S. 2006. *Fairness vs. Welfare*. Cambridge, Mass.: Harvard University Press.
Kaldor, N. 1939. 'Welfare Propositions in Economics', *Economic Journal*, vol. 49, p. 549.
Keynes, J.M. 1921. *A Treatise on Probability*. London: Macmillan.
Kornhauser, L.A. 1980. 'A Guide to the Perplexed Claims of Efficiency in the Law', *Hofstra Law Review* vol. 8, p. 591.
Kronman, A.T. 1980. 'Wealth Maximization as a Normative Principle', *Journal of Legal Studies*, vol. 9, p. 227.
Lawson, T. 1997. *Economics and Reality*. London: Routledge and Kegan Paul.
Lewis, D.K. 1969. *Convention: A Philosophical Study*. Cambridge, Mass.: Harvard University Press.
Luhmann, N. 1985. *A Sociological Theory of Law*. London: Routledge and Kegan Paul.
Malloy, R.P. 2000. *Law and Market Economy: Reinterpreting the Values of Law and Economics.* Cambridge: Cambridge University Press.
Mäki, U. 1998. 'Is Coase a Realist?', *Philosophy of the Social Sciences*, vol. 28, p. 5.
Meikle, S. 1979. 'Aristotle and Exchange Value'. In: F.D. Miller and D. Keyt eds. *A Companion to Aristotle's "Politics"*. Cambridge University Press: New York: 69–90.
Mercuro, N. and Medema, S.G. 1997. *Economics and the Law: From Posner to Post-Modernism.* Princeton: Princeton University Press.
Parsons, T. 1937. *The Structure of Social Action*. New York: Free Press.
Parsons, T. 1935. 'The Place of Ultimate Values in Sociological Theory', *International Journal of Ethics*, vol. 45, p. 282.
Polanyi, K. 1944. *The Great Transformation*. New York: Rinehart.
———. 1968. 'Aristotle Discovers the Economy'. In: G. Dalton ed. *Primitive, Archaic and Modern Economies. Essays of Karl Polanyi*. New York: Anchor Books.
Posner, R.A. 1975. 'The Economic Approach to Law', *Texas Law Review*, vol. 53, p. 205.
———. 1980. 'The Ethical and Political Basis of the Efficiency Norm in Common Law Adjudication', *Hofstra Law Review*, vol. 8, p. 487.
———. 1983. *The Economics of Justice*. Cambridge, Mass.: Harvard University Press.
———. 1987. 'The Decline of Law as an Autonomous Discipline: 1962–1987', *Harvard Law Review*, vol. 100, p. 761.
———. 1990. *The Problems of Jurisprudence*. Cambridge, Mass.: Harvard University Press.
———. 1992. *Economic Analysis of Law*. New York: Little Brown and Co.

———. 1993a. 'The New Institutional Economics Meets Law and Economics', *Journal of Institutional and Theoretical Economics*, vol. 149, p. 73.
———. 1993b. 'Ronald Coase and Methodology', *Journal of Economic Perspectives*, vol. 7, p. 195.
———. 2001. *Frontiers of Legal Theory*. Cambridge, Mass.: Harvard University Press.
Samuelson, P.A. 1938. 'A Note on the Pure Theory of Consumer's Behaviour', *Economica*, vol. 5, p. 61.
———. 1948. 'Consumption Theory in Terms of Revealed Preference', *Economica*, vol. 1, p. 243.
Sen, A.K. 1971. 'Choice Functions and Revealed Preference', *Review of Economic Studies*, vol. 38, p. 307.
Schlag, P. 1989. 'The Problem of Transaction Costs', *Southern California Law Review*, vol. 62, p. 1661.
Simmonds, N.E. 1984. *The Decline of Juridical Reason: Doctrine and Theory in the Legal Order*. Manchester University Press.
Smith, A. 1982. *Lectures on Jurisprudence*. R.L. Meek et al. eds. Indianapolis: Liberty Fund.
Soudek, J. 1952. 'Aristotle's Theory of Exchange: An Enquiry into the Origins of Economic Analysis', *Proceedings of the American Philosophical Society*, vol. 96, p. 45.
Tamanaha, B.Z. 1997. *Realistic Socio-Legal Theory: Pragmatism and a Social Theory of Law*. Oxford: Clarendon Press.
Teubner, G. 1993. *Law as an Autopoietic System*. Cambridge-Oxford: Blackwell.
Wittgenstein, L. 1953. *Philosophical Investigations*. Oxford: Blackwell.

Chapter 2
Cultural Transfer and Conceptualization in Legal Discourse

Anne Wagner, King Kui Sin, and Le Cheng

Henceforth, my dear philosophers, let us be on guard against the dangerous old conceptual fiction that posited a "pure, will-less, painless, timeless knowing subject" [which] demand[s] that we should think of an eye that is completely unthinkable, an eye turned in no particular direction, in which the active and interpreting forces, through which alone seeing becomes seeing something, are supposed to be lacking. . . . There is only a perspective seeing, only a perspective "knowing"; and the more affects we allow to speak about one thing, the more eyes, different eyes, we can use to observe one thing, the more complete will our "concept" of this thing, our "objectivity," be.

(Nietzsche 1967: 119)

It is neither the case that interpretation is constrained by what is obviously and unproblematically 'there', nor the case that interpreters, in the absence of such constraints, are free to read into a text whatever they like. . . . Interpreters are constrained by their tacit awareness of what is possible and not possible to do, what is and is not a reasonable thing to say, what will and will not be heard as evidence in a given enterprise, and it is within those same constraints that they see and bring others to see the shape of the documents for whose interpretation they are committed.

(Fish 1982: 555)

1. The Translabiliting Process – Towards Hybridization

While law shapes social knowledge within a specific language and culture, the importance of evaluating and finding significant frameworks in legal discourse and legal translation has become a priority. Knowledge has been organized into different disciplines over a long period of time. Transferring concepts from one language to another has become a challenge. These concepts can sometimes be fully or partially transferred from the source language to the target language. Translabiliting (Wagner and Gémar 2013: 731) is an 'act of cross-cultural communication, which implies matching cultural elements of two different languages rather than only considering the linguistic elements'. Conceptualizing knowledge in this way permits to evaluate the boundaries, the social control power from the source language and how concepts may expand into any other related knowledge from the target language. Therefore, 'cognitive exclusiveness' (Larson 1977) is a chimera. Indeed, the production of concept is itself bound up with societal consideration and law. Concepts cannot be abstracted from the social world (Gémar 1992: 377), and so their transferability into another linguistic framework is susceptible to criticism.[1] Foucault reveals the relationship between knowledge and power stating that power pervades the discourse:

> *We must cease once and for all to describe the effects of power in negative terms: it 'excludes', it 'represses', it 'censors', it 'abstracts', it 'masks', it 'conceals'. In fact power produces; it produces reality; it produces domains of objects and rituals of truth. The individual and the knowledge that may be gained of him belong to this production. (Foucault 1991: 194)*

Accordingly, creativity in law is crucial and permits the implementation of new concepts:

> *When I use a word, Humpty Dumpty said, in a rather scornful tone, 'it just means what I choose it to mean – neither more nor less'. The question is, said Alice, whether you can make words mean so many different things. (Carroll 1871)*

Translators are thus subject to stringent constraints at all levels (Gémar 1992: 376–377), and the act of transferring the source knowledge into the target knowledge is far from being such an easy task. Conceiving law as a symbol allows us to understand how that process works and how we can connect our life to the text of the law (Kevelson 1988: 4):

> *1. All communication is a process of exchange of meaningful signs, and signs and signs systems such as natural language mediate between communicating persons and those objects in the phenomenal, physical world of experience to which they refer.*
>
> *2. All human societies have developed complex systems of both verbal and nonverbal sign systems which are not static but which evolve continuously to correspond with and to represent changing social norms and the evolving, growing social consciousness of any given community.*

Likewise transferring legal knowledge is a discursive struggle where competing meanings from the Source language and the Target language are contested:

> *'The chief problem ... will always be, not the individual état de langue, but the relationship between different stages of a single language and between different languages, their similarities and their differences' (Hjelmslev 1970: 9).*

By concentrating on the discursive element rather than on the term itself, the process of translabiliting becomes easier and this interdisciplinary discipline implies 'an overlapping of segments of disciplines, a recombination of knowledge in new specialized fields' (Dogan 1997: 435), 'a hybrid discipline' (Gémar 2002: 173), leading to 'hybrid texts' (McAuliffe 2011: 99):

> *Intercultural communication gives rise to the development of new text types and genres. Particular stages of this development can be described as hybridisation. These are the stages at which the new text types and genres are not yet fully established themselves*

1 Criticism often comes from those who can't see the connection between the linguistic signs for the transferred concepts and the social world from which the concepts acquire their meaning. A case in point is the caustic criticisms of the Chinese version of Hong Kong laws prepared by way of translation in the run-up to 1997. Understandably, critics only saw the Chinese text of the law without seeing the social world from which the English common law derive its meaning. *See* Sin (1998).

as forms of communication in a sociocultural setting: they manifest linguistic and rhetorical features which are felt to be foreign.

1. Contamination of Law – A Series of Influences

The law is a symbolic construction and therefore rests on a variety of undertakings. What gives law its meaning is, for some, ideology; for others, it corresponds to the welfare of the majority. However, what is manifest is a conception of the law as a material structure that carries symbols of everyday life. The analyzes that are made in the law and semiotics movements show that the law's symbolism cannot be understood by reference only to itself, a strictly "legal" meaning. It is a symbol that conveys life, a symbol that in itself is contaminated with life, politics, morality, and so on.

1.1. Law Contaminated by Morality

In European jurisprudence, there is a concern with the relationship between the inside of the law and the outside of the law. In natural law theories, for instance, there is discussion about a distinction between law and morality. This might be viewed as an issue of sovereignty and the power to command. However, it is also a question of determining what can be placed within the law and what can be said to be the language of the law, that is, one of command and obedience (Fairclough 1989). In the natural law tradition, the law had to be read as governed by natural law with either religious values or secular values like the Universal Declaration of Human Rights. However, the relation was one in which law was part of morality, that is, law was contaminated by morality and was nothing else but morality (de Sousa Santos 1995; Unger 1977).

Positivism attempted to severe the relationship. In driving a wedge between law and morality, it took the fear of contamination to the extreme. Law, in the positivist tradition, is the command of the sovereign who has no sovereign to obey (Hart 1961). Its validity does not rest on an external measure.

The philosophical neo-Kantianism of the late nineteenth century, as well as the advent of positivism, was at the core of the development and systematization of language and law. The systematic determination of ideal speech (linguistics) and conduct (law) became the object of normative science. The studies of the time, especially those conducted by Saussure (1916: 118), showed the importance of using the prevailing philological and exegetical conceptions of language. The study of language was—and is still today—a unitarian science in which signs are elements of a code, subject to conventional regulations (Kevelson 1988).

There is a similar dualism in the advent of legal positivism. It can be found in the distinctions between legal system and judgment, legal validity and legal signifier, and norm and its practical application. These are always in conflict, the former being subjective and frequent, and the latter discretionary.

The linguistic theory of Saussure corresponds with the Kelsenian theory of the legal structure. For Kelsen (1953: 85), the grammar of law is the grammar of written text, and the formal limits of legal signifiers are the object of analysis. While Saussure wrote about *langue/parole*, Kelsen drew the distinction between *validity/legal volition*.

In summary, both studies – those of the linguist and those of the legal scholar – put an emphasis on abstract verification and on scientific description achieved with minimum normative requisites. Kelsen patently negates subjectivism, the social and the individual in favour of formalism and positivism. He explained legal science as a pure and united logic of norms.

In French scholarship, we find the works of Francois Gény (1922: 235), whose analysis of the free interpretation of the law became the basis for some analyses in the Latin American and American traditions. Gény drew the distinction between *legal science* and *legal technique,* borrowed from 'le donné' and 'le construit' of Bergson's philosophy (1930–1959). The former corresponds to natural law while the latter to positive law. Gény's work was dedicated to translating the given notion into a constructed one; that is, to the translation of this latent and spontaneous normativity which comes from society as a more formal and wisely organized normativity (positive law).

After the Second World War, with the critique of positivism in Germany, several authors proposed a different approach, in order to show the danger of preserving purity in the law. In a discussion famous in continental criminal law, Hans Welzel and Gustav Radbruch each proposed different approaches to the analysis of the law as a response to the horrors brought about by the law of the Nazi Regime (Welzel 1985; Radbruch 1986). While Welzel (1985) proposed an approach to the law from an ontological point of view, Radbruch (1986) proposed one in which universal values were taken into account within the law. To Welzel (1985), the law had to incorporate what he called the 'ontological structures'; in other words, reality had to be taken into account in the process of legislating about it. However, this approach did not say anything about the role of the law and the dangers of positivist approaches under a totalitarian regime (Muller 1901). Alternatively for Radbruch (1986), the law could not be analyzed as an autonomous structure, but should be analyzed with reference to external values. To Radbruch (1986) there was a supralegality that determine the status of the law. This supralegality was established in the values of the constitution or, in today's context, in the Universal Declaration of Human Rights.

The works on law of Robert Alexy (2002a; b) and Jurgen Habermas (1996) can be seen in this light, as an incorporation of non-legal elements in the discussion of the validity of law. Unlike Kelsen, Alexy and Habermas propose an argumentative theory of law in which the validity of law is given not only for the procedure of its production, but also for its position as a supralegal system underscoring the universal conception of human rights. However, what makes this approach different from the natural law tradition is the fact that these are not conceptual values but are incorporations of higher law in the spirit of democracy. To Alexy (2002: 127), 'the law has to incorporate the argumentative and the institutional procedure of the application of the law into a theory of the democratic constitutional state.' In his interpretation of Habermas (Alexy 2002a), he shows that the law is a case of the general practical discourse, that is, it is related to a democratic ethos and to moral practices of modern democracies (Alexy 1988: 232). Unlike natural law theories, these approaches to the law do not claim that the law is just another way of describing morality, but that the law is permeated by non-legal discourses and practices.

Other authors, like Luhmann (1985), insist in the incorporation of the outside of the law into the language of the law. Outside elements can be incorporated as long as the language and the code of the law is preserved. To Luhmann (1985), law and legal discourse cannot be permeated or confused with the outside of law. On the contrary, law is a subsystem of the social system that has its own binary code, where lawful/unlawful (recht/unrecht) under this code and everything is incorporated into the law. Law and particularly the legal system are autopoietic systems but not, as in the traditional theory of systems, closed systems. To say that the legal system is autopoietic means that the law creates and recreates itself, that its code is auto-reproductive, and that law imposes its own language whenever there is a relation with its outside (Luhmann 1985; Gimenez 1993). The outside of the law is its surrounding but once within the law it has to adopt its binary code. As is clear, this particular approach to the law is the result of the modern understanding of the state and society and, as Wallerstein (1999) would say, is the result of taking the nation-state as the unit of analysis.

1.2. Law as a Social Phenomenon

In the American tradition, perhaps the most important analysis of the law is that of the Realists. The works of Benjamin Cardozo and Oliver Holmes are seminal in the conception of the law as politics. Cardozo, whose work was based on the ideas of Francois Gény (1922), proposed that law is not the result of the written word in the statute but the result of real life. The law has to be interpreted in relation to everyday life, to capture its contamination by morality and politics.

This approach has been followed in the American tradition by critiques of the law like the Critical Legal Studies Movement, the Constitutive Approach, and the Legal Consciousness Studies. What makes these studies interesting for us is their understanding of the law as embedded in real life, as being something other than structure. But unlike the European tradition, this kind of analysis conceived of the law as being contaminated from outside and as being something else (politics, etc.). The European tradition, on the other hand, saw the outside of the law as a part of the law with proper codification.

The persistent conception of a legal order that is unified and definite excluded historical and sociological considerations. Law is a social phenomenon, and in order to be recognized by society, the statutes have to be intelligible and easy to understand (Hart 1953: 116). Hart's main preoccupation (1963) was the opacity of legal language, due to his idea that law is a system of rules, interconnected lexically and only able to be understood by legal experts. Only the system is capable of interpreting the system.

Hart's philosophy of language (1953) is based on a conventional view of the referent: this referent works as a function of the emitter's intent, and one affirmation is valid only when taken into consideration with the external world. The meaning of words depends, not only on the communication being transmitted, but also on the act and intent of the speaker (1961). This idea is in complete contradiction to the traditional idea *per genus et differentiam*. When Hart (1961) considers the problems of interpretation, he remains in between formalism (core of settled meaning) and realism (the penumbra of uncertainty).

Hart (1961) was criticized because he adopted a theory of an ingenuous language where the signifier is a fixed entity with a central and peripheral clarity, independent from the context and from the use of concepts. However, in contradictory terms, Hart (1961) also proposed a theory of legal pragmatics where the signifier is purely conventional. Indeed, the existence of '*core of settled meaning*' is based on the functioning of the legal system. This simply means that language does not have inherent qualities. Instead, its semantic characteristic is modified according to one's perception of it. The rules and its content are clear but the contingent effect of its use is not so visible. Indeed, the penumbra reflects the indeterminate feature of the object. Moreover, from time to time and from one case to another, the idea of the meaning of some terms as being 'settled' is questionable.

According to McCormick, the structure of legal language is formed by legal institutions, which are governed by overarching rules. These are divided into three types of rules: institutive (the ones which create the institution); consequential (the consequences in law of the existence of such an institution); and terminative (those which lead to the disappearance of such institutions) rules. The legal system thus represented closely resembles the syntagmatic level described by Greimas (1967), where the legal subjects evolve within a vital history represented by legal states (or consequential rules) and its transformations (or institutive and terminative rules). Such transformations are finalized by means of acts, and the person who carries them to an end is given qualification and obtains competence from them. This schema, in turn, parallels Hart's rules of recognition: the institutive and terminative rules recognized the examples of these institutions as legal in the processes known by Greimas as *vérification*. McCormick's point is without any doubt positivist, because it is based on the legal validity under which authority can be established. McCormick, however, explains that public and private institutions have the same structure with distinct contents, a matter, which Hart did not address.

But one of the questions that remain in this discussion about the law is: 'why do people obey the law?' (Tyler 2006). To positivists, the law is obeyed because it is the law and the command of the sovereign. To those from a Marxist tradition, the law is obeyed because, as a form of ideology, people are cheated into obedience (Stone 1985; Spitzer 1983: 103). Under the concept of hegemony, some scholars have found that the law is obeyed because people see in the law a source of legitimacy for the state and is seen as an instrument to convey the claims of the oppressed.

2. Legal Discourse Across Disciplines

Legal norms are expressed in words. Words must be capable of expressing law in a clear and understandable manner using different disciplines. Combining generalization and precision is one of the most serious challenges in law. Law refers to the diversity of former and actual social and professional practices. Words should be used to guide lay people as well as professionals with a sufficient degree of clarity. The language of the law has the capacity of creating, innovating, and distilling new ideas into a word. This capacity of distilling new meanings into former words and/or of creating new ones is crucial. The practical usefulness in the creation and application of law address the fundamental role of language in law and in the society. Law is embodied in language and thus language is the instrument and foundation of law.

Legal language is in constant interaction with general language usage. Influences are mutual. Law serves as one of the essential references for the explanation of words. Law is the result of creativity and has at its foundation human skills that have developed in the course of history. Likewise, it reflects and consolidates as well as forms and transforms—directly and indirectly—value perceptions that exist in the society and are historically changing (Gény 1922; Wagner 2005). Yet, scholarship has acknowledged that constructing the meaning of legal language is not alone subject to many societal mutations as legal language itself can be slippery, fluid, and highly unpredictable (Solan 1993; Nerhot 1993; Tiersma 2000).

2.1. Legal Language – A Language of Class

The language of the law should be understood by anybody, from a specialist to a lay man,[2] and avoid what Francis Bacon (in Mellinkoff 1963: 140) explained in his statement: 'The peculiar language of our law [. . .] a language wherein a man shall not be enticed to hunt after words, but matter.'

2 This is the natural conclusion from the fundamental presumption of law in the West that every person knows the law. Hence the legal principle, 'Ignorance of the law is no excuse'. This in turn presupposes that the law is intelligible to every person; in other words, the law is written in a language comprehensible to every person, lay people and legal professionals alike. For a detailed discussion of the issues relating to this principle, see Morrison (1989).

Indeed, the plural reality, which forms part of the silent dimension of the legal language, can be better understood with Sherry's (1996: 134) reflection: 'The globalization of culture means that we all live in 'translated' worlds, that the spaces of knowledge we inhabit assemble ideas and styles of multiple origins, as transnational communications and frequent migrations make every culture site a crossroads and a meeting place.'

Consequently, the explicit linguistics (Goodrich 1990: 115) or linguistics of practice (Vogel 1997) is a meeting place (Mounin 1963: 3), a place of interference (Weinrich 1953: 33) and a mode of cultural production (Wagner 1999): It is ' 'a transnational culture' as part of the processes by which 'newness enters the world' ' (Bhabha 1994: 212).

Likewise, legal language is considered a mere technicality, which is quite similar to a language of class.[3] Indeed the legal technician uses terms, which ideally fit into the context he studies and draws a distinction between their different interpretations. He adds a procedure and/or a gradation with the terms he uses. He refers to a language for specific purposes in which behind each technical noun, a legal concept, a procedure, a (several) legislative or jurisprudential reference(s) can be found.

As Hungerford-Welch (1999: 123–124) explained, 'words are very important to lawyers: they are the tools of our trade'. Consequently, guides have been written in order to express himself/herself or write with technical precision and accuracy (Conley 1998; Greene 1991). But does this mean that the legal discourse becomes more accessible to intelligent lay people? They simply provide a potential framework with which experienced people and law students have to comply in order to use the same standards in pleading and/or writing legal documents.

Given the causative link between law and technicality, we can talk about a language of class where lawyers and judges not only hunt after words but also after matter. From the lawyers' viewpoints, such a terminology justifiably 'increases the expense of lawyers who have to explain it to clients' (Harrison 1999: 1491). Thus, this specific language uses specified meanings, which mainly affects legal writing and clearly shows 'jargon of the worst sort' (Harrison 1999: 1491).

2.2. Textual Culture of Law

Sir Francis Bacon explained the multi-cultural origins of these *Laws of England* through an analysis of the deep and complex English historical elaboration:

> *It is true, they are mixt as our language, compounded of British, Roman, Saxon, Danish, Norman Customs. And as our language is so much the richer, so the laws are the more complete. (Mellinkoff 1963: 158)*

This quotation shows how close the link is between the development of English law and the various conquests on the English territory. Indeed within the English legal discourse, there remain visible vestiges of this past. The study of the historical circumstances therefore demonstrates how the discourse has evolved and enhanced itself over the centuries:

3 It must be noted here that the technicality of legal language does not and should not turn the law into a discipline, like physics or medicine, comprehensible only to experts. As noted above, the language of the law should be understood by every person. Thus, the technical meaning of "promise" in law, for example, renders "promise" incomprehensible to lay people who understand what "promise" means in ordinary language. For a detailed discussion of whether legal language is a technical language, see Morrison (1989).

> *Scandinavian words were borrowed most freely between the ninth century and the twelfth, French words during the twelfth, thirteenth, and fourteenth centuries, but Latin words have been making their way into English, throughout almost the whole period of its history. (Serjeantson 1968: 9)*

Moreover, when contemplating the legal circumstances of legal discourse development, Goodrich's reflection (1990: 115) seems elemental:

> *To know the law is not to know the words of the law, but the force and property of the words. The textual culture of law, indeed, brings with it an explicit linguistics, a linguistics of fidelity to sources, to originals, to supposed first usages and all that those usages implied.*

Consequently, a faithful analysis needs to be carried out by the discerning reader in order to fully understand the specific backgrounds of words within a specified context. This fragility in comprehension is all the more critical when people are confronted with cultural, legal or historical dimensions which they have not really fully mastered. So we need to invest in terminology, 'for it is worthwhile if it is validated and informed homogeneously' (Lebreton 1994: 87).

The language of the law is and always will be evolving in accordance with politics, social behaviours and historical circumstances. That is why we can say that each period of time contributed and continues to contribute to the construction of English legal architecture, leading to semantic variances. Owing to Peter Tiersma (1999: 1):

> *Our law is a law of words. Although there are several major sources of law in the Anglo-American tradition, all consist of words. Morality or custom may be embedded in human behavior, but law, virtually by definition, comes into being through language. Thus, the legal profession focuses intensely on the words that constitute the law, whether in the form of statutes, regulations or judicial opinions.*

The more complex the culture, the more important the institutional body, and the more complex the language used to codify it. As previously mentioned, the features of the language of the law derive not only from the legal institution itself but also from history, from social functions, actors, goals of the law and eventually linguistic usage. If law has to be simultaneously fixed and flexible (Wagner 2002), several communicational and institutional strategies are necessary in order to organise the linguistic means to enhance its understanding within the sociolinguistic community.

2.3. Hidden Dimension

Legal words have a peculiar tenacity with an ability to achieve stability within changing social and economic conditions (Gény 1922: 42). However, the illusion is of conservatism, rigidity, and uniformity for the social structure penetrates into the architecture of the English language of the law (Carbonnier 1978). This is the reason why every past and present society has had its own knowledge of words, and many have created or influenced words in order to reflect their particular standards and expectations (Hobbes 1971: 35). The French lawyer Gény (1922: 149) considers that law has its own "living reality" which is highly dependent upon a context.

Consequently, the English legal discourse reveals a complex network of interactions between the individual and his environment. Furthermore, there comes a linguistic insecurity as soon as someone is analyzing a former cultural notion. So, the legal discourse has to be construed within a specific period of time. The interpreter is then confronted with a web closely woven around production (Schauer 1992: 500–501; Aitchison 1991: 89–101), which Eco (1976: 86) describes as a multi-levelled maze, representing any legal situation. Historical knowledge can be gained only by seeing the past in its continuity with the present—which is exactly what the jurist does in his practical, normative work of 'ensuring the unbroken continuance of law and preserving the tradition of the legal idea' (Gadamer 1989: 327). Wittgenstein (1968: §129) reminds us:

> *The aspects of things that are most important for us are hidden because of their simplicity and familiarity. (One is unable to notice something -- because it is always before one's eyes.) The real foundations of his inquiry do not strike a man at all. Unless that fact has at some time struck him. -- And this means: we fail to be struck by what, once seen, is most striking and most powerful.*

The legal language is, then, a complex and interesting melting pot of intrinsic and extrinsic influences, coming from cultural practices evolving within space-time and stamped with modernity. Wherever one turns, individuals have maintained a written and hidden proof of this inheritance. It is only possible to decipher the language through an analysis of the historical and the silent dimensions. Indeed, Hall (1984: 35) has introduced the concept of silent language:

> *Culture acts directly and profoundly upon behaviours, and the mechanisms, which link them, are often untold and located far beyond the voluntary control of an individual.*

Given this criterion, lay individuals are in a state of perplexity because the language of the law has developed without taking into account everybody's personal background. And so, there is a clear-cut knock-on effect between non-practicing people and practitioners.

Let us examine the concept of *dwelling house* in various Acts. We can notice a shift in its definition. In compliance with the *Burial Act 1854, s.9* a vault 'means the building, so that the hundred yards therein mentioned have to be measured from the walls of the dwelling-house itself'; under the *Public Health Act 1936, s.43* a dwelling-house could 'either be private or not'; under the *Housing Act 1957, s.189* 'it includes any yard, garden, outhouses and appurtenances'; under the *Rent Act 1968, s.1* 'a dwelling-house means a house let as a separate dwelling or a part of a house being a part so let'.

Complainant is another example illustrating this trend. Indeed, under the *Sexual Offences (Amendment) Act 1976, s.3* it means 'a woman upon whom, in a charge for a rape offence to which the trial in question relates, it is alleged that rape was committed, attempted or proposed'. In other fields it simply means 'one who makes a complaint to the justices' (Burke 1977).

Even the simplest common word—*night*—can lead to semantic variances in legal documents and misunderstandings from a layperson's viewpoint. Under the *Night Poaching Act 1828, s.12* it is stated that 'the night shall be considered and is hereby declared to commence at the expiration of the first hour of sunset, and to conclude at the beginning of the last hour before sunrise'; under the *Customs and Excise Management Act 1979, s.1* 'night means the period between 11 p.m. and 5 a.m.'; under the *Highways Act 1980, s.329 (1)* it 'means the time between half an hour after sunset and half an hour before sunrise'.

Legal language roots meanings of words in relative stability—in a legal text. It strives for precision in language usage and in the context of the general polysemy of words it performs the tasks of explaining meanings of words. Although in law, the explanation of words is also part of the legal regulation that is endowed with the same legal force as any other part in the specific legal text, the binding character of language in law is nonetheless still indirect in the sense that its usage is not a general requirement for human communication in daily life. It becomes binding in situations that should be resolved in legal terms when it is applied as an instrument to specific reality.

> *Words have the meanings they have in a language because of their relations to other words, because of their contrasts and affinities, and because of the dense historical and social vocabulary they help to constitute and to which they belong. But they also have the meanings they have because of their relations to contexts of possible action and social practice. At the same time, the meaning of these actions and practices themselves depend upon the availability of a certain vocabulary of concepts and ideas. (Warnke 1992: 17)*

Likewise, if we consider the European perspective, legal communication is even more complex and needs to find out equivalences in meaning. Monjean-Decaudin (2010: 700) refers to the inevitable 'équivalence uniformisante' in the EU Legal order. MacAuliffe (2009: 107) points out that

> *EU law is a legal system built from approximations of law and language from different legal cultures and different legal languages, which come together to form a new supranational legal system with its own language.*

Legal language is a specific legal genre and its peculiarities include force, sanctions and status. Legal language is a prominent testimony of legal history, a source of the study of the society and culture which, alongside the message about a legal order that has existed or exists, includes indications how things, phenomena, processes are designated by words, what terms have been used in the creativity of law, in the practice of applying law, and in the doctrine of law:

> *Les mots sont intelligibles seulement si l'on admet l'hypothèse d'un contexte de production de l'intention, d'une pré-décision déjà en place de la part de la personne qui est en train de parler ou d'écrire [. . .] les sens ne sont pas enfouis dans les mots mais surgissent et deviennent clairs à la lumière des conditions de fond et d'intelligibilité qui les entourent. (Fish 1989: 150)*

3. Cultural Transfer of Concepts

Law is a social phenomenon having multiple (or comprehensive) philosophical, theoretical and historical roots. Meanings in law have cultural nuances according to the systems of lifestyle, values, traditions, and collective memory that are being examined. Law conveys testimony of the past but also an ongoing social process that could be adjusted within space and time. Likewise, law reflects human values, practices, and aspirations of changes as its boundaries are flexible and in constant evolution. As expressed by Cao (2007: 23), 'law and legal language are system-bound, that is, they reflect the history, evolution and culture of a legal system'. The concepts of a particular legal system, however, are not language-dependent. That is to say, they can be transferred from one language to another when carried out within a semiotic framework that facilitates the bridging of conceptual gaps between terms in the source language and their counterparts in the target language (Sin 2002).

It therefore seems logical to make prospective translators "fit" for a wide range of technical producing activities, providing them not only with a solid text-based competence, but also with a solid societal knowledge of both the source and target languages (Gémar 1992; Wagner and Gémar 2013: 738–739).

Concepts are part of the social phenomenon as they are units of meaning that can vary in their finality. Concepts serve as instruments for thinking and communication and allow expressing human thoughts, conclusions and suppositions in the source language. Consequently, the transfer process is not easy and translators have to distill a reasonable knowledge of the source language in the target language. Sin (1998: 136–137) points out:

> *All large-scale cultural transfers begin in the absence of a readily usable language. The first, and most natural, response of the native culture is to make an attempt to naturalize the foreign culture. Where it has a close affinity to the native culture, naturalization or minor adjustment may be adequate. But where it is one of great complexity, or radically different, the native culture will find it necessary at some point to change and adjust its language so as to make it [suitable for effecting such transfer].*

Cultural transfer, migration, or translatability is a priority and legal translators will have to fill the conceptual gap in the target language:

> *Translatability aims at comprehension, whereas encounters between cultures or interactions between levels of culture involve either assimilation or appropriation by making inroads into one another, trying to get out of a different culture or the different intra-cultural levels that seem attractive, useful, or is combated and suppressed for whatever reasons. (Iser 1994: 6)*

Provided below are two examples of concepts and the way legal translators should fix the semantic source, adjust it for the target language and if necessary build metalinguistic devices to fill the conceptual gap for the target language:

> *[. . .] translators are aware of the decisive part they have always played, without leaving the shadows themselves, to enable others to overcome the barriers of language and culture by way of the translators' skills as writers. (Correia 2003: 40)*

> *When the target language and the source language relate to different legal systems, absolute equivalence is impossible. For example, can the German word Ehescheidung be translated into French with divorce or into Italian with divorzio? We know that the grounds for divorce are different in Germany, France and Italy and further, that there are essential differences regarding the nature of the marriage, which is dissolved, specifically in the field of marital property law. [. . .] There is no absolute equivalence [. . .]. (De Groot 2006: 424)*

There is no absolute equivalence but a textual adjustment. It creates a living notion (Gény 1922) where:

> *concepts are more like chess pieces. They can be maneuvered to produce certain results but the players have a choice as to the move. Similarly, lawyers and judges often have a choice as to how they will move the concepts. (Farrar and Dugdale 1990: 78)*

Marriage is one of the most anchored concepts related to culture, society, and religion. It is considered as a cultural and Christian heritage. It is part of "cultural heritage", highlighting a distinction on the criterion of the composition of a couple. The assessment of the novelty "marriage" requires the identification of the concept, a sequential analysis of its development, and the cultural experience this word has in French language.

Marriage comes from the verb *marry*, which meant, in the 12th century, 'to bind women to men, and thus guarantee that a man's children were truly his biological heirs. Through marriage, a woman became a man's property'. "Marry" derives from the Latin *maritus* (husband). From a traditional etymology, *maritus* meant "male", but Alain Rey (editor of the dictionary *Petit Robert*) traces this word back to an Indo-European root, in Sanskrit *marya* (young man in love) and from the Greek *meirax*. Besides, Benoit De Boysson (2011) indicated that the term *mariage* comes not only etymologically from *maritare* (which means "male") but also from *matrimonium*, which means, in Latin, "marriage", and comes from *mater*, the mother. Etymologically, De Boysson (2011) concludes, 'marriage is a legal form by which a woman is preparing herself to become a mother by marrying a man'. Religion became involved in the institution of marriage when at the Council of Trent in 1563, the sacramental nature of marriage was written into canon law. However, same-sex couple marriage in history is rare, but known. The Roman emperor Nero, who ruled from AD 54 to 68, twice married men in formal wedding ceremonies, and forced the Imperial Court to treat them as his wives. In second and third century in Rome, homosexual weddings became common (Yalon 2002). Romans outlawed formal homosexual unions in the AD 342. But John Boswell's (1995: 199–217) research found evidence of homosexual unions after that period, including some that were recognized by Catholic and Greek Orthodox churches.

The history of the development of French national law in the area of conceptualization of family and marriage has evolved significantly. Modern cultural evolutions introduced the concept of "Civil Partnership" both for heterosexual and same-sex couple in the middle of the 20th century. With the introduction of civil partnerships, boundaries were reconsidered in terms of family concept where significant developments were experienced to comply with Human Rights frameworks encompassing the notion of family. They focused, mostly on the individual rights of man to participate, to create their own cultural identity, and have a family irrespective of their sexual orientation insofar as it did not infringe upon human rights of other individuals; however they could not enjoy the same rights as heterosexual couples in terms of parentage and inheritance.

The most recent evolution of the concept of marriage dates from November 2012, when the French government decided to vote a bill "mariage pour tous"—marriage for everybody irrespective of their sex. This text relies on the principle of equality before the law and permits same-sex couple to marry and enjoy the same rights and duties as heterosexual couples. This bill was passed and changes were made in the French civil code to replace the words "father and mother" with "parents", and "husband and wife" with "spouses" (Art. 4 of the French civil code).

An evolution of the concept of marriage also occurred in Hong Kong, a common law jurisdiction, when the Court of Final Appeal decided in 2013 (FACV No. 4 of 2012 on appeal from CACV No. 266 of 2010) that a post-operative male-to-female transsexual person who had undergone sex reassignment surgery (SRS) at hospitals be allowed to marry her male partner. Previously, she was refused to do so by the Registrar of Marriages on the ground that she did not qualify as a "woman" under Hong Kong's marriage law which solely adopted the biological criteria for assessing the sex of a person for the purposes of marriage as 'procreative intercourse was an essential constituent of a marriage at common law' (*Corbett v. Corbett*). Three points are worth noting in the decision of the Court of Final Appeal. First, as the right to marry is protected by the *Basic Law* of Hong Kong and the *Hong Kong Bill of Rights*, it must not be taken away by any marriage law. Second, the nature of marriage has undergone drastic changes in Hong Kong, so much so that procreation is no longer regarded as an essential constituent of marriage. Third, the biological status of a person's sex should not be fixed at birth and regarded as immutable. To put it in a nutshell, the decision has given new meaning to the common law concept of marriage and modified the conventional concept of sex as something inborn and immutable. Yet, unlike the latest French concept, marriage under Hong Kong laws remains marriage of opposite sexes. The two concepts, though close, are not equivalent.

Accordingly, legal language is bound to culture. In terms of translation, the translation of the concept "marriage", and for that matter, the concepts of sex (male, female, man, woman), might seem straightforward, but in terms of cultural transfer and in reference to the Christian or common law history, 'there cannot be equivalence of meaning between the law-in-translation and the original law' (Legrand 2005: 30). Translators will use a semi-equivalent in terms of linguistic word, but will not be in the capacity of 'translatabiliting' the full load of the concept into the target language, which can only be achieved through meta-translational devices (Sin 2013). The same idea was further developed (see Cheng and Sin 2008; Cheng, Sin and Cheng 2014), now labelled "the semiotic approach". They reiterated the simple truisms that a sign has no inherent meaning, that its meaning is given by the sign user, which can only be understood with reference to a particular sign system, and that meaning equivalence between different signs is established by certain linguistic devices at a meta-linguistic level (Cheng and Sin 2008: 33–45). Moreover, the choice of equivalence is not merely a linguistic and translational decision but a sociosemiotic and cultural mediation (Cheng, Sin and Cheng 2014; Wagner and Gémar 2013).

4. Conclusion

Translation is often seen as a mere process of transferring the source language to the target language. However, jurilinguistics is a more globalized transfer, which 'brings laws and legal cultures into more direct, frequent, intimate, and often complicated and stressed contact. It also influences what legal professionals want and need to know about foreign law, how they transfer, acquire and process information, and how decisions are made' (Gerber 2001: 950).

In this regard, the migration from one language to another is essential as it deals with the intrinsic value of the concept under consideration. This "migration", "transfer", "translatability", or "transplant" for others is a conscious adaptation process of the concept in the target language. There are recognized patterns of weakness in this process, as legal translators cannot consider only the social rule of the source language, but need also to consider its equivalence, semi-equivalence, or non-equivalence in the target language. Cultural transfer is a key element in legal language because 'the relationship between the inscribed words that constitutes the rule in its bare propositional form and the idea to which they are connected is largely arbitrary in the sense that it is culturally determined' (Legrand 2005: 36).

If no equivalence exists in the target language, the role of the legal translator becomes even more crucial. He will have to adapt the target language to make room for the source concept. Therefore a more comprehensive research agenda in the translation process will have to be established based on two criteria:

1. In the light of different legal cultures, research should be carried out regarding the way the concept has been transplanted in the target language. In terms of migration process, transfer process or adjustment process, accounts will be based on social and technical circumstances prevalent in each country's legal culture and legal system.

2. In the light of the fertilization of this translatability, with notions of power and prestige that have incubated in their new environment (the target language) should also be investigated. Sacco (1999: 398) rightly pointed out that 'every culture that has faith in itself tends to spread its own institutions. Anyone with the power to do so tends to impose his own upon others [. . .]. The desire arises because this work has a quality one can only describe as prestige'.

References

Aitchison, J. 1991. *Language Change: Progress or Decay?* Cambridge University Press.

Alexy, R. 1998. 'Jurgen Habermas's Theory of Legal Discourse'. In: M. Rosenfeld and A. Arato eds. *Habermas on Law and Democracy, Critical Exchanges*. Berkeley/Los Angeles/London: University of California Press.

——— 2002a. *The Argument From Injustice, A Reply To Legal Positivism*. New York/Oxford: Clarendon Press/Oxford University Press.

——— 2002b. *A Theory of Constitutional Rights*. New York: Oxford University Press.

Bergson, H. 1930–1959. *Oeuvres, Essai Sur Les Données Immédiates De La Conscience, Matière Et Mémoire, Le Rire, L'évolution Créatrice, L'énergie Spirituelle, Les Deux Sourcces De La Morale Et De La Religion, La Pensée Et Le Mouvant*. Paris: Presses Universitaires de France.

Bhabha, H. 1994. *The Location of Culture*. London: Routledge.

Boswell, J. 1995. *Same-Sex Unions in Premodern Europe*. New York: Vintage.

Burke, J. 1977. *Jowitt's Dictionary of English Law*. London: Sweet & Maxwell.

Cao, D. 2003. *Translating Law*. Clevedon, UK: Multilingual Matters.

Carbonnier, J. 1978. *Sociologie juridique*. Paris: Presses Universitaires de Franc.

Carrol, L. 1865. *Alice's Adventure in Wonderland*. London: Macmillan and Co.

Cheng, L., Sin, K.K. and Cheng, W. 2014. 'Legal Translation: A Sociosemiotic Approach'. In: A. Wagner and J.C. Gémar guest eds. *Decision-Making in Legal Translation, Interpretation and Speech Act – Legal Semiotic Cultural Mediation Techniques*. Special Issue, *Semiotica*.

Cheng, L. and Sin, K.K. 2008. 'Terminological Equivalence in Legal Translation: A Semiotic Approach', *Semiotica*, vol. 2008(172), pp. 33–45.

Conley, J. 1998. *Just Words: Law, Language and Power*. University of Chicago Press.

Correia, R. 2003. 'Translation of EU Legal Texts'. In: A. Tosi ed. *Crossing Barriers and Bridging Cultures: The Challenges of Multilingual Translation for the European Union*. Clevendon, UK: Multilingual Matters Ltd, pp. 38–44.

De Boysson, B. 2001. *Mariage et conjugalité: essai sur la singularité matrimoniale*. Lyon: Thèse – Université Jean Moulin.

De Groot, G. 2006. 'Legal Translation'. In: J. Smits ed. *Elgar Encyclopedia of Comparative Law*. Cheltenham, UK: Edward Elgar, pp. 423–433.

Dogan, M. 1997. 'The New Social Sciences: Cracks in the Disciplinary Walls', *International Social Science Journal*, vol. 49(153), pp. 429–443.

Eco, U. 1976. *A Theory of Semiotics*. Bloomington: Indiana University Press.

Fairclough, N. 1989. *Language and Power*. London: Longman.

Farrar, J.H. and Dugdale, A.M. 1990. *Introduction to Legal Method*. London: Sweet & Maxell.

Fish, S. 1982. 'Working on the Chain Gang: Interpretation in Law and Literature', *Texas Law Review*, vol. 60, p. 562.

———. 1989. *Respecter le sens commun*. Paris: LGDJ.

Foucault, M. 1991. *Discipline and Punish: The Birth of a Prison*. London: Penguin.

Gadamer, H.A.G. 1989. *Truth and Method*. 2nd rev edn. New York: Crossroad.

Gémar, J.-C. 1992. 'Traduction et Industries de la langue: nouveau défi pour le traducteur', *Meta: Journal des traducteurs/Meta: Translator's Journal*, vol. 37(2), pp. 374–378.
———. 2002. 'Le plus et le moins-disant culturel du texte juridique: Langue, culture et equivalence', *Meta: Journal des traducteurs/Meta: Translator's Journal*, vol 47, no. 2, pp. 163–176.
Gény, F. 1922. *Science et Technique en Droit Privé Positif, Tome 1*. Paris: Recueil Sirey.
Gerber, D.J. 2001. 'Globalisation and Legal Knowledge: Implications for Comparative Law', *Tulane Law Review*, vol. 75, p. 950.
Gimenez Alcover, P. 1993. *El Derecho En La Teoria De La Sociedad De Niklas Luhmann*. Barcelona: Instituto de Criminologia de la Universidad de Barcelona.
Goodrich, P. 1990. *Languages of Law: From Logics of Memory to Nomadic Masks*. London: Weidenfeld & Nicolson.
Greene, T. 1991. *The Language of the Constitution: A Sourcebook and Guide to the Ideas, Terms and Vocabulary Used by the Framers of the United States Constitution*. New York: Greenwood Press.
Greimas, A.J. 1967. 'Analyse Sémiotique d'un Discours Juridique'. In: *Sémiotique et Sciences Sociales*. Paris: Seuil.
Habermas, J. 1996. *Between Facts And Norms: Contributions to a Discourse Theory of Law And Democracy*. Cambridge, Mass.: MIT Press.
Hall, E.T. 1984. *Le langage silencieux*. Paris: Editions du Seuil.
Harrison, R. 1999. 'Linguistics and Litigation', *New Law Journal*, vol. 491, p. 1491.
Hart, H.L.A. 1953. *Definition and Theory in Jurisprudence*. London: Clarendon Press.
———. 1961. *The Concept of Law*. London: Oxford University Press.
———. 1963. 'A Description of Responsibility and Rights'. In: *Essays in Logic and Language*. pp. 146–166.
Hjelmslev, L. 1970. *Language: An Introduction*, F.J. Whitfield, trans. University of Wisconsin Press.
Hobbes, T. 1971. *Léviathan*. Paris: Tricaud.
Hungerford-Welch, P. 1999. 'Lawyers and the English Language', *New Law Journal*, January 29, 1999, pp. 123–124.
Iser, W. 1994. 'On Translability', *Surfaces*, vol. 4(307), pp. 5–13.
Kelsen, H. 1953. *La Théorie Pure du Droit*. Paris: Dalloz.
Kevelson, R. 1988. *The Law as a System of Signs*. New York: Plenum Press.
Larson, M.S. 1977. *The Rise of Professionalism: A Sociological Analysis*. Berkeley: University of California Press.
Lebreton, E. 1994. 'Investir dans la terminologie'. In: *Bons Termes*.
Legrand, P. 2005. 'Issues in the Translability of Law'. In: S. Bermann and M. Wood eds. *Nation, Language, and the Ethics of Translation*. New Jersey: Princeton University Press, pp. 30–50.
Luhmann, N. 1985. *A Sociological Theory of Law*. London/Boston: Routledge and Kegan Paul.
McAuliffe, K. 2009. 'Translation at the Court of Justice of the European Communities'. In: F. Olsen et al. eds. *Translation Issues in Language and Law*. Basingstoke: Palgrave, pp. 95–115.
———. 2011. 'Hybrid Texts and Uniform Law? The Multilingual Case Law of the Court of Justice of the European Union', *International Journal for the Semiotics of Law*, vol. 24(1), pp. 97–115.
Mellinkoff, D. 1963. *The Language of the Law*. London: Pluman.
Monjean-Decaudin, S. 2010. 'Territorialité et extraterritorialité de la traduction du droit'. *Meta*, vol. 55(4), pp. 693–711.
Morrison, M.J. 1989. 'Excursion into the Nature of Legal Language', *Cleveland State Law Review*, vol. 37(2), pp. 271–336.
Mounin, G. 1963. *Les problèmes théoriques de la traduction*. Paris: Gallimard.
Muller, I. 1901. *Hitler's Justice, the Courts of the Third Reich*. Cambridge, Mass.: Harvard University Press.
Nehrot, P. 1993. *Law, Writing, Meaning: An Essay in Legal Hermeneutics*. Edinburgh Press.

Nietzsche, F. 1967. *On the Genealogy of Morals*. W. Kaufmann and R.J. Hollingdale trans. New York: Random House.
Radbruch, G. 1986. *Derecho Legal y Derecho Supralegal*. Bogota: Temis.
Rosenfeld, M. and Arato, A. (eds). 1998. *Habermas on Law and Democracy, Critical Exchanges*. Berkeley/Los Angeles/London: University of California Press.
Sacco, R. 1991. 'Legal Formants: A Dynamic Approach to Comparative Law', *American Journal of Comparative Law*, vol. 39(II), p. 398.
de Saussure, F. 1916. *Cours de Linguistique Générale*. Paris: Payot.
Schauer, F. 1992. *Law and Language*. New York University Press.
Serjeantson, M.S. 1968. *A History of Foreign Words in English*. London: Routledge & Kegan Paul.
Sherry, S. 1996. *Gender in Translation*. London: Routledge.
Sin, K.K. 2002. Foreword to *English-Chinese Glossary of Civil and Commercial Law Terms*. Hong Kong: Department of Justice, pp. v–xi.
———. 2013. 'Out of the Fly-Bottle: Conceptual Confusions in Multilingual Legislation', *International Journal of Semiotica of Law, Language and Discourse*, vol. 26, pp. 927–951.
Solan, L. 1993. *The Language of Judges*. University of Chicago Press.
de Sousa Santos, B. 1995. *Towards a New Common Sense: Law, Science, and Politics in the Paradigmatic Transition*. New York: Routledge.
Spitzer, S. 1983. 'Marxist Perspectives in the Sociology of Law', *Annual Review of Sociology*, vol. 9, pp. 103–124.
Stone, A. 1985. 'The Place of Law in the Marxian Structure-Superstructure Archetype', *Law and Society Review*, vol. 19(1), p. 39.
Tiersma, P. 2000. *Legal Language*. University of Chicago Press.
Tyler, T.R. 2006. *Why People Obey the Law*. Princeton University Press.
Unger, R.M. 1977. *Law in Modern Society: Towards A Criticism of Social Theory*. New York: Free Press.
Vogel, K. 1997. 'L'interlangue, la langue de l'apprenant', *Langue Modernes*, vol. 2, p. 71.
Wagner, A. and Gémar, J.-C. (eds). 2013. 'The Process of Translabiliting: Translating and Transferring Law, its Concepts, Notions and Language', *International Journal for the Semiotics of Law*, vol. 26(4).
Wagner, A. 1999. 'Les maux du droit et les mots pour le dire', *Unesco ALSED-LSP Newsletter*, vol. 22(1/47), pp. 40–70.
———. 2002. 'The Legal Discourse of the Common Law: A Game of Chess', *International Journal for the Semiotics of Law*, vol. 15(4), pp. 345–360.
Wallerstein, I. 1999. *The End of the World As We Know It: Social Science For The Twenty-First Century*. Minneapolis: University of Minnesota Press.
Warnke, G. 1992. *Justice and Interpretation*. London: Polity Press.
Weinrich, U. 1953. *Languages in Contact: Findings and Problems*. Paris: Mouton, The Hague.
Welzel, H. 1985. *Derecho penal Aleman*. Buenos Aires: Editorial Depalma.
Wittgenstein, L. 1968. *Philosophical Investigations*. G.E.M. Anscombe trans. Oxford: Basil Blackwell.
Yalon, M. 2002. *A History of the Wife*. New York: HarperCollins Publishers.

Chapter 3
Lost in Translation? Linguistic Diversity and the Elusive Quest for Plain Meaning in the Law

Janet Ainsworth

1. Introduction

The task of the legal translator can be stated with simplicity: it is to take a legal text expressed in one language, and create an equivalent legal text in another language, such that a legal decision-maker, applying either text to a particular legal issue or dispute, will arrive at the same conclusion regardless of which text is used. As described, the task seems straightforward enough, but its simplicity is deceptive. It is by now nearly a cliché that legal translation is among the most challenging tasks that any translator can face (Correia 2002; Harvey 2002). This chapter will first articulate the nature of the special challenges presented to the translator of legal texts, then will go on to discuss some of the strategies employed to overcome those challenges, and finally, will suggest that the process of legal translation has consequences that go far beyond matters of ensuring legal equivalence. Choices made in the process of legal translation have ramifications for legal textual interpretation more generally and for the substance of legal decision-making in a globalized world.

2. Challenges of the Legal Translator

2.1. Challenges Arising from the Nature of Legal Language

This difficulty is the compounded product of several hurdles faced by the legal translator. First, legal language by its nature is notoriously difficult and opaque, presenting considerable interpretive difficulties even when the interpretive questions arise within a monolingual framework. Legal language is marked by its use of an obscure technical lexicon, adoption of ordinary words used in atypical senses as terms of art, archaic and foreign language-derived terminology, and complex syntactic structures and conventions (Danet 1980; Morrison 1989; Tiersma 1999). Some have gone so far as to say that legal language is intentionally incomprehensible to those without legal training in order to reserve access to the arena of legal knowledge and power solely to those admitted to the guild of legal practitioners (Mellinkoff 1963; Benson 1984–1985). Even without accepting the argument that legal language is deliberately made difficult for non-lawyers to understand, it is beyond dispute that that it is in fact difficult to make sense of legal language, and that consequently much of the professional training that would-be lawyers undergo is dedicated to the process of achieving mastery over the use and interpretation of legal language (Mertz 2007).

2.2. Challenges Arising from the Nature of Language

Second, the legal translator must face the ordinary problems inherent in all translation, namely that, contrary to popular belief, languages are not fully transparent and determinate systems for the transmission of propositional content. Even within a particular language, meaning is expressed in ways that are not hard-edged and precise but instead vague, allusive, and evocative. Language is thus by its nature indeterminate, unbounded, and imprecise, leading to inevitable instances of ambiguity and lack of clarity in meaning (See, e.g., Égré and Klinedinst 2011) Legal language, despite is surface appeals to precision and clarity, is no more determinate and certain in its meaning than any other form of language, and may in fact be even more indeterminate (Bix 1996: 178–193). Consider the fact that in many cases, lawyers and judges operating within a monolingual legal system cannot agree on the meaning to be given a legal text at issue. If that is true in the interpretation of a legal text in a single language, then how much more elusive the challenge of attempting to create perfect legal equivalency in two languages!

2.3. Challenges Arising from the Non-Commensurability of Languages

That task of translation—the attempt to reproduce meaning in one language into equivalent meaning in another language—is further complicated by the fact that languages are not fully commensurable systems of meaning (Ortega y Gasset 1937; Nida 1964). Language is inextricably bound up in the systems of meaning and practice that we call by the short-hand name "culture," and any attempt to transpose linguistic meaning from one culture-situated language into another is inevitably going to find things both lost and gained in translation (see generally Venuti 2000). In any language, the meaning of a word is built over time, with primary meanings accruing additional layers on connotation and nuance as a result of the ways in which the word has been used over historical time within its culture. Even assuming that the translator can find a word in the target language that seem to be the equivalent in its primary sense of the word in the source language, the connotations attached to that word are unlikely to be the same in each language.

2.4. Challenges Arising from the Non-Commensurability of Legal Systems

All of these problems are compounded by the fact that, unlike many registers of language for special purposes, there is often no unity in the underlying domain for which legal language registers have developed. When the professional language of say, a physicist, is translated from one language into another, both languages are attempting to communicate about the identical subject matter. However, when legal language is translated from one legal linguistic register into that of another language, those two linguistic registers may well have evolved to describe and manipulate entirely different kinds of legal orders and legal cultures (Šarčević 1985). To take an obvious example, legal terminology taken from a common law system like that of the United States or Great Britain is unlikely to have an appropriate terminological twin in the legal language developed within a civil law system such as those of Continental Europe (Triebel 2009: 169, 172–173). The gloss placed on terms taken from one jurisprudential system can render them dangerously misunderstood when transposed into the other. "False friends" in translation—similar appearing words that deceptively seem to have equivalent meaning in both languages because they have identical derivations or are literal lexical translations—are a pitfall in all translingual interpretation, but are particularly so when the translator is transposing common law language into civil law language or vice versa. Triebel (2009: 172–173) has noted that terms such as force majeure, good faith, vicarious liability, constructive knowledge, remedy, equity, deed, trust, consideration, breach, and negligence are all terms that have different meanings and salience in civil law versus common law usage, and a translation that ignores this does so at its peril.

3. Legal Terminology—Universal or Particularized?

Legal anthropologists have long struggled with the parallel problem of choosing a vocabulary with which to describe aspects of legal orders in non-Western societies. Some, like Bohannan (1969), insist the indigenous words for legal concepts be used as much as possible, because they believe that Western legal terminology is inescapably misleading in its connotations. Others, most notably Max Gluckman (1969), thought that a universally applicable legal terminology—which might or might not happen to correspond with Western legal language—could exist and could adequately describe non-Western legal practices. This debate over appropriate language is grounded in a yet deeper disagreement concerning the nature of law within a society. Those anthropologists siding with Bohannan assume that every culture and society has a unique legal order, with distinctive legal institutions, practices, and ideology that evolve in the context of its overall social order. Those scholars who agree with Gluckman, on the other hand, imagine that the legal order occupies the same structural niche in every society, so that the superstructural details of legal systems may vary dramatically from society to society, but the fundamental structural functions of all legal orders are universe and consistent.

Like Bohannan, I see any culture's legal order as a unique and finely tuned product of the cultural and historic context in which it is embedded. At the same time, legal discourse and practice act as a constituent thread in the fabric of meaning, belief, and social relations that make up each singular social world. In the words of Clifford Geertz (1983: 215), 'Law . . . is local knowledge, local not just to place, time, class, and variety of issue, but as to accent – vernacular characterizations of what happens connected to vernacular imaginings of what can.' In this regard, a culture's legal order is a highly particularized local form of discourse with a local legal sensibility that informs the practices and language through which that sensibility finds concrete realization. A legal order simultaneously encompasses systems of political arrangements, social relations, interpersonal interactional practices, economic processes, cultural categorizations, normative beliefs, philosophical perspectives, and ideological values. All of these aspects of a legal order are constituted through its legal discursive practices, and it is in these discursive practices that law provides an arena for contests over social meaning within a culture. In a study of cross-cultural dispute resolution, Sally Merry (1984: 2063) noted that the normative legal framework 'shapes the way people conceptualize problems, the ways they pursue them, and the kinds of solutions they look for.' It likewise shapes the language with which they interact in the law.

3.1 Adaptation and Meaning Lost and Gained in Translation

With this in mind, a translator might seek to take into account the cultural connotations of legal language in the process of translating a legal text derived from one cultural and social order into another. In this regard, Susan Šarčević (1985: 130) warns that adaptation—the use of a term within a translated text that it intended to take advantage of that term's supposed equivalent cultural salience in the target language to that of a term in the source text—can potentially lead to misinterpretation. Here I provide an example of such an adaptation, taken not from a legal translation but from a religious one. The important mystical passage in the Christian Bible in the Book of John Chapter One, Verse One, reads in its English version, 'In the beginning was the word, and the word was with God, and the word was God.' In this text, the English lexical term "word" is used to render the Greek original term, *logos*, which has a very close propositional meaning, even if the Greek philosophical connotation of *logos* is perhaps not fully expressed in that English language choice. When the Bible came to be translated into Chinese,[1] the translator needed to render the sense of that verse into a language in which the philosophical sense of *logos* had no direct Chinese equivalent. The translator could have made the choice that the English translator did, and use a Chinese word literally meaning "word." Instead the translator chose to render the passage as follows: 太初有道，道与神同在，道就是神。(tài chū yǒu dào, dào yǔ shén tòng zài, dào jiùshì shén): 'In the beginning was the *dao*, and the *dao* was with God, and the *dao* was God.'

By using the term *dao*, or way—a term laden with meaning from its long-standing historical use as a core philosophical term in both Daoism and classical Confucianism (Zhang 2002: 11–25)—the translator successfully got across the idea that *logos* meant much more than merely "word," but instead was a term steeped in deep and complex philosophical and religious significance. In that sense, one can say that *dao* was not as good a literal equivalent for *logos*, as the English term "word" is, but that it instead serves as what Eugene Nida ([1964] 2000: 128) called a dynamic equivalent, the closest natural rendering of *logos* within the cultural and linguistic context of a Chinese audience. But one must still ask, is this an equivalent translation of the text in question? By importing into the Chinese reader's understanding of the Biblical text all of the connotations inherent in the Daoist and Confucian use of the term *dao* built up over the centuries, hasn't the meaning of the Biblical passage become altered from the meaning that the original Greek text had? In other words, by preserving the cultural salience of the language used and invoking a spiritual and philosophical gloss on the translated text, meaning has been both lost and gained, or at least altered, by the Chinese translator. The mystical and religious register of the language has been captured, but perhaps at the expense of denotative and connotative meaning.

Just as religious doctrine can be threatened by adaptation in translation, so too can legal doctrine. Because law is a normative enterprise, adaptation within legal translation has the capability to both add and subtract meaning in the process. For example, the legal language used by the American legal system in defining the variety of crimes and culpabilities associated with homicide—the killing of a human being—is rich with differentiations, gradations, and categorizations corresponding to the law's nuanced set of judgments about comparative responsibility and culpability. Legal Spanish has a similarly rich and varied legal vocabulary regarding homicide, but because it originates in an entirely different legal normative order, the two legal language domains do not map onto each other in corresponding ways, complicating the appropriate way to translate that English legal language for Spanish speaking participants

1 The translation I am referring to here is the Chinese Union Version of the Bible, issued in 1919. It is still the most widely used translation of the Bible into Chinese, and has influenced several later versions that continue to use the language referenced here.

in the American criminal justice system (Mikkelson 1995). Similarly, the French legal term *bonne foi* incorporates both a subjective state of mind and an objective standard of the appropriateness of the behaviour in question, whereas the English equivalent "good faith" lacks that objective component of *bonne foi* (Kasirer 1999: 666). Functional equivalence in legal vocabulary from legal system to legal system would appear to be more the exceptional than the rule.

4. Is Legal Translation an Impossible Task?

The more one considers the challenges of legal translation, the farther its successful achievement appears to recede into impossibility. The role of law is, at least in part, to resolve disputes, including those made inevitable by the imprecision and ambiguity in the language in which the legal order constitutes itself. Generality is essential if legal language is to be of applicability beyond any particularized situation, and yet that very generality itself produces the vagueness and ambiguity in legal language that generates disputes and uncertainties. Legal translation turns out to be particularly fraught with difficulty precisely because legal texts have an inescapably instrumental character: they exist to actually do things that have concrete, dramatic, often far-reaching consequences in the real world. If the ideal legal translation is one that attains instrumental equivalence between texts, then fidelity in translating propositional content is a necessary but not sufficient condition for a successful translation. In addition, the texts must express the same cultural connotations given the norms and values and practices of each legal culture in order to generate identical legal outcomes. At the same time, inadvertent implication of unintended meaning through adaptation or adoption of "false friend" terminology must also be avoided. In the end, it may be unimportant whether language—the linguistic tokens used—or culture—the localized contextual implications habitually associated with those usages—is what creates the "lost in translation" problem for legal translators. Either way, ideal legal translation—or, at least accurate and faithful translation allowing translated texts to function as truly equivalent texts—seems forever outside our grasp.

5. Translation of Legal Texts Within the European Union: An Example of Success in Legal Translation?

Despite the formidable theoretical obstacles outlined here, legal translation cannot be impossible. The proof is all around us—in a globalized world, legal texts are translated and retranslated, and the translations made use of in legal proceedings in both national and international legal contexts. Take, for example, the legal system of the European Union—a transnational, multilingual legal system in which all enactments, regulations, and rulings are promulgated in all of the official languages of the member states. Although European Union legal instruments are originally drafted in one language, either English or French, and then subsequently translated into the 23 other official European Union languages, the drafting source text has no privileged legal status. All linguistic versions of any European Union legal text are considered equally authoritative and have identical legal status throughout the Union (*Skatteministeriet v. Codan*).

How then does the European Union deal with the inevitable situation in which the various linguistic versions of its legal texts fail to be precisely equivalent? When a dispute arises in which different linguistic formulations of a rule, if applied, would reach different conclusions in the dispute, the question of the relationship between linguistic and legal interpretation becomes paramount. The European Union court begins, as it must, with the proposition that the regulations, directives, and legislation that make up its law must be applied with reference to the texts of those enactments. 'The starting point for assessing [an enactment] must be its wording' (*Simutenkov v. Ministerio de Educacion y Cultura*). However, even in a monolingual legal system, the wording of a legal text is frequently susceptible to more than one construction of meaning, with even the simplest rules generating ambiguity in application. The famous Hart-Fuller debate, centering on the potential for ambiguity in the application of a simple rule such as 'No vehicles in the park', suggests that legal texts cannot be made determinate in their application (Hart 1958; Fuller 1958). Still more, when the text in question is present in a multiplicity of equally authoritative versions, it is inevitable that their application in concrete cases will lead to disparate conclusions. When the wording of a regulation gives varying results depending on which linguistic version is applied, the European Union court must determine how to resolve the inconsistency in the formulation of the law.

4.1. Interpretive Approaches to Resolving Ambiguity in the European Union

Several possible approaches that could be taken to resolving inter-textual ambiguity have been rejected. For example, one way to resolve ambiguity or inconsistency between linguistic versions of a rule might be to examine the language used in the original drafting of the rule, with the presumption that variance in later, target language versions is likely the result of inadvertent translation inaccuracies. This is not done, however. Perhaps the equality principle—that all member states have equal status and that no state or states should be elevated to a pre-eminent position—would be in jeopardy if the authoritative mother lode of European Union law were to be instantiated in one dominant language.

Where one particular version of a rule is an outlier, inconsistent with all or most of the other linguistic formulations of the rule, the European Union court sometimes takes that into account in rejecting the outlying version of the rule, but other times does not. For example, in *Lubella v. Hauptzollamt Cottbus*, a dispute over the scope of an import regulation, in which most linguistic versions of the regulations used a term that meant "sour cherries," but the German version used the word meaning "sweet cherries" instead, the court adopted the "sour cherry" reading despite the outlying German usage. On the other hand, in *Peterson v. Weddel & Co. Ltd.*, all linguistic versions of a rule except one, the Dutch version, were ambiguous as to whether a regulation in question applied to meat for human consumption or only to carcasses not intended for human consumptions. In that case, the court nevertheless applied the outlying Dutch version of the regulation in resolving the dispute.

Another possible interpretive strategy that has been largely rejected is to develop a European Union legal meta-language, with special terms evolving to reference particular legal principles and doctrines, such that, over time, the European Union's jurisprudence would be expressed in terms of a consistent body of legal language. Within the legal translation community in the European Union, some have welcomed the creation of a common European Union legal vocabulary as useful, and others panned it as a 'lazy and unreadable way of creating "equivalent" texts' (Buchin and Seymour 2002: 111). Useful or otherwise, the development of a coherent body of European Union-specific legal language has not occurred to any significant extent. Although a small number of meta-linguistic terms within European Union law have surfaced—for example, the term *acquis communautaire* to refer to the entire body of European Union statutes, regulations, and directives that are binding law for each member state—as a general matter, European Union laws are drafted in the various official languages often utilizing terminology derived from the national legal languages in question

(Lambert 2009: 87–88). However, the European Union court has firmly resisted the idea that, for those legal terms derived from national legal language, they should be interpreted consistently with the way in which they are given meaning within that national legal system (*Rockfon A/S v. Specialarbejderforbude*).

Instead, the European Union court has resorted to other interpretative strategies to resolve inter-linguistic inconsistencies and ambiguities. In one early case involving a conflict between the translated texts of a regulation, *North Kerry Milk Producers Ltd. v. Minister for Agriculture and Fisheries*, the European Union court was asked to resolve a dispute as to which of two possible operative dates—the manufacturing date or the marketing date—would trigger a payment. The English language version of the regulation supported one interpretation, and the French and Italian versions the other. The European Court of Justice declined the invitation to determine which of the translations of the regulations was to be given legal effect, stating: '[I]t is preferable to explore the possibilities of solving the points at issue without giving preference to any one of the texts involved.' Instead, the court looked at a variety of other regulations and tried to give a reading to the regulation in question that was consistent with those other texts, all the while acknowledging that 'one or more of the texts involved may have to be interpreted in a manner at variance with the natural and usual meaning of the words.' Relying on other legal texts to attempt to give meaning to the legal text at issue may have been an effective strategy in this early case, but as rules and regulations and directives have multiplied exponentially over the years, the question of which other rules are the appropriate rules to consider by analogy would threaten to explode every dispute about the interpretation of one rule into a meta-dispute about the application and interpretation of the rules purported to be analogous. Not surprisingly, this particular interpretive strategy has not been resorted to often as the body of European Union law has expanded in scope and volume.

Rather, the predominate interpretive strategy adopted by the European Union court to resolve cases of ambiguity and inconsistency has been to use a purposive approach, asking which interpretation best achieves what the court imagines to have been the intent of the legislation in question. As the court said in *Schulte v. Deutsche Bausparkasse*, 'Where it is difficult to interpret legislation from its wording alone, an interpretation based on purpose becomes fundamental. This is the case where the provision in question is ambiguous.' The European Union court used this purposive interpretive strategy in the case of *Commission of the European Union v. United Kingdom of Great Britain and Northern Ireland*. The dispute in question involved a regulation concerning whether fish caught in a joint fishing enterprise involving both European Union and non-European Union fishers should be subject to the payment of duty. Under the European Union system of tariffs, a duty would be levied on fish imported from outside the European Union, whereas European Union caught fish would be exempted from that taxation. In this particular case, fish were being netted by non-EU fishing vessels, dragged underwater to British fishing boats, and only then hauled onboard the British-flagged ships. The issue was whether these fish were EU-caught fish, not subject to duty, or non-EU-caught fish, on which duty would have to be paid. The British argued that the regulation in question supported its interpretation that the fish ought to be duty-free, since the English language regulations provided that 'products of sea-fishing and other products *taken from the sea* by vessels . . . flying [an European Union member's] flag' qualified for duty-free treatment. Since the fish in question were not 'taken from the sea' until they were hauled aboard the British-flag-flying trawlers, they ought to be considered as EU-produced fish, according to the British argument. To resolve this case, the court examined the other linguistic formulations of the regulations, and found that the French version, *extraits de la mer*, and the Greek, Italian, and Dutch versions were, like the English version, susceptible to the interpretation favoured by the British fishers. On the other hand, the German version, *gefangen*, was better translated as "caught," thus suggesting that the fish should be considered non-EU fish, since they were actually trapped and netted by non-EU fishers. Yet the court ultimately did not focus on a linguistic interpretation of the enactment or one which version ought to govern the case at bar. Instead it asked the question of which position would best satisfy what they presumed was the legislative intent of the duty-free provisions in general. It concluded that adopting the British interpretation would permit evasion of the tariff regulations on fish imported into the European Union as long as the non-EU fishers transferred the catch to an European Union-flagged vessel while netted but still in the water, and it presumed that the intent of the tariff regulations was to promote and protect European Union fisheries from non-European competitors. In other words, the precise linguistic formulation of the regulations was given no particular significance in the resolution of the case. Instead, the court felt free to construe what it presumed to be the overall legislative intent in the European Union tariff regulations.

4.2. De-Textualization in Resolving Inter-Textual Ambiguity

In effect, cases such as *Commission of the European Union v. United Kingdom of Great Britain and Northern Ireland* demonstrate that the European Union has attempted to avoid the inherent problems that translation theory tells us exist in legal translation by de-textualizing its legal system. That is, by giving the language of enactments only limited legal significance, the question of inter-linguistic equivalence becomes relatively unimportant to the functioning of the system. When the court is free to resort to its sense of the underlying purposes of the legal rule in question, the precise formulation of that rule bears less legal weight. Of course, no legal system can completely detach its adjudication from the linguistic formulation of its rules. The European courts may be free to decide that the "correct" interpretation of a regulation is that expressed in the Danish or French or Maltese versions as it will, but it cannot with legitimacy claim that a regulation on fisheries actually regulates dairies. De-textualization can thus only represent a partial de-coupling of decision-making from the written texts making up the *acquis communautaire*.

Can law really be de-textualized in this way, or does a de-textualization lead to a loss of legitimacy when the precise contours of legislative enactments are given such limited legal effect? One could well argue that the European Union's approach gives the courts the power to be the ultimate arbiter of the legal meaning of texts, almost entirely unconstrained by the texts of the enactments themselves. The answer to that question depends on the answer to another question: whether the words in which legal rules are expressed are merely the incidental way in which some pre-linguistic or meta-linguistic rule happens to be expressed, with the meta-linguistic rule being the "real" law and its linguistic expression merely a pale, second order approximation. If that is the case, then going behind the language of the rules—searching for some kind of legislative purpose or intent—raises no legitimacy problems. However, the process through which a court might determine the intent of the rule raises new issues, particularly if the text is displaced from the centre of the inquiry. It is unhelpful in most cases to try to ascertain the legislative intent with respect to a rule's application in a particular case. Not infrequently, the legislature enacting a rule had no intent with regard to its application in a particular circumstance because they had not imagined that circumstance in the first place. No code-drafting body—even the most clear-thinking and far-sighted one—can possibly anticipate every kind of dispute or issue that can arise; hence, the use of codes specifying general standards of conduct in place of itemized lists of instances of approved or disapproved conduct.

By de-textualizing the law, the jurisprudence of the European Union finesses the set of problems inhering in legal translation, but at the cost of rendering the texts of the law themselves practically irrelevant in resolving disputes. Of course, one can argue that de-textualization only has "bite" in those cases in which it happens that there are significant textual differences between the translated versions and in which those differences happen to make a difference in the resolution of a particular case. In other words, it could be argued that most cases will be "easy" cases in which there is no inter-linguistic inconsistency or ambiguity in applying the rule that governs the case. This is, in effect, the position taken by H.L.A. Hart (1958) in his famous 'No vehicles in the park' example, in which he argues that most purported violations of the rule will either clearly be violations or clearly not violations, and that the existence of penumbral cases—is a bicycle a vehicle? Is a toy car a vehicle? Should an ambulance responding to a medical emergency be sanctioned?—should not blind us to the fact that most rule applications turn out to be unproblematic. Similarly, it could be argued that only in marginal, penumbral cases will there be differences between language versions of European Union regulations that actually are determinative. Therefore, perhaps it should not trouble us that the European Union courts see themselves as free in those cases to construct a version of the rule in question that would appear to be the most appropriate one under the circumstances, detached from being moored in the language of the texts as enacted. Still, it is disquieting that the preservation of linguistic equality within the European Union's legal framework can only be achieved through the imposition of a kind of judicial supremacy that cannot easily be checked or constrained.

As a practical matter, it may be that conflicts between various language versions of European Union rules often go unrecognized and thus fail to lead to disputes because so much European Union law is actually adjudicated within the national court systems of the member states. It is true, under European Union law, the language used in European Union regulations and directives is not to be given meaning by reference to the interpretations given to identical terms when used in the national legal systems of the member states. However, given the fact that much European Union law is interpreted and applied by the national courts in member states, it is probably inevitable that, in those cases, such terms are understood in the light of their usage and meaning within the national legal system. Indeed, a member state's judge presiding within the national court system, familiar only with the European Union law as rendered in that member state's language, might well assume that the meaning of the European Union term was intended to be identical in meaning as usually accorded in the law of the home legal system. Only if someone called it to the judge's attention that the Bulgarian or Finnish or Spanish version of the legal text differed from the version in the national court's language would there even be an occasion to consider that a familiar legal term ought, perhaps, be given an unfamiliar meaning. Thus, in many instances, conscious de-textualization need not be resorted to at all in dispute resolution.

Nevertheless, the jurisprudence of the European Union, with its normative tendency to de-textualize legal decision-making, suggests that it cannot be pointed to as an example of a transnational legal system that has overcome the fundamental problems in effective legal translation, only one that has sidestepped them. Indeed, comparative legal theorists such as Pierre Legrand are deeply sceptical about the possibility that legal translation could ever result in transparent equivalency of legal texts. 'Even international conventions will not create legal uniformity given the inherently localized properties of language, culture and tradition', he wrote, because '[l]aw is a cultural phenomenon. . . . Therefore, differences across legal cultures can only ever be overcome imperfectly' (Legrand 2005: 42).

5. Globalization: Convergence in Legal Language?

Legrand (2005: 30–32) is likewise sceptical that globalization is leading to international legal convergence, as has been argued. Of course, there is no doubt that, with the growing interdependence of nations, economic legal frameworks in areas such as trade, finance, banking, securities regulation, corporations, and the like, have been imported wholesale by national governments needing to participate in increasingly globalized markets. Further, the interpenetration of those global markets into domestic economies has created pressure for the adoption into non-Western domestic legal systems of legal codes and practices that had their origins in Western civil and common law. Such legal transplants—the grafting of foreign legal forms and ideas into a legal system—have long been recognized as one way in which legal convergence might take place (Watson 1974). As non-Western nations increasingly import aspects of the legal institutions, regulations, and practices of Europe and North American into their national legal systems, it would be easy to assume that a transnational legal law—one very familiar to Western legal eyes—is inevitably the future of law. Yet, the same lessons learned from translation theory that so bedevil the attempts to create equivalence in texts in legal translation also suggest that the process of legal globalization will be more complex and less one-sided than the champions of legal convergence applaudingly predict and the critics of legal imperialism harshly denounce.

5.1 China as Example of Legal Transplantation—Western Law with Chinese Characteristics

Take the example of China as a case study of the degree to which legal transplantation need not necessarily lead to legal convergence. In recent years, China has adopted business regulations that are grounded in Western business law, in many cases adopting nearly verbatim many provisions from those statutory frameworks (Potter 2001). For example, the current contract law of China, for instance, is heavily influenced by the International Convention for the Sale of Goods and the UNIDROIT contract law principles (Chi 2010). It would be tempting to say, then, that Chinese business and trade law increasingly has taken on the characteristics of Western business law, and that its legal practices and doctrines have in effect been westernized. Certainly there is some grain of truth to this, as anyone doing business in China today can attest. But the story in the end will inevitably be more complicated than that. As John Gillespie (2008: 686) wrote in discussing the supposed westernization of law in East Asia, 'Social actors may unknowingly or deliberately invest borrowed ideas with new meanings to secure particular advantages.' Incorporation of foreign law into an existing legal culture is by no means a matter of passive adoption, and the law incorporated is by no means unchanged in the process of its incorporation. China has become a world player not merely on the world economic stage but on the world legal stage as well. As Chinese actors participate in the international legal arenas with greater frequency and greater clout, Chinese interpretations of legal texts will undoubtedly come to have increasing salience in constructing the meaning of those provisions. Donald Clarke (2006) has persuasively argued that the workings of many aspects of the contemporary Chinese legal system cannot be understood simply from the fact that many of the terminological and structural aspects of Western legal institutions and frameworks have been adopted into Chinese law. He views translations of Chinese corporate and business laws as problematic to the extent that they appear to incorporate concepts of rights and duties in an absolutist Western framework rather than in the pragmatic, sliding scale approach most natural in Chinese legal culture, and notes that one can already see ways in which Chinese legal concepts are subtly and not-so-subtly altering the meaning of the imported legal terminology. Frances Foster (2010) similarly sees a lack of congruence between the language of Western trust law incorporated into the Chinese statutes regarding trusteeship and the norms and values existent in Chinese legal culture, and she even suggests that the gloss put on that imported terminology and doctrine as Chinese trust law develops has the potential of influencing the direction of American trust law in the future. Given the reflexive role of language and culture in the construction of legal meaning, one might well ask how it could be otherwise. Legal evolution and change is unlikely to be a one-way street—from West to East. In a polyvocal, multilingual world, it is unlikely to be even a two-way street, and no one probably recognizes that fact with keener appreciation than legal translators.

6. Conclusion: Challenges in Legal Translation are a Microcosm of Challenges in Understanding the Nature of Legal Practice and Culture

What all of this suggests is that law cannot be understood without an appreciation of the nature of language, and that many jurisprudential issues turn out in the end to be language issues at base. Likewise, many problems that might appear to be technical linguistic problems turn out to be matters of the cultural construction of meaning at base. As much as we might wish it were otherwise, legal language can never attain its instrumental ideal of plain meaning, with all ambiguity and inconsistency banished. It is too inextricably bound up in the untidy enterprise of human culture for that. As a consequence, the elusive search for perfect equivalence in legal translation is likewise doomed to frustration. Nonetheless, the ways in which legal translators must struggle to provide an approximation of an ideal translation gives us a model for thinking about the nature of indeterminacy in law more generally as well as the nature and consequences of the global scale of legal transplantation and its impact on legal doctrine and practice in the future.

Cases Cited

Commission of the European Union v. United Kingdom of Great Britain and Northern Ireland [1985] ECR 1169.
Lubella v. Hauptzollamt Cottbus [1996] ECR I-5105.
North Kerry Milk Producers Ltd. v. Minister for Agriculture and Fisheries [1977] ECR 425.
Peterson v. Weddel & Co. Ltd. [1984] ECR 1567.
Rockfon A/S v. Specialarbejderforbude [1995] ECR I-4291.
Schulte v. Deutsche Bausparkasse [2006] All ER 420 (2005).
Simutenkov v. Ministerio de Educacion y Cultura [2006] All ER (EC) 420 (2005).
Skatteministeriet v. Codan [1998] ECR I-8679.

References

Benson, R.W. 1984–85. 'The End of Legalese: The Game is Over', *New York University Review of Law and Social Change*, vol. 13, pp. 519–574.
Bix, B. 1996. *Law, Language, and Legal Determinacy*. Oxford University Press.

Bohannan, P. 1969. 'Ethnography and Comparison in Legal Anthropology'. In: *Law in Culture and Society*. L. Nader ed. Berkeley: University of California Press, pp. 401–418.
Buchin, N. and Seymour, E. 2002. 'Equivalences or Divergences in Legal Translation?' In: A. Tosi ed. *Crossing Barriers and Bridging Cultures: The Challenges of Multilingual Translation for the European Union*. Clevedon: Multilingual Matters, pp. 111–116.
Chi, M. 2010. 'Application of the UNIDROIT Principles in China: Success, Shortcomings, and Implications', *Uniform Law Review*, vol. 15, pp. 5–35.
Clarke, D. 2006. 'Lost in Translation? Corporate Legal Transplants in China', George Washington University Law School Public Law and Legal Theory Working Paper No. 213. Available at: http://ssrn.com/abstract=913784.
Correia, R. 2002. 'Translation of EU Legal Texts'. In: A. Tosi ed. *Crossing Barriers and Bridging Cultures: The Challenges of Multilingual Translation for the European Union*. Clevedon: Multilingual Matters, pp. 38–44.
Danet, B. 1980. 'Language in the Legal Process', *Law and Society*, vol. 14(3), pp. 447–563.
Égré, P. and Klinedinst, N. 2011. 'Vagueness and Language Use'. In: P. Égré and N. Klinedinst eds. *Vagueness and Language Use*. Basingstoke: Palgrave Macmillan, pp. 1–24.
Foster, F. 2010. 'American Trust Law in a Chinese Mirror', *Minnesota Law Review*, vol. 94, pp. 602–651.
Fuller, L. 1958. 'Positivism and Fidelity to Law – A Reply to Professor Hart', *Harvard Law Review*, vol. 71, pp. 630–672.
Geertz, C. 1983. *Local Knowledge: Further Essays in Interpretive Anthropology*. New York: Basic Books.
Gillespie, J. 2008. 'Towards a Discursive Analysis of Legal Transfers into Developing East Asia', *New York University Journal of International Law and Politics*, vol. 40, pp. 657–721.
Gluckman, M. 1969. 'Concepts in the Comparative study of Tribal Law'. In: L. Nader ed. *Law in Culture and Society*. Berkeley: University of California Press, pp. 349–373.
Hart, H.L.A. 1958. 'Positivism and the Separation of Law and Morality', *Harvard Law Review*, vol. 71, pp. 593–629.
Harvey, M. 2002. 'What's So Special about Legal Translation?' *Meta*, vol. 47(2), pp. 177–185.
Kasirer, N. 1999. 'Lex-iconographie Mercatoria', *American Journal of Comparative Law*, vol. 47, pp. 633–676.
Lambert, J. 2009. 'The Status and Position of Legal Translation: a Chapter in the Discursive Construction of Communities'. In: F. Olsen, A. Lorz and D. Stein eds. *Translation Issues in Language and Law*. Basingstoke: Palgrave Macmillan, pp. 76–95.
Legrand, P. 2005. 'Issues in the Translatability of Law'. In: S. Bermann and M. Wood eds. *Nation, Language, and the Ethics of Translation*. Princeton University Press, pp. 30–50.
Mellinkoff, D. 1963. *The Language of the Law*. Boston: Little, Brown and Co.
Merry, S. 1987. 'Disputing Without Culture', *Harvard Law Review*, vol. 100, pp. 2057–2109.
Mertz, E. 2007. *The Language of Law School: Learning to 'Think Like a Lawyer'*. Oxford University Press.
Mikkelson, H. 1995. 'On the Horns of a Dilemma: Accuracy vs. Brevity in the Use of Legal Terms by Court Interpreters'. In: M. Morris ed. *Translation and the Law*. Amsterdam: John Benjamins Publishing, pp. 201–218.
Morrison, M.J. 1989. 'Excursions into the Nature of Legal Language', *Cleveland State Law Review*, vol. 37, pp. 271–290.
Nida, E. [1964] 2000. 'Principles of Correspondence'. In: L. Venuti ed. *The Translation Studies Reader*. London: Routledge, pp. 126–140.
Ortega y Gasset, J. [1937] 2000. 'The Misery and the Splendor of Translation'. In: L. Venuti ed. *The Translation Studies Reader*. Trans. E.G. Miller. London: Routledge, pp. 49–64.
Potter, P.B. 2001. *The Chinese Legal System: Globalization and Local Legal Culture*. London: Routledge.

Šarčević, S. 1985. 'Translation of Culture-Bound Terms in Laws', *Multilingua*, vol. 4(3), pp. 127–133.
Tiersma, P. 1999. *Legal Language*. University of Chicago Press.
Triebel, V. 2009. 'Pitfalls of English as a Contract Language'. In: F. Olsen, A. Lorz and D. Stein eds. *Translation Issues in Language and Law*. Basingstoke: Palgrave Macmillan, pp. 147–181.
Venuti, L. (ed.). 2000. *The Translation Studies Reader*. London: Routledge.
Watson, A. 1974. *Legal Transplants: An Approach to Comparative Law*. Edinburgh: Scottish Academic Press.
Zhang, D. 2002. *Key Concepts in Chinese Philosophy*. E. Ryden trans. New Haven: Yale University Press.

Chapter 4
Translation Equivalence as Legal Fiction[1]

Janny HC Leung

A translated text shall be the same as the original text. This simple and often assumed, but hardly incontrovertible, requirement provides the foundation of the language policy of many bilingual or multilingual jurisdictions (hereafter bilingual jurisdictions). An important question associated with the proposition persists, however, regarding the kind of equivalence that underlies the stated notion of "sameness." Bilingual jurisprudence assumes that a translation and its original will carry the same meaning. Yet such an assumption is frequently challenged by instances where textual differences are discovered that call for painstaking reconciliation based on interpretative principles. Although it is widely recognized outside the field of law that translations can hardly be perfect, bilingual legal systems rely on an unsafe assumption of translation equivalence, presumably because for law in particular the notion has a certain utility. Is textual equivalence, in these circumstances, a legal fiction (as historically "benefit of clergy", John Doe, and "steward of the Chiltern Hundreds" were, and others remain today)? If so, what function, as a part of legal reasoning, does this putative legal fiction serve? This chapter analyzes the specific nature and significance of translation equivalence as a legal fiction, as well as the purposes it may serve. That analysis is then used to illustrate broader issues regarding law, translation, and the relationship between the two.

1. Translation Equivalence as Imaginary

The usefulness and merit of a translation are often measured by its closeness to an original in terms of a number of variables, including form, content, style, function and effect.

While translation theories have tended primarily to emphasize formal and functional aspects of the notion of equivalence (Wolff 2011), there is general consensus that full equivalence—equivalence across all variables—is impossible (Bassnett 2000). The Italian proverb 'traduttore, traditore' (translator, traitor) encapsulates a frustration that almost unavoidably results. Just consider some word-pairs that appear very similar in conceptual meaning (e.g., "expert" and "connoisseur", or "mistake" and "error"): these words still inevitably differ in their associations, connotations, collocations and/or frequency of usage. Synonymy in the strictest sense (see 'absolute synonymy' in Lyons 1995), where alternative use of two distinct words in a given context generates the same effect, cannot be found within or between language systems (Jakobson 1959).

1 The author would like to thank Professor Alan Durant and Dr Frederick Blumberg for their invaluable feedback on an earlier draft of this chapter.

Since nobody has seen what a perfect translation looks like (assuming that perfection implies full equivalence), it seems reasonable to say that the ideal of equivalence is just that: something for which we strive without being able ever to realize it. Lack of realistic grounding for a view of perfection need not prevent an aspiration from being valuable, however: an unreachable goal may guide the translator in her work; and the resulting effect may be similar to how one might regard the concept of justice itself, as an end goal of law despite the fact that a shortfall between the two is frequently revealed.

In law, the presumption that bilingual and multilingual texts carry the same meaning is crucial to many contracts, statutes and treaties, to the degree that the principle has been codified in some legal texts of these kinds. But if equivalence exists only in our imagination, then such a legal presumption can appear somewhat risky. Could the legal understanding of textual "equivalence"' across languages be in some profound way different from that of a translator? If so, in what respect does such a legal understanding stand on safer ground? Alternatively, is "equivalence" a legal fiction, whose difference from reality forms the essence of its existence and function? Before we tackle these questions, let us first understand what legal fictions are and what they do.

2. Nature and Functions of Legal Fictions

In its broadest sense, fiction is the creation of a proposition or narrative that posits the existence of certain states of affairs which do not necessarily correspond to, or depict, actual states of affairs. The fiction is created and conveyed without the ultimate intention of deceiving the reader or listener as to the facticity of the states of affairs represented.

This concept of fiction is more commonly associated with literary arts than with legal discourse. Despite the stronger association with literature, however, lawyers and legal scholars have developed a specialized use for the term "legal fiction"—and for the concept throughout the historical development of common law, with particular legal fictions emerging, evolving, and receding in different periods according to their practical value.

Over time, the notion of "legal fiction" has come to include established concepts such as "implied conditions," "attractive nuisance," and "corporate personality." An "implied condition," for example, is taken to be part of a contract even if no party to the contract has ever considered it. According to the "attractive nuisance" doctrine, children are treated as invitees rather than trespassers on a property if that property contains objects that would entice them into it. The action of an agent is an action of the corporation. In each case, the legal fiction can be understood as purposeful make-believe, consisting of explicit or implied statements that are not literally true. Yet despite being counterfactual, those statements are not meant to deceive, so they cannot properly be understood as lies (Fuller 1967). The statements are not erroneous conclusions either, derived from misdirected argument or incorrect evidence, since they are devices that, through conscious pretense, allow judges to use settled law creatively to deal with unforeseen situations (such as new case facts, and potential new members of some given conceptual category) without having to bend the existing rule overtly (Fuller 1967; Schane 2006). This is why legal fictions are particularly associated with common law traditions, where the contribution they make to legal reasoning is most compatible with the notion of proper development of the law through judicial reasoning.

Although it is not difficult to illustrate the concept of legal fiction with typical examples, there is little agreement about the exact nature and scope of the overall class. Some early writers on the topic, such as Jeremy Bentham writing in the 18th century, treated the concept of legal fiction as some kind of professional disgrace. 'A fiction of law may be defined – a wilful falsehood, having for its object the stealing legislative power, by and for hands which could not, or durst not, openly claim it, – and, but for the delusion thus produced, could not exercise it' (Bowring 1843 vol. 1: 243). Bentham condemned legal fictions as 'lying', 'a wart', and 'a syphilis', since they deform the face of justice and carry into every part of the system 'the principle of rottenness' (Bowring 1843 vol. 5: 92). Equally famously, but writing nearly 100 years later, Henry Maine ([1861] 1917) ridiculed Bentham's sentiments. He saw practical value in legal fictions, in that they make possible the historical development of law. Maine drew on parallels between legal fictions and concepts such as equity and legislation, viewing all of these as deep-rooted principles and procedures of legal thought. Considering a legal fiction to be a device that brings law into harmony with society, rather than damaging that relation, Maine defines legal fiction as 'any assumption which conceals, or affects to conceal, the fact that a rule has undergone alteration, its letter remaining unchanged, its operation being modified' (Id.).

The varieties and scope of legal fictions have invited considerable interest. Baker (2001), for example, distinguishes between an evidential fiction[2] and a factual fiction,[3] as well as identifying what he calls the 'linguistic fictions' of deeming[4] and counterfactual presumption.[5] Baker argues that only the first two are genuine legal fictions. Deeming and presumption, by contrast, are for him rules of law, since they are not capable of being true or false (44). "Deeming", for example, is primarily a legal trope involving analogy: something is judged to be sufficiently similar to something else for a given legal purpose that it can be judged to be an (exceptional) member of that class. Opening up a contrasting view much earlier in the history of analyzing legal fictions, Finch (1759) had referred only to deeming and presumptions as legal fictions; and the Canadian Department of Justice similarly still regards legal fictions as serving primarily the basic purpose of deeming.[6] Other writers, such as Lon Fuller in his overview of the field in the 1930s ([1930–1931] 1967), have embraced all of these kinds of legal imagining as kinds of legal fiction.

Such debates are legally and philosophically important. But since the focus of this chapter is on understanding the nature, functioning and significance of translation equivalence in terms of the concept of legal fiction, rather than on the meaning or significance of the concept of legal fiction itself, Fuller's influential account of the concept will be taken as a principal reference point, with Baker's classification and others introduced where relevant to the discussion.

3. Equivalence as a Legal Fiction

Bilingual jurisdictions that uphold linguistic equality, such as Canada, Hong Kong, and the European Union, often have a rule called the "equal authenticity principle." According to this principle, the text of the law in each language is equally authoritative.

One corollary of an "equal authenticity principle" is some codified stipulation that different language texts will be considered as having the same meaning. For instance, Article 33(3) of

2 In these cases it is the evidence that is fictionalized, e.g., proof of adultery in divorce, or proof of reading skills to verify clergy identity.

3 In these cases, 'proof of a certain fact asserted in a lawsuit is completely dispensed with by the simple expedient of denying any means of disputing it' (Baker 2001: 41). Baker calls them classic fictions and cites the crown as an example of a fiction which has replaced that of the queen's two bodies following conventional usage.

4 Also called statutory fictions; a rule of law which seems to conflict with natural reality. It may be achieved by defining ordinary words with special legal meanings, or expanding a legal concept.

5 To treat X as Y for a particular legal purpose.

6 See http://www.justice.gc.ca/eng/dept-min/pub/legis/n8.html.

the Vienna Convention on the Law of Treaties (1969) states that '(t)he terms of the treaty are presumed to have the same meaning in each authentic text'. Similarly, Section 10B(2) of the Interpretation and General Clauses Ordinance in Hong Kong stipulates that '(t)he provisions of an Ordinance are presumed to have the same meaning in each authentic text'. Given that different language texts of the law are produced by means of translation, this presumption effectively says that a translation has the same meaning as its original, although terms such as "translation" and "original" themselves are generally avoided in the context of bilingual legislation (a point that will be elaborated in the next section).

Even these features of the notion of translation equivalence suggest that the concept might usefully be viewed as a legal fiction. That this could be so is not a new claim, of course (see, e.g., Cao 2010). However, discussion of this possibility, and its consequences, has so far remained rather simplistic, motivated chiefly by a perception that some particular assertion or presumption is false, even if not *consciously* false, while ignoring what may be a deeper work of concealment performed by the fiction in operation. Such deeper work of concealment springs from the fact that, while translated legislative texts are almost universally acknowledged as translations, and so are not facially deceptive, they may nevertheless obscure an extended exercise of legislative power by the courts.

How *far* the notion of legal fiction can be useful in understanding translation equivalence depends on more careful analysis, nevertheless. It is necessary, for example, to look more closely at those aspects of legal fictions that Baker and other writers have considered essential characteristics and to assess how far those characteristics are found in the treatment of translated legal texts. Such characteristics include at least the following: what might be called "basic properties" of translated legal texts, which may or may not qualify them as "fictitious" in a relevant sense; the functions served by the doctrine of translation equivalence (both overtly and covertly); some particular *kind* of legal fiction device in operation, as identified according to Baker's or some other system of classification; how safe or otherwise such a legal fiction would be, as judged for example against a standard of consciousness with which it is applied; and the future prospects for such a legal fiction, if considered against anticipated legal mechanisms by which it might be expected to be absorbed into other channels of legal reasoning or superseded by legislation. Each of these main considerations is now explored briefly in turn.

3.1. Basic Properties

If we accept the proposition that a translation and its original may only be truly the same in our imagination, then any presumption of textual equivalence must appear counterfactual. As the basis of such a presumption, relatedly, an "equal authenticity" principle therefore will have the most basic quality of a legal fiction: that of falsehood. There is another prototypical characteristic, too: that of pretense. Pretense is inevitable if the law is to act as though the fiction is real. For Fuller, it is the presence or absence of pretense that determines whether a legal fiction is 'dead or alive' (Fuller 1967: 19): the mental effort involved in pretense is not needed if a fiction is dead. When a legal fiction is "alive," on the other hand, judges are required to suspend their disbelief temporarily, and to pretend actively that original and translated texts do carry the same meaning. Such pretense has effects in areas beyond the stipulation of textual equivalence itself. It also plays a part in a kind of self-censorship in bilingual jurisdictions, which discourages legal practitioners from calling a translation a translation or referring to translation errors as translation errors (instead, one must call them, respectively, "text/

version" or "difference/discrepancy of meaning"[7]). In effect, such jurisdictions paint out the translation process and the people who do it from the image of law they create. One could also go further and argue that "authentication" (the legislative process through which a translation acquires the status of an authentic text) removes inferior connotations from the translated text which would otherwise subvert the principle of equal authenticity by suggesting that different language texts have unequal status. The effect, if not the purpose, of suppressing fuzziness in translation from the image of law is to strengthen the presumption of textual equivalence and so create a coherent narrative around this legal fiction.

3.2. Overt and Covert Functions

The positive claim usually made about legal fictions is that they are well adapted to solving problems which can arise when judges seek to apply an established statement of the law in dealing with new and complex fact-situations. Does the same or an equivalent role exist for translation equivalence in resolving legal problems?

First, we must note that a policy of legal bilingualism complicates understanding of what any given source of law really says. For any particular source, there are two or more authentic texts, both or all of them carrying the same authority but not automatically conveying the same meaning. Any textual discrepancy between them becomes a source of indeterminacy that can perturb a legal system founded on predictability, consistency of interpretation, and an underlying principle of legal certainty.

In such circumstances, the stipulation that guides bilingual statutory interpretation eases anxiety not only by insisting that the new text is as good as the old text but that the new text *is the same as* the old one. There is in effect just one version of the law, as if the jurisdiction were monolingual. To the extent that the goal of maintaining legal certainty is an important legal principle, the fiction accordingly seems an acceptable means of achieving that goal.

Legislators are unlikely, however, to be ignorant of difficulties involved in translation and the likelihood of textual discrepancies. Presumption of equivalence is scarcely irrefutable. Yet such presumption of equivalence will be upheld until all efforts to reconcile the meanings of the texts have been exhausted. Only when the presumption is rebutted in a given situation should one adopt the meaning which best serves the object and purpose of the law.[8] Oddly, at least at first sight, the importance of the presumption seems inversely proportional to the ease of overturning it. Rather than simply ensuring that judges keep the equal authenticity principle in mind, the presumption acts as an invisible bridge[9] which mutually binds two texts that would normally be considered discrepant; and the overarching prescription of textual equivalence exerts greatest force on occasions when a fact is assumed or known to be false (Fuller 1967).

7 E.g., 'A Paper Discussing Cases Where the Two Language Texts of an Enactment are Alleged to be Different', Law Drafting Division, Department of Justice, Hong Kong, May 1998.

8 For example, VCLT Article 33(4) states that 'where a comparison of the authentic texts discloses a difference of meaning which the application of articles 31 and 32 does not remove, the meaning which best reconciles the texts, having regard to the object and purpose of the treaty, shall be adopted.' Article 31 stipulates general rule of interpretation, such as how terms should be read with their ordinary meaning and the contextual factors that should be considered. Article 32 stipulates supplementary means of interpretation, including preparatory work of the treaty and the circumstances of its conclusion.

9 Baker (2001) says that 'We would only enter the realm of fiction if an invisible thumbprint alone were held to work the required magic' (47). The presumption seems to be that invisible thumbprint that may provide a shared meaning between texts when there is none.

A useful case in point is the Hong Kong case of *HKSAR v Tam Yuk Ha*, (1997) 2 HKC 531. The case concerned some metal trays and other items which the defendant had placed in front of her fresh provisions shop, and the question for the court was whether such placement constituted an offence under a bylaw which regulates unauthorized changes to building plans. The defendant's action fell within the scope of the bylaw if one considers the phrase "alteration or addition" in the English version. But such an interpretation appears contrary to intuition for any native speaker of Chinese if such placement is considered a "增建工程" (zeng jian gong cheng) (literally, "building additional construction or building works"), as in the Chinese version.[10] In order to preserve the presumption of textual equivalence, the appellate court departed from the ordinary meaning of the Chinese. Instead it relied on uncommon, outlier senses of the Chinese characters found in a dictionary, and interpreted the Chinese expression as being consistent with its English equivalent. On this basis, it was held that the law did cover the relevant facts of the case.

In cases such as *HKSAR v Tam Yuk Ha*, the presumption of textual equivalence affects—or reflects—judgments as to how equal two authentic texts are, and encourages readings that treat the texts as more equal than one normally would. In broader terms, an unacknowledged function of the presumption is to permit latitude in bending ordinary meaning by concealing a gap between theory and practice.

There is an additional layer of legal obscurity, which may be more disconcerting: the possibility of retrospective application of the law. The linguistic indeterminacy of bilingual legislation can make it more difficult than in a monolingual jurisdiction to predict legal outcomes, since harmonization of meanings across two or more "identical" texts may only be constructed when those texts are interpreted in the course of litigation, despite having come into force earlier. Following this line of argument, a codified presumption of equivalence appears to allow, or even invite, a shift in power from legislature to judiciary: the more textual discrepancies there are, the more scope there is for the courts to decide what the law really says. Such rebalancing of interpretation dynamics is not incompatible with the role of judges in common law systems. What is significant, however, is that the power shift brought about by such rebalancing is concealed by a stated commitment to a value that seems instead to limit latitude: that of textual equivalence.

3.3. Classification

What *type* of legal fiction, we can now ask, would a presumption of translation equivalence be, in Baker's or some other recognized classification? When the word "presumed" is used in stipulations of textual equivalence, it appears that such stipulation requires a counterfactual presumption. Such stipulation involves a 'linguistic fiction', in Baker's classification outlined above. But the fiction is also "statutory," in that it has been codified in international treaties and given effect in bilingual jurisdictions.

Recall that Baker (2001) himself sees 'nothing fictitious' in deeming and presumptions. All they do, as far as he is concerned, is to change the legal meaning of a word in such a way that it acquires a specialized legal purport instead of, or as well as, its more generally understood factual content (47). Legal thinking consists largely of concepts which are quite

10 In a related trial that took place earlier (*The Queen v. Tam Yuk Ha*, HCMA000933/1996), Justice Yeung has commented that 'No one who understands the Chinese language would, by any stretch of the imagination, come to the conclusion that the placing of metal trays and other items in front of the shop would be a 增建工程 (Zeng Jian Gong Cheng)'.

properly subject to redefinition. Fictions, on the other hand—as Baker points out—apply to facts, not matters of law.

It is relevant to map this type of classificatory argument onto the stipulation of translation equivalence with which this chapter began. That stipulation states that two authentic texts are presumed to have the same meaning. The wording is so simple that one wonders whether any legal concept is involved at all. What is hypothesized is merely a relationship between texts and, on an ordinary reading, such a relationship is a matter of fact. The adjective "same" does not seem to carry any technical legal meaning beyond its factual meaning. For that reason, the most likely candidate word as regards possible fit with Baker's classification of kinds of legal fiction is the word "meaning" itself. The ordinary meaning of this word "meaning" refers to what is expressed or represented. It is reasonable, accordingly, to infer that the stipulation does not presume that the authentic texts are identical in all their language properties (including informational, social, and affective content, style and collocation), and that the kind of equivalence at stake is not textual but legal. What is presumed might be taken to be the proposition that variant texts should achieve *the same legal effect*: that is, an application of any textual version of the same law to a case should lead to the same legal outcome.

In order to assess Baker's argument that presumptions are a rule of law (akin to deeming), and so not capable of being fictitious, we need to revisit the wider law-fact distinction. This distinction provides a means, widely recognized as "vexed" in accounts of common law reasoning, by which courts allocate decision-making power between judge and jury (Weiner 1966). Judges decide questions of legal principle and interpretation, which are matters of law, while jurors attend to the specific facts of a given case (for instance whether those facts have been sufficiently demonstrated by the evidence). As famously defined, law is 'a body of principles and rules which are capable of being predicated in advance and which are so predicated, awaiting proof of the facts necessary for their application', and fact is 'something which has happened or existed' (Bohlen 1924: 112). However, other than tautologically providing grounds for a strategic allocation of decision-making power, in many circumstances the notions of law and fact can seem not to reflect any principled, logical distinction. For instance, it is difficult if not impossible to see a clear boundary between law and fact capable of explaining why 'the excessiveness of punitive damages should be a question of law, while the amount of compensatory damages is a question of fact' (Thornburg 2010: 5). Such boundaries and distinctions are sometimes viewed instead as serving procedural needs, furthering the aim of ensuring consistency in application of the law.

How does this law/fact distinction affect the notion of translation equivalence? Beyond the conventional understanding that statutory interpretation rests squarely in the judge's domain, the question is whether there is any reason, other than procedural convenience, why presumption of textual equivalence involves a pure question of law? It should not be forgotten that the subject before the verb phrase "are presumed to have the same meaning" is algebraic, allowing for substitution into it of whatever words, phrases, or sentences are used in the legislative text in contention, irrespective of whether what is referred to involves terms from a treaty or the provisions of an ordinance.

In the reasoning applied in any given case, it is the scope of particular words, phrases or sentences that will determine whether a piece of legislation applies to the facts. The *Tam Yuk Ha* case can be used again to exemplify this. The scope of the phrase 'additional construction or building works/增建工程' determines whether the defendant will be found guilty if she placed the metal trays in front of her shop. In deciding cases such as this one, it is clear however that judges do not see themselves as dealing with technical legal meanings. Rather, their presumption of textual equivalence treats a factual relationship between words, phrases and sentences in two or more language versions; what makes this a question of law rather than of fact is only that the determination of the relationship affects the application of the law. Whether primary facts, fully found, come within a particular statutory description has accordingly been described as 'one of the worst grey areas' of the law/fact distinction (Ian 2007: 1), despite all the most important issues having been extensively tested in common law jurisprudence.

Because legislation must make reference to the world being regulated, it is inevitable that a stipulation of sameness of meaning will apply to words in legislative texts that have ordinary, non-technical meanings as well as to words that have established technical meanings. This observation is reinforced when judges, overcoming traditional reluctance, occasionally refer to dictionaries to delineate the scope of the words used in a legislative text under dispute, especially in cases where it has been submitted that there are discrepancies between the authentic texts. Deciding meaning may need to be the prerogative of a judge for procedural reasons; but this is hardly a "question of law" in any more analytic sense; and tension between these different understandings potentially creates a problem as regards legal certainty. For example, when laymen come across specific terms in legislative texts, there is no reason for them to believe that those terms should mean anything other than they normally mean (a belief strengthened by the interpretive doctrine of following plain meanings where available). Yet, as discussed above, the presumption of equivalence of meaning may encourage, even in some circumstances require, considerable bending of ordinary word-meanings in one language or another in order to secure a reasoned basis for the decision that the court presents as the correct one. A lay person might perceive this manipulation of meaning as a twisting of facts, or as a legal manoeuvre; and while this "laymen perspective" may be irrelevant as regards actual adjudication it may still be highly important as regards the legal principle of transparency and the notion of public understanding of and confidence in the justice system.

Given a fuzzy boundary between law and fact, as well as another fuzzy boundary between ordinary and legal meanings of words, the translation equivalence stipulation stands somewhere between Baker's category of "linguistic fiction" and his category of "factual fiction" (Baker 2001, discussed above). To understand translation equivalence as either completely a linguistic fiction or a factual fiction itself involves a form of obscurantism, leading to the next important consideration to address: that of the interpretive indeterminacy which the presumption entails.

3.4. Safety and Subjectivity

Fuller (1967) points out that a fiction 'becomes wholly safe only when it is used with a complete consciousness of its falsity' (1967: 10). Safety, in this context, involves sufficient distance from obviously associated risks such as that of dishonesty. But "consciousness," including consciousness of falsity, is an under-explored and yet important aspect of legal fictions. Falsehoods asserted *without* consciousness, for example, are simply erroneous statements. Falsehoods asserted *with* consciousness are either lies or fictions. Is a presumption of textual equivalence, we should therefore ask, a "safe" fiction in relation to these modalities?

As has been suggested above, there are various layers of possible disguise in the translation equivalence fiction. That fiction is built on a number of other positivistic fictions which include at least the following:

1. that legal texts have a plain, unique, and stable meaning (as contrasted with literary texts, translations of which are commonly regarded as different texts);
2. that meaning is capable of being represented in alternative written versions; and
3. that textual representations will be predictably interpreted as meaning the same thing on different occasions.

When case-facts force a spotlight on discrepant texts, and the various underlying fictions begin to crumble individually and cumulatively, the overall presumption steps in to bridge the gap between texts that opens up, in order to "achieve" (rather than simply reflect an already existing) equivalence.[11]

When problems arise between bilingual versions of legal texts, judges compare the relevant authentic texts and determine whether the two or more versions are equal. In this practice of analysis, an underlying assumption is involved that there *is* a truth of the matter, one way or the other, and that this truth can be discovered.

In his doctrine of the indeterminacy of translation, by contrast, Quine (1960) famously challenged that assumption. Based on his observation that the meanings of individual statements cannot be paired off with specific sets of experiences but are dependent on a language-specific system of reference, Quine dismantled the claim that meaning can be objective. Instead he argues that the meaning of a statement, including sameness of meaning in two different statements, is quite fundamentally not the sort of thing that one can be right or wrong about. In other words, there is no fact of the matter whether a source language (SL) text, and a target language (TL) text, mean the same thing. Quine's conclusion may not be convenient for court tasked with deciding particular cases rather than reflecting philosophically on problems of meaning. But it cannot easily be wished away by a simple act of presumption.

This is where judicial consciousness becomes important. Unlike classic legal fictions such as "attractive nuisance" or "implied conditions," the falsity of the fiction of textual equivalence highlighted by the work of Quine and many others since (and subscribed to by virtually all practising translators) rarely seems to enter judicial consciousness, at least as reported in proceedings whose insistence on the connectedness of facts, legal reasoning and outcome is essential in upholding the law. Some judges may genuinely believe they are locating an objective truth when comparing the sameness of texts. Others may feel they have arrived at a correct solution when a particular way of reconciling a particular discrepancy has been found. Either way, the underlying presumption generates not only external but also internal deception (Fuller 1967), and creates a false impression of legitimacy. The contrasting possibility, that there is no ready-made truth of fixed meaning but only active judgment, nevertheless repeatedly resurfaces in the frequency with which judges themselves disagree over the versions of truth on such matters that other judges have found.

There is a deeper danger inherent in the fiction of translation equivalence, as a result. This lies in only partial awareness of how the principle conceals the subjectivity involved in the exercise of judgment. The presumption only appears true if the texts in question are read in a certain way. More formally, but also more starkly, the translation equivalence stipulation might be said to allow *ad hoc*, subjective judgment on mixed questions of law and fact which are presented together as a legal issue that is thought to be answerable objectively by means of a close reading of texts.

Consider the *Tam Yuk Ha* case mentioned above once more. In that case, the judges looked up characters "建" (jian) and "工程" (gong cheng) in the phrase '增建工程' (zeng jian gong cheng) in a dictionary,[12] then looked up keywords contained in the dictionary definition of " 工程" (gong cheng)—that is, they looked up the meaning of words used as the meanings of other words—then selected among the listed senses of the characters involved and combined those senses (irrespective of collocational implications that might affect the suitability of those

11 When discrepancies are deemed as irreconcilable, the presumption is overturned; in such cases courts may consider the shared meaning of the texts or the object and purpose of the legislation.

12 The court relies on external authority when constructing the meaning of the Chinese expression concerned. It was further stated that 'unless the pertinent definitions of the Commercial Press, albeit published in 1987, can be demonstrated to be fundamental flaws, it would be quite unnecessary to proceed to consider a whole spectrum of meanings of these two characters.'

meanings in a given context) in order to arrive at a "consistent reading" of the discrepant texts. The overarching assumption that equivalence may be found via a close reading of texts in this way masks a series of opportunities for legal indeterminacy. Neither treating translation equivalence as a rule of law, nor as a matter of fact, properly acknowledges the indeterminacy implicit in the presumption. It might be more accurate to say that, before the court's judgment is handed down, the answer to the question it is addressing is neither already in existence nor clearly predicated.

3.5. Fading and Fixing

Let us next consider the fate of legal fictions: how they rise and wane over time in a legal system. Examining this aspect of legal fictions offers a way of posing the question whether the fiction of textual equivalence is likely to survive in the future development of bilingual and multilingual jurisdictions.

The usual starting point for considering this aspect of legal fictions is the idea that, if one views legal fictions as devices which assist the process through which the law (especially the common law) matures, then their role might be expected to diminish over time. In practice, legal fictions tend to be eliminated by two related processes: the process of "rejection" and that of "redefinition" (Fuller 1967). "Rejection" involves the discarding of fictitious statements such as removal of outdated evidential requirements that required the fiction in the first place. "Redefinition" allows necessary concepts, arguments and factual relations to enter into law as new meanings within the field's technical vocabulary, bringing about the death of the legal fiction concerned (in a process similar to how metaphors die through repeated usage and become 'ordinary' meanings). In some instances, legislative change is used to fill a gap that a fiction had previously filled; in other circumstances, there is no need for legislation and gradual processes of absorption and adaptation are sufficient.

Reflecting on how legal fictions work, Fuller suggests that 'the purpose of any fiction is to reconcile a specific legal result with some premise or postulate' (1967: 51). In the case of the presumption of textual equivalence, the fiction makes it possible to reconcile a potentially undesirable legal *result*—the indeterminacy of meaning of a particular piece of bilingual legislation—with a *premise*: that of equal authenticity. In other words, the fiction is need-driven, motivated by a policy imperative that is in some sense impossible to fulfill. The impossibility follows from the fact that bilingual legislative texts cannot be acknowledged to mean different things while at the same time claiming that they are equally authentic. Rejection of the presumption of equivalence would need to be accompanied by rejection of the equal authenticity principle itself. In many circumstances, the broader principle of equal authenticity may be essential politically, even if it leads to problems once developed into policy and enacted as law that has to be applied. Even so, rejection of an 'equal authenticity' principle need not be incompatible with a policy that still incorporates legal bilingualism: some bilingual jurisdictions (such as Belgium, Ireland, Malaysia and Malta) do designate one text as having more authority than another where a dispute between alternative versions arises (e.g., in Malta, Maltese shall prevail in case of conflict between the Maltese and the English texts of the law).

How *far* the fiction of translation equivalence could recede as a result of redefinition is unclear. Since this fiction is superimposed on other fictions, in ways described above, it is difficult to disentangle it without exacerbating contradictions inherent in those other fictions. One possibility might be to narrow the meanings of the word "meaning" itself in the stipulation of textual equivalence, for example, to "legal meaning," or alternatively to change the presumption so that it states that two authentic texts should be presumed 'to have the same legal effect'. Such redefinitions would substitute a more clearly legal relationship for an apparently factual relationship.

Whatever practical reforms might be attempted, however, as long as texts are contrasted in respect of their legal meaning, and a presumption of equivalence works either explicitly or implicitly to influence reasoning (so that meanings across texts will be harmonized to generate the same legal effect), the strain currently on alternative language versions of law will not disappear entirely (though it might be eased in terms of the extent of disguise involved).

Another practical possibility might be to ensure that the presumption as it stands is made rebuttable, in order to reduce its tendency to produce belief beyond an ordinary inference one might draw from the evidence available. This strategy would however seem to defy the purpose of having the presumption at all. As has been pointed out by Fuller, in more cases than not rebuttable presumptions tend to become increasingly limiting in the rebuttals they allow, and end up being conclusive presumptions (Fuller 1967). In any event, to the extent that a legal relationship remains subject to interpretation, the same degree of legal indeterminacy would still be present.

4. Implications for Legal Translation and Translation Theories

The kinds of argument under scrutiny in this chapter matter. They matter because the fiction of textual equivalence is crucial to the functioning of bilingual and multilingual law, in a world in which not only at national but also at international level bilingual and multilingual legal systems are becoming both more widespread and more important. They also matter because the principle of translation equivalence guides the reading of *all* legislative texts in a given jurisdiction, and so has more than isolated or limited effect. Whether, and if so in what ways, "equivalence" is a legal fiction should consequently form part of any successful theory of legal translation.

It is commonplace for translation theorists, for example, to refer to different *types* of equivalence in a translation, such as linguistic, conceptual and functional equivalence (Šarčević 1997). But the presumption of equivalence in law in particular pushes that established translation-theory concept into new and difficult territory. This is because law understandably allows little tolerance of discrepancy between a SL text and a TL text, and responds instead, as has been argued above, with a presumption that seeks to bridge the gap between the two.

No similar obsession with the ideal of translation equivalence is found in other fields. Nor is the same level of concern felt in relation to other translation genres, such as literary or journalistic translation. In work on literary translation, for instance, there is general recognition that refraction and the adaptation of a work of literature for a different audience will necessarily be involved in the process of translation (Lefevere 1982). Some literary genres, such as poetry, are notoriously difficult to translate precisely for reasons that push at the impossibility of equivalence rather than any presumption of it. Different genres in this way set different standards when it comes to what will count as their anticipated degree or kind of equivalence, or at least approximation. At present, however, there seems less readiness in translation to acknowledge the challenge presented by translating legal propositions in particular, which are often associated with clarity, precision, information or explicit performatives and can appear to be more concrete, stable and straightforward, possibly encouraging optimism as a result as regards translation equivalence.

Perhaps the most striking difference between translation of legal texts and of literary texts is that there is typically far greater recognition of the subjectivity involved in interpretation in literary translation, whereas in a legal context such recognition is regularly suppressed.

Combined with the kinds of indeterminacy of meaning already noted, the subjectivity revealed in translation of legal texts has far-reaching implications for translation theories in general. The indeterminacy which subverts translation equivalence has the effect of destabilizing the role of the translator as a sole agent, responsible for creating an equivalent effect by means of the translation, and adds a cloud of uncertainty over what kinds of functional or dynamic equivalence should be sought.

The legal translator simply has no control over reader experience and motivation, which together supply a crucial context in which the meaning of a translation will be determined. A translator may attempt to take into account, perhaps in collaboration with legislators, the policy concerns and legal effect that drive the enactment of the legislation, as a way of minimizing variance. But it is mistaken to assume that even legislators themselves can predict all the future circumstances that a piece of legislation is supposed to cover, utopian to suppose that equivalence becomes achievable once the purpose of a legal text is known, and naïve to imagine that subjectivity on the part of the reader can be eliminated.

Despite these difficulties, the impossibility of a perfect translation should not discourage the training of better translators and the production of better translations. Rather, the issues raised by translation equivalence should be a substantial topic in training programmes for legal translators, helping translators to understand the nature of language better and the task they have at hand.

5. Conclusion

As Fuller (1967) has put it, legal fictions represent 'the pathology of the law' (viii). As with counterparts in other areas of law, symptoms presented by the legal fiction of translation equivalence may be informative in the way that illness helps us to understand the body. In particular, the concealment work that the presumption of textual equivalence performs on the role of subjectivity in translation may illustrate a wider practice at work in legal rhetoric.

Alongside such general illustration, however, there are more specific features of translation equivalence that invite closer analysis. Unlike many legal fictions that have been studied, translation equivalence is not interesting simply because it provides a bold, innovative, or exemplary instance of the breadth and ingenuity of the legal imagination when faced with a challenge of reasoning. Rather, it is interesting because it is hideous, structurally complex, and exercises widespread but unacknowledged power. These are severe criticisms, and require comment. Translation equivalence is hideous because its fictitious aspect rarely enters judicial or public consciousness. It is structurally complex because it hovers somewhere between law and fact, and is embedded in a network of other presumptions that serve collectively to secure the authority of law. And its power is extensive, and conceals far-flung implications, because it goes beyond extending a piece of law to cover a new situation and plays a major part in governing the reading of all laws in bilingual and multilingual jurisdictions.

Although cases in which the presumption surfaces as an immediate problem may be exceptional, translation equivalence underlies all judgments of the courts in bilingual and multilingual jurisdictions and affects the esteem in which the law is held by different language-user groups. Legal fictions can alienate lay people from the law, and the legal fiction of textual equivalence in particular (if the arguments presented above are accepted) seems likely to create false expectations about the stability of law. Citizens in bilingual or multilingual jurisdictions will generally rely on one version of the law that they can comprehend in their own first (or only) language. They are unlikely to contemplate how the equivalence or non-equivalence of that version with one or more other texts of the same law might impact on what the law really says, how any variation between sources might apply to their present or anticipated behaviour, or how the law will be interpreted when its alternative textual versions are compared and explicated in the course of litigation.

Overall, we might say that translation equivalence intersects in significant ways with the established concept of legal fiction. It may nevertheless not be fully reducible to that concept. In fact, following Baker's logic, since "legal fiction" is itself a legal concept and since legal terms are subject to legal interpretation, there may be no truth regarding whether equivalence is or is not properly a legal fiction, either now or possibly ever. This chapter, accordingly, does not claim to have demonstrated that translation equivalence is a legal fiction. Rather, its analysis of such equivalence employing the concept of legal fiction draws attention to the functioning and implications of stipulations regarding meaning equivalence in law. Such analysis, it is hoped, may assist better understanding of the law, translation, and the unstable relationship between the two.

References

Baker, J.H. 2001. *The Law's Two Bodies: Some Evidential Problems in English Legal History*. Oxford University Press.

Bassnett, S. [1980] 2000. *Translation Studies*. Rev. edn. London and New York: Routledge.

Bohlen, F.H. 1924. 'Mixed Questions of Law and Fact', *University of Pennsylvania Law Review*, vol. 72, pp. 111–122.

Bowring, J. (ed.). 1843. *The Works of Jeremy Bentham (Principles of Morals and Legislation, Fragment on Government, Civil Code, Penal Law)*.

Cao, D. 2010. 'Judicial Interpretation of Bilingual and Multilingual Laws: A European and Hong Kong Comparison'. In: J. Jemielniak and P. Miklaszewixz eds. *Interpretation of Law in the Global World: From Particularism to a Universal Approach*, Berlin Heidelberg: Springer-Verlag, pp. 71–86.

Ellis-Jones, I. 2007. 'The Ever Elusive Fact/Law Distinction', *Local Government Law Journal*, vol. 13, p. 66.

Finch, H. 1759. *Law, Or, A Discourse Thereof*. Gale: Eighteenth Century Collections Online.

Fuller, L.L. 1967. *Legal Fictions*. Stanford University Press.

Jakobson, R. 1959. 'On Linguistic Aspects of Translation'. In: R.A. Bower ed. *On Translation*. Cambridge, Mass.: Harvard University Press, pp. 232–239.

Lefevere, A. 1982. 'Mother Courage's Cucumbers: Text, System and Refraction in a Theory of Literature', *Modern Language Studies*, vol. 12(4), pp. 3–20.

Lyons, J. 1995. *Linguistic Semantics*. Cambridge University Press.

Maine, H. [1861] 1917. *Ancient Law*. London: J.M. Dent & Sons; New York: E.P. Dutton.

Quine, W. 1960. *Word and Object*. Cambridge, Mass.: The MIT Press.

Šarčević, S. 1997. *New Approach to Legal Translation*. The Hague: Kluwer Law International.

Schane, S. 2006. *Language and the Law*. London/New York: Continuum.

Thornburg, E.G. 2010. 'Law, Facts, and Power', *Penn State Law Review*, vol. 114(1). Available at SSRN: http://ssrn.com/abstract=1540092.

Weiner, S.A. 1966. 'The Civil Jury Trial and the Law-Fact Distinction', *California Law Review*, vol. 54(5), pp. 1867–1938.

Wolff, L. 2011. 'Legal Translation'. In: K. Malmkjer and K. Windle eds. *The Oxford Handbook of Translation Studies*. Oxford University Press, pp. 228–242.

Chapter 5
Trying to See the Wood Despite the Trees: A Plain Approach to Legal Translation

Víctor González-Ruiz

1. The Communicative Flaws of Legal Language

In this chapter I will discuss an alternative approach to legal translation based on the arguments of the plain language movement, and will describe an experiment measuring how legal professionals perceive translations not written in the ordinary, traditional style.

In most English and Spanish-speaking countries, lawyers tend to use a language which is not easily understood by everyone participating in the system of the law (e.g., lay citizens affected by a particular legal speech act). This assertion derives not only from my own examination of legal texts and the way they are received by my relatives, friends, students and expert colleagues, but also from professional and scholarly research profusely carried out in the field of legal language. So far, anglophone authors have been the most prolific at studying whether there is actually a problem concerning lawyers' utterances, and which are the most pressing needs and deficiencies of legal communication. Mellinkoff (1963; 1982), Kimble (e.g., 1995; 2006), Tiersma (1999), Garner (e.g., 2001; 2011), Asprey (2003), Wydick (2005), Adler (2006), and Butt and Castle (2006), among others, have found that the English language used in the law is pointlessly convoluted, and most of them have put forward their own suggestions to amend its flaws. These contributions have gone hand in hand with the variety of professional associations which have advocated the reform of complex legal jargon and its associated modes of expression, such as the language used by civil servants (e.g., Clarity, Plain English Campaign, Plain English Commission and Plain Language Association International).

Although not so confidently as their anglophone counterparts, Spanish-speaking academics and professionals of the law have also acknowledged that legal Spanish features an ornate style which usually results in lack of clarity. Most significantly, the *Comisión para la Modernización del Lenguaje Jurídico*, an interdisciplinary expert committee backed by Spain's Department of Justice, have carried out several studies on the language used in a range of legal settings, and have concluded that lawyers and others involved in the application of the law need to dramatically improve the way they communicate (García de la Concha et al. 2011). As an example of similar public initiatives in the Spanish-speaking world, Mexico's Government also regard the discourse of their authorities as too elaborate and difficult to cope with, and have developed a set of reforming measures under the motto *Lenguaje ciudadano*, which includes the publication of a textbook which shows members of the civil service how to better inform Mexican citizens of their rights and obligations (Valdovinos Chávez et al. 2007).

The work carried out by all these experts (ranging from academics in the fields of linguistics and law, to practising lawyers and language consultants) provides authoritative evidence that those using the language of the law tend to overlook the principles of good expression. Despite their diverse historical backgrounds, the scenario seems to be the same in both English and Spanish-speaking systems. As regards legal English, Tiersma (1999) links its complex nature to the following characteristics:

- an excess of technical vocabulary;
- ever-present archaic, formal, and unusual words;
- frequent reliance on impersonal constructions;
- overuse of nominalizations and passives;
- excessive resort to certain modal verbs (e.g. 'shall');
- abundant instances of multiple negation;
- a textual form based on long and complex sentences; and
- a usually manifest poor organization.

These traits of legal language especially affect the comprehension of the ordinary lay public, for example when these must abide by the words of a binding consumer document or a set of jury instructions (i.e., according to Tiersma (1999), the two areas of legal language where citizens with no expert training are the main audience). However, even within the broad concept of 'internal legal language' (i.e., Tiersma's (1999: 211) label for the texts addressed primarily to legal practitioners), excessive obstacles to fluent communication may undermine the public's rights. As Tiersma (1999: 211) comments, 'it is not unreasonable to suggest that even internal legal documents be written in the most intelligible possible way, so that the client who paid to have the document prepared, and whose rights and duties are affected by it, knows what is being proposed on her behalf.'

Spanish-speaking legal professionals share with their English-speaking colleagues the taste for an elaborate and archaic-sounding style in their discourse. Among other findings in her thorough analysis of written legal discourse in Spain, Montolío Durán (2011) indicates that written texts suffer from rare vocabulary (including Latin phrases, archaic words and pompous formulas), complex syntactic structures, long sentences, and abundant instances of inadequate grammar, punctuation and cohesion. Similarly, Spanish lawyers tend to favour the complex over the simple in their oral performances (both in terms of syntax and vocabulary), regardless of the fact that the person they are speaking to cannot understand what they say, according to Briz Gómez (2011).

It is a matter of controversy whether lawyers have a right to speak and write as they do, however substandard their usage of language seems to be. In professional terms, their conventional discourse has proved successful at attaining business objectives—rarely has a pleading or an agreement been rejected on the grounds of poor grammar. However, experts concerned with the shortcomings of legal language have convincingly showed that, irrespective of its being a reliable business vehicle, there are no sound reasons to keep lawyers' expressions the way they have been for centuries (i.e., unclear, complex, and excessively formal), apart from the fact that they are conventional. This is a matter of concern particularly when this elaborate style threatens the right to understand of those most influenced by the machinery of the law (i.e., the millions of lay citizens living in any democratic country).

As to the significance of tradition in legal drafting, Wagner and Cacciaguidi-Fahy (2006: 20) refer to 'professional inertia and conservative attitudes', and 'a strong apprehension that the use of simple vocabulary may lead to added ambiguity in so far that departing from traditional legal language and style may result in flawed drafting'. In this respect, Butt and Castle (2006) find that what lies behind conventional legal drafting in common law countries is a combination of factors having little to do with professional rigour. These factors, which resemble the reasons come across by Conde Antequera (2009) in his analysis of the unclear linguistic behaviour of Spain's civil servants, are the following:

- traditional legal language is familiar and drafters are used to it;
- lawyers tend to be conservative, so they copy existing model forms and precedents, without paying much attention to the needs or circumstances of the particular client;
- the use of word processors allows for the indiscriminate copying of past texts;
- legal professionals wish to be members of a respected group, so they follow the language conventions of that group;
- they take for granted that conventional texts are unambiguous;
- where the overall length of documents (especially, in older times) or the time spent on a written task are relevant when calculating a fee, lawyers have an extra motivation to add pages to their writings; and
- lawyers draft their texts being aware that, at some time in the future, these may be scrutinized by a judge, so they stick to the most conventional and conservative style of drafting.

In such a scenario, it seems urgent to acknowledge that many instances of legal language amount to poor communicative acts for no good reason. Neither professional inertia, nor fear of departing from traditional models, justifies the drafting of legal texts which are incomprehensible for lay readers. This is why I find sensible to adhere to the position of plain language advocates, which support 'clear and effective communication' (Kimble 1995: 52) in legal writing, but are also keen to admit 'that technical terms and terms of art are sometimes necessary, and that some legal ideas can be stated only so simply' (Id. at 54). That is, they encourage a whole set of strategies to improve the way legal practitioners communicate (dealing not only with vocabulary and grammar, but also with text organization and layout), but they also accept that extreme care must be taken when drafting in order to deliver technically precise texts. This broad-minded stance towards drafting is something frequently overlooked by the critics of plain language, whose claims (e.g., that plain language is 'a kind of baby-talk', as reported by Asprey (2003: 11); that the status of legislative texts as *law* may be disguised by using plain language (Horn 2002); or that citizens do not wish to read the legislation that affects them (Hunt 2003)) seem to be mainly rooted in the angst for change.

2. A Functional Approach to Legal Translation

Traditional views on the language of the law have permeated the routine of many legal translators and translation trainers for centuries. Šarčević (1997) points out that the authoritative nature of legal texts placed them on a par with the Bible in the eyes of translators, thus allowing only for literal methods of language conveyance until the twentieth century. At this time, 'translators of lesser used official languages finally began to demand equal language rights, thus setting the stage for the development from literal to near idiomatic or idiomatic [. . .] translation' (Šarčević 1997: 23–24). However, the tendency to regard legal texts as sensitive objects not to be interfered with is still implanted in the minds of many translators. This inclination is closely linked to one of the arguments most frequently raised against plain language: legal texts are highly precise as they are because tradition is their source, and because they have proved to be effective throughout the centuries. In these circumstances, convention says that legal texts cannot be tampered with, nor when transferring them into a different language. This is why translators in this domain are required 'to reproduce the texts wholly and mechanically, to reflect it [*sic*] automatically as though they were a transparent pane of glass' (Vidal-Claramonte and Martín-Ruano 2003: 148). This stance on translation relies heavily on the simplistic assumption that legal language (or language in general, for that matter) is a straightforward container of information, 'a transparent vehicle of a stable reality or of evident, incontrovertible meanings' (149).

Translators, being aware of the canonical status attached to legal texts, are thus generally expected to pursue a neutral linguistic transcoding when addressing a task in this field. In my experience, as far as the translation of legal documents from English into Spanish is concerned, professionals do favour literal techniques aimed at replicating the surface of the source text. At the same time, however, they pepper their translations with typical formulas and vocabulary from target parallel texts, in an effort to make their texts more familiar and acceptable within the target system. This sometimes results in translations which, though outwardly reminiscent of original Spanish legal texts, abound in nonsensical syntactic and terminological calques due to the almost word-for-word approach of the translator. The fact that this behaviour and the reasons for it are frequently part of the (unconscious) set of preconceived ideas which unseasoned translation students bring with them at the start of their training period, reveals that the traditional stance on legal texts and legal translation belongs to the conventional worldview of most of us (whether experts or laypeople).

However deep-rooted these preconceptions are, an alternative model for the practice of translation in the legal domain is already part of the routine of many professionals. For this alternative model, the functional theories of translation (e.g., Reiss and Vermeer 1984; Holz-Mänttäri 1984; Nord 1991) provide a sound array of arguments, on which practitioners implicitly or explicitly base their translation decisions. The two most significant arguments in this respect are, first, that the *skopos* of a translation task justifies the application of any strategy (thus placing the literal method as just one option among others); and, second, that the concept of equivalence is replaced by the search of adequacy to a given function as the motor of the translator's actions. That is to say, professionals are no longer 'blind to the multiplicity of situations with which translators and interpreters have to deal nowadays' (Vidal-Claramonte and Martín-Ruano 2003: 154), and can see further than the mere uncritical conveyance of words and surfaces.

In this regard, Garzone (2000) classifies legal text types and situations which are relevant to translation. According to her, translators may come into contact with the following texts as part of their daily routine: (a) texts generated within the framework of a single national legal system; (b) documents drawn up in bilingual or bi-juridical countries; (c) 'hybrid texts' (i.e. most international instruments ratified by a number of countries, with EU legislation as a particular case); and (d) international private documents. Garzone (2000: 5–6) concludes that 'it is true that virtually in all categories discussed (with the exception of bilingual legislation) there are to be found translations that, not being authoritative, actually are only offers of information about an SL original', and that, as a consequence, are liable to the application of different translation strategies. This view, which draws on the distinction between documentary and instrumental translation by Nord (1991), means that the particulars of the translation project and the specific type of legal text will determine the 'crucial choices that will govern [the translator's] decisions down to the lower levels of the process. In this respect s/he will be guided prevalently by functional considerations' (Garzone 2000: 7).

This author considers that 'an examination of translators' behaviour in the legal field [. . .] shows that actual translating practice is routinely based on functional criteria' (Id. at 9). This should render invalid the criticism by scholars like Šarčević (2000), who dismisses functionalism as irrelevant to legal translation. In Šarčević's opinion, which focuses on the translation of texts in bilingual or multilingual scenarios and which relies on too narrow a concept of the functional theories, legal criteria (i.e., legal equivalence) should be given the primary role when selecting a translation strategy for legal texts. But this is something which suits the needs of documents that are to be valid in multilingual versions, but does not apply to other instances of legal translation.

Regarding functionalism as an optimum theoretical set of tools due to its comprehensive and flexible nature, translators should take the following as a working premise: when translating legal texts, they must attend first and foremost to the requirements of the given translation commission. This implies that no translation strategy should be ruled out before considering the circumstances of the particular project, and that all decisions should take into account the needs of the target readers. In the light of plain language advocacy, this means that translators should address their texts to 'a readership multiplied a thousand fold over the select group that was directly concerned with legal writings when the language of the law was in its infancy' (Mellinkoff 1982: 44), a readership that includes experts as well as non-experts. As a practical application of this thought, a practitioner facing the translation of a court statement of claim (in pending proceedings and where the defendant speaks a foreign language) should (a) use a language that will be understandable by all the potential recipients of the document (i.e. not only lawyers, judges, other court representatives and legal professionals, but also the lay person acting as the defendant and other members of the public that may become involved in the court proceedings at some time in the future); while (b) endeavouring to preserve the technical message of the text by availing of the strictly necessary legal terms.

As commented above, even legal texts originally intended for lawyers will at some point affect the interests of a lay reader (to start with, the client on whose behalf the lawyer takes action), so legal translators should always count inexpert members of the public among the likely recipients of a target text. By combining the versatile functional theories of translation with the principles that support plain language, translators could take a step forward and also challenge the communicative flaws of legal texts. In this sense, Kischel (2009: 9) points out that 'translation, as much of comparative law, can also be an eye-opener, a new point of reference. It can suddenly make one see the sometimes overly complicated, nearly self-serving nature of concepts which seemed so normal and necessary.'

Furthering this line of reasoning, Jacques Derrida's work serves Vidal-Claramonte and Martín-Ruano (2003: 155) as inspiration to challenge the concept of literal equivalence in legal translation and the status of legal texts as sacred objects: 'Deconstruction, in effect, encourages us to constantly reconsider the ethical implications of our decision-making, to endlessly search for the limitations of existing conventions, to persistently reflect on the limits, either self-imposed or norm-governed limits.' For legal translators, this appeal to critically revise existing conventions and norms should start by acnowledging that they ultimately translate for ordinary citizens. In the words of Mellinkoff (1982: 44–45), '[t]oday, as never before, the broad road to understandable legal writing is ordinary English composition. Depart from that road, and you risk being misunderstood by the people you want to reach – lawyers as well as non-lawyers.'

3. A Plain Language Approach to Translation Strategies

As previously noted, the plain language approach does not involve only the use of a more accessible language or a clearer document organization. In order to adequately convey the technical meaning intended by the text author, it is also essential to include the relevant set of inescapable legal terms. This is also valid in the field of translation, where professionals concerned with the search for clarity should hold precision as another major feature of their target texts. In practice, this means that translators will stick only to true technical terms and will dismiss conventional rare words and formulas with no precise sense attached. Critics of the plain language approach in the translation domain should be aware of this position, which only warns translators against the use of elaborate and usually incomprehensible language for the sake of tradition.

How this concern for clear language comes into being in the manifold projects that make up the workload of legal translators cannot be reduced to a set of procedures aimed at covering all or most translation situations. Following functional postulates, this would be in disagreement with the idea that the circumstances of any translation project are unique, and that translators should submit all decisions to those distinctive circumstances. However, in terms of delivering a reasonably clear target text, my proposal is that, whatever the situation involving a legal document, translation practitioners could always observe a number of principles on effective writing[1]. These principles should not deviate much from the basic rules of ordinary language: no valid argument to the contrary been raised, ordinary grammar and vocabulary will do in the composition of most legal texts and translations. As expressed by Mellinkoff (1963: vii): '[w]ith communication the object, the principle of simplicity would dictate that the language used by lawyers agree with the common speech, unless there are reasons for a difference'.

In the case of legal professionals, authors such as Wydick (2005) have suggested a set of guidelines for lawyers to draft in a clearer and more sensible fashion. Together with him, many others have also offered a hands-on approach to more effective drafting in the practice of the law (e.g., Mellinkoff 1982; Garner 2001; Asprey 2003; Adler 2006). Taking all these sources as a starting point, translators may easily follow suit and establish their own set of procedures to attain clarity. In González-Ruiz (2011; 2012), I present such a collection of strategies focused on two of the most significant flaws of legal writing: the use of very long and complex sentences, and the abundance of rare and ceremonial expressions. As has been said, these strategies are not intended to be a comprehensive aid kit for translators, but a group of guidelines which may be supplemented by translators themselves with findings of their own or with other suggestions by plain language advocates. In particular, according to González-Ruiz (2011; 2012), translation professionals in the legal domain are expected to improve their target texts by adhering to the following routines:

- identifying the key elements of a sentence (i.e., actor, action, and object) in order to ascertain its internal structure; by doing this, translators will unveil the pillars of long and ill-punctuated sentences;
- cutting up long sentences and using punctuation marks properly as a method to rearrange complex sentences without tampering with the "thread of sense" of the source text;
- repositioning long modifiers and parentheses to disentangle the matryoshka-styled structure of nested phrases;
- distinguishing authentic technical terms from merely ceremonial forms of expression devoid of precise meaning, and replacing the latter with plain alternatives;
- focusing on the language at the sentence level, without meddling with the arrangement of lists or paragraphs, so both source and target texts remain comparable in terms of referencing; and
- being constantly aware of the need to achieve clarity without neglecting precision.

Translators may put these suggestions into practice both when analyzing the source text and when producing their target text. As regards the former, these are scrutinising strategies designed for the "rebuilding" of the source text as an entirely comprehensible

1 If, in rare circumstances, the translator were asked to write the target text in an ornate style reminiscent of the traditional school of legal drafting (e.g., for literary purposes), then he or she would consciously ignore the suggestions for clarity.

working document. As to the latter, translators may use these actions, together with other basic principles of effective communication in their language, to deliver a text which is simple, compliant with the rules on good writing, attentive to the needs of its readers and, last but not least, technically precise.

Whether legal professionals will embrace plain language translations or will refuse them in favour of the traditional style of tried and tested documents remains to be seen. In 2004, I conducted an experiment concerning the assessment of two alternative Spanish versions of an Irish court-related text (one of them written in the traditional fashion, and the other one following the basics of plain language). Surprisingly, the group of lawyers participating in the investigation considered that, even though the plain language version was a better piece of writing, they preferred the conventional target text in professional terms (González-Ruiz 2005). One may read this result as a subtle admittance by lawyers that legal language is not about precision and communication, but about tradition and fossilized routines.

Contrary to what the outcome of this study suggested, legal professionals in other places have apparently given a welcoming reception to plain language. For instance, Kimble (2006; 2012) offers overwhelming evidence that, when given the choice, judges and lawyers from the US and other parts of the world prefer documents written in plain language. Likewise, Butt and Castle (2006) report that law societies and bar associations of several English-speaking countries have promoted the use of plain language among their members. Moreover, they offer a detailed account of the judiciary's support of plain language, and they conclude that 'surveys have shown that, given the choice, over 80 per cent of American judges would prefer to see pleadings in plain English rather than in traditional form' (Butt and Castle 2006: 110). Garner (2001) also finds that, when comparing a traditional provision in a fee agreement with a redrafted version of it in plain language, dozens of lawyer groups would view the plain text much more favourably.

This supporting evidence should encourage us, back in the translation domain, to keep challenging a legal tradition of flawed communication. With this object in mind, I performed a new experiment also intended to gauge the perception of plain language translations by practising lawyers. This is described in the next section.

4. Assessing the Acceptability of Plain Translations: An Experiment

What follows is a detailed account of a test administered to a group of Spanish lawyers with the purpose of measuring how keen these professionals are to the use of plain language in the translation of legal texts.

4.1. Subjects

The subjects were 30 Spanish lawyers (*abogados*) who, first, had graduated at a Spanish university and, second, now work in Spain or abroad. There were no restrictions on age or gender.

4.2. Instruments

Subjects were given a translated text written in Spanish (one of two alternative translations) and an accompanying questionnaire. They were supposed to read the text and, subsequently, complete the questionnaire.

The source text on which the translations are based is a paragraph of a clause from a US employment and non-competition agreement. The excerpt deals with the right which the company has to terminate the contract with the employee under certain circumstances. Under the supervision of a Spanish lawyer specialized in employment law, I wrote two separate translations of the same source text following different stylistic/linguistic criteria. In the first rendering (translation A), I literally followed the traditional and obscure style of the source text (i.e., I adhered to the prevailing trend of literalness in legal translation), and also imitated the patterns of Spanish "legalese." In the second translation (translation B), I used a set of plain language techniques, and prioritized clarity over legal language conventions in both languages. In the two versions, however, extreme care was taken to maintain the technical content of the piece by including the same set of actual terms of art. Finally, both translations were conceived as offers of information for target readers (i.e. both texts had an informative purpose).

4.3. The Source Text

The source text is a paragraph from a clause of a US employment and non-competition agreement. In order to contextualize the extract, the initial and final formulas of the agreement were also included:

> *EMPLOYMENT AND NON-COMPETITION AGREEMENT*
>
> *THIS EMPLOYMENT AND NON-COMPETITION AGREEMENT (the 'Agreement') is executed as of this first day of September, 2010, and effective as of September 15, 2010 (the 'Date of Hire'), by and between [. . .] (the 'Company'), and [. . .], an individual ('Employee').*
>
> *In consideration of the premises and the mutual agreements and covenants contained herein, and for other good and valuable consideration, the receipt and sufficiency of which is hereby acknowledged by the Company and Employee,*
>
> *IT IS HEREBY AGREED AS FOLLOWS:*
>
> *[. . .] 3.1 Right to Terminate.*
>
> *[. . .] (c) Termination by Company For Cause. Subject to Section 3.2, the Company may terminate Employee's employment and all of the Company's obligations under this Agreement at any time 'For Cause' (as defined below) by giving notice to Employee stating the basis for such termination, effective immediately upon giving such notice or at such other time thereafter as the Company may designate. 'For Cause' shall mean any of the following: (i) Employee's willful and continued failure to substantially perform the reasonably assigned duties with the Company which are consistent with Employee's position and job description referred to in this Agreement, other than any such failure resulting from incapacity due to physical or mental illness, after a written notice is delivered to Employee by the Board of Directors of the Company which*

specifically identifies the manner in which Employee has not substantially performed the assigned duties and allowing Employee thirty (30) days after receipt by Employee of such notice to cure such failure to perform, (ii) material breach of this or any other written agreement between Employee and the Company which is not cured within thirty (30) days after receipt by the Employee from the Company of written notice of such breach, (iii) any material violation of any written policy of the Company which is not cured within thirty (30) days after receipt by Employee from the Company of written notice of such violation, (iv) Employee's willful misconduct which is materially and demonstrably injurious to the Company, (v) Employee's conviction by a court of competent jurisdiction of, or her pleading guilty or nolo contendere to, any felony, or (vi) Employee's commission of an act of fraud, embezzlement, or misappropriation against the Company or any breach of fiduciary duty or breach of the duty of loyalty, including, but not limited to, the offer, payment, solicitation or acceptance of any unlawful bribe or kickback with respect to the Company's business. For purposes of this paragraph, no act, or failure to act, on Employee's part shall be considered 'willful' unless done, or omitted to be done, in knowing bad faith and without reasonable belief that the action or omission was in, or not opposed to, the best interests of the Company. Any act, or failure to act, expressly authorized by a resolution duly adopted by the Board of Directors or based upon the written advice of counsel for the Company shall be conclusively presumed to be done, or omitted to be done, in good faith and in the best interests of the Company. Notwithstanding the foregoing, Employee shall not be deemed to have been terminated For Cause unless and until there shall have been delivered to Employee a copy of a resolution, duly adopted by the Board of Directors at a meeting of the Board called and held for such purpose (after reasonable notice to Employee and an opportunity for Employee, together with Employee's counsel, to be heard before the Board), finding that in the good faith opinion of the Board of Directors Employee committed the conduct set forth above in (i), (ii), (iii), (iv), (v) or (vi) of this Section and specifying the particulars thereof in detail.

[. . .] IN WITNESS WHEREOF, the parties have executed this Agreement as of the day and year written above.

The excerpt deals with the right which the company has to terminate the contract with the employee under certain circumstances. It was provided by a Spanish professional translator who had worked on it as part of a completed project. As I discovered later, the text could also be found on the Internet as a model form, so I think it may be considered a reliable instance of current practice in contract (legal) drafting.

As regards its linguistic characteristics, this sample text features many of the conventions of legal discourse. To start with, it abounds in forms of expressions which are not frequent in common English: technical terms (e.g., "terminate", "fiduciary duty", "nolo contendere"); Old and Middle English words (e.g., "thereafter", "thereof"); expressions with deliberate vague meanings (e.g., "reasonable", "reasonably", "including but not limited to"); absolute and restrictive expressions ("all", "at any time", "any", "conclusively"); and coupled synonyms (e.g., "unless and until"). Leaving aside the use of an unusual vocabulary (understandably so in the case of genuine specialized terms), the author's attempts at extreme precision of expression are the most outstanding attribute of the text. This results in a convoluted and redundant style, which is evocative of traditional legal drafting and which, in my opinion, is its main shortcoming as an act of written communication. This complex style, which prevents the ordinary reader from understanding what it says after a careful first reading, is based on extremely long sentences (an average count of 103.4 words per sentence, with the longest sentence reaching 255 words), scarce or irregular use of punctuation, abundance of rare and ceremonial expressions, and redundancy in the use of key nouns (e.g., "Employee" and "Company") and certain adjectives (e.g., "such").

4.4. Target Text A

In agreement with the traditional approach to legal translation, the first criterion applied to translation A was to follow the style of the source text as closely as possible. This basically implied the imitation of the elaborate syntax of the English excerpt: on the one hand, target text A features the same number of sentences as in the source text (i.e., five, heading excluded), and a similar average word count (135.8 words per sentence); and, on the other hand, redundant and ceremonial forms of expression are reproduced in Spanish as literally as possible.

As a secondary strategy, I used the customary structure for agreements in the Spanish language (i.e., the distribution of contents into the *REUNIDOS, EXPONEN* and *CLÁUSULAS* sections), and dotted translation A with typical forms of expression which are recurrent in Spanish legal texts (as described, for example, by Alcaraz Varó and Hughes (2009)):

- nominalizations (e.g., *resolución, recepción, incumplimiento, traslado de una notificación*);
- complex verb-plus-noun phrases (e.g., *enviar una notificación* instead of *notificar, llevar a cabo una acción* instead of *actuar*);
- self-referential phrases (e.g., *en virtud de, a los efectos de*);
- uncommon terms devoid of technical meaning (e.g., *ut supra*); and
- capital letters in instances where Spanish rules advise against their use (e.g., *Fecha de Contratación, Causa Justificada*).

Together with the flourish these characteristics entail, I was particularly concerned with the need to insert the technical terms which were appropriate to the subject matter of the clause, in order to deliver a technically precise rendering. To sum up, target text A is a terminologically proper legal translation which literally conveys the style of the source text, and which emulates the conventions of legal Spanish by basically presenting an accustomed target-system structure and an unnatural and pompous language:

CONTRATO DE TRABAJO Y DE NO COMPETENCIA

Este Contrato DE TRABAJO Y DE NO COMPETENCIA (en adelante, el 'Contrato') se celebra el 1 de septiembre de 2010 y su fecha de entrada en vigor es el 15 de septiembre de 2010 (en adelante, la 'Fecha de Contratación').

REUNIDOS

DE UNA PARTE, [. . .] (en adelante, la 'Empresa').

Y, DE OTRA, [. . .], persona física (en adelante, el 'Empleado').

EXPONEN

QUE, a la vista de las circunstancias previas, y de los acuerdos y pactos mutuos incluidos en este documento, el valor y la pertinencia de los cuales reconocen tanto la

Empresa como el Empleado, estas partes desean iniciar una relación laboral de acuerdo con las siguientes

CLÁUSULAS

[. . .] 3.1 Derecho a resolver el Contrato

[. . .] c) Resolución por parte de la Empresa por una Causa Justificada. En virtud de la Cláusula 3.2, la Empresa puede resolver el Contrato de Trabajo del Empleado, así como renunciar a sus obligaciones según dicho acuerdo, en cualquier momento si se diera una 'Causa Justificada' (tal y como se define a continuación), mediante el traslado al Empleado de una notificación en la que se señale la razón de la resolución, siendo ésta efectiva inmediatamente en el momento de la recepción de dicha notificación o en el momento posterior que la Empresa determine. Por 'Causa Justificada' se entenderá alguna de las siguientes circunstancias: I) el incumplimiento intencionado y reiterado por el Empleado de una parte sustancial de las obligaciones que le hayan sido razonablemente asignadas en la Empresa, correspondientes al cargo y a la descripción del puesto de trabajo a los que se hace alusión en este Contrato, salvo, a título excepcional, el incumplimiento que se derive de la incapacidad debida a enfermedad física o mental, después de que le haya sido enviada al Empleado una notificación escrita por el Consejo de Administración de la Empresa en la que se especifique en qué sentido el Empleado no ha cumplido de forma sustancial las obligaciones asignadas y en la que se conceda al Empleado un período de treinta (30) días tras la recepción por éste de la notificación para rectificar dicho incumplimiento; II) el incumplimiento de alguna disposición sustantiva de este Contrato o de cualquier otro acuerdo celebrado por escrito entre el Empleado y la Empresa que no se haya rectificado en el período de treinta (30) días posterior a la recepción, por parte del Empleado, de la notificación escrita de dicho incumplimiento enviada por la Empresa; III) el incumplimiento de alguna norma escrita sustantiva de la Empresa que no se haya rectificado en el período de treinta (30) días posterior a la recepción, por parte del Empleado, de la notificación escrita de dicho incumplimiento enviada por la Empresa; IV) el comportamiento intencionado del Empleado que resulte, de modo grave y demostrable, perjudicial para la Empresa; V) la condena del Empleado por un tribunal de jurisdicción competente, o el reconocimiento previo del Empleado de su culpabilidad o de la condena, por la comisión de un delito; o VI) la comisión por el Empleado de un acto de fraude, de malversación de fondos o de apropiación indebida que vaya contra la Empresa, el quebranto de la buena fe o el incumplimiento de las obligaciones de lealtad, entre las que se incluyen, con carácter ilustrativo, el ofrecimiento, el pago, la pretensión o la aceptación de sobornos o actos similares de carácter ilegal vinculados a la actividad de la Empresa. A los efectos de esta Subcláusula, ninguna acción ni omisión del Empleado se considerarán 'intencionadas' a menos que la acción o la omisión se hayan llevado a cabo de manera consciente con mala fe y sin la creencia razonable de que la acción o la omisión tenían como objeto, o no se oponían a ello, el mejor interés de la Empresa. Toda acción u omisión que haya sido expresamente autorizada por una resolución debidamente adoptada por el Consejo de Administración o que se derive de las instrucciones escritas de los asesores jurídicos de la Empresa se entenderá, de modo concluyente, que ha sido llevada a cabo con buena fe y persiguiendo el beneficio de la Empresa. Sin perjuicio de lo anterior, no se considerará que el Contrato de Trabajo del Empleado ha quedado resuelto por una Causa Justificada a menos y hasta que se envíe al Empleado una copia de una resolución, que habrá sido debidamente adoptada por el Consejo de Administración en una junta de éste convocada y celebrada a tal efecto (tras

haber notificado al Empleado, con antelación razonable, la celebración de la junta y tras haber dado a éste, junto con su abogado, audiencia previa ante el Consejo), en la que se señale que, a discreción del Consejo de Administración, el Empleado cometió alguna de las conductas descritas en los subapartados I), II), III), IV), V) y VI) de esta Subcláusula, y en la que se especifiquen los detalles de esta circunstancia.

[. . .] EN PRUEBA DE CONFORMIDAD, las partes celebran este Contrato en la fecha ut supra. [. . .]

4.5. Target Text B

For target text B, I used the set of plain language techniques proposed in González-Ruiz (2011; 2012), which were briefly explained above. As a result, differences between translation B and target text A can be easily spotted. The most significant feature of the plain translation is that it consists of 19 sentences (compare to 5 sentences in the source text, heading excluded), with an average word count per sentence of 30.1 (compare to a mean count of 103.4 words in the source text). Another surface-level change was made to the layout (e.g., I rearranged the longest sentence in the excerpt, 255 words, by cutting it up in several subparagraphs, each of them clearly stating a separate possibility of misbehaviour by the Employee).[2] Long modifiers, in particular, were taken out of their place and into newly-formed and separate sentences.

In this process of 'carving' shorter sentences from their longer English-language counterparts, I faced the need of making implied and potentially ambiguous meanings explicit; I did this by adding relevant linking phrases, or by being straightforward when expressing senses which, though essential to the understanding of the provision, remained underdeveloped in the source text (e.g., the potential ambiguity of 'after a written notice is delivered to Employee', in 3.1(c)(i), was transformed into a clear statement of the time requirement in a separate sentence).

I also focused on avoiding the ceremony of tautologies, rare expressions and formulas, and refrained from being redundant and repetitive (e.g., by using pronouns to refer to the 'Company' and the 'Employee' in unambiguous contexts, and by not repeating identical information in successive sentences). Finally, I favoured subject-verb-object structures over the tendency to nominalize—so that the actor and the action are plainly identified—as well as an affirmative style over the use of multiple negation:

CONTRATO DE TRABAJO Y DE NO COMPETENCIA

Este contrato se celebra el 1 de septiembre de 2010 y su fecha de entrada en vigor es el 15 de septiembre de 2010 (en adelante, la 'fecha de contratación').

REUNIDOS

DE UNA PARTE, [. . .] (en adelante, la 'Empresa').

2 Although the set of strategies applied (González Ruiz 2011; 2012) expressly rules out the reshaping of source text paragraphs or lists in the target version, I made an exception in this instance for two reasons: (a) lawyers would not be provided with the source document and, as a consequence, they would not be able to set the source and target texts side by side; and (b) by opting for this solution for the longest and most complex sentence in the excerpt, the case for plain language would be strengthened through the display of its more far-reaching possibilities.

Y, DE OTRA, [. . .], persona física (en adelante, el 'Empleado').

EXPONEN

QUE, a la vista de las circunstancias previas y de los acuerdos mutuos incluidos en este documento, cuyo valor reconocen ambas partes, éstas desean iniciar una relación laboral de acuerdo con las siguientes

CLÁUSULAS

[. . .] 3.1 Derecho a resolver el contrato

[. . .] c) La Empresa podrá resolver el contrato por una causa justificada. De acuerdo con la cláusula 3.2, la Empresa podrá, en cualquier momento, resolver este contrato y renunciar a sus obligaciones según dicho documento si se diera una 'causa justificada' (según se define a continuación). Esto lo hará enviando al Empleado una notificación en la que se señale por qué la Empresa resuelve el contrato. Si esto ocurriera, el contrato quedaría resuelto en el momento de recibir esa notificación o en un momento posterior que la Empresa determine. Por 'causa justificada' se entenderá alguna de las siguientes circunstancias:

I. Cuando el Empleado incumpla, de manera intencionada y reiterada, una parte sustancial de las obligaciones que la Empresa le haya asignado según su cargo y según la descripción de su puesto de trabajo que se hace en este contrato. Se entenderá que esta circunstancia es una causa justificada si el Empleado incumple sus obligaciones después de que el Consejo de Administración de la Empresa le haya enviado una notificación por escrito. En ella, el Consejo especificaría por qué el Empleado no ha cumplido sus obligaciones, así como le concedería un período de 30 días a partir de la fecha en que reciba esa notificación para que rectifique su conducta. Este párrafo no tendrá efecto si el Empleado incumple sus obligaciones por alguna enfermedad física o mental.

II. Cuando el Empleado incumpla alguna disposición sustantiva de este o de cualquier otro acuerdo celebrado por escrito entre él y la Empresa, siempre que el Empleado no remedie esa situación en un plazo de 30 días después de haber sido notificado por escrito por la Empresa.

III. Cuando el Empleado incumpla alguna norma escrita sustantiva de la Empresa, siempre que el Empleado no remedie esa situación en un plazo de 30 días después de haber sido notificado por escrito por la Empresa.

IV. Cuando el comportamiento intencionado del Empleado dé lugar a un perjuicio grave y demostrable para la Empresa.

V. Cuando el Empleado sea condenado por un tribunal competente por haber cometido un delito, o cuando éste reconozca previamente su culpabilidad o su aceptación de la condena por ese delito.

VI. Cuando el Empleado cometa fraude, malversación de fondos o apropiación indebida contra la Empresa, o cuando quebrante la buena fe o incumpla su obligación de lealtad. El Empleado incumplirá esta última obligación cuando, por ejemplo, ofrezca, pague, pretenda o acepte sobornos o actos ilegales similares vinculados a la actividad de la Empresa.

A los efectos de esta subcláusula, se entenderá que el Empleado ha actuado o ha dejado de actuar de forma 'intencionada' si, conscientemente, se ha comportado de mala fe y creyendo que su conducta podía perjudicar a la Empresa. Por el contrario, se entenderá que el Empleado ha actuado o ha dejado de actuar con buena fe y a favor de la Empresa cuando su conducta esté expresamente autorizada por una resolución que haya adoptado de manera oportuna el Consejo de Administración, o cuando su conducta responda a las instrucciones escritas de los asesores jurídicos de la Empresa.

Sin perjuicio de lo anterior, este contrato sólo se considerará resuelto por una causa justificada cuando se envíe al Empleado una copia de la resolución adoptada por el Consejo de Administración. Esta resolución será adoptada por el Consejo en una junta convocada y celebrada a tal efecto. En ella, se señalará que, a juicio del Consejo de Administración, el Empleado ha cometido alguna de las conductas descritas en los apartados I, II, III, IV, V y VI de esta subcláusula, y se detallarán las circunstancias correspondientes. Esta junta, no obstante, sólo podrá celebrarse después de que se haya notificado al Empleado, con antelación razonable, su celebración y después de que se le haya dado a éste, junto con su abogado, audiencia previa ante el Consejo.

[. . .] EN PRUEBA DE CONFORMIDAD, las partes celebran este contrato en la fecha señalada al inicio del documento. [. . .]

4.6. The Questionnaire

The subjects were given only one of the two translations plus a questionnaire, which evaluated, on the one hand, what they generally expected of a legal translation and, on the other hand, how they perceived the target text. The questionnaire was the same for both versions, and consisted of eight Likert-type items, and a final box for optional extra remarks by the subjects. As regards personal data, they were only asked to provide the number of years they had been practising as lawyers. Each item consisted of a statement followed by a five-point scale, in which the numbers corresponded to the following meanings: 1 ('I strongly disagree'), 2 ('I disagree'), 3 ('I neither agree nor disagree'), 4 ('I agree') and 5 ('I strongly agree').

The items measured four factors: (a) what subjects generally expect of a legal translation (items 1 and 2); (b) what they think about the translator's specialized knowledge in the field of law (items 3 and 7); (c) to what extent they think that the translator is competent at writing in Spanish, and whether the language used is clear (items 4 and 6); and (d) whether they find the translation acceptable in professional terms (items 5 and 8). The statements in the items were as follows:[3]

- Item 1: When I commission the translation of a legal text, I expect the translator to literally follow the style of the source text.
- Item 2: When I commission the translation of a legal text which features an elaborate and unclear language, I am prepared to accept the translator to make the style of the source text plainer.
- Item 3: The author of this translation has an adequate knowledge of the field of law.

3 The questionnaire was presented in Spanish. This is my translation.

- Item 4: This translator has an excellent knowledge of the Spanish language, and uses it accordingly.
- Item 5: As an expert in the field of law, I find that this translation is acceptable from a professional point of view.
- Item 6: This translation features a language which is clear and easy to understand.
- Item 7: The translator has employed the correct terms regarding the rights and duties of the parties on the clause's particular subject.
- Item 8: If I needed the translation of a legal text in the future, I would have it done by this translator.

Bearing in mind the busy working hours of lawyers, the translated excerpt and the questionnaire were intentionally kept to a minimum, so that they could read the former and complete the latter in a total of approximately ten minutes.

4.7. Data Handling and Results

Once I had all tests completed, the numerical scores were processed in order to obtain, first, the average figure for each item, and then, the global result for each factor. The average number of years the participants had been practising as lawyers is similar for both target texts (12.4 for translation A, 11 for B), so no conclusions can be drawn as to the professional experience of the subjects. For the first factor – which did not gauge the effectiveness of either target text, but focused on lawyers' preconceived assumptions about legal translation – the results of the two items were kept separate for the sake of clarity:

Table 5.1 Results for factor on presumptions about legal translation

Item	Target text A mean	Target text B mean	Gobal mean (target texts A and B)
1	3.666	4.333	4
2	3	3.133	3.066

As regards what subjects generally expect of a legal translation, most participants agreed that they presumed that the translations they commission would literally follow the style of the original text. Consistently with this assumption, they seemed to be slightly at odds with the possibility of a translation featuring a plainer style than the one found in the source text. Generally speaking, these results are in line with González-Ruiz (2005), and with one of the basic principles that underlie the practice of legal translation—the literal approach.

For all the remaining factors, the participants clearly decided on the plain language translation as being more effective from the point of view of linguistic performance and legal knowledge, as well as more acceptable from a professional perspective:

Table 5.2 Results for factors on clarity, legal knowledge, and professional acceptability

Factor	Target text A mean	Target text B mean
Linguistc performance and clarity (items 4 and 6)	3.366	4.1
Specialized legal knowledge (items 3 and 7)	3.433	4.066
Professional acceptability (items 5 and 8)	3.533	4.1

In agreement with my previous study, subjects thought that translation B features a language which is clearer and easier to understand than the language in target text A. They also found that the translator of B shows greater linguistic skills than the author of A. This means that, as far as linguistic performance and clarity are concerned, the plain language translation was better rated than the conventional translation. However, in disagreement with my previous findings, the results of the last two factors indicate that, on the one hand, the author of the plain language translation was considered a more confident expert in the field of law, and target text B itself was better scored as an actual piece of professional legal translation. Thus, in response to the final item, subjects would rather commission a legal translation to the plain language translator than rely on the author of translation A.

5. Conclusion

Even though the size of this experiment (e.g., the small number of participants) provides statistical data which are insufficient to make any strong claim, the distance between the mean scores of both translations in all items signals an overall better appreciation of the plain language translation. According to the results, subjects found translation B a target text where language was more efficiently used, and where the legal content of the original agreement was conveyed in a more proper manner. These results confirm an incipient open-mindedness of Spanish legal practitioners towards the acceptance of clear and terminologically accurate translations, despite their apparent initial resistance and the underdeveloped status of the plain movement in Spain.

In principle, this outcome could amount to a contradiction when it is seen against the everyday routine of Spanish lawyers. Although, according to the results of this experiment, lawyers are capable of acknowledging the higher efficiency of plain language, they somewhat reject the idea of a translator employing plain language techniques, and they themselves tend to resort exclusively to conventional modes of writing in their professional practice. In this regard, I find that, as long as "gobbledygook" is the safest means for lawyers to achieving professional success, tentative attempts at plain language are likely to fail. Perhaps only the implementation of State or professional regulations making the use of plain language a requirement in legal texts could mark the beginning of a path forward for plain language defenders.

For legal translators, plain language arguments and techniques are valuable tools for their professional routine, but these still fall short of being a universal remedy for the difficulties the translation of the language of the law implies. Many of these difficulties, however, could be solved if all involved in communicating the law embraced the principles of clear language from the very inception of the source text. As to the remaining obstacles, I guess they are simply the charms of our trade.

References

Adler, M. 2006. *Clarity for Lawyers: Effective Legal Writing*. 2nd edn, London: The Law Society.

Alcaraz Varó, E. and Hughes, B. 2009. *El español jurídico*. 2nd edn. Barcelona: Ariel.

Asprey, M.M. 2003. *Plain Language for Lawyers*. 3rd edn, Annandale, Australia: The Federation Press.

Briz Gómez, A. (dir.). 2011. *Estudio de campo: Lenguaje oral (Comisión para la Modernización del Lenguaje Jurídico)*. Madrid: Ministerio de Justicia del Gobierno de España.

Butt, P. and Castle, R. 2006. *Modern Legal Drafting. A Guide to Using Clearer Language*. 2nd edn, Melbourne: Cambridge University Press.

Conde Antequera, J. 2009. *Lenguaje administrativo y Derecho: El lenguaje como aspecto de la actividad administrativa. Propuestas para un uso eficaz del lenguaje administrativo por el personal de las Administraciones Públicas*. Navarra: Aranzadi/Thomson Reuters.

García de la Concha, V. et al. 2011. *Informe de la Comisión para la Modernización del Lenguaje Jurídico*. Madrid: Ministerio de Justicia del Gobierno de España.

Garner, B.A. 2001. *Legal Writing in Plain English: A Text with Exercises*. Chicago and London: The University of Chicago Press.

Garner, B.A. 2011. *Garner's Dictionary of Legal Usage*. 3rd edn. Oxford University Press.

Garzone, G. 2000. 'Legal Translation and Functionalist Approaches: A Contradiction in Terms?', *La traduction juridique: Histoire, théorie(s) et pratique. Legal Translation: History, Theory/ies and Practice: Proceedings of the International Colloquium organized by the School of Translation and Interpretation of the University of Geneva and the Swiss Translators, Terminologists and Interpreters Association (ASTTI) (University of Geneva, February 17–19, 2000)*. Available at: http://www.tradulex.com/en/translators/Legal-Geneva2000 [Accessed 26 November 2012].

González-Ruiz, V. 2005. 'Translating the Unclear: How Spanish Law Professionals Accept Plain Translated Texts', *Folia Translatologica*, vol. 9, pp. 36–49.

———. 2011. 'The Application of Plain Language Techniques to Legal Translation', *Translation Studies in the New Millennium*, vol. 9, pp. 111–126.

———. 2012. 'A Plain Perspective on Legal Translation', *Clarity*, vol. 67, pp. 27–31.

Holz-Mänttäri, J. 1984. *Translatorisches Handeln: Theorie und Methode*. Helsinki: Suomalainen Tiedeakatemia.

Horn, N. 2002. 'A Dainty Dish to Set before the King: Plain Language and Legislation', *Fourth Biennial Conference Proceedings of the PLAIN Language Association International (Toronto, Canada – September 26–29, 2002)*. Available at: http://www.nald.ca/library/research/plain2/dish/1.htm [Accessed 19 June 2012].

Hunt, B. 2003. 'Plain Language in Legislative Drafting: An Achievable Objective or a Laudable Ideal?', *Statute Law Review*, vol. 2003.4(112), pp. 39–48.

Kimble, J. 1995. 'Answering the Critics of Plain Language', *The Scribes Journal of Legal Writing*, vol. 5(1994–1995), pp. 51–85.

———. 2006. *Lifting the Fog of Legalese: Essays on Plain Language*. Durham: Carolina Academic Press.

———. 2012. *Writing for Dollars, Writing to Please: The Case for Plain Language in Business, Government, and Law*. Durham: Carolina Academic Press.

Kischel, U. 2009. 'Legal Cultures – Legal Languages'. In: F. Olsen, A. Lorz and D. Stein eds. *Translation Issues in Language and Law*. Hampshire, UK: Palgrave Macmillan, pp. 7–17.

Mellinkoff, D. 1963. *The Language of the Law*. Boston: Little, Brown and Company.

———. 1982. *Legal Writing: Sense and Nonsense*. St. Paul, Minnesota: West.

Montolío Durán, E. (dir.). 2011. *Estudio de campo: Lenguaje escrito (Comisión para la Modernización del Lenguaje Jurídico)*. Madrid: Ministerio de Justicia del Gobierno de España.

Nord, C. 1991. *Text Analysis in Translation: Theory, Methodology and Didactic Application of a Model for Translation-Oriented Text Analysis*. Amsterdam: Rodopi.
Reiss, K. and Vermeer, H. 1984. *Grundlegung einer allgemeinen Translationstheorie*. Tübingen: Niemeyer.
Šarčević, S. 1997. *New Approach to Legal Translation*. The Hague, London and Boston: Kluwer Law International.
———. 2000. 'Legal Translation and Translation Theory: A Receiver-Oriented Approach', *La traduction juridique: Histoire, théorie(s) et pratique. Legal Translation: History, Theory/ies and Practice: Proceedings of the International Colloquium organized by the School of Translation and Interpretation of the University of Geneva and the Swiss Translators, Terminologists and Interpreters Association (ASTTI) (University of Geneva, February 17–19, 2000)*. Available at: http://www.tradulex.com/en/translators/Legal-Geneva2000 [Accessed 26 November 2012].
Tiersma, P.M. 1999. *Legal Language*. Chicago and London: The University of Chicago Press.
Valdovinos Chávez, C.M. et al. 2007. *Manual de Lenguaje Claro*. 3rd edn. México, D.F.: Secretaría de la Función Pública.
Vidal-Claramonte, M.C.Á. and Martín-Ruano, M.R. 2003. 'Deconstructing the Discourse on Legal Translation, or Towards an Ethics of Responsibility'. In: L. Pérez-González ed. *Speaking in Tongues: Language Across Contexts and Users*. Publicacions Universitat de València, pp. 141–159.
Wagner, A. and Cacciaguidi-Fahy, S. 2006. 'Searching for Clarity'. In: A. Wagner and S. Cacciaguidi-Fahy eds. *Legal Language and the Search for Clarity: Practice and Tools*. Bern: Peter Lang, pp. 19–32.
Wydick, R.C. 2005. *Plain English for Lawyers*. 5th edn. Durham: Carolina Academic Press.

Chapter 6
Minimal Unit of Legal Translation vs. Minimal Unit of Thought

Svetlana V. Vlasenko

Thought and word are not connected by a primary bond.
Lev Vygotsky, 1934/1979
The relevant unit of meaning for the translator
is not the word, but the message.

Eugene Nida, 1975

1. Introduction

Translation is all about natural languages processing, but the latter falls directly under the realm of thinking wherein a "thought" appears to be a unit worth dealing with whenever there is a need to see behind a word chosen or rejected. Thinking, however, does not *strictu sensu* falls under the domain of linguistics. Hence, translation studies represent a discipline at crossroads of a number of other disciplines; these are known to include three major fields of knowledge—linguistics, psychology, and semiotics—across their most prolific subfields, such as cognitive linguistics, psychosemantics, psychosemiotics, neurolinguistics, sociolinguistics, in couple with artificial intelligence, computer linguistics, cognitive psychology, ethnopsycholinguistics, as well as pragmatics, hermeneutics, and language philosophy, to name but a few.

Legal translation as part of a vaster cross-linguistic professional communication domain is, undoubtedly, a cognitively-conditioned linguistic intermediation activity as it profoundly draws on intensive processing of subject-specific knowledge via speech. Being by definition a mental exercise based on a remarkable cognitive effort, legal translation at the procedural level is like other types of translation[1]—unobservable and, therefore, scarcely explicable. However, pure linguistic assumptions on legal translation and its cognate mechanisms, such as associative imagery networking and abstract pattern-building, are seen subordinated to and determined by the national worldview schemata incorporated into respective national legal systems, legal traditions, and legal usage.

Given this, a major query in translating legal texts may be expected to relate to identifying particular kinds of knowledge engaged in conceptualizing legal practices, traditions, and usage and the respective mental networking which the legal translation necessitates for communicating such knowledge cross-linguistically. This is believed to necessitate identifying a "minimal unit of legal translation" as a step forward to advanced research on this intricate subfield within translation studies. Along with this, the legal translation theoretical framework may eventually benefit from the in-depth observations of several cases reviewed and detailed

1 Machine translation, also named "computer-aided" or "computer-assisted," remains outside the scope of this chapter.

below with the view of their possible extrapolation on and use in larger legal translation data analysis. Some regularities of the English-Russian legal languages switch, describing respective techniques employed, are also elaborated on and discussed in detail.

This chapter features a theoretical viewpoint on an elusive notion of a 'minimal unit of translation' which is believed to underlie a technical mastery of translation in general and legal translation, in particular. Consequently, it is hoped to bear relevance to the core legal translation studies issues. However, no essential conceptualization has been undertaken to date regarding a "unit of legal translation." This slows down the postulating of such crucial concepts for the legal translation theory and practice, as equivalence and semantic invariant, legal meaning nature and structure, practicable legal translation quality assessment criteria, and other vital issues.

Legal Translators[2] may be regarded as skillful masters conveying "stocks" and "flows" of human thoughts via linguistic tools across the versatile continuum of legal and related knowledge. Accordingly, the chapter attempts to define the tangibility of a "unit of legal translation" (ULT) as a primary measurement element correlating with the quantum of substance relevant for the Translator and identifiable at different levels of communicating the matter translated. In so doing, the legal translation theoretical framework is delineated from within several perspectives, including psycholinguistics and psychosemantics, with emphasis made on the reference theory as an indispensable descriptive instrument. Moreover, the background of the topic under study is the Translator's involvement in the cognitive shaping of the translation end-product by profiling the ongoing mental modelling of meaningful content and its verbalized contours.

The chapter title may mislead some of the readers whose expectations of detailed cutting-edge neurolinguistic or NLP findings applicable to translation studies might turn futile. Instead, the major accents are made on the mechanisms "jointly and severally" called *referencing* with the view of reconsidering the *referential meaning* and linking it to the *referential portraying*[3] of legal concepts. In its turn, the portraying is supposed to allow for establishing the scope of the legal Translator's *referential competence*[4] in conveying legal knowledge cross-linguistically. Both the procedural and end-product levels of legal translation can and should be merited with a thoroughly elaborated pragmatic footing.

2. Legal Canons vs. Linguistic Canons Dichotomy

Globalization has undoubtedly set up new environments for the existing legal languages by having them overhauled and readjusted towards meeting new realities and formats already in place in the dynamic multilingual world. National legal systems and the respective conceptual frameworks are being revised for accommodating innovations firmly positioned by the globalized setting. Both the lexis and terminological corpora are being renewed through integrating new concepts, which fit into national law systems more or less easily, altering the legal discourse parameters. If an English-speaking lawyer gets engaged in an international project entailing the studying of the Russian legal environments as the primary daily stint along with other work assignments. Would this necessitate the study of the Russian law enforcement

2 The word "Translator" is capitalized throughout the chapter with the view of facilitating the recognition of him/her as an actor in the ST decoding and TT generating processes and singling it out amidst the many same-root derivatives; it comprises "Interpreter" as well.

3 See the subheading "Referential Portraying of Legal Concepts" for details.

4 See the subheading "Referential Meaning and Referential Competence: in Search of Referential Equivalence" for details.

practices and/or the judicial system? Would acquainting with the translated Russian codes be sufficient for such a study? Or an encyclopedic outline by a legal scholar specializing in Russian law will suffice?[5] The Russian legal framework is known to be codified; it includes 20 codes encompassing major law fields and featuring law enforcement. The Russian Federation codes[6] cover the major socioeconomic relations across the national, regional and municipal levels, for instance, labor policies, entrepreneurship, budgeting, taxation, land use, water supply, forestry, penal procedure, etc.

Accordingly, under inevitable collisions of certain legal systems, such as Russian which is codified and Anglo-Saxon which is case-law–based, a response to a basic translation query of whether there are many readily available verbal correspondences between legal English and legal Russian is unlikely to be positive. Furthermore, another vital query may come to the fore regarding the pivotal issue of any translation: which language should and can be used for an English-speaking lawyer as the target? Should translation from legal Russian be made into legal English? Or should it be made into some sort of a general language comprehensible by the educated English-speakers? Should common sense preside over this dilemma or the "rule of law"? Can the Russian legal language serving country-specific legal settings be, literally speaking, translated to the English legal language serving principally different legal settings? Legalists make varied use of relevant doctrines for addressing similar queries; however, their doctrines cannot be straightforwardly customized and employed by legal Translators.

Professor E. Elhauge of the Harvard Law School dwells upon the importance of differentiating between the two key types of statutory interpretation customarily applied in law enforcement practices with the view of eliminating abundant ambiguities in invoking statutory default rules. These are linguistic and legal; the latter being also called "substantive." The two interpretation approaches are aimed at identifying the probable meanings from within the two distant perspectives, ideally, for ensuring the statutory interpretation consistency across the US courts. E Elhauge acknowledges 'the distinction between linguistics canons (which are supposed to help interpret the probable meaning of text) and substantive canons (which are supposed to further some substantive policy that judges have found persuasive)' (2008: 203) and expands on challenges associated with applying the distinction:

> *This standard distinction often will not track the underlying difference in default rule approach. Linguistic or textual canons may sometimes be applied to arrive at the best interpretation of meaning or best estimate of legislative preference. But often they intentionally deviate from the most likely meaning or preferences in order to elicit a more precise understanding of enactable preferences. Likewise, substantive canons may sometimes deviate from likely legislative preferences, as with the rule of lenity. (Ibid.)*

The legal scholar's concerns, despite the prioritized focus on these two types of cannons, are articulated but not meant to give practicable clues to legal Translators, thus remaining too inexplicit for the proper comprehension of what stands behind linguistics versus substantive canons distinction. Burdensome legal translation efforts clearly need a solid theoretical framework to rely on, the one which could encompass cannons well-defined and coordinated with the legal profession.

Similarly, although more relevant to the legal translation, Dr M.K. Treushnikov, Russian senior lawyer, expands on the legal translation practices by warning against what he calls a 'blind borrowing of separate foreign statutes or legal traditions' into other countries' national legal systems (2012: 28–30). The lawyer specifies his viewpoint by adding that studying foreign

5 See, for instance, WE Buttler (2008).
6 See, for instance, the following codes: CCRF 2007; CRCRF 2008; FCRF 2005; LCRF 2004; TCRF 2004.

judicial practices should aim at comprehending subtle technicalities and respective legal terminology for approximating them to unrelated legal systems based on the two principles: firstly, legal relevance for a given country and, secondly, practicability of applying a foreign legal institution or an institutional arrangement to the prior fixed legal setting deeply rooted in national history and culture. The lawyer's reasoning and his commonsense approaches are indisputable. In view of these concerns, identifying a unit of legal translation (ULT) is seen as one of the legal Translator's priorities calling for collaborative scrutiny and delineation on the part of legal translation scholars and translation analysis alike.

3. Linguistic and/or Extralinguistic Assumptions: Lacking a Trade-Off Between the Legal and Linguistic Professions

One brief example appears indicative of the growing significance of the legal translation quality with an implication that precedents of legal translation, particularly, of treaties, can be used further times and again, thus evidencing the need for inventorying the high-quality translation cases. A Moscow-based legal scholar believes that inadequacies in legal translation of international instruments may have "grave consequences" for the international status of the sovereign nation but can be attributable largely to translators' legal incompetence or the lack of translation vocation.

The referred event happened in April 2001[7] during the State Duma Budget and Security Committees Parliamentary Ratification Hearing, when a parliamentarian found a flaw in the Russian version of the 1990 Council of Europe Convention on Laundering, Search, Seizure and Confiscation of the Proceeds from Crime.[8] A technical concept from financial law central to the entire anti-money laundering (AML) legal framework was not translated properly: the ST in English contained *'fiscal offence'*[9] while the counterpart wording in the TT in Russian was *finansovyje prestuplenyja* (*'financial crime'*). An explanation given by the Russian Foreign Affairs Ministry in its official statement contained references to the Russian legislation as lacking the word "fiscal," therefore, the 'word 'financial' was quite justifiably used for translation purposes.' Additional references were made by Russian officials to the prior translation precedents of the ratified conventions dating 1957 and 1959 on related legal matters.[10] Both the Russian media and academia discussed the case at length. However, debatable is the issue of the legal meaning which may be expected to have been altered by the legal profession over the period since the 1950s referred to by the officials. Had an initial rendering remained unaltered, it would have implied reducing the range of offence committed and the entities liable under the said Convention, thus grossly downgrading the Convention ratification.

Some Russian legal scholars hold a tough view whereby all legal Translators must be knowledgeable in national and international law alongside in foreign languages, and should keep constant records of high-quality translation precedents. So doing suggests that updating those records is a must via choosing the best possible alternatives, if and when such options become available, then following those precedents in relevant contexts for ensuring consistency across the overall national legal translations corpora. Taking for granted the unsurpassed value of Translators' knowledge, these perfectionistic or, rather, uncompromising requirements by

7 Kizilova, L 2001, 'The Tongue Showed', in *Izvestyja* (Moscow), 11 April 2001.
8 The 1990 AML Convention. ETS 141. Ch. III, Sec. 5, Art. 18, Para 1(d).
9 Lyapunova, G 2001, 'Translators Declared Amnesty to Fraudsters. Russian Text of the Anti-Money Laundering Convention Has a Flaw,' in *Kommersant Daily*, No. 63, 10 April 2001.
10 RF MID Official Statement as of 10 April 2001, *Regarding Publications in Russian Newspapers on the Translation of the 1990 AML Convention into Russian.* ITAR-TASS Agency; Interfax.

the Russian lawyers should be made consistent with the reasonably feasible legal Translators' competences. Indeed, being knowledgeable in national and international law constitutes a profound task in itself, commensurate with an academic degree in law. To this effect, such task seems impracticable, specifically if coupled with the responsibility to ensure consistency across the national stock of legal terminology and/or legal texts corpora. Moreover, impracticability is doubled when it comes to uprooting the legal rules originating from one legal environment and implanting them in another.

The quoted case of the Russian translation of the 1990 AML Convention was quickly resolved by replacing *financovyje prestuplenyja* (*'financial crimes'*) with *fiskal'nyje pravonarušenyja* (*'fiscal offence'*), as appropriate. This case is hoped to call for an open dialogue and cooperative approach towards the more elaborate and thorough split of the mandates in the professional communication domains mediated by legal Translators. This debate definitely mirrors the lack of a reasonable trade-off between legal translators and lawyers.

Theoretically, however, the adjectives *fiscal* and *financial* holding hyponym–hyperonym relations may replace each other, if and only if such replacement complies with a firm in-depth grasp of the legal substance translated. Furthermore, deep-level comprehension involves referencing of the term to the domain-specific knowledge, i.e., an extralinguistic reality, wherein the rules of enclosing one section of reality within another are determined non-linguistically.

4. Legal Translation Proximity to Neurobiology of Consciousness: Brain and Justice Correlation

Consistently with the Peircean concept, translation at large is a universal cognitive phenomenon aimed at and focused on processing, elaborating, verifying linkages between texts or text units—textemes—as signs of mental imprints juxtaposing real/possible worlds reflected in Translators' minds. As such, translation relies on mental capabilities of the Translator who, along with other communicants, should be regarded not as a neutral buffer device impartially processing information flows representing outwardly generated knowledge but as a key processing device, the actor, whose performance gets vital for communicating the matter translated.

In view of this, the following questions may obviously be justified: Where do we play when dealing with a unit of verbalized legal thought? On a plane of thought, or on a plane of expression, or both? Whose playground does a thought—no matter legal, or chemical, or otherwise—occupy: that of a ST originator, or of the Translator, or both? What "place of residence" is a unit of translated thought domiciled in? Could a unit of translated thought be attributed to a fully-fledged mental event? Or part of it? Or, perhaps, if we rely on the frame semantics for purposes of our analysis, units of translated thought can be recognized to embody clustered referents standing for prototypical microevents or microsituations with bundles of associations zipped into gestalts and paving the plane of Translators' consciousness and, at the same time, storing less meaningful but more emotive traces in subconsciousness. Mental dimensions of professional translation activities will sooner or later be scrutinized and addressed by cognitivists and neuroscience researchers at least for furthering computer-assisted translation tools.

Reviewing conscious/unconscious brain functions, Italian neuroscientist A. Damasio comes to scrutinize over brain and justice correlation against the broad social behavior context (2012: 282–284). In so doing, the neuroscientist accentuates the moral behavior, specifically, the breaking of the social agreements, as featured and codified in laws. The following opinion is worthy quoting in the sense it captures the core of mental and/or cognitive perspectives on law-making, rule-making, and law enforcement practices by merging them into a novel and promising blend:

> *Civilization, and in particular the aspect of civilization that has to do with justice, revolves around the notion that humans are conscious. [. . .] By and large, cultures have evolved justice systems that take a commonsense approach to the complexities of decision-making and aim at protecting societies from those who violate established laws. Understandably, and with rare exceptions, the weight given to evidence coming from brain science and cognitive science has been negligible. (283)*

To this effect, a unit of legally relevant thought may be expected to change peoples' lives, get them imprisoned or released, defamed or praised. Most probably, no other profession than the legal one is so reliant on identifying its respective units of thought, if doing so is feasible cross-linguistically. Furthering his viewpoint, Dr Damasio makes a convincing statement on the significance of the professional neuroscience expertise for various legal purposes:

> *Now there is a growing fear that evidence regarding brain function, as it becomes more widely known, may undermine the application of laws, something that legal systems have by and large avoided by not taking such evidence into account. . . . The fact that everyone capable of knowing is responsible for his actions does not mean that the neurobiology of consciousness is irrelevant to the process of justice [. . .]. On the contrary, lawyers, judges, legislators, policy-makers, and educators need to acquaint themselves with the neurobiology of consciousness and decision-making. This is important to promote the writing of realistic laws and to prepare future generations for responsible control of their actions. (Ibid.)*

5. Translation Units: Whirlpool of Views and Approaches

5.1. Doing With or Without a "Unit"?

A profound communicative perspective given for translation in Hatim and Màson (1977) and an account of major translation/interpretation notions are summarized in their detailed glossary of terms. However, there are no UTs (1977: 213–226). Likewise, some prolific translation scholars do fairly well without the "unit," making no resort to them in elaborating translation paradigms despite profound research stances taken (see Eco 2003; Gutt 2010; Sorokin 2001).

Although not all translation scholars resort to the issue under analysis in striving to justify their methodologies cross-linguistically, nonetheless, a UT is believed to be indispensable for the translation studies in general, and a UT—for the legal translation, in particular. For reasons long-established, assessing translation quality rests upon assessing equivalence which, in its turn, depends on and is determined by a well-defined notion of equivalence, yet unavailable as a single standard definition. Equivalence-related matters require a toolkit, evidently, consisting of certain measurable, tangible units. Therefore, UTs have always been under the most pedantic analysis of the majority of translation studies scholars. Concerned with revising a much underestimated interdisciplinary nature of translation studies and an implicitly unfair overstating the significance of words in conveying the message, Schulte (1987) expresses the following convincing opinion:

Translators do not engage in the mere transplantation of words; [. . .] their interpretive acts deal with the exploration of situations that are constituted by an intense interaction of linguistic, psychological, anthropological, and cultural phenomena. (1987: 2)

According to the prolific American translation scholar E. Nida, 'in dynamic correspondences . . . the problems are related, not to specific units, but to the communication load carried by such units' (2003: 193). This view unambiguously asserts the units availability as translation tools by default.

5.2. Textualism Over Mentalism, or Form Over Substance

Noteworthy is Newmark's (1988: 285) standpoint as one of the most definitive examples of textualism, where he assesses a UT as being:

[. . .] the smallest segment of an SL text which can be translated, as a whole, in isolation from other segments. It normally ranges from the word through the collocation to the clause. It could be described as 'as small as is possible and as large as is necessary'. . ., though some translators would say that it is a misleading concept, since the only UT is the whole text.

A similar view is held by Bassnett, who firmly believes in the inevitability of the "blocking out" of translation in cases where the central problem turns out to be the determination of 'translation units' (2000: 117–118). Following Belloc's *On Translation* (1931), Bassnett (2000: 117–118) resolutely advocates an entire text as a UT by expanding as follows:

It must be clear at the outset that the text, understood to be in a dialectical relationship with other texts [. . .] and located within a specific historical context, is the prime unit. [. . .] If the translator takes each sentence or paragraph as a minimum unit and translates it without relating it to the overall work, he runs the risk of ending up with a TL text . . ., where the paraphrasable content of the passages has been translated at the cost of everything else.

Although the words "minimal" or "minimum"[11] accompany UTs somewhat occasionally, it stands to reason to postulate that any atomization of the phenomenon under study justifies the application of either to UTs by default. Interestingly, after some time without units, Hatim shifts his position to becoming a supporter of UTs as entire 'texts in communication' (2013: 39–40); he makes an assertion halfway in-between textualism and mentalism approaches discussed in this chapter:

From a text-linguistic perspective . . . the word or the sentence is no longer seen as an adequate unit of translation. . . . The parameters for a proper transfer of meaning across linguistic and cultural divides must instead be texts in communication, with words and sentences yielding not simply one definite meaning but rather an array of possible meanings. (39)

Furthermore, an awareness of an 'array of possible meanings' raises the degree of uncertainty when addressing the issue of the matter translated. The prevalence of textualism

11 "Minimal" and "minimum" units are treated as synonyms, with alternative uses being possible.

becomes less obvious when Malmkjær (1998), in an in-depth intradisciplinary overview of the UTs, indicates that they are believed to reside within the translation studies' process-oriented side and, following Lörscher, specifies as follows:

> *The unit of translation used by language learners tends to be the single word, while experienced Translators tend to isolate and translate units of meaning, normally realized in phrases, clauses or sentences. (1998: 286)*

The 'units of meaning' noted in the citation which starts with a "word" confuse the harmony of the suggested "form/substance" divide. Moreover, reflecting on the UTs, Malmkjær speaks of a 'strict opposition between translating word-for-word and translating sense-for-sense', the ongoing debates on the literal, surface meaning vs. a proposition, an idea-unit, or a sense-unit, affecting a 'reasonably sized portion of the text', which by no means preclude Translators or scholars to consider the entire text as a unit. In this analysis, Malmkjær relies on Catford (1965) and Toury (1986) to say that generally, 'the clause seems a sensible structure to aim for as translation unit, because it tends to be at clause level that language represents events', adding that 'the clause is a manageable unit of attentional focus' (Malmkjær 1998: 286–288).

To this effect, opting for idea-units or sense-units as propositions brings this reflection closer to mentalism. However, the eventual supporting of the form-over-substance dilemma suggests that the translation scholar holds the textualism approach. This directly follows from her remark that 'most comparative and introspective studies reveal that units can from time to time be isolated at every linguistic level' (286). There are other approaches to textualism and mentalism within one scholar's paradigm, evidencing that the dilemma is of extremely subtle and overly sensitive nature. For instance, Bell (1993) discriminates UTs in consistency with Newmark's vision, but presents interesting evidence in favor of cognitively conditioned syntactic segmentation of utterances, thus leaving more descriptive rather than prescriptive observations on UTs (29–31), and no simple answer to resolving the dilemma in question.

Synopsizing the UTs status cross-disciplinary after Malmkjær, Kenny (2011) classifies units into three types in line with the major translation studies areas: process-oriented, product-oriented, and computer-aided[12] (304–306). According to Kenny's classification, units which tend to be spotted within the process-oriented translation studies fall largely under the psycholinguistic and cognitive approaches, which in terms of our analysis represent the plane of thought, or mentalism approach[13] currently merging with phychosemantics. At this point, Kenny refers to quite a number of researchers who emphasize that identifying UTs correlates with translation expertise levels: the higher the expertise, the longer the UTs and the higher linguistic levels engaged in translating (305). Likewise, Jääskeläinen (2011) states: '[L]anguage learners and other non-experts in translation tend to work on the linguistic surface level, while professional translators and translation students exploit both textual and world knowledge to tackle translation problems' (129); the latter combination is clearly indicative of the integrated vision comparable with Vygotsky's stance (see below).

Among the process-oriented analysts, Kenny points at Bennett, who employs the term "translation atom" for a ST-segment which cannot be further split and thus must be rendered as a whole. Bennett also suggests the term "translation macro-unit" as a larger linguistic unit requiring Translator's intensive processing (Bennett, cited in Kenny 2011: 304).

Furthering Malmkjær's product-oriented studies framework for identifying UTs, Kenny relies largely on Toury's notion of "coupled pairs" embodying a basic "problem + solution"

12 Malmkjær's classification (1998) is extended by the last mentioned type, i.e., computer-aided translation studies. As noted above, this issue remains outside the scope of the chapter.

13 Detailed below under the subheading "Mentalism Over Textualism, or Substance Over Form."

translation principle (Toury 1988; 1995). As such, these coupled pairs, or 'individual coupled language pairs' (1995: 86), are enclosed into what he calls 'actual translation units'. Tracing units across Toury's classical work (1995) yielded also another type of unit, i.e., 'ultimate units of translational consideration' (Ibid. 200). In Kenny's opinion, Toury's units can be characterized by intensive dynamism and thus low predictability due to their high context dependency, and translators' subjectivity in equating those pairs (Kenny 2011: 305). If Toury's coupled pairs were treated as translators' decision-making imprints, it could have added extra evidence in favour of the process-oriented approach. Given Toury's contribution to elaborating the comprehensive translation studies paradigm, the mere availability of such combined standpoint once again proves the subtlety required for handling any dimensions regarding the UTs issue.

A pure textualism attitude is lacking in the product-oriented methods, consequently making such predominance less conspicuous across the research stances quoted so far. Remarkably, Kenny claims that the process-oriented analysts when segmenting UTs prioritize ST-segments, while the product-oriented researchers rely on TT-segments or entire TTs (2011: 305). Proving this standing, she quotes Malmkjær as saying that 'the unit of translation is the target-text unit that can be mapped onto a source-text unit' (1998: 286).

Coming back to Newmark's view on what he calls the 'unit of translating' (1988: 30–32), essential is his contradiction whereby 'normal translation sentence by sentence', done almost automatically, almost with no 'intercession of thought (scornfully referred to as *transcodage* by the ESIT school of Paris)', coexists with much stronger efforts caused by 'referential, cultural or idiolectal problem' signifying that the 'mental struggle between the SL words and the TL thought begins' (31). That is the exact point which necessitates shifting over to the mentalism approach for exploring the UTs.

5.3. Mentalism Over Textualism, or Substance Over Form

Mentalism and mentalizing are undoubtedly on the agenda for Translators when they traverse the text border to see the backyard of thoughts clustered or isolated but verbalized into text formats. Psychologists found their way to explain human interaction through brain/mind functioning, plainly indicating as follows:

> *The understanding of other people's mental life has been called a "theory-of-mind", although 'mind-reading' or 'mentalizing' skills are frequently used synonymously, depending on the user's theoretical convictions. In the last 25 years the question of how we develop mentalizing abilities has attracted great attention within philosophy, psychology, linguistics and primate studies. (Meristo 2007: 7)*

Any translation starts with perception of a ST-fragment or a SL-utterance. Studying perception *per se* falls more within general psychology, psycholinguistics, psychosemantics, as well as a bunch of cognitive sciences, such as cognitive psychology and cognitive linguistics; neurolinguistics, rather than the translation studies. However, perception is the onset, the very start of a sophisticated mental effort which stands behind translating. No categorization or conceptualization is possible unless the Translator becomes consciously or subconsciously aware of the *substance to be communicated.* Accordingly, we believe translation to be one of the mental mechanisms in-build into overall cognitive schemata innate in humans. For this reason, there is no exaggeration in highly meriting translation among the very basic and indispensable mechanisms intrinsic for human beings' cognitive faculties which underlie the core mental metabolism. This belief can be traced back to many a scholar, with Roman

Jakobson (1959) being one of them. Remarkable is a statement made in his symbolic essay over half a century ago:

> *In its cognitive function, language is minimally dependent on the grammatical pattern because the definition of our experience stands in complementary relation to metalinguistic operations – the cognitive level of language not only admits but directly requires recoding interpretation, i.e., translation. Any assumption of ineffable or untranslatable cognitive data would be a contradiction in terms. But [. . .] in what would call everyday verbal mythology [. . .], the grammatical categories carry a high semantic import. In these conditions, the question of translation becomes much more entangled and controversial. (1959: 236)*

It would be fair to suppose that translation is based on such cognitive mechanisms whose units may be a "span"—like a "reading span," measuring the working memory capacity available for remembering the words read (Field 2004: 211, 243)—or an "attention span," showing a "level" of short-memory engagement and memory store in general[14] and, additionally, in conjunction with mental efforts (Kahneman [1973] 2011: 31–38). The allocation of memory and attention is acknowledged as highly pertinent to interpreting (Chernov[15] 2004; Hatim, and Màson 1997), although translating deserves no less attentive treatment in terms of attention and memory store or use. This aspect appeared emphasized by Jakobson (1959: 236), who stressed attention-driven priorities on both ends of the translation process:

> *Languages differ essentially in what they must[16] convey and not in what they may convey. [. . .] Naturally, the attention of native speakers and listeners will be constantly focused on such items as are compulsory in their verbal code.*

Broadening his stance and favoring the elementary units' relevance for the cross-lingual perspective, Jakobson (233) expands as follows:

> *On the level of interlingual translation, there is ordinarily no full equivalence between code-units, while messages may serve as adequate interpretations of alien code-units or messages.*

Along with this well-defined perspective on units significance, Jakobson, though discussing the sound system of the language, makes a strong point about "auditory impressions" treated as 'units of understanding' which as such can be associated with mental impressions ''decomposable' and due to that found capable of being imprinted on our memory' (Id.).

Following the relevance theory of communication developed by Sperber and Wilson, as well as a notable shift in the overall linguistic research paradigm towards the Fodorian view on cognition and mental events, E.A. Gutt (2010) suggests the relevance theory of translation with the view of bridging the inevitable language and culture gaps. According to this method, the mentalism-driven approach was superseding the then dominant descriptive-classificatory approach, on the one hand, and the translational behaviorism,[17] on the other:

14 See Field (2004: 24, 78, 321) for details.
15 Alternative spelling—GV Černov—is also available in foreign bibliographical sources.
16 Italicized in the original (Jakobson 1959).
17 Gutt (2010: 198–201).

> *Relevance theory approaches communication from the point of view of competence rather than behavior: it tries to give an explicit account of how the information-processing faculties of our mind enable us to communicate with one another. Its domain is therefore mental faculties rather than texts or processes of text production and [. . .] the possibility of accounting for translation in terms of the communicative competence assumed to be part of our minds.* (2010: 21)

In particular, Gutt promotes the view outreaching the tangible faculties and resorting to the lesser tangible ones, such as 'intuition' or the 'cognitive environment of the receptor language':

> *Whatever decision the translator reaches is based on his intuition or beliefs*[18] *about what is relevant to his audience. The translator does not have direct access to the cognitive environment of his audience, he does not actually know what it is like – all he can have is some assumptions or beliefs about it.* (118)

Chernov treats the entire realm of speech activity associated with and involved in interpretation from within the psycholinguistic perspectives ([1987] 2004). Such prioritization can be easily attributed to the early 1970s when the newly emerged psycholinguistics was positioning itself in the Soviet Union and later in Russia as an independent and self-sufficient linguistics branch. Words like "mentalizing," "mental frames," "representation patterns," or "cognitive mapping" were not yet in use by Russian translation analysts at the time the scholar had been working on his monograph. However, such mechanisms and respective notions as *long-term working memory* and *memory overload, probabilistic inference, inferred meaning* and *situational inference, pragmatic meaning, value judgments,* etc., clearly emphasize Chernov's broad research scope and his exploration of the translation studies essentials not only from within the psycholinguistic, but also semiotic, hermeneutic, and cognitive perspectives.

Remarkable as it may seem, the number of "units" identified by Chernov as relevant for translation casts profound light on the scholar's perfectionism leaving no room for a simplistic approach. These units *inter alia* comprise: *semantic unit, unit of activity, unit of communication, unit of discourse, unit of information, unit of the Language of Thought*[19], *unit of meaning, unit of message, unit of speech,* and *unit of translation,* to name but a few.[20] Perception-wise, the scholar stresses that 'even though the word as such is never an object of translation, redundancy at this level is still significant for the perception of higher order units' (Id. at 172). Consequently, Chernov asserts an inseparable bond between the signifier and the signified, however, subject to Vygotskyan conditioning.[21]

6. In Pursuit of Semantic Contour: Referencing as Internalizing

Referencing falls within the primary translation procedures regardless of the subject-matter, genres, or ST types, since the ST comprehension starts with referencing ST-textemes as "units of understanding"[22] against the text-external contexts which may comprise prototypical events, state of affairs, or situations as the addressant's reflections on the real/possible world. The ST

18 Italicized in the original (Id. at 118).
19 Capitalized in the original (Chernov [1987] 2004: 266).
20 Chernov ([1987] 2004: 3, 7–9, 33, 65, 96, 101, 103, 170, 177–178, 206, 210).
21 See below under the subheading *Vygotskyan Stance.*
22 Jakobsonian units (1959: 233).

comprehension moves on to end up with TT generation in line with the text-external contexts of the addressee as anticipated and modelled by the Translator. The first procedure may be enclosed into what Burke names decontextualization, and the second, into recontextualization (2007: 10).

Among its other functions, referencing is aimed at allocating certain signs—verbal and/or nonverbal represented as texts or metatexts—on the knowledge continuum for generating referential knowledge. Referential knowledge is acknowledged to represent the world outside Translator's psyche: real, possible, desirable, or virtual, or else as reflected and/or reproduced and thus residing in his/her psyche. This knowledge is conveyed through the referential meaning. Following Wales, who shares Ogden and Richards' assumption that reference is used specifically for 'the mental image of the referent produced by the world and corresponds to Ferdinand de Saussure's signified' (de Saussure 2011: 360–361),[23] we see every reason to assert that internalizing as deep-level comprehension is reference-driven, inasmuch as referencing prompts categorization. In accord with the Russian psycholinguistic school, internalization is assumed to constitute the transitioning of accumulated world knowledge and associated imagery, as well as related imprints of practical experiences, into an individual mental representation structures reshaping the cognitive profile of an individual Translator over time (Vlasenko 2006: 82–84).

Taking a typical example of a SL-TL-switch can be suggestive of the units identifiable in rendering an English SL-texteme, *the US government social welfare package*, into Russian. With no grammaticalized gender or declination in the SL, this construction in cognitive terms presents a non-routine effort for the Russian Translator to process in the sense it is "inconvenient" for verbalizing, specifically due to the lack of explicit internal linkages. Here again undoubtedly relevant is Jakobson's opinion that when the 'information required by the English and Russian grammatical pattern is unlike, we face quite different sets of two-choice situations' (1959: 236). Indeed, to whom should the Translator be loyal when generating the TT-stretch: SL or TL?

There are at least four TL-renderings available upright. The listed Russian renderings are accompanied by their literal back-translations into English; these "transcripts" are marked by the "<<" symbol, indicating the reversed SL-message comprehension:

> *(a) gosudarstvennaja programma SŠA v oblasti social'noj zaščity naselenyja / po social'noj zaščite naselenyja << back-translated English transcript: the US government program on the social safety nets enabling social protection of the citizenry;*
> *(b) kompleksnij plan rukovodstva SŠA po ulučšeniju gosudarstvennoj systemy social'nogo obespečenija << an integrated plan adopted by the US officials on improving the government-driven social welfare system;*
> *(c) kompleksnyje mery pravitel'stva SŠA v oblasti soveršenstvovanyja social'nogo obespečenyja << integrated measures taken by the US government for the social welfare improvement in the field of social protection; almost a twin option – kompleks gosudarstvennych mer … << an action plan envisaging measures effected by the US government for … ; and*
> *(d) paket program SŠA po gosudarstvennym meram social'nogo obespečenija naselenija << the US package on government measures / steps to be taken for social protection of the citizenry; etc.*

These (a)–(d) optional renderings are all justifiable due to high predictability of their verbal realizations unfolding one after another. However, they are competing for being signifiers for the SL-texteme and mapping its referential range.[24] The renderings and their back translations

23 Wales mentions that sometimes referential knowledge is also named 'conceptual, cognitive or denotational' (2011: 360).
24 For details see Lyons (1981: 220).

help respond to the question relevant for the issue under analysis: whether units of translation are dispersed *pro rata* over units of thought or Jakabsonian's units of understanding.

In essence, the UTs non-linear ordering and their *non-pro rata* dispersion over meaningful units obviously follows from back translations. Given this, a major query in translating legal text segments may be expected to relate to particular kinds of referential knowledge, evidently shaped by a blend of the world knowledge and expertise.

7. Vygotskyan Stance: 'Unit of Verbal Thought in a Word Meaning'

Despite the ongoing developments in translation studies suggesting an upsurge in exploring the subject and many elaborate approaches and levels of understanding across countries and continents (e.g., Baker 1987; 1988; Bell 1993; Burke 2007; Eco 2004; 2012; Malone 1988; Milojević-Sheppard 1993; Nida 1975; 2001; Pym 2010; Shveitser[25] 1973; 1980; 1988; 1999; Toury 1986; 1988; Waard and Nida 1986; Wagner, Bech, and Martínez 2012), procedurally, translation studies are still in want of responses to the long-standing challenges, some of which are rooted in finding out why the need is persistently felt in identifying a suitable UT corresponding to a unit of thought to make as good a fit as practicable when producing a translation end-product.

Lev S. Vygotsky, a Russian psychologist acclaimed for his *Thought and Language* monograph ([1934] 1979),[26] treats thought and language as interrelated and mutually supportive systems, wherein the primacy of thought over language in no way overshadows their exclusively dissimilar functions.[27] Vygotsky affirms that people think in complexes based on networked associations which are eventually shaped into 'chain complexes' (Vygotsky [1934] 1979, cited in Field 2004: 325). Moreover, the scholar is known to have declared that 'thoughts are not expressed in words, but acquire existence in them', suggesting in addition that 'we might therefore speak about the becoming (the unity of existence and nonexistence) of thoughts in words' (Ibid.: 330). Also, the psychologist can be quoted as saying:

> *In essence, [. . .] we must agree that inner speech is not speech at all, but thinking and affective-volitional activity, since it includes in itself motives of speech and thought that is expressed in word. (Vygotsky [1934] 1979, cited in Veer and Valsiner 1991: 179)*

A "unit of thought" treated outside the neuroscience and related contexts may seem an idealized notion serving several ends. It is common knowledge that each language layer has units of its own allowing scholars to maintain a more or less precise inventory of trends and developments occurring inside or outside given or adjacent fields of study. A language theory enjoys impressive arsenals of units: phonemes, tonemes, morphemes, lexemes, grammemes, semantemes, sememes, syntagmemes, syntaxemes, tagmemes, textemes, etc., each of which is enclosed within a respective hierarchy arranged and used within a particular language-layer. The higher the level of language processing and the more technical the subject-matter—the higher the analytical abstraction. Discourse makes no exception and can be merited with a unit of its own, see *a minimal unit of discourse* in Yokoyama (1986: 3–5).[28]

25 Other spellings—Svejcer or Švеitser—can also be found in different bibliographical traditions in English and German publications.
26 Vygotsky's monograph, *Myšlenyje i jazyk*, was first published in Russian in 1934; its first translation into English appeared in Harvard in 1962; the quoted translation appeared in 1979.
27 See Field (2004: 324–325); Newman and Holzman (1993); and Veer and Valsiner (1991) for details.
28 See also *a unit of discourse* identified by Chernov (2004: 44, 65, 170).

A real need in singling out a 'minimal unit' seems to be felt in anticipation of an internal crunch within some research field, when routine research tools grow "older" and less responsive to obvious ontologically pressing challenges impeding intra-, inter-, and multidisciplinary solutions. An ongoing chain of unsettled problems in legal translation associated with individual/collective frustrated translation efforts, failed legal discourse, etc. prompt more finely-tuned toolkits to be identified as analytical tools. There are many units to measure all sorts of brain activity for various purposes; some of them are used for advancing applied research in quite different fields of research. A "concept" is claimed to consist of its minimal *units of meaning*,[29] linked together in a network (Field 2004: 225); *psycholinguistic units* were devised to tackle speech activity (Leontiev[30] 2007).

The indivisibility of language and thought is *a priori* and axiomatic (Field 2004; Jakobson 1990; Leontiev 2007; Zalevskaya 1995; et al.). Consequently, thoughts are enveloped into verbal codes which have their own units: words. Vygotsky persuasively warns us by indicating that 'thought and word are not connected by a primary bond'[31] and following up he locates a 'unit of verbal thought in a word meaning' (Ibid.: 120) with the following substantiation:

> *Since generalizations and concepts are undeniably acts of thought, we may regard meaning as a phenomenon of thinking. [. . .] Word meaning is a phenomenon of thought only in so far as thought is embodied in speech, and of speech only in so far as speech is connected with thought and illuminated by it. It is a phenomenon of verbal thought, or meaningful speech – a union of word and thought. (Ibid.)*

Assessing a UT as a fundamental issue for both translation theory and practice, French translation researchers Vinay and Darbelnet rejected an individual word as a UT candidate from the onset. In their opinion, a UT is a combination of a 'lexicological unit' and a 'unit of thought' which could be defined as 'the smallest segment of the utterance whose signs are linked in such a way that they should not be translated individually' (Vinay and Darbelnet, cited in Munday 2012: 92). Vinay and Darbelnet singled out units of translation: while the 1958 French edition had the list of UTs comprising individual words, grammatically linked groups, fixed expressions and semantically linked groups, the 1995 English version had an extended list of UTs comprising also longer units, such as subject and verb groups or enumerated objects given as single UTs.[32] Remarkable is the scholars' explicit striving to combine a thought with its verbal realization.

There are constituents of the mental representation structure recognized in the frame semantics for identifying mental structure units: frames, scenarios, scripts, and schemes (Minsky 1988; Johnson 1990). However, a referent is less merited within the mainstream translation studies research, being explored more frequently by philosophers and logisticians due to inexplicitness of available definition (Davis 2005; Kibrik 2011; Lebedev and Černjak 2001). It is noteworthy that communicants' attention may be treated in terms of reference. For instance, A.A. Kibrik, in analyzing reference in discourse in the cognitive interpretation perspective, defines "reference" as attention while referential choice as working memory activation (2011: 557); the scholar locates 'referents on the plane of thought, while referential devices – on the plane of talk' (97). The Russian linguist elaborates a theoretically-oriented cognitive approach to cross-linguistic aspects of reference along with an empirically-based analysis of the referent activation in working memory. Kibrik validates his arguments with

29 Cf. *units of meaning* identified by Malmkjær (1998: 286), mentioned above.
30 Spelt also as *Leontjev, Alexej*.
31 See Vygotsky ([1934] 1979: 119) for details.
32 See Munday (2012: 92) for details.

experimental data evidencing that almost every third word pronounced usually depends on the referential choice made by communicants. This stance complies with the mentalism approach.

It is no accident that we shifted over to the reference framework for analyzing legal translation technicalities. Sharing assumptions behind the mentalism approach, referent is postulated to be the very unit of thought which enables the Translator's decision-making aimed at spotting a unit of translation identifiable in the ST and conveyable to the TL.

8. Referential Meaning and Referential Competence: In Search of Referential Equivalence

The notion of 'referential equivalence' suggested in Eco (2004: 62–64) appears instrumental in so far as it ensures the minimizing of a semantic gap brought about by domain-specific and culture-specific connotations always implied in the SL and TL in bilingual communication. Referential equivalence is preceded by the concept of sameness in reference (14–17) denoting the evocation of the same effect for the TL-audience as was meant by the ST originator. Eco specifies the nature of the effect calling it 'psychological.' Hence, there is every reason to understand such effect as an 'emotional sensation,' or a communicative effect, if the communicative paradigm is relied on. In view of this, referential equivalence may be said to bridge the gap in those psycholinguistic translation theories, which attempted at explaining communicative effects purely in psychological terms (Sorokin 1974; Vlasenko 1993). The concept has undeniably conceptualized the linguistic tools employed for elaborating translation studies. Eco affirms the significance of reference by indicating:

> *One of the kinds of equivalence that could be judged for a translation was referential equivalence. In very simple terms, a translation should convey the same things and events as the original. [. . .] Reference in its strict sense, that is, an act by which, once one knows the meaning of the uttered words, one determines states of a possible world [. . .], and asserts that in a given spatio-temporal situation certain things or certain events happen.* (2004: 62)

Emphasizing reference as an act directed at identifying certain objects, situations, or events, state of affairs, etc. in a real, possible or virtual world narrated or otherwise actualized in a given text, its stretch or sequence, we believe that referencing and identifying referential meaning of verbal signs are the Translator's first and primary concerns—no matter conscious or subconscious and regardless of the type of discourse. Referencing necessitates contextualizing a verbal message. Quite a number of translation scholars pointed out the significance and indispensability of referencing in translation, stressing that different languages respond to slightly or grossly different referencing techniques. Referencing may be complicated by a frequent shortage of extralinguistic knowledge[33] and/or shared knowledge scarcity between the ST-originator and the target audience.

While some linguists treat reference as the text-internal cohesion device, the more traditional understanding of reference perceives it as the text-external device (Bell 1991: 154–156; DS 2011: 137, 150, 359–361). Being a traditional semantic instrument, reference stands for the relationship which holds between a word and what it points to in the real world (Baker 1997: 181). However, there is no unanimity where the reference points to. Besides, the world "real" for one communicant may be quite "unreal" for another communicant or a target

33 On knowledge in ST perception, see, for instance, Schäffner (1989).

audience. Can we expect a verbal sign or a combination of signs to point to an imaginative, make-believe, hypothetical, virtual object or event, state of affairs or abstract notions which are nonexistent? American philosopher W. Davis (2005) and Russian philosophers Lebedev and Černjak (2001) endeavoured to assess the ideational capacity of language and named it "referential capacity." They constitute that it forms part of ideational semantics. The scholars share the view, according to which 'we can and often do refer to things that do not exist' (Lebedev and Černjak 2001: 23; Davis 2005: 7).

Additionally, the concept of *referential competence* suggested here specifically for the legal translation paradigm was introduced by Eco (1999: 170–171); it was once again prompted by Eco's related notion '*the referential duty of the translator*' (2004: 64). In our understanding, referential competence allows for fixing the scope of the ST referentiality, as perceived by the Translator, against the TT. Also, it enables the Translator to allocate his/her referential coordinates on the ST's and/or TL's referential continuums, as appropriate. Such virtual allocation is important since any incoming message intended to be conveyed through interlingual translation is generated outwardly with the Translator having no 'direct access to the cognitive environment'[34] of either the SL-originator or the TL-audience. The Translator's "in-betweener status" calls for much more profound and meticulous study of the referential competence which has not been properly addressed so far.

A case of *damage + s ≥ compensation* may exemplify the validity of *referential competence*. Indeed, the formula is plain: *damage + s = damages*. Nevertheless, the resultant of "damages" has nothing to do with pluralia tantum for "damage." It has a different meaning: 'compensation' (Coulthard and Johnson 2007: 48), or, more precisely: 'a monetary remedy awarded by the court to a successful claimant' (Oliphant 2008: 295).

This case of the legal meaning conventionality challenges the regularity of the grammatical pattern employed by English for modelling pluralia tantum by adding *-s* suffix to the root. However, the so called plural form shifts the frame semantics of the legal term into a different representational format, yielding a semantic increment corresponding to the legal treatment of damage inflicted, rather than denoting a plural form *per se*. Consequently, we confront new semantic dimensions of this seemingly grammatical use. A quasi-plural of "damages" actualizes at least two implied sets of legally essential facts: first, the fact of damage suffered; second, the invoked liability to recover this damage. A shift in the semantic representation validates a conclusion that *-s* suffix, employed to form pluralia tantum as the grammatical norm would normally suggest, has not at all formed it, nor has the substance "damage" been multiplied in terms of quantity. Rather, a formally plural form emerges as a quasi-plural form and a "carrier" of different semantic schema which triggers a much more extended legal meaning comparable with the proposition. In other words, the pluralia tantum suffix shifts the word's denotational status from 'nominative' to 'propositional.' However, the problem seems to belong to a different domain.

It seems relevant to reiterate Jakobson's assumption, quoted above, that the 'grammatical categories carry a high semantic import' (1959: 236). In the same way, HG Schogt sees grammatical problems in translation as more serious than the lexical ones because, in his view, 'grammatical categories have an infinitely higher occurrence than lexical items' (1986: 1109). This example illustrates and, putting it precisely, necessitates the substantiating of a unit of legal translation. It would be fair to assess this case as indicative of (i) morphemic and grammatical levels of the ULT realization, (ii) the scenario level of thought representation in terms of frame semantics, or as (iii) the grammaticalization of pragmatic meaning.

Inasmuch as "compensation" may be rendered in other legal languages variously, consistently with respective regulations, there are reasons to recognize "damages" as, *inter alia*:

34 See a full citation above (Gutt 2010: 118).

(a) *damage recovery,* (b) *indemnification of damage incurred,* (c) *cost of damage reimbursement,* (d) *inflicted damage coverage,* etc. The referential equivalence seems barely feasible for objectifying multiple legal translation cases in dissimilar legal contexts deeply rooted in legal systems. The Translator's referential competence appears an adjustable concept to account for legal translation challenges since it clearly aids the Translator awareness/unawareness as an objective factor behind bridging those legal inconsistencies among foreign jurisdictions which are marked cross-linguistically. Some English–Russian correspondences[35] with "damages" in focus can be exemplified as follows:

- *inadequacy of damages ≥ (i) neadekvatnoje vozmeščenije [pričinjennogo] uščerba; (ii) nedostatočnaja kompensacyja ponesjonnych ubytkov; (iii) vozmeščenije [pričinjennogo] uščerba v nedostatočnom ob'jeme,* with an implication of an inappropriate indemnification amount estimated and awarded by the court;
- *damages at large ≥ (i) polnaja summa real'no ponesjonnych ubytkov; (ii) polnoje vozmeščenije [otvetčikom] pričinjennogo uščerba [ponesjonnogo iststom].*

Certainly, the English-Russian correspondences exemplified above illustrate Vygotsky's words on the lack of primary bond between the word and the meaning, entailing a negative response to a challenging legal translation query: Can the UTs be expected to be distributed over the relevant units of meaningful ideation on a *pro rata* basis? Unevenly spread over verbal units, the pieces of legal knowledge are obviously low predictable, unless the referential range is well-defined for the translated legal terms. Nevertheless, the predictability increases when the legal Translator is aware of the legal profession's conventions. For that reason, the legal language ought to be regarded as a professional convention-driven code provided conventional meanings fixed by the legal milieu in question are accessible to the Translator. What is left for the legal Translator is to access this referential convention with the legal profession. The knowledge of this convention can be considered indispensable for the legal Translator's referential competence. Ultimately, reasoning over a "unit of legal translation" suggests that the "damages" case signifies a referential convention[36] established by the English speaking lawyers on the onset of the profession. Clearly, it is getting increasingly obvious that the notion of referential equivalence appears crucial for legal Translators' competence fairly often conditioned by the knowledge of professional conventions.

9. Referential Portraying of Legal Concepts

Habitual referential expressions—nominal or pronominal—hold their referential status for the ST originator, but not necessarily for the target audience or a particular Translator who, in fact, is an "audience" himself/herself. At this very point, a concept of *referential portrait* shall be introduced (Zaitseva 1995). Working on the Transactional Discourse Model elaborated by Yokoyama (1986), whereby communicable knowledge is proven to be reallocated in discourse by and between discourse participants, Valentina Zaitseva, an American linguist, elaborated the concept of "referential portraits" for furthering the discourse analysis and ensuring better

35 Based on the specialized dictionary meaning; for details see ERBED 2000, 192; GFED 2003, 245; NFDER 2011, 188.

36 A notion of a "shared referential convention" is dwelt upon further in the chapter under the subheading *Referential Portraying of Legal Concepts.*

transparency of interlocutors' identities and shifts of identities in discourse-specific situations (1999a; 1999b).

Obviously, complex concepts abundant in and across the legal genres are in need of tools to finely-tune the semantic analysis. For so doing, we suggest the notion of *referential portraying,* which represents a conceptual blend of the two respective terms: *referential portrait,* described above, and *psycholinguistic portraying,* introduced by Russian psycholinguist Alexandra Zalevskaya (1995) for describing Russian general lexicon in speech realizations. The *referential portraying* is an analytical tool for the translation studies at large, as well as for a wide scope of its subject-specific applications, such as legal translation, financial translation, i.e., much beyond the literary or general discourse boundaries initially envisaged by Zaitseva and Zalevskaya.

9.1. "Disclosure": One Legal Concept—Two Opposite Referential Portraits?

The referential portraying of legal terminology is assumed to be legal Translator's strategic task and daily striving. A semantic analysis of the term "disclosure" consists of profiling the referential knowledge associated with the concept's core meaning by type of incremental information affecting its comprehension. The profiling may be based on definitions available in bilingual specialized dictionaries and encyclopedias, as well as legislative sources. Following the Yokoyama's graphic conventions detailed by Zaitseva, the following brackets are used for portraying semantic components enclosed in the referential knowledge to be conveyed by a legal concept under analysis:

- the figure brackets enclose verbalized referential knowledge
  { referential knowledge },
- the square brackets indicate referential specifications
  [extra referential knowledge, details, specifications], and
- the round brackets contain contextual additional information clarifying the context
  (contextual knowledge). (See Zaitseva 1999b: 511)

The referential portraying of legal concepts procedurally can rely on *referential frames. Referential frames* are seen as mental representations which may stand for stereotypical or idiosyncratic patterns of perception within a certain referential range known to communicants, i.e., shared by communicants, at any given time. In other words, *referential frames* are somewhat comparable with the psychological notion of "gestalts." As such, referential frames embody "ready-made templates" as basic units of knowledge and cannot be further split into minor meaningful units which the legal Translator is capable of assigning to the referent at any given time.

In essence, *referential frames* are introduced here to denote the most frequent and most probable referential templates correlating with mental representation units like frames or micro-scenarios and shaping referential portraits of concepts, similarly to "gestalts;" the latter might also correlate with bigger and more complex mental representation units, such as plans and schemes. As such, a referential frame shows the availability of one intake of referential knowledge stocked at the Translator's memory at a time and readily accessible for retrieval due to its recognisability. As such, a referential frame may be regarded as a unit of instantaneous thought, easily recognizable and retrievable from the memory. Also, a referential frame is associated with a verbal sign or signs like a text stretch or text sequences.

The referential portraying can be exemplified by the English legal concept "disclosure" used in a corporate context. The first most probable referential frame which may urge our association is the following:

> **Disclose (1) { statutory prescribed release of corporate information by** companies } with incremental referential specifications based on contextual details featuring the referential range of the concept under analysis,[37] namely:
> + [both positive and negative that might bear on investment decisions]
> + [by companies themselves to stockholders and investors to ensure equal access to information on the company's transactions]
> + [for financial reporting purposes as an accountability mechanism warranting the orderly functioning of the markets]
> + [in compliance with the transparency requirement for ease of understanding by providing relevant information on a full, clear, and timely basis that would enable detection of fraud or manipulation]
> + [as per the US Securities and Exchange Commission rules, other governmental regulations, and stock exchange requirements].

The referential specifications given above are assumed to be incremental because they prompt an increment in the constituent properties of the referential meaning, thus expanding the referential range of this legal concept. This first frame within the referential portrait may be added by two other referential specifications. First, "disclosure in civil litigation," understood as "the duty to discover evidence relevant to parties in civil litigation for revealing, proving or resisting the other party's claim."[38] The "duty to disclose" in civil litigation basically overlaps with the "corporate disclosure," particularly in the meaning of a mandatory obligation, which holds for the legally regulated relationship in question. Second, "information disclosure" in contract law seen in the same vein, i.e. as a mandatory commitment enforced for certain specific types of contracts.[39] Principally, we do not see the need in expanding this frame endlessly. Notably, the first referential frame might enter into an obvious contradiction with another concurrent referential frame, detailed below for the same concept.

> **Disclose (2) { unauthorized release of corporate information }** with incremental referential specifications based on contextual details featuring the referential range of the concept under analysis,[40] namely:
> + [through trading of yet unreleased information based on knowledge of material corporate developments (this is inside information)]
> + [including on major deals or latest earnings report which have not been announced publicly (these earnings may significantly differ from prior estimates)]
> + [for capitalizing on inside information like profiting from access to information

37 Based on the terminological dictionary meanings; for details see: Corporate Disclosure (NOCL 2008, 234–235); Disclosure (DFIT 2010, 190; ERBED 2000, 212); Disclosure in financial markets (NOCL 2008, 329–330); Financial public relations, Full disclosure (DFIT 2010, 260–261, 286); Disclosure of evidence, Disclosure order, Disclosure policy (NFDER 2011, 216); Transparency (DFIT 2010, 779), and (ABBYY 2011).

38 See NOCL (2008, 328–329) for details.

39 See (Ibid.: 584–585) for details.

40 Based on the terminological dictionary meanings; for details see: Disclosure, Disclosure document, Disclosed reserve (NFDER 2011, 216); Inside information, Insider (DBET 2012, 359); Inside(r) information, Insider dealings, Insider trading, Insider Trading Sanctions Act of 1984 (ERBED 2000, 365–366); Insider, Insider trading (DFIT 2010, 350; LD 2003, 259) and (ABBYY 2011).

unavailable publicly]
+ [abusing and noncomplying with state and federal law on corporate use of sensitive information by profiting personally from something that belongs to the corporation].

The two figures below illustrate referential frames in simple graphics, where legally conflicting contextual knowledge is given under each frame in the form of extra referential specifications enclosed in both round and square brackets. This is believed to show the subtlety of the proposed split. The concept demonstrates an inherent conflict of the referential knowledge immanent for its deep semantics.

9.2. "Disclosure" Concept in Corporate Settings: Conflicting Referential Frames Within One Referential Portrait

The "disclosure" concept is complex and sensitive to the legal context implying the possibility of applying two mutually exclusive legal treatments. Such context sensitivity of the concept may be mitigated by context transparency; while the availability of one overlapping referential property—"release of information"—may mislead the legal Translator, unless he/she is aware of the immanent semantic ambivalence. Despite its referentially conflicting nature and context-sensitivity, "disclosure" is comprehensible since no term is ever used alone for its own sake, save in the dictionary.[41] Thus, a conflicting set of referential frames within this term's semantics may not be regarded as a strong restraining factor for identifying its referential meaning in the course of legal translation.

Lebedev and Černyak suggest *reference* be treated for any given technical term of art as dependent on and bound by certain *communicative significance* recognized by expert community members. The scholars call such communicative convention a *general referential convention* (2001: 337–338). The latter is supposed to be known to each member in a given professional community. Evidently, it would be fair enough to call such expert community-specific convention a "shared referential convention" by analogy with the shared referent. Important as this standpoint may seem for the philosophical framework, it is no less valuable for the legal translation framework as it gives a major clue for comprehending technical legal concepts, i.e. a fundamental assumption of the prior established frame of reference (Vlasenko 2010b; 2011; Vlasenko and Suslov 2012).

10. Inventorying and Clustering SL-Signifiers for Referential Portraying of the Signified

10.1. Portraying the Bankruptcy/Insolvency Concepts

Legal concepts and their verbal "clothing" may be presumed to require special handling from the variety of perspectives, though what matters for such practical assignment as translation is a good dictionary. Dictionaries alone—even up-to-date and technically reliable—are insufficient for handling serious legal translation assignments. The legal Translator's worldview comprising the world knowledge, often referred to as background knowledge or encyclopedic

41 See also K. Malmkjær's comment on the translation-related regularities that 'in the preparation of bilingual dictionaries, the largest unit employed tends to be the phrase and the most common unit is the word' (1998: 286).

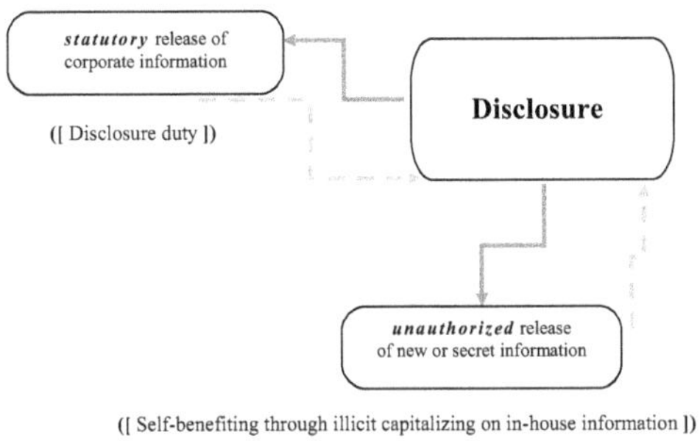

Figure 6.1 **Interrelation of conflicting referential frames with the *'disclosure'* core semantics**

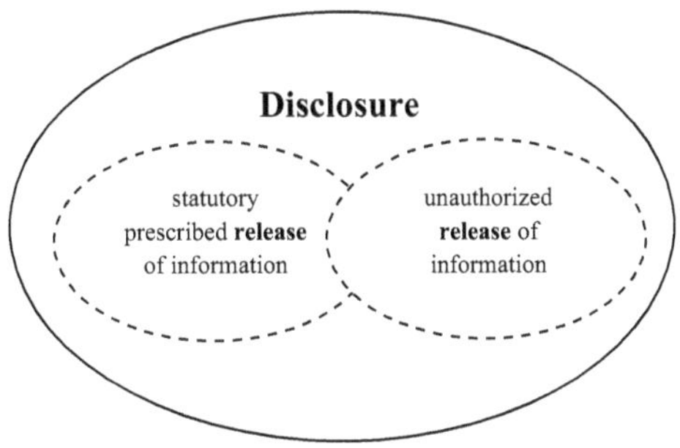

Figure 6.2 **Referential ambiguity: intersection of conflicting referential frames within one referential portrait**

knowledge, may not be sufficient for ensuring consistent SL-TL correspondences. An example described below suggests that regulations and statutory definitions should be considered as reference materials, alongside dictionaries, for identifying the referential range of properties for any given term or a terminological expression and conveying it cross-linguistically.

The term "bankruptcy" is a good example. Quite predictably, the term "bankruptcy" is treated differently in the English-speaking jurisdictions and the Russian jurisdiction; however, the difference persists even within the English-speaking jurisdictions—between the UK and the US. While British law treats "bankruptcy" as insolvency of an individual (UKIA 1986: X), US law applies it to both legal entities and individuals (U.S.C. 1926, 11 (109)). Russian bankruptcy law treats it broadly as the law of receivership setting forth specific procedures for regulating insolvency situations;[42] the coverage matters (Vlasenko and Galimov 2012: 23). Going into detail, Russia regulates "insolvency" and "bankruptcy" alike in cases of non-premeditated loss of creditworthiness; this makes itself conspicuous already in the title of the 2002 federal law 'On Insolvency (Bankruptcy)'. Where insolvency/bankruptcy implies fraud, it falls out of the said statutory provisions and is subject to regulation under the Russian Criminal Code;[43] where it implies premeditation, another article of the same Code applies.[44] Therefore,

42 The 2002 Federal Law 'On Insolvency (Bankruptcy)' (thereafter – RFLIB No.127-FZ dd.26.10.2002).
43 The Russian Federation Criminal Code, Art. 195.
44 The Russian Federation Criminal Code, Art. 197.

"insolvency" and "bankruptcy" being a twinned synonymic pair in the Russian legal language in consistency with the Russian regulatory framework, in legal English it becomes split into British legal English and American legal English options: "insolvency" in the UK law (UKIA 1986) and "bankruptcy" in the US law (U.S.C. 1926: 9).

The semantic analysis of "bankruptcy" and "insolvency" concepts is based on a number of proven lexicographic sources: Russian–English and English–Russian law and finance dictionaries,[45] as well as English specialized encyclopedic and/or terminological dictionaries.[46] However, for legal translation purposes dictionary meanings intended mostly for general public require adjustment to meanings based on the statutory definitions available. Alongside the usual pile of dictionaries for arriving at the referential equivalence between SL-textemes and TL-textemes, regulations must be used as sources not only of rules, but also of definitions.

10.2. Lack of Intralingual and Interlingual 'Shared Referential Convention': Legal Russian vs. Legal British English vs. Legal American English

The above described case of comparing "insolvency" and "bankruptcy" concepts reveals both an intralingual (British English vs. American English) and interlingual (English vs. Russian) disparity in the referential portraits of these concepts. Figure 6.3 illustrates this conceptual incongruity stemming from the unavailability of the shared referential convention regarding the international homonyms under analysis and entailing a clear referential nonequivalence.

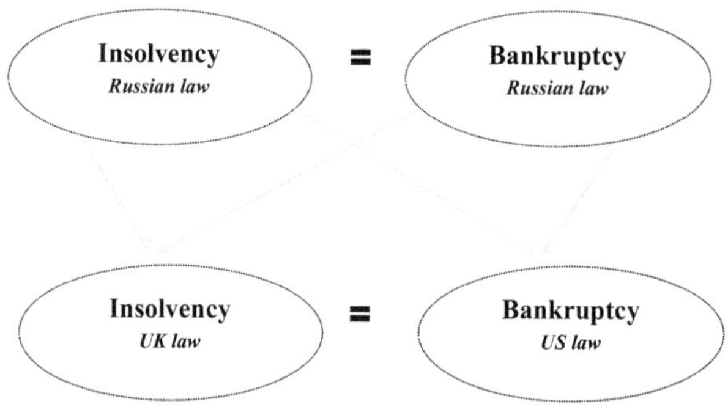

Figure 6.3 Conceptual incongruity: lack of intra- and interlingual referential equivalence

Nida (2003) draws distinctive features regarding the referential meanings by noting that these meanings can be characterized as:

- extralinguistic, extrasomatic, and situational,
- referring primarily to the cultural context identified in the text/discourse,
- representing those generally thought of as 'dictionary meanings' (2003: 70).

45 Among other dictionaries see, for instance: (ERBED 2000; GFED 2003; NFDER 2011).
46 Among other dictionaries see, for instance: (DBET 2012; DFIT 2010; LD 2003; NOCL 2008).

As follows from this viewpoint made by the translation studies patriarch, translation practices should incorporate a default assumption for legal translation encompassing that the legal Translator depends on both the quality of specialized dictionaries and encyclopedias and their explanatory potential and linguistic evidence, as well as on knowing the statutory definitions stored in accessible databases.

At this point, our analysis may rely on two more opinions regarding dictionaries and encyclopedias. The subject of dictionaries' and encyclopedias' quality cannot be overestimated as both lexicographic sources are routinely used by all Translators internationally regardless of language pairs. Rey (1996) indicates that encyclopedias may analyze concepts, but describe classes of referents in the form of imagery to convey cultural sets of information and knowledge (1986: 201). Eco (1986) assumes dictionaries are intended to provide 'mere' linguistics information while encyclopedias—pieces of world knowledge, adding that, quite evidently, the latter correlates with referents or classes of referents (1986: 201). Given Rey's and Eco's trustworthy views, dictionaries and encyclopedias are believed to be stocks of precedent technical knowledge based on stored expertise arranged domain-specifically, whose quality distinctly affect the legal Translator's performance and end-product quality.

10.3. An "Insolvency Practitioner" Concept and its Verbal "Clothing"

Less transparent referentially is an "insolvency practitioner" concept subordinated to the insolvency/bankruptcy subject domain and the same law field. An "insolvency practitioner" denotes an administrator of debtor's assets and, even when detailed, requires additional efforts for internalizing. Specialized dictionaries show quite a remarkable variety of signifiers for this single concept. The English synonymic chain comprises 18 members, whose synonymic relations vary from absolute to similar in meaning; the chain is pooled into the following abundant array:

> *administrative receiver, appointed trustee, arbitration manager, assignee in bankruptcy, bankruptcy commissioner, bankruptcy registrar, bankruptcy trustee, co-administrator, liquidator, manager in receivership, managing trustee, official assignee, official receiver, receiver, referee, trustee in bankruptcy, sequestrator, trustee of bankrupt's estate (based on ABBYY 2011; GFED 2003; NFD 2011 (I); Vlasenko and Galimov 2012: 22–25).*

None of the statutory naming variants are found in the above array, except for one: "'liquidator," which corresponds to both the British and American statutory prescribed terminology. Moreover, hyperonyms comprising all of the statutory fixed terms across all the stages of insolvency/bankruptcy proceedings—*nominee, supervisor, administrator* in UK law (UKIA 1986) and *examiner, trustee* in US law (U.S.C. 1926)—happen to be missing in the dictionary-inventoried stock of English–Russian correspondences. Given this, a major query in translating legal texts can be expected to relate to particular kinds of referential knowledge similar to the world knowledge and/or the expert knowledge, or rather, to an expert-community convention regarding the naming of certain legal phenomena, institutions, etc. It is exactly at this point that a legal Translator may become aware of not knowing a general referential convention and, therefore, being challenged by a ULT. An on-going mental metabolism through mental networking is what the legal translator is engaged in for identifying ULTs corresponding to conceivable stretches of legal thought.

Following Dascal (1986), an array of signifiers is nothing but 'the external clothing of thoughts' (1986: 761). The above array can be clustered based on various criteria. Nonetheless, the mere availability of such a variety merits the status of a referential range[47] for the concept under analysis. It shows the possibility for legal concepts to routinely correlate with multiple signifiers contradicting traditional but obsolete provisions in the terminology studies. Subscribing to J. Lyons opinion, whereby the actual reference depends upon a variety of contextual factors, we admit that synonymic variety itself is indicative of the need in the enhanced pragmatic approach to define meanings for any of the synonymic chain members based on their text-external linkages. For that reason, it seems justifiable to speak about referential portraying of a legal concept each time a Translator "departs" from the text into the respective context for establishing the boundaries of meaning corresponding to a UT or a ULT, as appropriate.

A major idea behind this inventoried stock of terminological expressions capturing the bankruptcy/insolvency subdomain can be defined as the prerequisite for legal translation. In other words, the availability of different sets of knowledge in a single legal concept by far exceeding the pure linguistic knowledge, no matter how perfect and impeccable it might be, clearly positions legal translation among the most challenging translation activities. Thus, the choice of a ULT by any one Translator seems to correlate with the SLT complexity; however, what such correlation is based on necessitates additional research.

To a large extent, translation process draws on Translator's referential competence shaped by the existing referential knowledge. Essentially, English legal terminology is networked in the way which rests on multiple signification of a single concept. Therefore, signifiers, when pooled together, produce chains denoting legal concepts whose referents may become blurred or indeterminate due to such multiplicity of 'names' (Vlasenko 2006: 63, 69–70; 2010a; 2012). For that reason, translation efforts may be regarded as decision-making process under varying degrees of uncertainty with scoping for meaning predictably slowed down due to the multiplicity of verbalization options. Searching for a stopgap solution under multiple referential portraits and their constituent frames correlating with different verbal signs for a given technical concept is likely to be complicated. Moreover, opting for a definite verbalization pattern may be still more complicated if the referential range is blurred due to a nontransparent context which may and often does cause Translator's confusion at the final choice stage.

When dealing with semantically complex concepts and their multiple SL-wordings, keeping track of signifiers, maintaining their registry or inventory as a constantly updated stock by chain-linking or clustering should be regarded as a routine task for the legal Translator. Unless such "stocks" of verbalized legal thoughts are regularly maintained, identifying an appropriate TL-texteme correlating with a translated concept will predictably entail extra cognitive effort. As indicated above, legal concepts encountered in a ST are believed to correlate with certain "templates" of legal thought—referential frames—activated during their retrieval by the Translator at the recognition and comprehension stages. In practical terms, multiple synonymy cases where SL-concepts are overly verbalized either in the source or in the receptor language may entail the activation of the entire cohort, hindering Translator's swift response to the translated message.

47 Lyons' term "referential range" is used several times across the chapter; it is first discussed above the subheading *In Pursuit of Semantic Contour: Referencing as Internalizing* in relation to the "damages" example.

11. Conclusion

This chapter was intended to provide a new insight into the cognitively conditioned mechanisms associated both with the product-oriented side and the process-oriented side of legal translation, the later predominated. In so doing, the major recourse was made to the referential theory of meaning. The major emphasis was made on revising the status of 'translation units' admittedly regarded as one of the core concepts in the legal translation studies paradigm and identifying the status of "units of legal translation" via exploring numerous theoretical dimensions and analytical contexts, scholarly approaches and opinions available internationally both intradisciplinary and interdisciplinary. Since no units have been identified for the legal translation so far, the efforts in this regard are hoped to merit the novelty.

Additionally, the chapter also aimed at structurizing a legal meaning based on the reference theory explored and detailed for the legal translation purposes, expanding the use of referential knowledge in the legal translation studies and legal discourse analysis, and showing this knowledge to be a pillar for the legal Translator's referential competence, as well as reference equivalence cross-linguistically. These issues are assumed to relate to a unit of legal translation as a starting point of studies.

In general, translation units are inconspicuously present in Translator's decision-making, thus affecting translation practices. UTs mark a single "mentally digestive intake" for any one Translator at both text level and cognitive level. Obviously, more experimental and empirical data from such fields as neurolinguistics, cross-linguistic pragmatics, psychosemiotics, and cognitive psychology are needed for backing up the legal translation theoretical footing. In view of this, a ULT concept is suggested as an instrumental tool for the follow-up legal translation research.

Particular efforts were made to categorize a 'unit of legal translation' through profiling several cases of the English–Russian legal correspondences covering morphemic, lexical, and grammatical levels of equating SL and TL legal meanings. These translation cases trigger a deeper understanding of the close interrelation between ULTs and the legal translation equivalence issue. The alternative translation solutions as "competing wording options" are described as driven by the cognitively conditioned mechanisms of referencing and inferencing. The conclusions drawn from these particular instances can be extrapolated on larger selections of legal translation data for verification based on other language pairs.

A minimal ULT is postulated to be a SL-texteme representing the plane of expression, the signifier, identifiable by the legal Translator as correlating with a certain set of his/her expert knowledge as part of the professional worldview at any given time. The other side of the "bond," in Vygotsky's terms, is a referent or a range of referents corresponding to SL-textemes. As shown above, referents can stand and do stand for abstract concepts. As such, they can be described in terms of referential portraits; referential portraying method is suggested for exploring the complex legal concepts. In turn, the portraits are presumed to be capable of further decomposition into referential frames as micro-gestalts. These structures represent the plane of thought, the signified, and constitute the "concealed" part of a minimal ULT; they correlate with certain SL- or TL-texteme(s) on the plane of expression. The pair is knotted and is likely to be one of the most probable candidates for the prioritized translation studies research issues in the foreseeable future.

As noted above, a semantic analysis of the legal translation cases was conducted based on the analytical tools as currently available in or stemming from the reference theory. The concept of a *referential frame* as an elementary unit of instantaneous thought readily retrievable from the Translator's memory due to its "gestalt" nature appears basic for structurizing the legal meaning and should be presumed to:

a. be a quantum of communicated substance and a constituent of the referential knowledge;
b. form a core of the Translator's referential portraying capabilities underlying the Translator's referential competence;
c. imply knowledge of the referential convention shared by the professional community in question which is a prerequisite for the quality translation end-product; and
d. more often than not, correlate with more than one verbal sign in both the SL and the TL in legal knowledge domains.

Given diverse legal translation data quoted above,[48] a ULT is never one and the same for any given text or utterance, or even for different fragments within one and the same ST handled by one and the same Translator. Since units identified by legal Translators are different, the very notion of a "unit of legal translation" clearly projects itself on the plane of thought correlating with the legal translation techniques and technicalities on the plane of expression. ULTs are complex speech activity units whose identification is based on the multiple-choice decision-making under varying degrees of uncertainty. Also, ULTs are marked by high context sensitivity. The latter requires legal Translators be familiarized with professional community conventions, eventually ensuring his/her referential competence.

As a final point, a unit of legal translation is the resultant of the ST complexity, its genre, type, and of higher layers of knowledge represented in it. Such a perspective, being pragmatic in its essence, features prerequisites which comprise, but are not limited to, comprehension as part of the subject-matter categorization and interiorization as the exact comprehension by the legal Translator of the substance communicated. Accordingly, the tangibility of a ULT is subtle since it is presumed to be a standard elementary constituent or, putting it otherwise, a primary measurement element identifiable by the legal Translator as conveying a relevant substance. Singling out ULTs may prove low feasible due to subjectivity and language-pair-dependency.[49] Singling out units of legal translation and tracing their dependence on various language pairs may definitely ensure more or less standard renderings in certain types of statutory texts or international legal instruments intended to regulate crucial issues in increasingly globalized world. However, assuming ULTs being standard for any given language pair at this point in time is by far premature.

By way of a finishing touch, there is a big temptation to answer the question on whether we departed farther in understanding the translation process and translation end-product; at least to the extent Quine (1959: 171–172) did that half a century ago when he wrote:

> *Cassirer, Sapir, and latterly B.L. Whorf have stressed that deep differences of languages carry with them ultimate differences in the way one thinks, or looks upon the world. I should prefer not to put the matter in such a way as to suggest that certain philosophical propositions are affirmed in the one culture and denied in the other. What is really involved is difficulty or indeterminacy of correlation.*

48 In particular, the case of The 1990 AML Convention translated into Russian quoted in the beginning of the chapter.
49 See, for instance, Vlasenko and Galimov (2012) for English–French–Russian correspondences.

Acknowledgements

The chapter has been prepared within the framework of the 2012–2013 Interdisciplinary Research Project *Law Universe and Law Texts: Challenges for Cross-Language Communication*, sponsored by the Academic Foundation at The Higher School of Economics National Research University (NRU HSE), Moscow, Russia.

Grateful acknowledgements should be made to my academic mentor, Professor Alexandra Superanskaya, Institute of Linguistics, Russian Academy of Sciences (Moscow), for consultations in cross-linguistic aspects of terminology studies.

Special thanks should go to Professor Olga T. Yokoyama, PhD (Harvard), Department of Applied Linguistics, University of California (Los Angeles), and Valentina Zaitseva, PhD (Harvard), Department of Slavic Languages and Literatures, University of Washington (Seattle), for updating me on their recent elaborations in the cognitively conditioned pragmatics of discourse.

The author owes thanks to the colleague, experienced translator with years of responsible translation/interpretation engagements, Ekaterina Grouzdeva (Russia).

List of abbreviations

SL – source language
SL-texteme – source-language texteme: any verbal sign, such as a word, a word combination or a text stretch or sequence in the ST under analysis
ST – source text, text in a source language
TL – target language
TL-texteme – target-language texteme: any verbal sign, such as a word, a word combination or a text stretch or sequence in the TT under analysis
TT – target text, text in a target language
UT – unit of translation, translation unit
ULT – unit of legal translation

References

Baker, M. 1997. *In Other Words: A Coursebook on Translation*. New York: Routledge.
Baker, M. (ed.). 1998. *Routledge Encyclopedia of Translation Studies*. London and New York: Routledge.
Baker, M. and Saldanha, G. (eds). 2011. *Routledge Encyclopedia of Translation Studies*. 2nd edn. London and New York: Routledge Taylor and Francis Group.
Bassnett, S. 2000. *Translation Studies*. Rev. edn. T. Hawkes ed. London and New York: Routledge.
Bell, R.T. 1993. *Translation and Translating: Theory and Practice*. G.N. Candlin ed. London and New York: Longman Group UK Ltd.
Burke, P. 2007. 'Cultures of translation in Early Modern Europe'. In: P. Burke and R. Po-Chia Hsia eds. *Cultural Tradition in Early Modern Europe*. Cambridge University Press, pp. 7–38.
Buttler, W. 2008. 'Russian Law'. In: P. Cane and J. Conagham eds. *The New Oxford Companion to Law*. Oxford University Press, pp. 1038–1039.
Catford, J. 1965. *The Linguistic Theory of Translation*. London: Oxford University Press.
Chernov, G.V. 1978. *Teorija i praktika sinkhronnogo perevoda* (*The Theory and Practice of Simultaneous Interpreting*). Moscow: Mezhdunarodnyje otnoshenyja.

———. 1987. *Osnovy sinkhronnogo perevoda (Fundamentals of Simultaneous Interpreting)*. Moscow: Vysshaya shkola.

———. 1988. 'Kontekstno-svobodnaja i kontekstno-svjazannaja implikativnos't i problemy perevoda' ('Context-Free and Context-Bound Implications and Translation Problems'). In: A.D. Shveitser ed. *Tekst i perevod (Text and Translation)*. Moscow: Nauka, pp. 51–63.

———. 2004. *Inference and Anticipation in Simultaneous Interpreting: A Probability–Prediction Model*. Amsterdam and Philadelphia: John Benjamins Publishing Company.

Coulthard, M. and Johnson, A. 2007. *An Introduction to Forensic Linguistics: Language in Evidence*. New York: Routledge.

Damasio, A. 2012. *Self Comes to Mind: Constructing the Conscious Brain*. London: Vintage Books.

Dascal, M. 1986. 'Pragmatics'. In: T.A. Sebeok, P. Bouissac et al. eds. *Encyclopedic Dictionary of Semiotics, in 3 Vols*. Berlin, New York, Amsterdam: Mouton de Gruyter, pp. 2, 751–761.

Davis, W.A. 2005. *Nondescriptive Meaning and Reference: An Ideational Semantics*. Oxford University Press.

Eco, U. 1986. 'Dictionary vs. Encyclopedia'. In: T.A. Sebeok, P. Bouissac et al. eds. *Encyclopedic Dictionary of Semiotics, in 3 Vols*. Berlin, New York, Amsterdam: Mouton de Gruyter, pp. 2, 201–206.

———. 1999. *Kant and the Platypus: Essays on Language and Cognition*. A. McEwen trans. London: Secker & Warburg.

———. 2004. *Mouse or Rat? Translation as Negotiation*. London: Weidenfeld Nicolson.

———. 2012. *Experiences in Translation*. A. McEwen trans. Toronto, Buffalo, London: University of Toronto Press.

Elhauge, E. 2008. *Statutory Default Rules: How to Interpret Unclear Legislation*. Cambridge and London: Harvard University Press.

Field, J. 2004. *Psycholinguistics: Key Concepts*. London and New York: Routledge.

Gutt, E.A. 2010. *Translation and Relevance: Cognition and Context*. Manchester and Boston: St. Jerome Publishing.

Hatim, B. and Màson, I. 1997. *The Translator as Communicator*. London and New York: Routledge.

Hatim, B. 2013. *Teaching and Researching Translation*. 2nd ed. Harlow: Pearson Education Ltd.

Jääskeläinen, R. 2011. 'Studying the Translation Process'. In: K. Malmkjær and K. Windle eds. *The Oxford Handbook of Translation Studies*. Oxford University Press, pp. 123–138.

Jakobson, R. 1959. 'On Linguistic Aspects of Translation'. In: R.A. Brower ed. *On Translation*. Cambridge, Mass.: Harvard University Press, pp. 232–239.

———. 1990. *On Language*. L.R. Waugh and M. Monville-Burston eds. London, England and Cambridge, Mass.: Harvard University Press.

Johnson, M.G. 1990. 'Language and Cognition in Products Liability'. In: J.N. Levi and A.G. Walker eds. *Language in the Judicial Process*. New York and London: Plenum Press, pp. 291–308.

Kahneman, D. 2011. *Thinking, Fast and Slow*. London: Penguin Books, Pearson.

Kenny, D. 2001. *Lexis and Creativity in Translation: A Corpus-Based Study*. Manchester, UK and Kinderhook, New York: St. Jerome Publishing.

———. 2011. 'Unit of Translation'. In: M. Baker and G. Saldanha eds. *Routledge Encyclopedia of Translation Studies*. 2nd edn. London and New York: Routledge Taylor and Francis Group, pp. 304–306.

Kibrik, A.A. 2011. *Reference in Discourse: Cross-Linguistic Aspects of Reference*. Oxford University Press.

Leontiev, A.A. 2007. *Psicholingvističeskyje edinici i poroždenyje rečevogo vyskazivanyja (Psycholinguistic Units and Speech Generation)*. 4th edn. Moscow: URSS Publishers.

Lebedev, M.V. and Černjak, A.Z. 2001. *Ontologičeskyje problemi referencii (Ontological Problems of Reference)*. Moscow: Praxis.

Lyons, J. 1981. *Language, Meaning and Context*. London: Fontana.
Malone, J.L. 1988. *The Science of Linguistics in the Art of Translation: Some Tools from Linguistics for the Analysis and Practice of Translation*. Albany: State University of New York Press.
Malmkjær, K. 1998. 'Unit of Translation'. In: M. Baker ed. *Routledge Encyclopedia of Translation Studies*. London and New York: Routledge, pp. 286–288.
Meristo, M. 2007. *Mental Representation and Language Access: Evidence From Deaf Children With Different Language Backgrounds*. Unpublished doctoral dissertation. Göteborg University.
Milojević-Sheppard, M. 1993. *Morpho-Syntactic Expansions in Translation from English into Slovenian as a Prototypical Response to the Complexity of the Original*. München: Sagner.
Minsky, M. 1988. *The Society of Mind*. Touchstone Book. New York, London: Simon & Schuster, Inc.
Munday, J. 2012. *Introducing Translation Studies: Theories and Applications*. 3rd edn. London and New York: Routledge.
Newmark, P.P. 1988. *A Textbook of Translation*. London: Prentice Hall.
Nida, E.A. 1975. 'Words and Thoughts'. In: S.A. Dil ed. *Language Structure and Translation: Essays by Eugene A. Nida*. Stanford University Press, pp. 190–199.
———. 2001. *Contexts in Translating*. Amsterdam and Philadelphia: John Benjamins Publishing Co.
———. 2003. 'Referential and Emotive Meanings'. In: *Toward a Science of Translating: With Special Reference to Principles and Procedures Involved in Bible Translating*. The Hague: Brill Academic Publishers, pp. 70–119.
Oliphant, K. 2008. 'Damages'. In: P. Cane and J. Conagham eds. *The New Oxford Companion to Law*. Oxford University Press, pp. 295–296.
Pym, A. 2010. *Exploring Translation Theories*. London and New York: Routledge.
Quine, W.V. 1959. 'Meaning and Translation'. In: R.A. Brower ed. *On Translation*. Harvard University Press. Cambridge, Mass., pp. 148–172.
Rey, A. 1986. 'Dictionary'. In: T.A. Sebeok, P. Bouissac et al. eds. *Encyclopedic Dictionary of Semiotics, in 3 Vols*. Berlin, New York, Amsterdam: Mouton de Gruyter, pp. 2, 200–201.
Schäffner, C. 1989. 'An Account of Knowledge Use in Text Comprehension as a Basis for Frame-Based Interference'. In: *Interferenz in der Translation*. Leipzig: VEB Verlag Enzyklopeidie, pp. 65–72.
Schogt, H.G. 1986. 'Translation'. In: T.A. Sebeok, P. Bouissac et al. eds. *Encyclopedic Dictionary of Semiotics, in 3 Vols*. Berlin, New York, Amsterdam: Mouton de Gruyter, pp. 2, 1107–1111.
Schulte, R. 1987. 'Translation Theory: A Challenge for the Future', *Translation Review*, vol. 23, pp. 1–2.
Sorokin, J.A. 1974. 'Issledovanyja vnejazykovoj obuslovlennosti psicholingvističeskich javlenyj' ('Research on Extralinguistic Determination of Psycholinguistic Phenomena'). In: A.A. Leont'ev ed. *Osnovy teorii rečevoj dejatel'nosti* (Foundations of Speech Activity Theory). Akademija Nauk SSS, Institut jazykoznanija (Institute of Lingustics, USSR Academy of Sciences). Moscow: Nauka, pp. 220–233.
———. 2001. 'Perevodčeskyj triptich' (Translation Triptych). In: A.I. Novikov ed. *Problemy prikladnoj psicholinguistiki* (*Applied Linguistics Problems: Collected Papers*). Moscow: Azbukovnik, pp. 261–276.
Svejcer, A.D. 1973. *Perevod i lingvistika* (*Translation and Linguistics*). Moscow: Voenizdat / 1987. *Ubersetzung und Linguistik*. (German trans). Berlin: Akademie Verlag.
Šveitser, A.D. 1980. 'O vzaimodejstvyji raznourovnevych sredstv vydelenyja temy i remy vyskazyvanyja' ('On Different Levels of Identifying Theme and Rhyme Interaction'), *Zeitschrift fur Phonetik, Sprachwissenschaft und Kommunikationsforschung*, vol. 33(3), pp. 405–409.

———. 1988. *Teoryja perevoda: status, problemi, aspekty* (*Translation Theory: Status, Problems, Aspects*). Moscow: Nauka.

———. 1999. 'Perevod i lingvistika: evolucyja svyazej' ('Translation and Linguistics: Evolving Relationship'), *Teoryja perevoda i metodika podgotovki perevodčikov: sbornik materialov conferencii (18 February 1999), Voennyj universitet Ministerstva oborony Rossiji* (Translation Theory and Translation Training Methodology: Moscow Conference Proceedings. RF Defence Ministry Military University 18 February 1999). Moscow: VUMO, pp. 254–257.

Toury, G. 1986. 'Translation. A Cultural-Semiotic Perspective'. In: T.A. Sebeok, P. Bouissac et al. *Encyclopedic Dictionary of Semiotics, in 3 Vols.* Berlin, New York, Amsterdam: Mouton de Gruyter, pp. 2, 1111–1124.

———. 1988. 'The Coupled Pair of "Solution + Problem" in Translation Studies', *Translation Theory in Scandinavia: Scandinavian Symposium on Translation Theory (SSOT) III Proceedings.* P.N. Chaffey et al. eds. pp. 1–23.

———. 1995. *Descriptive Translation Studies and Beyond.* Amsterdam and Philadelphia: John Benjamins.

Treushnikov, M.K. 2012. 'Evolucyja rossyjskogo graždanskogo sudoproizvodstva v načale XXI veka' ('Russian Civil Procedure Evolution at the Early XXI Century'). D. Maleshin ed. *Graždanskyj proces v meždunarodnom dialoge: evrazyiskyj kontekst, in Vsemirnaja konferencyja Meždunarodnoj associacii processual'nogo prava* (*Civil Procedure in Cross-Cultural Dialogue: Eurasia Context: IAPL World Conference on Civil Procedure*). Moscow, Russia 18–21 September 2012. Moscow: International Association of Procedural Law, Statut, pp. 28–30.

van der Veer, R. and Valsiner, J. 1991. *Understanding Vygotsky: A Quest for Synthesis.* Oxford and Cambridge: Blackwell.

Vlasenko, S.V. 1993. 'On Pragmatic Aspects of Translation'. *Translation – The Vital Link: XIII International Federation of Translators World Congress: FIT Proceedings, in 2 vols.* Brighton, UK 6–13 August 1993. London: Institute of Translation and Interpreting, pp. 1, 642–648.

———. 2006. *Professional Translation Practices in the English–Russian Language Pair.* Moscow: Wolters Kluwer.

———. 2010a. 'Referencyja i referencial'nost' v mežjyazykovom perevode' ('Reference and Referentiality in Interlingual Translation'), *Vestnik Moskovskogo universiteta. Seryja 22: Teoryja perevoda* (*Moscow University Journal. Series 22: Translation Theory*), vol. 4, pp. 3–28.

———. 2010b. 'Text kak objekt referencii' ('Text as Referencing Percept'), *Voprosy psicholingvistiki* (*Journal of Psycholinguistics, Institute of Linguistics, Russian Academy of Sciences*), vol. 1(11), pp. 115–132.

———. 2011. 'Juridičeskyj perevod v aspekte coreferentnosty terminov prava' ('Legal Translation in the Law Terminology Co-Reference Perspective'), *Voprosy filologyji* (*Journal of Philology, Institute of Linguistics, Russian Academy of Sciences*), vol. 3(39), pp. 89–100.

Vlasenko, S.V. and Galimov, A.R. 2012. 'Koncept "bankrotstvo" v koordinatach pravovoj lingvistiki: russko-anglo-francuzskyje approximacii' ('"Bankruptcy" Concept within the Legal Linguistics Coordinates: Russian–English–French Approximations'), *Vestnik Tverskogo gosudarstvennogo universiteta. Seryja Philologyja. Linguistika i mežcul'turnaja kommunikacia* (*Tver State University Journal of Philology. Linguistics and Cross-Cultural Communication*), vol. 10(2), pp. 21–28.

Vlasenko, S.V. and Suslov, R.E. 2012. 'Dynamika razvityja sovremennogo anglyjskogo jazyka i voprosy terminologičeskoj abbreviacii na primere jazykov prava i meždunarodnoj torgovli' ('Dynamic Changes in Current English Usage and Terminological Abbreviations Exemplified by Languages of Law and International Commerce'). *Dynamičeskyje processy v germanskich jazykach* (*Dynamic Processes in Germanic Languages: Fourth Linguistic Readings in Honoured Memory of Professor V.N. Jartseva. Proceedings*). Moscow: Institute of Linguistics, Russian Academy of Sciences, pp. 163–179.

Vygotsky, L.S. [1934] 1979. *Thought and Language* (*Myšlenyje i jazyk*). E. Hanfmann and G. Vakar eds and trans. Cambridge, Mass.: The M.I.T. Press.
Waard, J. and Nida, E.A. 1986. *From One Language to Another: Functional Equivalence in* Bible *Translating*. Nashville: Nelson Publishers.
Wagner, E., Bech, S. and Martínez, J.M. 2012. *Translating for the European Union Institutions*. 2nd edn. Manchester, UK and Kinderhook, New York: St. Jerome Publishing.
Yokoyama, O.T. 1986. *Discourse and Word Order*. Amsterdam/Philadelphia: John Benjamins Publishing Company.
Zaitseva, V. 1995. 'Particles and Subtext: Coding Referential Portraits of the Interlocutors'. In: O.T. Yokoyama ed. *Harvard Studies in Slavic Linguistics*. Harvard University Press, pp. 3, 213–233.
———. 1999a. 'Referential Knowledge in Discourse: Interpretation of {I, YOU} In Male and Female Speech'. In: M. Mill ed. *Slavic Gender Linguistics*. Amsterdam and Philadelphia: John Benjamins Publishing Company, pp. 1–26.
———. 1999b, 'Šiftery Jakobsona v glagolach recevogo deistvyja' ('Jakobson's Shifters in Speech Act Verbs'). In: H. Baran et al. eds. *Roman Jakobson: Teksty, documenty, issledovanyja* (*Roman Jakobson: Texts, Documents, Studies*). Moscow: RGGU, pp. 508–518.
Zalevskaya, A.A. 1995. 'Psichologičeskoyje portretirovanyje leksiki: opyt eksperimentalnogo issledovanyja' ('Psycholinguistic Portraying: Experimental Research'). In: *Psichologičeskyje issledonanyja : slovo i tekst : sbornik naučnyck trudov* (*Psycholinguistic Research: Word and Text: Collected Papers*). Tver State University, pp. 38–47.

Statutes and Regulations Cited

The 1990 AML Convention: *1990 Council of Europe Convention on Laundering, Search, Seizure and Confiscation of the Proceeds from Crime*, Council of Europe. Strasbourg, 8.XI.1990. European Treaty Series - No. 141 (ETS 141. Chapter III, Section 5, Article 18, Paragraph 1(d)). Available at: http://www.conventions.coe.int/Treaty/en/Treaties/Html/141.htm [Accessed 22 December 2013].
CCRF: 2007. Government of Russia. *Civil Code of the Russian Federation Part 4*. 2007. Parallel Russian and English Texts status juris: 20 May 2007. W.E. Buttler trans. and ed. Moscow: YurInfoR-Press.
CRCRF: 2008. Government of Russia. *Criminal Code of the Russian Federation*. 2008. Parallel Russian and English Texts status juris: 1 February 2008. W.E. Buttler trans. and ed. Moscow: Zertsalo.
FCRF: 2005. Government of Russia. *Family Code of the Russian Federation*. 2005. Parallel Russian and English Texts status juris: 1 September 2004. W.E. Buttler trans. and ed. Moscow: YurInfoR-Press.
LCRF: 2004. Government of Russia. *Land Code of the Russian Federation*. 2004. Parallel Russian and English Texts status juris: 20 March 2004. W.E. Buttler trans. and ed. Moscow: YurInfoR-Press.
RFLIB No.127-FZ dd. 26.10.2002: The 2002 Russian Federal Law *"O nesostojyatel'nosti (bankrotstve)"* (On Insolvency (Bankruptcy)). No.127-FZ dated 26.10.2002. Available at: http://pravo.gov.ru/proxy/ips/?docbody=&nd=102078236&intelsearch=%CE+%ED%E5%F1%EE%F1%F2%EE%FF%F2%E5%EB%FC%ED%EE%F1%F2%E8 [Accessed 15 September 2013].
TCRF: 2004. Government of Russia. *Tax Code of the Russian Federation*. 2004. Parallel Russian and English Texts status juris: 20 May 2004. W.E. Buttler trans. and ed. Moscow: YurInfoR-Press.

UKIA 1986, X: Government of the United Kingdom. *UK Insolvency Act 1986*. Chapter X. 1986. Available at: http://www.legislation.gov.uk/ukpga/1986/45/part/IV/chapter/X [Accessed 10 November 2013].

USC 1926: Government of the United States of America. *United States Code 1926*. Chapters 9, 11. 1926. Available at: http://www.law.cornell.edu/rules/frbp; http://www.law.cornell.edu/uscode/text/18/part-I/chapter-9?quicktabs_8= 1#quicktabs-8 [Accessed 10 November 2013].

Dictionaries and Encyclopedias

ABBYY 2011: ABBYY LINGVO x5: Electronic Multilingual Dictionary, ABBYY Software Ltd., 2011. Available at: www.Lingvo.ru [Accessed 30 July 2013].

DBET 2012: Friedman, J.P. (gen ed.). *Dictionary of Business and Economics Terms*. 5th edn. New York: Barron's Educational Series, Inc.

DFIT 2010: Downes, J. and Goodman, J.E. *Dictionary of Finance and Investment Terms*. 8th edn. New York: Barron's Educational Series, Inc.

DS 2011: Wales, K., *A Dictionary of Stylistics*. 3rd edn. London: Pearson Education Ltd.

ERBED 2000: Fjedorov, B.G. *English–Russian Banking and Economic Dictionary*. St. Petersburg: Limbus Press.

GFED 2003: Pivovar, A.G. (ed.). *Great Financial and Economic Dictionary*. 2nd rev. edn. Moscow: Ekzamen.

LD 2003: Gifis, S.H. *Law Dictionary*. 5th edn. New York: Barron's Legal Guides Inc.

NFDER 2011: Faekov, V.Y. *New Finance Dictionary*, in 2 vols. 2nd edn Moscow: International Relations Publishing House.

NOCL 2008: Cane, P. and Conagham, J. (eds), *The New Oxford Companion to Law*. Oxford University Press.

Sebeok, T.A. (gen ed.), Bouissac, P. et al. (eds). *Encyclopedic Dictionary of Semiotics*, in 3 vols. Berlin, New York, Amsterdam: Mouton de Gruyter.

Media Sources

Kizilova, L. 2001. 'Pokazaly jazyk. Urok anglyjskogo. *Konvencyja po bor'be s otmyvanyjem deneg netočno perevedena*' ('The Tongue Showed. An Lesson of English. The Money Laundering Convention Translated Imprecisely'), *Izvestyja*, 11 April. Available at: http://pressarchive.ru/izvestiya-moskva/2001/04/11/209772.html [Accessed 15 October 2013].

Lyapunova, G. 2001. 'Perevodčiki objyavily amnistyju mošennikam. V russkyj tekst konventsyji ob otmyvanyji deneg vkralas' ošibka' ('Translators Declared Amnesty to Fraudsters. Russian Text of the Anti-Money Laundering Convention Has a Flaw'), *Kommersant Daily*, No. 63, 10 April. Available at: http://www.kommersant.ru/daily/5901 [Accessed 10 October 2013].

Russian Federation Ministry of Foreign Affairs. Official Statement. 2001. *Zajavlenyje MID Rossyji 'V svyazi s publikatsyjami v rossyjskikh gazetakh otnositel'no perevoda na russkyj jyazyk teksta Konventsyji ob otmyvanyji dokhodov ot prestupnoj dejatelnosty' ('Regarding Russian Newspapers' Publications On the Translation into Russian of the 1990 Convention on Laundering of the Proceeds from Crime')*. 10 April. In: ITAR-TASS Agency (V.A. Khrekov), Interfax (A.I. Korzun). Available at: http://www.mid.ru/brp_4.nsf/76bbf733e3936d4543256999005bcbb7/65f25fed3ab8d29943256a2a0050c0e8?OpenDocument [Accessed 10 October 2013].

Chapter 7
Parameters for Problem-Solving in Legal Translation: Implications for Legal Lexicography and Institutional Terminology Management

Fernando Prieto Ramos

1. Introduction

Legal terminology is undoubtedly a hallmark of legal discourses and a key component of quality control and competence evaluation in legal translation. The culture-bound and evolving nature of most legal concepts, the complexity of their semantic layers and the various degrees of asymmetry between their native legal systems and sources explain the added difficulty of terminological work in this area and the prominent attention devoted to it in Legal Translation Studies (LTS). Terminological problems illustrate the need to analyze changing situational factors and macrotextual parameters for decision-making at microtextual level. The enormous variability of such factors and their distinctive legal dimension call for specific methodologies. The integration of those variables into universally-applicable conceptual paradigms remains a major challenge. As Garzone (2000: 395) put it, 'most studies have had their starting point in a specific experience in one area of this very broad field, so that the theoretical concepts proposed, however viable, have tended to be all but comprehensive in their scope of application.'

Against this background, an integrative methodological model will be presented (section 2) which has been defined and tested in different professional settings of legal translation. Recognizing that terminological decisions cannot be isolated from the overall conditions of the translation process, this model serves as the basis to contextualize and identify the requirements for translation-oriented legal lexicography (section 3). Particular emphasis will be placed on international institutional settings, since they constitute benchmarks in terminological work for international specialized communication and provide accessible resources (both multilingual corpora and terminology databases) produced under and for identifiable communicative conditions (section 4). Legal terminological entries in that context will be scrutinized with a view to determining the extent to which they respond to legal translators' needs (section 5). This analysis will allow for the comparative qualitative assessment of terminological practices as reflected in illustrative United Nations (UN) and European Union (EU) databases.[1]

1 Throughout this chapter, the term "international organizations" is meant to comprise both intergovernmental organizations (such as the UN) and supranational organizations (such as the EU).

2. An Integrative Model for Problem-Solving in Legal Translation

As pointed out by Šarčević (1997: 47), 'despite the inflation of equivalence types', translators have been 'guided more or less by their own intuition' in legal translation problem-solving for many years. Although this has been gradually addressed in formal training, methodological gaps among trainees and practitioners are still rife within this field (see Prieto Ramos 2013b). Theories of legal translation have become increasingly elaborate in highlighting contextual factors and the relevance of comparative legal analysis for the application of translation techniques (e.g., Šarčević 1985; Weston 1991; Harvey 2000; Megale 2008). However, these elements are not always integrated into operational models encompassing key parameters for decision-making.

The holistic proposal represented in Figure 7.1 responds to the need for further synthesis and systematization of such parameters, from macrotextual to microtextual levels of translation-oriented analysis in professional practice. It addresses all stages of the translation process and considers the essential aspects for identifying and solving legal translation problems in widely varying translation scenarios. The approach begins with the definition of the overall translation strategy of adequacy with regard to the *skopos*, which is determined by the components of the relevant communicative situation (including purpose, target readers and time). Given the variability of conditions of legal communication, this dynamic concept of adequacy to the *skopos* (Nord 1991; 1997) has been praised as a useful general framework in legal translation (e.g., Prieto Ramos 1998; Dullion 2000; Garzone 2000). Nonetheless, while modern functionalist notions are nowadays widely accepted in LTS, their combination with legal pragmatic considerations into more specific methodological models remains a persistent challenge.

In the integrative model proposed, the *definition of the overall translation strategy* is based on:

a. The analysis of the translation brief and the communicative situation, including the type and general conditions of translation (extratextual constraints, legal effects, applicable quality standards or requirements), and the relation between ST (source text) and TT (target text) communicative situations. This will determine whether the TT will be an instrumental translation (Nord 1991) with the same function as the ST (e.g., an international treaty to be authenticated in different languages) or a documentary translation "reflecting" the ST for a different purpose (e.g., the translation of a marriage certificate needed in probate proceedings).
b. The legal macro-contextualization of the translation process according to three parameters: legal systems involved (if more than one), branches of law, and legal text-type and genre. These parameters help to delineate, respectively, the following legal communicative conditions, which can be plotted as situational "coordinates": linguistic and jurisdictional, thematic and normative, procedural and discursive (see Prieto Ramos 2011a).

The information elicited in this dual analysis is essential in order to situate the translational action, to define its adequacy requirements, and to prioritize certain translation techniques in problem-solving at a microtextual level. In the case of inter-systemic terminological problems, *translation-oriented analysis* focuses on elucidating the exact meaning of legal concepts (i.e., their semantic layers based on relevant legal sources), their relation to the main legal function of the text, and the extent to which they adhere to well-established culture-bound or system-specific terminological patterns. This is followed by a further dual analysis for *reformulation*:

(a) Definition of the substrategy of microtextual adequacy (subordinated to the overall adequacy strategy) on the basis of receivers' needs and expectations in terms of identification

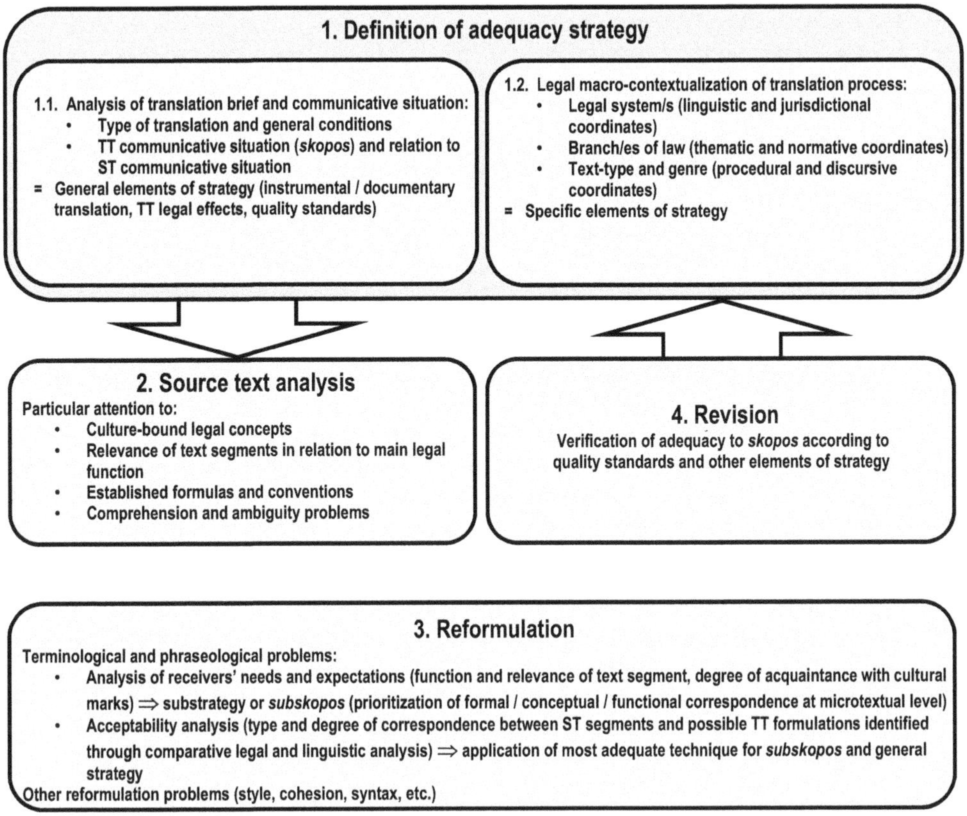

Figure 7.1 Outline of Integrative Methodological Model

and comprehension of culture-bound concepts, considering their function and relevance within the text and the receivers' degree of acquaintance with such cultural marks. As a result, a type of correspondence between ST and TT segments can be prioritized in the search for adequacy: more or less neutral, formal or functional, with more or less focus on the source system (SS) or the target system (TS).

(b) Acceptability analysis of the terms or formulations that can meet those needs with a view to selecting the most adequate technique (or combination of techniques) when more than one option would be viable. Such options are identified through comparative legal and linguistic analysis (see Spanish-English, English-Spanish, and French-Spanish examples analyzed in detail in Prieto Ramos 1998; 2013b).

Three interrelated implications emerge from the above:

1. *Contextualizing the translational action entails determining the role of legal translation itself in the relevant scenario.* Legal translation fulfills its mediating role in different ways depending on whether it takes place between different legal systems or within national or international multilingual systems. For instance, in the first context, the role of legal translation will commonly be to offer culture-bound SS information to TS receivers without replacing SS distinctive cultural marks with TS ones. As rightly put by Biel (2009: 187), this usually implies 'a hybrid where the source language text is

accessed through target language knowledge structures.' In the case of rulemaking in the second context, translation itself contributes to building shared concepts with the support of mechanisms for the conciliatory interpretation of multilingual instruments (see, e.g., Cao 2010).

2. *Legal translation as the search for adequacy under specific legal communicative coordinates is always possible*. Defining the *skopos* and the conditions for adequacy reinforces the idea of professional problem-solving centered on the systematic analysis of variables rather than the perception of an alienating practice of looking for universally-valid equivalents or pre-established solutions that do not exist in all instances, which would thus render legal translation virtually impossible. This idea is frequently found among outsiders to LTS and even among translation scholars. However, adequacy is always possible, whether it means rendering cultural specificities accessible to "foreign eyes" or articulating multilingual concepts with new shared semantic layers or made compatible under shared legal frameworks for the sake of legal certainty and processes of legal convergence. In other words, legal translation overcomes challenges for effective legal communication in its various facets, and legal asymmetries are acknowledged as an inherent part of that equation rather than a deterministic cause of impossibility of legal translation.
3. *No translation technique is a priori more adequate than another*. This can only be determined through a contextualized analysis of acceptability in which the consideration of functional equivalents on the basis of comparative law is part of the decision-making process and is not an end in itself. As opposed to certain interpretations of the *skopos* theory as systematic adaptation to the TS, the major value of this theory precisely lies in its flexibility as a general framework to justify the application of all kinds of translation techniques in light of the TT communicative situation. This approach overcomes the problematic nature of "equivalence" as a broad and undetermined concept. For example, in the translation between two legal systems, when the TT receivers need and expect the cultural specificity of a particular ST term to be identified in the TT, ST-oriented formal correspondence must be prioritized and adequate solutions might include borrowing the ST term, a literal translation and/or a "neutral" descriptive (or conceptual) formulation. In that case, functional equivalents will not meet adequacy requirements if they lead to the replacement of an SS cultural mark with a TS-specific one (see, e.g., Prieto Ramos 1998). Overall, the more unique the original term and the more distant the SS and the TS are from each other, the more challenging the acceptability analysis might prove.

Comparative legal and linguistic analysis is necessary when the relevant terminological correspondence is not already established (or even mandatory) in a given translation context (e.g., terminology specific to certain international organizations). This implies identifying possible functional equivalents; even if they might not exist or be congruent enough with the ST concept, or "neutral" enough to meet formal or conceptual correspondence priorities, this information is very valuable in the search for the most adequate translation solution. In this sense, comparative law, like legal hermeneutics, provides a useful means of grasping legal semantic elements in the analysis of acceptability, but decision-making still depends on the macrotextual and microtextual parameters outlined above. Therefore, generalizations on preferable techniques in legal translation must be circumscribed to specific scenarios. What really matters is the contextualization and coherent reasoning of decisions about acceptability rather than the label ascribed to each technique in different taxonomies.

3. Implications for Translation-Oriented Legal Lexicography

In light of the above, this section will consider how legal terminological work should be tackled and what information should be offered in order to meet translators' needs. If we focus on inter-systemic terminological problems, three stages may be identified which are to be addressed in terminological work: (1) analysis of the ST term; (2) comparative legal and linguistic analysis; and (3) analysis of acceptability of reformulation options (to the extent possible).

In the *analysis of the ST term*, conceptual features must be identified drawing on sources of law in the relevant legal system: legislation, case-law, scholarly writings, customary law (Constantinesco 1974: 135). The characteristics or 'intensions of concepts' (Sandrini 1996: 343) defined by their legal content are the basis for *comparative legal and linguistic analysis*. 'When searching for equivalents in the target legal system, translators should approach the matter as if they were solving a legal problem', i.e., 'they should identify the nature of the issue at hand and determine how that issue is dealt with in the target legal system' (Šarčević 1997: 235). This leads to the search for functional equivalents, which coincides with the predominant functional approach in comparative law (e.g., Vanderlinden 1995). Even within the framework of more conceptually-oriented approaches in comparative law (e.g., Brand 2007), legal function must necessarily remain a key feature in establishing comparability and communicative bridges.

In the comparative analysis, each term must be scrutinized as part of the conceptual network of its legal system and branch of law, as applied and construed in its historical context. This is essential in order to take account of the polysemic and evolving nature of many legal terms (e.g., the use of "trust" in different branches of law in a particular jurisdiction).

Considering all the semantic layers involved, it is widely accepted that total equivalence between terms from different legal systems is rare, and 'most functional equivalents fall into the category of partial equivalence' (Šarčević 1997: 214), i.e., a question of degrees between non-equivalence and near equivalence. As expressed by Sandrini (1999: 105), total equivalence would require 'complete identity of moral values, legal provisions, interpretation rules and forms of application of laws – but this [. . .] would mean the same legal framework.' Therefore, in inter-systemic terminological work, "functional equivalents" usually imply near equivalence, i.e., correspondence between essential conceptual features of legal terms rather than absolute equivalence. The main challenge is to determine the degree of equivalence from which a term can be considered a functional equivalent. Understandably, there is no consensus around this question.

As mentioned in section 2, even when functional equivalents are identified, they are not necessarily adequate translation solutions. Comparative law is an instrumental tool for gaining insights to be used in the crucial stage of *analysis of acceptability* of translation options (see Figure 7.1). This analysis, which characterizes translation-oriented legal lexicography, must integrate pragmatic considerations on specialized language use through the lens of target needs and expectations. It is also this orientation that marks the difference with comparative lawyers (see Engberg 2013). When that work is carried out by a terminologist or lexicographer in order to inform translators' decisions, it follows that s/he should be guided by problem-solving parameters in legal translation. The more clearly s/he can define macro-contextual variables and analyze receivers' needs and expectations, as proposed in our model, the more relevant information about acceptability s/he might be able to provide. While the translator will have the final say depending on microtextual considerations (within the given macro-contextual variables and constraints), such considerations can be more or less predictable in specific contexts, thus enabling the terminologist to propose certain equivalents or reformulation options. However, s/he 'should not seek artificial one-to-one equivalences' (Sandrini 1999: 110).

Consequently, bilingual or multilingual resources for inter-systemic legal terminology transfer are expected to be more descriptive than prescriptive, unless they are the result of a standardization effort based on recognized terminological authority within a particular scope. The final product should include the following core information:

1. *Information on legal macro-contextualization*: legal systems involved, branch/es of law and, whenever possible, legal text-type/s and genre/s (see Figure 7.1). The better defined these parameters are, the more focused the comparative and acceptability analyses may be. While the last parameter might remain undefined to the terminologist, specification of the legal systems is vital when dealing with international languages used in more than one national system. Otherwise, it may be necessary to analyze a diversity of applicable rules and discourse patterns at national level. Likewise, imprecise definition of the branch of law would have serious implications for the scope of the legal analysis and the information to be offered on polysemic terms.
2. *Comparative legal and linguistic information relevant for translation decision-making, including reformulation options.* In practice, this means providing the results of an acceptability analysis, or facilitating this analysis to the translator to the extent possible, i.e. selection of translation options depending on receivers' needs and expectations, and, where appropriate, differences between near equivalents as regards legal content and linguistic use. For Šarčević (1989), this information should cover three essential aspects: scope of application, structure/classification and legal effects of both the SS term and the TS term. In any case, translation proposals and comments on adequacy apply to one direction in the translation from the SS term into the TS and might not work in the opposite direction, i.e. each direction requires an acceptability analysis depending on legal realities and implications.
3. *Information on sources.* The relevance and reliability of sources used in legal and linguistic analysis are critical throughout the process and directly affect the reliability of the final product itself. Sources must be indicated in some form or another, either in individual entries (whenever possible) or as part of methodological information. In the case of legal sources, the right balance must be found between legal definitions, judicial interpretation and scholarly discussions, depending on the concept and the legal system (see Garner 2003 in relation to the *Black's Law Dictionary*). For instance, case-law would be generally expected to play a more relevant part in analyzing common law concepts than civil law concepts. Examples of use in context in relevant corpora of texts of legal implementation (e.g., institutional document series or private legal instruments) are also paramount in decisions on adequacy, and therefore constitute important information sources to be provided.[2]

Formal requirements and space constraints will determine how explicit and concise certain elements must be kept. Contextual and methodological information (including general indications or guidelines on linguistic issues and legal sources) might be provided in introductory sections or user manuals, as traditionally recommended in legal lexicography (e.g., Groffier and Reed 1990: 107–108). In fact, in translation-oriented legal lexicography, this kind of introduction or manual should ideally go beyond methodological guidance and offer an overview with as much useful information as possible on the conceptual network examined and the results of comparative legal analysis, before presenting individual entries. This holds

2 On the integration of discursive resources as lexicographical data for legal translation, see Leroyer and Rasmussen (2010).

good, in particular, for terminological resources on specific legal subjects or branches (e.g., Peñaranda López 2011).

Furthermore, appropriate metalanguage on legal translation (e.g., on proposed translation techniques) should ideally be used, particularly in comments on the acceptability of reformulation options for different translation scenarios. Any relevant taxonomy in this respect may be briefly described in the introduction or user manual for ease of reference. Illustrative texts are also welcomed in the case of terminological work on specific text-types or genres (for example, as part of annexes). Since, nowadays, terminological resources are expected to be available in electronic format (preferably online), relevant sources or texts could be easily accessible if hyperlinks are integrated into the tool. The electronic format is obviously an advantage for faster retrieval, for regularly updating terminological entries and for more dynamic adaptation to user needs in general.

Even if we disregard these *desiderata* and focus on the core information outlined above, bilingual and multilingual legal lexicographical resources have often fallen short of translators' needs to a lesser or greater extent. As a result, and excluding rare or partial exceptions, they have traditionally been regarded as resources of limited usefulness and reliability in legal translation, in particular when they just provide lists of translation suggestions with no hint regarding contextualization, conceptual analysis or acceptability in cases of asymmetry. As noted by de Groot and van Laer (2008: 8), this kind of resource only has 'some use as a starting point of one's own investigations in order to discover an equivalent term in the target legal system vocabulary, an appropriate description of the source term in the target system terminology or an informative neologism' (see also evaluations of bilingual legal dictionaries by, e.g., Kim-Prieto 2008 and Thiry 2009).

4. Legal Terminology Management in International Institutional Settings

Translation teams at international organizations are keenly interested in the integration of sound terminology management into their services:

a. they deal with high volumes of translation, and terminological consistency is vital in that context, especially in large organizations with various translation teams at different agencies or duty stations;
b. they play a benchmark role by establishing terminology in international law (as intertwined with several branches of law), and disseminating specialized uses in languages that often comprise more than one national legal order;
c. institutional translators, like so many of their peers, usually work under time pressure, and terminological resources can critically hasten their translation-oriented research.

Terminology managers at international organizations (regardless of the job title of those responsible for terminology work) are well-positioned to address these challenges and overcome the shortcomings of traditional legal lexicographical resources. They can have access to in-house expertise in translation and other fields, they can avail of sophisticated technological tools, and can define the situational factors conditioning the translation process.

Indeed, in most of such organizations, great effort has been made to accommodate and develop computer-assisted translation tools, including electronic corpora and term banks. These resources do not only facilitate in-house translation work, but they can also be useful to and guide other translators and language users. Open-access resources make it possible to trace the conditions of translation and terminological work, and therefore to assess the quality of such resources with regard to translators' needs. Terminological databases reflect institutional translation practices since they are usually built through the extraction, analysis and validation of terms from texts translated for the organization in question.

As pointed out in section 2, in the context of international rulemaking, translation itself contributes to building the shared concepts that underpin the international legal system in the different official languages. Conceptual unity, terminological harmonization and formal concordance are prioritized in that process (Prieto Ramos 2011b). As opposed to oversimplistic generalizations on international settings of legal translation, these also include procedures for monitoring rule implementation (e.g., UN bodies responsible for monitoring the application of human rights treaties), as well as procedures for settling disputes on legal interpretation and compliance (e.g., the World Trade Organization's dispute settlement procedures).[3] Such procedures, which generate a high amount of translation work, entail the interaction between international law and national levels of implementation, i.e. not only international legal concepts, but also national ones.

When translating these system-bound terms for international language communities, functional equivalents valid in one national system alone are normally ruled out. Neutral conceptual or literal formulations will rather take priority to facilitate the widest possible comprehension, while borrowings might be part of the solution if the SS-term cultural specificity is to be identified, as long as this technique is compatible with the institutional translation policy. In the search for maximum accuracy and consistency, it is indeed mandatory to follow internal translation conventions according to the hierarchy of institutional texts.

As a general rule, the above translation patterns are mirrored in terminology databases. Three groups of terms can be identified in these resources:

(1) Terms designating shared concepts created in the international system and recognized as established terminology within the specific scope of competence of a particular organization. Once coined in the different languages, this terminology is generally followed by other specialized language users, for example, terminology on the law of the sea used by the International Law Commission (e.g., "extended continental shelf"/"*extensión de la plataforma continental*"/"*plateau continental élargi*" or "*plateau continental étendu*") or terminology on international tariff regulations at the World Trade Organization (e.g., "tariff escalation"/"*progresividad arancelaria*"/"*progressivité des tarifs*").

(2) Terms previously existing in some jurisdiction or legal tradition and borrowed to be used with a shared meaning in the international system. This usually implies adding a new layer of legal content to the original term and transferring it to other languages involved in the translation process, i.e. secondary term formation (Sager 1990: 80; see, e.g., Peruzzo 2012 on the EU-Italian terms adopted for originally-English terms on victims' rights in criminal proceedings, such as "restorative justice"). Since English is nowadays the predominant language of international negotiation and drafting of original texts, common law tends to be a major source of concepts transposed internationally (see, e.g., Drohla 2008 and Hernández 2010). At the same time, international legal discourses in English, as appropriated by the international community, are characterized by hybridity (see, e.g., Trosborg 1997) as a result of their detachment from a particular legal culture and their permeability to different legal norms.

When the original term is used by different organizations, institutional translation proposals may be divergent, even if the concept remains essentially the same. This is the case, for example, of procedural law concepts borrowed from common law, such as "due process", or financial law terminology originally coined in English and then transferred to

3 On the scope and conditions of institutional legal translation at international level, see Prieto Ramos (2014).

other languages as neologisms (see, e.g., Prieto Ramos 2013a). In such instances, it might prove difficult to propose a single reference target language (TL) equivalent when expert uses informing terminological work are still unclear or scattered to support the preference for a term. In turn, the lack of intra- and inter-institutional terminology harmonization can lead to "terminological congestion", thus contributing to the insufficient entrenchment and standardization of a single TL term.

(3) Terms designating culture-bound or system-specific concepts to be identified as such in the international context, for example, names of national judicial institutions, pieces of legislation or other legal singularities mentioned in texts on law enforcement or dispute settlement. The interaction between international and national law mentioned above explains the keen interest to include this terminology in databases. The focus shifts from harmonizing shared concepts to describing national or regional specificities systematically for translation purposes at the relevant organization, i.e., offering translation proposals and/or information for translation decision-making according to relevant contextual variables. In other words, this terminology tends to be representative of classical problems of asymmetry in legal lexicography and requires sufficient knowledge of legal translation methodology. For this reason, terms from this group have been selected for further analysis.

5. Illustrative Legal Terminological Entries

We will focus on the third group of terms to briefly analyze the content of legal terminological entries in two institutional databases: IATE, covering terminology used in EU institutions and agencies; and UNOGTerm, the terminological database of the United Nations Office at Geneva. Both are web-based tools developed by language services with the primary objective of assisting institutional translators and language staff in their tasks. Given the inter-institutional nature of IATE, its entries systematically specify the institution from which input is retrieved in the lists of search results. In the case of UNOGTerm, the tool coexists with UNTERM, another UN database developed for the entire organization. However, in practice, UNOGTerm is the primary reference for all UN translators with regard to UNOG's main subject matters, including human rights and the International Law Commission.

Let us now examine a few illustrative entries on national courts dealing with criminal cases: "magistrates' court" and "Court of Appeal" (in England and Wales), and "*tribunal de police*" and "*tribunal correctionnel*" (in France). The reliability and usefulness of entries will be assessed in the context of the translation into Spanish of reports on criminal proceedings (EU) and human rights treaty implementation (UN), i.e. for European receivers in the first case (IATE) and for the entire Spanish-speaking world in the second case (UNOGTerm).

Most *macro-contextualization information* can be obtained from the entries, including domain information. An important exception arises in the case of UNOGTerm entries: the source term and its legal system cannot always be clearly identified by the translator. For instance, the entry below ("*tribunal de police*") contains functional equivalents for Chile and Uruguay but no information on legal systems for the French or the English terms:

tribunal de police
UNOGTerm entry number: 28456
Domain: *Human rights*

Subject: *Human rights-General*
French
tribunal de police
English
police court
Spanish
juzgado de policía local
Note: *(Chile)*
Tribunal de Faltas
Note: *(Uruguay; hay solamente un tribunal de este tipo)*

At the same time, the entries for these two terms in Spanish include exactly the same entry number and information, but languages are presented in a different order, which raises doubts about the language pair and translation direction for which the entry was originally created. In fact, given the asymmetry between concepts in this subject area, not knowing the translational direction considered in the acceptability analysis critically limits the reliability of entries. The same problem applies to the entry for "court of appeal", which offers a list of related terms (seven in English, eight in French, six in Spanish) with no indication of connection between them.

As regards *comparative legal and linguistic analysis, translation options and sources*, the information offered by UNOGTerm is clearly more limited. Apart from the lists of terms in each entry, the only information provided are "remarks" or "notes" in some cases, mostly to indicate the system to which the term refers and, in two instances, to include short descriptive elements: one for "*tribunal correctionnel*" (with no source), and another one for "court of appeal" (followed by the source: literally, "*(Black)*").[4] No information is provided on reliability or validation of the terms examined.

IATE systematically indicates the source of original and target language terms, as well as a reliability value for each term and the date of registration of terminological information. These two elements are also extremely useful on account of the diversity of EU institutions contributing to the database and the dynamic nature of terms (particularly, changes in judicial organization in this case). A definition of the original term and the source of this definition are usually provided too. Notes are sometimes added (in our entries: a cross-reference to "*tribunal de grande instance*" from "*tribunal correctionnel*", and a short comment on SS-TS comparison in the TL information in "*tribunal de police*"). Definitions of the TL terms and examples of use in context are occasionally offered, albeit not in the entries analyzed.

However, the diversity and reliability of sources vary considerably from one IATE entry to the other, for instance: a dictionary reference under "*tribunal correctionnel*"; rather than a source, a comment on the creation of a "*tribunal de police*" exclusively with criminal jurisdiction; in the case of "court of appeal", the only entry referring to England and Wales (as updated in August 2012) combines a definition from *Wikipedia* with a link to an official webpage of the UK Ministry of Justice. Interestingly, the Spanish term under the same entry is a translation proposed by an oral source at the Spanish Labor Ministry in 2003. Likewise, the Spanish formulations proposed for "*tribunal correctionnel*" and "*tribunal de police*" are suggestions from an external sworn translator (and law graduate) in the first case, and a law professor in the second one. All this information is validated and considered reliable with a 3-value on a 1–4 scale.

The search results for "magistrates' court" (or "magistrate's court") are not useful since, in the entries retrieved, the term does not really refer to the English system but to original names

4 The only source identified as a specific field in the entries analyzed features a UN document symbol for the Russian term under "*tribunal correctionnel*".

of courts in other languages and systems. Nonetheless, *"justicia de paz"* (UNOGTerm) and *"juzgado de paz"* (IATE) are included as possible equivalents in those entries. Unfortunately, if translators look for a reference on the English court name elsewhere within the EU institutions, they will find a false friend, *"tribunal de magistrados"* (*"magistrado"* meaning senior judge in Spanish), on the webpages of the European Judicial Network (EJN).[5] The same false friend is found in approximately two thirds of translations of the term in publicly accessible UN documents (as of October 2012).

The translation proposals in the other entries (Table 7.1) show that (misleading) approximate functional equivalents in the Spanish judicial system are avoided in IATE entries. However, the translation proposals are inadequate and incoherent in the case of French criminal courts: a literal translation for *"tribunal de police"* (*"tribunal de policía"*) which can be misleading for Spanish readers, and conceptual renderings (*"juzgado/tribunal de lo penal"*) which are too general to distinguish the original term from other criminal courts. UNOGTerm seems to focus on the reverse as it prioritizes functional equivalence between national realities, even though this may run contrary to the need for conceptual solutions for the entire Spanish-speaking world. In the case of "court of appeal", since the term is not only a system-bound name but also a more general concept in several legal cultures, the only difficulty lies in finding the most adequate conceptual formulation for the TL receivers. This is not facilitated by the list of options provided by UNOGTerm.

Except for this "transparent" concept, borrowings might be part of translation solutions for the terms analyzed, together with some descriptive formulation, in order to meet both identification and comprehension needs. However, borrowings are avoided in both databases. In contrast, they are systematically employed at the Court of Justice of the EU for national court names. Borrowings are not unknown of in UN translations either, and some example can be found in UNOGTerm (e.g., Canada's 'Court of Queen's Bench', partially reproduced in Spanish as 'Queen's Bench'), but they seem to be used as a last resort.

Table 7.1 Translation suggestions in illustrative entries

	IATE	UNOGTerm
tribunal de police	tribunal de policía	juzgado de policía local (Chile) Tribunal de Faltas (Uruguay)
tribunal correctionnel	juzgado de lo penal tribunal de lo penal	tribunal correccional (Perú)
court of appeal	tribunal de apelación audiencia territorial	tribunal de alzada corte de alzada corte de apelaciones tribunal de apelación tribunal de segunda instancia tribunal ad quem

Overall, if we focus on the quality of the content as the 'foremost criterion in the appraisal of the value and utility of a terminological tool' (de Bessé and Pulitano 1996: 44), both databases have considerable shortcomings from the perspective of translators' needs in the examples analyzed. In spite of some useful definitions provided by IATE, the link between SL term and translation suggestions is not clear, and there is no hint of systematic comparative and

5 Available at: http://ec.europa.eu/civiljustice/org_justice/org_justice_eng_en.htm.

acceptability analysis, except for a very general comment confirming that *"tribunal de police"* is a French criminal court which does not exist in Spain (IATE entry). Otherwise, translation recommendations by individuals consulted by IATE and national functional equivalents provided by UNOGTerm would be just a first step in the translator's research. More information on the courts' composition, jurisdiction and position within judicial hierarchies would be necessary in the comparative analysis for decision-making.

6. Conclusion

Translation-oriented legal terminology work constitutes a major methodological minefield which encapsulates the interrelation of parameters for problem-solving in legal translation. The variability and legal dimension of such parameters remain a characteristic challenge in the field. Legal terminology management for translation cannot be isolated from the legal and discursive variables which frame that mediation. The methodological model presented above responds to the need for their practical integration and systematization. It is premised on the perception of legal translation as an expert activity aimed at defining and meeting adequacy conditions in each communicative situation, rather than searching for off-the-shelf, all-purpose binary "equivalents".

Indeed, translation-oriented legal terminology work cannot be effectively tackled without acknowledging that legal translation itself can serve different communicative purposes, and these most often include conveying legal singularities. Legal translators must delve into legal conceptual asymmetries through comparative analysis in order to determine the acceptability of any possible reformulation options depending on receivers' needs and expectations. Translation-oriented legal lexicography must be shaped accordingly, elicit information relevant to that end, and even offer valid solutions when situational conditions are sufficiently defined. These requirements have not often been met by traditional bilingual and multilingual legal lexicographical resources.

Translators at international organizations are not exempt from the challenges of legal asymmetries, and the terminological problems that these pose are also captured in institutional documents and terminology databases. Beyond the standardization of terms that designate shared concepts in different areas of international and supranational law, terminology managers must also deal with national legal concepts. These constitute a source of time-consuming translation problems for which terminological assistance is most needed and adequate solutions are a quality marker. The purposes and situational factors conditioning the translation process are clearly established in that context, which places institutional terminologists in a strategic position to provide relevant information on term content and acceptability. Our analysis of some illustrative entries on national criminal courts in IATE and UNOGTerm shows that progress has been made in facilitating searches with new online tools, but the content of entries generally falls as short of translators' needs as traditional lexicographical resources. The lack of systematic translation-oriented analysis leads to some inadequate and/or inconsistent translation proposals, while the information provided on legal content and sources relevant to acceptability analysis is also limited, particularly in UNOGTerm.

Advances in legal translation methodology can and must contribute to improving legal lexicographical practices if they are to address translators' needs. As evidenced in our research, their successful integration into applied terminological work requires interdisciplinary expertise combining terminology management and legal translation competence, including comparative law methodology and corpus analysis. However, profile requirements and quality standards may not be raised without previous acknowledgment of strengths and weaknesses, and their practical impact. Since terminological work is always work in progress and a sound investment for translation quality and effective translation management, it is never too late to improve professional resources for translators in this field.

References

Biel, Ł. 2009. 'Organisation of Background Knowledge Structures in Legal Language and Related Translation Problems', *Comparative Legilinguistics*, vol. 1, pp. 176–189.

Brand, O. 2007. 'Conceptual Comparisons: Towards a Coherent Methodology of Comparative Legal Studies', *Brooklyn Journal of International Law*, vol. 32(2), pp. 405–466.

Cao, D. 2010. 'Judicial Interpretation of Bilingual and Multilingual Laws: A European and Hong Kong Comparison'. In: J. Jemielniak and P. Miklaszewicz eds. *Interpretation of Law in the Global World: From Particularism to a Universal Approach*. Heidelberg: Springer, pp. 71–86.

Constantinesco, L.J. 1974. *Traité de droit comparé*. Paris: Librairie générale de droit et de jurisprudence.

De Bessé, B. and Pulitano, D. 1996. 'Which Terms Should Firms or Organisations Include in Their Terminology Banks?: The Case of the Canton of Berne'. In: H. Somers ed. *Terminology, LSP and Translation: Studies in Language Engineering in Honour of Juan C. Sager*. Amsterdam: John Benjamins, pp. 35–46.

De Groot, G.R. and van Laer, C. 2008. *The Quality of Legal Dictionaries: An Assessment*. Maastricht Faculty of Law Working Paper. Maastricht University Law School.

Drohla, J. 2008. 'The Languages of Public International Law: Power Politics under the Cloak of Cultural Diversity?'. In: *Droit international et diversité des cultures juridiques – International Law and Diversity of Legal Cultures*. Paris: Societé française pour le droit international, Pedone, pp. 153–182.

Dullion, V. 2000. 'Du document à l'instrument: les fonctions de la traduction des lois'. In: *La traduction juridique: Histoire, théorie(s) et pratique / Legal Translation: History, Theory/ies, Practice*. Bern and Geneva: ASTTI and ETI, pp. 83–101.

Engberg, J. 2013. 'Comparative Law for Translation: The Key to Successful Mediation between Legal Systems'. In: A. Borja Albi and F. Prieto Ramos eds. *Legal Translation in Context: Professional Issues and Prospects*. Bern, Berlin, Brussels, Frankfurt am Main, New York, Oxford and Vienna: Peter Lang, pp. 9–25.

Garner, B. 2003. 'Legal Lexicography: A View From the Front Lines', *English Today*, vol. 19, pp. 33–42.

Garzone, G' 2000. 'Legal Translation and Functionalist Approaches: a Contradiction in Terms?' In: *La traduction juridique: Histoire, théorie(s) et pratique / Legal Translation: History, Theory/ies, Practice*. Bern and Geneva: ASTTI and ETI, pp. 395–414.

Groffier, E. and Reed, D. 1990. *La lexicographie juridique: principes et methods*. Cowansville (Québec): Éditions Yvon Biais.

Harvey, M. 2000. 'A Beginners Course in Legal Translation: the Case of Culture-Bound Terms'. In: *La traduction juridique: Histoire, théorie(s) et pratique / Legal Translation: History, Theory/ies, Practice*. Bern and Geneva: ASTTI and ETI, pp. 357–369.

Hernández, G.I. 2010. 'On Multilingualism and the International Legal Process'. In: H. Ruiz-Fabri, R. Wolfrum and J. Gogolin eds. *Select Proceedings of the European Society of International Law*. Oxford: Hart Publishing, pp. 441–460.

Kim-Prieto, D. 2008. '*En la tierra del ciego, el tuerco es rey*: Problems with Current English-Spanish Legal Dictionaries, and Notes toward a Critical Comparative Legal Lexicography', *Law Library Journal*, vol. 100(2), pp. 251–278.

Leroyer, P. and Rasmussen, K.W. 2010. 'Accessing Discursive Data Types in Legal Translation Dictionaries: The Case of *Sans Préjudice de*'. In: D. Giannoni and C. Frade. *Researching Language and the Law: Textual Features and Translation Issues*. Bern, Berlin, Brussels, Frankfurt am Main, New York, Oxford and Vienna: Peter Lang, pp. 157–178.
Megale, F. 2008. *Teorie della traduzione giuridica. Fra diritto comparato e «Translation Studies»*. Napoli: Editoriale scientifica.
Nord, C. 1991. *Text Analysis in Translation: Theory, Methodology, and Didactic Application of a Model for Translation-Oriented Text Analysis*. Amsterdam and Atlanta: Rodopi.
———. 1997. *Translating as a Purposeful Activity*. Manchester: St. Jerome Publishing.
Peñaranda López, A. 2011. *El proceso penal en España, Francia, Inglaterra y Estados Unidos: descripción y terminología*. Granada: Comares.
Peruzzo, K. 2012. 'Secondary Term Formation Within the EU: Term Transfer, Legal Transplant or Approximation of Member States' Legal Systems?' *Journal of Specialised Translation*, vol. 18, pp. 175–186.
Prieto Ramos, F. 1998. 'La terminología procesal en la traducción de citaciones judiciales españolas al inglés', *Sendebar*, vol. 9, pp. 115–135.
———. 2011a. 'Developing Legal Translation Competence: An Integrative Process-Oriented Approach', *Comparative Legilinguistics*, vol. 5, pp. 7–21.
———. 2011b. 'El traductor como redactor de instrumentos jurídicos: el caso de los tratados internacionales', *Journal of Specialised Translation*, vol. 15, pp. 200–214.
———. 2013a. 'Traducción institucional y (co)gestión de neologismos: entre la armonización y la congestión terminológicas', in *Comunicación y transmisión del saber entre lenguas y culturas*, ed. C Sinner, Peniope, Munich, pp. 387–400.
———. 2013b. '¿Qué estrategias para qué traducción jurídica?: por una metodología integral para la práctica profesional'. In: I. Alonso Araguás, J. Baigorri Jalón and H. Campbell eds. *Translating the Law: Theoretical and Methodological Issues / Traducir el Derecho. Cuestiones teóricas y metodológicas*. Granada: Comares, pp. 87–106.
———. 2014. 'International and Supranational Law in Translation: From Multilingual Lawmaking to Adjudication', *The Translator*, vol. 20(2) (forthcoming).
Sager, J. 1990. *A Practical Course in Terminology Processing*. Amsterdam and Philadelphia: John Benjamins.
Sandrini, P. 1996. 'Comparative Analysis of Legal Terms: Equivalence Revisited'. In: C. Galinski and K.D. Schmit eds. *Terminology and Knowledge Engineering (TKE '96)*. Frankfurt am Main: Indeks, pp. 342–351.
———. 1999. 'Legal Terminology: Some Aspects for a New Methodology', *Hermes*, vol. 22, pp. 101–112.
Šarčević, S. 1985. 'Translation of Culture-Bound Terms in Laws', *Multilingua*, vol. 4(3), pp. 127–33.
———. 1989. 'Conceptual Dictionaries for Translation in the Field of Law', *International Journal of Lexicography*, vol. 2(4), pp. 277–293.
———. 1997. *New Approach to Legal Translation*. The Hague: Kluwer Law International.
Thiry, B. 2009. 'Análisis crítico de algunos diccionarios jurídicos publicados', *Entreculturas*, vol. 1, pp. 443–468.
Trosborg, A. (ed.). 1997. 'Translating Hybrid Political Texts'. In: *Text Typology and Translation*. Amsterdam and Philadelphia: John Benjamins, pp. 145–158.
Vanderlinden, J. 1995. *Comparer les droits*. Diegem: E. Story-Scientia.
Weston, M. 1991. *An English Reader's Guide to the French Legal System*. New York and Oxford: Berg Publishers Ltd.

Chapter 8
Structuring a Legal Translation Course: A Framework for Decision-Making in Legal Translator Training

Catherine Way

Translation studies have come a long way since the first tentative steps to define our field of studies (Holmes [1972] 1988). The last thirty years have seen an exponential growth of publications and research projects in our dynamic field, drawing on many other disciplines in an attempt to discover how translation and translators really work. It was not until the 1990s, however, that calls for more attention to be paid to training were really heard (Kiraly 1995).

Training translators has become an important area of research as we attempt to prepare our graduates to enter the professional market. Many authors have dedicated time and effort to improving training, particularly over the last decade (e.g., Kiraly 2000; Hatim 2001; Baer and Koby 2003; González Davies 2004; Kelly 2005; and Gile [1995] 2009). Many of these authors reflect the important shift in translator training, to process-oriented models rather than product-oriented models (Gile [1995] 2004; Kussmaul 1995).

Undoubtedly, one of the prominent areas of research in translator training has been the search for a definition of translation/translator competence, with a view to guiding us through the complicated path of designing specific objectives for each course, in our teaching practices and in designing classroom activities. In this paper we intend to combine recent training approaches by attempting to construct a framework for decision making in the translation classroom, based upon translator competence.

1. Translator Competence

Whilst many contributions have been made to defining translator competence[1], four of the most recent proposals (Neubert 2000; Kelly 2002, 2005 and PACTE 2000, 2002, 2005, 2008, Pym 2003) are of interest to us in this chapter. An interesting comparison of these four approaches can be found in Hague, Melby and Zheng (2011).

Pym's definition of translation competence, often considered to be a minimalist approach, focuses on the results once translator competence has been acquired, describing it as 'the ability to generate a series of more than one viable target text (TTI, TT2 … TTn) for a pertinent

1 Amongst the main contributions to the definition of translator competence we will find Krings (1986); Ammann (1990); Gile (1995); Hurtado (1996); Kiraly (1995; 2000); Kussmaul (1995); Robinson (1997); PACTE (1998; 2003); Kelly (1999; 2002; 2005); Neubert (2000); Pym (2003); and Orozco (2000).

source text (ST)' and 'the ability to select only one viable TT from this series, quickly and with justified confidence' (Pym 2003: 489). Despite the fact that Pym's definition is true in essence, it is less helpful than the more detailed approaches which divide translator competence into subcompetences or partial competences. These subcompetences have proved to be a valuable tool in establishing specific training objectives and, I also believe, when trying to perform effective assessment of our trainees (Way 2006, 2008: 91). Neubert defined *translational competence* (2000: 6–10) as integrating five competences: (1) language competence; (2) textual competence (3) subject competence (4) cultural competence; and (5) transfer competence. Whilst Neubert's model does not define the competences exhaustively, PACTE and Kelly models are much more detailed. The PACTE group has proposed a translation competence model with five subcompetences: (1) bilingual subcompetence; (2) extralinguistic subcompetence; (3) knowledge about translation subcompetence; (4) instrumental subcompetence; and (5) strategic subcompetence (PACTE 2008: 106). Kelly (2002: 9–20; 2005: 32–33) proposed a model in which she described translator competence as the macrocompetence which constitutes the set of skills, knowledge and attitudes which professional translators use in their daily translation tasks as experts. This macrocompetence is divided into the following seven subcompetences with their respective components: (1) Communicative and textual competence; (2) Cultural competenc; (3) Subject area competence; (4) Instrumental and professional competence; (5) Psycho-physiological or attitudinal competence; (6) Interpersonal competence; and (7) Strategic competence.

The models proposed by Kelly and PACTE have progressed beyond the earliest linguistic models such as Neubert's to include elements that come into play in the decision making process of the translator and which influence his/her metacognitive ability to justify strategies and decisions. According to Hague, Melby and Zheng (2011: 250):

> *Pym's minimalist approach describes an overarching expectation – what professional translators are expected to be able to do – while the subcompetence approaches describe how translators accomplish what they are expected to do. Consequently, we see no reason to argue with Pym, Neubert, PACTE, or Kelly, despite apparent differences. The granular approach of the subcompetence models simply allows trainers to identify discrete abilities that Pym's approach assumes.*

My research and training uses the model proposed by Kelly (2002: 9–20; 2005: 32–33) where the subcompetences are obviously inter-related and each is necessary for translator competence to function correctly[2]. Nevertheless, it is strategic competence which coordinates how the other subcompetences work when completing a given translation task. Kelly (2002: 17–18) organizes the subcompetences in graphic form as a pyramid in order to illustrate this idea of an overarching strategic macrocompetence which combines all the other subcompetences to allow organizational and planning skills, problem identification and problem-solving to come into play through decision making. This translator competence model provides us with a basis to establish learning outcomes, to structure a decision making framework and to assess the completion of our goals.

1.1. Research on Translator Competence

The AVANTI research group and the PACTE research group have been particularly active in researching not only the elements which constitute translator competence, but also, more

2 See, for example, Chesterman (1997) and Jääskelainen (1989).

recently, how different subcompetences are acquired. Authors such as Kelly (2002; 2005), PACTE (2000; 2001; 2002; 2003; 2005; 2009; 2011), Way (2002; 2004; 2006; 2008; 2009) and Valderrey (2005)[3] have continued to research different aspects of translator competence in order to observe how subcompetences are best acquired. The different translator competence models have also been used to research assessment, especially by Olivia Fox (2006), who has proposed a colour-coded marking system which highlights the competences that are lacking in the errors corrected in students' work, and by Way (2008; 2009). More recent studies approach interpersonal competence by researching collaborative work in translation classrooms (Huertas Barros 2013) or psychophysiological competence by researching student confidence when performing their translation tasks (Haro Soler 2013). Central to much of this research is functionalism (Chen 2008) and the belief that the translator is inevitably visible since, as Honig (1998: 12–13) rightly points out, functionalism avoids rules in favour of decision making strategies which begin by defining the *skopos* in order to choose the best strategies to meet the target reader's needs. These decisions, whether made consciously or not, are what justify the use of one strategy rather than another. Indeed, Hatim and Mason (1990: 3–4) defined translation as:

> *(. . .) a process, involving the negotiation of meaning between producers and receivers of texts. In other words, the resulting translated text is to be seen as evidence of a transaction, a means of retracing the pathways of the translator's decision-making procedures.*

In recent years, and particularly whilst training novice translation lecturers, I have noticed that a recurring theme has been the difficulties encountered when attempting to enable trainees to establish an overarching framework for decision making rather than specific decision making processes for individual translation problems. Mayoral (2007) suggested some time ago that translator training should be structured around problem solving and not by field or language combination, although in practice this is rarely administratively viable.

The framework of decision making, which brings into play different subcompetences to solve different problems, and hence strategies, is, therefore, central to the translation process. The question is, how do we stimulate our trainees to create their own personal framework of decision making?

2. Translator Training and Decision-Making

The new pedagogical approaches to translator training in recent years have brought to the fore the importance of trainees being able to recognize the factors that have an impact on their translation decisions (Kiraly 2000; González Davies 2004). Nevertheless, despite the obvious importance of decision making in the translation process it has received scant attention, which is surprising given that translators face an endless stream of decisions on a daily basis.

Several authors have dedicated time to this question since Jumpelt (1961) described translation as a decision making process involving choices between variables, similar to the choices in a chess game, for example. Later, Levy (1967: 156) used game theory to analyze translation with the "minimax" strategy used by the translator in an attempt to achieve the maximum of effect with minimum effort. Holmes ([1972] 1988) developed Levy's use of game theory suggesting a hierarchical system of correspondences in translation decision making.

3 Way (2002; 2004; 2006; 2008; 2009) and Valderrey (2005) have worked specifically in the field of translator competence and legal translation.

Other authors used different approaches, such as Toury (1985; 1995), who discussed decision making from the focus of norms and strategies, Séguinot (1991), who looked at cognitive processes by observing decisions taken in the translation process, Wilss (1994), who considered translator behaviour and proposed problem-solving steps to be used in translator training, and Lörscher (1991; 1995), who viewed strategies to be problem-solving mechanisms. All of them have discussed different areas of decision making in an attempt to understand the translation process. In the 1980s and 1990s research using "Think-Aloud Protocols" or TAPs (see, for example, Tirkkonen-Condit; 1992) delved further into decision making and it also appeared in works by authors such as Laviosa (1998) and Baker ([1998] 2011) in the corpus-based approach to Translation Studies. However, as Darwish (1999) rightly points out, the question of decision-making has been discussed mainly at the level of individual decisions and not as an overarching activity that governs the whole translation process. Thus he has approached this question from the perspective of constraints on the translation process by discussing the difference between constraints and norms and highlighting how understanding constraints on the translation process affect translation decisions and problem-solving strategies (Darwish 1999: 3).

Of particular interest for my proposal is Levy (1988: 38), who described decision making as the need to choose between a number of alternatives or solutions. Evidently, any choice will then influence subsequent choices in the translation as translators take into account the target audience's expectations. Levy's suggestion (1988: 48) that translators use the 'minimax strategy', choosing the solution which requires minimum effort for maximum effect is undoubtedly true. Also, for Wilss (1994: 131):

> *Decision-making in translation amounts to an information-processing concept that describes decision-making behaviour in terms of an interaction between the translator's cognitive system; his linguistic, referential, socio-cultural and situational knowledge bases; the task specification; and the text type-specific problem space. All four factors together enable the translator to build up an internal problem representation which, once constructed, will profoundly influence the translator's subsequent decision-making performance, taking account of probability ratings which are an important element in many translational decision-making settings.*

Therefore, decision making plays a vital role in the translator's performance (process) and the end translation product. In fact, if we consider our assessment methods, what we are often measuring is the success or failure of our trainees' decisions. The move from product-oriented to process-oriented approaches means that at different stages of training we place more emphasis on assessing the process than the final product itself, but both still rely heavily on the trainees' decision making.

In training, particular attention has to be paid to the elements which influence decision making behaviour or pre-choice behaviour as described by Wilss (1998):

> *in other words, the factors which favour one choice over another, rather than merely the choices themselves, that is to say, the process rather than just the product. These choices or decisions are constructed on our knowledge base and personal values or preferences: for example – our initial choice to translate literally, semantically, communicatively, etc.*

Our knowledge base includes the theories from which we draw our translation strategies, which are then used as problem solving solutions in a series of steps throughout the text (Darwish 1999: 18). Each step defines part of the framework which will then influence other decisions in the process and this must be made explicit to trainees.

Decision making and problem solving are obviously intertwined (Wilss 1998: 57), thereby bringing into play both declarative/theoretical and operative/practical knowledge as suggested by González Davies and Scott-Tennent (2005: 161): in order to solve a problem we must make a decision.

Pavlović (2010) has performed research into decision making in L1 and L2 translation processes in order to determine, among other things, the types of translation problems students encounter when translating comparable texts in two directions, the number of tentative solutions they consider per problem in each direction, and how they decide which of the tentative solutions to select for the final version of their translation. She also makes reference to internal and external resources and how they are used (Pavlović 2010: 65). The classification she presents of the novice translators' justifications when questioned about solutions include the vague 'it sounds better' or 'it's not said that way' which we often hear in translation classrooms.

This raises the question of the use of what is normally referred to as 'intuition' or the ability to intuitively choose the correct/best solution. This area is often neglected as it obliges us to delve into the internalized or automatic responses, rather than the more easily assessable external resources used. In decision making we perform a conscious act based on reflection and thought, whilst a reflex action, which is often our first impulse, is unconscious (see Robinson 1997). This does not mean that the reflex act may not be the best solution, as our prior experience often leads us to internalise previous decision making in a similar context, transforming it into an automatic response. As Konečný (2008: 42) puts it:

> *However, contemporary translation studies seeks to transcend this static concept [intuition]: "What may seem automatic behaviour may well be the result of previous controlled learning" (González Davies and Scott-Tennent 2005:161). Indeed, a more modern outlook on the handling of language approaches intuition as the result of a gradual shift from controlled processes which – through sufficient practice and experience – become internalized, eventually reaching a point where it is "difficult for the translator to verbalize what or why a solution has been applied, producing what may seem like non-reflective behaviour (intuition)" (González Davies and Scott-Tennent 2005: 162). This is then precisely what Anthony Pym refers to as the "apparent automatism" (Pym 2003: 489) involved in the process of generation and selection.*

Scaffolding and classifying problems and processes enables students to progressively acquire the necessary skills to justify their decisions, eliminating the vague justifications mentioned above, by basing their decision on a particular subcompetence skill, and to understand which subcompetence has not been activated appropriately, whilst at the same time enabling trainers to assess constructively. Thus, decision making becomes internalized and offers the tools to better visualise, understand and justify decisions throughout training and in professional practice. Translator trainers, then, need to help trainees create a decision making framework which will gradually enable them to internalise problem solving strategies through structured, controlled training. These processes will then become automatic to a certain extent, facilitating their work as a translator. It is these initially controlled processes that we attempt to convey to our trainees, so that they can internalise certain mechanisms to provide solutions as reflex actions or habits and reduce their decision making load, and thus their uncertainty and lack of confidence.

3. Decision Theory

As Wilss (1994: 140) reminded us:

> *[T]he decision making aspect of translation has been relegated to the fringe of research, and rarely has decision theory been called upon to support translation theorists and translation practitioners with findings useful for systematically improving translator performance.*

Decision theory, however, has a lot to offer translator training. Hastie (2001) defines a decision as:

> *The conceptual (perhaps defining) template for a decision includes three components: (a) courses of action (choice options and alternatives), (b) beliefs about objective states, processes, and events in the world (including outcome states and means to achieve them), and (c) desires, values or utilities that describe the consequences associated with the outcomes of each action-event combination. Good decisions are those that effectively choose means that are available in the given circumstances to achieve the decision-maker's goals.*

If we relate this to the process of translation, the course of action will include possible translation strategies or, for example, choices between terms; beliefs which will include our personal view of translation, theoretical basis and personal worldview; and desires, values or utilities which will include our estimation of the outcome of our decision making and the effects it will have. Even if we put the three elements in play, there will always be uncertain events beyond our control, such as the degree of knowledge the target text reader may have about the source text content (such as a particular legal system or legal concept from another culture).

Hastie (2001) distinguishes between decision making and judgement:

> *Decision making refers to the entire process of choosing a course of action. Judgement refers to the components of the larger decision-making process that are concerned with assessing, estimating, and inferring what events will occur and what the decision-maker's evaluative reaction to those outcomes will be.*

Particularly in early stages of translator training, we tend to assess the accuracy of a particular judgement and the criteria used to implement it. In other words, when looking at how trainees choose which action to take we are really assessing their judgement. What concerns us in training is where our trainees acquire the information about alternatives, consequences, and events, and how they use this information, besides how their personal preferences and values come into play.

Arsham (2002: 62) describes six key stages in a decision making process:

1. Identification of the problem [often the most difficult stage- if not completed properly the results will be unsatisfactory].
2. What is the goal?
3. Possible Actions: Pending your theory on determining the goal will have a huge influence on the types of action that make sense. Actions are primarily determined by the goal you wish to achieve.
4. Predict Outcome: [Calculate the results based on input].

5. Pick the Best Alternative: Is the best alternative simply the predicted outcome which maximizes goals or does it merely provide empirical results for comparison.
6. Implement Decision.

For Arsham (2002), this implies a series of steps in the decision making process: understanding the situation and decision; understanding what matters in order to establish criteria on which to make the decision; searching for options by being aware of the possible options; choosing the best option in order to satisfy as far as possible what matters; and implementing the decisions. If we adapt Arsham's proposal to translation the steps required would be:

- Establishing the communicative situation or *skopos*—the overarching decision.
- Identifying and categorising the translation problems—in order to select the subcompetence skills required to find a solution for each of them.
- Analysing possible solutions or strategies and their effects in the Target Text.
- Choosing the best alternative or solution for each problem.
- Implementing the chosen course of action, once the decision has been taken, and assessing the possible effects of the solution selected.

This requires declarative/theoretical and operative/practical knowledge. In other words, knowing what theoreticians suggest for dealing with a type of problem may not suffice if I am not aware of the practical consequences of a given decision in a particular translation. So how can trainees be guided to know which is the best possible solution when faced with a given problem? Evidently, understanding what the problem is correctly is the first step, but theoretical knowledge of translation problem types and suggested solutions is useless if applied inappropriately. Thus, trainees need to combine their theoretical and practical knowledge and gain experience through practice by facing and solving problems in a scaffolded, repeated way. Obviously, the greater our competences, experience and knowledge as translators, the easier the decision making process will be.

The field of translation studies has tended to dwell on decision-making for isolated translation problems (institutional names, metaphor, etc.) rather than establishing an overarching framework. Decision theory can help us to organize the presentation of translation problems to trainees by categorising decision making situations. Whilst revising approaches from other fields to decision making (business, public administration), an interesting proposal by Snowden and Boone (2007) outlined a leader's framework for decision making. Snowden and Boone decided to use a perspective based on complexity science, an approach which as recently been reflected in Translation Studies too (see Kiraly 2013; Marais 2014). Snowden and Boone (2007: 2) developed the Cynefin framework for leaders[4] which suggests five contexts for decision making defined by the nature of the relationship between cause and effect: Simple, complicated, complex, chaotic and disorder. The first four "require leaders to diagnose situations and to act in contextually appropriate ways", whilst the fifth, disorder, comes into play when it is difficult to decide which of the first four contexts predominates. The authors provide a guide for leaders which outlines the characteristics of each of the first four contexts; describe the leader's job; highlight danger signals or elements to be avoided; and suggest responses to the danger signals, or ways of avoiding the dangers outlined (Snowden and Boone 2007: 7).

4 '. . . (*Cynefin*, pronounced ku-nev-in, is a Welsh word that signifies the multiple factors in our environment and our experience that influences us in ways we can never understand.' (Snowden and Boone 2007: 2).

If we apply their categories to translation we will find that *simple contexts*, as the name denotes, involve stable problems where clear cause and effect relationships are evident. This would imply situations in which translation norms or accepted behaviour would apply. In this context the decision maker must consider or identify the problem, categorize it, and then resolve it by using established practices. Despite its name, a simple context may still be problematic if the problem is not identified correctly or if the decision maker falls foul of what the authors call 'entrained thinking' (Snowden and Boone 2007: 2): in other words, by implementing a conditioned response that has been acquired through previous experience or training and success, or they may become complacent when facing apparently familiar problems (see Robinson's example of an alarm system (1997: 106)). For *complicated contexts*, on the other hand, multiple right answers may exist to the problem, requiring the decision maker to analyze the possible solutions before implementing them, which will often be time consuming as more than one right answer may be viable. These problems should be introduced gradually in translation courses as they require greater diagnosis skills and expertise. *Complex contexts* involve problems with large numbers of interacting elements which are dynamic and nonlinear and imply that minor changes may produce disproportionately serious consequences, often impeding predictions of the outcome. They are unpredictable and often require creativity and innovative approaches. These problems are less common in translation than interpreting, but may be occasionally found. *Chaotic contexts* are full of unknowns because of constantly changing circumstances and are described by (Snowden and Boone 2007: 5) as 'the domain of rapid response', likening these contexts to the events of 9/11. These contexts involve high tension, multiple decisions and are characterized by a lack of time, as is the case in interpreting. Contexts with *disorder* are extreme, again often as in interpreting, and are unpredictable (Snowden and Boone 2007: 4).

We can use this classification to select translation problems for our courses, progressively increasing the complexity of the problems posed and of the decisions to be taken. If structured carefully, they can also exemplify the dangers of only making decisions based on past patterns of success and failure, rather than on a clearly defined framework of decision making: for example, it is not uncommon for trainees on introductory legal translation courses to rely heavily upon glossaries, understood as lists of static equivalences without contextualization. If the trainee does not reflect carefully upon the source text and *skopos*, we will find then misusing a term which was used successfully as appropriate in another context. Interestingly, Snowden and Boone (2007: 5) also state that in decision making, '[c]onditions of scarcity often produce more creative results than conditions of abundance.' This is also true for translation, where occasional activities without Internet access (excess of information) often produce surprising results and reinforce trainees' confidence in their internal resources.

4. Creating a Framework for Guided Decision Making

Building a framework for guided decision making, especially in initial stages of translator training, must, then, be central to our teaching. Legal translation courses are often structured according to the degree of abstraction of legal terms and concepts, used to identify a text as being more or less specialized. The framework suggested here, however, provides a sequencing pattern of increasing difficulty dependent on the activation of all the subcompetences and not just subject area competence.

When training legal translators we assume, to varying degrees, that our trainees have already acquired a certain degree of core knowledge, both in Translation Studies and Law. Unfortunately this is not often the case and we may face classrooms with varied degrees of knowledge (law graduates with little or no translation theory background or translation students with little or no knowledge of law).

Our training, based on the competence model mentioned earlier (Kelly 2002; 2005), of communicative and textual competence, cultural competence, subject area competence, instrumental and professional competence, psycho-physiological or attitudinal competence, interpersonal competence and strategic competence, must juggle all of these at the same time, whilst also introducing a decision making framework through practice. This is what many novice translator trainers find to be their hardest task.

The first three competences (communicative and textual competence, cultural competence, subject area competence) have received more attention in research into translator training than the last three (instrumental and professional competence, psycho-physiological or attitudinal competence, interpersonal competence and strategic competence). This is probably due to the difficulties involved in observing how these transversal competences are acquired, which is far more complex. It is, however, by paying particular attention to strategic competence through the creation of a framework of decision making that trainees may make the best use of their other competences. This problem-solving and decision-making framework will enhance their analysis and evaluation skills by providing trainees with the confidence and autonomy to bring all their subcompetences into play with maximum benefit.

The reason for using a pedagogy based on a decision making framework is that it is a vital tool which will enable trainees to develop self-confidence in their decision making ability (Way 2002; 2004). This provides the foundations for them to become confident, autonomous professional translators, capable of adapting to new situations.

In order to do this we require a participatory learning environment which promotes active learning (learning to learn) through problem-based activities. The presentation of translations performed with real translation briefs in groups using project management (Way 2009) provides a basis for the clear division of tasks by subcompetence(s) and the justification of translation solutions to be debated in the classroom, reinforcing the possibility of more than one solution based on valid criteria. The use of brainstorming for decision making and problem solving is a valuable tool in these activities. By incorporating teamwork, the trainees learn to apply their subcompetences in different stages of the translation task and thereby systematise the translation process.

4.1. Establishing the Decision Making Framework

Uncertainty is probably the greatest dilemma faced by our trainees. In introductory legal translation courses our trainees are normally still unsure of their theoretical translation basis and often frightened of the task of approaching texts in a field which is unfamiliar to them. They need to learn to apply the knowledge already acquired and incorporate new knowledge and skills through their translating experience in the classroom (both personal and observed in their fellow trainees). This will enhance their judgment and decision making skills so that they can reduce the uncertainty factor when choosing between alternative solutions. As trainees progress to more advanced courses, they will acquire the practice and expertise required to operate flexibly and confidently in the future.

Trainers must provide room for each student to create their own personal framework, rather than being prescriptive. In fact trainees are often more prescriptive themselves due to their earlier learning experiences. How do we go about this? Below is a suggested structure which bears in mind the following factors.

- First, we need to organize our course around a structure of decision making contexts based on different tasks.
- Basing our courses on pre-existing knowledge is vital. Hence, in a legal translation course we can begin by using the relatively familiar field of Family Law (for example) to lead trainees gently into the specialized field of legal translation.
- Initially we will be introducing new concepts (subject area and cultural competence), new text types and discourse (communicative and textual competence), requiring research and IT skills (instrumental and professional competence) based on collaborative activities (psycho-physiological or attitudinal competence, interpersonal competence and strategic competence).
- Group presentations using the Project Management Sheet (Way 2009) require the trainees to identify the different problems faced in each different task (project manager, researcher, terminologist, translator, editor, reviser), to analyze and classify the problems, to determine which skills or tools are required needed to solve the problems, to present the different alternative solutions, to justify their choice of solution, the reliability of their sources and in conjunction with the rest of the class to evaluate the proposed solution.

The framework we propose is based on scaffolding in an attempt to both provide support for trainees whilst allowing them to develop their own decision making by guiding them towards becoming autonomous at the same time. Therefore it includes careful selection of tasks to provide problems based on trainees' knowledge and skills; a degree of continuity provided by some task repetition and problem repetition, building upon acquired knowledge as the course progresses; the use of support and encouragement emphasising positive rather than negative aspects of trainees' work (particularly in early training stages); the ability to adapt to new situations created by trainees' needs as the course progresses (for example by returning to an earlier task if reinforcement is needed); and a gradual reduction of the role of the trainer permitting trainees to assume an ever increasing role. Ideally, by the time students finalise each course the trainer's role should be reduced to a minimum. The use of Snowdon and Boone's classification (2007) combined with a translator competence model will enable us to structure the gradual progression from simple to more complex decisions.

Each year provides us with a new group of trainees and tried and tested materials will need to be adapted so that we ensure that trainees feel both challenged and yet secure enough to be able to perform optimally. This will require the trainer to establish an overall plan based on the final course objectives and learner outcomes, a progressive plan which establishes the stages and steps involved in each activity or translation task and, on a more immediate basis, the ability to react to problems which may arise at any point in the course. Inevitably, the clearer all of this is to all participants, the greater the possibilities of success. Trainees need to know what is expected of them (in each activity and at the end of the course), when (a clear calendar of activities with reasonable time scales), why (the purpose of each activity) and how the course plans to lead them towards the final objective (precise explanations of work methodology).

Table 8.1 Legal Translation Decision Making Framework

Class	Content	Activities	Subcompetences (See list below)	Decision making context: Simple	Decision making context: Complicated	Decision making context: Complex
1	Introduction Programme (objectives) Diagnostic test Bibliography Translator Competence Group organization Project management	Establish clear objectives Discuss documentary sources and required competences for the course Reinforce collaborative learning basis and tasks required for specialized translation	4, 5, 6, 7			
2	Legal systems and sources of Law	Introduction to legal systems Discussion of differences between legal systems and sources of Law in each system	2, 3, 4, 5, 6, 7 Group presentations based on research	Emphasis on only 2 legal systems (e.g., Spain and England and Wales)	Emphasis on 2 legal systems, but broadened to different legal cultures (e.g., Spain, Mexico, Argentina and England and Wales, Ireland, USA)	Broaden the discussion and examples to more than 2 systems (Spain, Mexico, China, India)
3	Legal texts and legal language	Introduction of legal text typology Introduction to legal discourse	1, 2, 3 Group presentations based on research	Introductory courses a basic overview	Broaden scope of possible text types and legal discourse—different varieties of legal Spanish and legal English—England and Wales, Ireland, USA	Broaden scope of possible text types and legal discourse—different varieties of legal Spanish and legal English (England and Wales, USA, English as a lingua franca for other legal systems and cultures
4	Legal Translation	Introduction to the theory of legal translation	1, 4, 5 Group presentations based on research	Basic introduction to legal translation theory	Legal translation theory including Discourse Analysis	Legal translation theory including Critical Discourse Analysis

5	Family Law	Introduction to the basic concepts and organization of Family Law	1, 2, 3 Group presentations based on research	Basic introduction to Family Law in 2 legal systems – Spain, England and Wales	Broaden scope of legal systems—different approaches to Family Law Spain— England and Wales, Ireland, USA	Broaden scope of legal systems—different approaches to Family Law Spain—England and Wales, Ireland, USA and other legal systems and cultures of non-anglophone countries
6	Translation 1 Newspaper text on marriage in Spain for UK audience	Guided group translation of basic informative text for lay audience	1, 2, 3, 4, 5, 6, 7 Group presentations using project management	Informative text, simple discourse, audience of 1 legal system, some cultural and thematic problems	Informative text, simple discourse, audience of 2 legal systems, some cultural and thematic problems	Informative text, simple discourse, audience of 2 or more legal systems, some cultural and thematic problems
7	Translation 2 Newspaper text on marriage in Spain for UK audience (introduction of new elements e.g., same sex marriage)	Guided group translation of basic informative text for semi-specialized audience	1, 2, 3, 4, 5, 6, 7 Group presentations using project management	Informative text, simple discourse, lay audience of 1 legal system, introduction of more cultural and thematic problems (e.g., terminological and conceptual differences describing the same situation)	Informative text, simple discourse, specialized audience of 2 legal systems, more cultural and thematic problems (e.g., terminological and conceptual differences describing the same situation)	Informative text, simple discourse, expert audience of 2 or more legal systems, some cultural and thematic problems (e.g., terminological and conceptual differences describing the same situation)
8	Translation 3 Newspaper text on marriage, divorce and/or nullity in Spain for UK audience	Guided group translation of basic informative text for expert audience	1, 2, 3, 4, 5, 6, 7 Group presentations using project management	Informative text, simple discourse, audience of 1 legal system, introduction of more cultural and thematic problems (e.g., Canon Law/religion and marriage)	Informative text some opinion, complicated discourse, audience of 2 legal systems, more cultural and thematic problems (e.g., Canon Law/religion and marriage)	Informative text, complex discourse, audience of 2 or more legal systems, some cultural and thematic problems (e.g., Canon Law/religion and marriage)

9	Translation 4 Law manual on requirements for marriage in Spain 2 briefs	Guided group translation of basic informative text for lay/specialized audience (1. Secondary school students, 2. Law students)	1, 2, 3, 4, 5, 6, 7 Group presentations using project management	Informative text, simple discourse, lay audience of 1 legal system, introduction of more textual and linguistic problems (e.g., need for explicitation)	Informative text some opinion, complicated discourse, specialized audience of 2 legal systems, more textual and linguistic problems (e.g., need for explicitation or not)	Informative text, complex discourse, expert audience of 2 or more legal systems, textual and linguistic problems (e.g., need for explicitation or not)
10	Translation 5 Women's Guide to Rights and Obligations in Marriage 2 briefs	Guided group translation of basic informative text for lay/specialized audience (1. Multicultural audience living in Spain, 2. University Feminist Research Group)	1, 2, 3, 4, 5, 6, 7 Group presentations using project management	Brief 1 Informative/operative text, simple discourse, audience of more than 1 legal system, introduction of more cultural and thematic problems (e.g., need for explicitation)	Brief 2 Informative/operative text, simple discourse, audience of more than 1 legal system, introduction of more cultural, thematic, lingustic problems (e.g., need for explicitation or not)	Multicultural audience Lingua franca
11	Translation 6 Spanish Civil Code for Judge(s)	Guided group translation of a specialized (legislative) text	1, 2, 3, 4, 5, 6, 7 Group presentations using project management	Informative/operative text, complicated discourse, audience of 1 legal system, introduction of more textual and linguistic problems (e.g., complicated legal discourse) and cultural and thematic problems (e.g., need for explicitation)	Informative/operative text, complicated discourse, audience of more than 1 legal system, introduction of more textual and linguistic problems (e.g., complicated legal discourse) and cultural and thematic problems (e.g., need for explicitation)	Multicultural audience Lingua franca
12	Revision of legal translations	Introduction to basic parameters for revision	1, 2, 3, 4, 5, 6, 7 Group presentations	Revision of a legal translation from Spain for England	Revision of a legal translation from Spain for England and Wales and Ireland	Revision of a legal translation from Spain for a multicultural audience

Let us see how the problem solving framework mat be developed and which activities may be included.

1. Communicative and textual competence
2. Cultural competence
3. Subject area competence
4. Instrumental and professional competence
5. Psycho-physiological or attitudinal competence
6. Interpersonal competence
7. Strategic competence

4.2. Adapting the Decision Making Framework

Translator trainers may use this framework to design the course content and establish progression. Emphasis will clearly be placed on different subcompetences at different stages of their training. The suggested framework is, however, flexible too, catering to different trainee profiles by, for example, simply changing the brief for one text which will increase the difficulty or scope of a given decision making context or will introduce different subcompetence requirements. The same course materials may also be adapted to different decision making contexts for different student groups, such as Law graduates or Translation undergraduates at different training stages. Progression may also be adapted by reinforcing certain decisions by repetition or by introducing added difficulty to others, depending on how a given group is coping with the problems posed. It is also possible to introduce texts that may pose a particularly problem on one subcompetence level (e.g. subject area competence), yet still be able to use the text at an early stage by providing greater support materials and explanations to obviate this added difficulty in that one subcompetence area alone.

5. Conclusion

This proposal, in line with Kiraly's 'emergent post-modern approach' to translator training (Kiraly 2013: 198) combines the more reductionist two-dimensional competence models with a decision-making framework stemming from complexity studies (Snowden and Boone 2007), in line with the complexity perspective suggested by Marais (2014: 5) in the search for the '*emergence* of translator competence' described by Kiraly (2013: 203). Furthermore, this proposal, when applied in more advanced training stages, is leading to new research into the difficult step towards acquiring expertise.

If we bear in mind that our different backgrounds and experiences inevitably affect the way in which we make decisions, it is not surprising that no two translations are identical. This implies that when training future translators we must be prepared to assist them in forging their own decision making framework and not a unique solution to all problems. The advantage of focusing on the creation of a decision making framework, that emphasises the process rather than the product, is that this can help trainers to see where trainees have problems and also ensure that what the trainees learn may be applied in new situations encountered after training in professional practice.

Experience has demonstrated that even students who excel may not always be confident about why or how they have made a successful translation decision. By explicitly pointing out successful decisions based on specific skills in a particular subcompetence, they will become aware of the reasons underlying both their successful and their less successful decisions, thereby allowing them to detect strengths and weaknesses and to analyze their own personal decision making framework.

References

Ammann, M. 1990. *Grundñagen der modernen Translationstheorie – Ein Leitfaden für Studieren.* Heidelberg: Universität.

Arsham, H. 2002. 'Overcoming Serious Indecisiveness: How People Avoid Making Serious Decisions', *Iraniha.* Available at: http//home.ubalt.edu/ntsbarsh/opre640/partxiii.htm [Accessed April 2002].

Baer, B.J. and Koby, G.S. (eds). 2003. *Beyond the Ivory Tower: Rethinking Translation Pedagogy.* Amsterdam and Philadelphia: John Benjamins.

Baker, M. 2011. *In Other Words: A Coursebook on Translation.* 2nd edn. London and New York: Routledge.

Chen, S. 2008. 'Cultural Presupposition and Decision-Making in the Functional Approach to Translation', *Journal of Humanities and Social Sciences,* vol. 4(1), pp. 83–89.

Chesterman, A. 1997. *Memes of Translation: The Spread of Ideas in Translation Theory.* Amsterdam and Philadelphia: John Benjamins.

———. 2000. 'Teaching Strategies for Emancipatory Translation'. In: C. Schäffner and B. Adab eds. *Developing Translator Competence.* Amsterdam and Philadelphia: John Benjamins, pp. 77–90.

Darwish, A. 1995. *A Model for Designing Decision-Based Translation Tests.* Available at: http://www.at-turjuman.com/ [Accessed 30 November 2013].

———. 1999. *Towards A Theory of Constraints in Translation.* Available at: http://www.translocutions.com/translation/constraints_0.1.pdf [Available at: 30 November 2013].

Fox, O. 2006. 'Criterion Referenced Assessment in a Process-Oriented, Competency-Based, Multilingual, Multicultural Translation Classroom'. In: C. Way, G. Soriano, D. Limon and C. Amador eds. *Enhancing the ERAMUS Experience: Papers on Student Mobility.* Granada: Atrio, pp. 211–221.

Gile, D. [1995] 2009. *Basic Concepts and Models for Interpreter and Translator Training.* Amsterdam and Philadelphia: John Benjamins.

González Davies, M. 2004. *Multiple Voices in the Translation Classroom: Activities, Tasks, and Projects.* Amsterdam and Philadelphia: John Benjamins.

González Davies, M. and Scott-Tennent, C. 2005. 'A Problem-Solving and Student-Centred Approach to the Translation of Cultural References', *Meta,* vol. 50(1), pp. 160–179.

Hague, D., Melby, A. and Zheng, W. 2011. 'Surveying Translation Quality Assessment: A Specification Approach', *The Interpreter and Translator Trainer,* vol. 5(2), pp. 243–267.

Haro Soler, M. del Mar. 2013. *La confianza del estudiantado de Traducción en su capacidad para traducir: su desarrollo en la formación en Traducción.* Unpublished Masters dissertation. Universidad de Granada.

Hastie, R. 2001. 'Problems for Judgement and Decision Making', *Annual Review of Psychology,* Available at: http://www.annualreviews.org/doi/abs/10.1146/annurev.psych.52.1.653 [Accessed 30 November 2013].

Hatim, B. 2001. *Teaching and Researching Translation.* Harlow and New York: Longman.

Hatim, B. and Mason, I. 1990. *Discourse and the Translator.* London: Longman.

Holmes, J.S. [1972] 1988. 'The Name and Nature of Translation Studies'. In: *James S. Holmes, Translated! Papers on Literary Translation and Translation Studies*. Amsterdam: Rodopi, pp. 67–80.
Hųnig, H.G. 1998. 'Positions, Power and Practice: Functionalist Approaches and Translation Quality Assessment'. In: C. Schaeffner ed. *Translation and Quality*. Philadelphia: Multilingual Matters, pp. 6–34.
Huertas Barros, E. 2013. *La competencia interpersonal en la formación de traductores en España: un estudio empírico-descriptivo del trabajo colaborativo durante la primera etapa de formación en Traducción e Interpretación*. Unpublished PhD dissertation. Universidad de Granada.
Hurtado Albir, A. 1995. 'La didáctica de la traducción. Evolución y estado actual'. In: P. Fernández Nistal and J.M. Bravo Gozalo eds. *Perspectivas de la Traducción Inglés/Español: Tercer Curso Superior de Traducción*. Valladolid: Instituto de Ciencias de la Educación, pp. 49–74.
———. 2007. 'Competence-Based Curriculum Design for Training Translators', *The Interpreter and Translator Trainer*, vol. 1(2), pp. 163–188.
Jääskeläinen, R. 1989. 'Translation Assignment in Professional Versus Non-Professional Translation: A Think-Aloud Protocol Study'. In: C. Séguinot ed. *The Translation Process*. Toronto: H.G. Publications, pp. 87–98.
———. 1990. *Features of Successful Translation Processes: A Think-Aloud Protocol Study*. Unpublished Licenciate thesis. University of Joensuu, Savonlinna School of Translation Studies.
Jumpelt, R.J. 1961. 'On the Objectivization of Translation'. In: A. Chesterman ed. *Readings in Translation*. Helsinki: Oy Finn Lectura Ab.
Kelly, D. 1999. *Proyecto docente e investigador*. Universidad de Granada.
———. 2002. 'La competencia traductora: bases para el diseño curricular', *Puentes*, vol. 1, pp. 9–20.
———. 2005. *A Handbook for Translation Trainers: A Guide to Reflective Practice*. Manchester: St. Jerome.
Kiraly, D. 1995. *Pathways to Translation: Pedagogy and Process*. Kent, Ohio: Kent State University Press.
———. 2000. *A Social Constructivist Approach to Translator Education: Empowerment from Theory to Practice*. Manchester: St. Jerome.
———. 2013. 'Towards a View of Translator Competence as an Emergent Phenomenon: Thinking Outside the Box(es) in Translator Education'. In Kiraly, D. et al .(eds): *New Prospects and Perspectives for Educating Language Mediators*. Tubingen: Narr Verlag, pp. 197–224.
Konečný, D. 2008. *The Problem of Non-Literary L2 Translation*. Master's Diploma thesis. Masaryk University.
Krings, H.P. 1986. 'Translation Problems and Translation Strategies of Advanced German Learners of French'. In: J. House and S. Blum-Kulka eds. *Interlingual and Intercultural Communication*. Tubingen: Gunter Narr, pp. 263–275.
Kussmaul, P. 1995. *Training the Translator*. Amsterdam and Philadelphia: John Benjamins.
Levy, J. 1967. 'Translation as a Decision Process'. In: *To Honor Román Jakobson*. Vol II. The Hague: Mouton, pp. 1171–1182.
———. 1988. 'Translation as a Decision Process'. In: A. Chesterman ed. *Readings in Translation Theory*. Finland: Oy Finn Lectura Ab, pp. 37–52.
Lörscher, W. 1991. *Translation Performance, Translation Process, and Translation Strategies. A Psycholinguistic Investigation*. Tubingen: Gunter Narr.
———. 1991. 'Thinking-Aloud as a Method for Collecting Data on Translation Processes'. In: S. Tirkkonen-Condit ed. *Empirical Research in Translation and Intercultural Studies: Selected Papers of the TRANSIF Seminar*. Tubingen: Gunter Narr Verlag, pp. 67–77.
———. 1992. 'Investigating the Translation Process', *Meta*, vol. 37, pp. 426–429.

———. 1995. 'Process Oriented Approaches to Translation and the Development of Translation Competence'. In: A. Neubert, G. Shreve and. K. Gommlich eds. *Basic Issues in Translation Studies*. Kent, Ohio: Institute of Applied Linguistics, pp. 113–122.

Marais, K. 2014. *Translation Theory and Development Studies: A Complexity Theory Approach*. New York and London: Routledge.

Neubert, A. 2000. 'Competence in Language, in Languages, and in Translation'. In: C. Schaeffner and B. Adab eds. *Developing Translation Competence*. Amsterdam and Philadelphia: John Benjamins, pp. 3–18.

Orozco Jutorán, M. 2000. *Instrumentos de medida de la adquisición de la competencia traductora: construcción y validación*. Doctoral thesis. UAB.

PACTE 1998. 'Procesos de aprendizaje y evaluación en la adquisición de la competencia traductora', EST Congress, Granada, Spain. Granada: EST/Universidad de Granada.

———. 2000. 'Acquiring Translation Competence: Hypotheses and Methodological Problems of a Research Project'. In: A. Beeby, D. Ensinger and M. Presas eds. *Investigating Translation: Selected Papers from the Fourth International Congress on Translation, Barcelona, 1998*. Amsterdam and Philadelphia: John Benjamins, pp. 99–106.

———. 2002. 'Exploratory Tests in a Study of Translation Competence', *Conference Interpretation and Translation*, vol. 4(2), pp. 41–69.

———. 2003. 'Building a Translation Competence Model'. In: F. Alves ed. *Triangulating Translation: Perspectives in Process Oriented Research*. Amsterdam and Philadelphia: John Benjamins, pp. 43–66.

———. 2005. 'Investigating Translation Competence: Conceptual and Methodological Issues', *Meta*, vol. 50(2), pp. 609–618.

———. 2008. First Results of a Translation Competence Experiment: Knowledge of Translation and Efficacy of the Translation Process'. In: J. Kearns ed. *Translation and Interpreter Training: Issues, Methods, Debates*. London and New York: Continuum, pp. 104–26.

———. 2009. 'Results of the Validation of the PACTE Translation Competence Model: Acceptability and Decision Making', *Across Languages and Cultures*, vol. 10(2), pp. 207–230.

———. 2011. Results of the Validation of the PACTE Translation Competence Model: Translation Project and Dynamic Translation Index'. In: S. O'Brien ed. *Cognitive Explorations of Translation*. London and New York: Continuum Studies in Translation, pp. 30–53.

Pavlović, N. 2010. 'What Were They Thinking? Students' Decision Making in L1 and L2 Translation Processes', *Hermes, Journal of Language and Communication Studies*, vol. 44, pp. 63–87.

Pym, A. 2003. 'Redefining Translation Competence in an Electronic Age: In Defence of a Minimalist Approach', *META*, vol. 48(4), pp. 481–97.

Robinson, D. 1991. *The Translator's Turn*. Baltimore: Johns Hopkins University Press.

———. 1997. *Becoming a Translator: An Accelerated Course*. London: Routledge.

Séguinot, C. 1991. 'A Study of Student Translation Strategies'. In: S. Tirkkonen-Condit ed. *Empirical Research in Translation and Intercultural Studies*. Tubingen: Narr, pp. 79–88.

Snowden, D.J. and Boone, M.E. 2007. 'A Leader's Framework for Decision Making', *Harvard Business Review*, November 2007. Available at: http://www.mpiweb.org/CMS/uploadedFiles/Article%20for%20Marketing%20-%20Mary%20Boone.pdf [Accessed 30 November 2013].

Tirkkonen-Condit, S. 1992. 'The Interaction of World Knowledge and Linguistic Knowledge in the Process of Translation: A Think-aloud Protocol Study'. In: B. Lewandowska-Tomaszczyk and M. Thelen eds. *Translation and Meaning: Part 2*. Maastricht: Rijkshogeschool Maastricht, Faculty of Translation and Interpreting, pp. 433–440.

Toury, G. 1985. *In Search of a Theory of Literary Translation*. Tel Aviv: Porter Institute.

———. 1985. 'A Rationale for Descriptive Translation Studies'. In: T. Hermans ed. *The Manipulation of Literature: Studies in Literary Translation*. London: Croom Helm, pp. 16–41.
———. 1995. *Descriptive Translation Studies – and Beyond*. Amsterdam and Philadelphia: John Benjamins.
Valderrey Riñones, C. 2002. *Análisis descriptivo de la traducción jurídica (francés-español): aportes para su mayor sistematización*. Doctoral thesis. Universidad de Salamanca.
———. 2005. '¿Cómo ser un traductor jurídico competente? De la competencia temática'. In: M.E. García, A. González Rodríguez, C. Kunschak and P. Scarampi eds. *Actas de las IV Jornadas sobre la Formación y Profesión del Traductor e Intérprete Calidad y Traducción: Perspectivas Académicas y Profesionales*. Madrid: UEM.
Way, C. 2002. 'Traducción y derecho: iniciativas para desarrollar la colaboración interdisciplinar', *Puentes*, vol. 2, 15–26.
———. 2004. 'Making Theory Reality: An Example of Interdisciplinary Cooperation'. In: G. Androulakis ed. *Proceedings of "Translating in the 21st Century: Trends and Prospects"*. Aristotle University of Thessalonica, Greece, 27–30 September 2002. Thessalonica: Faculty of Arts AUTH, pp. 584–592.
———. 2006. 'Evaluación efectiva: el talón de Aquiles'. In: S. Bravo Utrera and R. García López eds. *Estudios de Traducción: Problemas y Perspectivas*. Spain: Universidad de Las Palmas de Gran Canaria, pp. 755–762.
———. 2008. 'Systematic Assessment of Translator Competence: In Search of Achilles' Heel'. In: J. Kearns ed. *Translator and Interpreter Training: Issues, Methods and Debates*. London: Continuum, pp. 88–103.
———. 2009. 'Bringing Professional Practices into Translation Classrooms'. In: I. Kemble ed. *The Changing Face of Translation*. Portsmouth: University of Portsmouth, pp. 131–142.
———. 2012. 'A Discourse Analysis Approach to Legal Translator Training: More Than Words', *International Journal of Law, Language and Discourse*, vol. 2.4, pp. 39–61.
Wilss, W. 1994. 'A Framework for Decision-Making in Translation', *Target*, vol. 6(2), pp. 131–150.
———. 1998. 'Decision Making in Translation'. In: M. Baker ed. *Routledge Encyclopedia of Translation Studies*. London and New York: Routledge, pp. 57–60.

PART II
LEGAL TRANSLATION IN PRACTICE

Chapter 9
EU Legislative Texts and Translation

Colin Robertson [1]

1. Introduction

The aim of this chapter is to provide information about the translation of European Union (EU) legislative texts.[2] The emphasis is mainly on the texts that are translated, but they are placed within a broader setting to reveal the precise legal and linguistic ambition of EU legislative texts, which has implications for choice of term and allocation of meaning. The voice is of a practitioner in legal-linguistic revision (lawyer-linguist) who has worked with EU legislative texts for many years, and there is an emphasis on legal and structural issues at the expense of more specifically language issues such as how to render particular words and sentences from language A to language B, C, or D. The reason is that such information is more widely available. Furthermore, if one is familiar with EU texts, their structure, styles and ambitions, as well as the tools for extracting and comparing documents, it becomes easier to address individual linguistic questions through comparative study of the many thousands of pages of EU acquis in each of the increasing number of EU languages. EU legislative texts are frequently hyper-complex and technical, and they aim at the highest levels of legal precision compatible with a multilingual and multicultural drafting environment shared between member states, which have diverse systems of law to be accommodated. The nodal point on which the EU arrangements turn is language and by extension drafting and translation, and EU legislative translation needs to be seen in that light. It is law-making for 27, and more, European states written in their languages. The translator does not usually think of her/himself as a drafter but with EU legislative texts it is translators who draft the language versions, from a source language, of legislative texts, which become legally operational and determining for the national legislative systems. Thus it is desirable from the outset to place the EU legislative translator, alongside the legislative drafter and the legal-linguistic reviser, as part of a combined multilingual EU legislative team.

From the point of view of discussing EU legislative translation, there are many issues to be addressed. On the one hand, there are all the standard issues and problems that routinely face the translator in terms of linguistic knowledge of source and target language, pitfalls of grammar and syntax, false friends and problems of terminology, turn of phrase, syntax and meaning. For EU legal texts, if one is familiar with the databases, such as EUR-Lex,[3] it is straightforward to access any language version of a published text on any subject and to search for individual terms and expressions in any language and to make comparisons between language versions simply by switching language code within the same site. On the other hand,

1 Formerly in the Council of the European Union. The views expressed are solely those of the author.
2 The reference date is January 2013 for the number of member states. Croatia became a member state in 2013 bringing the number to 28.
3 Available at: http://eur-lex.europa.eu/fr/index.htm [Accessed 27 November 2012].

EU legal texts are technical acts constructed in special ways and they are designed to achieve precise effects while at the same time fitting within the whole structure of EU law, its concepts, and the mass of other legal texts that go to form the whole system. Their aim is to achieve precise effects within the world of international relations, business and commerce. They use language and create concepts in ways that are adapted to the needs and context of the European Union and take care of its multilingual dimension. We are in the field of legal language, abounding with abstract legal concepts. Legislative texts constitute a genre, and within it is the sub-genre of legislative texts of the European Union. For the theoretician, we could suggest it is part of the field of applied linguistics (Cook, Davies and Elder 2004; Wiśniewski 2007; Richards and Schmidt 2011)[4] and legal linguistics (Galdia and Marcus 2009[5]; Mattila 2006[6]) where language is used for specific, special or specialized purposes (LSP) (Hoffmann, Kalverkämper, Wiegand and Ernst 1998; Swales 1992). English for specific purposes (ESP) (Hutchinson and Waters 1987) is a branch of the field relating to one language, but it is a language that is now used for a significant amount of drafting within the EU, including legislative texts. English has become a leading international language and is widely used across cultures round the world and that has resulted in a widening of the styles, syntax and terminology as speakers from different languages adapt it to their own experience. This also has impacts in the field of legal language, for example in EU legislative drafting by non-native speakers (Robertson 2010a).[7] Thus, in addition to the topic of translation in general, there is a large dimension of learning in order to cope with and adapt to the form of English used in the EU legislative texts. It is proposed to handle this by discussing issues by reference primarily to the English terms and, later on, looking at the parts of typical EU legislative acts from an English-language perspective, including some standard provisions laid down in drafting guidance.

Although we are in the field of the language of law (Bhatia 1987), EU law is not the same law as that of the national, or domestic, systems of law with which one is normally most familiar, with the traditional branches and structures such as we find in civil law systems or common law systems (David and Brierley 1985; Glenn 2010; Payne 1976). EU law, and its legal language, are different and have quite different aims. (Foster 2009; Berry and Hargreaves 2007; Glanert 2008). In particular, it is teleological and the purpose of a text can have an influence on meaning, as can be studied from the cases of the Court of Justice of the European Union. The underlying concept is that of change and a dynamic process. It can be seen as a new genre (Robertson 2012). The cultural reference points are different since they derive from all the member states and their languages, and the aims, objectives and methods are also different in subtle ways because the context is one of international relations and international co-operation and the application of economic theory. In addition, the EU texts are written by persons of all nationalities and they bring with them the expressions and choices of syntax of their mother-tongue language. For all these reasons, language itself is used in subtly different ways in EU legal texts. These are all factors that the EU legislative translator has to adjust to. The act of translation crosses boundaries of language, concepts and culture. In the EU there are currently

4 See also http://www.appliedlinguistics.org/ [Accessed 27 November 2012].

5 Reviewed at: http://www.bsos.umd.edu/gvpt/lpbr/subpages/reviews/mattila0607.htm [Accessed 27 November 2012].

6 Note also http://www.mastersportal.eu/students/browse/programme/14752/legal-linguistics.html [Accessed 27 November 2012].

7 See http://old.unifg.it/esp/abstracts_7.asp [Accessed 28 November 2012].

23 languages,[8] with more in the pipeline,[9] and the 27 member states[10] are each rich in history and traditions, so the cultural diversity goes wide. This makes EU language and translation relevant for a wider study of language as part of translation studies (Baker and Saldanha 2008; Baker 2009; Munday 2008).[11]

The EU is constructed on differences. They constitute the threads that are brought together and bound into the skein of texts that are multilingual and multicultural but form part of a single system of law-making. The EU treaties create the primary structure and lay down the foundation concepts and methods, including a framework for producing EU secondary-level legislative texts, whose function is to implement and flesh out the structures and approaches laid down in the treaties. The need for a high level of quality in all language versions of the texts has led to the recruitment of lawyer-linguists to check, revise and generally supervise the linguistic "finalisation" (French: "*mise au point*") of EU legislative texts in all languages (Šarčević and Robertson 2013; Robertson 2010b). Their work feeds into EU translation and constitutes a significant influence, because the revisers help fix the terminology, ensure legally accurate texts and participate in the production and constant updating of the guides and manuals on legislative drafting in the EU languages which are in turn followed by translators, who themselves do not require to have legal qualifications to work on the texts.

How does EU legislative translation fit within a general picture of legal translation? Clearly the starting point is with the specialized field of translation of legal texts, with everything that implies in terms of knowledge about the significance of abstract legal concepts, legal methods and the features and styles of legal language, having regard to source and target languages and their attached cultures. Thus we can examine different types of legal text and identify some specific features of EU legislative texts that need to be reproduced in translation. However, there is also the question of what one is translating for, the purpose of the text and the needs of the user. This question in an EU context is allied to the status of the source and translated texts and that in turn can be highlighted through a selection of diverging scenarios involving translation of a legislative type of text to find out what the EU legislative translator needs to achieve. The approach enables us to see the scenarios that most nearly represent that of EU legislative translation, or rather to affirm that there are different functional needs for such translation. It helps us to understand the level of linguistic precision to be attained and the context for handling EU translation problems, especially those related to terminology.

Translators work with texts and need to understand the environment, or context, in which those texts are created, as this determines many of their aspects, such as name, type, function, structure, terminology, syntax, and meaning. The EU context is created by international treaties agreed between European states. The EU treaties set the agenda, indicate the goals and generate the terms and concepts that are reproduced in secondary level texts which must be followed faithfully if consistency of meaning is to be maintained. The treaty texts are themselves the subject of translation and revision, but strictly they are not "*legislation*". They rather resemble "*contracts*" between states, as they contain the term "*agreed*", but not the legislative term "*enact*" or its EU equivalent "*adopts*", as we can see from the whole structure,

8 Bulgarian, Czech, Danish, Dutch, English, Estonian, Finnish, French, German, Greek, Hungarian, Irish, Italian, Latvian, Lithuanian, Maltese, Polish, Portuguese, Romanian, Slovak, Slovenian, Spanish, and Swedish.

9 Croatian from 2013.

10 Austria, Belgium, Bulgaria, Cyprus, the Czech Republic, Denmark, Estonia, Finland, France, Germany, Greece, Hungary, Ireland, Italy, Latvia, Lithuania, Luxembourg, Malta, the Netherlands, Poland, Portugal, Romania, Slovakia, Slovenia, Spain, Sweden, and the United Kingdom; Croatia accedes in 2013.

11 For EU-related information, see http://ec.europa.eu/dgs/translation/publications/studies/index_en.htm [Accessed 28 November 2012].

as well as the opening wording of the Treaty on European Union (TEU) in its published consolidated form.[12] It starts with a preamble listing the heads of state of the member states and then sets out a series of *recitals* stating the reasons and objectives of the treaty; the preamble concludes with the following words:

> *'HAVE DECIDED to establish a European Union and to this end have designated as their Plenipotentiaries: (List of plenipotentiaries not reproduced)*
>
> *WHO, having exchanged their full powers, found in good and due form, have agreed as follows:*
>
> *TITLE I COMMON PROVISIONS' . . . (followed by the articles)*

However, although they are in the form of contracts, the treaties are contracts to create *legislative acts* through institutions created and financed by the member states. These acts of the institutions are devolved acts and in that sense at a "*secondary*" level. They are the core EU legislative instruments and constitute the "bread and butter" of EU legislative translation and revision work. To understand the EU legislative translation tasks one must know these texts in their intimate details of construction and terminology.

EU law is multilingual. That is the reason why translators are employed. (Robertson 2013). The EU linguistic regime prescribes the production of texts in the EU languages. Article 55(1) of the *Treaty on European Union* (TEU) and Articles 342 and 358 of the *Treaty on the Functioning of the European Union* (TFEU) provide the foundation, together with *Regulation No 1* which has been updated with each accession to add more languages.[13] At the time of writing the number of languages is 23, but from 1 July 2013 this is to increase to 24 with the addition of Croatian as a result of the accession of Croatia.[14] Article 4 of Regulation No 1 says that '*Regulations and other documents of general application shall be drafted in the official languages[]*', and that is taken as applying to EU legislative texts generally. Thus, they are to be drafted in all EU languages and, pursuant to Article 5 of Regulation No 1, published in the Official Journal of the European Union.[15] The language arrangements applying to the Court of Justice of the European Union and cases brought before it are different.[16] (On legal translation at the Court, see the Court website at *http://curia.europa.eu/*; Mulders 2008; McAuliffe 2010).

Translators are employed by EU institutions and other agencies. In the course of their work they are called on to translate legal texts but the focus here is on the context of the creation of legislative texts by the EU institutions engaged in law-making. The EU institutions are listed in Article 13 TEU: European Parliament, European Council, Council, European Commission, Court of Justice of the European Union, European Central Bank, Court of Auditors. They all[17] employ translators, but only some employ lawyer-linguists. Details on each institution can be obtained via the general EU portal *http://europa.eu/* in all languages. The institutions mainly

12 Official Journal C 326 of 26 October 2012.

13 For the current consolidated version of Regulation No 1, see http://eur-lex.europa.eu/LexUriServ/LexUriServ.do?uri=CONSLEG:1958R0001:20070101:EN:PDF [Accessed 30 November 2012].

14 Available at: http://www.eubusiness.com/europe/croatia/accession-1 [Accessed 28 November 2012].

15 There are derogations for technical reasons for Irish and Maltese; see paragraph 7.2.4. of the Interinstitutional Style Guide, available at: http://publications.europa.eu/code/en/en-370204.htm [Accessed 30 November 2012].

16 Available at: http://curia.europa.eu/jcms/jcms/Jo2_10739/?hlText=languages [Accessed 30 November 2012].

17 But note that the European Council uses the services of the Council.

engaged in making legislative texts are first the European Commission,[18] whose task is to prepare proposals in all languages, second the Council of the European Union,[19] which was formerly the sole legislator, and remains so for certain acts, but now shares the task of co-legislator with, third, the European Parliament.[20] The Commission and Council are based in Brussels, but the European Parliament has premises in Brussels, Luxembourg, and Strasbourg. The European Central Bank, based in Frankfurt, also enacts legal acts by virtue of Article 132 TFEU and Article 34 of Protocol No 4 on the Statute of the European System of Central banks and of the European Central Bank.[21] Each of these institutions employs translators, but also lawyer-linguists who are *'specialized lawyers with high-level language abilities and are usually employed in the legal service of the respective institution'* (Šarčević and Robertson 2013).[22]

The lawyer-linguists play a key role in the preparation of EU legislative texts in all languages, but here the emphasis is placed primarily on the texts themselves, whether it be for translation or revision. EU translators do not require legal qualifications and recruitment takes place via open competitions organized by the European Personnel Office (EPSO) based in Brussels.[23] It also organises competitions for lawyer-linguists and information can be obtained from the same source. The recruitment requirements for lawyer-linguists for each institution, including the Court of Justice, are discussed in Šarčević and Robertson (2013). However, whether it be translator or lawyer-linguist, the skills required centre on language and translation abilities, from at least two foreign languages. Usually recruitment is for a limited number of posts and the candidates who achieve the highest scores are placed on a reserve list. Being included on a list does not confer a right to employment but renders one eligible for being recruited. A notice of competition sets out the conditions applying to the particular competition, the qualifications required, the tests to be sat and the choices of languages for them. It also indicates the grade for recruitment. The general conditions of employment, together with salary scales, etc., are laid down in the *Staff Regulations of Officials of the European Communities and Conditions of employment of other servants of the European Communities*,[24] which should be consulted to obtain an overall picture. The Staff Regulations are in all languages and constitute an EU legislative text. Technically, it is in a separate category from other EU legislative texts because it contains specialized concepts and terms related to EU Civil Service employment and it also follows certain styles of construction that place it in a subgenre of its own.

2. EU Language

Each EU official language derives from the relevant national language of the EU member state(s) having it as official language. At the time of accession, bringing with it a new language, the national language of the acceding state in its legal form is carried over into the EU context

18 Available at: http://ec.europa.eu/index_en.htm [Accessed 30 November 2012].
19 Available at: http://www.consilium.europa.eu/ [Accessed 30 November 2012].
20 Available at: http://ec.europa.eu/index_en.htm [Accessed 30 November 2012].
21 On the ECB, see http://www.ecb.int/home/html/index.en.html [Accessed 30 November 2012].
22 For a short film on Council lawyer linguist work, see http://www.youtube.com/watch?v=n3c80Xpords [Accessed 8 March 2013].
23 For details of competitions, consult the EPSO site: http://europa.eu/epso/ [Accessed 30 November 2012].
24 For the latest consolidated version, see http://ec.europa.eu/civil_service/docs/toc100_en.pdf [Accessed 30 November 2012].

and adapted to the EU's specialized needs.[25] The Publications Office[26] produces a style guide for each language in the form of an Inter-Institutional Style Guide.[27] This is an invaluable source of guidance for the EU translator because it provides a mine of information, in particular as regards historical information relating to past texts which is otherwise difficult of access. However, the task for a new language is to work from the existing EU languages and texts and construct new patterns, terminology, and templates in the new language. English language versions are frequently used for that purpose, but older ones derive mainly from prior French texts, and all the other languages need to be consulted to see the approaches followed by them as for interpretation by the courts meaning is drawn from all the language versions and not just the source drafting language. For that reason, the choices by translators come into comparison with the original drafting.

Over time the EU has developed its own specialized terminology and jargon[28] sometimes referred to as "*eurospeak*". Broadly, it is reflected in hybridity of speech terms and patterns from the different languages. It abounds in "*false friends*". Since the main working language in the EU was French, and it remains very strong, many of the false friends derive from French. That is especially the case for English, which is currently the language for drafting of up to 90 percent of EU texts. The phenomenon carries over into drafting EU legislative texts so that a translator may be translating into a third language (or back into French) a text written in English containing words and expressions borrowed from French and used with the wrong meanings in English. The Commission identified the problem and issued guidance in its pamphlet, *How to Write Clearly* (European Commission 2011). Among others, it listed, and explained, the following French terms frequently misused: *actuel, adéquat, assister à, attribuer, compléter, délai, élaborer, éventuel, prévu, important, matériel, opportunité.*[29] These terms can creep into draft legislative texts in English. The hawk-eyed lawyer-linguists seek to remove them from the source texts where possible, but where they remain, the problem for the translator into a third language is to identify whether the term is meant to have an original French meaning or an English meaning, and if so which one. A broad language knowledge, plus cultural EU awareness and thinking carefully what the piece of text is aiming to achieve are essential abilities. The peculiar features of EU English are discussed by Mollin (2006).

The EU has given rise to a huge number of concepts and expressions, with terms to match.[30] Terminology is a large topic for EU translation as new concepts keep coming along and need to be accommodated. Words like "*comitology*", "*gender mainstreaming*", or "*flexicurity*" come to mind. For the most part new terms derive from the member states and enter a domain that is the subject of EU legislation for the first time, or being extended. They may arrive first in one language, for example English as international language and drafting language, and then have to be translated into the other EU languages. That can pose problems. For example, "*gender mainstreaming*": one must first understand the concept aimed at and then figure out how to reproduce the idea in other languages. To find the solutions adopted, one can look up the IATE terminology database[31] or make a search in EUR-Lex,[32] by selecting English language, word-

25 For a discussion on EU legal translation in preparation for accession from a Croatian perspective, see Šarčević (2001).
26 Available at: http://publications.europa.eu/index_en.htm [Accessed 30 November 2012].
27 Available at: http://publications.europa.eu/interinstitutional_style_guide/index_en.htm [Accessed 30 November 2012].
28 See also http://news.bbc.co.uk/2/hi/europe/3595155.stm [Accessed 30 November 2012].
29 For a longer list, see http://www.realfrench.net/pdf/false.pdf [Accessed 30 November 2012].
30 For a long list of terms, see http://www.eubusiness.com/topics/eulaw/key-eu-terms [Accessed 30 November 2012].
31 Availableat:http://www.professional-translations.ro/DLFiles/SDL_Trados_2007_TranslatorsWorkbench.pdf [Accessed 30 November 2012].
32 Available at: http://eur-lex.europa.eu/fr/index.htm [Accessed 30 November 2012].

searching under the relevant words combined with another term such as *"question"* (because it has been used in questions by members of the European Parliament) to obtain "hits", locating the places where the term is used and switching language code to see what was said in the same place in the text. Doing that for Spanish gives: *'Integración de la perspectiva de género'*. While the expression does not take the same form, it has become a term equivalent. If the terms are embedded in legislative acts, they become legislative also and are the starting point for judicial interpretation and determining effects and meaning. It then becomes important to use the same matching terms wherever possible in the multilingual EU legislation. The translator's freedom of choice in varying the target language terms according to personal preference becomes narrowed down. The problem is to know how far terms have become established in this way and how much latitude remains for different approaches. There is no simple answer. Some terms, like the names of legal acts, EU bodies and key concepts have become fixed, whereas other terms more closely connected to general language allow of variation.

EU legislative texts are constructed in particular ways, derived originally from national, notably French, models and adapted to EU needs. Efforts are made at standardization across all languages where possible. This is reflected in terminology, syntax, punctuation and orthographic details reproduced across all languages such as using commas in place of full-stops (in English) for fractions of numbers such as "5,34", or a space in place of a comma (in English) to indicate thousands and millions (for example, "53 400 000"). In this way, all the language versions follow the same standardized approach and that facilitates the work of the readers and users and cross-cultural communication. Placing all this in a multilingual and multicultural context leads to a certain hybridity and the construction of a new genre. EU language, while deriving from civil law roots is not entirely civil law in style, and when drafted in English as a source language, is certainly not common law in style (Robertson 2012). The jump from national to EU context is not innocuous. Words change context and hence meaning in subtle ways. The meaning of terms is created by context, definitions of them, and through a network of interlinking texts that cross-refer inter-textually with each other. EU concepts are created in one language and then represented in 23 languages in parallel. Thus the concept of EU *"regulation"* has a matching word for it in each language as can be seen from a EUR-Lex search.

The "correct" term must be used in translation where it is technical; there is no choice, and so it is for a vast list of EU concepts. This tends to make EU translation mechanistic but also facilitates computerization. The EU institutions have taken a lead in developing translation tools and software and making them widely available. The Commission DG Translation website contains a mass of information for every EU language.[33] The use of SDL Translator's Workbench[34] is ubiquitous and forms part of a range of tools that are used routinely by EU translators that include SDT tools, as well as terminology tools such as Eurodicautom, Multiterm, EC Systran, and Euramis (Lavigne 2001). Of the terminology databases IATE has become perhaps the most significant. It exists in two forms, one for inside use and another made available to the public via internet.[35] Words and expressions once established become fixed as standardized EU term equivalents and are repeated throughout subsequent texts. This is facilitated by the computer tools used. The phenomenon of standardization extends to whole phrases, sentences and paragraphs of equivalent texts in each language. When looked at it in this way, EU text construction starts to resemble *"lego-type"* construction through the

33 Available at: http://ec.europa.eu/dgs/translation/index_en.htm [Accessed 30 November 2012].

34 Available at: http://www.professional-translations.ro/DLFiles/SDL_Trados_2007_TranslatorsWorkbench.pdf [Accessed 30 November 2012].

35 Available at: http://iate.europa.eu/iatediff/SearchByQueryLoad.do;jsessionid=9ea7991930d68674b42743ef4738a516e9c9bec6f3a1.e38KbN4MchyMb40SbxyRaN0Lc3z0?method=load [Accessed 30 November 2012].

use of standardized blocks of text, using the translation memory programmes. The role of translator shifts to that of text editor and reviser. English language translators in institutions have found themselves adapting to the high degree of drafting in English by providing internal text editing for non-native speakers. The lawyer-linguists are also engaged in the task of text editing, but they have the task of checking and adapting the legal aspects of the texts too.

EU legislative texts are replete with standard expressions and formulations. They are established in one language, generally French for the legal ones in the treaties, and translated and aligned in the other languages. The legislative acts are constructed in particular ways, using standard formulae covering the different parts of the structure of the act: titles, citations, recitals, enacting provisions (articles), and annexes. The way that EU secondary legislative acts are to be constructed has been laid down in guidance. The main guidance is in the *Interinstitutional Agreement of 22 December 1998 On Common Guidelines for the Quality of Drafting of Community Legislation.*[36] This is backed up by the *Joint Practical Guide.*[37] These are in the EU languages. They are aimed at drafters, but should be familiar also to EU legislative translators and revisers. They contain broad and general guidance. For specific detailed textual guidance on what wording to insert one looks to the Council Manual of Precedents which sets out the types of EU legislative acts, their forms and a range of detailed points relating to their construction and wording. The Manual exists in each language and the approaches followed by that language are set out in the relevant language version. A recent version of the Manual has been placed online.[38] It is not the latest version used internally as the guidance is continuously updated but it gives extensive information. The Commission also has guidance available online, for example *Legislative Drafting. A Commission Manual*[39] and the *English Style Guide,*[40] which is a handbook for authors and translators in the European Commission (see also Robinson (2008) on EU legislative drafting and Robertson (2010a)). Inspiration for the solution of new problems is drawn from national and international law-drafting practice, adapted to the specific EU needs and context, to create models which are reviewed and reproduced in all languages and subsequently inserted into the Manual as a source of reference for the future. New terms are also inserted into the terminology databases, translator memory, and so on. These standard terms and formulae perhaps reduce variety over time, but they greatly enhance legal certainty and facilitate a shared common understanding as to effects across languages. They are a tool for precision as they are each constructed with special care.

One question that might be asked, especially for an enquirer fresh from translation college, concerns the translation methods and theories followed. To such a question the answer proposed here is simply that the EU context is so innovative that it would be unwise to allow oneself to become dominated by ideas of theory and the question is not addressed here. In EU legislative translation, theory is the daughter of practice. If we manage to identify tasks, contexts and needs, the implications for theory can be left to emerge by themselves. Of course, the approaches do fit within patterns identified and described within Translation Studies, and knowledge of the alternative strategies possible do indeed help solve problems, but the viewpoint proposed here is simply that EU translation is a pragmatic activity and the needs of the moment and the text in hand tend to impose the type of solution to be adopted. The EU environment is one of innovation, and that includes language. One must be free to think

36 Available at: http://eur-lex.europa.eu/LexUriServ/LexUriServ.do?uri=CELEX:31999Y0317(01].:EN:HTML [Accessed 30 November 2012].
37 Available at: http://eur-lex.europa.eu/en/techleg/index.htm [Accessed 30 November 2012].
38 Available at: http://ec.europa.eu/translation/documents/council/manual_precedents_acts_en.pdf. [Accessed 30 November 2012].
39 Available at: http://ec.europa.eu/governance/better_regulation/documents/legis_draft_comm_en.pdf [Accessed 30 November 2012].
40 http://ec.europa.eu/translation/english/guidelines/documents/styleguide_english_dgt_en.pdf.

the previously unthought and to break new ground; that is the essence of EU work and it extends to translation. In the debate on "elegance" and "faithfulness" the priority is fidelity, as language versions of texts must align in their legal effects and concepts must match across languages. But fidelity does not exclude elegance; the translator has sometimes an advantage over the drafters who work in committees on a source text. The biggest single problem for the new EU language and the new EU translator is simply adapting to the vast range of specialized EU terminology. But there are plenty of colleagues willing and able to help.

3. Legislative Translation: Three Scenarios

EU legislative texts are legal texts, but what does it mean, in particular, to say that they are "legal"? EU texts are also economic, agricultural, customs-union, competition, environmental, because they treat of subjects in those domains. What do we mean by "law", and more particularly what is "EU law"? As noted earlier, it is not the same as the law we find in the domestic systems of law of the member states. These questions are fundamental because law serves a purpose and it functions, inter alia, through language and legal texts. One needs to be clear about the nature of law, in particular EU law, the purpose of legal texts in general, and EU legislative acts in particular, as well as the individual text worked on. There are, of course different types, or genres, of legal text and sub-genres (Bhatia 1987). Take for example a will written by a person to pass on property after death. Or a commercial contract between two companies for the supply of goods. Or again, a judgment in a court case between two parties. These are all legal texts, but we do not think of them as being "legislative" or as legislation. For such texts we think of a parliament, a ruler, a body promulgating decrees or laws that set down commands, rules or norms to prescribe what is, or is not, to be done by people with respect to the matter dealt with in the text. The prescriptions are backed up by sanctions in the event of non-compliance and it is that fact which gives legislative texts their particular character.

In general, when thinking about law-making, it is in a national state context where a legislature in a country enacts a law in accordance with a legislative procedure. Unless you come from a multilingual country, it would not occur to you that there is any place for translation in such a set of arrangements. Thus, the idea of there being a role for translation within the legislative process is not evident for everyone. The European Union, however, is not a country. It is not a sovereign state but an international organization created by European states to assist them in the conduct of their activities together. Does it have a "legislature"? Does it have "laws"? Does it have "legislation"? These questions can legitimately be asked, but the practical answer is that the EU makes texts which have such ambition and uses the terminology of legislation to discuss them. Thus Article 289 TFEU contains the expressions *'ordinary legislative procedure'* in paragraph 1 and *'legislative acts'* in paragraph 4. In paragraph 2, there is specific linking to particular types of act, namely *'regulation, directive or decision'* and the mention that the adoption of these acts under certain circumstances is to constitute a *'special legislative procedure'*. It is not proposed to enter into a discussion of EU legislative procedures here, other than to say that EU translators and lawyer-linguists form part of the process for generating and revising (Robertson 2010b) legislative acts in the EU languages. Much modern EU legislation is authored by the European Parliament and Council jointly, through co-decision (Maury 2007; Guggeis and Robinson 2012), which constitutes the *'ordinary legislative procedure'* as opposed to the *'special legislative procedure'* of Article 289(2). From the point of view legal-linguistic revision and the alignment of the language versions, the process contains a degree of 'co-drafting' and 'co-revision' (Gallas 1999). It is not bi-jural legislation as practised in Canada,[41] but it goes in that direction. The roles of drafter, translator and reviser blur and shift towards a more team-oriented approach. What then is the nature of the task facing the EU legislative drafter, translator and reviser? To give an idea of the context and degree of precision aimed at, we can imagine three scenarios involving translation of a legislative, or equivalent, text.

Scenario one: a court case involves a foreign element and the court orders the translation of a foreign law. It wants to know what the law says, what the words mean and what are the legal effects. An official translation is made; some concepts are unknown to the court and the translator (let us say) finds it useful to insert footnotes and comments, with source-language terms alongside descriptive words in brackets so as to convey the full meaning. The text is used only for this information purpose and goes no further.

Scenario two: an international agreement is written in one language. Only that version is "authentic" and may be used for interpretation by a court. However, a translation is needed in other languages for official purposes of domestic law as it is intended to adopt the agreement and implement it in national law. The translator has an eye on the source culture and the target culture, which are different; comments and footnotes are not possible.[42]

Scenario three: a law is drafted in language A and translated into language B. The legal system is officially bilingual and language version B has the same status as language version A as an authentic text to be interpreted on its own. Both texts form part of the same legal system. Either text can be used interchangeably. The terms in each text need to match up with each other and the references in each version are to the same "objects" and concepts. One system expressed in two languages.

With EU legislative translation we are within the scope of *scenario three*, except that there are 23/24 language versions. In that respect the EU system is like a single national system of law and each language expresses the same EU message (Gallas 1999). We see this by comparing the language versions of any EU legislative text. Nonetheless, the EU situation is more complicated, because there is not just a dimension resembling *scenario three* but also a dimension resembling *scenario two* built into the same texts, insofar as the EU text is created so as to function simultaneously within all the member state national legal systems. EU law has no meaning or function outside that purpose. We see this duality most clearly with EU directives where an EU text is expressly created for the purpose of being a source text for the creation, as necessary, of national law. However, unlike *scenario two*, it is the same body, or author, that creates each language version and the EU texts are legally tied together as individual strands of a single comprehensive multilingual text, which brings us back to *scenario three*. To illustrate the approach, here is a short example from the multilingual signature page[43] to the Final Act to the Treaty of Lisbon:

41 Available at: http://canada.justice.gc.ca/eng/dept-min/pub/hfl-hlf/b1-f1/bf1g.html [Accesed 30 November 2012].

42 An example of this scenario is with Hague Conventions on Private International Law (Available at: http://www.hcch.net/index_en.php] [Accessed 30 November 2012]), with conventions in two languages, English and French.

43 Available at: http://eur-lex.europa.eu/LexUriServ/LexUriServ.do?uri=OJ:C:2007:306:0231:0271:EN:PDF [at Page 238] [Accessed 5 December 2012].

Съставено в Лисабон на тринадесети декември две хиляди и седма година.
Hecho en Lisboa, el trece de diciembre de dos mil siete.
V Lisabonu dne třináctého prosince dva tisíce sedm.
Udfærdiget i Lissabon den trettende december to tusind og syv.
Geschehen zu Lissabon am dreizehnten Dezember zweitausendsieben.
Kahe tuhande seitsmenda aasta detsembrikuu kolmeteistkümnendal päeval Lissabonis.
Έγινε στη Λισσαβώνα, στις δέκα τρεις Δεκεμβρίου δύο χιλιάδες επτά.
Done at Lisbon on the thirteenth day of December in the year two thousand and seven.
Fait à Lisbonne, le treize décembre deux mille sept.
Arna dhéanamh i Liospóin, an tríú lá déag de Nollaig sa bhliain dhá mhíle a seacht.
Fatto a Lisbona, addì tredici dicembre duemilasette.
Lisabonā, divtūkstoš septītā gada trīspadsmitajā decembrī.
Priimta Lisabonoje du tūkstančiai septintųjų metų gruodžio tryliktą dieną.
Kelt Lisszabonban, a kétezer-hetedik év december tizenharmadik napján.
Magħmul f'Lisbona, fit-tlettax-il jum ta' Diċembru tas-sena elfejn u sebgħa.
Gedaan te Lissabon, de dertiende december tweeduizend zeven.
Sporządzono w Lizbonie dnia trzynastego grudnia roku dwa tysiące siódmego.
Feito em Lisboa, em treze de Dezembro de dois mil e sete.
Întocmit la Lisabona la treisprezece decembrie două mii șapte.
V Lisabone dňa trinásteho decembra dvetisícsedem.
V Lizboni, dne trinajstega decembra leta dva tisoč sedem.
Tehty Lissabonissa kolmantenatoista päivänä joulukuuta vuonna kaksituhattaseitsemän.
Som skedde i Lissabon den trettonde december tjugohundrasju.

The EU directive speaks in two directions: "internally" as EU law and "externally" towards the national systems. The drafters, translators and revisers sit at the point of discomfort between these two directions.

Sometimes an EU legislative act is drafted in language A, sometimes in language B, but perhaps also in language C or D.[44] It is a matter of convenience and practicality which language is chosen as source, and the choice can switch during the different gestation stages of a text. The draft serves as a model to be reproduced and aligned on through translation and revision by all other EU languages. The EU legislative text is produced in all EU languages in parallel so that all language versions are ready for adoption and signature at the same time. They are written, studied and worked on by experts, officials and politicians from all 27 member states (28 including Croatia), as well as the EU administrative, drafting, legal, translation and revision staff. Text amendments may be proposed in any EU language. The final checking and review of all language versions by lawyer-linguists, working with subject-matter experts, ensures as far as possible an overall consistency and equivalence in message for all languages.

4. EU Legislative Texts

It is difficult in a short chapter to dwell on all the terminology and concepts that have been generated over the years in each of the domains of policy in which the EU has been active, and

44 English, French, and German principally.

there is also the internal edifice comprising the EU institutions, the procedures they follow and the relationships with the member states, not to mention the array of legal concepts that have been developed over the years in EU law, which can all be accessed via the EU portal http://europa.eu/. If one knows where to look, the terms can be researched, examined and compared. More complicated is the work of term creation, but it is not discussed here (see Cabré 1998). However, the most difficult aspect is to be able to form an understanding of the nature of the EU legislative acts, what each seeks to do, how they are structured and what wording must be used in their construction. This takes us into legislative drafting, but if one has an understanding it becomes much easier to find one's way around the texts and to see how the diverse elements fit together to create the whole "picture" of the act. This is important for translation, and especially for revision where the legal-linguistic reviser analyzes the act from different perspectives such as law, language, policy and the intended action (Robertson 2010b) to ensure that it "functions" on each level. The translator of the target language starts where the drafter leaves off, but the EU translator and reviser as participants in the multilingual legal system are also checking the source language text for possible errors, inconsistencies or problems that may arise for "their" own language. Familiarity with the texts and their construction and styles is essential for them too.

If we think in terms of the authors of EU legislative texts, we need to address three broad categories of text: first, those that are made between the member states as international agreements which carry the title "treaty" and found EU law;[45] second, the acts authored by the institutions created by the treaties some of which are specifically labelled as *"legislative"*, to which could be added special ad hoc categories such as where the representatives of the governments of the member states meet within the Council to adopt an act; third, there are international agreements entered into by the EU, with or without the participation of the member states as joint signatories, with third countries. This last category again is more properly seen in terms of international contracts. We will concentrate on the second category and restrict attention to the texts designated as "legislative", and within that category we will narrow down essentially to one type, the regulation, but with a few words in particular on directives.

When it comes to deciding which act to use and how to construct it in each language through drafting or translation, internal guidance exists and there are templates for each type of text. Examples of published acts can be readily identified from a search of the EUR-Lex database on-line and studied for their details. Most of this guidance is internal to the institutions. However, some has been made publically available on-line, for example the Commission Manual on Legislative Drafting[46] (European Commission Manual 1997) and the Council Manual of Precedents (Council Manual 2010/2011). In both cases these are *not* the most recent editions, but they nonetheless provide a picture of the EU legislative acts and how they are constructed. It is proposed now to take a look at some of the acts referred to in the Council Manual, but on the basis that the information is primarily *historical* and does not necessarily reflect the latest state of the art. Indeed, with time the divergences from current practice are likely to increase. The Council Manual was originally drafted in French and is revised in French as source language. The English version referred to here is a translation. Thus one can see that when EU legislative texts are drafted in English as source language, the starting point is often not "English English" but "French English", or if you like "EU English".

45 Available at: http://eur-lex.europa.eu/en/treaties/index.htm [Accessed 3 December 2012].

46 Available at: http://ec.europa.eu/governance/better_regulation/documents/legis_draft_comm_en.pdf [Accessed 3 December 2012].

The online text of the Council Manual is an English 2011version of a French 2010 edition; hence the date reference to 2010/2011.[47]

In the Foreword the Manual states:

> *The aim of this manual is to harmonise the finalisation of texts of final legal acts drawn up in the official languages of the institutions of the European Union as well as to provide those responsible for drafting acts or proposals for acts with a guide to Council practice.*
>
> *The types of legal act provided for in the Treaties are relatively few in number. The principles of those acts are defined in Articles 288 to 299 of the Treaty on the Functioning of the European Union (TFEU). The formal structure of regulations, directives and decisions is governed by Annex VI to the Council's Rules of Procedure (OJ L 325, 11.12.2009, p. 36). No particular form is prescribed by those texts for recommendations or opinions.*

The Manual is divided into two parts. Part 1 'sets out all the types of acts concerned in schematic form, showing the usual methods of presentation and the most common formal provisions.' Part II 'contains general information, in particular, on the structure of acts and how they should be drafted.' The Manual exists in all the EU languages. A Croatian version is in the course of preparation. Part 1 starts by making a distinction between legislative acts and non-legislative acts. The former are acts covered by Article 289 TFEU as being adopted in accordance with the 'ordinary legislative procedure' or the 'special legislative procedure', with the former involving 'co-decision' by the European Parliament and the Council, in accordance with Article 294 TFEU and the latter being acts adopted by one institution 'with the participation' of the other. As to which procedure is relevant, the answer is found each time in the wording of the treaty and it is not proposed to dwell on the question.

Three types of act are listed in Part 1 of the Manual under both types of legislative procedure: *regulations, directives and decisions*. These are three of the acts listed in Article 288 TFEU which states:

> *To exercise the Union's competences, the institutions shall adopt regulations, directives, decisions, recommendations and opinions.*
>
> *A regulation shall have general application. It shall be binding in its entirety and directly applicable in all Member States.*
>
> *A directive shall be binding, as to the result to be achieved, upon each Member State to which it is addressed, but shall leave to the national authorities the choice of form and methods.*
>
> *A decision shall be binding in its entirety. A decision which specifies those to whom it is addressed shall be binding only on them.*
>
> *Recommendations and opinions shall have no binding force.*

There is an overlap between "legislative acts" in the strict sense and "non-legislative" acts because one finds the same three types of act listed also as "non-legislative" in the Manual; the difference essentially being one of procedure. As well as those acts, the non-legislative

47 The first edition was drawn-up by former Council lawyer-linguist Gérard Losson.

acts include *"recommendations"*. However, other types of act are listed: acts adopted by the European Council, decisions of the Representatives of the Governments of the Member States, and decisions of the Council and the Representatives of the Governments of the Member States. We will concentrate on the three ordinary-legislative-procedure acts, and of those, the regulation.

Regulations, directives and decisions are all subject to the Interinstitutional Agreement of 22 December 1998 on common guidelines for the quality of drafting of Community legislation (Interinstitutional Agreement 1998).[48] Article 7 states: 'All Community acts of general application shall be drafted according to a standard structure (title – preamble – enacting terms – annexes, where necessary).' The first part of the text is the title and on this Article 8 of the Interinstitutional Agreement states:

> *The title of an act shall give as succinct and full an indication as possible of the subject matter which does not mislead the reader as to the content of the enacting terms. Where appropriate, the full title of the act may be followed by a short title.*

If we turn to the Manual, we find that there is a standard formula to be inserted, according to the treaty base which is indicated by acronyms: '*REGULATION (EU) [(EU, EURATOM)] No . . . /2010 OF THE EUROPEAN PARLIAMENT AND OF THE COUNCIL of . . . (date)*' and an open part which says what the act is about and is adapted according to the subject matter of the text. (See the Official Journal for actual examples.)

After the title we find the name(s) of the authors; in the above example it is that of the two legislative institutions, but for other texts we may find another institution named, most notably the Commission which itself produces a large number of EU legal acts. There is a matching signature by an authorized representative at the end of the text, again according to a standard formula.

The third standard item in the EU legislative text comprises the "citations". Article 9 of the Interinstitutional Agreement says that: '*The purpose of the citations is to set out the legal basis of the act and the main steps in the procedure leading to its adoption.* The citations are important legally as they indicate the devolved power to make the act. From a linguistic point of view, one should note the absence of a verb. The citations do not "do anything"; they merely record what "*is*". Here are two examples: '*Having regard to the Treaty on the Functioning of the European Union, and in particular Article(s) . . . thereof,* and '*Having regard to the proposal from the European Commission*'.

The citations form part of the "preamble" to an act, the introductory part. The other part of the preamble is formed by "recitals". Again the Interinstitutional Agreement gives guidance[49] in Article 10:

> *The purpose of the recitals is to set out concise reasons for the chief provisions of the enacting terms, without reproducing or paraphrasing them. They shall not contain normative provisions or political exhortations.*

The recitals are numbered (Article 11). They can be long, stretching to dozens or even a hundred numbered recitals according to the size of the act. The main linguistic feature of them is to avoid the use in English of the verb "shall" as a verb of obligation. The obligations are set out in the enacting provisions and the function of the recitals is to set out background, the

48 On drafting, see also the Interinstitutional Agreement on Better Law-Making. Available at: http://europa.eu/legislation_summaries/institutional_affairs/decisionmaking_process/l10116_en.htm [Accessed 6 December 2012].

49 See also the Joint Practical Guide, which explains the Interinstitutional Agreement.

purposes of the text and the main provisions. In that respect verbs linked to "fact" are normal, together with conditional verbs such as "ought", "should", "must". Where there is reported speech of a text using *"shall"*, this is usually rendered as *"is to"* or *"are to"*. Sometimes one finds the text of articles reproduced as recitals with just the verb *'shall'* changed to its recitals equivalent *"should"*. The reason is that the articles are usually drafted first and the recitals afterwards.[50] The standard-wording part of the recitals is minimal. With respect to regulations, the Manual simply indicates:

> *Whereas:*
>
> *(1) [Begin with a capital letter]. . . .*
>
> *(2) [Begin with a capital letter]. . . .*
>
> *() [Begin with a capital letter]. . . .,*

The legislative "enacting formula" is short. In the case of regulations: *'HAVE ADOPTED THIS REGULATION:'*. It is followed by the enacting provisions which comprise articles. These may be grouped into higher levels of generality, as parts, chapters, titles, sections and also into lower subdivisions as paragraphs, points, indents. This is all explained in the Manual in Part 2. The Interinstitutional Agreement, in Article 12 observes:

> *The enacting terms of a binding act shall not include provisions of a non-normative nature, such as wishes or political declarations, or those which repeat or paraphrase passages or articles from the Treaties or those which restate legal provisions already in force. Acts shall not include provisions which enunciate the content of other articles or repeat the title of the act.*

This information, and the guidance following is primarily aimed at drafters and we need not dwell on it further as it is quite technical. Once again the template in the Manual is very brief, being simply an opening: *'Article 1'*. The closing formula for the regulation is fairly standard. It deals with when the act comes into force and who is bound. Thus we find the following formulae:

> *This Regulation shall enter into force on . . .*
>
> *[This Regulation shall enter into force on the (. . .) day (following that) of its publication in the Official Journal of the European Union.]*
>
> *[It shall apply (from . . .) (until . . .)]*
>
> *[It shall expire on . . .]*
>
> *This Regulation shall be binding in its entirety and directly applicable in all Member States.*

50 For more on citations and recitals see the Interinstitutional Style Guide. Available at: http://publications.europa.eu/code/en/en-120200.htm [accessed 3 December 2012].

> *[This Regulation shall be binding in its entirety and directly applicable in the Member States in accordance with the Treaties.]*

Normally a regulation binds everyone, but the wording *'in accordance with the Treaties'* in the last sentence signals that there are special provisions and that there is a departure from the standard rule. The reason for the departure is generally explained in the recitals, often towards the end. The important point here is that often what seems a fairly "innocent" little expression worded in a general way is connected to very major significance. In this case, it is that certain Member States are completely excluded from the scope of the act. The recent EU Regulation on Succession comes to mind as the act does not apply to Denmark, Ireland or the UK.[51] This is explained in Recital (83) of the Regulation, but is not stated explicitly in the articles. Subtle details, such as we have here, explain why it is necessary to pay attention to every nuance and word; there are legal implications.

The last part of the legislative act is the annex. Not all acts have an annex. Technically it is an extension of an article; one could have an article full of technical details running to many pages, but it is simpler to assign the technical information to a place at the end. However, each annex must be referred to in an article so as to make it part of the act, through being incorporated in the "single sentence" which is the concept that underlies the construction of an EU legislative act and influences punctuation, another whole topic in itself. The Interinstitutional Guidelines (Article 22) state:

> *Technical aspects of the act shall be contained in the annexes, to which individual reference shall be made in the enacting terms of the act and which shall not embody any new right or obligation not set forth in the enacting terms. Annexes shall be drawn up in accordance with a standardised format.*

In practice the structure of annexes is variable, so long as each is consistent and coherent. Their purpose is technical and they frequently contain terminology of the utmost degree of specialization and technicality. The templates in the Council Manual with respect to directives and decisions are broadly similar to those for regulations and there is no need to repeat them. However, when one enters into the details, there are differences.

This brings us to Part 2 of the Manual, which starts by explaining the changes brought about by the Treaty of Lisbon and then proceeds to set out detailed remarks on each part of the legislative act which supplements Part 1. It explains how titles are constructed (Council Manual: 58) and the system for numbering acts which forms part of the title, as well as how to describe the subject-matter and references to other acts in the title. This is technical information but it must be "correct" and the translator must follow with absolute fidelity, using the standard forms where laid down verbatim. Issues for citations and recitals are discussed, and of these the ways in which to cite other acts is prominent; one needs to be able to know exactly which act and which part of it is being referred to. The form of citations is discussed (Manual: 77), as well as punctuation (here in English) and footnoting. Similarly as regards recitals (Manual: 79), with explanations about their contents, purpose, form, punctuation, etc.; information that is essential for drafting. There is similarly extensive treatment with respect to the enacting terms (Manual: 83), covering general issues. Thus:

The enacting terms form the legislative part of the act. This means that:

51 Regulation (EU). No 650/2012 of the European Parliament and of the Council of 4 July 2012 on jurisdiction, applicable law, recognition and enforcement of decisions and acceptance and enforcement of authentic instruments in matters of succession and on the creation of a European Certificate of Succession *O J L 201, 27.7.2012, p. 107.*

– the enacting terms of a binding act should not contain provisions of a non normative nature, such as wishes or political declarations, those which repeat or paraphrase passages or articles from the Treaties or those which restate legal provisions already in force,

– in English, the auxiliary "shall" is generally used in enacting terms. However, in resolutions and, generally speaking, in the annexes to all acts, the "will" or "must" form is to be preferred to the "shall" form.

Furthermore:

The enacting terms are, as far as possible, drafted in accordance with a standard structure:
– subject matter and scope,
– definitions,
– rights and obligations,
– provisions on the delegation of powers to the Commission or provisions conferring implementing powers,
– procedural provisions, including:
(i) procedures concerning delegated acts
(ii) procedures concerning implementing acts,
– implementing measures,
– transitional and final provisions.
They are divided into articles, and, depending on their length and complexity, into titles, chapters and sections. Articles may (each) have a title showing their purpose and chapters and sections should (each) have such a title. (Manual: 83)

Certain words should be avoided, such as "*above-mentioned*" or "*set out below*". The guidance also covers annexes, footnoting, how to refer to the Official Journal and sets out a series of standard paragraphs that are relevant in different circumstances. Of these, the provisions relating to directives are noteworthy. The purpose of a directive is to bring about changes in national law. The Manual (98) says:

Transposition of directives

The transposition of a directive by Member States comprises the adoption, publication and entry into force of the provisions of national law.

(a) Some directives fix separate dates for adoption and publication, on the one hand, and application, on the other;

(b) Most directives simply give one overall date by which Member States are to comply with their provisions (thus leaving Member States to determine the course to be taken by the various stages of transposition).

Rather than a final date (introduced by wording such as "at the latest on", "by" or "before", all of which offer some flexibility as regards timing) sometimes a single, fixed date is used; this obliges all Member States to apply the directive's provisions from the same date.

The forms listed above should be examined in each case to ascertain which is the most appropriate.

There are different forms of wording possible for the transposition of directives: Here is one example proposed:

1. Article . . .

1. Member States shall bring into force the laws, regulations, and administrative provisions necessary (take the necessary measures) to comply with this Directive by . . . (with effect from . . .) (within a period of . . . as from the date of its entry into force (adoption)). They shall immediately inform the Commission thereof.

When Member States adopt those measures, they shall contain a reference to this Directive or shall be accompanied by such reference on the occasion of their official publication. The methods of making such reference shall be laid down by Member States.

2. Member States shall communicate to the Commission the text of the (main) measures of national law, which they adopt in the field covered by this Directive.

(The Commission shall inform the other Member States thereof.)

Only the English versions of the wording have been given here and we should remind ourselves that these texts are translations from French. The same guidance and equivalent textual provisions exist for each EU language and are explained in the Manual for each language. There is a vast amount more in the Manual of Precedents, but the foregoing is sufficient to provide a flavour of the EU legislative environment from a drafting point of view. It is one of extreme precision, extreme detail and minute attention to the slightest nuances and variation. The translator may not think it necessary to know how a source text has been written and constructed, but with EU legislative texts it is different, for each language expresses the single EU message and there is an absolute need for alignment. The translator is obliged to follow the exact wording that has been prescribed in the Manual. The languages function "horizontally", like an army marching in step. It is the work of the lawyer-linguist to check this is achieved but equally it is the work of the EU legislative translator on whom the legal-linguistic revisers rely. The keyword is teamwork and this extends to all the participants in the EU legislative process, wherever situated. The clients for the texts are throughout Europe and the wider world.

5. Conclusion

This chapter has sought to give a flavour of EU legislative translation. The notion of "legislative" text is one that is probably best regarded as in a state of evolution. The Treaty of Lisbon introduced changes and as can be glimpsed from the description of legislative and non-legislative texts and the range of variants of the latter, which seem to overlap with the former, there is still work in hand to review and restructure the internal arrangements. The EU system, curiously enough, bears a certain resemblance to the common law approach to the extent that frequently it is a case of a problem arising, a pragmatic solution being found, and only later is it possible to come back and reorganize the internal arrangements. The process requires time, and it also requires the consent of the member states, implying careful intercultural negotiations.

The emphasis here has been placed on the texts, and in particular those that are "legislative" within an EU sense. Specifically translator-related information relating to the act and process of translation has been back-grounded as there is extensive coverage in the literature on translation. The EU translator context has been evoked, without going into detail, and here the best approach is to consult the translation websites of the EU institutions, in particular that of Commission DG Translation and the EU Translation Centre[52] in Luxembourg which covers the translation needs of a range of EU bodies. Similarly, the whole field of terminology has been evoked without going into detail. The IATE database provides many answers here, as does that ultimate source of information the Internet. The text here has remained pedantically English-oriented, but in the EU context English is both a translation language and a drafting language. There are traps in using it as a source and the EU translator needs to become skilled at spotting them and realizing that the intended meaning may be clearer from another language, or that variations in terms in English texts may correspond to a single term in French. This chapter could be rewritten in other EU languages and the references given to guidance and manuals, and quotations, would be replaced by the equivalent terms and expressions and convey the same EU information. So many difficulties exist, but there is also the pleasure for the translator in being engaged in a shared Europe-wide activity, learning new languages, exchanging experiences, remaking history and building together a common shared multilingual future. That, after all, is why the EU legislative texts are the way they are, and why the EU legislative translators and revisers play such an important role.

References

Baker, M. 2009. *Translation Studies*. New York and London: Routledge.

Baker M. and Saldanha, G. 2009. *Routledge Encyclopedia of Translation Studies*. Abingdon: Routledge.

Berry, E. and Hargreaves, S. 2007. *European Union Law*. Oxford: Oxford University Press.

Bhatia, V.K. 1987. 'Language of the Law', *Language Teaching*, vol. 20(4), pp. 227–234.

Cabré, T. 1998. *Terminology: Theory, Methods and Applications*. Amsterdam: John Benjamins.

Cook, V. n.d. 'What *Is* Applied Linguistics?' Available at: http://homepage.ntlworld.com/vivian.c/Writings/Shorts/WhatisALl.htm [Accessed 27 November 2012].

Council of the European Union. *Directorate for the Quality of Legislation*. 2011. Manual of Precedents for acts established within the Council of the European Union. Available at: http://ec.europa.eu/translation/documents/council/manual_precedents_acts_en.pdf. Accessed 9 March 2013].

David, R. and Brierley, J.E.C. 1985. *Major Legal Systems in the World Today: An Introduction to the Comparative Study of Law*. London: Stevens.

Davies, A. and Elder, C. 2004. *The Handbook of Applied Linguistics*. Malden: Blackwell.

European Commission. 1997. *Legislative Drafting. A Commission Manual*. Brussels: European Commission. Available at: http://ec.europa.eu/governance/better_regulation/documents/legis_draft_comm_en.pdf [Accessed 9 March 2013].

European Commission. 2011. *How to Write Clearly*. Brussels: European Commission. Available at: http://ec.europa.eu/languages/documents/publications/write-clearly_en.pdf [Accessed 9 March 2013].

52 Available at: http://cdt.europa.eu/FR/Pages/Homepage.aspx [Accessed 3 December 2012].

European Parliament, the Council of the European Union and the Commission. 1998. Interinstitutional Agreement on Common Guidelines for the Quality of Drafting of Community Legislation. 22 December. Available at: http://eur-lex.europa.eu/LexUriServ/LexUriServ.do?uri=CELEX:31999Y0317(01):EN:NOT [Accessed 9 November 2011].

Foster, N. 2009. *Foster on EU Law*. Oxford: Oxford University Press.

Galdia, M. 2009. *Legal Linguistics*. Oxford etc.: Peter Lang.

Gallas, T. 1999. Coredazione e Traduzione Giuridica nella Legislazione Multilingue, in Particolare Quella Comunitaria. In: *43 Quaderni di Libri e riviste d'Italia, la Traduzione, Saggi e documenti (IV)*, pp. 135–147.

Glanert, S. 2008. 'Speaking Language to Law: The Case of Europe', *Legal Studies*, vol. 28, pp. 161–171.

Glenn, H.P. 2010. *Legal Traditions of the World*. Oxford: Oxford University Press.

Guggeis, M. and Robinson, W. 2012. 'Co-Revision: Legal-Linguistic Revision in the European Union Co-Decision Process'. In: C.J.W. Baaij ed. *The Role of Legal Translation in Legal Harmonization*. Alphen an den Rijn: Kluwer Law International, pp. 51–81. Available at: http://www.europarl.europa.eu/aboutparliament/fr/0080a6d3d8/Ordinary-legislative-procedure.html [Accessed 5 November 2012].

Hoffmann, L., Kalverkämper, H. and Wiegand, H.E. (eds). 1998. *Fachsprachen / Languages for Special Purposes.Ein internationales Handbuch zur Fachsprachenforschung und Terminologiewissenschaft / An International Handbook of Special-Language and Terminology Research*. Berlin: De Gruyter Mouton.

Hutchinson, T. and Waters, A. 1987. *English for Specific Purposes*. Cambridge: Cambridge University Press.

Lavigne, E. 2001. 'Translation Tools in the Translation Service of the European Commission'. In: S. Šarčević ed. *Legal Translation: Preparation for Accession to the European Union*. Rijeka: Faculty of Law, University of Rijeka, pp. 65–74.

Mattila, H.E.S. 2006. *Comparative Legal Linguistics*. Aldershot: Ashgate.

Maury, J.-P. 2007. *Institutions européennes. La procédure de codécision*. Available at: http://mjp.univ-perp.fr/m/codecision.htm [Accessed 5 November 2012].

McAuliffe, K. 2010. 'Language and the Institutional Dynamics of the Court of Justice of the European Communities: A Changing Role for Lawyer-Linguists?' In: M. Gueldry ed.. *How Globalizing Professions Deal With National Languages: Studies in Cultural Conflict and Cooperation*. Lewiston, Queenstown, Lampeter: The Edwin Mellen Press, pp. 239–263.

Mollin, S. 2006. *Euro-English: Assessing Variety Status*. Language in Performance Series. Tübingen: Günter Narr.

Mulders, L. 2008. 'Translation at the Court of Justice of the European Communities'. In: S. Prechal and B. van Roermund eds. *The Coherence of EU Law, The Search for Unity in Divergent Concepts*. Oxford: Oxford University Press, pp. 45–59.

Munday, J. 2008. *Introducing Translation Studies. Theories and applications*. London and New York: Routledge. Available at: http://www.nhh.no/Files/Filer/institutter/fsk/Synaps/28–2013/Robertson_28_2013.pdf.

Payne, M. 1976. 'Hart's Concept of a Legal System', *William & Mary Law Review*, vol. 18, p. 287. Available at: http://scholarship.law.wm.edu/wmlr/vol18/iss2/4 [Accessed 28 November 2012].

Richards, J. and Schmidt, R.W. 2011. *Dictionary of Language Teaching and Applied Linguistics*. Harlow: Longman.

Robertson, C. 2010a. 'Legislative Drafting in English for Non-Native Speakers: Some Do's and Don'ts (With Reference to EU Legislation)'. In: M. Gotti and C. Williams eds. *ESP Across Cultures. Special issue: Legal English across cultures*, vol. 7. Bari: Edipuglia.

———. 2010b. 'Legal-Linguistic Revision of EU Legislative Texts'. In: M. Gotti and C. Williams eds. *Legal Discourse across Languages and Cultures*. Bern: Peter Lang, pp. 51–73.
———. 2012. 'EU Legal English: Common Law, Civil Law or a New Genre?' *European Review of Private Law*, vol. 20(5/6), pp. 1215–1240.
———. 2013. 'How the EU Functions in 23 Languages', *SYNAPS*. Available at: http://www.nhh.no/Files/Filer/institutter/fsk/Synaps/28–2013/Robertson_28_2013.pdf [Accessed 17 November 2013].
Robinson, W. 2008. 'Drafting of EU Legislation: A View from the European Commission', *Rivista di Diritto Pubblico Italiano, Comunitario e Comparato*. Available at: http://www.federalismi.it/ApplOpenFilePDF.cfm?artid=9008&dpath=document&dfile=08012008032419.pdf&content=Drafting+of+EU+legislation:+a+view+from+the+European+Commission+-+dottrina+-+dottrina+-+ [Accessed 26 January 2012].
Šarčević S. (ed.). 2001. *Legal Translation. Preparation for Accession to the European Union*. University of Rijeka.
Šarčević, S. and Robertson C. 2013. 'The Work of Lawyer-Linguists in the EU Institutions'. In: A. Borja Albi and F. Prieto Ramos eds. *Legal Translation in Context. Professional Issues and Prospects*. Oxford etc.: Peter Lang, pp. 181–202.
Swales, J.M. 1992. 'Language for Specific Purposes'. In: W. Bright ed. *International Encyclopedia of Linguistics*, vol. 2. New York, Oxford: Oxford University Press, pp. 300–302.
Wiśniewski, K. 2007. *Applied Linguistics*. Available at: http://www.tlumaczenia-angielski.info/linguistics/applied-linguistics.htm [Accessed 27 November 2012].

Chapter 10
Phraseology in Legal Translation: A Corpus-Based Analysis of Textual Mapping in EU Law

Łucja Biel

1. Introduction

Legal language is notorious for its formulaicity, perceived by outsiders as a vice (petrification, lack of spontaneity) while by insiders as a virtue (standardization). Formulaicity institutionalizes the discourse by limiting drafters' creativity and idiosyncrasy. It is to a large degree created and strengthened by phraseology—fixed recurrent patterns at the textual, grammatical, and collocational level. Little research has been conducted to investigate how phraseology behaves in legal translation and whether translation is able to retain the same level of formulaicity. The aim of this chapter is to fill in this gap by providing a conceptual framework based on the existing literature and by exploring translated legal phraseology against the background of nontranslated law in an empirical corpus-based study.

2. Developments in Phraseology

A recent surge of interest in phraseology has been triggered by corpus-based methodologies, which have shifted attention from a word to a pattern. As a result, the traditional approach to phraseology with idioms as the prototype was replaced by the frequency-based approach comprising lexicogrammatical patterns which would be regarded as free or peripheral within the traditional approach but met a recurrence threshold (Nesselhauf 2005: 12; Granger and Paquot 2008: 28–32). In the frequency-based approach phraseology is a broader category which includes collocations, multi-word lexical units, and lexical bundles (defined as 'sequences of words that tend to co-occur, irrespective of their idiomaticity and whether or not the sequence of words constitutes a grammatical unit', cf. Biber et al. 2007: 58–59), which are more frequent and cognitively salient in specialized languages than idioms or proverbs.

Another offspring of the corpus revolution was interest in specialized phraseology from the field of Terminology. Terminology shifted away from Wüster's General Theory of Terminology (GTT), a dominant approach for a few decades, towards approaches which incorporate social, cognitive and communicative aspects into the study of terms. Although the main object of study of Terminology has remained unchanged, terminologists started to extend the concept of a term by accounting for phraseology, in particular collocates of terms. It was triggered by phraseologically-oriented postulates raised by terminologists: to analyze, through corpora, how terms behave in context and to study the relation between terms and phraseology (L'Homme *et al.* 2003: 156; Cabré Castellví 2003: 168); to study how collocations affect term use and formation (Antia *et al.* 2005: 3); to include phraseology and other semantic relations (synonymy, antonymy) in the description of terminology (Rogers and Wright 2006: 114), including grammatical and lexical collocations and maxims of law for legal terminography (Tessuto 2008: 293); and to develop data models for capturing collocational knowledge in termbases (Heid 2001: 806). These postulates have contributed some important knowledge on specialized phraseology.

3. Legal Phraseology

The dominant perspective of legal language studies has been terminological rather than phraseological; therefore, phraseology has usually been treated perfunctorily, notably exceptions being Kjær's pioneer papers (1990; 2007) and, more recently, Goźdź-Roszkowski's (2011) work on multi-word patterns across legal genres and Pontrandolfo's (2011) study of phraseology in translated criminal judgments.

Kjær proposes a classification of norm-conditioned legal word combinations, depending on the correlation between the stability of combinations and legal constraints: (1) prefabricated word combinations directly prescribed by law; (2) word combinations only indirectly prescribed by law; (3) word combinations based on implicit quotation from other text in a genre chain in the legal domain; and (4) habitually used routine phrases (1990: 28–29). Her classification emphasizes the systemic nature of legal phraseology and intertextuality of legal texts, showing the link between law and lower-ranking texts in the hierarchy of legal genres: '[c]oherence of the system is based on the intertextual relations between legal texts, obtained by reproduction (implicit quotation) and recontextualization of words and phrases' (2007: 513). In respect of legal phrasemes, Heid *et al.* note that, in contrast to other LSPs, some word combinations which are significant for the legal domain do not contain terms (2008: 133). It should also be noted that legal language clusters may be very long, ranging from phrases, sentences, to entire clauses or parts of documents, known as boilerplate clauses (Tiersma 1999: 59).

Kjær's classification is however not fully applicable to the language of the law and needs adapting to the primary and constitutive genre of legal language, which is the object of this study. I find more useful a simpler typology proposed by Kjær: (1) multi-word terms; (2) collocations with a term; and (3) formulaic expressions and standard phrases (2007: 509–510). Drawing on these two classifications and on the corpus-based analyses conducted for the purposes of this study, I propose the following classification of phrasemes in the language of the law to account for additional categories which are statistically significant. The classification should be viewed as existing on a **phraseological continuum** with fuzzy boundaries between each category, ranging from the global textual level to the local microlevel: text-organizing patterns, grammatical patterns, term-forming patterns, term-embedding collocations, and lexical collocations. All types of phrasemes contribute to the make-up of the legislative text at the macrostructural and microstructural level, providing a stable matrix to be filled with details.

- **Text-organizing patterns**: repetitive global textual patterns which are often prescribed in drafting guidelines. They form a matrix of a legal text, emphasizing its ritualized nature. Typical text-organizing patterns include a title of the document, citations, transitions between sections, enacting formulas, amending and closing formulas. They have a high frequency in the corpus because they are consistently repeated in legislative instruments with very low variation. This group may be illustrated by the opening metasentence and closing part of EU instruments (Table 10.1).

Table 10.1 Examples of text-organizing patterns: opening and closing sections of EU instruments

English version of an EU instrument	Polish version of an EU instrument
THE COMMISSION OF THE EUROPEAN COMMUNITIES, *Having regard to the Treaty ...,* *Having regard to ...,* *(Having consulted ...)* *(Acting in accordance with ...)* *Whereas:* *(1)* *(2) ...,* *HAS ADOPTED THIS REGULATION:* *Article 1*	*KOMISJA WSPÓLNOT EUROPEJSKICH,* *uwzględniając Traktat ...,* *uwzględniając ...,* *(po konsultacji z ...)* *(stanowiąc zgodnie z ...),* *a także mając na uwadze, co następuje:* *(1) ...* *(2) ...,* *PRZYJMUJE NINIEJSZE ROZPORZĄDZENIE:* *Artykuł 1*
This Regulation shall enter into force on the third day following its publication in the Official Journal of the European Union. *This Regulation shall be binding in its entirety and directly applicable in all Member States.* *Done at Brussels, 30 June 2006.* *For the Commission* *XYZ* *Member of the Commission*	*Niniejsze rozporządzenie wchodzi w życie trzeciego dnia po jego opublikowaniu w Dzienniku Urzędowym Unii Europejskiej.* *Niniejsze rozporządzenie wiąże w całości i jest bezpośrednio stosowane we wszystkich państwach członkowskich.* *Sporządzono w Brukseli, dnia 30 czerwca 2006 r.* *W imieniu Komisji* *XYZ* *Członek Komisji*

- **Grammatical patterns**: genre-specific recurrent grammatical patterns, for example patterns and lexical bundles which express deontic modality (*shall, must, should, may*), if-then mental models of legal reasoning and other conditional clauses (*if, in the event that, in case, unless, otherwise, provided that*), purpose clauses (*with a view to –ing, in order to, to this end*), the passive voice and other impersonal structures (Table 10.2).

Table 10.2 Examples of grammatical patterns in EU instruments

English version of an EU instrument	Polish version of an EU instrument
The fishing quota allocated to the Member State ... shall be deemed to be exhausted from the date set out in that Annex.	*Kwotę połowową przyznaną na 2006 r. państwu członkowskiemu ... uznaje się za wyczerpaną z dniem określonym w tym załączniku.*
The successful tenderer must accept the lot as established if the final result of the sample analyses indicates a quality ...	*Oferent, którego ofertę przyjęto, musi przyjąć partię taką, jaka jest, jeśli wynik ostateczny analiz wykonanych na próbkach wykazuje jakość ...*
If the fixing of a minimum price ... would lead to an overrun on the maximum quantity available to a Member State, an award coefficient may be fixed at the same time for the quantities offered at the minimum price in order to comply with the maximum quantity available to that Member State	*W przypadku gdy ustalenie ceny minimalnej ... doprowadziłoby do przekroczenia maksymalnej ilości dostępnej dla państwa członkowskiego, oprócz ustalenia tej ceny można zastosować współczynnik redukcji udzielonych zamówień na poziomie ceny minimalnej, tak aby nie przekroczyć maksymalnej ilości dostępnej w danym państwie członkowskim.*

- **Term-forming patterns (multi-word terms)**: collocates of a generic term which form more specific multi-word terms of varying degrees of terminologicality (cf. Shelov, quoted in Thelen 2002: 196), the typical most productive patterns tend to be Adj+N and N+N, but in practice multi-word terms may be structurally very complex (*common draft terms of cross-border merger*) (see Table 10.3 for more examples). Multi-word terms may be seen as frozen collocations due to their high structural stability (cf. Biel 2012). They constitute single choices, but their meaning tends to be compositional, transparent and analysable.

Table 10.3 Examples of term-forming patterns in EU instruments.

English version of an EU instrument	Polish version of an EU instrument
registered office	*siedziba statutowa*
European public limited-liability company	*europejska spółka akcyjna*
cross-border merger of limited liability companies	*transgraniczne łączenie się spółek kapitałowych*
merger by the formation of a new company	*łączenie przez zawiązanie nowej spółki*
share exchange ratio	*stosunek wymiany akcji*
common draft terms of cross-border merger	*wspólny plan połączenia transgranicznego*
persons acting in concert	*osoby działające w porozumieniu*

- **Term-embedding collocations**: collocates of terms which embed terms in cognitive scripts and the text, evidencing combinatory properties of terms (see Table 10.4). They establish links between terms and elements of conceptual frames. While term-forming collocations, such as Adj+N and N+N, indicate subtypes of the objects denoted by the node or their typical properties, N+V term-embedding collocations denote "what one can typically do with (or to) the object denoted by the base noun" (Martin, quoted in Heid 1994: 238), as well as the manner of such action. Subtype-denoting collocations are often subject to terminologization and form distinct terms. In the group of term-embedding collocations the N(term)+V structure may be expected to be prototypical. Such collocations form the skeleton of legal rules by providing action and enabling terms to enter into relations. They play an important role in establishing the conceptual system of the domain: they map links to related domains and indicate elements of conceptual frames (Meyer and Mackintosh 1994: 346). As such, collocations organize a text, dividing it into units of meaning (Teubert 2010: 357). It should be borne in mind that the separation of terms from collocations is arbitrary to a certain degree (for more discussion, see Heid 2001: 791; L'Homme et al. 2003: 156).

Table 10.4 Examples of term-embedding collocations in EU instruments

English version of an EU instrument	Polish version of an EU instrument
to hold shares	*posiadać udziały*
company being dissolved without going into liquidation	*spółka rozwiązana bez przeprowadzenia postępowania likwidacyjnego*
securities conferring the right to vote at general meetings of the company being acquired *To confer the right to vote* *To vote at a general meeting* *To acquire a company*	*papiery wartościowe przyznające prawo głosu na zgromadzeniu wspólników spółki przejmowanej* *przyznać prawo głosu* *głosować na zgromadzeniu* *przejąć spółkę*
pro-rata issue of securities	*proporcjonalny przydział papierów wartościowych*
judgment declaring a merger void	*wyrok uznający łączenie za nieważne*
the proper completion of the pre-merger acts and formalities	*należyte dopełnienie czynności i formalności poprzedzających połączenie*

- **Lexical collocations:** routine formulae at the microstructural level which are not built around terms. They include in particular inter/intratextual referential patterns, such as collocates of editing units, other recurrent patterns referred to by Bhatia as qualifications (cf. 2006: 2) and non-terminological lexical bundles (see Table 10.5). In contrast to term-embedding collocations and multi-word terms, recurrence is an important criterion in their identification.

Table 10.5 Examples of lexical collocations in EU instruments

English version of EU regulation	Polish version of EU regulation
Notwithstanding the third paragraph of Article 16 of Regulation (EEC) No 2131/93	*Na zasadzie odstępstwa od art. 16 akapit trzeci rozporządzenia (EWG) nr 2131/93*
In accordance with the procedure referred to in Article 25(2) of Regulation (EC) No 1784/2003	*Zgodnie z procedurą, o której mowa w art. 25 ust. 2 rozporządzenia (WE) nr 1784/2003*
Subject to this Regulation	*jeżeli niniejsze rozporządzenie nie stanowi inaczej*
Export licences shall be valid from their date of issue within the meaning of Article 9 of Regulation (EEC) No 2131/93 …	*Pozwolenia na wywóz są ważne od daty wydania w rozumieniu art. 9 rozporządzenia (EWG) nr 2131/93 …*
The costs of taking the samples and conducting the analyses provided for in Article 5, with the exception of those referred to in Article 6(3), shall be borne by	*Koszty związane z pobraniem próbek i analizami przewidzianymi w art. 5, poza tymi, o których mowa w art. 6 ust. 3, ponosi*

The empirical study will focus on the hitherto neglected component of the phraseological continuum: lexical collocations. In this group collocations of editing units were selected as one of the key generic features of the language of the law due to their high frequency.

In corpus-based approaches **collocations** are defined quantitatively/statistically (cf. McEnery *et al.* 2006: 82 for more details) as strings of words that co-occur on a frequent basis. Collocations are 'diagnostic, vital elements' and 'powerful indicators of register' (Partington 1998: 17, 20). A number of studies have confirmed that collocations behave differently in general language and specialized languages (cf. Meyer and Mackintosh 1994; Heid 1994; L'Homme 2000) and these claims may be extended to legal language. For example, LSP collocations are more restricted and show lower variation, polysemy and synonymy and they tend to center around nouns (terms). On the other hand, properties that seem to be more pronounced in legal language are:

- a system-bound nature of collocations, e.g. *to register articles of association* (UK) versus *to file articles of incorporation* (US), however, to a smaller degree than terms are;
- lower variation and synonymy than in other LSPs combined with increased stability due to institutional standardization and the prescribed hierarchy of terminological and phraseological choices imposed by higher-ranking statutes;
- fixedness of legal collocations with limited substitutability of constituents; and
- lower importance of frequency in the case of term-embedding collocations which are sanctioned by law.

4. Phraseology in Translation

Models of translation competences have recently started to account for phraseology, even though it is still treated as part of terminological or other competences. Phraseology has been perceived as a criterion in the assessment of translation quality (Colson 2008: 201); being recognized—in particular collocations—as a source of difficulty in translation and a frequent error (cf. Newmark 1981: 180). Collocational patterns differ across languages and are partly arbitrary (cf. Baker 1992: 48); collocational ranges of equivalent words do not match totally (Larson [1984] 1998: 159).

Translators are expected to ensure what Gouadec refers to as '**phraseological conformity**', i.e., TL phraseology, sentence structure and text organization which are typical of a genre, text type and professional group (2007: 23). The common consensus is that equivalence at the phrase level should produce unmarked, domesticated collocations in translation. As stressed by Hatim and Mason, 'the collocations should in general be neither less unexpected (i.e. more banal) nor more unexpected (i.e. demanding greater processing effort) than in the ST' (1990: 205). In particular, translators should not calque SL collocation patterns if it produces untypical collocations in the TL; however, it is not infrequent to find odd collocations in translations (Baker 1992: 55). Similarly, the legal translation literature recommends translating collocations and other phraseological patterns functionally to answer reader expectations and conform to the TL legal style (Kierzkowska 2002: 123; Orozco and Sánchez-Gijón 2011: 27). In particular, the literal translation of legal collocations is discouraged (Kierzkowska 2002: 123). However, legal translation may legitimately produce unnatural or untypical collocations in certain situations which will be described below.

One of the strongest causes of distortions is **interference**. During the translation process the source language may adversely affect the assessment of collocation typicality. Translators may also confuse SL and TL collocational patterns (Baker 1992: 54; Hatim and Mason 1990: 204) due to the complexity of bilingual processing which 'interferes with or upsets the spontaneous, or 'ideally monolingual' processing of a native speaker' (Mauranen 2007: 44). Another cause of distortion is 'the tension between accuracy and naturalness' when a translator has to choose between a typical and an accurate collocation (Baker 1992: 56). This tension seems to be lower in the translation of law: if an unmarked TL equivalent implies a change in meaning, the translator should opt for a less typical but accurate collocation, even if it sounds awkward. However, in most cases unnatural collocations will result from conceptual lacunas between the legal systems and the need to convey elements of the SL frame which are absent in the

TL. In such a case the translator has to approximate the missing element by a neologism or a possible but rare collocation (cf. Biel 2012).

Collocational distortions may also be discussed in the context of translation universals, that is, distortions typical of the translation process itself (cf. Baker 1996). Mauranen's **untypical collocation hypothesis** suggests that translations contain collocations which are possible but rare in the TL, have few combinations which are frequent in nontranslated TL, have more varied, less stable and less frequent patterns (cf. 2006: 97). Tirkkonen-Condit's unique items hypothesis proposes the underrepresentation of typical TL phraseological unique items which are not prompted in translation (cf. 2004: 178). On the other hand, the normalization hypothesis (translators tend 'to exaggerate features of the target language and to conform to its typical patterns' (Baker 1996: 183)) and Toury's law of growing standardization (translators tend to choose 'more habitual options offered by a target culture' (1995: 268)) draw attention to another aspect of untypical distribution—namely, overrepresentation of collocations due to the exaggeration of typical TL patterns by translators. A few words of warning should be given in respect of the translation universals:

1. they still have a status of a hypothesis;
2. the evidence is inconclusive and contradictory; and
3. most empirical studies of collocations have been carried out on translated literature, which is hardly representative of and generalizable to all translators' behaviour, especially legal translators.

5. Translated EU Law

EU translation is a classic example of institutional translation. The EU culture of translating is promoted through style guides, terminological databases and other resources that facilitate standardization of translation in line with institutional policies. One of the main factors which impacts EU translation is the **multilingualism** policy, under which EU-wide legislation is adopted in all 23 official languages, all language versions being equally valid and authentic and presumed to have the same meaning. Translated EU legislation has an authoritative status, which is known as the principle of equal authenticity (Šarčević 1997: 64). To make EU multilingualism feasible, the language of source texts is adjusted at the drafting stage to make them translatable into other languages and minimize translation problems. In consequence, the language of EU instruments has a hybrid form resulting from the interplay between EU intraculture and national cultures, involvement of non-native speakers, complex drafting process comprising multilingual translation, institutionally controlled language of source and target texts, high standardization of textual patterns and terminology, as well as semantic and syntactic simplification. All these factors contribute to what Koskinen refers to as 'the extreme visibility of the "translatedness" of the texts' (2000: 61).

In view of the aforementioned properties of EU translation, more research is needed into the language of EU legislation to verify which levels are affected by visible "translatedness". The next section will investigate whether collocational patterns of editing units in translated EU law differ from those that may be found in naturally occurring language, that is, nontranslated national law, and if they do, in what way. It is believed that such studies may help develop aids for translators to reduce the foreignness of translation wherever possible.

6. Corpus Design

The methodology applied in this project combines Baker's pioneer method of studying translated language against nontranslated one on comparable monolingual corpora (cf. Baker 1996); however, I also use a parallel corpus of the JRC Acquis in English to analyze SL interference in line with recent methodological postulates (cf. Bernardini and Zanettin 2004: 59). The main corpora used in the study are: the Polish JRC Acquis Corpus of translated EU law and the Polish Law corpus of nontranslated legislation compiled by the author:

- **The JRC Acquis Corpus** was built by the European Commission's Joint Research Centre (JRC). Version 3.0 of JRC-Acquis was downloaded as an independent Polish corpus from the JRC website http://optima.jrc.it/Acquis/, converted, cleaned of some noise and sorted manually to isolate two types of instruments: resolutions (**R-Acquis**) and directives (**L-Acquis**). The entire texts were used in the corpus.
- **The Polish Law Corpus** (PLC) is a reference corpus for translated Acquis. It contains nontranslated Polish legislation in force as of 1 August 2011. The files were downloaded from the online legislation database *Lex Omega*. The corpus was designed to cover the full range of primary legislation of general application passed by the Polish Parliament, i.e., the Constitution and acts of parliament (*ustawa*), which have a supreme status over secondary and tertiary legislation passed by other bodies under their authority.

Table 10.6 shows basic statistics for the corpora.

Table 10.6 Corpus design

Name of the corpus	Texts	Tokens	Types
PL JRC Acquis: Regulations (R-Acquis)	8821	14.7 million	176,038
PL JRC Acquis: Directives (L-Acquis)	1962	7.2 million	128,071
Polish Law Corpus (PLC)	755	6.8 million	68,513

Owing to the different sizes of the corpora, all frequencies obtained in the study were normalized to 1 million words. The software used for corpus analysis is Wordsmith Tools, Version 6.0.

7. Collocations of Editing Units: Textual Mapping Through Inter- and Intratextuality

The Acquis and PLC keyword lists contain editing units, names of instruments, and components of patterns which refer to such units. References to editing units serve the function of navigation within the same instrument and establishing links to relevant sections of other instruments. The referencing keywords are very salient due to their top positions and high frequency in the corpora, indicating that (1) referencing patterns differ in translated and nontranslated language; (2) referencing patterns are one of the most distinctive features of the language of the law.

The basic editing unit both in EU law and in Polish law is *artykuł* (article). One of the most noticeable differences is that Polish law shows a strong preference for the abbreviated form *art.*, while translated EU law opts for the full form *artykuł*. The same applies to a lower ranking unit *ustęp*, the abbreviated form of which *ust.* is preferred in nontranslated law. The most frequent editing units, *art.*, *artykuł* and *ust.*, were selected for collocational analysis.

The next table shows top left collocates of the most frequent editing unit *art.* (article) in the corpora. The collocational range of the second most frequent editing unit *ust.* (paragraph) is similar to that of *art.*, although the collocates have markedly lower frequencies.

Table 10.7 Direct collocational environment of *art.*: left collocates (normalized occurrences per 1 million words)

	Patterns	Translated EU law		Nontranslated PL law
		R-Acquis	L-Acquis	PLC
1	*w art.* [in article]	2716	2372	5365
2	*przepis* art.* [provisions of article]	235	202	674
3	*na podstawie art.* [on the basis of article]	166	90	367
4	*z zastrzeżeniem art.* [subject to article]	10	16	137
5	*w trybie art.* [under article, lit. in the manner of article]	1	0	40
6	*zgodnie z art.* [according to article]	878	537	153
7	*w rozumieniu art.* [within the meaning of article]	153	137	112
8	*jego/jej art.* [its article]	701	344	0
9	*na mocy art.* [pursuant to article]	207	108	1
10	*do/dla celów art.* [for the purposes of article]	30	23	0
11	*bez uszczerbku dla art.* [without prejudice to article]	26	29	0

Table 10.7 shows marked differences in how *art.* is embedded in text in translated and nontranslated language. Translated language has a number of patterns which are absent in nontranslated law. Furthermore, nontranslated law contains a pattern which is not prompted in translated language (*w trybie*) and, hence, may be regarded as a unique item.

The top collocate in all the corpora is *w art.* [in article] (1), which is two times more frequent in PLC than in the Acquis; it will be further analyzed below. The second most frequent collocate in nontranslated language is *przepis* art.* [provisions of the article] (2), again with a markedly lower frequency in translated law. It mainly combines with *stosuje się / nie stosuje się* [apply / do not apply], to indicate the scope of application of an article. Translated language does not frequently precede *artykuł* with *przepisy* and uses more varied synonymous collocates instead: *zapis artykułu* and *postanowienia art.* (which is reserved for contractual provisions in correct legal Polish). The remaining collocates (3–11) are mostly complex prepositions whose function is to establish legal authority or resolve conflict; they will be discussed below. The collocate *jego/jej art.* [its article] (8), which is absent in PLC, is triggered by the text-organizing pattern used in preambles of EU instruments:

> EN version: Having regard to the Treaty . . ., and in particular Article 285(1) **thereof**
>
> PL version: uwzględniając Traktat . . ., w szczególności **jego** art. 285 ust. 1
> Backtranslation: [having regard to the Treaty . . ., in particular **its** Article 285 paragraph 1].
>
> Its use in a highly repetitive textual pattern contributes to its high frequency in translated law.

8. Hypertextuality

Let us now analyze the most salient pattern *w art./ust.* [in article/paragraph] (Table 10.8). This pattern is embedded in non-finite clauses which function as place adverbials pointing to relevant articles/paragraphs where a concept is specified in greater detail. As such, they ensure precision of information and eliminate ambiguity by referring to a specific place within the same or a different instrument. Secondly, they condense information by providing a hyperlink to a place where such information is specified in detail or defined, allowing the reader to focus on new information introduced in a given legal rule.

> EN version (EU): They shall be informed of the time-frame, as well as the means at their disposal for fulfilling the obligation to submit the elements as referred to in Article 4 of Directive 2004/83/EC. This information shall be given in time to enable them to . . . comply with the obligations described in Article 11.
>
> PL version (EU): Są one informowane o terminach, a także przysługujących im środkach, służących spełnieniu obowiązku przedstawienia elementów, o których mowa w art. 4 dyrektywy 2004/83/WE. Informacje te są udzielane w takim terminie, aby umożliwić tym osobom . . . wypełnienie obowiązków, o których mowa w art. 11.

There are two types of references: intratextual ones within the instrument and intertextual ones to external instruments. In this example the first reference is intertextual to a different directive which lists the elements that substantiate the application for international protection. Instead of repeating the elements, the instrument provides a hyperlink which defines the elements in question:

> *The elements . . . consist of the applicant's statements and all documentation at the applicants disposal regarding the applicant's age, background, including that of relevant relatives, identity, nationality(ies), country(ies) and place(s) of previous residence, previous asylum applications, travel routes, identity and travel documents and the reasons for applying for international protection.*

The second reference is intratextual, referring the reader to the next article which lists the obligations of applicants for asylum. This confirms that legal texts behave as a 'non-linear "hypertext" weighed down with a large number of references' which function as shortcuts (Mattila 2006: 78). Such references, referred to by Bhatia as textual mapping, have a generic function of ensuring that law is all-inclusive, clear and precise (1998). They are cohesive devices which provide texture to legal texts; they are 'used for text-cohering' (Bhatia 1998). In the case of EU discourse, intertextuality is much more complex than in national legislation because an EU instrument has:

- standard references to other instruments in the system of EU law that provide a legal basis, amend, are amended or referred to for other reasons (these references may be conceptualized as **vertical intertextuality**);
- primary intertextual links to all authentic language versions of the same instrument (which may be conceptualized as **horizontal intertextuality**). Horizontal intertextuality makes EU instruments different from a typical translation which has a primary intertextual link to a single ST.

Coming back to the *w art./ust.* bundle, Table 10.8 shows the most frequent patterns which are used for textual mapping: intratextuality and vertical intertextuality. It should be noted that functionally, all the structures listed in Table 10.8 are synonymous; however, they differ in terms of their degree of conventionality and combinatory properties.

Table 10.8 Top left collocates of *w art.* and *ust.* (normalized occurrences per 1 million words)

	Patterns	Translated EU law		Nontranslated PL law
		R-Acquis	L-Acquis	PLC
1	o któr* mowa w art. [which (is) referred to in article]	416	229	3380
	o któr* mowa w ust. [which (is) referred to in para]	98	92	3725
2	określony w art. [specified in article]	1067	1020	770
	określony w ust. [specified in para]	345	375	408
3	wymieniony w art. [listed in article]	136	100	228
	wymieniony w ust. [listed in para]	36	54	125
4	przewidziany w art. [provided for in article]	370	274	44
	przewidziany w ust. [provided for in para]	41	66	13
5	ustanowiony w art. [laid down in article]	196	307	1
	ustanowiony w ust. [laid down in para]	20	31	0
	TOTAL	**2725**	**2548**	**8694**

A closer analysis of collocational environment shows further differences between the corpora. The first most noticeable difference is that references to an article and a paragraph through this bundle are three times more common in nontranslated Polish law than in EU law. Polish law shows a clear preference for a single pattern, *o któr* mowa w art./ust.* [which (is) referred to in article/para] (1), the frequency of which is several times higher than that of any other pattern and which is severely underrepresented in translated law: it is 10 times less common in R-Acquis and 16.5 times less common in L-Acquis. The most frequent collocate of the pattern in Polish law is *ust.* [paragraph], which provides a very local reference to a paragraph within the same article. The second top collocate of a slightly lower frequency is *art.* [article], which refers to an article within the same or a different instrument; however, intratextual references are more common. By contrast, references to a paragraph are very rare in the Acquis compared to the Polish Law Corpus, which indicates that Polish law more frequently builds local intratextual references within the same article.

The most salient pattern in translated law is *określony w art.* [specified in article] (2), which is overrepresented compared to the Polish Law Corpus. Patterns 1, 4 and 5 have similar distribution in translated law; however, *przewidziany w art.* [provided for in article] (4) is insignificant and *ustanowiony w art.* [laid down in article] (5) is absent in nontranslated law. Another underrepresented pattern in translated law is *wymieniony w art.* [listed in article] (3).

The differences may be attributed to SL interference and little effort on the translators' part to normalize references to the textual mapping conventions of Polish law. Since such patterns have a low degree of terminologicality, translators may have approached them as patterns which can be translated literally from English. The second reason for high variation of the navigational patterns in translated law as shown in Table 10.8 is the fact that such references are not controlled institutionally by standardization in *Vademecum tłumacza*[1], a style guide for Polish translators published by the Directorate General for Translation. The next table shows the most frequent corresponding patterns which embed an *article* in the English version of EU law.

Table 10.9 Direct collocational environment of *article* in the English section of JRC Acquis (normalized occurrences per 1 million words)

Pattern	EN R-Acquis	EN L-Acquis
referred to in article	987	685
laid down in article	334	404
provided for in article	291	145

In contrast to Polish law, which predominantly uses a single referencing pattern, the English version of EU law is more varied in this respect. The main pattern is *referred to in article/paragraph*, which ranks high in the English Acquis cluster list. It is followed by *laid down in* and *provided for in* . . . . Other patterns may also be found, such as *set out, listed, defined, specified, mentioned, indicated, described, prescribed, imposed in Article/Paragraph*, although their frequency is markedly lower. Therefore, English-language EU instruments show lower formulaicity of patterns comprising the bundle *in article/paragraph*; such lower formulaicity is mirrored in the Polish translated version of EU law contrary to the conventions of Polish law.

1 http://ec.europa.eu/translation/polish/guidelines/documents/styleguide_polish_dgt_pl.pdf.

9. Legal Authority

As already noted, some of the collocates of editing units are used to establish legal authority. The most frequent patterns are formed with complex prepositions: *na podstawie* [on the basis of], *zgodnie z* [according to], *na mocy* [pursuant to], etc. There is a marked asymmetry in the distribution of these complex prepositions, which is mainly due to different patterns of establishing legal authority in translated and nontranslated law.

Table 10.10 Collocates of editing units, which establish legal authority (normalized occurrences per 1 million words)

Patterns	Translated EU law		Nontranslated PL law
	R-Acquis	L-Acquis	PLC
1. *na podstawie* [on the basis of]	**983**	**723**	**1730**
~ *art., ust., przepisów, ustawy*	288	190	935
2. *zgodnie z* [according to]	**2722**	**3155**	**688**
~ *art., ust., przepisami*	1869	1558	450
3. *na mocy* [pursuant to]	**595**	**435**	**47**
~ *art., ust., przepisów*	418	306	16
TOTAL (patterns referring to editing units):	**2575**	**2054**	**1401**

The predominant pattern in nontranslated law is *na podstawie art., ust., przepisów, ustawy*, etc. (1), which is circa four times more frequent than in translated law. The second pattern *zgodnie z* is used two times less frequently. The analysis of collocational environment of these two patterns shows that their use is complementary rather than interchangeable; for example, *na podstawie* collocates most frequently with the verb *wydać* [issue] while *zgodnie z* collocates with *ustalić* [determine]. In addition, *zgodnie z* collocates more frequently on the right with *przepisy* [provisions], next with *art.* [article], which is reversed in *na podstawie*. The last pattern *na mocy* (3) is hardly ever used for referential purposes in nontranslated law. Translated law shows a very strong preference for the second pattern, *zgodnie z*, which is significantly overrepresented due to interference and the literal translation of *in accordance with* and *according to*. The English pattern, as noted by Bhatia, raises an expectation of obligation (1998). The second most frequent pattern *na mocy* is also strongly overrepresented in translated law and is prompted by *pursuant to* (which 'raises an expectation of rights depending on the individual's choice' (Bhatia 1998)). The least frequent pattern, which establishes legal authority in the Acquis is *na podstawie*, which is relatively rarely prompted in translated language, even though it is a strong generic feature of Polish law.

10. Legal Scope: Conflict Avoidance or Resolution

Another group of collocates of editing units which may be singled out are *z zastrzeżeniem* [subject to] and *bez uszczerbku dla* [without prejudice to]. They correspond to *subject to* and *without prejudice to*, the function of which is to define the legal scope of a provision by avoiding or resolving potential conflicts between editing units or legal norms (cf. Bhatia 1998).

Table 10.11 Conflict resolving collocates of editing units

Patterns	Translated EU law		Nontranslated PL law
	R-Acquis	L-Acquis	PLC
1. *z zastrzeżeniem* [subject to]	121	158	501
~ *art., ust., pkt., lit., przepisów*	51	71	449
2. *bez uszczerbku dla* [without prejudice to]	170	263	2
~ *art., ust., przepisów ...*	86	114	0

Polish law shows a clear preference for *z zastrzeżeniem* (1) and does not use the other pattern for referential purposes. Translated law uses both patterns but more often resorts to *bez uszczerbku dla* (2), which is untypical for Polish law and is a literal translation of *without prejudice to*.

11. Conclusion

The analysis confirms that collocations of editing units used for textual mapping are genre-specific features of the language of the law due to their high frequency and salience. It has been demonstrated that Polish law relies more on intratextual references to achieve internal cohesion and precision while EU law tends to rely more on intertextual links and seldom uses local intratextual references.

One of the main findings is that translated law uses untypical collocational patterns and is marked by a lack of phraseological rigor. The referencing patterns in translated language are significantly more varied and are a close reflection of SL patterns with little effort on the part of translators to overcome interference. It significantly decreases the textual fit of translated law to nontranslated legal language in the area where difference may not be attributed to the multilingalism-related constraints, conceptual lacunas or asymmetry between languages. The departure from the TL conventions is unjustified—natural referencing patterns in the Polish version of EU law would not interfere with the uniform application of EU law in the Member States.

The departure from the TL referencing conventions may be confusing to the reader and may cause some interpretative doubts concerning legal relationships between articles. Another consequence is the reduced formulaicity of translated law. Recurrent patterns save cognitive effort during processing and facilitate concentrating on new information. As argued by Partington, prefabricated units allow writers 'to balance new information with old information, novelty with habit, (prefabs contributing to the second items of these pairs) to cut down processing effort' (1998: 20). In this context, the high stability of patterns in Polish law (strong preference for a single pattern) is more functional and effective: it saves processing effort and facilitates segmenting the text into new and old information. The mundane repetition of a single textual-mapping pattern emphasizes its status of a qualification/addition and removes this information into the background. Lower formulaicity of translated law reduces its functionality and may adversely affect effectiveness of communication.

References

Antia, B.E. et al. 2005. 'Shaping Translation: A View from Terminology Research', *Meta: Translators' Journal*, vol. 50(4). Available at: http://www.erudit.org/revue/meta/2005/v50/n4/019907ar.pdf [Accessed 14 March 2012].

Baker, M. 1992. *In Other Words: A Coursebook on Translation*. London and New York: Routledge.

———. 1996. 'Corpus-Based Translation Studies: The Challenges That Lie Ahead'. In: H.L. Somers ed. *Terminology, LSP and Translation. Studies in Language Engineering in Honour of Juan C. Sager*. Amsterdam/Philadelphia: John Benjamins, pp. 175–186.

Baroni, M. and Bernardini, S. 2003. 'A Preliminary Analysis of Collocational Differences in Monolingual Comparable Corpora'. In: D. Archer, P. Rayson, A. Wilson and T. McEnery eds. *Proceedings of the Corpus Linguistics 2003 Conference. UCREL*. Lancaster: Lancaster University, pp. 82–91.

Bernardini, S. and Zanettin, F. 2004. 'When Is a Universal Not a Universal? Some Limits of Current Corpus-Based Methodologies for the Investigation of Translation Universals'. In: A. Mauranen and P. Kujamäki eds. *Translation Universals. Do They Exist?* Amsterdam/Philadelphia: John Benjamins, pp. 51–62.

Bhatia, V.K. 1998. 'Intertextuality in Legal Discourse', *The Language Teacher*, vol. 22.11. Available at: http://jalt-publications.org/tlt/articles/2427-intertextuality-legal-discourse [Accessed: 8 August 2014].

———. 2006. 'Legal Genres'. In: K. Brown ed. *Encyclopedia of Language and Linguistics*. 2nd ed. Oxford: Elsevier, pp. 1–7.

Biber, D., Johansson, S., Leech, G., Conrad, S. and Finegan, E. 2007. *Longman Grammar of Spoken and Written English*. Harlow: Longman.

Biel, Ł. 2012. 'Areas of Similarity and Difference in Legal Phraseology: Collocations of Key Terms in UK and Polish Company Law'. In: A. Pamies, J. Manuel Pazos Bretaña and L. Luque Nadal eds. *Phraseology and Discourse: Cross-Linguistic and Corpus-based Approaches*. Baltmannsweiler: Schneider Verlag, pp. 225–233.

Cabré Castellví, M.T. 2003. 'Theories of Terminology. Their Description, Prescription and Explanation', *Terminology*, vol. 9(2), pp. 163–199.

Colson, J.P. 2008. 'Cross-Linguistic Phraseological Studies: An Overview'. In: S. Granger and F. Meunier eds. *Phraseology. An Interdisciplinary Perspective*. Amsterdam/Philadelphia: John Benjamins, pp. 191–206.

Gouadec, D. 2007. *Translation as a Profession*. Amsterdam/Philadelphia: John Benjamins.

Goźdź-Roszkowski, S. 2011. *Patterns of Linguistic Variation in American Legal English: A Corpus-Based Study*. Frankfurt am Main: Peter Lang.

Granger, S. and Paquot, M. 2008. 'Disentangling the Phraseological Web'. In: S. Granger and F. Meunier eds. *Phraseology: An Interdisciplinary Perspective*. Amsterdam/Philadelphia: John Benjamins, pp. 27–49.

Hatim, B. and Mason, I. 1990. *Discourse and the Translator*. Harlow: Longman.

Heid, U. 2001. 'Collocations in Sublanguage Texts: Extraction from Corpora'. In: S.E. Wright and G. Budin eds. *Handbook of Terminology Management. Application-Oriented Terminology Management*, vol. 2. Amsterdam/Philadelphia: John Benjamins, pp. 788–808.

Kierzkowska, D. 2002. *Tłumaczenie prawnicze*. Warszawa: Tepis.

Kjær, A.L. 2007. 'Phrasemes in Legal Texts'. In: H. Burger, D. Dobrovol'skij, P. Kühn and N.R. Norrick eds. *Phraseology/Phraseologie: An International Handbook of Contemporary Research / Ein internationales Handbuch der zeitgenössischen Forschung*. Berlin/New York: Walter de Gruyter, pp. 506–516.

Kjær, A.L. 1990. 'Context-Conditioned Word Combinations in Legal Language', *Journal of the International Institute for Terminology Research*, vol. 1(1–2), pp. 21–32.

Koskinen, K. 2000. 'Institutional Illusions: Translating in the EU Commission', *The Translator*, vol. 6(1), pp. 49–65.

Larson, M.L. [1984] 1998. *Meaning-Based Translation: A Guide to Cross-Language Equivalence.* Lanham: University Press of America.

L'Homme, M.-C. 2000. 'Understanding Specialized Lexical Combinations', *Terminology*, vol. 6(1), pp. 89–110.

L'Homme, M.-C., Heid, U. and Sager, J.C. 2003. 'Terminology during the past decade (1994–2004): An Editorial Statement', *Terminology*, vol. 9(2), pp. 151–161.

Mattila, H.E.S. 2006. *Comparative Legal Linguistics.* Aldershot: Ashgate.

Mauranen, A. 2006. 'Translation Universals'. In: K. Brown ed. *Encyclopedia of Language and Linguistics*, vol. 13. Oxford: Elsevier, pp. 93–100.

Mauranen, A. 2007. 'Universal Tendencies in Translation'. In: G.M. Anderman and M. Rogers eds. *Incorporating Corpora. The Linguist and the Translator.* Clevedon: Multilingual Matters, pp. 32–48.

McEnery, T., Xiao, R. and Tono, Y. 2006. *Corpus-Based Language Studies: An Advanced Resource Book.* London and New York: Routledge.

Meyer, I. and Mackintosh, K. 1994. 'Phraseme Analysis and Concept Analysis: Exploring a Symbiotic Relationship in the Specialized Lexicon', *Euralex 1994 Proceedings*. Amsterdam. W. Martin et al. eds. Amsterdam: International Congress on Lexicography, pp. 339–348. Available at: http://www.euralex.org/elx_proceedings/Euralex1994/ [Accessed 1.06.12].

Nesselhauf, N. 2005. *Collocations in a Learner Corpus.* Amsterdam/Philadelphia: John Benjamins.

Newmark, P. 1981. *Approaches to Translation.* London/New York: Prentice Hall.

Orozco, M. and Sánchez-Gijón, P. 2011. 'New Resources for Llegal Translators', *Perspectives: Studies in Translatology*, vol. 19(1), pp. 25–44.

Partington, A. 1998. *Patterns and Meanings: Using Corpora for English Language Research and Teaching.* Amsterdam/Philadelphia: John Benjamins.

Pontrandolfo, G. 2011. 'Phraseology in Criminal Judgments: A Corpus Study of Original vs. Translated Italian', *Sendebar: Revista de la Facultad de Traducción e Interpretación de Granada*, vol. 22, pp. 209–234.

Rogers, M. and Wright, S.E. 2006. 'Approaches to Terminological Theories: The Anglo-Saxon Approach'. In: H. Picht eds. *Modern Approaches to Terminological Theories and Applications.* Bern: Peter Lang, pp. 107–134.

Šarčević, S. 1997. *New Approach to Legal Translation.* The Hague: Kluwer Law International.

Tessuto, G. 2008. 'Legal Concepts and Terminography: Analysis and Application'. In: V.K. Bhatia, C.N. Candlin and P.E. Allori eds. *Language, Culture and the Law: The Formulation of Legal Concepts Across Systems and Cultures.* Bern: Peter Lang, 283–302.

Teubert, W. 2010. 'Our Brave New World?' *International Journal of Corpus Linguistics*, vol. 15(3), pp. 354–358.

Thelen, M. 2002. 'Relations Between Terms: A Cognitive Approach. The Interaction between Terminology, Lexicology, Translation Studies and Translation Practice', *Linguistica Antverpiensia*, vol. 1, pp. 193–209.

Tirkkonen-Condit, S. 2004. 'Unique Items – Over- or Under-Represented in Translated Language?' In: A. Mauranen and P. Kujamäki eds. *Translation Universals: Do They Exist?* Amsterdam/Philadelphia: John Benjamins, pp. 177–184.

Toury, G. 1995. *Descriptive Translation Studies and Beyond.* Amsterdam/Philadelphia: John Benjamins.

Chapter 11
Translating International Arbitration Norms into the Italian Language and Culture

Maurizio Gotti

The last few decades have witnessed a great development in the process of globalization in the legal field, where an international perspective has become more and more widespread (Gotti and Williams 2010). Nowadays many of the texts in use at a local level are the result of a process of translation or adaptation of more general documents formulated at an international level. This is the consequence of the fact that in the context of co-operation and collaboration in international trade, law too is fast assuming an international perspective rather than remaining a purely domestic concern.

An excellent example of the globalizing process taking place in the legal system is constituted by international commercial arbitration. In the last few decades, all over the world arbitration has become more and more common as a legal instrument for the settling of commercial disputes. The very wide acceptance of this adjudging procedure has been promoted by the growing internationalization of commercial exchanges, which involves an ever-increasing number of trade disputes (Bernstein et al. 2003 and Berger 2006). The high recourse to international arbitration has given rise to a widely felt need for greater harmonization of the procedures followed, which has led to the elaboration of the *UNCITRAL Model Law*[1] to be used as a starting document by most of the member countries when producing their own individual statutory provisions for commercial arbitration. Indeed, this model has been adopted by a large number of countries all over the world. As the Model Law and its connected arbitration rules were created with the purpose of achieving the highest degree of harmonization,[2] the single countries have been recommended to make as few changes as possible when incorporating them into their legal systems. However, the adoption of this Model Law has not guaranteed complete uniformity among the various national legislations, as the different countries have used this model in different ways, depending upon their national requirements, concerns, cultures, legal systems, languages, and other constraints. Indeed, in the process of adoption

---

1 The *UNCITRAL* Model Law (United Nations document A/40/17, Annex I) was adopted on 21 June 1985 by the Commission on International Trade Law (UNCITRAL) and is available at: http://www.uncitral.org/uncitral/en/uncitral_texts/arbitration/ 1985Model_arbitration.html. The UNCITRAL Arbitration Rules (AR), are available at: http://www.uncitral.org/english/texts/arbitration/arbitrul.htm.

2 An explanatory note to the UNCITRAL provisions specifies that: 'The Model Law constitutes a sound and promising basis for the desired harmonization and improvement of national laws [. . .]. It is acceptable to States of all regions and the different legal or economic systems of the world [. . .]. It is advisable to follow the model as closely as possible since that would be the best contribution to the desired harmonization and in the best interest of the users of international arbitration, who are primarily foreign parties and their lawyers' (Document A/CN.9/264: *UNCITRAL Yearbook 16*, 1985).

of this model, the English language text of the UNCITRAL has often had to be translated into the local languages, a procedure which has implied not only the adaptation of the original discourse to the typical features and resources of the national tongues, but also its adjustment to the cultural needs and legal constraints of each specific country.

It is the aim of this chapter to investigate the adoption of the *UNCITRAL Model Law* in the Italian context and to examine in particular the adaptations that have been made to the model document in the process of translation/localization of this text.[3] The texts analyzed here will be drawn from Italian legislation on international arbitration based on the Model Law on International Commercial Arbitration (ML) and the UNCITRAL Arbitration Rules (AR); in particular, the analysis will focus on the Italian arbitration law inserted in the Code of Civil Procedure (CCP, arts. 806–840).[4] In order to highlight the differentiations and adaptations to a particular context, the Italian text taken into consideration will be compared to that of the United Nations, with the aim of offering a more detailed understanding of linguistic and textual phenomena closely linked to cross-cultural translation.

1. Translating Legal Texts in a Multilingual/Multicultural Context

The increasing need at an international level for accurate and authoritative translation of legal texts and documents across languages relies on the need for them to convey appropriately in both languages the pragmatic and functional intentions and implications of the original text (Šarčević 1997; Gotti and Šarčević 2006). Although all legal documents in all languages address common issues, they do so in distinctive and also in overlapping ways, because of the different languages in which they are constructed and the cultural differences of the societies in question and of their legal systems. Indeed, legal terminology is so culture-bound (the reasons being at the same time historical, sociological, political and jurisprudential) that a satisfactory translation of all the legal terms of one text from one context to another is at times impossible. David (1980: 39) underlines this difficulty with a few examples:

> *To translate into English technical words used by lawyers in France, in Spain, or in Germany is in many cases an impossible task, and conversely there are no words in the languages of the continent to express the most elementary notions of English law. The words common law and equity are the best examples thereof; we have to keep the English words [. . .] because no words in French or in any other language are adequate to convey*

3 This process of adoption and adaptation of the UML has been the object of analysis of two international research projects, one entitled *Generic Integrity in Legislative Discourse in Multilingual and Multicultural Contexts* (available at: http://gild.mmc.cityu.edu.hk/) and the other *International Commercial Arbitration Practices: A Discourse Analytical Study* (available at: http://enweb.cityu.edu.hk/ arbitrationpractice/), both led by Prof. Vijay Bhatia of the City University of Hong Kong. These projects have investigated the linguistic and discoursal properties of a multilingual corpus of international arbitration laws drawn from a number of different countries, cultures, and socio-political backgrounds, written in different languages, and used within and across a variety of legal systems. Some of the results of the project are presented in Bhatia, Candlin and Gotti (2003), Bhatia, Candlin and Engberg (2008), Bhatia, Candlin and Gotti (2010), and Bhatia, Candlin and Gotti (2012).

4 More specifically, articles 806–831 constitute the legislative and procedural framework for arbitration *per se*, while 832–840 contain special provisions for international controversies. The texts taken into consideration are available at http://www.camera-arbitrale.com/codice.htm; an English translation, offered by the Milan Chamber of National and International Arbitration, is available at http://www.camera-arbitrale.com/eng/rifarb.htm; it is the version referred to in this chapter.

> *the meaning of these words, clearly linked as they are to the specific history of English law alone.*

The adoption of a particular term instead of another may give rise to ambiguity and misinterpretation. Several examples of this are given by Fletcher (1999), who examines the translation into various languages of the English text of the European Convention on Human Rights. For instance, the translation provided for the expression *fair and regular trial* into *juicio justo y imparcial* (Spanish) and *procès juste et équitable* (French) is not satisfactory, as the use of the non-equivalent adjectives *regular* (English)/*imparcial* (Spanish)/*équitable* (French) can easily show. The same could be said for the rendering of the concept of *reasonableness,* basic in common law systems, where expressions such as *reasonable steps, reasonable measures, reasonable person* and *proof beyond a reasonable doubt* frequently occur. This concept, instead, when translated into languages spoken in countries adopting a civil law system is considered too vague and its rendering as *ragionevole, raisonnable* or *vernünftig* often gives rise to criticism and dissatisfaction. Other excellent examples of translation discrepancies can easily be found in texts relating to the process of building a common European legal framework. For example, translators into English find it difficult to express such culturally-specific French collocations as *acteurs sociaux, acteurs économiques, acteurs institutionnels, acteurs publics, acteurs politiques,* which have no direct equivalent in the target language (Salmasi 2003: 117), and they sometimes transliterate terms or create calques from one language into another, relying on the false premise of a very close relationship between similar lexemes in different languages (see the examples of *transmettre/transmit* and *prévoir/foresee* in Seymour 2002). Indeed, in Europe the legal drafting issue has become extremely important with the elaboration of a multilingual legislation concerning the European Union. This depends on the fact that the official languages of the European Union are those of its Member States, and as new countries join the Union, their languages are added to the number. This is part of a precise policy aiming to build a community of peoples respecting and safeguarding at the same time the existing variety of customs and cultural identities, a principle based on the conviction that the languages of Europe are part of its immense and diverse cultural heritage, and therefore it is considered the duty of the Union to guarantee their preservation. The European authorities are aware of these problems and greater and greater emphasis is being laid on the quality of legislation drafting at supranational level. An example of this is the 'Declaration on the Quality of the Drafting of Community Legislation' which is an important part of the Treaty of Amsterdam (1998); this document explicitly states that 'the quality of the drafting of Community legislation is crucial if it is to be properly implemented by the competent national authorities and better understood by the public and in business circles'. This has led to much greater uniformity in the translation of European directives into the various languages of the Union and to more marked homogeneity and interdependence of the resulting texts. This new approach to the translation of European directives has also served a harmonising function, in the sense that from the adoption of the texts of the European Union greater uniformity has derived in the use of terminology as well as a higher degree of conceptual homogeneity, which is then transferred into local legal practices (Šarčević 2010). However, these efforts and initiatives in better drafting procedures have not solved all discrepancy problems, as the final texts are also conditioned by the different rhetorical traditions pertaining to the cultural systems involved, thus often leading to diverging constructions and therefore to conflictual interpretations, with the risk of raising legal controversies. For this reason it is commonly suggested that translators working in this field should have two different types of competence: not only linguistic but also legal (Robertson 2010).

2. Topical Aspects

As illustrated in Table 11.1, the coverage of the Italian text (CCP) and the original Model Law (ML) is very similar in terms of topical content. For this reason, article headings and clauses often overlap, despite understandable terminological and juridical differences between the two documents. The organization of content, however, reflects the different context in which they are embedded: most CCP provisions apply also to domestic commercial arbitration, with only the last three chapters dealing specifically with international awards. On the other hand, ML approaches the matter more systematically, with no allowance for domestic cases.

Table 11.1 Comparison of United Nations (ML) and Italian (CCP) statutory provisions on international commercial arbitration (from Giannoni 2003: 224–225)

ML	CCP
CHAPTER I. GENERAL PROVISIONS Article 1 – Scope of application Article 2 – Definitions and rules of interpretation Article 3 – Receipt of written communications Article 4 – Waiver of right to object Article 5 – Extent of court intervention Article 6 – Court or other authority for certain functions of arbitration assistance and supervision	CHAPTER I. ARBITRATION AGREEMENT AND ARBITRATION CLAUSE Article 806 – Arbitration agreement Article 807 – Form of the arbitration agreement Article 808 – Arbitration clause Article 809 – Number and appointment of arbitrators
CHAPTER II. ARBITRATION AGREEMENT Article 7 – Definition and form of arbitration agreement Article 8 – Arbitration agreement and substantive claim before court Article 9 – Arbitration agreement and interim measures by court	CHAPTER II. THE ARBITRATORS Article 810 – Appointment of the arbitrators Article 811 – Replacement of arbitrators Article 812 – Capacity to act as arbitrator Article 813 – Acceptance by and duties of the arbitrators Article 814 – Rights of the arbitrators Article 815 – Challenge of arbitrators
CHAPTER III. COMPOSITION OF ARBITRAL TRIBUNAL Article 10 – Number of arbitrators Article 11 – Appointment of arbitrators Article 12 – Grounds for challenge Article 13 – Challenge procedure Article 14 – Failure or impossibility to act Article 15 – Appointment of substitute arbitrator	CHAPTER III. THE PROCEEDINGS Article 816 – Proceedings Article 817 – Objection of lack of jurisdiction Article 818 – Interim measures Article 819 – Incidental issues Article 819-bis – Connected cases Article 819-ter – Hearing of witnesses
CHAPTER IV. JURISDICTION OF ARBITRAL TRIBUNAL Article 16 – Competence of arbitral tribunal to rule on its jurisdiction Article 17 – Power of arbitral tribunal to order interim measures	CHAPTER IV. THE AWARD Article 820 – Time limit for the decision Article 821 – Relevance of the expiry of the time limit Article 822 – Rules for the deliberation Article 823 – Deliberation of and requirements for the award Article 824 – Place of rendition Article 825 – Filing of the award Article 826 – Correction of the award
CHAPTER V. CONDUCT OF ARBITRAL PROCEEDINGS Article 18 – Equal treatment of parties Article 19 – Determination of rules of procedure Article 20 – Place of arbitration Article 21 – Commencement of arbitral proceedings	CHAPTER V. MEANS OF RECOURSE Article 827 – Means of recourse Article 828 – Recourse for setting aside Article 829 – Grounds for setting aside Article 830 – Decision on the recourse for setting aside Article 831 – Revocation and third party opposition

Article 22 – Language
Article 23 – Statements of claim and defence
Article 24 – Hearings and written proceedings
Article 25 – Default of a party
Article 26 – Expert appointed by arbitral tribunal
Article 27 – Court assistance in taking evidence

CHAPTER VI. MAKING OF AWARD AND TERMINATION OF PROCEEDINGS
Article 28 – Rules applicable to substance of dispute
Article 29 – Decision making by panel of arbitrators
Article 30 – Settlement
Article 31 – Form and contents of award
Article 32 – Termination of proceedings
Article 33 – Correction and interpretation of award; additional award

CHAPTER VII. RECOURSE AGAINST AWARD
Article 34 – Application for setting aside as exclusive recourse against arbitral award

CHAPTER VIII. RECOGNITION AND ENFORCEMENT OF AWARDS
Article 35 – Recognition and enforcement
Article 36 – Grounds for refusing recognition or enforcement

CHAPTER VI. INTERNATIONAL ARBITRATION
Article 832 – International arbitration
Article 833 – Form of the arbitration clause
Article 834 – Norms applicable to the merits
Article 835 – Language of the arbitration
Article 836 – Challenge of arbitrators
Article 837 – Deliberation of the award
Article 838 – Recourse

CHAPTER VII. FOREIGN AWARDS
Article 839 – Recognition and enforcement of foreign awards
Article 840 – Opposition proceedings

ML opens with a definition of legal scope, status and interpretation (Chapter I) and then follows a chronological progression from the drafting of a commercial contract to the eventual recourse against the award. The communicative rationale that underlies CCP is traceable in a roughly chronological sequence not dissimilar to the Model text (Chapters I–V). The remaining articles are simply a list of points integrating or derogating the aforementioned provisions. Within this framework, varying emphasis is given to each aspect, with some provisions occurring only in one of the two laws. CCP, for instance, gives hardly any terminological definitions, whereas ML has no provision for time-limits or overdue awards. The amount of legal mapping clearly depends on the different origin of these two texts, rather than their purpose.

A complementary view of the topical aspects of the two texts may derive from the analysis of content as opposed to grammar words (cf. Brennan and van Naerssen 1989). Figures 11.1 and 11.2 show the most frequent content words in each text.

There is a considerable degree of semantic similarity between the two lists, which overlap in nine instances: parte/i = party/ies; articolo/i = article/s; lodo/i = award/s; compromesso = agreement; capo/i = paragraph; arbitrato = arbitration; procedimento = proceedings; tribunale = court; arbitrale = arbitral. Interestingly, they are all nouns with the exception of the last item. At the same time, ML has a far stronger clustering of lexis at the top of the list—a finding consistent with the wider range of legal terminology observed in CCP (cf. below).

In terms of word count, the picture is that summarized in Table 11.2. Compared to CCP, ML is longer and more structured, with 44 per cent more articles and 30 per cent more words overall.

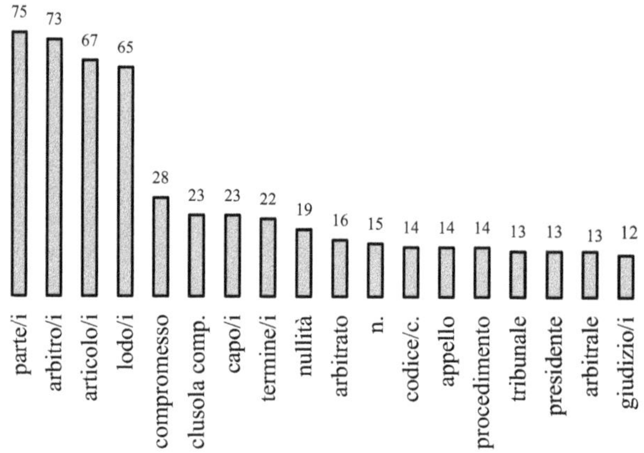

Figure 11.1 CCP content words with ≥10 occurrences (from Giannoni 2003: 230)

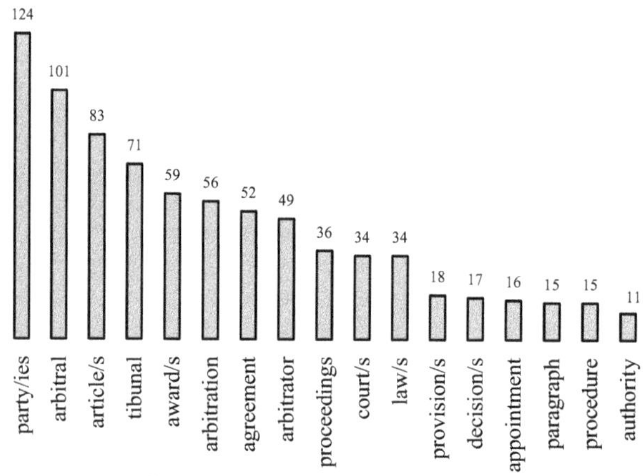

Figure 11.2 ML content words with ≥10 occurrences (from Giannoni 2003: 230)

Table 11.2 Quantitative data (from Giannoni 2003: 226)

	ML	CCP
Articles	36	25
Sentences	156	135
Sentence length (word range)	7–74	9–62
Total length (words)	5,291	4,067

The greater length of ML—in terms of number of articles and words—seems in line with the preference for precision and detailed guidelines built into the common law tradition (Campbell 1996).

3. Linguistic Aspects

The analysis of the arbitration texts in the two languages (English and Italian) also shows examples of discrepancy due to different legal discursive conventions. This can be seen, for example, in the way juridical obligation is signalled. This concept is traditionally expressed by modal *shall* in English legal discourse:

> *(1) The appointing authority shall, at the request of one of the parties, appoint the sole arbitrator as promptly as possible. In making the appointment the appointing authority shall use the following list-procedure, unless both parties agree that the list-procedure should not be used or unless the appointing authority determines in its discretion that the use of the list-procedure is not appropriate for the case [. . .]. (AR 6.3)*[5]

Italian legal discourse, instead, usually adopts a present indicative to state legal provisions,[6] thus emphasising the actuality and applicability of the legal provision and also implying that the law draws its force from the natural order of things rather than an order imposed by human agents:

> *(2) Gli arbitri, sentite le parti, provvedono entro venti giorni. (CCP 826.2)*
>
> *[The arbitrators take the necessary action within twenty days, after hearing the parties]*
>
> *(3) Gli arbitri redigono il lodo in tanti originali quante sono le parti e ne danno comunicazione a ciascuna parte mediante consegna di un originale, anche con spedizione in plico raccomandato, entro dieci giorni dalla data dell'ultima sottoscrizione. (CCP 825)*
>
> *[The arbitrators draft the award in as many originals as the number of the parties and give notice of it to each party by handing over an original or sending it by registered mail within ten days of the date of the last signature]*

Another cause of variation in the linguistic realization in different languages is the greater degree of concern for clarity of expression. This is very high in the UNCITRAL text, which pays great attention to conceptual and terminological unambiguity. This feature can be associated to the emphasis normally placed by common law legislation on precision and detail for action in specific circumstances (Campbell 1996). Another reason for this greater need for clarity is the broader scope of the Model Law, which targets the whole international community and as such is potentially more prone to misinterpretation. This explains why ML devotes various parts of its text to very detailed terminological explanations:

> *(4) 'Arbitration agreement' is an agreement by the parties to submit to arbitration all or certain disputes which have arisen or which may arise between them in respect of a defined legal relationship, whether contractual or not. An arbitration agreement may be in the form of an arbitration clause in a contract or in the form of a separate agreement. (ML 7.1)*

---

5 Emphasis added, as in all quotations in this chapter.

6 This preference for the present tense is also part of the drafting tradition of another country belonging to the civil law system, that is, France. As Garzone's (2003: 206) analysis shows, the simple present indicative—rather than the deontic modal *devoir*—is the form customarily used to convey both the prescriptive and the performative functions of normative and legislative texts.

CCP, instead, gives hardly any terminological definitions. This is also due to the fact that the monocultural background of CCP is in fact less likely to require such specifications. Indeed, in the Italian text there are cases in which specifications remain implicit or refer vaguely to "law" in general:

> *(5) se nel procedimento non sono state osservate le forme prescritte per i giudizi sotto pena di nullità. (CCP 829.7)*
> *[where the formalities laid down for proceedings under penalty of nullity have not been observed]*
>
> *(6) Gli arbitri debbono pronunciare il lodo entro il termine stabilito [. . .] dalla legge; (CCP 813)*
> *[The arbitrators shall render their award within the time limit set [. . .] by law;]*

This different degree of precision is also visible in the lexis found in the two texts, the Italian one employing a wider range of words. Indeed, types in CCP account for 20 per cent of tokens, as compared to 14 per cent in ML. This greater lexical variety of CCP also accounts for a higher proportion of polysemous items in its specialized lexis. This evidence suggests that English legal discourse is more lexically restricted and specific than Italian, which results from the layering of the formal, specialized and bureaucratic registers of language (Petta 1994).

As regards archaic or literary expressions, CCP contains fewer of these items than its counterpart: the only instances are *alcuno* (for *nessuno* [nobody]), *allorché* (for *quando* [when]), *ove* (for *dove* [where]), *pronunzia* (for *pronuncia* [pronunciation]) and the crystallized form *per iscritto* [in writing]. ML has *agreed upon* (for *agreed on*), *commencement* (for *beginning*), *furnish* (for *produce*), *notwithstanding* (for *regardless of*) and compound pronouns *thereof, thereon* and *thereto*. These forms are related to the register of legal writing rather than its terminology: at the same time, however, outdated expressions in ML underline the timeless quality of statutory provisions. Surprisingly, CCP has no Latin expressions except for the terms *bis, ter, quater, quinquies* used in the numbering of additional statutory articles. Instead in ML there are two terms in this class: *interim* and *ipso jure*; the complementary binomials (Gustafsson 1984) *de jure or de facto* and *ex aequo et bono* complete the list. Incidentally, the English text also includes a French expression (*amiable compositeur*) borrowed from the language of international arbitration.

4. Textual Aspects

Although the coverage of the contents of both ML and CCP is very similar, the Italian law is more comprehensive, as it deals both with national and international arbitration, while the Model Law does not apply to domestic controversies. Moreover, the Italian text displays a high degree of intertextual linking as this new law is embedded in the extant body of legislation, and therefore has to be interpreted in the light of hundreds of other texts of greater or equal authority. The sources of some of these references are explicitly mentioned in the text (cf. quotation 7 below), but in other cases the links to other documents remain implicit, as in quotation 8, where references to other parts of the Civil Code (c.c.) or Penal Code (c.p.) are given in brackets:

(7) La clausola compromissoria contenuta in condizioni generali di contratto oppure in moduli o formulari non è soggetta alla approvazione specifica prevista dagli artt. 1341 e 1342 del Codice civile. (CCP 833.1)
[An arbitration clause contained in general conditions of contract or standard forms shall not be subject to the specific approval provided for in Arts. 1341 and 1342 of the Civil Code]

(8) Gli arbitri possono essere sia cittadini italiani sia stranieri. Non possono essere arbitri i minori (c.c. 2), gli interdetti (c.c. 414; c.p. 32), gli inabilitati (c.c. 415), i falliti, e coloro che sono sottoposti a interdizione dai pubblici uffici (829 n. 3; c.p. 28, 23, 31.). (CCP 812)
[The arbitrators may be Italian or foreign nationals. Minors (c.c. 2), persons under a legal incapacity (c.c. 414, 415; c.p. 32), bankrupts and those who have been disqualified from holding a public office (829 n. 3; c.p. 28, 23, 31) may not act as arbitrators]

In ML, instead, reference is usually internal and has the function of facilitating 'textual mapping' (Bhatia 1987). This is achieved mainly through the use of complex prepositional phrases, such as *under, in accordance with* or *according to*:

(9) The award shall state the reasons upon which it is based, unless the parties have agreed that no reasons are to be given or the award is an award on agreed terms under article 30. The award shall state its date and the place of arbitration as determined in accordance with article 20(1). (ML 31.2–3)

Other typical realizations include past-participle clauses such as *referred to* and *specified in*:

(10) Where an action referred to in paragraph (1) of this article has been brought, arbitral proceedings may nevertheless be commenced or continued, and an award may be made, while the issue is pending before the court. (ML 8.2)

(11) any party may request the court or other authority specified in article 6 to take the necessary measure, unless the agreement on the appointment procedure provides other means for securing the appointment. (ML 11.4)

Intra-textual links also occur in CCP, as can be seen in the following case:

(12) La clausola compromissoria deve risultare da atto avente la forma richiesta per il compromesso ai sensi dell'articolo 807, commi primo e secondo. (CCP 808.1)
[The arbitration clause shall be contained in a document meeting the formal requirements for an arbitration agreement according to Art. 807, first and second paragraphs]

However, these devices are less frequent in the Italian text, this being linked to the fact that this law is firmly embedded within the Code of Civil Procedure and its authority, whereas ML is a stand-alone law with no inherent intertextual linking.

The analysis of the two texts has shown a great reliance of ML on the traditional features of common law legal discourse. A relevant aspect of this legal drafting tradition is the use of coordination; indeed, the two texts have a comparable amount of parallel coordination (with 55 *e(d)* in CCP, 59 *and* in ML), while alternative coordination is considerably more frequent in the UNCITRAL text, with 172 occurrences of *or* as compared to 70 of *o/oppure*. The pervasiveness in ML of this second type of binomial is particularly evident inasmuch as it links whole paragraphs rather than single words. Alternative/complementary options with *or* are frequently used in the UNCITRAL text, and the way in which they are usually punctuated and paginated emphasizes their function of making the provisions both more inclusive and semantically transparent.[7] Here is a particularly striking example:

> *(13) Grounds for refusing recognition or enforcement*
>
> *(1) Recognition or enforcement of an arbitral award, irrespective of the country in which it was made, may be refused only:*
>
> *(a) at the request of the party against whom it is invoked, if that party furnishes to the competent court where recognition or enforcement is sought proof that:*
>
> *(i) a party to the arbitration agreement referred to in article 7 was under some incapacity; or the said agreement is not valid under the law to which the parties have subjected it or, failing any indication thereon, under the law of the country where the award was made; or*
>
> *(ii) the party against whom the award is invoked was not given proper notice of the appointment of an arbitrator or of the arbitral proceedings or was otherwise unable to present his case; or*
>
> *(iii) the award deals with a dispute not contemplated by or not falling within the terms of the submission to arbitration, or it contains decisions on matters beyond the scope of the submission to arbitration, provided that, if the decisions on matters submitted to arbitration can be separated from those not so submitted, that part of the award which contains decisions on matters submitted to arbitration may be recognized and enforced; or*
>
> *(iv) the composition of the arbitral tribunal or the arbitral procedure was not in accordance with the agreement of the parties or, failing such agreement, was not in accordance with the law of the country where the arbitration took place; or*
>
> *(v) the award has not yet become binding on the parties or has been set aside or suspended by a court of the country in which, or under the law of which, that award was made; or*
>
> *(b) if the court finds that:*
>
> *(i) the subject-matter of the dispute is not capable of settlement by arbitration under the law of this State; or*
>
> *(ii) the recognition or enforcement of the award would be contrary to the public policy of this State. (UML 36)*

7 The advantages of good paragraphing are thus pointed out by Driedger: '[It] provides a visual aid to comprehension by breaking up solid blocks of type; it delivers the sentence in packages, so to speak, making it easier for the mind to grasp the whole. It does visually what the reader would do mentally without it.' (Driedger 1982: 78)

By arranging content schematically, the drafter can construct a denser, more cognitively demanding text such as the one cited above. ML incorporates no less than ten bi/multinomials of this type, while CCP only has four. The prevailing pattern in Italian is simply coordination with *or* at word level:

(14) La parte che intende far eseguire il lodo nel territorio della Repubblica è tenuta a depositarlo in originale o in copia conforme, insieme con l'atto di compromesso o con l'atto contenente la clausola compromissoria o con documento equipollente, in originale o in copia conforme, nella cancelleria della pretura nella cui circoscrizione è la sede dell'arbitrato. (CCP 825)
[The party intending to have the award enforced in the territory of the Republic shall file the original award or a certified copy thereof, together with the original arbitration agreement or document containing the arbitartion clause or an equivalent document, or a certified copy thereof, with the Registry of the Magistrate's Court [Pretura] of the district in which the arbitrator has its seat]

(15) Il lodo può esssere corretto, su istanza di parte, dagli stessi arbitri che lo hanno pronunziato, qualora questi siano incorsi in omissioni o in errori materiali o di calcolo. (CCP 826)
[On the request of a party, the award may be corrected by the same arbitrators who have rendered it, where there have been omissions, material errors or miscalculations]

5. Cultural Aspects

Even from a very superficial analysis of the arbitration texts in the two languages, it is easy to realize that the cultural environment has greatly influenced the outcome of the translation/adaptation process. Indeed, it is often impossible to guarantee a perfectly homogeneous process, as the various legal patterns of the countries involved re-emerge in some of the procedures described or in a few of the principles set out. Some of the differentiations in the formulation of legal norms may depend on diverging cultural implications involved in dispute resolution or on the different legal system adopted (e.g., common law versus civil law). One of the main features of the common law system is the greater degree of autonomy enjoyed by the judge (cf. Borris 1994). Similarly, in the arbitration process the arbitrator plays a very active role due to the fact that no jury is involved in the proceedings and that the majority of the disputes in international commercial arbitration are of a technical and complicated nature. Moreover, the arbitrator often makes proposals for an amicable settlement of the dispute if he sees any feasible solutions. It is important, therefore, that the decision-making process should be totally transparent and that the arbitrator should be impartial and independent. This need is particularly felt in the Italian context, where the custom of non-standard arbitration has often been regarded as too sensitive to the parties' interests and pressures (Ceccon 2000: 12), and provides an explanation for the specific norms that the Italian arbitration law has laid down to regulate the challenge of appointed arbitrators. In particular, these norms contain specific reference to such important issues as the arbitrator's competence, impartiality and independence, which are largely modelled on the Criteria of Arbitral Ethics *(Criteri di Deontologia Arbitrale)* enacted by the Italian Arbitration Association in 1999 (cf. Bartolini and Delconte 2001). In the UNCITRAL text, instead, this issue is considered in very general terms:

(16) In making the appointment, the appointing authority shall have regard to such considerations as are likely to secure the appointment of an independent and impartial arbitrator and shall take into account as well the advisability of appointing an arbitrator of a nationality other than the nationalities of the parties. (AR 6.4)

Instead, the reasons for challenging an arbitrator included in CCP are more specific as they consist of several items:[8]

(17) Un arbitro può essere ricusato:

1) se non ha le qualifiche espressamente convenute dalle parti;

2) se egli stesso, o un ente, associazione o società di cui sia amministratore, ha interesse nella causa;

3) se egli stesso o il coniuge è parente fino al quarto grado o è convivente o commensale abituale di una delle parti, di un rappresentante legale di una delle parti, o di alcuno dei difensori;

4) se egli stesso o il coniuge ha causa pendente o grave inimicizia con una delle parti, con un suo rappresentante legale, o con alcuno dei suoi difensori;

5) se è legato ad una delle parti, a una società da questa controllata, al soggetto che la controlla, o a società sottoposta a comune controllo, da un rapporto di lavoro subordinato o da un rapporto continuativo di consulenza o di prestazione d'opera retribuita, ovvero da altri rapporti di natura patrimoniale o associativa che ne compromettono l'indipendenza; inoltre, se è tutore o curatore di una delle parti;

6) se ha prestato consulenza, assistenza o difesa ad una delle parti in una precedente fase della vicenda o vi ha deposto come testimone. (CCP 815)

[An arbitrator may be challenged if he or she:

1) lacks the qualifications indicated by the parties;

2) has an interest in the case;

3) (or his or her spouse) is a relative, or lives with, a party, one of its legal representatives or its counsel;

4) (or his or her spouse) is involved in a case pending against, or has a serious enmity with, one of the parties, one of its legal representatives or counsel;

8 Also in the Arbitration Law of the People's Republic of China the grounds for challenging the appointment of arbitrators are mentioned in very specific terms, and are exemplified in a close relationship with any 'one litigant' or 'the attorney', 'private meetings with the litigants or with their attorneys' or acceptance of 'invitation of the litigants or their attorneys to dine' or acceptance of 'gifts' (Bhatia, Candlin and Wei 2001: 10).

5) is an employee or a partner or does business which might affect his or her independence vis-à-vis one of the parties, with a company controlled by that party, with its controlling entity or with a company subject to its common control; furthermore, if he or she is a guardian or a curator of one of the parties; or

6) has given advice, assistance or acted as counsel to one of the parties in a prior phase of the same case or has testified as a witness.]

It is self-evident that the choice of an arbitrator is of immense importance: s/he must be a figure of sufficient professional standing to satisfy the parties of his/her competence in resolving the issue(s) and add personal credibility to the legal validity of the procedure. These qualities are of particular importance in a country such as Italy, where for many years arbitration was considered as a secondary, alternative tool, appropriate only for the resolution of minor disputes. As a consequence, the drafters of the Italian Code of Civil Procedure have decided to provide detailed specifications as regards the qualifications of an arbitrator.

6. Conclusion

The comparison between CCP and ML has shown that—as the former derives from the latter—the two texts are obviously very similar in terms of topical content and coverage. This is confirmed by an analysis of content-word clustering, with most top occurrences overlapping both semantically and grammatically. The use of lexis also points to interesting differences in legal discourse, with Italian employing fewer archaic or literary expressions and a wider range of words: types in CCP account for 20 per cent of tokens, as compared to 14 per cent in ML. Moreover, the proportion of legally marked terms in Italian is more than twice that observed in English.

The investigation of intertextual linking has also shown that—particularly in the Italian text—the reader is repeatedly referred to other texts which constrain and frame interpretation. This finding is probably linked to the fact that the arbitration law is firmly embedded within the Code of Civil Procedure and its authority, whereas ML is a stand-alone law with no inherent intertextual linking. Both texts do, however, signal that certain expressions should be understood in the light of a given statutory provision.

Although these findings cannot be generalized, they suggest interesting divergences between the common law tradition reflected in the UN document and the civil law perspective adopted by Italian legislators. Whereas the former favours precision and detailed guidelines for action in specific circumstances, the latter takes a more systematic approach, with arbitration firmly embedded within the country's highly codified domestic legislation. This is confirmed by the wealth of intertextual references found in CCP.

As can be seen from the analysis carried out in this chapter, the phenomenon of legal translation in a multilingual/multicultural contest is greatly influenced by the linguistic constraints and legal traditions of the local communities to which the translation is addressed. As language is inseparable from set cultural implications and is deeply involved in social norms, translations into different local discourses often demonstrate that linguistic and cultural adaptations are bound to arise. Indeed, variations in the formulation of legal norms are to be attributed to the different cultural traits and legal traditions of the communities for which they are meant. This can be seen, in particular, in the analysis of the specificity of information included in the two texts taken into consideration here, which differ significantly, due to differences in socio-cultural expectations and practices that constrain social behaviour in local contexts. A relevant case in point was seen in the comparison of the article concerning the grounds for challenging the appointment of arbitrators: the UNCITRAL text is expressed in more general terms, while in the Italian arbitration law the constraints are specified in greater detail.

The investigation of the process of translation/adaptation of the UN Model Law to the Italian reality has shown that, in spite of the growing efforts of the international community to guarantee greater and greater harmonization in legislation and procedures, local constraints and specific cultural aspects still represent a relevant conditioning factor. This is clearly visible in the normative resulting text, which shows discrepancies deriving not only from differing legal and cultural systems, but also from the use of different linguistic codes. The interpretation of this adaptation of the UN Model Law to a specific national reality is in line with the findings of other scholars (e.g., Vermeer 1996), who have pointed out further cases in which the source text offers the input on the basis of which a new autonomous text is created taking into consideration mainly the needs of the final users. The resulting Italian text has shown to possess clear features of "hybrid" (Trosborg 1997) discourse, deriving from the process of adjustment and adaptation of a text issued by an international organization to the legal and socio-cultural traits of the national target users. Indeed, the differentiations among them is the result of the conscious and deliberate decisions operated by the drafters of the local document, and its final form shows that it is 'arrived at as an outcome of negotiations between cultures and the norms and conventions involved' (Trosborg 1997: 146).

The analysis of the arbitration texts carried out here has shown that, although the Model Law has been created with the purpose of achieving the highest degree of harmonization, total harmonization has not been realized, with the consequence that it is no longer unanimously perceived as a final and attainable goal. Indeed, the current prevalent interpretation of the harmonization process emphasizes a common understanding of the meaning of terms and practices rather than total adoption and blind acceptance of proposed models (Borris 1999). In spite of the desire to make international arbitration procedures 'unbound' (Paulsson 1981) by local constraints, linguistic, social and cultural aspects still represent an important conditioning factor in the translation/adaptation of the legal discourse concerning this mediating practice.

References

Bartolini, F. and Delconte, R.C. (eds). 2001. *Il codice dell'arbitrato* [*The Arbitration Code*]. Piacenza: La Tribuna.

Berger, K.P. 2006. *Private Dispute Resolution in International Business: Negotiation, Mediation, Arbitration*. The Hague: Kluwer Law International.

Bernstein, R., Tackaberry, J., Marriott, A.L. and Wood, D. (eds). 2003. *Handbook of Arbitration Practice*. London: Sweet & Maxwell.

Bhatia, V.K. 1987. 'Textual-Mapping in British Legislative Writing', *World Englishes*, vol. 1(1), pp. 1–10.

Bhatia, V.K., Candlin, C.N. and Wei, S. 2001. *Legal Discourse in Multilingual and Multicultural Contexts: A Preliminary Study*. Research Group Report. Hong Kong: City University of Hong Kong.

Bhatia, V.K., Candlin, C.N. and Engberg, J. (eds). 2008. *Legal Discourse Across Cultures and Systems*. Hong Kong: Hong Kong University Press.

Bhatia, V.K., Candlin, C.N. and Gotti, M. (eds). 2003. *Legal Discourse in Multilingual and Multicultural Contexts: Arbitration Texts in Europe*. Bern: Peter Lang.

———. 2010. *The Discourses of Dispute Resolution*. Bern: Peter Lang.

———. 2012. *Discourse and Practice in International Commercial Arbitration*. Farnham: Ashgate.
Borris, C. 1994. 'Common Law and Civil Law: Fundamental Differences and their Impact on Arbitration', *Arbitration*, vol. 60(2), pp. 78–85.
Borris, C. 1999. 'The Reconciliation of Conflicts Between Common Law and Civil Law Principles in the Arbitration Process'. In: S.N. Frommel and B.A.K. Rider eds. *Conflicting Legal Cultures in Commercial Arbitration: Old Issues and New Trends*. The Hague: Kluwer Law International, pp. 1–18.
Brennan, M. and van Naerssen, M. 1989. 'Language and Content in ESP', *ELT Journal*, vol. 43(3), pp. 196–205.
Campbell, L. 1996. 'Drafting Styles: Fuzzy or Fussy?', *ELaw. Murdoch University Electronic Journal of Law*, vol. 3(2). Available at: http://www.murdoch.edu.au/elaw/issues/v3n2/ campbell. html.
Ceccon, R. 2000. 'La Corte Arbitrale di Venezia, una nuova istituzione per attrarre l'arbitrato internazionale in Italia [The Venice Arbitration Chamber, A New Institution to Attract International Arbitration to Italy]'. In: *Le prospettive dell'arbitrato interno ed internazionale: il Regolamento della Corte Arbitrale di Venezia*. Turin: Giappichelli, pp. 7–12.
David, R. 1980. *English Law and French Law*. London: Stevens.
Driedger, E.A. 1982. 'Legislative Drafting Style: Civil Law *versus* Common Law'. In: Jean-Claude Gémar ed. *Langage du droit et traduction/The Language of the Law and Translation*. Montreal: Linguatech/Conseil de la Langue Française, pp. 63–81.
Fletcher, G.P. 1999. 'Fair and Reasonable: A Linguistic Glimpse into the American Legal Mind'. In: Rodolfo Sacco and Luca Castellani eds. *Les multiples langues du droit européen uniforme*. Turin: L'Harmattan Italia, pp. 57–70.
Garzone, G. 2003. 'Arbitration Rules Across Legal Cultures: An Intercultural Approach'. In: V.K. Bhatia, C.N. Candlin and M. Gotti eds. *Legal Discourse in Multilingual and Multicultural Contexts: Arbitration Texts in Europe*. Bern: Peter Lang, pp. 177–220.
Giannon, D.S. 2003. 'The UNCITRAL Model and Italian Statute Law: A Linguistic and Topical Desciption'. In: V.K. Bhatia, C.N. Candlin and M. Gotti eds. *Legal Discourse in Multilingual and Multicultural Contexts: Arbitration Texts in Europe*. Bern: Peter Lang, pp. 221–246.
Gotti, M. and Šarčević, S. (eds). 2006. *Insights into Specialized Translation*. Bern: Peter Lang.
Gotti, M. and Williams, C. (eds). 2010. *Legal Discourse Across Languages and Cultures*. Bern: Peter Lang.
Gustafsson, M. 1984. 'Syntactic Features of Binomial Expressions in Legal English', *Text*, vol. 4(1–3), pp. 123–141.
Paulsson, J. 1981. 'Arbitration Unbound: Award Detached from the Law of its Country of Origin', *International and Comparative Law Quarterly*, vol. 30, pp. 358–387.
Petta, P. 1994. 'Il linguaggio del legislatore [The Legislator's Language]'. In: *Quaderni Regionali*, pp. 1303–1316.
Robertson, C. 2010. 'Legal-Linguistic Revision of EU Legislative Texts'. In: M. Gotti and C. Williams eds. *Legal Discourse Across Languages and Cultures*. Bern: Peter Lang, pp. 51–73.
Salmasi, S. 2003. 'English as a *Lingua Franca* at the European Union: The Undertakings of Pride?', *Recherches Anglaises et Nord-Américaines*, vol. 36, pp. 113–120.
Šarčević S. 1997. *New Approach to Legal Translation*. The Hague: Kluwer Law International.
———. 2010. 'Creating a Pan-European Legal Language'. In: M. Gotti and C. Williams eds. *Legal Discourse Across Languages and Cultures*. Bern: Peter Lang, pp. 23–50.
Seymour, E. 2002. 'Euro-English: The New Pidgin?', *Terminologie et traduction*, vol. 3, pp. 22–32.
Trosborg, A. 1997. *Rhetorical Strategies in Legal Language: Discourse Analysis of Statutes and Contracts*. Tübingen: Gunter Narr.
Vermeer, H.J. 1996. *A Skopos Theory of Translation (Some Arguments For and Against)*. Heidelberg: Textcontext Wissenschaft.

Chapter 12
Translating Domestic Legislation: A Comparative Analysis of English Versions of Brazilian Law on Arbitration

Celina Frade

The insertion of Brazil in the legal international community has resulted in some practical advances concerning how our legal practice and domestic legislation are to be produced and understood by non-native legal practitioners. As a Portuguese-speaking monolingual country, wherein English bears the status of foreign language, legal translation[1] is still a non-standardized, subjective and irregular activity mostly performed by lawyers who also speak English rather than legal linguists, experienced legal translators or professional drafters.

On the whole, legal translation in Brazil can be performed in two ways: the translation of documents in a foreign language into Portuguese and the translation of domestic-oriented documents into a foreign language. In both cases, versions can be either authoritatively binding or non-binding according to their communicative purpose, the target audience and the context of situation wherein the documents are to be produced and used (see Frade 2014). In both cases, the role of translator is key to 'mobilize translation competence to perform legal translation tasks in the legal setting for intercultural and interlingual communicative purposes' (Cao 2007: 39).

This chapter provides a comparative analysis of two English versions of the Brazilian law on arbitration—Law 9.307/1996[2]—in the light of the concept of generic integrity and consistency. The versions are available in institutional websites and, though neither of them has established possible *skopoi*,[3] I will assume that they are intended to be understood by foreign legal practitioners as parallel informative texts. The issue posed here is a practical one: is literal translation to be adopted in order to keep the generic integrity of the original legislation in Portuguese or can the translator appropriate of some conventions of legislative drafting[4] so as the translated version is used in non-domestic settings? I have focused the

---

1 In this chapter, "translation" refers to the process performed by the translator to translate a source text into a target text and "version" refers to the product of translation.

2 Law 9.307/96 was partly based on the UNCITRAL Model Law. Available at: http://www.uncitral.org/pdf/english/texts/arbitration/ml-arb/06–54671_Ebook.pdf [Accessed 12 January 2014]. The original Portuguese version of the law was published in the Official Gazette [*Diário Oficial*] dated 24 September 1996. Available at: http://www.planalto.gov.br/ccivil_03/leis/l9307.htm [Accessed 17 January 2014]. See also a contrastive analysis between both laws in Frade (2004).

3 The Greek term *skopoi*, plural of *skopos*, means "the prospective use[s] of the target text" in translation (Kocbek 2009: 47).

4 In this chapter, legislative drafting refers particularly to English legislative drafting in the common law tradition in the United States, except otherwise stated.

analysis on some particular formal and linguistic elements displayed in the data: title, the enacting clause, terms of authority, and collocations.

Results evidenced that the versions are hybrid texts as not only do they maintain part the generic integrity of the original version in Portuguese but appropriate of some generic resources from legislative drafting as well. Lack of consistency and non-familiarity with conventions of legal drafting and the creation of neologisms posed the analyzed between and within versions. We conclude summarizing the study and suggesting alternatives for legal translators in task of translating across unrelated legal systems and languages.

1. Legislative Texts Across Legal Systems

Legal systems vary according to the origins and historical developments they encode. Likewise, legislative writing displays variations as expressed in particular conventions of description and argument in the use of law languages as, for example, across the two main contemporary legal systems: common law and civil law.[5]

In common law, legislative drafting is distinguished from other legal writing insofar as it is guided by drafting manuals containing 'the exact parts, formats, styles, and sometimes language prescribed by state commissions or statutes for the bills [the professional drafters] draft' (Child 1992: 177–178). The text, and not its intent, is the most important source of interpretation, what prevents the judges from a free interpretation. Some generic formalities of legislative texts include the title with the purpose of the subject, the enacting clause and the material organized within sections into self-contained and all-inclusive sentences.

On the other hand, the civilian tradition of legislative drafting established a systemic and principled legal method framed by political histories, which led to codifications of law. Its style is usually plain and reader-friendly (though formal), with short and simple sentences, and seems to rely heavily on cross-referencing to other legislations or codes, and tacit shared knowledge of civil lawyers who use the text as a guide only (Maley 1987; Bhatia 1993). The role of the civil law court is to treat the text as a guide only and to establish the details of its application in specific cases.

As genres, legislative texts bear generic integrity which 'is essentially constructed in the context of the goals of the professional / . . . / culture' with which they are often associated (Bhatia 2004: 123). Generic integrity includes both text-internal text-external indicators: the former refers to the construction and interpretation of the legislative text in question and the latter is related to its wider cultural and professional context of use by the legal community in which it is inserted. (Id.).

As a pragmatic consideration, a legislative text can be regarded 'a rule-enacting document, that its promulgation by the legislature is a speech act with the illocutionary force of enacting' (Kurzon 1986: 9). The entire legislation and many of the sentences in the text may also have a status as speech acts containing explicit or implicit performatives and '"the various felicity conditions such as the authority of the speaker and the function of the relevant convention' (Kurzon 1986; Cao 2007: 115).

Although each legal system has its own drafting tradition and stylistic conventions, legislative texts are mostly descriptive, prescriptive and relatively uniform with some permissible variations on how to make law (Gotti 2009: 278). Nevertheless, one of the most highly valued principle in legal drafting—consistency—is to be achieved during all the process

5 See Campbell (1996) and Frade (2014).

of drafting legislative texts: in any well-drafted legal document, 'the drafter always say the same thing the same way and different things differently' (Child 1992: 376).

In regard to legal translation, a translational approach to legislative writing will also vary depending on the circumstances and purposes of the communicative situation evaluated by the translator. The claim is also that legislative translation should be consistent: it does not matter the translator's choices as long as he/she observes them consistently. In this case, consistency can be achieved at different levels by observing the relatedness of conventions of form and substance of legislative drafting of the languages and/or legal systems included and their culture-specific contexts.

2. Translating Domestic Legislation

Legal translation has been considered a highly sensitive area mainly due to 'profound differences in categories and concepts between legal systems' (Garzone 2000: 4). Although traditional translation theory still aims at 'preserving the letter of the original as much as possible', more recent approaches have assumed more communicative and pragmatic factors placing it 'as a communicative and intercultural action' (Garzone 2000: 1–5).[6]

The translation of domestic legislation is needed within both bilingual and multilingual, and monolingual jurisdictions, with possible situations which include the translation between related and unrelated languages (Cao 2007; Kocbek 2009). There are two types of translated domestic legislation: one that is used for normative purposes in multilingual jurisdictions where two or more languages are the official languages, as in Canada and Switzerland; and other that is used for informative rather than normative purposes in monolingual jurisdictions, as in Brazil. In the latter case, 'the translated text does not have any legal force, and the original law and the translated text are not equal' (Cao 2007: 103). However, the most difficult situation will be translating domestic legislation between unrelated legal systems and languages. In this case, the translator should be able to establish the *skopos* and the kind of translation required, and also to identify 'sources of translational difficulty to be expected' in a given legal setting (Kocbek 2009: 49–53).

On a generic viewpoint, Bhatia (2004: 198) argues that translated texts should 'maintain the generic integrity of the source text in its recontextualized form, so that one can convey not only the textual meaning, but also the more conventionalized generic meaning of the source text.'

Another sensitive issue in legal translation is the role of the legal translator and his/her competence and proficiency to "adapt" non-official translated versions of domestic legislation. The feature of "adaptation" should be part of the translator's choice of entextualization elements to meet the demand of the target audience which may have a different legal view, 'a different knowledge of the world' and a different legal document experience in the light of the translated text (Trosborg 1994: 23).[7] For some authors, legal translators should preserve the 'textual symmetry to the extent possible' securing the user 'confidence not literal translations' (Šarčević 2008: 295); others claim that the translator 'in her/his interpreting efforts, is constantly at risk or overstepping the limits of her/his professional competence' (Garzone 2000: 3). And, as pointed out by Kocbek (2009: 53), the translator should always evaluate the relatedness of

6 See also Trosborg (1994; 1997), Campbell (1996), Cao (2007), Šarčević (2008), Garzone (2008), and Frade (2014).

7 Entextualization is the process 'by which a discourse is lifted out of its original interactional context of production and reception and is inserted, via successive and/or simultaneous decontextualizations and recontextualizations, in alternative contexts' (Vigouroux 2009: 617). For other approaches and applications of this concept in legal translation, see Frade (2014).

the legal systems and also 'take into account the connectedness of the languages involved in the translation'. In short, translating domestic legislation constitutes part of 'the workload of the practicing legal translator' (Cao 2007: 103), bilingual lawyers, and, particularly, academic lawyers.

3. Method and Material

The analysis comprises two English versions of the Brazilian law on arbitration—Law 9.307/96. Version 1 was retrieved from the Brazilian Committee of Arbitration (CBAr, in Portuguese) website, unidentified translator; Version 2 was retrieved from the Brazilian Association of Arbitration Students (ABArb, in Portuguese), translated by a Law student and revised by 'Brazilian legal practitioners in the field of domestic and international commercial arbitration'.[8] As stated previously, I will assume that the versions were produced to be read by foreign legal audiences for informative purposes.

It is worth a brief description of the original textual organization of Law 9.307/96 as the source text of the translation. It displays a rhetorical 4-move arbitration interchange pattern following the norms and guidelines of Decree 4.176/2002,[9] which provides for the elaboration and drafting of Brazilian normative acts. The layout is meant to serve as a visual device to identify and separate the component parts of the substantive statements presented in a rather arbitrary order. The body of the text is organized in seven chapters, forty-one articles and forty-nine paragraphs; the articles are numbered in ordinal numbers and the paragraphs are marked with a symbol (§) preceding an ordinal number. All-caps headings are given only to the chapters and there are no subheadings for the articles. As usual in civil law legislation, Law 9.307/96 does not have a definition section and terms are defined, when necessary, within the body of the document with no initial capitalization, as types of adjective statements 'to assist the reader with following the legislation' (Cao 2007: 104).

The comparative analysis between the English versions is focused on the consistency of use of some particular features of the translated versions, as follows: titles, the enacting clause, terms of authority and collocations. Also, the maintenance (or not) of the generity integrity of the versions is considered in relation to the original version in Portuguese and the UNCITRAL Model Law. Examples extracted from the data are displayed in tables for ease of comparison.

4. English Versions of Law 9.307/2007 on Arbitration

The analysis include some required elements in legislative texts—titles and the enacting clause—and some optional ones inserted in the substantive body of the texts (chapters and articles)—terms of authority and collocations. Although not particularly approached here, some issues on consistency in the selection of terms and syntactic construction of the clauses were also raised out of the examples provided.[10]

8 Both versions are available at http://cbar.org.br/site/eng/brazilian-legislation/law-9-307-96-english/ [Accessed 13 October 2013] and http://abearb.org/arquivos/138/abearb---bal-final.pdf [Accessed 17 January 2014], respectively.

9 Available at: http://www.planalto.gov.br/ccivil_03/decreto/2002/D4176.htm [Accessed 17 January 2014].

10 Titles and numbers of clauses and sections of the examples were omitted when not relevant for the analysis in question.

4.1. Titles

In legislative drafting, titles are constitutionally required to express their subject and purposes 'designed to put people on notice of the content of legislation' (Child 1992: 197). On the contrary, Brazilian legislation is referred to by a main title containing its number and date of enactment in all-caps, underlined bold centered, and in a large font. The purpose of the law is stated in an epigraph or short title below the main title.

Table 12.1 Main title

Version 1	Version 2
BRAZILIAN ARBITRATION ACT *Law nº 9307, 23 September 1996* *- Regarding Arbitration -*	BRAZILIAN ARBITRATION LAW (Published in the Official Gazette of the Federal Executive, Section I, on September 24, 1996, page 18897) Law No. 9.307, September 23, 1996 *Provides for arbitration.*

In the translation, both versions followed the requirement of legislative drafting by stating the purpose of the law in the main title. They bear at least two epigraphs each containing the number and date of the enactment of the law whereas Version 2 also adds the place it was published and its purpose again, as in the original. The result is a hybrid way, 'both mixed and embedded' (Bhatia 2004: 58), of presenting the law to fit conventions of legal drafting and to comply with the guidelines set forth in Decree 4.176/2002 as well. The translated title with the purpose of the law can be also explained by reference to how the law is commonly known amongst Brazilian legal experts.

The terms "act" and "law" are used interchangeably in the titles without any significant change in meaning. Definitions of both terms in Portuguese and English dictionaries seem to corroborate the idea that there is actually no relevant difference in meaning between them, as shown in Table 12.1.[11]

Table 12.2 Definitions

Portuguese	English
Ato – documento público que expõe a deliberação de uma autoridade. **Lei** – regra escrita de alcance geral, emanada pelo poder legislativo do Estado e promulgada pelo presidente da República.	**Act** – the formal product of legislature or other deliberative body. **Law** – a statue or a law passed by a legislative body.

According to Decree 4.176/2002, however, "normative acts" imply a more generic term, which includes 'laws, provisionary measures and decrees'. Therefore, "law" could be more appropriately and consistently used in the titles for at least two reasons: to follow the

11 Portuguese definitions are available at houaiss.uol.com.br [Accessed 17 January 2014]; for English definitions, see *Black' s Law Dictionary* (2006).

UNCITRAL Model Law as an established convention and also to be consistent with the use of "this law" (never "this act") as internal reference throughout the body of the text.

Titles also identify and express the subject of the sections divided in numbered chapters, articles and paragraphs (symbol §).

Table 12.3 Subtitles

Version 1	Version 2
CHAPTER I GENERAL PROVISIONS	Chapter I General Provisions
Article 1 – Persons capable of entering into contracts may settle through arbitration disputes related to freely transferable patrimonial rights.	Art. 1 Persons capable of contracting may refer to arbitration disputes related to disposable patrimonial rights.
Article 2 – At the parties' discretion, arbitration may be in law or in equity. § 1 – The parties may freely choose the rules of law applicable in the arbitration, as long as their choice does not violate good morals and public policy. § 2 – The parties may also stipulate that the arbitration shall be conducted under general principles of law, customs, usages and the rules of international trade.	Art. 2 The arbitration may be conducted under rules of law or of equity, at the parties' discretion. First Paragraph. The parties may freely choose the rules of law applicable to the arbitration provided that their choice does not violate good morals or public policy standards. Second Paragraph. The parties may also establish for the arbitration proceedings to be conducted under general principles of law, customs, usages and international rules of commerce.

The titles of the chapters are translated *ipsis litteris* from the original version and differ only as to the use of the definite article "the" in Version 1, as in "The Arbitrators" (Chapter III), "The Arbitral Proceedings" (Chapter IV) and "The Award" (Chapter V).

Both versions follow the original organization of the sections, with some variations concerning the identification of the articles: while Version 1 displays "Article X" and the symbol § to identify paragraphs, Version 2 displays the abbreviated form "Art. X" and replaces the paragraph symbol for the title "First Paragraph", and so on.

4.2. The Enacting Clause

In legal drafting, the enacting clause usually reads: 'Be it enacted by the Senate and House of Representatives of the United States of America in Congress Assembled, That. . . .' It is prescribed in a passive imperative and, according to Child (1992: 197), 'failure to use the prescribed language can render the legislation invalid'.

Kurzon (1986: 12) claims that legislative texts are explicit performatives in nature as indicated in the "enacting formula" and in the direct link between the formula and the entire text that follows. Similarly, Dorsey (2006: 157) points out that: 'The clause is the signal to the reader that what follows is what is proposed to be given effect. The matter before the clause is not given in effect. While the clause and the matter that follows the clause are given effect.' In civil law legislation, there is neither prescription for enacting clauses nor any reference of their performative nature. However, they 'may be considered implicit performatives, since it is only the situation – the promulgation of the law – not the linguistic form, that allows for a performative interpretation' (Kurzon 1986: 12).

Table 12.4 The enacting clause

Version 1	Version 2
THE PRESIDENT OF THE REPUBLIC Let it be known that the National Congress decrees and I ratify the following law:	The PRESIDENT OF THE REPUBLIC. I hereby make known that the National Congress decrees and I sanction the following Law:

The versions differ as to the structure of the enacting clauses. In Version 1 the enacting formula is a probate declaration—'Let it be known that . . .'—which is quite unique; and, in Version 2, the explicit performative 'I hereby make known that . . .' is used.

Both enacting clauses may be regarded as macro speech acts which combine three types of speech acts and the two performers of the act contained in the formula. Both declarative formulas—'Let it be known . . .' and 'I hereby make known . . .'—are presented in the beginning of the law in which the grammatical and real subject is "the President of the Republic" who declares something. The National Congress performs one of its attributions to decree the law and then the President of the Republic also performs his/her other attributions to sanction or ratify the law.

The versions display an apposition indicator—'the following'—instead of the traditional form "that". According to Kurzon (1986: 11), the predicate 'the following Law/law' is a place holder, since 'the real subject, extra-posed to the end of the sentence is the entire text of the law', as in Version 1 ('Let it be known that the National Congress decrees and I ratify the following law: [*the entire body of the law that follows*]') and in Version 2 ('I hereby make known that the National Congress decrees and I sanction the following Law: [*the entire body of the law that follows*]').

In Version 2, the adverb "hereby" is 'a marker of a performative and, more specifically a legal performative' (Mellinkoff 1963: 305; Kurzon 1986: 7). Once again, it seems that there is an attempt to comply with the enacting formula of common law legislative drafting without being aware of its being 'an optional element in a performative' (Kurzon 1986: 6).

The performative verbs in the versions are not the conventional ones used in common law statutes, for example, "declare" rather than "make known", "enact" rather than "decree", "ratify", and "sanction". One possible explanation for such variation may be that such terms derive from Latin, the same family as Portuguese. Nevertheless, enacting clauses in Brazilian legislation could be consistently translated into the conventionalized formula 'Be it enacted by the . . .' without losing the generic integrity of the law as a whole.

4.3. Terms of Authority

In legislative drafting, the convention regarding terms of authority is to use "shall" to order or command and "may" to allow. Likewise, "shall not" expresses prohibition and "may not" negates discretionary authority and by convention (Child 1992: 204).[12] Although such terms may still cause interpretive problems as they are inherently ambiguous, the convention remains (Dorsey 2006: 190).[13] An alternative could be to replace the modals by more precise indicatives such as "is required to" instead of "shall" and "is free to" or "is authorized to" instead of "may", for example.

12 See Kurzon (1986).
13 See also Child (1992) and Mellinkoff (1993).

In Brazilian legislation, there is no convention or regulation regarding the use of terms of authority. To express obligation/liability, for example, performative markers, such as *dever*, *poder*, are used interchangeably with descriptive forms of performative verbs in the present or future tense, as underlined and explained in the examples below drawn from the original version of Law 9.307/96.

> *Art. 1º As pessoas capazes de contratar poderão valer-se da arbitragem para dirimir litígios relativos a direitos patrimoniais disponíveis. (modal "poder" in future tense)*
>
> *§ 1º A cláusula compromissória deve ser estipulada por escrito, podendo estar inserta no próprio contrato ou em documento apartado que a ele se refira. (modal "dever" in present tense)*
>
> *§ 1º O compromisso arbitral judicial celebrar-se-á por termo nos autos, perante o juízo ou tribunal, onde tem curso a demanda. (performative ver "celebrar" in future tense)*
>
> *Art. 31. A sentença arbitral produz, entre as partes e seus sucessores, os mesmos efeitos da sentença proferida pelos órgãos do Poder Judiciário e, sendo condenatória, constitui título executivo. (performative verb "produzir" and non-performative verb "constituir" in present tense)*

In consequence, not only are inconsistency and ambiguity prone to be found in original versions of Brazilian legislations but in translated versions as well.

Except for "may", which is rather consistently used in both versions, 'shall" is often mistakenly substituted by "will", particularly in Version 2. It can be explain by the translator`s choice for literal translation of the future tense in Portuguese into its equivalent form "will" in English. It is worth pointing out though that some authors do not even consider "will" as a term of authority (see Dorsey 2006; Child 1992). Similarly, the modal "must" mistakenly replaces "shall" to express command in both versions. While Child (1992: 294) claims that "must" is a term of authority 'to create a mere condition precedent' (which is not the case in the versions), it is not even used in everyday English significantly.

4.4. Collocations

Collocations can be described as 'the habitual cooccurrence of words, which / . . . /must be compatible within a certain semantic range' (Gläser 1995: 54). In legislative drafting, collocations consist of fixed lexical combinations hardly ever found in legal dictionaries, including nouns, verbs and adverbs, and the so-called binomials and multinomials.[14]

In legislations, lexical collocations are of three types: a) a verb and a noun/pronoun; b) a verb 'meaning essentially *eradication* and/or *nullification*' and a noun and c) and adjective and a noun (Benson, Benson and Ilson 1986: xxx–xxxii).

14 Grammatical collocations were not considered in the present analysis as the subject deserves a study on its own.

Table 12.5 Terms of authority

Version 1	Version 2
The parties may submit their disputes to arbitration by virtues of the arbitration agreement, which may be in the form of either an arbitration clause or a submission agreement. *(compromisso)*	The interested parties may submit the resolution of their disputes to an arbitral tribunal through an arbitration agreement, which may take form of either an arbitration clause or a submission agreement. *(compromisso)*
The arbitration clause shall be in writing and it can be inserted in the main contract or in a document to which it refers.	The arbitration clause must be in writing, either inserted in the contract itself or in a separate document referring to it.
If the arbitration clause makes reference to the rules of a particular arbitral institution or specialized entity, the arbitration shall be commenced and conducted in accordance with such rules; / . . . /	If the parties refer to rules of an arbitral institution or specialized entity in the arbitration clause, the arbitration will be commended and conducted pursuant to such rules, / . . . /
The submission agreement (*compromisso*) must contain: / . . . /	The submission agreement must provide: / . . . /
If the motion is granted, the suspect or impeded arbitrator will be removed and replaced in accordance with Article 16 of this Law.	If the motion is granted, the disqualified or challenged arbitrator will be discharged and replaced in accordance with Article 16 of this Law.
The arbitral ward shall be made in writing.	The decision of the sole arbitrator or of the arbitrators must be made in writing.
The arbitrator or the arbitral tribunal shall decide within ten days, through and addendum to the award, which shall be communicated to the parties in accordance with Article 29.	Within ten days, the sole arbitrator or the arbitral tribunal will decide this matter, through an addendum to the award, which will be sent to the parties in accordance with Art. 29.
The denial of the request for recognition or enforcement of a foreign arbitral award based on formal defects does not prevent the interested party from renewing the request once such defects are properly cured.	The denial of recognition or enforcement of a foreign award based on formal procedural flaws does not preclude the interested party from renewing its request, once such defects are properly corrected.

Table 12.6 Lexical collocations

Type 1	Type 2	Type 3
to conduct the arbitration to submit a dispute to arbitration to commence arbitration to make an award to appoint arbitrators to terminate the arbitration to grant a motion to set aside the arbitral award	to settle a dispute through arbitration to challenge an award/an arbitrator to violate good morals and public policy to fail to provide . . . to disagree on . . . to withdraw oneself from the office	Transferable/disposable patrimonial rights Adhesion contracts arbitration agreement the adhering party the interested party submission agreement arbitral proceedings notified party arbitral tribunal sole arbitrator sworn translations duly certified copy the defaulting party coercive or injunctive orders inalienable rights

Most collocations in the versions belong to the individual subject area of arbitration. They incorporate both conventional phrases and neologisms to designate procedures and concepts wherein 'the coinage of word-like phrases (nominations) is a prime requirement' (Gläser 1995: 50). In all types, the terms 'entail the self-explanatory meaning of their constitutions' (Gläser 1995: 50), as in Type 2, where the verbs nullifies the action expressed by the following noun.

Nevertheless, the versions also contain "violations of collocability" not accepted as conventions, such as *to initiate arbitration; *to render an award; *to conclude the submission agreement and *at the beginning of the arbitration, indicating mostly the literal translation of their equivalents in Portuguese. As the UNCITRAL Model Law displays very similar lexical collocations, it also seems that the translator established a one-to-one correspondent translation based upon an allegedly equivalence of collocations between the model law and its equivalent in Portuguese.

Much has been written about the conventional use of binomials and multinomials in legal English in search of precision, accuracy and all-inclusiveness.[15] In short, while binomials consist of pairs of words or pairs of syntactic sequences connected by a lexical link—usually "and" or "or"—multinomials are extended nominal binomials with 'an enumerative sequence [which] may contain several members' of the same category (Gustafsson 1975: 17). Historically speaking, binomials are explained by collocations where the first term, usually derived from Latin-French source, is more common, and sometimes more formal than the second one, which is mostly derived from German (Motos and González-Jover 2009: 73).

Brazilian legislation makes little use of collocations which, in general, do not share the same rhetorical and historical values as in common law tradition. The use seems to be more concerned with 'a way of guaranteeing that the text covers all intended cases or eventualities' (Motos and González-Jover 2009: 75).

Binomials and multinomials appear quite often in the versions though displaying discrepancies as to use of "and" and "or" to connect the constituents, and their reversibility and regularity of terms. They were literally translated from the original law in Portuguese which in turn also displays discrepancies in regard of both phenomena. On the other hand, other binomials and multinomials seem to have been translated due to the familiarity with their use in legal drafting keeping the same conventional structure, such as in "null and void", "costs and expenses, and "resident and domiciled".

Coincidently, some consistency in the use of binomials and multinomials in the versions can be seen in relation to terms which embody uniform legal concepts with 'corresponding terminological counterparts' (Chromá 2009: 30) in English, such as "recognition and enforcement", "submission agreement or the arbitration clause", "existence, validity and effectiveness", and "nullity, invalidity or ineffectiveness".

The lack of consistency and misuse of such type collocations can be explained by the fact that they are not part of the set of conventions of Brazilian legislative drafting. Also, the creation of neologisms, new binomials and multinomials, out of restricted civil law legal concepts with no equivalent to their counterparts in legal English should be considered more carefully, as in "[the judge] in fact and in right/ [the judge] in fact and right", "ex officio or at the parties' request/a party's request or *ex officio*".

4.5. Discussion

As can be seen from the analysis above, it is evidenced that both English versions of Law 9.307/2007 on arbitration display discrepancies and lack of consistency between and within

15 See Mellinkoff (1963), Gustafsson (1975), Bhatia (1993), and Frade (2004).

Table 12.7 Binomials and multinomials

Version 1	Version 2
CHAPTER ONE	
[rules of] law or of equity	in law or of equity
equity, good morals and public policy	good morals or public policy
law, customs, usages and the rules of international trade	law, customs, usages and international rules of commerce
CHAPTER TWO	
an arbitration clause or a submission agreement	an arbitration clause or a submission agreement
a particular arbitral institution or specialized entity	an arbitral institution or specialized entity
commenced and conducted	commenced and conducted
by mail or through any other means of communication	by mail or through any other means of communication
null and void	----
existence, validity and effectiveness	existence, validity and effectiveness
one or more persons	one or more persons
[executed by] two witnesses or by public notary	[signed by] two witnesses, or by public deed
name, profession, marital status and domicile	name, profession, marital status and domicile
arbitrator or arbitrators	arbitrator or arbitrators
[if the arbitrator] dies or becomes unable to [act as such]	[if any arbitrator] dies or becomes incapable of [ruling]
the arbitrator or the chairperson of the arbitral tribunal	the arbitrator or the chairperson of the arbitral tribunal
CHAPTER THREE	
[proceed] diligently, efficiently, independently	[behave in an] impartial, independent, competent, diligent and judicious manner.
[cover] expenses and services	[cover] expenses and sections
duties and liabilities	duties and responsibilities
impartiality and independence	impartiality and independence
suspect or impeded [arbitrator]	disqualified or challenged [arbitrator]
removed and replaced	discharged and replaced
[the judge] in fact and in right	[the judge] in fact and right
CHAPTER FOUR	
the sole arbitrator or the arbitral tribunal	the arbitrator or the arbitral tribunal
jurisdiction, suspicion or impediment	jurisdiction, suspicion or impediment
nullity, invalidity or ineffectiveness	nullity, invalidity or ineffectiveness
ex officio or at the parties' request	a party's request or *ex officio*
testimonies by parties and witnesses	statements by parties and witnesses
CHAPTER FIVE	
[signed by] the arbitrator or all arbitrators	[signed by] the sole arbitrator or by all arbitrators
is unable to or refuses to [sign]	is unable to or refuses to [sign]
costs and expenses	costs and expenses
obscurity, doubt or contradiction	obscurity, doubt or contradiction
null and void	null and void
unfaithfulness, extortion or corruption	unfaithfulness, extortion or corruption
CHAPTER SIX	
recognition and enforcement	recognition and enforcement
recognized and enforced	recognized and enforced
the original arbitration agreement or a duly certified copy	the original or a duly certified copy of the arbitration agreement
under the law to which the parties have subjected it or [ ]	under the law to which the parties have subjected it or [ ]
under the law of the country where the award was made	under the law of the country where the award was rendered
submission agreement or the arbitration clause	submission agreement or the arbitration clause
resident or domiciled	

them. In general, both translators made use of literal translation 'to legitimate the texts by their entextualization choices in spite of inconsistencies displayed all over the final products' (Frade 2004). Also, the translators appropriated of sets of uniform legal concepts and conventions which have corresponding counterparts in the UNCITRAL Model Law, as is the case of the main title, the enacting clause and some types of collocations, 'assuming an international perspective rather than remaining a purely domestic concern' (Gotti 2009: 277).

The result is the production of two hybrid texts sharing their own original genre characteristics with the ones of the text that influenced them in the first place, the UNCITRAL Model Law (Bhatia 2004: 58). This perception seems to extend to procedures in line with Gotti (2009: 280) that argues that 'when the language chosen for an international arbitration case is English, there is a tendency to adopt procedures typical of common law countries'.

As far as legal interpretation is concerned, the versions provide much room for misunderstanding and misinterpretation even for informative purposes. The most problematic area is the use of terms of authority which have no specific cultural value or identity as in our legal system. The constant variation of terms to express the same concepts of obligation, command or permission, for example, surely results in ambiguity. It seems to prove that Brazil has been using model laws, such as the UNCITRAL Model Law, in different ways depending on its own national requirements, culture, legal system and other constraints (Gotti 2009: 296).

While specialized dictionaries fail to take into account most of the generic, pragmatic and rhetorical legal features of collocations, terms of authority, legal vagueness, grammatical structures, examples and restrictions (Ahoda 2009: 262), traditional translation theories no longer seem to cope with the myriad of legal discursive and generic surrounds which extends from national to global time-spatial scale conducted in English. Therefore, legal translators must adopt a multidisciplinary approach 'which addresses the various aspects of intercultural legal communication by uniting the findings of comparative legal science, translation studies and contrastive linguistics' (Kocbek 2009: 60) to improve their drafting skills of domestic documents aiming at high-quality English translation. All is needed is the acquisition of such skills in the course of academic education and continuing professional education and practice.

To conclude, legal translation should be neither a matter of the translator's personal choices as to lexical and grammatical structures without any compliance with principles of consistency and conventions nor the mere replication of source texts into versions from unrelated legal systems and languages. The aim is to consider a systematic process of legal translation for global use so as to minimize socio-cultural variants and to promote the pragmatic conditions for the harmonized and "common sense" English as *lingua franca* without excluding potential reciprocal influences of or resistance to one hegemonic legal system upon others.

5. Conclusion

Apart from being a sensitive area *per se*, legal translation involving unrelated legal systems and languages poses an extra burden to the translator as to maintain the generity integrity of the source text by adopting a one-to-one correspondent translation or else to assume the responsibility for potential consequences of appropriating of generic features of other legal systems.

As suggested by the title of the chapter, it approached some critical elements regarding two versions of the Brazilian law on arbitration—Law 9.307/96—for informative purposes, that is, they are non-binding. The analysis showed at least three strategies employed by the translator: literal translation based on the generic features of the original version of the law in Portuguese; the appropriation of some generic features and conventions set forth in the

UNCITRAL Model Law and the creation of unrelated legal neologisms to both legal systems (civil law x common law) and languages (Portuguese x English).

The consequence was the production of two hybrid texts without any linguistic and generic consistency since the translator relied on 'stylistic variation in the choice of words or patterns of expression [which] must be avoided' (Cao 2007: 27). Moreover, lack of consistency was seen in relation to an existing model law as the translated corresponding terms were not employed consistently. And lastly, the creation of neologisms resulted in an unfamiliar variation, which can potentially introduce extra uncertainty or ambiguity.

Our present challenge is to provide Brazilian legal translators with specific multi-disciplinary training actions so as they can no longer rely solely on literal translation to produce versions of our legislations in English. As suggested by several linguistic and translation experts in Šarčević (2009), legal translators should search for more suitable approaches to translation to include socio-cultural factors in legislative drafting aimed at different target audiences at supranational level, whether binding or not.

References

Aohda, M.M. 2009. 'The Bilingual Legal Dictionary and the Translator'. In: S. Šarčević ed. *Legal Language in Action: Translation, Terminology, Drafting and Procedural Issues*. Zagreb: Nakladni zavod Globus, pp. 261–276.

Benson, M., Benson, E. and Ilson, R. 1986. *The BBI Dictionary of English Word Combination*. Amsterdam, Philadelphia: John Benjamins Publishing Company.

Bhatia, V.K. 1993. *Analysing Genre: Language Use in Professional Settings*. Longman: London.

———. 2004. *Worlds of Written Discourse. A Genre-Based View*. London: Continuum.

Black's Law Dictionary. 2006. Third Pocket Edition. St. Paul, Minn.: Thomson/West.

Campbell, L. 1996. 'Drafting Styles: Fuzzy or Fussy?', *E Law: Murdoch University Electronic Journal of Law*, vol. 3(2). Available at: http://www.austlii.edu.au/au/journals/MurUEJL/1996/17.html [Accessed: 8.8.14).

Cao, D. 2007. *Translating Law*. Clevedon: Multilingual Matters Ltd.

Chromá, M. 2009. 'Semantic and Legal Interpretation: Clash or Accord?'. In: S. Sarčevic ed. *Legal Language in Action: Translation, Terminology, Drafting and Procedural Issues*. Zagreb: Nakladni zavod Globus, pp. 27–42.

Dorsey, T.A. 2006. *Legislative Drafter's Deskbook: A Practical Guide*. Alexandria, Virginia: The CapitolNet.

Frade, C. 2014. 'Legal Translation in Brazil: An Entextualization Approach', Wagner, A. and Gémar, J. eds., *Legal Translation and Jurilinguistics: Globalizing Disciplines. Retrospects and Prospects, International Journal for the Semiotics of Law*, vol. 27(4).

Frade, C. 2004. 'Generic Variation Across Legislative Writing: A Contrastive Analysis of the UNCITRAL Model Law and Brazil's Arbitration Law', *Hermes, Journal of Linguistics*, vol. 32, pp. 45–75.

Garzone, G. 2008. 'International Commercial Arbitration Rules as Translated/Re-written Texts: An Intercultural Perspective'. In: Bhatia V.K., Candlin, C.N. and Allori, P.E. eds. *Language, Culture and the Law: The Formulation of Legal Concepts Across Systems and Cultures*. Bern: Peter Lang, pp. 47–73.

Garzone, G. 2000. 'Legal Translation and Functionalist Approaches: A Contradiction in Terms?', International Colloquium on Legal Translation: History, Theory/ies, and Practice. Geneva, Switzerland, 17–19 February 2000. Available at: Tradulex.org http://www.tradulex.org/Actes2000/Garzone.pdf [Accessed 8 October 2011].

Gläser, R. 1995. *Linguistic Features and Genre Profiles of Scienfic English*. Frankfurt am Main: Peter Lang.

Gotti, M. 2009. 'Legal Drafting in an International Context: Linguistic and Cultural Issues'. In: S. Šarčević ed. *Legal Language in Action: Translation, Terminology, Drafting and Procedural Issues*. Zagreb: Nakladni zavod Globus, pp. 277–299.

Gustafsson, M. 1975. *Binomial Expressions in Present-Day English: A Syntactic and Semantic Study*. Turku: Turun Yliopisto.

Kocbek, A. 2009. 'A Targeted Approach to Legal Translation'. In: S. Sarčevic ed. *Legal Language in Action: Translation, Terminology, Drafting and Procedural Issues*. Zagreb: Nakladni zavod Globus, pp. 43–62.

Kurzon, D. 1986. *It is Hereby Performed . . . Legal Speech Acts*. Amsterdam/Philadelphia: John Benjamins Publishing Company.

Maley, Y. 1987. 'The Language of Legislation', *Language in Society*, vol. 16, pp. 25–48.

Mellinkoff, D. 1963. *The Language of the Law*. Boston: Little, Brown and Company.

Mottos, R.M. and González-Jover, A.G. 2009. 'Anisomorphism in the Translation of Legal Texts'. In: S. Sarčevic ed. *Legal Language in Action: Translation, Terminology, Drafting and Procedural Issues*. Zagreb: Nakladni zavod Globus, pp. 63–87.

Šarčević, S. (ed.). 2009. *Legal Language in Action: Translation, Terminology, Drafting and Procedural Issues*. Zagreb: Nakladni zavod Globus.

Šarčević, S. 2008. 'Translation in International Arbitration'. In: Bhatia, V.K., Candlin, C. and Engberg, J. eds. *Legal Discourse Across Cultures and Systems*. Hong Kong: Hong Kong University Press, pp. 291–308.

Trosborg, A. 1994. 'Translation Studies: Some Recent Developments', *Hermes: Journal of Linguistics*, vol. 12, pp. 9–28.

———. 1997. *Rhetorical Strategies in Legal Language: Discourse Analysis of Statutes and Contracts*. Tübingen: Gunter Narr Verlag Tübingen.

Vigouroux, C.B. 2009. 'The Making of a Scription: A Case Study on Authority and Authorship', *Text and Talk*, vol. 29(5), pp. 615–637.

Chapter 13
Translation of Japanese Laws and Regulations

Kayoko Takeda and Yasuhiro Sekine

1. Introduction

As part of the Japanese government's endeavour to make the Japanese legal system more transparent to the world, a government-led initiative to translate Japanese laws and regulations (cabinet orders, ministry ordinances, etc.) was launched in 2004. Some Japanese laws had been translated into English, but it had been done in a fragmented way by different ministries and agencies, and by the private sector, resulting in, inconsistencies in the translation of legal terms, and difficulty in locating the translated texts. Therefore, in tandem with the actual work of translating laws and regulations, this project has been focusing on establishing infrastructure for ongoing efforts to provide reliable translation of Japanese laws in a centralized way with a standard bilingual glossary in place, and for easy access to the translation.

Roughly speaking, there have been two types of studies on this translation project: studies focusing on the general background, issues and future directions of the project (e.g., Chiyo 2005; Kashiwagi 2006; Yamamoto 2006; Matsuura 2010); and studies mainly addressing technical aspects of its translation database system (e.g., Toyama et al. 2006; Toyama et al. 2011; Sekine 2012; Sekine et al. 2012). In order to provide a fuller understanding of the Japanese law translation project, an attempt is made here to engage in a critical analysis of translation issues with the project by drawing on prior scholarly discussions on legal translation and a historical perspective on aims and methods of law translation in Japan.

This chapter first introduces law translation in 19th-century and post-war Japan, focusing on the purposes of law translation and the effect of translation on the development of Japanese legal language. It then shifts the focus to the current law translation project. Its background and aims are introduced, followed by a discussion on the law translation database system and some of the problems with translations contained in the system. Further, possible solutions to the problems are suggested, such as the use of a translation memory. In conclusion, the importance of the government's commitment to the continuous effort to provide quality translation of Japanese laws is reiterated.

2. Historical Background

In the late 19th century, as Japan reopened its door to the world after more than 200 years of seclusion policy, intense efforts to catch up with the West began. Setting up Western-influenced political, military, and industrial systems involved a tremendous amount of translation activity (e.g., Kondo and Wakabayashi 2008; Yanabu 2010). Law-related matters were not an exception. There was a great deal of translation work in connection with the establishment of a modern legal system. Another period of extensive translation activity took place in occupied Japan after World War II. For the demilitarization and democratization of Japan, the Superior Commander of the Allied Powers (SCAP) propelled legal reforms, including the establishment of a new constitution. As was the case in other areas of the occupation operations, translation was an integral part of the efforts to draft and revise laws.

The following provides a brief overview of major translation projects in both eras, highlighting the distinct nature of how translation was used. In addition, it discusses the impact of law translation in those periods on the development of legal language in Japan.

2.1. Law Translation in the 19th Century

As Japan ended its isolationist policy and transitioned from the feudal Shogunate system to the emperor-centred Meiji government in the second half of the 19th century, there was a great deal of translation activity, which included the translation of laws and scholarly texts on law in the West. In 1865, a Chinese translation of *Elements of International Law* by H. Wheaton (first published in 1836) was released in Japan, with *kunten* (guiding marks for rendering into Japanese). Subsequently, several versions of Japanese translation from this Chinese version, and from the original English text, were published in the late 19th century, along with translation of other texts on international law. They became essential references as the new Meiji government fervently carried out various initiatives to modernize Japan and revise unequal treaties the Tokugawa Shogunate had concluded with Western countries (Ozawa 2010). Also, the above-mentioned Chinese translation (by an American missionary) became a useful resource for translators to devise Japanese translations of English legal terms (Ibid.).

The government modelled its modern legal system on European codified law and sought advice from foreign jurists, especially those who were invited from France and Germany. There was even a failed attempt by Shimpei Eto (Justice Minister, 1872–1873) to use a hastily prepared Japanese translation of the Code of Napoleon as a new civil code by simply replacing 'France' and 'French' with 'Japan' and 'Japanese' (Röhl 2005: 24). In many cases, however, the Japanese translations of drafts written in French or German by foreign advisors were used as the bases for creating laws, including the Penal Code, the Civil Code, and the Constitution of Japan (Ozawa et al. 2010). Before reaching enactments in the 1870s–1890s, those drafts went through a number of revisions by Japanese jurists and officials to 'Japanize' the texts to reflect Japanese traditions and customs, in consultation with foreign advisors (ibid.).

2.2. Law Translation in Occupied Japan

According to Takayanagi (1968), legislation enacted during the occupation of Japan (1945–1952) can be divided into three categories: (1) legislation based on SCAP orders; (2) legislation based on drafts made by the Japanese government, reviewed and approved by SCAP; and (3) legislation based on drafts made by SCAP but amended by Japanese, with SCAP approval. In either case, a significant amount of translation activity took place for the establishment of a new legal system in post-war Japan. It was a high-pressure operation for the Japanese government since SCAP demanded accuracy and promptness of translation of all legislative drafts and deliberations (Sekiguchi 2012). Individual ministries and agencies prepared translations, but it was the Central Liaison Office (a Japanese government organization established to liaise with SCAP) and the Cabinet Office who then reviewed (and corrected, if necessary) the translations and submitted them to SCAP for review and approval (Ibid.).

The most prominent case of law translation concerned the Constitution. A mostly American group assembled by SCAP drafted a new Japanese Constitution in English in a week and handed it to the Japanese government on 13 February 1946. With a few changes made through negotiations with SCAP, the Japanese government announced the Japanese version of a summary of the finalized draft on 3 March 1946. The translated text was then stylized to be close to spoken Japanese (rather than the traditional literary style) in response to calls for readability of law, and also to smooth out the 'translation flavor' (McNelly 1987: 145). After deliberations at the Diet, while in close consultation with SCAP, the Constitution was enacted on 3 May 1947. Since the Constitution is regarded as the Supreme Law of the nation, its translation-derived language has also influenced the language used in the subsequent laws that were newly drafted or revised. Although these new and amended laws were heavily influenced by US law, the nature of Japanese law as part of the Civil Law system (as a result of adopting French and German laws in the Meiji era) did not change much (Oda 2009). This mixture of the influence of Civil Law and US Common Law traditions still remains in the Japanese legal system, which is considered one of the challenges for legal translators (e.g., Kashiwagi 2006; Matsuura 2010).

2.3. Translation as a Base for Drafting a Law

Law translation in 19th-century and post-war Japan raises interesting points for two areas of study in legal translation: one is the purpose of legal translation, and the other is the difficulty of legal translation. In classifying legal translation by the purpose of target texts, Cao (2007: 10–12) presents three categories: normative, informative, and general legal or judicial. The first two types concern translation of national legislation, which is the focus of this chapter. While a normative purpose means to produce translation that is equally authentic as the source text, an informative purpose indicates that the translation is produced solely to inform the target readers, such as foreign lawyers and comparativists (Ibid.). Similarly, Šarčević (2012: 190–191) refers to the communicative purpose of a legal translation as authoritative (having the force of law) or non-authoritative (without the force of law).

As a nation of monolingual jurisdiction, Japan never required the translation of laws for normative or authoritative purposes. Law translation for information only, however, has been used from ancient times (generally to learn from Chinese laws) to the present day. The phenomenon of translations used as bases for drafting laws in the Meiji and post-war eras, however, does not seem to fit into either of the categories. Those translations themselves were not authoritative, but they were not quite for information only, either, since they became or formed authoritative legal texts. In particular, during the occupation period, virtually all laws had Japanese and English versions, whichever was originally used as source text. Although only the Japanese versions were legally binding in Japanese society, they had to be approved by SCAP who relied on their English versions. In other words, English translation was more than a reference – it had a "performative" effect in the process of drafting laws.

Presumably, this type of translation activity can take place under similar circumstances, such as newly independent countries modelling their legal systems on those of other countries, and the colonizer imposing their laws on the colonized. This particular purpose of law translation seems to have received little attention in prior examinations on legal translation, but should be included to enrich the discussion of how law translation is used.

Another noteworthy aspect of using translations as bases for drafting laws is the effect of translation-derived legal terms and writing style on the subsequent development of legal language in the national language. Studies on peculiar terms and complex sentences used in Japanese laws cite translation in the Meiji era as one source of these oddities (e.g., Hayashi and

Aomi 1981; Aoki 2000; Okawara 2012). In those days, translators had to invent new Japanese words by combining idiographic Chinese characters to render totally unfamiliar concepts found in French and German laws. Words so derived can be unintelligible for laypersons, yet they are still used in contemporary legal texts. In fact, 70 per cent of the major legal terms in Japanese are said to originate in German (Furuta 2004). Also, law translation generally sacrificed readability for the sake of being "faithful" to the original sentence structures in French, German or English, and this tradition of writing complex, long sentences has a bearing on how legal texts are drafted even now (Aoki 2000).

The issue of translation affecting legal language is not unique to Japanese. Tiersma (1999), for example, refers to traces of translation from Latin and Law French in discussing unusual sentence structures and archaic language as sources of difficulty in comprehending legal texts in English. The crossing of incongruous legal systems, cultures and languages has been examined as sources of challenges in legal translation (e.g., Cao 2007; Šarčević 2012). In addition, source text "embedded" with translation from a mixture of legal traditions can pose lexical and semantic complexities, which translators may have to tackle as the first challenge in the translation process.

3. Current Project of Translating Japanese Laws

In 2004 the Japanese government embarked on a project to promote the translation of Japanese laws and regulations as part of its Judicial System Reform. To support this ongoing effort, an online translation database system was launched in 2009. Since then, it has been attracting a lot of traffic from all over the world (Sekine 2012).

The following presents the background and overview of this translation project and the features of the database system. It then discusses some of the problems with translations in the database and looks into possible causes of the problems.

3.1. An Overview of the Project

Following the Japanese government's decision to advance the translation of Japanese laws in 2004, the Study Council of Promoting Translation of Japanese Laws and Regulations into Foreign Languages (hereafter, Study Council) conducted comprehensive studies on the development of infrastructure for law translation. Its final report in 2006 recognized the need for Japanese laws to be easily and accurately understood in the globalized world, and pointed to the following as significant to promoting the translation of Japanese laws: to facilitate smooth international transactions and increase the international competitiveness of Japanese companies; to promote foreign investment in Japan; to assist the construction of legal systems in developing countries (by referencing Japanese laws); to enhance the understanding of Japan in the international community; and to support foreigners living in Japan (Study Council 2006).

English translations of some Japanese laws had existed before this project, but they were produced in a decentralized way by different ministries and agencies, and by private entities, which resulted in quality issues, inconsistencies in document formats and the translation of legal terms and phrases, and difficulty in locating and accessing the translated texts. The report concluded by urging the government to establish a foundation for continuous efforts to produce reliable translation (into English, first) and provide easy access to the translations (Ibid.).

To this end, it was suggested that: (1) translation "rules" should be established; (2) priority should be given to essential laws whose translation can become a basis for future translation of other laws and regulations; (3) a centralized website should be launched for easy access to the translations; (4) and a system should be developed for the continuous maintenance and updating of existing translations and a standard bilingual dictionary for legal terms (Ibid.).

In response, a provisional website was built in 2006 within the Cabinet Secretariat's website. At the outset, it provided English translation of 14 Japanese laws and the first version of a standard Japanese-English legal term dictionary, which contained about 3,300 terms.

3.2. The 'Japanese Law Translation' Database

In 2009, a full-fledged website called 'Japanese Law Translation'[1] was launched by the Ministry of Justice, with 164 translated laws. In this database system English translations of laws are compiled in a centralized location, and the user has free, easy access to the translations and the 'Standard Legal Term Dictionary', a Japanese-English glossary of legal terms. It currently offers 270 Japanese laws with English translation. In addition, English translation of over 1,600 titles of laws is available, though their contents have not been translated.

Figure 13.1 Home page of 'Japanese Law Translation". Reproduced with permission from the Ministry of Justice

As shown in Figure 13.1 above, the JLT offers three main search functions: 'Law Search', 'Dictionary Search' and 'Keyword in Context Search'. Law Search enables users to search

1 Available at: http://www.japaneselawtranslation.go.jp/?re=02.

laws by keywords, a title, a law number, a category and a responsible ministry. With Dictionary Search, users can search for legal terms from the Standard Legal Term Dictionary, which translators are supposed to follow as "rules". The entire content of the dictionary is downloadable. Keyword in Context Search automatically extracts a list of occurrences of words or phrases with their contexts, in Japanese and English, which are displayed in parallel. (See Toyama et al. (2011) for detail.)

Since its introduction in 2009, the system has been accessed over 110,000 times every day on average from all over the world (Sekine 2012). The laws accessed most frequently are the Commodity Exchange Act, the Companies Act, the Civil Rehabilitation Act, the Banking Act, and the Small and Medium-Sized Enterprise Cooperatives Act, among others (Sekine 2013). It is assumed that there is consistent demand for information on Japanese laws in Japan and internationally, especially business-related laws.

3.3. Problems with Translation

There are two types of problems associated with translations stored in the database system: quantity and quality. The problems of quantity concern the number of translated laws. As of 30 November 2012, the JLT provides English translation of 270 laws, and this number is increasing daily. However, compared to the total number of laws currently in effect in Japan, which is over 7,700, the number of laws that have been translated is still low. It seems far from enough to satisfy the demand, as evidenced in a number of requests submitted via the website from users who ask for more translations of laws (Sekine et al. 2012). The 'Translation Development Plans' (a list of laws to translate chosen by the government every year) are grossly behind schedule, as more than 300 planned translations from 2007 to 2011 have not been released yet.

The problems of quality refer to the accuracy and consistency of translation. Quality issues have been raised by users through the feedback feature of the JLT, and by the system administrator who reviews translations before feeding them into the database (Ibid.). Users have reported over 100 quality issues since the release of the system in 2009 (Sekine et al. 2012). Generally, the problems can be divided into three categories: translation errors, careless mistakes and inconsistent translations.

In many cases, translation errors seem to be caused by translators' lack of legal knowledge. In the following example, the error occurred probably because of the translator's unfamiliarity with a certain legal term.

> 三　第二十二条（第四十二条において準用する場合を含む。）の規定による立入り若しくは検査を拒み、妨げ、若しくは忌避し、又は質問に対して陳述をせず、若しくは虚偽の陳述をしたとき。
>
> *(iii) When any officer or employee refused, or disturbed, or recused the entry or inspection pursuant to the provision of Article 22 (including the cases where it is applied mutatis mutandis pursuant to Article 42), or did not give statement to the question, or gave false statement.*
>
> *(Professional Engineer Act, Article 63, paragraph (1), item (iii))*

The word "忌避 (*kihi*)" in the source text is translated as "recuse" in the target text. The Japanese word "*kihi*" can be translated as "recuse" or "evade", depending on the context. In other words, the English words "recuse" and "evade" can be translated into one Japanese word, "*kihi*", although these two English words have totally different meanings from each other. When "*kihi*" means to escape from an obligatory inspection like in the example above, it should be translated as "evade", but when "*kihi*" means to challenge a judge as incompetent, "recuse" should be used. Usually, the word "*kihi*" is not used in daily life, but it needs to be translated discriminately by paying attention to the legal context. This is yet further evidence for why a legal translator needs to have a basic knowledge of laws and be familiar with the legal terminologies of both the source language and target language (e.g., Cao 2007; Lawson 2007; Wolff 2011; Šarčević 2012).

Careless mistakes are often found in grammar, spelling, formats and numbers. The mistakes found most frequently are in the numbering expressions for law (Sekine 2013). The rules for translating the numbering expressions of Japanese law are specified in the Standard Legal Term Dictionary, which is reviewed and approved by the Japanese Law Translation Council, a group of government-appointed jurists. As shown in Table 13.1 below, the numbering formats are complicated, but it is very important to adhere to the rules because those numbers are tied to specific information within and among laws. A mistake in numbering format may direct a user to the wrong information.

Table 13.1 Examples of numbering expressions rules

Japanese	English
第一編、第二編、第三編 . . .	Part I, Part II, Part III . . .
第一章、第二章、第三章 . . .	Chapter I, Chapter II, Chapter III . . .
第一節、第二節、第三節 . . .	Section 1, Section 2, Section 3 . . .
第一款、第二款、第三款 . . .	Subsection 1, Subsection 2, Subsection 3 . . .
第一目、第二目、第三目 . . .	Division 1, Division 2, Division 3 . . .
第一条、第二条、第三条 . . .	Article 1, Article 2, Article 3 . . .
1 2 3 . . . (paragraph in title)	(1) (2) (3) . . .
一二三. . . (item in title)	(i) (ii) (iii) . . .
イロハ. . . (sub-item level 1 in title)	(a) (b) (c) . . .

Mistakes are also found in other numbers: days, months, years, dates, amounts of money, and so on (Ibid.). In Japanese law, numbers are usually expressed in Chinese numerals. Conversion from Chinese to Arabic numerals seems to cause mistakes, and conversion from the Japanese calendar system (based on the reigns of emperors) to the Gregorian calendar can also result in mistakes.

Inconsistency in translation can be a serious problem in law. As indicated in a number of manuals for legislative drafting (e.g., Hirsch 1989; European Commission 1997), the same term should be used consistently to express a given concept. Legal texts are intricately linked with each other in intra-document and inter-document ways. To understand a certain legal matter, it may not be enough to understand a single provision or even a whole law. It may be necessary to understand related provisions among related laws systematically. Inconsistent translations between law texts may hinder this systematic understanding. The consistency issue also affects productivity of translation work. It can be confusing and time consuming if the translator, in searching for the previous translation of a given phrase in the database, faces a number of different translations and has to choose just one. In the following example, a very simple sentence used in many laws is linked with thirty different translations in the database. Some of them are shown here.

この法律は、公布の日から施行する。
This Act shall be enforced from the date of promulgation.
This Act shall come into effect as from the date of promulgation.
This Act shall come into effect as of the date of promulgation;
This Act shall come into effect as of the day of its promulgation.
This Act shall come into effect on the day of promulgation.
This Act shall come into force as from the date of its promulgation.
...

Inconsistency in the translations of law titles can present even more serious problems. If the title of a law is translated in more than one way, they may be recognized as different laws. In the following example of a law title, the database contains six different translations.

一般社団法人及び一般財団法人に関する法律
Act Concerning General Corporations and General Foundations
Act on General Associations and Foundations
Act on General Associations and Incorporated Foundations
Act on General Incorporated Association and General Incorporated Foundation
Act on General Incorporated Associations and General Incorporated Foundations
General Incorporated Associations/Foundations Act

Although the JLT has been accessed by many users and is generally recognized as a useful resource for jurists and translators (e.g., Kamiya 2009; Lawson 2010), problems with translation, as indicated above, can defeat the original purpose of the project, i.e., to present Japanese laws so that they may be understood "easily and accurately". In the next section, an attempt is made to identify and analyze some causes of the translation problems with the JLT project.

3.4. Causes of Translation Problems

The root cause of these problems probably relates to the government's procurement system for law translation in Japan. There is no single organization that manages the project of translating laws as a whole and is responsible for the final checking of translation. Instead, individual ministries and agencies are responsible for the translation of their laws, and they usually outsource the translation work to the private sector through competitive bidding. Although a government guideline for outsourcing is in place to secure reliable translation and it does refer to translation requirements and qualifications of translators and revisers, contractors seem to be chosen by price in many cases (Sekine 2012). This situation can result in variation in translation quality, redundancy of translation efforts, and inconsistencies in the translation of legal terms and phrases.

Discussions on the poor quality of Japanese law translation generally point to two major culprits: absence of input from English-native legal experts and 'unnecessarily' difficult law texts in Japanese. It has been pointed out that English translation of Japanese laws is often crude, unreliable, not very readable (Chiyo 2005), even 'unintelligible gibberish' (Lawson 2007: 189). Although there have been strong calls for collaboration between Japanese-native and English-native experts in law translation (e.g., Chiyo 2005; Kashiwagi 2006; Kawano 2006; Lawson 2007; Transparency of Japanese Law Project, International Finance Law Group (hereafter, TIFLG) 2008), law translation seems to be carried out often by Japanese-native speakers with little input from English-native expert translators and lawyers, resulting in unreliable translation with poor grammar and awkward expressions (e.g., Lawson 2007; 2010).

The lack of sustained collaborative work between Japanese-native and English-native experts can be attributed to cost and availability issues (e.g., Kashiwagi 2006; Lawson 2007), but also, as Lawson (2007) implies, to the attitude and culture of some Japanese-native translators.

The other issue is that of the Japanese law texts themselves. As discussed earlier, Japanese law has been influenced by both Civil Law and Common Law traditions, and is filled with German and French-derived words that were invented in the late 19th century. Consequential complexities of semantics and syntax in Japanese law can indeed be a challenge for translators. Lawson (2007: 195) calls some expressions in Japanese law 'unnecessarily impenetrable'. According to a report by TIFL (2008), one of the "positive" aspects of translating Japanese law into English is that it has exposed how poorly law is written in Japan and how difficult it is to understand Japanese law and this exposure might stimulate discussion on the use of plain Japanese in law. Long nested sentences written in archaic language can not only result in incomprehensible translation, but they can also negatively affect the productivity and motivation of translators.

4. Directions for Solving Problems

As Kashiwagi (2006) indicates, the Japanese government passed the point of no return in its effort to promote the translation of Japanese laws. Laws are frequently amended, and new laws are enacted in great number every year. The JLT would not serve sufficiently without continuous and prompt updates of translations and the dictionary. Since the website is open to the public, the quality of translation can be assessed and compared with that of law translation in other countries by global users. Translation problems should be urgently addressed to keep the JLT relevant and hold a good standing in the international legal community. Some approaches to solving translation problems are suggested below.

4.1. Translation Memory

The current problems with law translation can be reduced to some extent by the use of advanced tools for improving the quality, efficiency and consistency of translation. For instance, automatic conversion programs can be developed for numbering expressions, and for converting the Japanese calendar into the Gregorian, and Chinese numerals into Arabic ones. In particular, active use of a translation memory (TM) should be considered as a key to the successful operation of the overall translation project. A translation memory is a database that stores segments (usually sentences) of source texts and their corresponding segments of target texts from previous translations. Since it enables the efficient recycling of previous translations, the use of a TM can save time and money. A TM can also be helpful in enforcing consistency of translation. The types of texts best suited for working with a TM are said to be those which are repetitive or which will be updated or revised (e.g., Bowker and Fisher 2010). Since laws are generally written in formulaic ways and often revised, translation of laws can benefit from the use of a TM.

In fact, in bilingual and multilingual jurisdictions such as Canada, Switzerland, Hong Kong and the European Union (EU), where a large amount of high quality translations of laws are continuously required, various technologies and tools have been applied for translating laws (e.g., Bowker 2002; see relevant pages of EC DGT's website[2]). The most prominent example

2 Available at: http://ipsc.jrc.ec.europa.eu/index.php?id=197.

may be "Euramis" (European Advanced Multilingual Information System), an integrated translation memory database system for EU laws and other documents. This TM system is available for translators of EU institutions for continuous improvement of productivity and consistency of translation.

Problematic aspects of a TM have been discussed, such as transmission of translation errors and the "sentence salad" effect (e.g., Bowker 2002; 2005; Pym 2008). It is possible that translation errors are propagated by the use of a TM. However, now that all the translated laws in Japan are exposed online and there is a system to receive user feedback on the JLT, there may be more opportunities to capture and correct translation errors. The sentence salad effect is a phenomenon observed when a TM contains multiple text types, resulting in patchwork-like, incoherent translation. This problem seems to carry less relevance to a TM for laws since it generally deals with a specific type of document.

4.2. Translator Training

Translator training should be an integral part of the effort to improve the quality, efficiency and consistency of law translation. For instance, if a TM is fully incorporated into the JLT system, some initial training should be provided to translators to promote its use, just as European institutions do with their translators. In order to advance the use of a TM among translators even with no prior TM experience, it is important to demonstrate the benefits of working with a TM for Japanese law translation. (A test version of a TM for translating Japanese law[3] has been available since September 2011 (Sekine et al. 2012).)

Training sessions and workshops for other types of skills and information should be encouraged as well, such as sharing useful resources for legal information and productivity tools, and learning from legal experts on comprehending and drafting of laws. JATLAW, a subgroup of the Japan Association of Translators, has been leading this effort by organizing several seminars a year with guest speakers from the government, industry and academia. These types of translator-led initiatives are promising not only for improving their skills, but also for enhancing their collective presence in the world of legal translation.

These gatherings may also nurture a collaborative culture through interactions between English-natives, Japanese-natives, translators, legal professionals and government officials. Back in the Meiji era, Japanese linguists, scholars and officials worked closely with German and French jurists, and during the occupation period a large amount of translation went back and forth between the Japanese government and SCAP for drafting, revisions and approval of laws. In a way, these experiences represent collaborative efforts between Japanese-natives and non-Japanese natives, involving legal experts. In fact, the quality of English translation produced during the post-war era may have been higher than that of translation in the JLT system, because it *had to* be understood by SCAP. It may be worthwhile to revisit and learn from the process and product of law translation in the past. (The Japanese Legal Information Institute (JaLII) at Nagoya University posts the Official Gazette English Edition from the occupation era on its website[4] for possible use in law translation and other projects.)

In addition to workshops and seminars, webinars and other types of distance learning opportunities would serve people who cannot attend those meetings. Easy, open access to online legal information, such as JALII, would be helpful as well. Continuous updates of such information would be most welcome by legal translators.

3 Available at: http://itrd.crestec.co.jp/transmemoryweb/.
4 Available at: http://jalii.law.nagoya-u.ac.jp/project/jagasette.

4.3. Plain Japanese in Law

Legal language has been one of the target areas of the plain language movement (see Adler (2012) for an overview of the case of English). For instance, the Australian government already has a manual in place for legislation in plain English.[5] In Japan there have been calls for making legal language more understandable for laypeople, but such calls have not led to a concerted effort or movement yet. The only exception may be the project of critically reviewing courtroom language in preparation for the *saiban-in* (lay judge) system, carried out by the Japanese Federation of Bar Associations (JFBA). As the conclusion of the project, two books were published in 2008: one is the final report of this study, which included recommendations for lawyers on the handling of difficult legal terms before lay judges (JFBA 2008a); and the other is for explaining courtroom language in plain Japanese for laypersons (JFBA 2008b).

In the context of law translation, nothing concrete seems to be happening in the movement to make law language closer to spoken language or more comprehensible (thus, more translatable). Rather, there have been some suggestions to make Japanese law translation more understandable by adding annotations to explain difficult terms and concepts in context (e.g., Kashiwagi 2006; TIFLG 2008), and attaching a translation of "Outline" and/or "Reasons" of the bill for a given law, which is written in ordinary language in a concise and formulaic manner (Matsuura 2010).

A more radical way to address this issue may be to produce translation that is more target-oriented or readability-oriented, instead of adhering to the tradition of strict literalism. As the Ministry of Justice clearly states, the translations contained in the JLT are 'to be used solely as reference material to aid in the understanding of Japanese laws and regulations', and are not legally enforceable.[6] This is typical "non-authoritative" "for information only" translation. An argument can be made here that in order to achieve the communicative purpose (i.e., to promote the understanding of Japanese law) translation should be allowed to have 'some wiggle-room' (Wolff 2011: 241) for readability and comprehensibility. This would require a careful balancing act by legal translators who generally strive for precision. It is hoped that the approach to translating Japanese law is revisited from the perspective of its communicative purpose, with due attention to the feedback from the receiving end of the translation.

Given the absence of strong activism to promote plain Japanese in the legal context, it may be a long way to implementing plain Japanese in the drafting of laws. Such effort, however, should lead to higher productivity and cost savings in the work of translating Japanese laws (e.g., Lawson 2007; TIFLG 2008).

5. Conclusion

This chapter has presented a historical overview of law translation in Japan, and the current government project to translate Japanese law into English. A new perspective was proposed for discussion on the purposes of legal translation by drawing on how law translation was used in the Meiji and post-war periods in Japan. Also, some problems with translation in the JLT were analyzed, and possible solutions to them were suggested, such as the use of a TM.

In conclusion, it should be emphasized that the Japanese government's commitment is the key to the JLT's success. The JLT has been up and running and attracting a great deal of

5 Available at: http://www.opc.gov.au/about/draft_manuals.htm.
6 See 'About Law Data' in JLT: http://www.japaneselawtranslation.go.jp/law/about_lawdata/?re=02 [Accessed 30 November 2012].

traffic since its introduction in 2009. There is no turning back for the government now. As over 100 amendments and new laws are enacted every year (Hoseishitsumu-yogo 2012), the law translation project must keep going. Since the JLT provides free, open online information, quality issues and delays with translation are easily exposed and these problems can negatively affect the Japanese standing in the international network of legislative information. All the possible solutions laid out above would not work without the government's initiative. There may be much to learn from other countries with similar law translation projects. In Korea, for instance, a single government entity manages the translation of all laws. As of November 2012, it has produced English translation of more than 900 laws and Chinese translation of 11 laws. It is hoped that the Japanese government will secure resources to continue providing reliable translation of Japanese laws in order to keep the JLT relevant and contribute to the international sharing of legal information.

References

Adler, M. 2012. 'The Plain Language Movement'. In: P.M. Tiersma and L.M. Solan eds. *The Oxford Handbook of Language and Law*. Oxford: Oxford University Press, pp. 67–83.

Aoki, H. 2000. 'Horitsu-gainen o honyaku suru muzukashisa: <tentative> to 'misui' [Difficulty of translating legal concepts: 'tentative' and 'misui']', *Hitotsubashi ronso*, vol. 124(4), pp. 495–505. Available at: http://hermes-ir.lib.hit-u.ac.jp/rs/bitstream/10086/10474/1/ronso1240400310.pdf [Accessed 30 November 2012].

Bowker, L. 2002. *Computer-Aided Translation Technology: A Practical Introduction*. Ottawa: University of Ottawa Press.

———. 2005. 'Productivity vs. Quality: A Pilot Study on the Impact of Translation Memory Systems', *Localisation Focus*, vol. 4(1), pp. 13–20.

Bowker, L. and Fisher, D. 2010. 'Computer-Aided Translation'. In: Y. Gambier and L. Van Doorslaer eds. *Handbook of Translation Studies*. Amsterdam and Philadelphia: John Benjamins, pp. 60–65.

Cao, D. 2007. *Translating Laws*. Clevedon: Multilingual Matters.

Chiyo, M. 2005. 'Nihon horei no gaikokugo-yaku seibi no kadai [Issues of Translating Japanese Laws into Foreign Languages]', *Reference*, vol. 2005(7), pp. 6–23. Available at: http://www.ndl.go.jp/jp/data/publication/refer/200507_654/065401.pdf [Accessed 30 November 2012].

European Commission. 1996. *Legislative Drafting: A Commission Manual* [Online: European Commission]. Available at: http://ec.europa.eu/governance/better_regulation/documents/legis_draft_comm_en.pdf [Accessed 30 November 2012].

Furuta, H. 2004. *Honyakugo toshiteno nihon no horitsu yogo* [Japanese Legal Terms as Translated Words]. Tokyo: Chuo University Press.

Hayashi, O. and Aomi, J. (eds). 1981. *Ho to nihongo* [Law and Japanese]. Tokyo: Yuhikaku.

Hirsch, D. 1989. *Drafting Federal Law*. Washington, D.C.: US Government Printing Office. Available at: http://www.llsdc.org/attachments/files/92/Drafting-Fed-Law.pdf [Accessed 30 November 2012].

Hoseishitsumu-yogo, K. 2012. *Jobun no yomikata* [How to Read the Text of Law]. Tokyo: Yuhikaku.

Japanese Federation of Bar Associations. 2008a. *Saiban-in jidai no hotei yogo: hotei yogo no nichijogoka ni kansuru PT saishu hokokusho* [Courtroom Language in the Lay Judge Era: PT Final Report on Making Courtroom Language Daily Language]. Tokyo: Sanseido.

———. 2008b. *Yasashiku yomitoku saiban-in no tameno hotei yogo handbook* [Handbook of Understanding Courtroom Language for Lay Judges]. Tokyo: Sanseido.

Kamiya, S. 2009. 'Laws, Legal Terms Get Official Translation', *The Japan Times*, 6 September. Available at: http://www.japantimes.co.jp/text/nn20090610f1.html [Accessed 30 November 2012].

Kashiwagi, N. 2006. 'Horei gaikokugo-yaku seibi no suishin ni kansuru totatsu-ten to kongo no kadai [Achievements and Future Issues of Promoting Translation of Laws and Regulations into Foreign Languages]', *Jurist*, vol. 1312, pp. 2–9.

Kawano, T. 2006. 'Soto-kara nihon-ho wa do mieteiruka: tokutei ryoiki kenkyu "Transparency of Japanese Law" dai-1-kai symposium no gaiyo' [How Does Japanese Law Look from Outside: Special Area Study "Transparency of Japanese Law', a summary of the first symposium], *Jurist*, vol. 1312, pp. 30–36.

Kondo, M. and Wakabayashi, J. 2008. 'Japanese Tradition'. In: M. Baker and G. Saldanha eds. *Routledge Encyclopedia of Translation Studies*. London and New York: Routledge, pp. 485–494.

Lawson, C. 2007. 'Found in Translation: The "Transparency of Japanese Law Project" in Context' *Journal of Japanese Law*, vol. 24, pp. 189–99. Available at: http://sydney.edu.au/law/anjel/documents/ZJapanR/ZJapanR24/ZJapanR24_16_Lawson.pdf [Accessed 30 November 2012].

———. 2010. 'Legal Translation Tools for Everyone', *51st Annual Conference of American Translators Association*. Denver, Colorado, 28 October 2010.

McNelly, T. 1987. 'Kanri sareta kakumei [Controlled Revolution]'. In: Y. Sakamoto and R.E. Ward eds. *Nihon senryo no kenkyu* [Studies on the Occupation of Japan]. Tokyo: University of Tokyo Press, pp. 133–176.

Matsuura, Y. 2010. 'Nihon horei hanketsu no honyaku to nihon ho no tomeika [Translation of Japanese Laws, Regulations, and Case Laws, and Making Japanese Law Transparent]', *Jurist*, vol. 1394, pp. 24–28.

Oda, H. 2009. *Japanese Law*. 3rd edn. Oxford: Oxford University Press.

Okawara, M. 2012. 'Horitsu no kotoba [Language of Law]'. In: T. Hashiuchi and S. Hotta eds. *Ho to gengo* [Law and Language]. Tokyo: Kuroshio Shuppan.

Ozawa, T. 2010. 'Kokka kiko [The National System]'. In: H. Asako, T. Ito, N. Ueda and F. Jinbo eds. *Nihon Hoseishi* [History of the Japanese Legal System]. Tokyo: Seirin-Shoin, pp. 251–269.

Ozawa, T., Asako, H., Koyanagi, S. and Ito, T. 'Kindai-ho no keisei [Formation of Modern Law]'. In: H. Asako, T. Ito, N. Ueda and F. Jinbo eds. *Nihon Hoseishi* [History of the Japanese Legal System]. Tokyo: Seirin-Shoin, pp. 251–328.

Pym, A. 2008. 'On Toury's Laws of How Translators Translate'. In: A. Pym, M. Shlesinger and D. Simeoni eds. *Beyond Descriptive Translation Studies*. Amsterdam and Philadelphia: John Benjamins, pp. 317–328.

Röhl, W. 2005. 'Generalities'. In: W. Röhl ed. *History of Law in Japan Since 1868*. Leiden and Boston: BRILL, pp. 1–28.

Šarčević, S. 2012. 'Challenges to the Legal Translator'. In: P.M. Tiersma and L.M. Solan eds. *The Oxford Handbook of Language and Law*. Oxford: Oxford University Press, pp. 187–199.

Sekiguchi, T. 2012. 'Shusen renraku chuo jimukyoku ni yoru kaku-sho-kan no renraku chosei: ho-kankei shiryo no eiyaku sagyo o jirei toshite [Coordination Between Ministries by the Central Liaison Office: A Case Study of English Translation of Law-Related Documents]', *Rekishigaku-kenkyu* [Study of History], vol. 896, pp. 22–32.

Sekine, Y. 2012. 'The Development of Translation Memory Database System for Law Translation (in Japanese)', *Invitation to Translation Studies*, vol. 7, pp. 79–88. Available at: http://honyakukenkyu.sakura.ne.jp/shotai_vol7/No.7–04-Sekine.pdf [Accessed 30 November 2012].

Sekine, Y., Ogawa, Y., Toyama, K. and Matsuura, Y. 2012. 'Development of Translation Memory Database System for Law Translation', *Paper to the Law via the Internet*. 7–9 October 2012. Ithaca, NY: Cornell University.

Sekine, Y. 2013. *A Study on Technologies for Translating Japanese Laws*. Forthcoming master's thesis (unpublished). Rikkyo University, Tokyo.

Study Council for Promoting Translation of Japanese Laws and Regulations into Foreign Languages. 2006. *Final Report*. [Online: Cabinet Secretariat, Japan]. Available at: www.cas.go.jp/jp/seisaku/hourei/report.pdf [Accessed 30 November 2012].

Takayanagi, K. 1968. 'Some Reminiscences of Japan's Commission on the Constitution'. In: D.F. Henderson ed. *The Constitution of Japan: Its First Twenty Years*. Seattle and London: University of Washington Press, pp. 71–88.

Tiersma, P.M. 1999. *Legal Language*. Chicago and London: University of Chicago Press.

Toyama, K., Ogawa, Y., Imai, K. and Matsuura, Y. 2006. 'Application of Word Alignment for Supporting Translation of Japanese Statutes into English', *JURIX 2006: The Nineteenth Annual Conference on Legal Knowledge and Information Systems*. Paris, France, 7–9 December 2006.

Toyama, K., Saito, D., Sekine, Y., Ogawa, Y., Kakuta, T., Kimura, T. and Matsuura, Y. 2011. 'Design and Development of Japanese Law Translation Database System', *Paper to the Law via the Internet*. The University of Hong Kong, 8–10 June 2011.

Transparency of Japanese Law Project, International Finance Law Group. 2008. International Workshop: Nihon-ho no eiyaku wa nihon-ho no tomeika ni tsunagaruka [Does English translation of Japanese law lead to the transparency of Japanese law?], *Kokusai shoji homu* [International Commercial Law], 36(3), 327–338.

Wolff, L. 2011. 'Legal Translation'. In: K. Malmkjær and K. Windle eds. *The Oxford Handbook of Translation Studies*. Oxford: Oxford University Press.

Yamamoto, T. 2006. 'Horei gaikokugo-yaku suishin no tame no kiban seibi ni kansuru seifu no torikumi [The Government's Efforts Concerning the Infrastructure for Promoting Laws and Regulations into Foreign Languages]', *Jurist*, vol. 1312, pp. 10–17.

Yanabu, A. 2010. 'Nihon ni okeru honyaku [Translation in Japan]'. In: A. Yanabu, A. Mizuno and M. Naganuma eds. *Nihon no honyaku ron* [Japanese Discourse on Translation]. Tokyo: Hosei University Press, pp. 1–34.

Chapter 14
Important Translation Strategies Used in Legal Translation: Examples of Hooper's Translation of the Ottoman Majalla into English

Rafat Y. Alwazna

The need for legal translation and qualified legal translators has drastically increased, particularly in this globalized world. This unequivocally explains the reason behind the increasingly growing interest in the translation of legal texts by both linguists and lawyers (Šarčević 2000) as legal translation has become a practically pressing need at current times (Wolff 2011: 232). Today, issues of nation, language and translation have been of paramount importance for the sake of world communication, and translation with no doubt is crucial for the living of texts and pivotal for intercultural communication (Bermann 2005: 1, 6). Legal texts, without being translated into different legal systems, become restricted in world understanding (Cao 2007: 2).

This chapter deals primarily with the methods and strategies that translators of laws follow and adopt when coping with legal translation. It starts by offering a succinct account of the translation theories that have been adopted and are still being applied to legal translation, showing three different camps of scholars with regard to the validity of applying such translation theories to legal translation. Important methods and strategies often used in the translation of laws are then presented, discussing each strategy in the light of its validity to legal translation and in view of different opinions of various scholars in this field regarding the useful application of these strategies to legal translation. This presentation includes literal translation, free translation, functional approach to translation, transliteration/transcription, loan translation, adaptation, description by definitions, and explanations/lexical expansion, as well as descriptive substitution. The chapter then reaches its pivotal practical part, discussing and analyzing three different legal Articles (101, 102, 123), taken from the Ottoman Majalla and translated by Hooper (1933) from Arabic into English, in an attempt to explore and analyze the translation methods and strategies adopted by the translator in his translation of the aforementioned articles. In each article, the ST in Arabic will first be presented, followed by the TT in English, which is then followed by discussion and analysis. It can be claimed that a single small legal text may merit a diverse set of translation strategies depending on the differences in the legal rules between the source legal system and the target legal system and the difference in the language of law peculiar to each legal system alongside the type of the target audience.

1. Translation Theory and Legal Translation

Translation theories have been applied by both linguists and lawyers to legal translation, amongst these theories are Catford's situation equivalence (Kielar 1977: 33), Nida's formal correspondence (Weisflog 1987: 187, 191) and Vermeer's skopos theory (Madsen 1997: 17–26). However, the application of translation theories to legal translation is still a disputable matter. While there are some legal translators who see the validity of applying translation theories to legal translation, others argue that translation theories are not applicable to legal translation (Šarčević 2000; Weston 1991). The latter view is perhaps expected as legal translation generally demands special translation techniques, methods and strategies which are practice-oriented (Šarčević 2000). Theorists holding this view claim that legal language is characterized by special qualities which distinguish it from ordinary language (Garzone 2000: 395). This makes legal translation distinctive and difficult in practice (Harvey 2002: 177). A third view does not see that legal translation should be given a special status and linguistic uniqueness which take it outside of general translation theory, and that theorists who believe in the special status of legal translation have misconceived the whole idea and are ipso facto mistaken (Garzone 2000: 395; Wolff 2011: 230).

One important task that should be performed by translation theorists is to establish identifiable criteria to scaffold translators to choose the right translation strategy for a particular translation project (Šarčević 2000). Selection of the appropriate translation strategy has long been hinging upon text type whose creation is contingent upon the subject matter (Šarčević 2000). Another element of text typology propounded by Reiss (1971: 32) is the function of the text type. The new focus on the function of the text has given rise to the promotion of the pragmatic aspects of the text at the expense of linguistic theories of translation (Šarčević 2000). Communicative factors of reception have become the main basis on which the translated text is created, thus the translator becomes a text producer rather than an ST reproducer (Šarčević 2000).

2. Methods/Strategies Adopted in Legal Translation

As all translators, legal translators encounter both linguistic and cultural issues and problems when rendering a particular legal text from one legal system into another. Linguistic differences found between two specific legal languages may be solvable as most of the translations require grammatical transformation. However, if linguistic items carry legal concepts peculiar to the SL legal system, which are not present in the TL legal system, fundamental issues and problems may arise. Similarly, if the ST is replete with culture-specific terms, which are particular to the source language culture, and are not ipso facto found in the target language culture, thorny issues and complex problems may emerge. Šarčević (1985: 127) asserts that legal translators should surmount cultural obstacles between the SL and the TL. She goes on to point out that in the case of culture-specific terms, adequate TL equivalent for the SL lexical item is usually not possible (128).

2.1. Literal Translation versus Free Translation

Legal translators have long been committed to the principle of fidelity to the source text for the sake of preserving the letter of the law (Šarčević 1997: 16; Poon 2005: 316; Wolff 2011: 236), thus they endeavour to reproduce the form and content of the source text as closely as possible in the target language (Hjort-Pedersen and Faber 2001: 379; Šarčević 1985: 127). In other words, legal translators are required to achieve denotative equivalence, which can only be accomplished by preserving the ST lexical, syntactic and stylistic features as closely as possible in the TL (Šarčević 1985: 128; Newmark 1981: 47). Winter (1964: 76) contends that the transfer of denotative meaning can be achieved satisfactorily, though this process may involve some difficulties. Newmark (1981: 11) and Šarčević (1985: 130) reach the agreement that in rendering the laws of the source language country into another language, legal translators should not make changes on the text to suit the laws of the target language country. It is commonly known that legal language is sensitive and sacred (Wolff 2011: 229). This view of adopting literal translation for the translation of legal texts dates back to the time of the Roman Empire, which imposed the use of formal correspondence when dealing with the translation of legal and biblical texts (Šarčević 1997: 23–48). This approach to legal translation is regarded by Taylor (1997) as a kind of positivism, which claims that legal meaning is wholly derived from a direct reading of the letter of the law. This type of legal meaning is detached from its political, social and economic context. Indeed, positivism views law, which is laid down in legal documents, as being equal to the law in action (Wolff 2011: 237). Any sacrifice in the accuracy of meaning is not only deemed by positivism a liberty, but also wrong in the eyes of law (Kasirer 2001: 331).

Similarly, lawyers view the source text with reverence and necessitate adherence thereto in legal translation (Kasirer 2001: 332; Šarčević 1985: 128). They oblige legal translators to follow literalism and reproduce both form and content of the ST in the TL, fearing that the TT could deviate from the ST, which may pose a real problem that may affect uniform interpretation and application (Šarčević 1998: 282). Therefore, literal translation was the common strategy used by both legal translators as well as lawyers and is still in use by some of them at current times (Šarčević 2000; Wolff 2011: 228). For instance, Weisflog (1987), who is a lawyer translator, strongly advocates the strategy of literal translation for legal texts regardless of text type and function. He believes that legal translators should adhere to literal translation and should not be given any freedom to change the form and/or the content whether the texts they work on are national legislations, international treaties, conventions or instruments of primary or secondary community law.

Having considered the distinctive nature of legal texts, it is generally accepted that content should always be prioritized over form in legal translation. The issue of whether authenticated translation should be literal or free is debatable. In practice, there is clear variation in methods and strategies adopted in different jurisdictions, even if the texts are identical. Gutt (1991, 19) contends that the decision of adopting a translation strategy that is source-language-oriented or target-language-oriented is not an easy task, rather it is a discretionary choice. Along similar lines, Hjort-Pedersen (1996, 370) confirms, after conducting an empirical study of Danish and English wills, that legal translators should not always trust source-language-oriented strategy, but they are indeed entitled to produce natural communicative legal text. Rossel (a law professor) challenges the method of literal translation. He has translated the German text of the Swiss Civil Code into idiomatic French. He has been accused of altering the letter of the law, however, Rossel has defended his position, stating that he has translated the text in question with the use of high quality language. He goes on to argue that French-speaking population living in Switzerland are entitled to see their laws written in such natural and idiomatic French (Šarčević 1997: 36–40; Šarčević 1998: 282).

Koutsivitis (translator at the EU Commission) accentuates the concept of sense-for-sense translation, confirming that the task of the legal translator is to convey the sense of the source text in the target language. Giving credence to idiomising translation, he points out that EU translators are given leeway to be creative in the target language (Šarčević 2000). This is supported by Pescatore (former justice at the European Court of Justice), who takes this theme further, explaining that the optimum way of EU translators is to produce a text in the target language which reads as if it were originally written in that very language (Šarčević 2000). Within the same line of thought, it is claimed that a faithful translation should not eliminate the role of the target language (Legrand 2005: 38); rather, it should relay the target language concepts and follows its discursive structures (Lewis 2004: 262). Wolff (2011) claims that legal translation theory should go beyond its current restricted limitations, adopting free translation that completely respects the contextual essentials of the text (230). He goes on to argue that translation based on linguistic fidelity to the source text, which does not give the legal translator leeway to be creative in producing integral and expressive target legal text, fails to achieve the essential point of legal translation (235).

It is indeed the Canadians who have applied this concept by developing techniques and strategies of bilingual drafting (Šarčević 1997). This is owing to the fact that Canada is both bilingual and bilegal as it follows more than one law. The conflict that exists between the civil law followed in the French-speaking province of Quebec and the common law adopted in the English-speaking province has unquestionably played a pivotal role in making Canada an interesting centre for legal translators (Šarčević 1998: 283). Francophone translators who are responsible for translating federal legislations have been given a leeway to produce texts formulated in a natural, pure, communicative, and idiomatic French in response to the demand made by the people of Quebec province for language equality. This has given rise to the introduction of methods of bilingual drafting, which has made considerable changes to the role and task of the legal translator (Ibid.).

It can be argued that co-drafting has given translators in charge of federal legislations in Canada a kind of freedom, which did not exist before. In the past, translators of law in Canada did not enjoy any freedom in legal translation, and they ipso facto had practically no decision-making role. They were committed to follow the letter of the law and were not allowed to omit any words in the source text, even if their existence in the target text is superfluous (Id. at 287). However, things have completely changed in co-drafting. The freedom, which has been given to translators of federal legislations, has played a substantial role in encouraging legal translators in Canada to be creative in the target language. However, it should be clarified that the freedom that has been given to legal translators has not been at the expense of the translator's reliability (Id. at 284). The Canadian Parliament has equally approved and authenticated both the English and the French texts of federal legislations. This is due to the fact that the English and the French texts of federal legislations are seen to have the same legal content, convey the same legislative intent and consequently produce the same legal effect (Didier 1990: 221). No doubt that the present Canadian model serves as an inspiring source for translators of law all over the globe (Šarčević 1998: 290).

2.2. Functional Approach to Translation

It can be claimed that translation strategy for a particular translation project is chiefly adopted on the basis of the type of audience whom the translation is targeting, thus giving rise to the fact that the same text can be translated differently depending on the type of audience to whom the translation is directed (Šarčević 2000; Šarčević 1985). This may require the translator to make noticeable changes with regard to the lexical, syntactic as well as the stylistic features of the target text to suit the target audience (Šarčević 1985: 127). There has then been a shift towards the purpose or the communicative function of the target text. A number of theorists believe that legal translation AS other areas of translation is receiver oriented (Šarčević 2000: 329; Wolff 2011: 229). In other words, the legal target text needs to be adapted to live up to the target reader's expectations (Stolze 2001: 302; Chroma 2004: 202; Wolff 2011: 229). Taking on board that legal translation is receiver/oriented, the main focus here becomes on the interpretation and application of the parallel texts by the court (Šarčević 1998: 284). Taylor (1997) argues that functional equivalence is the strategic approach which is often employed within the European comparative law sphere to convey legal concepts across legal systems and legal cultures.

In skopos theory proposed by Vermeer (1998: 41–45), the functional approach to translation aims at producing a text which lives up to the cultural expectations of the target reader. This theory has developed translation theory by providing traditional translation with a new alternative (Šarčević 2000). While traditional translation focuses on reproducing the form and content of the source text in the target text with the function of the source text kept intact in the target text, Vermeer's skopos theory clearly marks shift in the translation focus where translation function becomes different from that of the source text. Different from traditional translation, the functional approach to translation claims that the same text can be translated differently on the basis of the communicative function of the translated text. Following Vermeer's skopos theory, the translator is given a leeway to produce a text which largely differs from the original text in both form and content (Šarčević 2000).

Vermeer's claim that his theory can be applied to all texts has been heavily criticized by a number of scholars, such as Šarčević (1997: 18–19, 65–66, 71, 104–106, 108–110), Madsen (1997: 17–26), and Nord (1997: 109–122). His notion that translation strategy used in contracts is chiefly determined by function fails to take account of the fact that legal texts are subjected to the rules of law which govern their use. Selection of appropriate translation strategy for a particular legal text is contingent upon legal considerations (Šarčević 2000: 332; Wolff 2011: 238). Šarčević (1997: 18–19, 69) and Madsen (1997: 17) reach the same conclusion concerning the translation of contracts; they both confirm that the decision as to whether or not adherence to the target language formulae is appropriate is primarily determined by the type of law governing that contract, but not by function.

Šarčević (2000) claims that communicative factors of reception influence translation strategy in plurilingual jurisdictions. Authenticated translations, which are vested with the law force, enable the mechanism of a particular law to be implemented in several languages. One important feature of authenticated translations according to the theory of original texts is that they should be as precise and inviolate as the original text(s) (Šarčević 2000). Indeed, authenticated translations are not at all viewed as "mere translations"; rather, they are seen as original texts (Šarčević 1997: 20).

Unlike Vermeer's skopos theory, which entails shift in function between source text and target text, there is no shift in function in authenticated translations of legislation (Id. at 21). Nevertheless, authenticated translations of legislations are done differently in different jurisdictions, which leads to the fact that adopting a unified translation strategy based chiefly on function for all legislative texts is unquestionably inadequate. In order to lay down a set of criteria for determining the translation strategy used in legal translation, it is of utmost importance to analyze the communicative factors in each legal situation (Šarčević 2000).

Other pivotal translation strategies are provided by Šarčević (1985: 128), which can be adopted by legal translators, particularly when confronted by lexical-semantic problems arising from SL culture-specific terms. These are shown below.

2.3. Transliteration/Transcription

Transliteration is a commonly used translation strategy, and has been widely adopted by legal translators in Quebec who were in charge of translating the French statutes for English-speaking audience who were familiar with the legal terminology specific to Quebec (Ibid.).

Transliteration points to the transcription of the SL term with the use of the TL alphabets where the SL term appears as a loan word in the TL, and is often placed between inverted commas or is italicized. This strategy is adopted if the SL term has already been culturally borrowed by the TL and has therefore become part of the TL legal terminology, or if the legal meaning of the SL term is fully understood from the context (Ibid.). These conditions for transliteration have been met in Quebec. However, this type of transliteration may make the comprehension of the French statutes more complicated for the readers who are not familiar with the legal terminology of Quebec (Russell 1979: 216). Consequently, legal translators, who translate for audience belonging to diverse legal cultures, are likely to avoid the use of transliteration, which may cause misunderstanding for the readers who are not versed in the legal system of the SL country (Šarčević 1985: 129). This fact is particularly relevant to the case of minority languages.

Conversely, it can be argued that transliteration can also be exercised even if the SL term has not been naturalized in the TL legal terminology, nor is its legal meaning fully fathomed from the context. After the translator transliterates the SL term, he/she is required to provide the reader with a definition and explanation of the term in question so as to familiarize him/her with the legal meaning of the term and the legal concept implied by the term concerned. This description by definitions and explanations indicated by Šarčević (1985) is another translation strategy that can be adopted along with transliteration, and will be tackled below. This description can be contained within the body of the target text, i.e. after the transliterated SL term and placed in brackets. Alternatively, it can be put as a footnote or as an endnote, which usually tails the target text. Another option which some legal translators sometimes resort to is to write a linguistic commentary or linguistic analysis in which they explore and analyze the crucial linguistic and cultural issues and problems that they have encountered during the translation process, and explain the strategies that they have adopted to overcome the complex problems that they have faced throughout the translation project.

2.4. Loan Translation

Loan translation is another strategy often exploited by legal translators. New legal terms are first introduced to a particular legal system, conveying legal concepts. These legal terms are then naturalized into the legal system to which they have been introduced, before they are translated into other foreign languages (Šarčević 1985: 129). For instance, Yugoslav legal translators make use of loan translation to resolve lexical-semantic problems in lieu of the use of transliteration (Ibid.). In the case of loan translation, a compound expression is rendered verbatim into the TL. Literal translation is adopted when the source term is clearly comprehended by the reader. Legal translators need to be fully cognizant of the legal terminology specific to the TL so as to avoid producing loan translations which may relay different legal concepts in the TL. Exceptions are only allowed if the context refers to a foreign concept (Ibid.).

In crude terms, legal translation team are usually commanded by a particular country's authority to produce an official translation of the laws implemented in the country concerned. When this legal translation team officially make use of a loan translation for a particular culture-specific term, this loan translation becomes recognizable, and other legal translators become obliged to adopt this very loan translation. Conversely, legal translators should reject the use of loan translation for terms which have no historical connotations in the target audience. For the sake of accuracy and precision in legal translation, the use of loan translation is at times favoured over a TL equivalence, especially if the latter fails to impart the importance of the SL message conveyed by the SL term (Šarčević 1985: 129). It is worth noting that loan translation is widely adopted in Quebec, even when there are equivalent terms in the English common law for the French civil law terms (Id. at 130). However, it should be pointed out that loan translations for culture-specific terms, which are not fully comprehended by the target reader, and are not followed by description by definitions and explanations may well cause undertranslation. This means that a certain amount of information content of the SL term will be lost during the translation process. If the target text is full of undertranslation, it will be rendered incomprehensible (Ibid.).

2.5. Adaptation

Another strategy which is adopted by translators, though its use is controversial within the realm of translation theory is adaptation. Using this translation strategy, the SL term is formulated so as to convey a particular message that can be found in the social reality of the target language and can have the same function (Šarčević 1985: 130–131). In other words, the translator resorts to make use of a cultural equivalent. In a more restricted sense, adaptation is no longer deemed translation as it is a kind of cultural transplantation (see Dickins, Hervey and Higgins 2002: 32). Kade (1980: 152–158) clearly differentiates between translation and adaptation, stating that in the case of translation, the translator is required to reproduce the information content of the source text, while in the case of adaptation, the translator adapts the source text to live up to the culture of the target language through making changes on the information content of the text in question. This distinction becomes evident when back-translation test is exercised on the target text. Back-translation test will clearly reveal considerable divergence between the source and target text due to the fact that cultural equivalent usually has one-to-one equivalent in the source language (Šarčević 1985: 131).

Šarčević (1985: 131) points out that since there must be no difference in legal meaning in legal translation between the source text and the target text, the use of adaptation is considered misleading and should be completely shunned by legal translators when dealing with the translation of laws. If cultural equivalents are nonetheless utilized in a particular legal text, they should serve as a lexical expansion (Ibid.).

2.6. Description by Definitions and Explanations/Lexical Expansion

Another important strategy often adopted by legal translators to compensate for undertranslation is known as lexical expansion. Using this strategy, extra detail is added to the target text, either in the body of the text per se, as a footnote, as an endnote or in the glossary (Ibid.). Lexical expansion usually takes the form of definitions and explanations, and is an extensively used strategy by legal translators who particularly work on laws comprising a number of culture-specific terms. As indicated earlier, when dealing with transliteration, the extra detail can also be included in a linguistic analysis or linguistic commentary to explain all the tiny detail attached to these culture-specific terms and how they have been dealt with in the translation. As Yugoslav legal translators, who translate for readers with diverse cultural and social backgrounds practise definitions and explanations, it is clear that their definitions and explanations are SL-oriented, with no clear attempt made to adapt the information content to the TL reader. Following this path, these definitions and explanations become restricted in effect and function, which resides only in enabling the target reader to fully comprehend their intended meaning (Ibid.).

By contrast, translators who translate for audience with a particular cultural and social background, i.e., translating into their mother tongue, tend to orient their definitions and explanations towards the TL reader. Consequently, such definitions and explanations become comprehended by the TL reader, who is not versed in the SL legal concepts, but who is fully aware of the same field in the TL country (Šarčević 1985: 131). This practice lies in the use of TL cultural equivalents to stand for the SL legal concepts in lieu of describing them with the use of SL legal terms. This gives rise to the adoption of a comparative approach in the field of legal translation, which runs in line with Kielar's (1977: 153) claim. Such TL-oriented extra detail unquestionably enhances the comprehensibility of the target reader, though cannot completely manage to bridge the gap in the background knowledge of the target reader (Šarčević 1985: 131).

2.6.A. Translation Couplet

Another kind of lexical expansion often utilized by legal translators who translate for specific relationship is known as translation couplet. This type of lexical expansion is advantageous as it keeps the loan translation intact in the TT, with inserting some additional detail (Ibid.). In spite of the fact that translation couplet is a type of overtranslation, or what can be referred to as translation gain, it is, however, distinguishable from adaptation, albeit both may involve the use of cultural equivalents. Although some translators tend to include translation couplets within the target legal text itself, this is deemed a controversial matter among translators who translate laws (Ibid.).

A commonly used practice of translation couplet, which is frequently exercised by legal translators, lies in the use of loan translation, followed by the transliterated SL legal term in brackets. This practice has been also exercised in the English translation of the statutes of Quebec where couplet translations have been contained within the text per se, e.g. *bailiff (huissier)* (Šarčević 1985: 131; Russell 1979: 214). The other kind of translation couplet resides in the use of the loan translation followed by the TL cultural equivalent put in brackets. An example for this can clearly be shown in *work organization (firm)* (Šarčević 1985: 131).

2.6.B. Translation Triplet

Another kind of lexical expansion is called translation triplet. This type of lexical expansion is resorted to if Loan translation needs to be further clarified to avoid any possibility of double meaning (Šarčević 1985: 131–132). Triplet translation is composed of the loan translation, the SL legal term in brackets and the cultural equivalent also in brackets.

2.7. Descriptive Substitution

The last strategy stated by Šarčević (1985) is descriptive substitution, which is followed by translators of laws. It is used as a part of translation couplet, which consists of the transliterated SL term, followed by descriptive substitution in brackets. It is adopted when there is no one-to-one correspondence between the SL culture-specific term and the TL legal terminology which can designate the same legal concept. In other words, this strategy is resorted to by legal translators when literal translation of a culture-specific term becomes impossible, thus ruling out the possibility of adopting loan translation (1985: 132). This strategy provides a kind of description of the form and/or function of the legal concept concerned, albeit it cannot be regarded as a cultural equivalent. Indeed, descriptive substitution is barely adopted in the translation of legal texts (Ibid.). This is due to the fact that descriptive substitutes are often inaccurate and lengthier than the equivalent SL legal term, which may lead to the practice of paraphrases rather than descriptive substitution. Hence, descriptive substitution should only be made use of when the SL culture-specific legal term can never be rendered into the target language by any other strategy (Ibid.). When adopted at the first time, translation couplet is used consisting of the SL legal term, followed by the descriptive substitute in brackets. Failing to do that, the SL legal term cannot be identified if back-translation is carried out (Ibid.).

The different methods of lexical expansion explained above are deemed various options available to the legal translator working on translating laws, their use is usually contingent on the translator's readiness and his/her ability to adapt the TL to fit the target reader's comprehension. It can be claimed that in legal translation, the translator's first task is to reconvey the content of the SL into the TL. Given that the target reader's understandability is regarded as a pivotal factor in specifying whether or not the translation is successful, legal translators cannot wholly disregard this significant factor. Even when choosing the most appropriate strategy that can best fit the translation of culture-specific legal terms which convey specific legal concepts, the target reader's comprehension should always be taken into account by the legal translator (Ibid.). When the target reader manages to fully comprehend the TT, he/she will be in a good position to receive the right legal result that the legal text in question is aiming to produce.

The legal translator is required to adhere to the ST as closely as possible so as to achieve the goals of the SL country law. This means that forms or strategies of overtranslation that would alter the content of the ST should be avoided, such as adaptation, descriptive substitution as well as translation couplets and triplets that comprise cultural equivalents. At the same time, the legal translator should compensate for any undertranslation that takes place as a result of loan translation through adopting forms or strategies of overtranslation to be exercised outside the ST. These forms or strategies represent all types of lexical expansion, such as adaptation, description by definitions and explanations, translation couplets, translation triplets and descriptive substitutions (Šarčević 1985: 132). Given that the extra supplementary detail targets the improvement of the reader's comprehension, this kind of detail will be more beneficial to the reader as long as it is TL-oriented (Ibid.).

3. Examples of Hooper's Translation of the Ottoman Majalla into English

In this section, selected examples of three legal Articles (101, 102, 123) translated by Hooper (1933) will be presented, after introducing the source text from the Ottoman Majalla. This is followed by some explanations to specify the strategy(s) that Hooper (1933) has adopted in his translation. Examples presented in this section are taken from the Ottoman Majalla, the book of sale. It is worth stating that the Ottoman Majalla (Majallat Alaḥkām Al ʿadliyya) is deemed the first attempt to codify Islamic Law according to the Ḥanafī School of Law concerning civil transactions and jurisdictions (Alshashrī 2005: 14). It was compiled by a committee of different Ḥanafī scholars during the Ottoman age so as to be followed in the courts of the Ottoman State (Alnadawī 2004: 178–179).

> *Article 101*
> *'(Māda 101). Alaījābu alawwalu kalāmun yaṣduru min aḥadi al ʿāqidayni liajli inshāʾi altaṣarruf wa bihi yūjabu wa yathbutu altaṣarruf' (Almajalla 1877: 22–23).*

'(Article 101). Offer is the statement made in the first place with a view to making a disposition of property and such disposition is proved thereby' (Hooper 1933, vol. I: 31).

Considering the translation of Article 101 from Arabic into English made by Hooper (1933), different points and remarks can be raised. The translator has not translated the second word in the Arabic article "alawwal" the literal rendering of which into English is "the first". The ST phrase "min aḥadi al'āqidayn" the literal rendering of which into English is "by one of the two contracting parties" has also not been translated into English, though it has been compensated for by the phrase "in the first place". This means that Hooper (1933), beside his use of literal translation in his translation of some terms in the article above, such as "alaījāb, offer; kalām, statement; yaṣdur, made", though the last example has undergone grammatical transposition see Dickins, Hervey and Higgins 2002: 16); changing a verb from an active voice in the ST to a passive voice in the TT, has adopted a strategy known as translation by omission. This strategy requires the deletion of some textual elements from the TT, which are present in the ST (Id. at 23). The use of such a strategy unequivocally causes translation loss in economy, which affects the complete transfer of the information content from the ST into the TT, though this matter is of an utmost importance in legal translation. The translator could have kept the omitted textual elements intact in the TT without affecting the style and naturalness of the TL, however, he has preferred to dispense with them.

The ST phrase "liajli inshā'i altaṣarruf" has been rendered into English as "with a view to making a disposition of property". Again, the translator has adopted literal translation in translating terms, such as "inshā', making; altaṣarruf, disposition". However, strangely enough, the translator has rephrased the prepositional phrase "liajl" as "with a view to", though he could have translated it verbatim as "for" or "to", etc. It is generally agreed that descriptive paraphrase, which is a strategy adopted for achieving free translation, is resorted to when there is no one-to-one correspondence between the ST and the TT (see Dickins, Hervey and Higgins 2002: 16–17). Another strategy also adopted by the translator is known as translation by addition. This strategy demands inserting textual elements in the TT, which are not present in the ST (Id. at 24). The term "property" is the textual element added to the TT, which does not exist in the ST. This addition is required by the English structure as the mention of the term "disposition" on its own in such construction does not relay a clear message, rather creates a stilted ill-formed English construction. Consequently, the addition of the term "property" to the TT is necessary to produce a tight, coherent and well-formed English construction. The use of such strategy has led to overtranslation or what is known as translation gain.

The ST phrase "wa bihi yūjabu wa yathbutu altaṣarruf" has been translated into English as "and such disposition is proved thereby". The translator at the outset has rendered the Arabic cohesive device "wa", which is known as connective or conjunction (see Baker 1992: 190) into an equivalent English cohesive device "and", adopting in this very instance literal translation. He has then changed the syntactic nature of the ST from an active construction to a passive construction in the TT by foregrounding the term "disposition", whose Arabic equivalent, "altaṣarruf", is backgrounded in the ST. This change in voice is necessary due to the linguistic differences between Arabic and English as the former can start with either a noun or a verb, and it has started with a verb in this particular instance, while the latter must start with a noun unless the sentence is imperative. The translator has translated the two Arabic verbs "yūjabu wa yathbut" into a single English verb "prove", which is the literal rendering of the second Arabic verb "yathbut", thus giving no textual equivalent to the First Arabic verb "yūjab", which could have been rendered into English as "be obligatory". Hence, the translator again has made use of translation by omission, presuming that the English verb "prove" is able to convey the meaning of both the Arabic verbs "yūjabu wa yathbut" and that inserting an English equivalent for the Arabic verb "yūjab" is superfluous. The Arabic prepositional phrase "bihi", which is composed of the preposition "bi", the literal rendering of which into English is "by" and the pronoun "hi", the literal rendering of which into English is "it", is foregrounded in the ST. The ST writer has used another cohesive device known as pronominal reference, i.e., replacing a particular noun, in this particular instance the term "Alaījāb", with a suitable pronoun "hi" (Baker 1992: 181). The translator has translated the foregrounded prepositional phrase "bihi" into a backgrounded adverbial legal phrase "thereby". The English phrase "thereby" is equal to "by it", thus using the same cohesive device adopted in the ST by substituting the term "offer" by the pronoun "it", then changing the typical English phrase "by it" to a more legal-sounding phrase "thereby". Hence, the translator has made use of the same cohesive device as that utilized in the ST in order to arrive at the same result without affecting the flow of the English legal text.

Having a close look at the strategies adopted by the translator to achieve translating the aforementioned article into English, it is clear that the translator has used multiple translation strategies to render the article in question into acceptable legal English. Literal translation, though sometimes with grammatical transposition, translation by omission, free translation, translation by addition, change in voice, use of specific cohesive devices, such as connectives and pronominal references are a diverse set of translation strategies that the translator has exploited in order to translate the article concerned. The question that may be raised is concerning the reasons behind the use of translation by omission, free translation and translation by addition as such strategies should be generally avoided in legal translation. The use of translation by addition in this instance is justified as it is related to language norms and structure requirements. However, the use of translation by omission in several instances and the use of free translation in one instance in the translation of the article concerned are, in my view, problematic and should have been avoided. This is due to the paramount importance of the complete transfer of the information content in translation, particularly in legal translation, in addition to the high necessity of following literal translation in legal translation, particularly when this is a possible practice. Nonetheless, it can be argued that the legal effect produced by the TT article is the same as that conveyed by the ST article, which is the most important goal in legal translation (See Alwazna 2013a; Alwazna 2013b).

> *Article 102*
> *'(Māda 102). Alqabūlu thānī kalāmin yaṣduru min aḥadi al'āqidayni liajli inshā'i altaṣarruf wa bihi yatimmu al'aqd'. (Almajalla 1877: 23)*
>
> *'(Article 102). Acceptance is the statement made in the second place with a view to making a disposition of property. The contract becomes completed thereby'. (Hooper 1933 vol. I: 31)*

Studying the translation of Article 102 from Arabic into English made by Hooper (1933), it is evident that the translator has adopted nearly the same strategies that have been adopted in the previous article. After his literal translation of the term "alqabūl" as "acceptance", he has not rendered the second word in the Arabic article "thānī", the literal rendering of which into English is "second", thus adopting translation by omission. Literal translation has been applied to the translation of the term "kalām" as "statement" and the term "yaṣdur" as "made", with some grammatical transposition being made on the second term to change it from a verb in the active voice in the ST to a verb in the passive voice in the TT, a grammatical transformation that has also been exercised in Article 101 on the same term. The ST phrase "min aḥadi al'āqidayn", the literal rendering of which into English is "by one of the two contracting parties", which has been mentioned in Article 101 of the ST, but has not been translated in the TT, has also been repeated in Article 102 of the ST, but has been omitted in the TT, albeit compensated for by the phrase "in the second place", which is the same practice as that exercised in Article 101. Clearly, the translator has used translation by omission in this article to dispense with the same textual elements that he has omitted in Article 101, though he could have translated these textual elements literally to the TL. This, as indicated earlier, causes translation loss in economy. In other words, there has been incomplete transfer of the information content from the ST to the TT, which should generally be avoided in translation, particularly in legal translation. It appears that the translator believes that inserting the omitted elements in the TT is unnecessary due to the insignificance of these textual elements on the target reader's comprehension of the whole article according to his concluded presumption.

The ST phrase "liajli inshāʾi altaṣarruf" has been translated into English as "with a view to making a disposition of property". The translator here has adopted exactly the same strategies as those used in Article 101. He has started by using free translation; exercising descriptive paraphrase to rephrase the meaning of the Arabic prepositional phrase "liajl" as "with a view to", though there is an English equivalent for this phrase, i.e., "to", "for", etc., and these are widely used in Arabic-English legal translation. Literal translation has been applied to the translation of the term "inshāʾ" as "making" and the term "altaṣarruf" as "disposition". However, the translator has inserted an additional textual element in the TT, i.e., "property", which does not exist in the ST, thus using translation by addition. The use of this strategy is justifiable as the failure of adopting such a strategy will lead to an incomplete English structure. This strategy, however, has also brought about overtranslation, or what is called translation gain, which should generally be avoided in legal translation.

The ST phrase "wa bihi yatimmu alʿaqd" has been rendered into English as "the contract becomes completed thereby." It is worth noting at the outset that the translator has started a new sentence, thus breaking the article into two sentences, a practice which does not exist in the ST article, nor has it been exercised by the translator himself in Article 101. This strategy of sentence break is a new strategy adopted by the translator in Article 102, but not in Article 101. It seems that the translator has not seen the need for applying this strategy in Article 101 as the last part of Article 101 deals with the term "disposition", which has also been mentioned previously within the same article. Consequently, it has been appropriate to repeat stating the term "disposition" in the same sentence, rather than inserting two different sentences, in each of which the same term is mentioned. Conversely, in Article 102, it is clear that the last part of the article deals with how the contract is concluded and has not comprised the term "disposition", which has been mentioned in the first part of the article. Hence, a sentence break has been exercised as a new proposition has been introduced in the second sentence of Article 102. This strategy has obviated the need for translating the Arabic cohesive device "wa", the literal rendering of which into English is "and". The Arabic cohesive device is intended to link the preceding discourse with the following one, however, this is not required in the English TT once a sentence break has been exercised. Therefore, the strategy of sentence break has caused the translator to make use of another strategy, i.e. translation by omission, the use of which in this very instance is justifiable and acceptable.

The ST prepositional phrase "bihi", which is composed of a preposition "bi", the literal rendering of which into English is "by" and the pronoun "hi", the literal rendering of which into English is "it", has been backgrounded in the TT and translated into English as "thereby". It is evident that the ST author has used pronominal reference as a cohesive device where the pronoun "hi", which represents the term "Alqabūl" has been used instead of the term "Alqabūl". This is due to the fact that the term "Alqabūl" has been used at the beginning of the article, therefore, the author has replaced the term in question by the pronoun in order to avoid repetition. The same practice has also been applied by the translator, albeit at the end of the article. He has utilized the pronoun "it", which stands for the term "acceptance", which has been mentioned at the outset of the article. Consequently, the translator has substituted the term concerned by the pronoun preceded by the preposition "by". He has then changed the prepositional phrase "by it" to the phrase "thereby" so as to produce a more-sounding legal construction.

The ST verbal phrase "yatimmu al'aqd" has been translated into English as "the contract becomes completed". It is obvious that the translator has changed the word order of the ST sentence from verb subject (vs.) to subject verb compliment (svc). This is due to structure requirements as English always starts with a noun unless the sentence is imperative. Conversely, Arabic can start with either a noun or a verb, depending on the textual element which is being emphasized in the discourse. The Arabic verb "yattim", when rendered into English, needs verb to "be" or "become" in addition to an adjective, e.g., "completed", "concluded", etc. In other words, there is no English verb that can relay the whole sense of the Arabic verb on its own, but it requires to be supported by an adjective. Hence, the translator has no choice but to paraphrase the meaning of the verb "yatimm" using to English textual elements, i.e., "becomes completed". He has made use of literal translation in rendering the term "al'aqd" into English as "the contract".

Having considered the translation strategies used by the translator in rendering Article 102 into English, it is evident that the translator has adopted nearly the same strategies he has used in translating Article 101, with very minimal differences. Literal translation, translation by omission, translation by addition, free translation, sentence break, change in voice and word order as well as use of a pronominal reference as a cohesive device are amongst the crucial translation strategies adopted in translating the article in question. It seems that the use of all strategies exploited by the translator has been justifiable, with the exception of free translation in a single instance and translation by omission. The translator has adopted free translation twice; one is when dealing with the translation of the Arabic verb "yattim", and this has been acceptable as there is no one-to-one correspondence between Arabic and English in this very translation situation. However, the translator has also made use of free translation when rendering the Arabic prepositional phrase "liajl", when he could have easily used literal translation. Translation by omission has been adopted by the translator in more than one instance, with unjustifiable use thereof, in my view. This springs from the fact that a complete transfer of the message content is highly necessary in translation, particularly in the translation of laws. However, it should be noted that the translator, with all strategies he has resorted to, has managed to produce the right legal result for proper and uniform application, which is the end result sought from the translation of laws.

Article 123
'(Māda 123). Alsalamu bay'u mu'ajjalin bimu'ajjalin ay an yakūna almabī'u mu'ajjalan wa althamanu mu'ajjalan ḥālan'. (Almajalla 1877: 24)

'(Article 123). Sale by immediate payment against future delivery consists of paying in advance for something to be delivered later, that is to say, to purchase something with money paid in advance, thereby giving credit'. (Hooper 1933 vol. I: 33)

With meticulous study of the translation of Article 123 from Arabic into English made by Hooper (1933), it goes without saying that the translator has made use of different strategies, some of which have not been adopted in the previous two articles. He has rendered the term "alsalam" into English as "sale by immediate payment against future delivery", though the term in legal English, which is commonly employed to stand for the term "alsalam" is "forward sale", albeit unused by the translator. Hence, the translator has avoided using the English legal term often adopted to stand for the term concerned, and has instead favoured explaining the term "alsalam" using typical English words, thus adopting the strategy known as description by definitions and explanations. The translator could have used the English legal term, which is usually utilized in this legal translation situation, alongside description by definitions and explanations, thus informing the target reader of the English legal term often adopted in such a legal translation situation, in addition to clarifying the legal meaning of the Arabic term in question. Moreover, the translator has made use of description by definitions and explanations in a place which is different from the one in which it is usually used. The translator has explained the Arabic term within the target text, without even using bracketing. However, explanatory detail specific to a particular ST term, if used within the target text, is usually bracketed. Also, it can be used as a footnote, an endnote, in the glossary or as part of linguistic analysis/commentary that can tail the target text.

The ST phrase "bayʿu muʾajjalin bimuʿajjal" has been rendered into English as "consists of paying in advance for something to be delivered later". It is clear that the translator has not translated the term "bayʿ" literally as "sale". This is probably owing to the fact that he has already mentioned the term "sale" at the beginning of the article when translating and explaining the meaning of the term "alsalam", which is a kind of sale. Therefore, the translator has preferred to dispense with the term "sale" as it has been mentioned previously in the article in order to avoid repetition. This is an important aspect of English language norms compared to Arabic, as clarified by Baker (1992: 207), who points out that Arabic prefers more repetition than English. The translator has ipso facto adopted the strategy of translation by omission in accordance with the English language norms in this particular instance. The translator has employed the verb "consist" in lieu of the verb "is", which conveys an important message to the target reader that the term "alsalam", as a kind of sale, consists of different constituents. However, what follows the verb "consist" is a kind of description of the term "alsalam", but not parts or constituents. It seems that the translator has viewed the phrases "paying in advance" and "for something to be delivered later" as two different constituents, rather than a description and clarification of the meaning of this type of sale. He could have employed verb to be "is" in order to avoid any possible ambiguity this may cause to the target reader. Hence, the translator has employed free translation in this specific instance. The term "muʾajjal" has been backgrounded and rephrased in English as "for something to be delivered later", while the term "bimuʿajjal" has been foregrounded and rephrased in English as "paying in advance". This foregrounding/backgrounding process and paraphrase have been necessary as the English structure requires them to be exercised on the target text so as to produce a natural, well-constructed legal English text. Failure to apply foregrounding/backgrounding practice alongside free translation in this particular translation situation would result in creating a stilted, ill-formed and cumbersome legal English construction.

The ST phrase "ay an yakūna almabīʿu muʾajjalan wa althamanu muʿajjalan ḥālan" has been rendered into English as "that is to say, to purchase something with money paid in advance, thereby giving credit". The translator has translated the Arabic conditional "ay" with the use of the English phrase "that is to say", surrounded by two comas so as to show the target reader that what follows is explanatory detail interpreting what precedes this very phrase. Another phrase employed in English to achieve the same purpose is "in other words", albeit less legal than the one employed by the translator. A third option is the use of the abbreviated form "i.e.", which means "that is to say", though contracted. The translator has avoided the use of the aforementioned contracted form as this does not run in line with the language of law.

The ST phrase "an yakūna almabīʿu muʾajjalan wa althamanu muʿajjala" has been freely translated into English as "to purchase something with money paid in advance", where a more literal rendering of the previous ST phrase may read as "the delivery of the sold property shall be delayed, while the consideration/price is paid in advance". Thus, the translator has adopted free translation, though he could have been more literal. Within this technique, the translator has also made use of other strategies. He has not rendered the term "almabīʿ" literally as "the sold property", rather he has replaced it by a general word "something", thus employing the strategy of substitution. Again, it seems that the translator could have been more literal in the translation of the aforementioned term, however, he has preferred to use substitution, thus using a general word "something" instead of adopting the exact English term often adopted in this legal translation situation, i.e., "the sold property". Another clearly noticeable use of this strategy is the use of the verb "purchase" as a translation of the ST verb "yakūn", which literally means "be". Again, what has been said about the previous instance can also apply to this specific instance though it can be well understood that these are the inevitable results of adopting free translation.

The ST term "muʾajjal" has not been translated literally as "delayed, etc."; however, its meaning can be implicitly fathomed from the text "with money paid in advance". When the price is paid in advance, the item will be delivered thereafter. Hence, the translator has made use of translation by omission on the grounds that the textual element omitted can well be understood from the context. Another use of substitution appears in the translation of the term "althaman", the literal rendering of which into legal English is "the price, the consideration, etc.", as "money". In this particular instance, the translator has substituted a general word "althaman", which could be money or any other item deemed equivalent to the sold property, with a more specified term as "money". This is followed by a literal rendering of the term "muʿajjal" as "paid in advance".

The ST adverb "ḥālan", the literal rendering of which into English can read as "with immediate effect, on the spot, instantly, etc.", has not been translated into English, nor could its meaning be inferred from the context. The target reader will understand that the price in the sale of "alsalam" should be paid prior to the delivery of the sold property. However, there is no information content in the TT, informing the target reader that the payment of the price should not only be made in advance, but also with immediate effect, i.e. after the mutual agreement made by the two contracting parties to conclude this type of sale, as could be understood from the ST. Hence, the translator has adopted translation by omission, dispensing with the translation of the ST adverb "ḥālan", when he could have inserted a textual element in the TT to stand for the ST adverb in question.

The phrase "thereby giving credit" has been inserted in the TT, though it has no equivalent in the ST. In other words, the translator has added this phrase to the TT, though it is not present in the ST, probably as a kind of compensation for the ST adverb "ḥālan" which has not been translated into the TT. This phrase is directly related to the price of "alsalam" which the buyer is required to pay in advance. The word "thereby" means "by it, i.e., the price which has been paid in advance". The phrase "giving credit" means "the buyer has given a loan". Consequently, the whole phrase "thereby giving credit" can be interpreted as "by paying the price in advance, the buyer has given a loan". Of course, this loan will be paid back upon the delivery of the sold property. In other words, the buyer will lend the seller something by paying him/her the price in advance, and the seller will pay back the loan when he/she delivers the sold property to the buyer. Needless to say, this phrase has not been inserted in the ST, which confirms that the translator has added it as a compensation for the ST adverb "ḥālan", which has not been rendered into English, and as an explanatory detail to further interpret the nature of the type of sale known as "alsalam" around which Article 123 revolves. Thus, the strategy of description by definitions and explanations has been adopted at the end of this article to further elaborate on the nature of "alsalam". It goes without saying that the strategy of description by definitions and explanations, albeit used in a very narrow sense in legal translation within the target text, should be avoided in legal translation within the target text if not bracketed. Moreover, this strategy, if used in legal translation, will be primarily adopted to resolve the problem of untranslatability of a particular SL culture-specific legal term, as indicated by Šarčević (1985). Nevertheless, the translator has made use of the strategy in question to interpret the preceding phrase, or probably the entire article, though the meaning of the article is to a good extent clear to the Islamic Law specialists. Again, the translator may have had in mind other types of audience who are non-specialists of Islamic Law, though he could have had a footnote to insert this type of detail, as generally practiced by translators of laws.

Examining the strategies adopted by Hooper (1933) in the translation of Article 123 into English carefully, it seems that the translator has made use of a diverse set of different strategies to deal with various issues and problems that have confronted him. Amongst these strategies used by the translator are description by definitions and explanations, translation by omission, free translation, foregrounding/backgrounding practice, substitution and literal translation. Description by definitions and explanations has been used to explain an ST term and to interpret a phrase or probably the whole article, though it should be used only for the first purpose. When employed within the target text, it has to be placed in brackets, a practice which has not been exercised by the translator. Translation by omission, although should generally be shunned in legal translation, has been adopted logically to avoid repetition. It has also been used by the translator to dispense with the translation of a very important adverb in the ST, i.e. "ḥālan", though, in my view, the use of this strategy for this specific instance has not been successful. Free translation has been exercised in a number of instances for restructuring purposes, though the translator could have been more literal in some of them. For the same reason, the translator has also practised the strategy of foregrounding/backgrounding. Substitution has been exercised in a number of instances, such as replacing a more specific term with a general one and vice versa, though, in my view, there is no real need for substitution as there is an equivalent term in the TL for the term used in the ST. There is also some use of literal translation in the article in question. Indeed, although the translator has relied on a number of different strategies, some of which are generally agreed upon by law translators, while others are not suitable in my opinion, he has, however, managed to produce the appropriate legal result sought from the translation of this particular article.

4. Conclusion

Legal translation has become a clearly crucial means for global communication as the whole world is in a pressing need for legal translation without which dealing between world countries, particularly in business and economy would completely be hindered. Some translation theories have been varyingly applied to legal translation, such as situation equivalence, formal correspondence and skopos theory, with existing differences among scholars concerning the validity of implementing such translation theories to legal translation. Three prominent views of scholars can be generally identified. While some scholars believe in the importance of applying the aforementioned theories to legal translation, others rule out the possibility of applying such theories to legal translation, arguing over the merit of dealing with legal translation with more careful treatment and devising other theories to legal translation which are practice-oriented. The last view of scholars obviates the need for viewing legal translation as having a special status and that legal translation should be treated within the realm of general translation theories.

There are a number of methods and strategies which have been followed and adopted in the field of legal translation, albeit with varying degrees of acceptability and restriction. Amongst these important methods and strategies are literal translation, free translation, functional approach to translation, transliteration/transcription, loan translation, adaptation, description by definitions and explanations/lexical expansion as well as descriptive substitution. Each method and strategy has its own merits and demerits and can be used in particular legal translation situations and under specific conditions. Failure to adopt the right strategy for a particular legal translation situation would unquestionably affect the formal usability of the translated text. Given that legal translation is of a sensitive and sacred nature, the translator of laws should exert every effort to make use of the appropriate translation strategy for each legal translation situation, dealing with each legal translation situation on its own merit. As clearly shown in the discussion and analysis of the translation of Hooper, a legal article consisting of three to four lines may warrant a diverse set of translation strategies to achieve its translation purpose. This may be due to the difference in legal rules that govern both the source legal system and the target legal system, the difference in how each legal language specific to each legal system is structured, the type of audience to whom the legal translation is directed and how much information he/she needs in order to be as informed as the reader of the original text.

References

Alnadawī, A.A. 2004. *Alqawā'id Alfiqhiyya*. Damascus: Dār Alqalam.

Alshashrī, A.S. 2005. *Taqnīn Alsharī'a bayn Altaḥlīl Wa Altaḥrīm*. Riyadh: Dār Alfaḍīla.

Alwazna, R.Y. 2013a. Testing the precision of legal translation. In L. Cheng, L. Hale, Q. He, L. Sun et al eds. *Proceedings of The Third International Conference on Law, Translation and Culture*. Paper presented at The Third International Conference on Law, Translation and Culture, Hangzhou, China, 31 May–2 June. Marietta, GA: The American Scholars Press, pp. 251–256.

———. 2013b. Testing the Precision of Legal Translation: The Case of Translating Islamic Legal Terms into English. *International Journal for the Semiotics of Law*, special issue *The Process of Translabiliting: Translating and Transferring Law, Its Concepts, Notions and Language*, vol. 26(4), pp. 897–907.

Asir, Y. (ed.). 1877. *Almajalla*. 3rd edn. Beirut: Maṭba'at Alādāb.

Baker, M. 1992. *In Other Words: A Coursebook on Translation*. London: Routledge.

Bermann, S. 2005. 'Introduction'. In: S. Bermann and M. Wood eds. *Nation, Language and the Ethics of Translation*. Princeton, NJ: Princeton University Press, pp. 1–10.

Cao, D. 2007. *Translating Law*. Clevedon: Multilingual Matters.

Chroma, M. 2004. 'Cross-Cultural Traps in Legal Translation'. In: C.N. Candlin and M. Gotti eds. *Intercultural Aspects of Specialized Communication*. Bern: Lang, pp. 197–221.

Dickins, J., Hervey, S. and Higgins, I. 2002. *Thinking Arabic Translation: A Course in Translation Method: Arabic to English*. London: Routledge.

Didier, E. 1990. *Langues et langages du droit*. Montreal: Wilson & Lafleur.

Garzone, G. 2000. 'Legal translation and functionalist approaches: A contradiction in terms?', *ASTI/ETII*, pp. 395–414.

Gutt, E.A. 1991. *Translation and Relevance: Cognition and Context*. Oxford: Blackwell.

Harvey, M. 2002. 'What's So Special About Legal Translation?', *Meta*, vol. 2, pp. 177–185.

Hjort-Pedersen, M. 1996. Legal Translation and the Principle of Relevance. *Metalingua*, vol. 15, 361–371.

Hjort-Pedersen, M. and Faber, D. 2001. Lexical Ambiguity and Legal Translation: A Discussion. *Multilingua*, vol. 20(4), pp. 379–392.

Hooper, C A. 1933. *The Civil Law of Palestine and Trans-Jordan*. 3 vols. Jerusalem: Azriel Printing Works.

Kade, O. 1980. *Die sprachmittlung als gesellschaftliche erscheinung und gegenstand wissenschaftlicher untersuchung*. Leipzig: Veb.

Kasirer, N. 2001. 'Francois Geny's Libre Recherche Scientifique as a Guide for Legal Translation', *Louisiana Law Review*, vol. 61, pp. 331–352.
Kielar, B. 1977. *Language of the Law in the Aspect of Translation*. Doctoral dissertation. Warsaw University.
Legrand, P. 2005. 'Issues in the Translatability of Law'. In: S. Bermann and M. Wood eds. *Nation, Language and the Ethics of Translation*. Princeton, NJ: Princeton University Press, pp. 30–50.
Lewis, P.E. 2004. 'The Measure of Translation Effects'. In: L. Venuti ed. *The Translation Studies Reader*. 2nd edn. New York: Routledge, pp. 256–275.
Madsen, D. 1997. 'Towards a Description of Communication in the Legal Universe', *Fachsprache*, vol. 19(1–2), pp. 17–27.
Newmark, P. 1981. *Approaches to Translation*. Oxford: Pergamon.
Nord, C. 1997. *Translating as a Purposeful Activity*. Manchester: St. Jerome.
Poon, W. 2005. 'The Cultural Transfer in Legal Translation', *International Journal for the Semiotics of Law*, vol. 18, pp. 307–323.
Reiss, K. 1971. *Moglichkeiten und grenzen der ubersetzungskritik*. Munchen: Hueber.
Russell, R. 197). 'The Statutes of Quebec: Linguistic Interference', *Meta*, vol. 24(1), pp. 213–217.
Šarčević, S. 1985. 'Translation of Culture-Bound Terms in Laws', *Multilingua*, vol. 4(3), pp. 127–133.
———. 1997. *New Approach to Legal Translation*. The Hague/London/Boston: Kluwer Law International.
———. 1998. 'Creativity in Legal Translation: How Much is Too Much?' *EST Congress*. Granada, Spain. In: A. Chesterman, N.G. S. Salvador and Y. Gambier eds. *Translation in Context: Selected Contributions from the EST Congress*. Amsterdam/Philadelphia: John Benjamins Publishing Co., pp. 281–292.
———. 2000. 'Legal Translation and Translation Theory: A Receiver-Oriented Approach', *Legal Translation: History, Theory/ies and Practice, International Colloquium*. Geneva, Switzerland, February 2000.
Stolze, R. 2001. 'Translating Legal Texts in the EU', *Perspectives*, vol. 9, pp. 301–313.
Taylor, V. 1997. 'Beyond Legal Orientalism'. In: V. Taylor ed. *Asian Law Through Australian Eyes*. Sydney: Law Book Company , pp. 47–62.
Vermeer, H. 1998. 'Starting to Unask what Ttranslatology is About', *Target*, vol. 19(1), pp. 41–68.
Weisflog, W.E. 1987. 'Problems of Legal Translation', *XIIth International Congress of Comparative Law*. Schulthess, Zürich: Swiss Report pp., 179–219.
Weston, M. 1991. *An English Reader's Guide to the French Legal System*. Oxford: Berg.
Winter, W. 1964. 'Impossibilities of Translation'. In: W. Arrowsmith and R. Shattuck eds. *The Craft and Context of Translation*. Paper presented at a Symposium. Garden City, N.Y: Doubleday, pp. 68–82.
Wolff, L. 2011. 'Legal Translation'. In: K. Malmkjaer and K. Windle eds. *The Oxford Handbook of Translation Studies*. Oxford: Oxford University Press, pp. 228–242.
Zhao, Y. 2000. 'Legal Translation in the Legislative Genre', *Journal of Translation Studies*, vol. 4, pp. 19–44.

Chapter 15
On the Translation of the Criminal Procedure Law of the PRC

Lijin Sha and Jian Li

1. Introduction

In Mainland China, the legislative texts are translated mainly for informative purposes. In other words, the translated versions are not authoritative and have no binding effect. It is not permissible to use the translated versions as one type of authority resource. However, the lack of legal effect of the translated versions never downplays the urgency and importance of producing "satisfactory" English versions of Chinese legislative texts. Since China's accession to the WTO in 2001, the Chinese government has promulgated or amended volumes of statutes designated to implement China's commitments. In this study, the Criminal Procedure Law of the People's Republic of China (CPL) is taken as an example, because CPL is a yardstick to measure the *status quo* of human rights in China. For the first three decades of its existence since 1949, the People's Republic of China (PRC) had neither a general Criminal Law nor a general Criminal Procedure Law. The post-Mao leadership, however, saw a need for a firmer legal foundation for China's criminal law regime, and quite quickly (in 1979) promulgated both a Criminal Law and a Criminal Procedure Law (CPL). The 1979 CPL was substantially revised in 1996 in order to bring its provisions in line both with the vast changes in Chinese society that had taken place since the original law was promulgated and with demands for greater rationalization. On the whole, the revised CPL is more hospitable to defendants' rights. It allows earlier access to lawyers, and makes court proceedings somewhat more transparent than before (Hecht 1996). In amendments to the CPL in March 2012, there are several points deserving considerable attention. For the present study, we took two English versions of the CPL (1997), one from the National People's Congress and the other compiled by the Chinese Scholar in the USA, and analyze the parts corresponding to which the Chinese articles are still effective in the CPL (effective 1 Jan 2013). We also use the English version translated by Li Changshuan as a reference in our discussion. As will be shown in this study, what an appropriate approach to legal translation is, is not just an issue of the translation quality but an issue of better reflecting the reality of rule of law in Mainland China.

2. Problems in the English Translation of CPL

There are problems of different kinds in the original Chinese version of the CPL, which may cause problems and difficulties in the English translation of the CPL. For the present study, we only focus on the problems that occur in the translated version. The major problems identified in the English translation can be categorized into three types: informality, inaccuracy, and inconsistency.

2.1. Informality

If we understand the language of the law as a particular type of social dialect, the features of legal register should be the primary consideration in legal translation. As noted in *Systemic Functional Linguistics* (Halliday and Matthiessen 2004), the contextual dimensions of register of a genre govern the semantic and grammatical organization of language itself. For example, in Article 53 of the CPL (1997), the Chinese expression 保证金 ("baozhengjin") have at least two English versions. As shown below, one is "guaranty money", the other "bail".

> 第五十三条
> 人民法院、人民检察院和公安机关决定对犯罪嫌疑人、被告人取保候审，应当责令犯罪嫌疑人、被告人提出保证人或者交纳保证金。(emphasis added)
>
> *Article 53 (NPC 2004)*
> *If the People's Courts, the People's Procuratorates or the public security organs decide to allow a criminal suspect or defendant to obtain a guarantor pending trial, they shall order the criminal suspect or defendant to provide a guarantor or pay guaranty money.* (emphasis added)
>
> *Article 53 (Luo 2000)*
> *The people's courts, the people's procuratorates, and the public security organs shall order the criminal suspect or the accused to provide a guarantor or pay bail when deciding to release the criminal suspect or the accused on bail.* (emphasis added)

From a semiotic perspective, we can assign any Interpretant, the legal expression in the target text, to a given Representamen, the legal expression in the source text (Cheng and Sin 2008), as long as the two are defined within the same Semantic Reference Scheme (Sin and Roebuck 1996), but when there is more than one Interpretant for the same Representamen, we have to deliberate and decide. The awareness of registral characteristics should be highlighted in translating legal texts, of which one of the typical features is formality. In other words, daily spoken language is not expected to be taken into legal language. One can easily identify that "bail" is a better choice within this context to function as an exact equivalent for the Chinese expression 保证金 ("baozhengjin"), because "bail" is more technical within the legal register than "guarantee money".

2.2. Accuracy

Accuracy in legal translation is the key criteria, because a mistranslation of even one word may cause a lawsuit. For example, in Article 42 of the CPL, the Chinese expression 物证 ("wuzheng") were translated as "material evidence" in the NPC version but as "physical evidence" in Luo's version; also in the same article, 勘验、检查笔录 ("kanyan\jianchabilu") were translated as "records of inquests and examination" in the NPC version but as "transcripts of inspection and examination" in Luo's version.

第四十二条
证明案件真实情况的一切事实，都是证据。证据有下列七种：
（一）物证、书证；（二）证人证言；（三）被害人陈述；（四）犯罪嫌疑人、被告人供述和辩解；（五）鉴定结论；（六）勘验、检查笔录；（七）视听资料。以上证据必须经过查证属实，才能作为定案的根据。(emphasis added)

Article 42 (NPC 2004)
All facts that prove the true circumstances of a case shall be evidence. There shall be the following seven categories of evidence:
(1) material evidence *and documentary evidence;*
(2) testimony of witnesses;
(3) statements of victims;
(4) statements and exculpations of criminal suspects or defendants;
(5) expert conclusions;
(6) records of inquests and examination*; and*
(7) audio-visual materials.

*Any of the above evidence must be verified before it can be used as the basis for deciding cases. (*emphasis added*)*

Article 42(Luo 2000)
Any facts which may prove the factual situation of cases are evidence. The categories of evidence may be listed as follows:
(1) Physical evidence *and documentary evidence;*
(2) Testimonies of witnesses;
(3) Statements of victims;
(4) Confessions and exculpations by the criminal suspects or the accused;
(5) Conclusions of expert evaluators;
(6) Transcripts of inspection and examination*; and*
(7) Audio and video materials.

*However, the evidence must be examined and proved to be true before any of it can be used as the basis for determining cases. (*emphasis added*)*

"Material evidence" may be interpreted as "key evidence", so such a translation is ambiguous. As to the translation of "kanyan\jianchabilu", Luo's translation is obviously more accurate than the NPC's translation, because "bilu" is indubitably "written records" or "transcripts" rather than "records" in a wider sense. While realizing the importance of legal translation, we should also emphasize the necessity of accurate communicative function for legal translation.

2.3. Consistency

In a particular field like law, a term is expected to have one meaning only. Monosemy is a central principle for law. The ideality of monosemy of legal terms implies that one Representamen in the same context is not expected to have two Interpretants (Cheng and Sin 2008). Monosemy of legal terms require the consistency in legal translation. Ideally, there should be only one translation for the same legal term within the same context. But we can still notice some inconsistency of the English translations in the same version (NPC) of the CPL. For example,

"重大" (zhongda) are rendered in different Chinese translation such as "major", "grave", "prominent", and "high-profile", which are of near synonymy but not of exact equivalence.

3. Approaches to Legal Translation

Traditionally, the two major approaches in translation have been literal and free. The literal approach has been particularly popular among many translators of classic literature, religious texts, and political documents. On the one hand, they value greatly the form of the source text, and on the other hand, they do not want to bring about divergent interpretations of the source texts. In essence, proponents of the literal approach have been quite willing to sacrifice the formal elements of the target language—and even the intelligibility of the target language text—for the sake of preserving what they regard as the integrity of the source text. The literal approach has deep roots in the history of translation in China. In East Jin Dynasty, Dao'an (AD 314–385), a well-known monk, was the representative of those who firmly advocated literal translation. Since he feared that free translation might not be true to the original, he advocated strict literal translation so as to preserve the true features (Ma 2004). In Tang Dynasty, the famous Buddhist monk, Xuan-zang, in the seventh century set down the criterion that translation 'must be both truthful and understandable to the populace' (Jin and Nida 1984) in an attempt to reconcile the literal and free approaches to produce the best translation. In the 19th century, the triple criteria of 'faithfulness, intelligibility, and elegance' (Jin and Nida 1984) were put forth by Yan Fu, a famous translator of western works in late Qing Dynasty. The first criterion, "faithfulness" (to the source text), emphasizes the literal approach. Although there are sometimes stylistically and rhetorically awkward renderings in literal translating, one must recognize that a relatively literal rendering works well on many occasions.

In her paper 'Legal Translation and Functional Approaches: a Contradiction in Terms?', Garzone (2000) briefly reviewed the common typologies of legal translations and the translational procedures routinely implemented in actual practice, based on pragmatic criteria, e.g., considering the legal force of the original and of the translated text respectively. The first category she reviewed is the texts generated within the framework of a single national legal system. She concludes that the approach adopted in the translation of this category of legal texts is usually literal, and that sometimes a "strict literal" approach should be prescribed. Given the distinctive quality of Chinese legal concepts and the terse nature of Chinese language, there may be situations where a literal approach can be taken. There have been occasions where foreign newspapers use the "political-legal system" to translate "政法系统" ("zhengfaxitong"), as police, procurators, and courts are collectively known. This somewhat strict literal rendering is acceptable due to the fact that "政法系统" ("zhengfaxitong") covers a wide spectrum of institutions and any explanatory translation is inadequate. As a result, the term "political-legal system" is invested with meaning with reference to China's unique legal system.

However, the literal approach has never been free from criticism. 'The real problem is that those who advocate literal translation do not realize that the whole is greater than the sum of the parts' (Jin and Nida 1984). Furthermore, the literal approach is never a cure-all in the translation of Chinese legislative texts. Sometimes it is inappropriate. Consider the legal term "监视居住" ("jianshijuzhu") as an example. The term is literally translated into "residential surveillance" on many occasions, which is inadequate to convey the legal meaning of this term. In Article 57 of the 1996 *CPL*, it is provided that:

> *A criminal suspect or defendant under residential surveillance shall observe the following provisions:*
> *(1) not to leave his domicile without permission of the executing organ or, if he has no fixed domicile, not to leave the designated residence without permission;*
> *(2) not to meet with others without permission of the executing organ;*
> *(3) to be present in time at a court when summoned;*
> *(4) not to interfere in any form with the witness when the latter gives testimony; and*
> *(5) not to destroy or falsify evidence or tally confessions.*
> *In the Decision of the National People's Congress on the Amendment of the Criminal Procedure Law of the People's Republic of China, the term is redefined, with two requirements added: "(2) not to meet or correspond with anyone without the prior approval of the enforcement authority;" "(6) to surrender his passport or other border crossing documents, and identification documents and driver certificates, to the enforcement authority." (trans. Li Changshuan)*

It is clear that the term "监视居住" refers to a compulsory measure enforced by the Public Security Organ, which deprives the criminal suspect or defendant of his or her freedom. The criminal suspect or defendant is actually in a state of house arrest and cannot even "correspond" with the outside. However, the term "surveillance", according to the Black's Law Dictionary (Garner 2009), means 'police investigative technique involving visual or electronic observation or listening directed at a person or place (e.g., stakeout, tailing of suspect, wiretapping). Its objective is to gather evidence of a crime or merely to accumulate intelligence about suspected criminal activity'.

In this regard, though the term is translated in a strict literal way, its legal meaning is lost. A more appropriate rendering may be "residential confinement". In acknowledging that literal approach is acceptable and achievable, we should also be aware of the inadequacy of this literal approach in translating Chinese legislative texts. Given the absence of legal effect of the translated versions of Chinese legislative texts, there may be situations where a certain degree of free approach can be taken, in that the only aim is informing the recipient of the content of the original legal texts. In fact, the crux of the issue is not the dichotomy between "literal approach" and "free approach", and "the Middle Way" is to establish semantic equivalence between Chinese culture-laden concepts and the English language. By "equivalence", we do not mean one-to-one correspondence in the narrow field of standardized terminology, but "total equivalence in legal meaning".

Let's take "立案" ("li'an"), for instance. The term occurs 17 times in the provisions of the Chinese version of 2012 CPL. In accordance with Article 110 of the 2012 CPL,

> *A people's court, People's Procuratorate or public security organ shall, within the scope of its jurisdiction, promptly examine the materials provided by a reporter, complainant or informant and the confession of an offender who has voluntarily surrendered. If it believes that there are facts of a crime and criminal liablity shall be held, it shall* <u>file a case (立案)</u>. *(*<u>emphasis added</u>*)*

"立案" ("li'an") is mostly rendered into "file a case" in its English version, which is absurdly misleading. In common law countries, the term "filing a case" means filing the document that initiates legal proceedings in a court. For a case in a trial court, the document filed is usually called a complaint or petition. In most cases, you must pay a filing fee when you file the document that may initiate a lawsuit. Either you or your attorney may file a document through mail or in person. However, the legal meaning of "立案" ("li'an") is totally different from "filing a case". First, it is the "政法系统" ("zhengfaxitong"), as police, procurators, and courts are collectively known, that has the right of "立案" ("li'an"). Second, according to the CPL, two conditions must be met: there are facts of crime, and the facts of crime have to be criminally liable in accordance with the law. Clearly, there is a distinction between "立案" ("li'an") and "to file a case", as the term of "立案" ("li'an") bears the Chinese characteristic of law, and can not be mechanically and literally translated by simply using an English equivalent "to file a case".

In the English version of the CPL translated by Washington University School of Law, the term "立案" ("li' an") is rendered as "to open a case", with an explanatory note that 'opening a case here means a public security organ or a People's Procuratorate to start a case for criminal prosecution'.

The term "审查起诉" ("shenchaqisu"), which occurs 12 times in the Chinese version of 2012 CPL, is another culture-embodied concept which refers to the proceeding activity conducted by the People's Procuratorate. Articles 169 and 171 of the 2012 CPL shed more light on the legal meaning of this term:

> *Article 169:*
> *'A People's Procuratorate shall make a decision within one month on a case that a public security organ has transferred to it with a recommendation to initiate a prosecution; an extension of a half month may be allowed for major or complex cases.'*
>
> *Article 171:*
> *'In examining a case, the People's Procuratorate may request a public security organ to provide the evidence that is essential to the trial in court.*
> *In examining a case that requires supplementary investigation, the People's Procuratorate may remand the case to a public security organ for supplementary investigation or conduct the investigation itself. . . . With respect to a case for which supplementary investigation has been conducted, if the People's Procuratorate still believes that the evidence is insufficient and the case does not meet the conditions for initiation of a prosecution, the People's Procuratorate may decide not to initiate a prosecution.'*

According to Articles 169 and 171, it is obvious that "审查起诉" refers to the decision-making process of the People's Procuratorate as to whether or not to initiate a prosecution. The power of making "审查起诉" ("shenchaqisu") lies exclusively in the People's Procuratorate. In the *Decision of the National People's Congress on the Amendment of the Criminal Procedure Law of the People's Republic of China*, "审查起诉" ("shenchaqisu") has been translated into "review and prosecution". However, according to *Black's Law Dictionary* (2009), "review" is 'used especially for the examination of a decision of a court or an administrative agency by a court or an administrative agency at a higher level.' In this regard, the choice of the word "review" is inappropriate, and the meaning of "审查起诉" in the context is distorted. A more proper rendering may be "examination before prosecution".

When it comes to the translation of culture-laden legal concepts, legal translators are more likely to go to extremes. To recklessly find an English equivalent in the common law system is one extreme, and to literally render a concept into English without adequate thought on its legal meaning is the other extreme. As the two examples above demonstrate, legal translators are apt to become "extremists" and as a result they either give a confusing association or distort the real meaning of the Chinese legal concepts. While nothing is perfect, to go to extremes is by no means a perfect solution. As a matter of fact, what we pursue is a path between the extremes—the Middle Way without detriment to the legal meaning. At this juncture, we should ask a question: can we blaze a trail toward semantic equivalence?

Nothing is a sign unless it is interpreted as a sign (Peirce 1931–1958: vol. 2 172). The value of a sign depends on its relations with other signs within the system – a sign has no absolute value independent of its context (Saussure 1983: 80). A cup itself may be named as "tea cup" when drinking tea, while the same cup may be called "wine cup" when drinking wine. As we have mentioned, the legal concept with Chinese characteristics, "政法系统" ("zhengfaxitong") is rendered as "political-legal system", which in normal sense is a weird translation. Although the term "political-legal system" as a sign itself does not carry any inherent meaning, and its meaning can only exist in the relationship with other signs or sign systems (Cheng and Sin 2009), it is invested with meaning with reference to China's unique legal system. Given the terse nature of the Chinese language, one Chinese legal term may refer to many legal concepts and one Chinese legal concept may be referred to by many legal terms.

4. Conclusion

As a special language text involving standardized concepts, the scope of interpretation in legal documents is very narrow, and the (translator's) task is to limit possible responses to the one interpretation/response intended by the drafter of the text. However, this is not easily attainable when it comes to translation of Chinese legislative texts into English. A subject much overlooked in studies of the translation of LSP-texts (Language for Specific Purpose) is the study of underlying processes and rules as a prerequisite for the understanding of these texts. Concerning legal language, familiarity with underlying legal procedures is a prerequisite for the understanding of legal documents, just as the translation of, for example, technical texts may require knowledge of mechanical processes. So far, very little attention has been paid to the importance of underlying semantic knowledge of such processes to translation (Nielsen 1994).

Legal translators in China apparently give little attention to this prerequisite and are too arbitrary in producing a rendering which is far away from the meaning of the source text. In Hong Kong, there have been cases in which a defendant could have been guilty under a law in English but innocent according to its Chinese version. But any deviation or confusion caused by the translation is subject to the judicial interpretation in Hong Kong, which is vital for the efficient operation of bilingual legal system. Although in Mainland China we don't have to worry that any discrepancy between the Chinese text and the English text of a law will cause judicial problems, it is by no means acceptable for legal translators to produce reckless translation.

As we have exemplified by data from the CPL, use of the literal approach as the conventional wisdom in legal translation is a double-edged sword that should be used with caution. On the one hand, the fact that many Chinese legal concepts are culture-laden implies the necessity of a literal approach. On the other hand, the inherent requirement for preservation of legal meaning in legal translation reveals the inadequacy of the literal approach. The crux of the issue is not whether to stick to the literal approach, but how to think beyond and seek a solution to this dilemma. From a semiotic perspective, we have exemplified that the goal of semantic equivalence is not only worthy to pursue but also attainable in the translation of Chinese legislative texts. However, in order to achieve this goal, legal translators should demand more of themselves than ever before. As we have demonstrated by examples, translation based only on strictly linguistic understanding of the legislative texts is inadequate, and will cause misconception.

References

Cheng, L. and Sin, K.K. 2008. 'Terminological Equivalence in Legal Translation: A Semiotic Approach', *Semiotica*, vol. 172, pp. 33–45.

———. 2009. 'Legal Terms Across Communities: Divergence Behind Convergence in Law'. In: A. Wagner and V.K. Bhatia eds. *Diversity and Tolerance in Socio-Legal Context: Explorations in the Semiotics of Law*. London: Ashgate, pp. 181–190.

De Saussure, F. 1983. *Course in General Linguistics*. London: Duckworth.

Garner, B.A. (ed.). 2009. *Black's Law Dictionary*. 9th edn. Eagan: Thomson West.

Garzone, G. 2000. 'Legal Translation and Functionalist Approaches: A Contradiction in Terms?', *ASTTI/ETI*, pp. 395–414.

Halliday, M. and Matthiessen, C. 2004 *An Introduction to Functional Grammar*. 3rd edn. London: Arnold.

Hecht, J. 1996. *Opening to Reform? An Analysis of China's Revised Criminal Procedure Law*. New York: Lawyers Committee for Human Rights.

Jin, D. and Nida, E.A. 1984. *On Translation: With Special Reference to Chinese and English*. Beijing: China Translation & Publishing Corporation.

Luo, W. 2000. *The Amended Criminal Procedure Law and the Criminal Court Rules of the People's Republic of China: With English Translation, Introduction, and Annotation*. New York: William S. Hein & Co.

Ma, Z. 2004. *A Brief History of Translation in China: The Part Before the May 4th Movement of 1919*. Beijing: China Translation & Publishing Corporation.

Nielsen, S. 1994. *The Bilingual LSP Dictionary—Principles and Practice for Legal Language*. Tubingen: Gunter Narr.

Peirce, C.S. 1931–1985. *Collected Papers of C.S. Peirce (8 Vols)*. Cambridge: Harvard University Press.

Sin, K.K. and Roebuck, D. 1996. 'Language Engineering for Legal Transplantation: Conceptual Problems in Creating Common Law Chinese', *Language & Communication*, vol. 3, pp. 235–254.

Further Reading

1 See National People's Congress of the People's Republic of China. 2004. Available at: www.npc.gov.cn [Accessed 1 July 2012].

2 See Luo (2000). Although various versions of the English translation of the Chinese Criminal Procedure Law have been available in print or on the Internet, none of these English translations are annotated with the official interpretations except the one by Luo (2000), so such a book enables us to better understand the true intent of the legislature.

3 At the time of publication, the English version of Criminal Procedure Law by the NPC was not available.

4 See Li Changshuan Space. Available at: http://i.chaoxing.com/14717691/blog_2c6315932c624ea8.html [Accessed: 08.08.14].

5 Li Changshuan is an associate professor in the Graduate School of Translation and Interpretation, Beijing Foreign Studies University.

Chapter 16
The New Czech Civil Code – Lessons from Legal Translation – A Case-Study Analysis

Marta Chromá

1. Introduction

Bilingual translation of legislation has always been, and will continue to be, a challenge for any legal translator regardless of the proximity of the source legal system to the target legal system and the typological distance between the source and target languages. This chapter will introduce a project for translating the new Czech Civil Code into English, focusing on its preparatory stage, namely determining the scope and depth of a jurilinguistic comparative analysis that precedes the translation, selecting a relevant research methodology and providing practical examples of its application.

1.1. Language of Legislation

Legislation is the most important source of law in the continental legal family, to which Czech law belongs. The language of statutes in its original or restated wording is used in other "derived" documents (text types or genres) and legal communication, whether falling into private or public law, and constitutes a jurilinguistic foundation for the respective branch of law.

The language of law has undergone gradual development on two levels: purely linguistic (for example the disappearance of certain morphological or syntactic features in the general language over a certain time) and jurilinguistics, determined by the direction and development of the system of law in question. The former reflects the natural evolution of the language as determined by the social and cultural environment in which the language serves as a basic means of interaction between members of that linguistic community. The latter encompasses the conceptual structure of the legal environment, the related body of legal institutions and terminology, approaches to, and prevailing modes of, legal interpretation, and the impact of wider historical, social, cultural, geographical, and international contexts upon the legal system.

The legislature in most countries, irrespective of the nature of the legal system, declares its objective to produce legislative texts that could be interpreted and understood by all recipients in the way intended by the legislature despite a variety of audiences for their texts (cf. Bell 1999: 73–75; Jackson 1999: 21–22). As '[legal] texts are to be interpreted in their ordinary, natural meaning, as they would be understood in the wider community' (Charnock 2007: 22), the clear, unambiguous, formally transparent, consistent and semantically predictable language of a statute is the main factor facilitating (desirably) uniform interpretation and subsequent (desirably) uniform application of the statute. More or less binding technical rules for legislative drafting are adopted, whatever format they may acquire (manual, guide, guidance, etc.).[1] The main purpose of the drafting rules is to standardize the language of the legislation, to remove linguistic ambiguities usually leading to legal misinterpretation, and to write a formally consistent and coherent 'statute book that is easy to use for regular users of legislation',[2] whatever professional background they may have. Contemporary manuals of legislative drafting in English-speaking countries more or less follow basic principles established within Plain English Campaign[3] launched in the 1970s. Observing the whole issue "from outside", we tend to maintain the position of Phillips (2003: 40), claiming that 'there is no reason to believe that verbal simplicity delivers linguistic clarity" and that "simplicity, itself, is a fluid, far from simple, concept'.

1.2. Translation of Legislation

The reasons for translating national legislation into other languages vary. There are several circumstances determining the decision to translate, and the approach to translation, of which two appear to be essential:

(a) Translated legislation is to serve the same purpose as the original, i.e., to be binding and to have the same legal force. This is usually the case in monojural countries (having one legal system) with bilingual or plurilingual environments (having more than one official language) such as Switzerland, Malta or Ireland;[4] all national laws in such countries are available in all official languages and citizens may rely on any of the official language versions. Although translation of EU law falls into this category, the situation within the European Union is much more complex.[5] Its specificity lies in its specifically developed (and developing) uniform law, i.e., it is a monojural and yet multilingual entity with 23 official languages and 23 "equally authentic" texts of every law (whether in the form of a treaty, regulation, directive, recommendation, or decision).[6]

(b) Translated legislation is to serve primarily as a source of information on legal issues for interested persons who have no or limited command of the language of the original. This is usually the case of a monolingual legal environment, i.e., having just one official (national) language which is not widely spoken by the international community. A translated text may not be ordinarily relied upon in judicial proceedings in such country. Its procedural applicability in private documents would also be limited, since the original (local) linguistic version generally prevails in the event of any conflict. In this sense and in most countries,

1 Such drafting rules are regularly followed when new laws are prepared, or existing legislation is to be amended, by a government (government bills). However in the Czech Republic, the observance of the rules tends to be weaker if drafts have been prepared by individual members of Parliament within their legislative initiative. There are no professional drafters employed by the Czech Parliament (such as those working for the Parliamentary Counsel Office in Westminster); government bills are prepared by legislative departments of the respective ministries or government agencies and bills tabled by individual members are quite often drafted by their assistants whatever professional background they may have.

2 *OPC Drafting Manual*. 2012. Australian Government, Office of Parliamentary Counsel, p. 6. Available at: http://www.opc.gov.au/about/draft_manuals.htm [Accessed 13 March 2013].

3 See, for example, http://www.plainenglish.co.uk/; http://www.plainlanguage.gov/; http://www.plainlanguageaustralia.com/about_pl.html; http://www.opc.gov.au/plain/docs.htm.

4 For drafting and/or translating such legislation, compare Šarčević (2000: 36–41, 49–53).

5 For the specificity of EU translation see Doczekalska (2009).

6 For various aspects of translating law within the EU, see Baaij (2012).

no translation of their legislation into a language other than the official language would be promulgated as "official".[7]

However, should a translation of any national law into an unofficial foreign language be published locally, whether in a printed or electronic format, it tends to assume, to a certain extent, one of the basic roles of original legislation: its language (irrespective of the quality of the translation) becomes a source for drafting in, or translating into, that foreign language other "derived" documents dealing with the subject of the respective law.

While translation of legislation into one or more official languages in a country, as outlined under (a), would be under the supervision and/or management of a relevant executive body (e.g., a ministry, a government agency) and their respective legislative drafting rules would apply essentially in the same manner as they apply to the original, a translation under the circumstances described in the case (b) would usually depend upon the individual initiative of, for example, a law publisher, the local bar association or, marginally, an academic institution.

In a monojural and monolingual country with historically limited international contacts and historically limited needs for translating their laws to other languages (such as the former Czechoslovakia and the Czech Republic today), people in charge of practical arrangements for translating legal texts, whether at the level of the Executive branch or a private entity (e.g., a law publisher), have traditionally minimum or no knowledge of relevant theoretical issues of legal translation and their awareness of potential pitfalls and traps of incorrect translation is usually non-existent. Even after almost 25 years of democracy and an internationally open society, what prevails in the Czech Republic is the misconception about a translator's sufficient competences.[8] It is generally reduced to purely linguistic competence in both languages (the source language and the target language).[9] The requirement of a translator's relevant knowledge of the source legal system and the target legal system is disregarded, as is the ability of the translator to identify a conceptual relationship between the systems and the competence to select relevant jurilinguistic means to reflect differences and similarities. As a result of ignoring the requirement of such specific expertise, any project aimed at translating statutes, whether governmental or private, is substantially underfunded, and accordingly the quality of the final translational product tends to be substandard and far from being "easy to use" by its potential recipient.

1.3. The Process of Translation

The practice of translating legislation into foreign languages dates back to Ancient Rome. As early as in 529 AD, allowing for the translation of the Digest into Greek in his *constitutio Tanta* promulgating the Digest (as part of *Corpus iuris civilis*) Justinian ordered: '. . . and We again forbid all persons now in existence as well as those who are to come to write any commentaries on these laws, unless someone may wish to translate them into the Greek language and this

7 The distinction between (a) and (b) corresponds to the distinction between instrumental and documentary translation respectively; cf. Trosborg (1997: 154–155, referring to Nord (1991: 72)).

8 Cf. Cao (2007: 39–48) and her dichotomy between translation competence and translation proficiency a legal translator should achieve in order to produce as high quality a translation as practicable.

9 Such approach is partly caused by the content of university programmes in translation studies primarily considered to be a linguistic discipline: students are trained to be near native speakers in their non-native languages, they are introduced to basic translational typology and may acquire basic translational skills, but they are lacking sufficient knowledge or even awareness in the subject-area they are to translate from one language into another. As a result they tend to fully rely on language converting source language terms into to-be target language terms without understanding what message they may convey.

translation We desire to be literal, or such as are called 'according to the foot',[10] to be employed in the interpretation of the laws; . . .".[11] Justinian was well aware of problems potentially triggered by the interpretation of his laws and its subsequent translation into Greek as the only permitted language for translation.[12]

The genesis of the theory of legal translation resembles that of theories of translation of any professional, i.e., non-literary, texts. The study of translation extends from source text (ST) orientation theories to a target text (TT) focus, from purely linguistic theories to pragmatic and semiotic views on translation, including the attention paid to the role of an ultimate recipient of the translated text in the very process of translation. Discussions have frequently spiralled around "invisibility" or "visibility" of the translator in a translated text, i.e., to what extent translation should read fluently (like a piece of domestic culture), or should remind the reader of its foreign origin.[13]

What is common to all types of non-literary translation, whether covering medicine, mechanical engineering, chemistry, architecture or any other professional subject-areas, and what has been often omitted in different translation theories, is that a translator should understand the subject of a text and should have at least an elementary awareness of the whole subject area. Otherwise the translator's performance become superficial and is reduced to transferring words (lexical units) from a source language to a target language, fully relying on bilingual dictionaries or terminological glossaries of variable quality.[14]

Law has been confined to a geographically delimited area by its nature, history, culture and tradition on the one hand, and by language on the other, thus becoming unique. In this sense, law establishes a dual semiotic system. Translation of a legal text into another language essentially means that a text composed in one dual semiotic system is to be "replaced" by a text written in the target language and communicating legal issues in a manner that should be comprehensible in the target legal system (i.e., in the other dual semiotic system). Wagner (2003: 178) points out that 'to use legal language accurately, translators must understand all the mechanisms of the law, the way legal texts are drafted, interpreted and applied in practice. So, technical drafting competence includes the ability to use rhetorical, terminographical and semantic devices in both the source and the target languages'. Thus, the requirement of a translator's sufficient legal knowledge, or at least legal literacy, of both the source law and the target law is of utmost importance.

One of the basic postulates of the theory of legal translation, heavily supported by practice, has been that translators of legal texts are able to transfer into another language only what they understand in the source text, or how they construe the signification and meaning of the source text message. Although most translators in the Czech Republic are not lawyers by education and their approach to interpretation to a legal text is essentially that of an informed or legally literate lay person, they, rather unintentionally, implement a technique of statutory interpretation termed "grammatical" or "literal" in common law (or "linguistic" in Czech jurisprudence). Unlike lawyers who usually interpret law in order to apply it, translators must interpret a legal text in order to "just" convey the information into another language. There will be others (e.g., recipients of the translation) who, having interpreted the translated legal text, may apply it and act accordingly. Translators, much more frequently than lawyers and

10 *Kata poda* in Greek.
11 The English translation is available at: http://droitromain.upmf-grenoble.fr/Anglica/Digeste_Pre3_Scott.gr.html [Accessed 26 August 2013].
12 My thanks for this retrospective note extend to Professor Michal Skřejpek, one of the leading experts in Roman Law in Central Europe.
13 Cf. Venuti ([1995] 2008); Pym (1996); or Lane-Mercier, G. (1997).
14 For an analysis of dictionaries for legal translation, see De Groot et al. (2008); or Van Laer and Van Laer (2007).

due to the translators' limited legal knowledge, may face situations where the grammatical meaning of a provision seems ambiguous or obscure, and not clear. As defined by Bennion (2009: 36): '[the grammatical meaning] is clear when apart from legal consideration, there is no real doubt about it. It is ambiguous when grammatically capable of more than one meaning. It is obscure when the language is disorganized, garbled or otherwise semantically confused or opaque.'

It is not just the clear, unambiguous, formally transparent, consistent and semantically predictable language of a legal text which would enable the translator to rightfully interpret it. There are historical, social, cultural and philosophical contexts determining the meaning of the legal text, its segments and the substance of the law, which should be considered by a translator who is searching for the adequate wording of the target legal text. The primary task for the translator of a legal text is not to "just translate" the source legal text from the source language into the target language (cf. Joseph 1995: 33–34), but to transmit the meaning of the source legal text and its segments into the target language in such a way that the target legal text, as a whole and in all its parts, makes (legal) sense to the ultimate recipient, approximating the sense of the source legal text as perceived by its intended (original) recipient. This is what can be termed the semiotics of legal translation.[15]

2. Project

In 1989, after fifty years of totalitarian regimes, Czechoslovakia began to restore democracy and ideological liberty. Three years later the country split into two independent states, the Czech Republic and the Slovak Republic. One of the basic principles of establishing the new democratic society after 1989 was the principle of continuity of law, i.e. the most ideologically striking legislative provisions in statutes were repealed, some provisions were amended to reflect changes in the society, and others remained intact. Simultaneously, the process of legal reconstruction was launched. Of the three pillars supporting most democratic societies in continental Europe—a Constitution for the general system of government, a Civil Code governing private law, and a Criminal Code facilitating the safe and regular functioning of society—the Civil Code took the longest to conceive. It was adopted by the Czech Parliament in 2012 to become effective on 1 January 2014.

2.1. Legislative Background

The previous legislation—the 1964 Civil Code—was amended many times since 1990 in order to remove socialist ideological principles. However, basic institutions, concepts, and terminology were well established not only in Czech law, but also in their European application. Even after 1989, amended 59 times (including two repealing judgments of the Constitutional Court), the 1964 Civil Code had formed a certain conceptual environment governing a major part of Czech private law and reflected European legislation either through its direct applicability or its transposition. Certain methods and techniques were chosen during the last twenty three years for the translation of the 1964 Code, or its individual provisions, into English so that its English-speaking recipients could understand the law and could act accordingly. At the same

15 For more on the semiotics of legal translation, see Chromá, M. (forthcoming), 'Making sense in legal translation', *Semiotica*, vol. 2014.

time, English terms used in European private law were incorporated into Czech in a manner that was linguistically and legally compatible with the 1964 Code.

The process of legislative drafting of the new law, as well as its outcome—the 2012 Civil Code—is regarded as unprecedented by Czech lawyers. In 1999, the Czech Government launched its plan to newly codify the entire branch of private law.[16] As a result and after 13 years of legislative work, three new codes were passed by Parliament, namely the 2012 Civil Code,[17] the 2012 Business Corporations Act,[18] and the 2012 Private International Law Act.[19] Intended as a fundamental reform of private law in the Czech Republic, the 2012 Civil Code, with its 3,080 sections, has stirred up a lot of emotions. The legal community has been split in their approach to the Code, particularly due to political haste in the legislative process resulting in the short interval (*vacatio legis*) between the force and effect of the Code (just one year), which has resulted in in a fair amount of legal chaos for both lawyers and the general public. Many lawyers from all branches of law and various legal professions (academics, the judiciary, the bar association) have claimed that the adoption of such a Code is far from being positive for the development of modern Czech private law since it will evidently lead to years of legal uncertainty until the first conclusive judgments are delivered settling the most conspicuous interpretive issues.

2.2. Linguistic Background

As suggested earlier, only language that is clear, unambiguous, formally transparent, consistent, and semantically predictable may lead to the undisputable interpretation of statutory provisions and their intended application. Such linguistic quality is difficult to identify in the Code: a structurally complex language, having its roots in codes passed in the 19th century and redrafted in the first half of the 20th century[20] and which were based on the Code Napoléon and primarily the Austrian ABGB (*Allgemeines Bürgerliches Gesetzbuch*), is considered one of its main problems.[21]

16 The first governmental attempts to codify private law according to the principles of a democratic society were pursued as early as in 1991, but they were postponed with the split of Czechoslovakia at the end of 1992. The Ministry of Justice of the Czech Republic presented another codification project in 1996 (Zoulík 1996) but again to no effect.

17 Act no. 89/2012 Sb., the Civil Code. The number of the Code was intentionally chosen as reminiscence of the Velvet Revolution in 1989.

18 Act no. 90/2012 Sb., to govern business corporations and cooperatives (the Business Corporations Act).

19 Act no. 91/2012 Sb., to govern private international law.

20 The most apparent inspiration for the drafters of the 2012 Civil Code was the draft of a Civil Code submitted for adoption to the Czechoslovak Parliament in 1937. Due to the Munich Agreement in 1938, World War II and the post-war Communist take-over of Czechoslovakia, the draft was never considered and remained in the parliamentary archives.

21 While drafting the new Code, the Ministry of Justice requested from the Institute of the Czech Language of the Czech Academy of Sciences an opinion on the Czech language used in the draft. The opinion (just one and a half pages), signed by the Head of the Institute and returned in November 2008 (unpublished), was quite reserved in general (with some explicitly negative comments on the syntax and certain grammatical issues) emphasizing that "it should be kept in mind that it is a specialist text which should be sufficiently precise and unequivocal and whose good and thorough understanding usually requires, as a matter of principle, certain intellectual labour. However, requirements for the extent of such labour must not be inadequate and the understanding of the text must not rely on specialist knowledge which is not generally shared." (Translated from Czech by the author of this chapter.) Moreover, comments on the comprehensibility of the terminology used were rather cautious leaving it up to drafters to decide what is terminologically appropriate.

Although many of the grammatical features typical of pre-WWII Czech have been adapted to the recent usage, most readers do not perceive the language of the Code as being up-to-date. In any case, the choice of lexical units (other than pure legal terminology) along with their lexical and grammatical patterns (collocations and correlations) renders the text of the Code linguistically outdated or even obsolete. Substantial conceptual shifts and novelties in legal institutions tend to be often denoted through semantic shifts in existing terms, by reintroducing Czech terminology used before World War II and, marginally, by developing brand new legal terms. Considering the fact that the concepts and language of a Civil Code in continental countries form the foundations of private law and that hundreds of other laws use that terminology to further develop any particular issue, such a radical change in terminology and language, as introduced in the 2012 Civil Code, will make the existing special laws in the Czech Republic, including those implementing European law, conceptually and terminologically inconsistent (or even incompatible) with the Civil Code. The more or less compact language of Czech private law in the 21st century is to be pervaded with legal concepts and their linguistic designation mostly developed and used before World War II.

3. Methodology of Translation

In analyzing the difficulties arising when English is used as a language of contract, Volker Triebel (2009: 149) notes: 'Legal English and common law grew up together. Many English legal terms and concepts can only be understood against a common law background.' This conclusion applies to legal English in general. Whatever variety of legal English one encounters, it always stems from the "original" legal English, i.e., that of common law. Certain jurilinguistic aspects may be expanded upon, some pushed out, and others added. The scope of modification of, or even departure from, classical common-law English would depend on the philosophical and conceptual remoteness from the common law of the respective legal system, using English as its official language.

The preparatory stage of translating the new Czech Civil Code into English requires identification of all available legislative sources, whether originally drafted in English and based primarily on civil law, or quality translations into English of civil legislation; all sources should be subject to a comprehensive analysis and conceptual comparison with the English of common law.

3.1. Sources

Translation of the new Czech Civil Code into English requires extensive comparative research focusing on the conceptual analysis of terminology used in the 1964 Czech Civil Code and in the new code. Such analysis may indicate whether certain conceptual patterns and terminology used in the English translation of the 1964 Code may be used in the translation of the 2012 Code (e.g., as functional or partial equivalents). The concepts and structures missing in the 1964 Code should be transmitted into English and localized within the existing legal concepts and terms in such a way that their translation would make sense to an English-speaking recipient (usually a foreigner living, working and/or doing business within the context of Czech law). This would apply to the majority of all terms as one may reasonably assume from the total number of sections, i.e., 880 in the 1964 Code and 3,080 in the 2012 Code.

The recurrence in the 2012 Code of legal concepts instituted by the ABGB, and possibly by the Code Napoléon, would require that corresponding legislative texts in English be identified and a legal and linguistic comparative analysis of such texts be made. Since Czech law belongs to the continental legal family, it would be desirable to build upon native English legislative sources based on the continental legal tradition. In this respect, the Louisiana Civil Code[22] and the English version of the Quebec Civil Code[23] appear to be linguistically and legally the most reliable sources of potential translational equivalents. Both codes are derived from the French *Code civil*, although both have undergone certain legal and linguistic development during their existence, as has the *Code civil* itself.

Another valuable source may be high-quality translations of civil codes of other European countries or countries that have built their system of law on the continental legal tradition. A high quality translation of a continental civil code into English is a text not only written with no grammatical errors at any level (this requirement is usually tacitly presumed), but primarily a text from which a preceding legal and linguistic comparative analysis between the source and target legal systems can be made. As a result, the translation makes legal sense to a recipient knowledgeable of the potential drawbacks of translating civil law into English.

In addition to the Austrian ABGB whose only publicly available translation into English dates back to 1866,[24] the German BGB (*Bürgerliches Gesetzbuch*) is also close to the Czech system of private law. The translation of the BGB into English has been under the supervision of the German Federal Ministry of Justice and has been regularly updated in line with the latest amendments to the BGB.[25] Another continental civil code deserving attention in our project is the Dutch Civil Code. There are two freely accessible translations of the DCC into English, one on the Internet,[26] the other in a printed version.[27] Having compared the two translations, and after consulting a Dutch legal academic, we have chosen the printed version ("Warendorf") as a more reliable source. The main reason is that the provisions in various parts of the Code translated by Warendorf made more legal sense in English, but still explain the relevant continental substance. On the other hand, the Internet translation of the DCC was appended with certain explicative notes in most provisions. The line between the original wording of the law and its explication is very often quite opaque. In addition, the translators of the Internet version sometimes resort to creating new, "artificial" terms, such as "keepership" for regular "detention" in Article 3.5:107, making the interpretation of the respective provision difficult.[28]

22 Available at: http://www.legis.state.la.us/lss/lss.asp?folder=67 and http://www.law.lsu.edu/index.cfm?geaux=clo.lcco, the latter being maintained by the Center of Civil Law Studies of the Louisiana State University and supported by many commentaries and explanations of the continental legal system in the common law environment of the USA.

23 Available at: http://www.justice.gouv.qc.ca/english/sujets/glossaire/code-civil-a.htm; the accuracy and preciseness of English in the Code has been subject to permanent supervision (and possible rectification, if required) within the bijuralism policy and related comparative jurilinguistic projects launched and maintained by the Canadian Department of Justice, of which the Civil Code of Québec has been part.

24 *General Civil Code for all the German Hereditary Provinces of the Austrian Monarchy*. Translated by Joseph m. Chevalier de Winiwarter, Doctor in Law, Advocate in Vienna, and Legal Adviser to Her Britannic Majesty, Embassy at Vienna. Vienna 1866. Sold by Rudolph Lechner, Bookseller to the University.

25 Civil Code in the version promulgated on 2 January 2002 (Federal Law Gazette [*Bundesgesetzblatt*] I page 42, 2909; 2003 I page 738), last amended by Article 1 of the statute of 27 July 2011 (Federal Law Gazette I page 1600). Bundesministerium der Justiz. Translation provided by the Langenscheidt Translation Service. Translation regularly updated by Neil Mussett. Available at: http://www.gesetze-im-internet.de/englisch_bgb/ [Accessed December 2012].

26 Available at: http://www.dutchcivillaw.com/civilcodebook033.htm [Accessed July 2012].

27 Warendorf et al. (2009).

28 See Chromá (forthcoming 2014).

There are countries outside Europe that have systems of law historically based on the continental (i.e., Roman law) tradition, such as Japan or the Philippines.[29] Both systems regulate private law through their civil codes, and both have their codes translated into English and freely available to the public. Surprisingly, the first translation of the then new Japanese Civil Code (1896) was made in 1898.[30] A new translation of the latest version of the Civil Code of Japan is available on the webpage of the Ministry of Justice.[31] Simple comparison of the two English texts of the Japanese Civil Code shows that, despite a span of more than 100 years, the translations are a solid example of propositional synonymy in almost every provision (with the exception of provisions non-existent in the 1896 version): the Japanese source text for translation is the same (the 1896 Civil Code of Japan), and the English outcome is in two legally identical and linguistically similar (synonymic) versions.

3.2. Technicalities

What we consider extremely valuable with respect to the newer translation of the Civil Code of Japan into English is its bilingual format. A provision in Japanese is immediately followed by its translation into English. This is the format we prefer in publishing any translation of legislation, and it may also be useful in private transactions (e.g., making two language versions of a contract). Paralleling the source legal text and its translation not only saves time when looking up a respective phrase in the source language, but also may serve certain "educational" purposes, such as increasing the foreign language awareness and knowledge of communication partners, helping law students acquire relevant terminology in a foreign language or providing foreigners with a basic conceptual source of local law.

The last issue in the context of translating legislation that is to be accessible to the public (whether electronically or in a printed format) is the authorship of translation. From the legal perspective, the outcome of translating (i.e., transformation of a text written in one language into a text written in another language) is subject to copyright as any other text. This is one reason why the name of the translator (or translators, or the translation agency in charge of the respective translation) should be revealed and, depending on the format of the translation, published accordingly. The other reason is that the translator's quality performance (or the professional standing of a translation agency) may be subject to public scrutiny, which is desirable particularly with respect to translating national legislation into other languages.

The translated civil codes we have worked with show that when a translation is published as a printed book, the translator is clearly indicated (with the exception of the Czech Republic). The translation is produced as part of the person's special commission,[32] academic performance,[33] or professional specialization.[34] Translations of civil codes posted on Internet

29 The Civil Code of the Philippines is available at: http://www.lawphil.net/statutes/repacts/ra1949/ra_386_1949.html. The English translation of the Code provides a good picture of the regulation of private law despite some terms that make not much sense, such as '[the parent or guardian] or *person having legal charge*' in the context of annulment of marriage.

30 *The Civil Code of Japan*. Translated by Dr Ludwig Lönholm, Professor at the Imperial University of Tokyo. Yokohama, Shanghai, Hong Kong & Singapore: Kelly & Walsh Lim. Available at: https://ia600407.us.archive.org/10/items/cu31924069576704/cu31924069576704.pdf.

31 Available at: http://www.moj.go.jp/content/000056024.pdf.

32 Joseph M. Chevalier De Winiwarter, translator of the ABGB in 1866, acted as a legal adviser to the British Embassy in Vienna.

33 Dr Ludwig Lönholm, translator of the Japanese Civil Code in 1898, was Professor of Law at the Imperial University in Tokyo.

34 The Dutch Civil Code, published in English by Kluwer Law International in 2009, was translated by lawyers (Hans Warendorf, Richard Thomas and Dr. Ian Curry-Sumner) specialized in translating

websites rarely contain the name of translators; exceptions include the BGB (see n. 24) and the English version of the French *Code civil*.[35] It should be noted in this context that no translation of legislation published in the Czech Republic has been authored, whether as a book printed by an established publishing house, or electronically on official websites of government agencies (such as the Czech National Bank) or as a part of law databases maintained by legal publishers. Moreover, one international publisher can publish translations of legislation that are rather inconsistent in quality in the individual countries, indicating that there is no uniform corporate policy for legislative translation. The excellent quality of the English translation of the Dutch Civil Code already mentioned (Warendorf) published by Wolters Kluwer, the Netherlands, is in sharp contrast to the poor quality of the translation of the Czech Criminal Code and the Criminal Procedure Code published as a book by Wolters Kluwer, the Czech Republic, without providing the names of the translators.

3.3. Comparative Jurilinguistic Analysis

Translating legal texts into English requires that a translator make a qualified decision with respect to a variety of legal English issues. Eversheds LLP (2011) suggests[36] that '70 countries use English as an official language in government, courts, media and education' (2011: 6). This implies that there are more varieties of legal English than just those used in traditional English-speaking countries whose system stems from common law. In addition, there is the English of international public law and the English of European Union law, each being an autonomous variety.

There are certain "varieties" of legal English established by translation from various legal systems and languages into English. Such "translational varieties" are usually confined to employing specific terminology, which is determined partly by the specificity of the local legal order. Its concepts may be difficult to transmit to another language, and translators tend to resort to prima facie equivalents, irrespective of their conceptual substance. One can hardly expect the five degrees of damage stipulated in the Czech Criminal Code ('damage not insignificant'; 'damage not small'; 'larger damage'; 'considerable damage'; 'damage of a large extent') to be perceived by native or non-native speakers of English in a uniform way without, for example, referring to specific sums.[37] Local translational "habits" may also contribute to a local "translational variety" because translators can be strongly influenced by translations that already exist in the respective area and use the same terminological equivalents or patterns in their product. They usually dispense with any adequate conceptual analysis between the terms in the source legal texts and their potential equivalents in the target law. The term "joint-stock company" used for the Czech "akciová společnost" is just one example illustrating such an approach.[38] The regular and widely known English terms "stock corporation" or "public

Dutch legislation into English, who have been recently working on translating the civil law of Suriname into English.

35 The French Civil Code may be retrieved from the official site of the French Government at http://www.legifrance.gouv.fr. The Code was translated by Georges Rouhette, Professor of Law, with the assistance of Dr Anne Rouhette-Berton, Assistant Professor of English.

36 Eversheds LLP (2011).

37 Even associating the degrees with a concrete amount of Czech crowns converted into US dollars did not persuade a US court to extradite a Czech citizen, accused of serious fraud in the Czech Republic, back to the Czech Republic, as the amounts in USD were too low to constitute a crime in the US (see Chromá 2005).

38 See Act No. 513/1991 Sb., the Commercial Code. The name of the law is another example of a local translational habit: immediately after its adoption (1991), the Czech "obchodní zákoník" was translated as the Commercial Code into English irrespective of the fact that the adjective "commercial"

limited company" could have been used instead since the Czech type of business entity is almost identical in its essential elements with entities denoted by the US and British terms, respectively. The English term "joint-stock company", if considered within common law, is rather a terminological historism denoting an unincorporated entity established to pool the share capital of individual shareholders usually with unlimited liability.

Lawyers tend to be rather sceptical about the quality of legal translation, as expressed by Kischel (2009: 7), with a certain undertone of resignation: "[T]he question in legal translation is not which translation is right, but, more modestly, which one is less wrong.' Whatever the prevailing opinion and practice might be, translators are never relieved from their responsibility and commitment to produce as good a translation as practicable under the given circumstances.[39]

The decision relating to "which legal English" should be used may often be motivated by an envisaged ultimate recipient of the translated text. Estimating the potential recipient of a translation and adapting the language accordingly is easier in private transactions where the contact and/or communication between the parties who speak different languages can be quite close. The misunderstandings caused by the obscure language of a translation can be swiftly explained if need be, and misapplication of the legal text can essentially be avoided. A similar situation may arise when a judgment or any other binding decision is translated into English for the purposes of one particular case, such as extradition proceedings: it is known from the beginning for which jurisdiction such decision is to be translated, and the jurilinguistic choice can be directed accordingly.

English translations of any legal documents, whether legislation or judgments for law reports, to be published with no particular recipient in mind, i.e., those intended for the interested (legal) public who does not speak the language of origin, should always be preceded by an extensive analysis. Immediate clarification of the ambiguous or opaque language of a translation is usually impracticable. The analysis should be aimed at choosing the best possible "variety" of legal English at all levels—grammatical (morphology and syntax), semantic and conceptual (relevant terminological choice), textual (relevant text types/genres) and pragmatic (considering potential addressees). We will concentrate on the first two overlapping levels, keeping in mind the pragmatics of translation.

---

conceptually applies to obligations and the Czech Code contained a major part governing business entities (unlike the Uniform Commercial Code in the USA, which inspired the first Czech translators of "obchodní zákoník"). Subsequently, the register of Czech companies is called the "Commercial Register" in English. In the early 1990s, English translations of newly emerging Czech legislation had to be done quickly: no Internet sources were available, and the sources in Czech libraries were very limited and insufficient for pursuing a deep conceptual analysis of Czech terms and their potential equivalents in English. These English terms (as well as dozens of others) have existed (and survived) for more than 20 years in cross-border and global business transactions with a Czech party, thus establishing themselves as what can be called "legal and linguistic *realia*" (i.e., items perceived from the outside as typical of, and special for, the Czech system).

39 I recently took part in a meeting convened by the Czech Ministry of Justice (the contracting party) and a translation agency that won a government public tender for translating the new Czech Civil Code into four international languages. Documents for the invitation to bid had clearly indicated that their drafters (from the contracting Ministry) had no knowledge of the specificity of legislative translation. In addition (or rather as a result), the project had been significantly underfunded. The translation agency won because it had offered a bidding price lower than the maximum price set in the tender documentation. Since there were doubts regarding the competence of the engaged translators, a question was raised at the meeting whether the agency was prepared and able to produce quality translations of the Code. The frank response of the owner of the agency that 'the quality will correspond to the amount of money of the bid' might seem logical from the owner's perspective but, objectively, was striking and strongly indicated that the translation quality was not the agency's ultimate goal in establishing their reputation.

3.3.1. *Grammatical Analysis*

We have examined in this analysis modality, gender neutrality, and presumptions as they are used in legislation originally drafted in English. In addition, the conjunction "rather than" relevant in translating certain phrases from the Czech Civil Code into English was dealt with to ascertain its prevailing meaning in legislative texts.

3.3.1.1. *Modality*

The meaning of modality for the purposes of translation is reduced to linguistic devices indicating the degree of (normative) force a respective legislative provision is to express and the way in which the provision should be evaluated. Jackson (1999: 17) notes that 'there is a widespread view that legislative language is reducible to norms expressed in terms of three deontic modalities, that which is required, prohibited and permitted.' The correct choice by translators from amongst *shall, may, may not, must,* or any other relevant modal auxiliary would render possible the correct interpretation of a translated proposition.

Legislative drafting manuals in English-speaking countries could be a helpful source of information for identifying a contemporary approach to expressing requirements, prohibitions and permissions, primarily regarding the use of *shall,* in statutes within the Anglo-American system of law. We examined the modality issue in recent versions of legislative drafting guidelines for legislators in the United Kingdom—Drafting Guidelines 2011[40] (OPC-UK), Australia—the OPC Drafting Manual 2012[41] (OPC-AU), and two US states[42]—the Idaho Legislation Drafting Manual 2013[43] (ID) and the Colorado Legislative Drafting Manual 2012[44] (CO). The Canadian Drafting Conventions[45] (CDC-CA) and the House Legislative Counsel's Manual on Drafting Style 1995[46] (US) were taken into account in analyzing certain issues.

"SHALL" No other modal auxiliary stirs up debates among lawyers, legal linguists and translators as much as *shall.* Butt and Castle (2004: 99) note that '*shall* is the hallmark of traditional legal writing. Whenever lawyers want to express themselves in formal style, *shall* intrudes.' Garner (2001: 105), in a chapter entitled 'Delete Every *Shall*', complains: 'But legal drafters use *shall* incessantly. They learn it by osmosis in law school, and the lesson is fortified in law practice. Ask a drafter what *shall* means, and you'll hear that it's a mandatory word – opposed to the permissive *may.*' Kimble (2007: 42) resigns, claiming that 'lawyers are uneducable on *shall* and we should give up.' Translators essentially follow linguistic patterns in legal texts they are to translate. If they have to translate English texts with abundant

40 Published by the Office of the Parliamentary Counsel, Cabinet Office, London, UK; available at: https://www.gov.uk/government/publications/the-office-of-the-parliamentary-counsel-guidance [Accessed September 2013].

41 Published by the Office of Parliamentary Counsel of the Australian Government; available at: http://www.opc.gov.au/ [Accessed September 2013].

42 The National Conference of State Legislature provides a list of, and links to, all legislative drafting manuals available in the individual US states, available at: http://www.ncsl.org/legislators-staff/legislative-staff/legal-services/bill-drafting-manuals.aspx.

43 Published by the Idaho Legislative Services Office; available at: http://legislature.idaho.gov/about/draftingmanual.pdf [Accessed September 2013].

44 Prepared by the Office of Legislative Legal Services, an agency of the Colorado General Assembly; available at: http://www.state.co.us/gov_dir/leg_dir/olls/LDM/OLLS_Drafting_Manual.pdf [Accessed September 2013].

45 Available at: http://www.ulcc.ca/en/uniform-acts-new-order/drafting-conventions/546-josetta-1-en-gb/uniform-actsa/drafting-conventions/66-uniform-drafting-convention.

46 Prepared by the Office of the Legislative Counsel of the US House of Representatives; available at: http://www.house.gov/legcoun/pdf/draftstyle.pdf [Accessed September 2013].

examples of *shall* into other languages, one may expect them to use or overuse this auxiliary in their translations from those languages into English simply because '*shall* is the hallmark of traditional legal writing'.

A comparison of the two translations of the Japanese Civil Code with respect to the use of *shall* shows quite a surprising result: the translation of 1898, composed of 1146 articles, contains just 34 occurrences of *shall* (expressing an obligation in most cases), whilst the new translation posted on the website of the Japanese Government, with just 724 articles (excluding BOOK IV on Family) contains *shall* in every article at least once in all possible meanings of the auxiliary.[47] The following examples illustrate this difference.

Example 1

(1898) '1. The enjoyment of private rights begins at birth.'

(new) '1. The enjoyment of private rights *shall* commence at birth.'

Example 2

(1898) '421. The provisions of the preceding article apply correspondingly, where the parties have agreed beforehand that compensation shall be made in something other than money.'

(new) '421. The provisions of the preceding Article *shall* apply mutatis mutandis to the cases where the parties agree in advance to allocate anything other than money to the compensation for damages.'

Both occurrences of *shall* in the new translation are typical cases when the modal auxiliary may be omitted without changing the sense of the provision. The use of *shall* in Article 421 in the old translation (1898) implies a future obligation agreed by the parties.

However, it should be noted that legislative drafting manuals are divided on whether *shall* should maintain its position or whether it should be removed from the repertoire of the language of statutes altogether. Whilst the Australian and British manuals insist on dispensing with this modal auxiliary,[48] all US legislatures preserve its role as indicating 'that something is mandatory [. . .]' and further instruct their drafters (ID: 31): 'As to a public official, *shall* is used to impose a duty, direction or command unless the context indicates that the legislature wished discretion to be exercised. Use *shall* to prescribe a rule of conduct, but not to declare a legal result.'

The position of *shall* has been weakened also in drafting private documents (at least in countries that have removed it from their legislative drafting). In 2010, the ambiguity of *shall* was highlighted in the case *BW Gas AS v. JAS Shipping Ltd.* [2010] EWCA Civ 68. The British Court of Appeal ruled that the phrase 'The BUYER shall supply and deliver to the BUILDER all of the items' did not impose an obligation on the Buyer to deliver these items; the court provided quite an extensive jurilinguistic analysis supporting its decision. Long before that judgment, Allen & Overy's English law banking practice had advocated the use of *must* to impose obligations rather than *shall*, which could lead to interpretive ambiguity in legal documents. The firm had adopted this principle of excluding *shall* not only in its overall

47 See an analysis of *shall* in Garner (1995: 939–940).

48 Garner (1995: 940) calls this approach the 'ABC rule', as it has been most strongly advocated by some Australian, British, and Canadian drafters; Garner suggests that 'lawyers are not educable on the subject of *shall*, so the only solution is complete abstinence.' However, the Canadian Drafting Conventions for bilingual legislative drafting provide (Rule 24(3)) that '*Shall* is used to impose a duty or (with *not* or *no*) a prohibition.'

drafting guidelines, recommending to their lawyers to avoid *shall* in their drafting, but has also extended this recommendation to their English translators.[49]

Translators have several options for avoiding *shall* in translation. The guidance provided by the UK drafting rules (OPC-UK) can be useful and inspiring (p. 14):

> 18 There are various alternatives to *shall* which can be used, depending on context.
> *must* in the context of obligations (although *is to be* and *it is the duty of* may also be appropriate alternatives in certain contexts);
> *there is to be* in the context of the establishment of new statutory bodies etc.;
> use of the present tense in provisions about application, effect, extent or commencement;
> *is amended as follows* in provisions introducing a series of amendments;
> *is repealed* in the context of free-standing repeals;
> *is to be* in the context of provisions relating to statutory instruments (and, if appropriate, *may not* as an alternative to *shall not*).

What might be surprising is the use of *is to* recommended in order to replace *shall*. In the OPC-AU, p. 19, Australian drafters are advised to 'say *must* or *must not* when imposing an obligation, not *shall* or *shall not*. If you feel the need to use a gentler form, say *is to* or *is not to*, but these are less direct and use more words.' A quick scan of the Australian Corporations Act 2001 suggests that *is to* is widely used; however, considering Example 3, one may have doubts as to what extent such substitution helps clarify the meaning and whether *is to* is not becoming a source of ambiguity, having led to the disqualification of *shall* in drafting.

Example 3

Section 5H
'(1) ... if a law of a State or Territory in this jurisdiction:
(b) specifies:
(i) the day on which the body *is to be* taken to be registered (the registration day) or the manner in which that day *is to be* fixed; and
(ii) the type of company the body *is to be* registered as under this Act;
...
(3) If the company:
(a) *is to* be a public company; and
(b) *is to* have a constitution on registration;
a copy of the constitution must be lodged before the registration day.'

Section 45A
'(4) For the purposes of this section, the question whether a proprietary company controls an entity *is to be* decided in accordance with the accounting standards made . . .'

Section 109
'(1) Except so far as the contrary intention appears, a provision of this Act *is to be* interpreted in such a manner that . . .'

Section 111J
'(1) . . . . The guide then *is to be* read as if it were so modified.'

49 See 'Discussion Paper' written by Philip Carstairs in March 2010 (an internal document, courtesy of Allen & Overy's Prague Office).

Without being knowledgeable of the intended sense of *is to* declared in the drafting rules, one might encounter interpretive difficulties trying to establish its precise meaning in the above provisions. The semantic range spans a duty (§§45H, 109), a condition (§5H(3)), express intention (§5H (1)(b) (i) and (ii)), and direction (§111J).

The British Defamation Act 2013 seems to be more accurate and unequivocal when using *is to*.

Example 4

Section 6

'(7) Nothing in this section *is to be* construed – . . .

(8) The reference in subsection (3)(a) to "the editor of the journal" *is to be* read, in the case of a journal with more than one editor, as a reference to the editor or editors . . .'

Section 12

'(3) If the parties cannot agree on the wording, the wording *is to be* settled by the court.'

Section 16

'(6) In determining whether section 8 applies, no account *is to be* taken of any publication made before . . .'

Interpretation of *is to* in the above provisions seems to be unambiguous in imposing a duty upon anyone involved. However, the context is relevant as the clarity of its meaning is supported by a rather rigorous formulation of the whole provision.

Since *shall* may be understood in many, sometimes even opposing manners, and *is to* as its substitute may occasionally lead to interpretive ambiguity, translators should be heedful of potential risks either auxiliary may produce when their English translation is interpreted by its ultimate recipient. Moreover, a continental law statute translated into English will bring about interpretive uncertainty caused primarily by conceptual differences in the legal institutions of continental law conveyed into English (originating in common law). There is no reason to increase the risk of misinterpretation by using equivocal auxiliaries. Translators should consider the scope of normative modality in the source text and choose other auxiliaries whose interpretation is more predictable. Most provisions in the new Czech Civil Code determine what the law is and what the law requires. In such provisions, and in provisions about application or effect (as suggested by the OPC-UK), the simple present tense should be used. In cases where a requirement imposing a duty is expressed by the auxiliary "musí" in Czech, *must* would be used in English. Statutory permission indicated by Czech "může" will be translated by its legal and linguistic equivalent *may*. Prohibition imposed on animate objects by Czech "nesmí" will be *may not* (e.g., 'Unless approved by court, a curator may not give the consent to changing the personal status of an individual under curatorship.'). Where prohibition is imposed on an inanimate object, *must not* will be used in English (e.g., 'The interpretation and application of a legal regulation must not be in contradiction to good morals and must not lead to cruelty and recklessness offending common human feelings.').

3.3.1.2. Gender Neutrality

Traditionally, laws governing the interpretation of the language of statutes in common law countries contain a gender clause: (i) 'words importing a gender include every other gender' (§23(a) of the [Australian] Acts Interpretation Act 1901, as amended); (ii) ' . . . unless the contrary intention appears¾ (a) words importing the masculine gender include the feminine; (b) words importing the feminine gender include the masculine' (§6 of the [British] Interpretation

Act 1978, as amended); (iii) 'words importing female persons include male persons and corporations and words importing male persons include female persons and corporations' (§33(1) of the [Canadian] Interpretation Act 1985, as amended); or (iv) 'every word importing the masculine gender only may extend to and be applied to females and things as well as males; every word importing the feminine gender only may extend to and be applied to males and things as well as females; and every word importing the neuter gender only may extend to and be applied to natural persons as well as things.' (Colorado Revised Statutes C.R.S. §2-4-103). Whatever phrasing is preferred, most statutory provisions used the masculine *he* as an assumed "generic" pronoun covering both male and female individuals.

Attempts to write legal documents without specifying the natural gender of parties or other actors within legal transactions were traceable in private documents, such as contracts, much earlier than in academic publications or even statutes. Discussions over possible solutions aimed at eradicating gender specificity from texts dealing with, and applicable to, both genders, have been rather emotional. Decades ago, Fillmore (1978: 157) sarcastically complained about the conflicts experienced by anyone 'who took seriously the effort to "desex" English':

> *Since the system of pronouns in English is a closed class of words in which singularity for humans cannot be separated from sex, there is no way of choosing an anaphoric pronoun for an indefinite human antecedent without offending somebody. 'They' offends the grammarians, 'he' offends the feminists, 'he or she' offends the stylists, 'she' is downright hostile, and 'it' just cannot be taken seriously. We could get out of this by speaking Chinese, but that's bound to offend some people, too.*

All modern instructional legislative drafting documents attempt to practically illustrate how the gender neutrality principle can be applied in the language of statutes. The Canadian Drafting Conventions enjoin that 'sex-specific references should be avoided'; other manuals prefer using gender-neutral language wherever possible. The OPC-AU attempts to refute a traditional claim that gender-neutral English in legislation makes statutory language clumsy and advocate their approach (14):

> *We have found that this approach does not make provisions more cumbersome or lead to a proliferation of 'his and hers' etc. throughout new legislation as drafters tend to use the description of the relevant person (e.g. the taxpayer's) instead. In many cases this makes the provision clearer than if just 'his' was used and may also avoid ambiguity where there is more than one person referred to in the provision.*

Translators transferring the source legislative text into English may divide this assertion into two main areas: (a) gender-neutral nouns, and (b) achieving gender neutrality in pronouns. Needless to say, the second category is much more difficult as pronouns by nature are words used to replace nouns. Should we succeed in finding a gender-neutral noun, we usually fail in pronouns since neither Czech nor English (to limit the choice of languages to our project) have developed a special gender neutral pronoun (singular) to refer to a human being who is, by nature, either male or female. Moreover, each language—Czech and English—belongs to a different language type (synthetic and analytic respectively) with different morphosyntactic structures. It is quite clear that the methods of making the statutory language used in English gender neutral need not work in Czech, and vice versa. For example, unlike English, Czech has grammatical gender *she* for a "person" or a "party", which are frequently used nouns in the legal context. As the aim of our project is to translate the Czech code into English, recommendations provided in legislative drafting manuals in English-speaking countries should be taken into account.

The OPC-UK (18–24) provides useful guidelines on how to achieve the desired degree of gender neutrality in legislative drafting, which are more than inspiring for translating statutes into English. The following six techniques are just a selection of suggested solutions from drafting manuals that may be applicable to translating the Czech Code into English.

1. Repeat the noun rather than using a pronoun;
2. Substitute *the* or *that* for the personal pronoun;
3. Use *he or she;*
4. Change to a plural noun followed by *they;*
5. Omit the pronoun;
6. Use a present or past participle.

The examples of rephrasing translated statutory provisions into gender neutral wording suggest that a combination of more techniques should normally be used for one provision. The combination of numbers shows which techniques from the list above apply to the respective provisions. Words in brackets were used in the original translation before adapting it to a gender neutral language; the adapted wording is in italics.

Example 5

A. 1+1+3

'A person becoming the holder of an ownership right in good faith and in a lawful and genuine manner is deemed to be the owner against a person retaining [his] *a* thing *of that owner,* or disturbing [him] *the owner* otherwise without having any legal ground for that or [his] *his or her* legal ground is of the same value or weaker.'

B. 1+3

'Where the legal order makes a certain consequence dependent upon someone's knowledge, such knowledge is deemed as that which would be reasonably acquired by a person acquainted with the case in consideration of all circumstances which must have been obvious to [him] *that person* in [his] *his or her* capacity.'

C. 5+1

'A possessor may resist arbitrary disturbance by repossessing, during the disturbing act, a thing removed [from him] unless doing so [he] *the possessor* exceeds the limits of self-defence.'

D. 4+5

'Protection extends to the life and dignity of [an individual] *individuals,* [his] *their* health and right to live in a favourable environment, [his] *their* reputation, integrity, privacy and [his] expressions of a personal nature.'

E. 4

'Other persons in family or other relationship are considered persons close to each other if harm suffered by one of them would be perceived by the [other] *others* as [his] *their* own harm.'

F. 3+6+1+3+6

'A person believing, upon convincing grounds, that [he] *he or she* holds the right [he has] exercised, is a possessor in good faith. A person is a possessor in bad faith if [he] *the person* knows, or should, due to the circumstances, be aware that [he] *he or she* exercises the right not [belonging to him] *acquired.*'

G. 2+1
'The owner of land acquires the ownership of what has accrued to [his] *the* land as a result of sowing the seeds of another or planting the plants of another; however the plants become [his] property *of the owner of the land* after they grow roots.'

H. 5+3
'No person may suffer unreasonable harm due to [his] insufficient age, mental state or due to [his] dependence; no person may take unreasonable advantage from [his] *his or her* own incapacity to the detriment of others.'

As can be seen from the examples and as emphasized in legislative drafting manuals dealing with gender neutrality in statutory English, translators [drafters] should be flexible and evaluate the potential of each technique keeping in mind that the goal in translating [drafting] is to assure clarity and to avoid ambiguity. In addition, translators are responsible for as precise a "transfer" as possible of the legal information from a source language to the target language, i.e., translators are not drafters and are always bound by the legal content of the source text in formulating the foreign language version.

Our own experience suggests that, should it be desirable to rephrase the translated provisions of the Czech Code in order to produce English that is perceived as more gender neutral, translators would probably complete such an adaptation after the translation has been completed. The reason for proceeding in such a way is that Czech in statutes is not gender neutral and fully relies on the grammatical gender of nouns and on the singular of nouns of the masculine gender perceived by lawyers as a "generic" gender in legislation. As translators should focus on transferring the correct meaning of the source language provisions into the target language, they would concentrate on transmitting the normative sense of provisions (selecting proper terminological equivalents and relevant phrases in the target language). Naturally, most translators of legal documents into English know that they should use gender neutral nouns such as "chairperson", "businessperson", "spouse", "sibling", "grandparent", "individual", etc., and they would do so in the course of their translation. In addition, as also suggested by the OPC-UK (19), "testator", "manager", or "director" would be regarded as gender-neutral, despite the existence of their female counterparts ("testatrix", "manageress", or "directress"). The gender neutral rephrasing made after the translation has been completed would relate primarily to pronouns in order to make the gender neutral modification coherent throughout the whole translated text. Of course, it is always possible to make an explicit (foot) note at the beginning of the translated text stipulating that 'words importing the masculine gender include the feminine and the neuter and vice versa'.

3.3.1.3. Presumptions in Law

Drafters of the new Czech Civil Code in their commentaries for Czech lawyers and for the general public rather strictly claim that they were consistent in distinguishing in the language of the Code between a rebuttable presumption, an irrebuttable presumption and legal fiction.

Translators usually do not think of the legal substance of presumptions when they are to transfer their linguistic expression into another language. They often tend to "slide down the linguistic surface" and use phrases in the target language giving the linguistic impression of correspondence with phrases in the source language. Most non-lawyers would see no difference in the legal meaning of "presumption" in phrases "presumption of innocence" (rebuttable presumption) and "presumption of knowledge" (irrebuttable presumption) unless they knew that the latter may be viewed from another angle as "ignorance of law is no defence".

Formulating presumptions apparently poses no problem for lawyers within the Anglo-American system of law since no textbook on legal writing we were able to trace on the book market contains a chapter, or even brief instructions, on what linguistic verbal patterns should be used to express presumptions. The legislative drafting manuals we worked with either remain silent in this respect or provide some unintentionally guidance when explaining other features.

Phrases establishing rebuttable presumptions are the easiest of the three to translate. Rebuttable presumptions (also called disputable or conditional presumptions) express inference drawn from certain facts that establish a prima facie case.[50] Such presumptions may be defeated by introducing sufficiently persuasive contrary evidence and become part of the law of evidence (cf. Phillips 2003: 29).

A rebuttable presumption may be illustrated by the following examples.

Example 6

A. '(2) Any person may apply to the High Court for a declaration that the missing person *is presumed to* be dead.' (Section 1 of the Presumption of Death Act 2013, UK)

B. '(2) For the purposes of any proceedings under this Part –
(b) a document purporting to be such a certificate *is to be deemed to be* one unless the contrary is proved.' (Section 13 of the Antarctic Act 2013, UK)

C. '(1) If a child is born to a woman while she is married, the child *is presumed to be* a child of the woman and her husband.' (Section 69P of the Family Law Act 1975, AU)

D. '(1) Parenting time shall be granted in accordance with the best interests of the child. It *is presumed to* be in the best interests of a child for the child to have a strong relationship with both of his or her parents.' (Section 7a. of the Child Custody Act of 1970, Michigan, USA)

As can be seen from the examples, there are two phrases used to express a rebuttable presumption: *is deemed to* and *is presumed to*. Either verbal phrase may be, and quite often is, appended with a clause expressly supporting the rebuttable nature of a presumption, e.g., "unless there is sufficient evidence (to the contrary)" or "unless the contrary is shown/proved". Translator can quite easily conclude that these two phrases could be used interchangeably and would always be interpreted in a way that the presumption would be rebutted should there be persuasive evidence to the contrary. However, it may be quite a misleading assumption, particularly regarding *is deemed to* as the following examples show.

Example 7

A. '(2) Where the Attorney-General intervenes in any proceedings, the Attorney-General shall *be deemed to* be a party to the proceedings with all the rights, duties and liabilities of a party.' (Section 91 of the Australian Family Law Act 1975, as amended)

B. '(12) In relation to any time after the day on which the clinical commissioning group ceases to be subject to any conditions or directions, the group *is to be deemed to* have been established by virtue of an application granted under section 14C of the 2006 Act.' (Section 8 of Schedule 6 to the British Health and Social Care Act 2012)

50 *Black's Law Dictionary* (2009: 1306).

C. '(a) Upon merger pursuant to this chapter, a surviving domestic or foreign corporation or other business entity shall *be deemed to* have assumed the liability of each disappearing domestic or foreign corporation or other business entity that is taxed under Part 10 . . .' (Section 1107.5 of the California Corporations Code)

All occurrences of *be deemed to* express an irrebuttable presumption and declare what the law is in such situations. An irrebuttable presumption, also termed "conclusive", "absolute", or "mandatory", cannot be overcome by any additional evidence or argument. The proof of certain facts makes the existence of the assumed fact beyond dispute. Conclusive presumptions refer to rules of law and must be accepted to be true without any possibility of rebuttal.[51] Therefore, it is extremely important for translators to use phrases in the translation that would lead their interpreter in the correct legal direction.

Some legislative drafting manuals recommend replacing *is deemed to* with *is* (e.g., the South Dakota Drafting Manual p. 29, the Massachusetts Legislative Research and Drafting Manual, 5th edn. 2010 p. 27, or Colorado p.124). In such a case, the provisions change to a declaration of what the law is and not what is (conclusively) presumed that the law may be. The OPC-AU instructs its drafters to replace *shall be deemed to be* with *is taken to be*, or *is treated as*, or *is regarded as*. Peter Quiggin PSM, current First Parliamentary Counsel in the Office of Parliamentary Counsel of the Australian Government, has noticed with respect to the above Example 7A: 'If we were drafting section 91(2) today we would say 'the Attorney-General *is taken* to be a party'. This has been our practice for about 25 years.' He added that, even though the participle *deemed* is no longer used in modern legislative drafting in Australia, provisions containing conclusive presumptions are commonly referred to as *deeming* provisions.[52] In addition, the participle *deemed* is used as a pre-modifying attribute, suggesting that the following noun must be accepted to be true. This is illustrated by Section 82 of the British Health and Social Care Act 2012: the conclusive presumption regarding the licence holder in subsection (2) is expressed as *deemed breach* used in the section heading:

Example 8

'82 *Deemed* breach of requirement to be licensed

(1) This section applies where a licence holder –

(a) in providing a health care service for the purposes of the NHS, carries on a regulated activity (within the meaning of Part 1 of the Health and Social Care Act 2008), but

(b) is not registered under Chapter 2 of Part 1 of that Act in respect of the carrying on of that activity.

(2) The licence holder *is to be regarded* as providing the service in breach of the requirement under section 81 to hold a licence.'

Irrebuttable or conclusive presumptions in the Czech Code are indicated by the verbal phrase "platí, že", literally translated as "it applies that". However, this phrase, if used in certain provisions of the Code, need not unequivocally imply a conclusive presumption. One more possibility to express this type of presumption seems to be useful for translators, namely using the phrase *be/is conclusively presumed to*; for legally literate readers, its interpretive potential is semantically reduced to an irrebuttable presumption. The phrasing is shown in two examples of statutory provisions:

51 *Black's Law Dictionary* (2009: 1305).
52 Private correspondence of the author of the chapter.

Example 9

A. '(3) This section does not apply in relation to any articles or products in respect of which, at the time when they were sold, let for hire or offered or exposed for sale or hire, the corresponding design concerned was excluded from registration by regulations made under the Designs Act 1906 or the Designs Act 2003, and, for the purposes of any proceedings under this Act, a design shall *be conclusively presumed* to have been so excluded if: . . .' (Section 77 of the Australian Copyright Act 1968, as amended)

B. '(3) Where an advertisement is published which indicates, or might reasonably be understood as indicating –
that employment to which the advertisement relates is open only to a person who is, or is not, a member of a trade union, . . .

a person who does not satisfy that condition . . ., and who seeks and is refused employment to which the advertisement relates, *shall be conclusively presumed* to have been refused employment for that reason.' (Section 137 of the British Trade Union and Labour Relations Act 1992)

The third category of legal presumptions encompasses legal fiction. A legal fiction is a statement about some event or occurrence that is not true as a matter of historical fact but that is accepted as true for the convenience of administering a legal rule in a given context or for the broader policies underlying the law (Bouvier 2011: 849). Or, as explained by a former British Parliamentary Counsel, 'a fiction is an artificial way of proceeding (and therefore in general to be avoided) but is sometimes justified; it is often a short way of applying a whole body of existing law or producing a legal result that would otherwise be difficult to express or involve tedious length.'[53] He provides two examples from recent British legislation:

Example 10

A. '(2) The amendment made by this section *is treated as* having come into force on 16 January 2012, but, in relation to any time before 22 November 2012, section 987A of CTA 2010 *has effect as if* paragraph (a) were omitted.' (Section 38 of the Finance Act 2013)

B. '5. A consular marriage *is valid in law as if* the marriage had been solemnized in the relevant part of the United Kingdom with a due observance of all forms required by the law of the relevant part of the United Kingdom.' (Schedule 6 of the Marriage (Same Sex Couples) Act 2013)

It should be noted, however, that the phrase *is treated as* is considered as expressing a conclusive presumption in the OPC AU mentioned above. On the other hand, the Legislative Drafting Manual of the United States Senate (1997: 72) instructs drafters to use *shall be treated as* (along with *is deemed to be*, or *is considered to be*) for a legal fiction. There is no need, for the purposes of translation, to analyze and identify the fluid legal line between a conclusive presumption and a legal fiction. Translators are usually guided by the phrases in the source text they intend to translate into English. Drafters of the Czech Civil Code have declared two phrases to express a legal fiction, either "hledí se na" (literary translated as "is seen as") or

53 Geoffrey Sellers, former Parliamentary Counsel, the Office of the Parliamentary Counsel, the Cabinet Office, London, UK; the explanation is taken from private correspondence of the author of the chapter.

"považuje se za" (literally translated as "is considered as"). It appears to be impossible to identify any contextual rule (whether legal or semantic) in the Czech Code why the former phrase is used in a particular provision and why the latter in another provision. The drafters in their commentary to the Code have not indicated any traceable pattern. Should translators follow the same "dual" approach, there are more English phrases available: *is treated as*, or *is regarded as*, or is *considered to be*. Due to syntactic structures in the Czech Code denoting legal fictions, the phrases *be valid as if* or *have effect as if* seem unlikely to be used as an equivalent in the translation of the Czech Code into English. Moreover, purely semantically, they are closer to the Czech phrase "platí, že" declared to express a conclusive presumption in the Czech Code.

In conclusion, having analyzed all three of the legal presumptions as expressed in English, we have selected the following phrases for the translation of the Czech Code; the sections referred to are sections in the Czech Civil Code:[54]

> Rebuttable presumption *is presumed to* as in Section 4:
> 'Every legally competent individual *is presumed to have* the reason of an average person and the ability to use it with ordinary care and diligence, and everyone may reasonably expect this in legal transactions.'
>
> Irrebuttable presumption *is taken to* or *is conclusively presumed to* as in Section 436:
> 'A person empowered to make juridical acts on behalf of another, is a representative of that person; the representation gives rise to rights and duties directly for the person represented. If it is not apparent that a person is acting on behalf of another, the person *is taken to / conclusively presumed to* be acting on his or her own behalf.'
>
> Legal fiction *is regarded as* as in Subsection 1043(2) and *is considered to be* as in Section 681:
> '(2) If the right of ownership has been acquired by one person gratuitously and by another for value, the gratuitous acquisition *is regarded as* the weaker ground.'
> 'A marriage *is considered to be* valid unless judicially declared invalid. If a marriage has been declared invalid it *is considered as* having never been contracted.'

It would be advisable for translators of the Czech Civil Code into English to make explicit comments in the translation (as an introductory part or footnote on the first page or the first occurrence of any of the three presumptions) on the linguistic manner in which rebuttable and irrebuttable presumptions and legal fictions are to be phrased in English. Explanatory (interpretive) remarks in this regard would direct the ultimate recipient of the translated Code to the proper interpretation of its provisions in English.

3.3.1.4. "RATHER THAN"

In English, the quasi-coordinator[55] *rather than* is most frequently used in two meanings: (1) in comparative forms for saying that one thing (action, event) is preferred to another (e.g., We should focus on quality rather than on quantity.); and (2) having the prepositional role of *instead of*, or as a conjunction, in saying that one thing, action, or event, and not the other, is, was, or will be relevant (e.g., happy rather than angry). Interpretation of either meaning is supported by the context. In legal contexts, the second meaning (X not Z) absolutely prevails

54 We would like to thank Geoffrey Sellers for all valuable comments regarding the wording of the translated provisions as may be perceived by a common law lawyer.

55 Quirk et al. (1992: 982).

and the first meaning is absent in legislation. Usage is shown in both legislative provisions (Example 11) and other legal texts (Example 12):

Example 11

'(2) A person may be regarded as having abused his position even though his conduct consisted of an omission *rather than* an act.' (Section 4 of the British Fraud Act 2006)

'(1) . . . (b) the matter needs to be dealt with urgently, or there is some other compelling reason for the matter being dealt with at the directors' meeting, *rather than* by a general meeting called under subsection 195(4).' (Section 196 of the Australian Corporations Act 2001)

Whilst *rather than* shown in A has a prepositional character and theoretically might be replaced by *instead of*, in B it enables an elliptical usage of a subordinate clause without a verb ("*rather than* [being dealt with] by a general meeting"). Whatever grammatical expression it may acquire, the function of *rather than* is rejection in all the four provisions, i.e., "X and not Y".

Example 12

'. . . malice is an essential element of, for example, conspiracy which requires proof of an intention to injure the claimant *rather than* to promote the defendant's legitimate interests.'[56]

'The Limitations Act "bars" (*rather than* completely discharges) a right of action if the promisee fails to assert it within the time specified.'[57]

The parts after *rather than* in both sentences refer to an earlier assumption which is rejected; hence *rather than* is again equivalent to "and not".

There are just three occurrences in the Czech Civil Code where *rather than* would be used in its English translation for the Czech combined conjunction "spíše než". The only meaning in Czech is that something should be perceived as more likely than something else, i.e., expressing preference. The following provision is Section 574 of the Czech Code: its Czech wording and the literal translation in parentheses are under A; the final translation into English is under B.

Example 13

'Na právní jednání je třeba *spíše* hledět jako na platné *než* jako na neplatné.'
(Literal translation: It is necessary to see juridical acts as valid rather than invalid.)

'Juridical acts should be construed as valid *rather than* invalid.'

This provision declares a general principle that legal transactions are to be considered primarily as valid. However, the tenor of the Czech provision may be confusing for translators as "je třeba hledět" semantically implies recommendation rather than a duty. Moreover, the verb "hledět na" is designated by the drafter of the Czech Code as denoting a legal fiction, which is definitely not applicable to this particular section (thus indicating its inconsistent use by drafters).

56 Riches et al. (2009: 331).
57 Smyth et al. (2004: 133).

As can be seen in B, the implied declaratory character of the provision is preserved in "should be construed"; in addition, "should" may be replaced with "is to be" and other verbs may stand for "construe" (e.g., interpret, consider). As a result, we can create propositional synonyms "is to be interpreted", "should be considered", etc.

The following two uses are in Sections 1258 under A, and 1747 under B. Its preferential nature is strengthened by its position as part of rebuttable presumptions; unless evidence proves to the contrary, the determinant before *rather than* applies.

Example 14

> 'Where the content or scope of servitude is not expressly determined, the content or scope is determined in compliance with local custom; should there be no local custom the scope and content are presumed to be less *rather than* more.'
>
> 'In a gratuitous contract, the debtor is presumed to have intended to be obligated less *rather than* more.'

It should be noted that the interpretation of these two clauses might be perceived as unusual by a common law lawyer, not because of the improper translation, but because of the civil law substance of these provisions.

Although the strict semantic and legal content of the Czech "spíše než" differs from the prevailing legal interpretation of *rather than* in English, this jurilinguistic discrepancy should not lead to improper application of the provisions if the English version is relied on. The provision in Example 13 is a declaration of a generally known and accepted principle. The understanding of the other two provisions in Example 14 would depend on the contextual interpretation of rebuttable presumptions whose formulation includes *rather than*.

3.3.2. Conceptual Analysis

Many lawyers practising locally and having limited contact with foreign law tend to confine the language of law to terminology. The more they communicate with legal professionals from other countries in languages and legal systems that are foreign to them, the more they realize that terminology creates only part of the legal language (no more than 30 per cent in legislation[58]). In informal, verbal interaction, if lawyers or any other partners in communication do not know a proper term in another language, they can replace it with a conceptual explanation, definition, or situational description. Exceptionally, and in some contexts (usually when the source and target legal systems and languages are not remote), a loan translation (or calque) of a source language term might help. However, translators of written legal texts should be as precise and accurate as possible in the selection of equivalent terms and should not resort to approaches acceptable in informal discussions.

Attaining equivalence in the translation of legal terms in legislation should follow the conceptual analysis of a particular term. Translation may not only require a comparative conceptual analysis of the source term and its potential equivalent in the target language and/or legal system, but also comparative research into the wider extra-linguistic and possibly extra-legal context. Concepts as mental representations (units of knowledge) are essentially context-bound. Terms, strictly speaking, are their spelling or sound forms (lexical units). Šarčević (2000: 238) divides content elements of a legal concept into essential and accidental.

58 Cf. Chromá (2004: 16).

Measuring the extent and proportion of both types of elements she determines (a) 'near equivalence' (a source language concept and its selected target language equivalent share all essential and most accidental elements); (b) 'partial equivalence' (the concepts share most essential and only some accidental elements); and (c) 'non-equivalence' (concepts in the source language and target language share a few or none of their essential elements and no accidental characteristics). Measuring what is "most" and "a few", and whether "all" means absolutely all characteristics, usually depends on the experience of translators and their ability to identify the elements in respective concepts. Decision-making is often quite hard should we consider philosophical and conceptual differences between, for example, common law and continental law and between languages conveying either legal system.

A conceptual analysis in legal translation starts with identifying the concept in source law represented by a respective source language term. Translators then attempt to find a corresponding concept in the target law and a relevant term in the TL, or they may guess what a suitable term in the target language may be and identify the concept behind it. Next, the translators should decide, balancing the essential and accidental elements of the source and equivalent concepts, whether the required conceptual equivalence has been, or can be, achieved. If not, the translators would determine whether any substitute steps should be taken to convey the message from the ST to the TT in an intended manner determined by the purpose of translation. Substitute steps usually include selecting a suitable functional term, i.e. a term having the same function in the target legal system as the SL term has in the source legal system, but semantically they need not correspond. Non-equivalence could be compensated for by an explanatory or descriptive equivalent.

The new Czech Civil Code has introduced many new concepts and older concepts that revive the central European legal tradition in Czech private law. Thus the primary orientation in searching for relevant English equivalents would be towards authentic English texts governing continental law as has been already explained in Section 3.1 of this chapter.

The following selection of Czech terms to be translated into English are just a marginal sample of terminology created to illustrate the approach to the conceptual analysis of potential equivalents of Czech terms spread over 3,080 sections of the Code. The first four examples show a conceptual analysis and/or clarification of the meaning of the Czech terms; as soon as the meaning is clear, their English counterparts can be easily found. The other Czech terms must be subject to a comparative conceptual analysis in both languages and legal systems. The heading of each part (1 to 15) is composed of a Czech term and its section in the Czech Code (in parentheses), followed by its German (G) and French (F) terminological counterpart, if available and applicable.

1. "Právní osobnost" (§15); G – Rechtsfähigkeit; F – personnalité juridique

In the 1964 Civil Code, the same concept was termed 'způsobilost mít práva a povinnosti' (literally the 'capacity to have rights and duties'); 'právní subjektivita' was used for the same concept in legal theory. As declared by the drafters of the new Code, the reason for introducing this new Czech term was to depart from the socialist terminology of private law heavily influenced by Russian concepts and terms. Both former Czech terms were regularly translated as *legal personality*. The English term is a precise equivalent of the newly introduced Czech term, and one may presume that it should pose no problem for translators to select the right English equivalent. In such a situation, translators should realize that the Czech concept was simply "renamed" and that they should preserve for the "new" Czech term the English equivalent of the former. The only decision translators should make regarding the English equivalent is whether to use *legal personality* or *juridical*[59] *personality*. The former seems to be prevalent in original common law contexts, whilst the latter seems to prevail in continental law English and various translations into English.

2. "Svéprávnost" (§15); G – Geschäftsfähigkeit; F – capacité

This term was used in Czech legislation before World War II and, as such, reintroduced into the new Czech Code in order to free legal Czech from the socialist terminology of the Russian origin. It is to replace "způsobilost k právním úkonům" (literally the "capacity to make legal acts"), which was ordinarily translated as *legal capacity* or *legal competence*. These English terms will continue to serve as equivalents for the reintroduced "svéprávnost", and translators should be aware that the concept once again remains the same. It is only the linguistic designation that has changed, and the English equivalents need not be altered.

3. "Dočasný vlastník" (§1303)

What is confusing in this terminological phrase is the premodifying attribute 'dočasný'. The phrase is literally translated as *temporary owner*, which makes no legal sense in the context of the provision. The Czech phrase originated in the beginning of the 19th century when the first commentaries on the Austrian ABGB were published in Czech. At that time, the meaning of "dočasný" in general Czech was "existing at the time of the action". However, the meaning has significantly shifted over almost two centuries and today it is perceived exclusively as *temporary*. Translators relying on their interpretation of the language of the provision would hardly suspect that "dočasný" has any meaning other than what they are used to in other Czech legal texts. Section 1110 in the German BGB dealing with a similar issue and translated into English speaks about *current owner*, which can be freely used as an equivalent phrase for translating the Czech phrase into English. Another possibility is to use just *the owner* without any attribute, since the context of the provision implies what owner is meant.

4. "Doložení času" (§550)

Not only literal but also regular translation of this phrase is *proving time*. However, such an interpretation would make little or no sense in many provisions. It was necessary again to trace the earlier meanings of "doložení" in Czech legal texts (along with its verbal and attributive forms "doložit" and "doložený") in phrases with "čas" (*time*). The usage before World War II quite clearly shows that the legal meaning of the whole phrase was *stipulating time*, which would be a suitable equivalent in English (allowing for its forms as a verb and participle).

5. "Opatrovník" (§457); "poručník" (§928); G – Pflegschaft, Vormund; F – curateur, tuteur

These legal concepts, as applied in Czech law and most continental jurisdictions, originated in Roman law as "cura" (instituting "opatrovník") and "tutela" (instituting "poručník"). The Czech Code provides that if a child has no parents a court appoints a "poručník" to stand "in loco parentis" in order to exercise duties collectively termed "parental responsibility" (i.e., to raise a child, to act as the child's statutory representative, and to manage the child's property). The concept of "opatrovník" is wider as it applies to both minors and adults incapable of caring for their person or property. The appointment of an "opatrovník" is more restrictive (including its duration) as it applies to a particular assignment. Most frequently, a court appoints an "opatrovník" for procedural issues (*ad litem*) if there is no statutory representative to defend the person's rights.

59 Law dictionaries (e.g., *Black's*, *Bouvier*, or *Curzon's*) suggest that the primary meaning of *juridical* relates to the administration of justice or judicial proceedings.

Having analyzed various sources, a terminological split between common law English and continental law English can be seen. The Louisiana Civil Code and the Quebec Civil Code distinguish between *curator* and *tutor*, and their definitions correspond to those of "opatrovník" and "poručník" respectively. Interestingly, the English translation of the BGB uses the dichotomy of *guardian* for "Vormund" and *curator* for "Pflegschaft". The same approach to English equivalence was chosen in the 1898 translation of the Japanese Civil Code, in the 1866 translation of the Austrian ABGB (using "Kurator" to mean "Pflegschaft"), and in the translation of the Dutch Civil Code (Warendorf). *Black's Law Dictionary* defines the term *curator* (as understood in continental law) as 'a guardian who manages the estate of a minor, an absent person, or an incapacitated person'. The term *tutor* (applicable to continental law) is explained as 'a guardian of a minor appointed to have the care of the minor's person and estate'. Entries relating to *guardian* in *Black's* clearly suggest that, in common law, this term contextually covers both concepts distinctly designated in continental law. Considering the potential *guardian*'s interpretive ambiguity, our solution is to maintain the English terminology of continental law (as used in Louisiana or Quebec), i.e., *curator* for the Czech "opatrovník" (including *curator ad litem* for Czech "kolizní opatrovník"), and *tutor* for "poručník". The respective terms will be *curatorship* and *tutorship*. Since the Czech Code uses different designations of the other parties to those relationships ("opatrovanec" and "poručenec"), it would be logical to refer to them as *person under curatorship* and *person under tutorship* in order to indicate the specific type of relationship. Using one (common law) term, *ward*, for both types may be quite confusing, particularly when the Czech Code provides for various aspects of both concepts in one clause.

6. "Fundace" (§303); G – Fundation

The drafters of the Code use this archaic[60] Czech word to institute a new generic term covering all (in fact, two) legal entities established by property endowed and assigned for a particular purpose, and not by an association of persons. Etymologically, the term dates back to medieval Czech. It not only designates money or property bestowed on an institution with a specifically declared objective, but also serves as a synonym for *foundation*. In addition, the Code subdivides "fundace" into "nadace", traditionally translated as *foundation*, and "nadační fond", traditionally translated as *endowment fund*. It practically means that no entity will have the word "fundace" in its name, and the term just designates the legal type of entity as opposed to *corporation*. Neither the codes we have worked with (whether originally drafted or translated), nor the law dictionaries provide a generic term covering both foundations and endowment funds. Thus the English equivalent should be tailored from words whose combination can serve as a statutory term and essentially transfer the meaning of the Czech term, namely *endowed institution*.

7. "Rozhrady" (§1024); G – Abmarkungen; F – mitoyenneté)

The Czech term "rozhrady" (the plural form of "rozhrada") has been reintroduced into private law after a lapse of sixty years, during which time it almost disappeared from general Czech as well. It is a generic designation covering fences, walls, bounds, ditches and similar natural objects and artificial arrangements indicating a boundary between plots of land. *Black's Law Dictionary* defines *boundary* as 'a natural or artificial separation that delineates the confines of real property', giving an example of a creek serving as a boundary between the two properties. The translation (1898) of the Japanese Civil Code (§229) provides for 'boundary marks, fences, walls and ditches made on the boundary line . . .', apparently distinguishing between *boundary marks* on the one hand and fences, walls and ditches on the other. The English translation

60 Used in formal Czech before WWII; however, the term was missing in the draft Civil Code of 1937, as even then it was perceived as obsolete.

of the BGB uses two terms, i.e., *boundary marker* in §919, and *boundary installations* in §921 ('a space, border, corner, a ditch, a wall, hedge, fence or another structure'). Article 784 of the Louisiana Civil Code seems to provide some terminological clarification: 'A boundary is the line of separation between contiguous lands. A boundary marker is a natural or artificial object that marks on the ground the line of separation of contiguous lands.' The Austrian ABGB (1856 translation) prefers *landmark* to *boundary marker* and uses the singular of *boundary* in the abstract meaning of the border around a parcel. Section 854 provides for '[f]urrows, fences, hedges, planking, walls, private brooks, canals, places and other similar *partitions* [Scheidewände], which are to be found between neighbouring parcels of ground . . .'. From a purely semantic perspective, the Czech *rozhrady* and English *partitions* are fully equivalent. However, the drawback of the term *partitions* to serve as a statutory term (including a section heading) in the translation of the Czech Civil Code is that this plural form is quite rarely (if at all) found in this particular meaning in legal contexts. The usual legal understanding of *partition* is the division of co-owned property into separate assets for each owner, which is not relevant in section 1024 of the Czech Code. Thus, it is advisable to use a functional equivalent (i.e., a semantically different term with the same jurilinguistic function in the given context), such as *boundaries*. The translated provision would then read: 'Fences, walls, bounds, ditches and other similar *natural or artificial boundaries* between neighbouring plots are presumed to be common.' The section heading would be *Boundaries*.

8. "Přestavek" (§1087); G – Überbau; F – empiètement (in Quebec)

The literal translation would be 'building over'. Conceptually, it means a situation where an inconsiderable part of a structure encroaches upon the neighbouring plot of land. There are similar provisions in the Louisiana Civil Code ('a landowner constructs in good faith a building that encroaches on an adjacent estate'), the Quebec Civil Code ('an owner has, in good faith, built beyond the limits of his land on a parcel of land belonging to another'), and the German BGB ('the owner of a plot of land, when erecting a building, built over the boundary, but this was neither intentional nor the result of gross negligence, the neighbour must tolerate the encroachment'). The act of encroachment (an interference with or intrusion onto another's property) is considered primary in formulating relevant provisions in all the three codes. The Czech term "přestavek" (also the section heading) expresses that a structure has been "over-built", i.e., designates the technological, not legal, aspect of the action. In order to make the interpretation of the Czech provision in English clearer, the legal substance should be preferred in translation, and the wording of the provision of the Czech Code may read: 'Where a permanent structure built on his or her own land by the owner encroaches upon a small part of the neighbouring plot, the *encroached part* of the neighbouring plot becomes the property of the owner of the permanent structure; this does not apply to an owner who has not erected the structure in good faith.' The phrase *encroached part* elliptically stands for 'a part covered by an over-built portion of the structure', which would be a literal translation from Czech. 'Přestavek' in the section heading may simply be *Encroachment*, indicating an unlawful act by its nature which should be legally tolerated under certain circumstances.

9. "Právo stavby" (§1240); G – Erbbaurecht; F – droit de superficie (Switzerland)

This term literally means "the right of building". It is a special right *in rem*, held by a builder, entitling the builder to erect a structure on or below the surface of a plot of land of another. The right may be created for a maximum of 99 years and is to be recorded in the Land Register. The right may be acquired by a contract, acquisitive prescription, or by the decision of a public authority. Moreover, the Code stipulates that this right is immovable property. The Quebec Civil Code contains many provisions governing *superficies* (a Latin term denoting a special real right to the structures and plantings on a plot of land owned by another). The same term is used in the 1898 translation of the Japanese Civil Code. The Dutch Civil Code (Book 5, Art. 101) provides for the *right of superficies* (to own or to acquire buildings, works or vegetation in, on or above an immovable thing owned by another). Both concepts by nature are close to the Czech term in that it is a right relating to the land or the surface of the land of another. What significantly differs is that the Czech right is confined just to the activity of building (constructing) something on the land of another, or to the result of such activity (a permanent structure for any purpose). Moreover, the right need not be exercised at all and may be an object of inheritance. Considering all features of the Czech concept, the English equivalent of the term "právo stavby" should be tailored to cover two essential elements—a type of superficies confined to building, i.e., a *superficiary right of building*.

10. "Reálné břemeno" (§1303); G – Reallast

The Czech Code reorganizes the structure of rights to use and control the land of another: there is the generic term of *easement* covering all rights (and relating duties) of that type, which is subdivided into *servitudes* and "reálné břemeno". Whilst a *servitude* is defined as a duty of the owner of a servient plot to suffer activities of the owner of the dominant land (i.e., not to do anything and to remain passive), a "reálné břemeno" binds an owner of the servient land to do or to provide something for the benefit of the owner of a thing subject to the "reálné břemeno". In this respect, it is a personal right, and not a real right. Examples are to keep a well in good repair for another owner or to provide a portion of harvest or timber to the entitled owner. A person benefitting from a "reálné břemeno" is entitled to performance. The person has a right to compensation only if, for any reason, the performance has been defaulted. Should the compensation not be paid, the thing to which the "reálné břemeno" is attached may subsequently be subject to garnishment. The legal classification contained in the Czech Code is not similar to that in the Louisiana Civil Code or the Quebec Civil Code. Both provide that, under *servitude*, 'the owner of the servient estate is not required to do anything. His obligation is to abstain from doing something on his estate or to permit something to be done on it.' (LA, Art. 651). This is a definition fully corresponding to the Czech "služebnost". The English translation of the Austrian ABGB (§482) uses the term *easement* [Dienstbarkeiten, Servituten] in the meaning of *servitude*, preferred in Louisiana and Quebec. The same terminological preference (*easement*) can be traced in the Dutch Civil Code (Book 5, Art. 70–84), stipulating only a duty to suffer something or refrain from doing something. The German concept of "Reallast" in the BGB (§§1105–1111), translated as *charge on land*, corresponds to the Czech "reálné břemeno", in that 'recurring acts of performance are to be made from the plot of land to the person in whose favour the encumbrance is created' (§1105 BGB). The German 'Subjektiv-persönliche Reallast' as a charge on land existing in favour of a particular person (§1111) is a *personal charge on land* in English. The equivalent *charge on land* with any premodifier, if used outside the BGB, would be correctly interpreted under the BGB only if appended with the relevant definition. The meaning of *charge on land* varies among common law jurisdictions. The *Bouvier Law Dictionary* explains it as an obligation amounting to a lien on a parcel of land (as security). *Black's Law Dictionary* provides seven meanings of *charge* with just one in the area of property law, namely an encumbrance, lien, or claim (with respect to property). The British Land Charges Act of 1972 provides for six classes (A to F) of more or less historically determined land charges (such as rent, annuity, puisne mortgage, an owner's charge, equitable charge, restrictive covenants, and equitable easements), none of which approximates the meaning of the Czech "reálné břemeno" or the German "Reallast", but all of which denote some kind of encumbrance of real property. The legal meaning of the common law term *charge* is much wider as it serves more as a generic term covering all types of burden imposed upon (real) property. Considering all of the jurilinguistic circumstances, it appears quite clear that any reasonable English equivalent for "reálné břemeno" may be chosen or tailored in the English translation of the Czech Civil Code as the Code contains the definition of the concept. However, if the English equivalent is chosen from English terms existing in common law and is used in legal documents drafted in English and derived from the Czech Civil Code, such equivalent should always be appended with the relevant part of the explanation of the concept behind the English term, distinguishing this concept from whatever may exist in common law, such as "the duty to do or to give something". One more aspect seems to be relevant in selecting an English equivalent, i.e., a certain degree of terminological consistency in explaining continental law or central European law in English. Since the concept of "reálné břemeno" is identical with the German "Subjektiv-persönliche Reallast", and there is a quality English translation of the BGB, it would be advisable to use the same term—*personal charge on land*—for the translation of the Czech term "reálné břemeno".

11. "Závdavek" (§1808); G – Angeld, Angabe; F – arrhes

This is an old Roman law concept ("arha") meaning money given as evidence of a completed bargain. The concept is encompassed in most continental jurisdictions. It is regulated in the Louisiana Civil Code, but missing from the Civil Code of Quebec. The triple purpose of this concept in Czech law is (a) to serve as proof that a contract has been made, (b) to secure the obligations of the contract (as a security deposit), and (c) to serve as a penalty should a party, which has provided the "arha", fail to perform its part of the contract (in such case, the defaulting party is obliged to return to the innocent party double the amount of the deposit). The Austrian ABGB (§908, translation of 1856) and the LA Civil Code (Art. 2624) use *earnest money*. The German BGB (§336) prefers *earnest* as the equivalent. *Black's Law Dictionary* provides two separate entries for *earnest* and *earnest money*. The term *earnest* (with the first known occurrence in the 13th century) is defined in one meaning as 'a nominal payment or token that serves as a pledge or a sign of good faith, especially as the partial purchase price of property'. Its second meaning is identical with *earnest money*, i.e., these two terms may be entirely synonymous in some contexts. The term *earnest money* (dating back to the 16th century) is defined as 'a deposit paid (often in escrow) by a prospective buyer (especially of real estate) to show a good faith intention to complete the transaction, and ordinarily forfeited if the buyer defaults; . . . in the real estate context it is generally a percentage of the purchase price . . .' *Black's* provides synonyms for *earnest money*, such as *bargain money*, *caution money* (where *caution* means the security given), or *hand money*. The *Bouvier Law Dictionary* adds one more synonym—*down payment*, and explains the concept as 'a deposit made as partial payment of a contract'. Considering all nuances in the definitions, our preference would be *earnest money* because of its wider semantic application.

12. "Výprosa" (§2189); G – Bittleihe; F – prêt précaire

This reintroduced Czech law term comes from the Roman law *precarium*. It is very close to the contract of *borrowing* in that a lender provides to the borrower, for free, a non-consumable thing which must be returned to the lender. What differs from an ordinary borrowing is the indeterminate time in *precarium*, which means that the contract terminates at the will of the lender. *Black's Law Dictionary* defines *precarium* as: (1) a gratuitous grant of the enjoyment of property, revocable at will; and (2) the property so granted. It also provides the term *precarious loan* for (1) a loan that may be recalled at any time; and (2) a loan in danger of not being repaid. The attribute *precarious* in general English tends to suggest something uncertain, insecure or unstable. However, what is "uncertain" in its combination with "loan" is only the time by which the thing borrowed should be returned to the lender. The Austrian ABGB (§974) uses in both the German text and its English translation the word *precarium* (in German alternatively "Bittleihe (Precarium)"); in the English translation, only "*precarium*" is used in inverted commas). The German BGB contains no concept of "Bittleihe". There are a few ways of ascertaining an English equivalent for the Czech "výprosa": (1) As the concept is unusual in common law, the Latin *precarium* may be preserved in English translation; (2) The term *precarious loan* may be used with the risk of the concept being incorrectly interpreted as the second meaning of this phrase provided above (i.e., a loan in danger of not being repaid); and (3) The essential elements of the concepts are determined and translated accordingly: the act is gratuitous, it is a type of loan, and may be revoked at any time by the lender. As a result, a *gratuitous loan at will* would be coined and could be easily distinguished from another gratuitous loan, namely a *loan for use* (Latin *commodatum* applicable to non-consumable things but with the time fixed; in Czech "výpůjčka" in §2193 of the Czech Code), and from a *simple loan* (Latin *mutuum* applicable to money or other fungible goods; in Czech "zápůjčka" in §2390 of the Czech Code).

13. "Pacht" (§2332); G – Pacht; F – bail emphytéotique

This traditional central European concept has been reintroduced into Czech private law after a lapse of more than 70 years. However, it should be noted that an object of the Czech "pacht", as restored in the new Civil Code, may be any thing, whether movable or immovable, corporeal or incorporeal, and not just land which was traditionally presumed in Roman law under *emphyteusis*.

The Austrian ABGB regulates "Pacht" in Sections 1091 and the following. In its 1856 translation, the term *lease* is used as an English equivalent. The German BGB provides for "Pacht" in Sections 581 and the following; the English equivalent is *usufructuary lease*. In Louisiana and Quebec, the concept of "Pacht" seems to be concealed within their term *conventional usufruct*. The 1898 translation of the Japanese Code uses the term *emphyteusis* (with *emphyteuta* as a designation for the person) for 'a right to carry on agriculture or cattle raising on the land of another on payment of a rent'. The translators of the Dutch Civil Code (Warendorf et al.) use *agricultural lease* as an equivalent for the Dutch "Pacht" (Art. 311 of Book 7). *Black's Law Dictionary* explains *emphyteusis* as where 'one person delivers to another (*emphyteuta*) a tract of land, either in perpetuity or for a long period of time, in exchange for the obligation to cultivate the land and to pay annual rental'. *Usufruct* is defined as 'a right for a certain period to use and enjoy the fruits of another's property without damaging or diminishing it, but allowing for any natural deterioration in the property over time'.

Considering the essential elements of the Czech "pacht", namely a lease of a thing, whether movable or immovable, the right not only to use, but also to enjoy the thing (i.e., to take civil and natural fruits) as it is in *usufruct*, the equivalent used for "Pacht" in the translation of the BGB—*usufructuary lease*—appears to be a suitable English equivalent for the Czech "pacht". In addition, it allows for terminological extensions: *usufructuary lessor* for the Czech "propachtovatel", *usufructuary lessee* for "pachtýř", and *usufructuary rent* for "pachtovné", although where the context explicitly indicates that *usufructuary lease* is involved, the parties would be simply called *lessor* and *lessee*, and the money paid in return would be referred to as *rent*.

14. "Výměnek" (§2707); G – Ausgedinge; F – vente en viager (both are only partial equivalents)

Historically, this concept resembled that of the Austrian or German "Ausgedinge". Whilst the content of the German concept has narrowed and it is implied in different legal terms today, the reintroduced "výměnek" in the new Czech Civil Code remains conceptually intact. The Code provides for two types of contract under a generic heading of 'Purveyance Contracts'. These are (a) an annuity contract (as an agreement by which a party binds itself to make periodic payments to a designated recipient), and (b) a contract of "výměnek". The latter denotes a contract whereby the owner of an immovable, as a transferor, reserves for itself or a third person the right to civil or natural fruits, certain performance or purveyance, for the duration of life or for a fixed period of time, and the transferee agrees to provide them. Such a right becomes effective upon the transfer of the immovable to the transferee. It may include the right of dwelling in a marginal part of the house transferred (similar to the British "granny's flat" or German "Altenteil"), providing certain services (such as attending the transferor in regular intervals) or supplying certain goods (such as one ton of potatoes from the transferred farm once a year). As there is no suitable English term in original laws drafted in English or in English translations of legislation, it appears to be unavoidable to coin a new term which would suggest at least some essential elements of the Czech concept. The substance of the concept consists of the right arising from a contract, created as a reservation (i.e., set aside for a specific purpose), with the primary purpose of taking fruits from the transfer of the immovable. As a result, there may be a term *contractual (conventional) reservation of usufruct;* another possibility could be a *contractually (conventionally) reserved usufruct.* Alternatively, *usufruct* could be replaced with *(the) right of enjoyment.* However in all cases, the contextualizing attributes *contractual* (*conventional*) or *contractually (conventionally)* may be eliminated as the wording of the statutory provision in the Czech Code expressly determines the contractual framework of the reservation.

15. "Společnost" (§2716); G – Gesellschaft; F – société

This Czech term will undoubtedly lead to confusion not only with translators but also with the Czech-speaking public. The reason for such confusion would be that there is one Czech term "společnost" having three legal meanings: (a) a society as a community of people with a common culture, traditions, etc.; (b) a type of incorporated business entity; and now also (c) a conventional association of persons aimed at achieving common purposes, but not possessing legal personality. In the 1964 Civil Code, a similar grouping was termed "sdružení" and was traditionally translated as *association*. Nevertheless, the new Czech Civil Code provides a wider definition and requires that the English equivalent be revised. Both the ABGB and the BGB use *partnership* in their English translation of "Gesellschaft". "Maatschap" in the Dutch Civil Code (Art. 1655, Book 7A) is also *partnership* in its English version. The official English translation of the French Civil Code (posted on the website of the French Ministry of Justice) uses *firm* for "société" in Art. 1832. It should be noted that the English word *firm* usually denotes entities having the legal form of a partnership. However, the Quebec Civil Code (§2186) distinguishes between a *partnership* and an *association* in that the former is established in order to achieve pecuniary profits, the latter as a not-for-profit entity. In Louisiana, a *partnership* has legal personality. Considering the selection of English terms in original English legislation or equivalents in translations, the term *partnership* and *partner* (Czech "společník") should be used in the translation of the Czech Code. The provision would read: 'Where several persons bind themselves by a contract to associate as partners in order to achieve a common purpose in activities or things, a partnership is established.' In this respect, the interpretation of the English translational equivalent will be easier than the original, ambiguous Czech term "společnost".

4. Conclusion

Translating legal texts from various languages into English has always been a hard task. Although English serves as almost a global language in interaction between partners who are native speakers of other languages and who try to establish working communication, there is not one "uniform" legal English to acquire for translating foreign legislation. Moreover, English as the language of law would always stem from common law since the system of common law is the natural and genuine cradle of legal English.

Translation of legislation into English is even harder as the language of statutes (whether original or translated) should be clear, unambiguous, formally transparent, consistent and semantically predictable in order to facilitate their uniform interpretation and subsequent uniform application. Rules for and approaches to statutory interpretation may also differ between English-speaking and non-English-speaking jurisdictions. In addition, the first role of translators in the process of legal translation is that of interpreters. Their ability or inability to fully understand the source legal text predetermines the quality of legal translation and its potential for correct interpretation.

The described project deals with the preparatory stage of translation of the new Czech Civil Code into English. Although the Czech Code was declared to be a modern statute of continental private law, it was drafted in a structurally complex language, having its roots in codes drafted in the 19th century and redrafted in the first half of the 20th century. The first task for translators is to understand the various peculiarities of Czech, in combination with understanding the new or reintroduced legal concepts. Next, translators should pursue a comparative jurilinguistic analysis: they should decide what variety of legal English should be used to preserve the underlying philosophy of continental law. This includes studying various original English legislative sources and legislation translated into English. The purpose is to identify the main English legislative drafting rules, i.e., primarily the technical language of legislation. The final step at the preparatory stage of translation is a comparative conceptual analysis in order to identify the conceptual differences between Czech legal terms and their potential English counterparts with the aim of selecting adequate terminological equivalents.

From a quantitative standpoint, the work spent on the analysis took more than one year, with six months of rather intensive research. Our experience suggests that translating provision after provision of 3,080 sections of the Czech Civil Code can take four months as a full time activity (8 hours a day, 5 days a week). It should be followed by, or paralleled with, proofreading and editing by a native English-speaking lawyer who has some experience with Czech law (e.g., practising in the Czech Republic, not necessarily speaking Czech). This requirement is important in order to formulate Czech legal nuances in English in a way that would make sense in English, and at the same time, would approximate the legal sense of the Czech provision.

References

Baaij, C.J.W. (ed.). 2012. *The Role of Legal Translation in Legal Harmonization*. Alphen aan den Rijn: Kluwer Law International.

Bell, J. 1999. 'Statutes, Text and Operative Enactments'. In: Hanneke van Schooten ed. *Semiotics and Legislation*. Liverpool: Deborah Charles Publications, pp. 71–79.

Bennion, F. 2009. *Understanding Common Law Legislation: Drafting and Interpretation*. Oxford: Oxford University Press.

Butt, P. and Castle, R. 2004. *Modern Legal Drafting: A Guide to Using Clearer Language*. Cambridge: Cambridge University Press.

Cao, D. 2007. *Translating Law*. Clevendon, Buffalo, Toronto: Multilingual Matters Ltd.

Charnock, R. 2007. 'Lexical Indeterminacy: Contextualism and Rule-Following in Common Law Adjudication'. In: A. Wagner, W. Werner and D. Cao eds. *Interpretation, Law and the Construction of Meaning*. Dordrecht: Springer, pp. 21–48.

Chromá, M. 2004. *Legal Translation and the Dictionary*. Lexicographica, Series Maior. Tübingen: Max Niemeyer Verlag.

———. 2005. 'Indeterminacy in Criminal Legislation: A Translator's Perspective'. In: V.K. Bhatia, M. Gotti, J. Engberg and D. Heller eds. *Vagueness in Normative Texts*. Linguistic Insights: Studies in Language & Communication. Bern: Peter Lang, pp. 23, 379–412.

De Groot, G.-R. and Van Laer, C.J.P. 2008. 'The Quality of Legal Dictionaries: An Assessment', Unpublished working paper. Maastricht Faculty of Law, p. 6.

Doczekalska, A. 2009. 'Drafting of Translation – Production of Multilingual Legal Texts'. In: F. Olsen, A. Lorz and D. Stein eds. *Translation Issues in Language and Law*. Basingstoke: Palgrave Macmillan, pp. 116–135.

Eversheds LLP. 2011. *Legal Drafting in English: The Big Picture on the Small Print*. London: Eversheds. Available at: http://www.eversheds.com/documents/Legal-drafting-in-English.pdf [Accessed September 2013].

Fillmore, C.J. 1978. 'On the Organization of Semantic Information in the Lexicon'. In: D. Farkas, W.M. Jacobsen and K.W. Todrys eds. *Papers from the Parasession on the Lexicon*. Chicago: Chicago Linguistic Society, pp. 148–173.

Garner, B.A. 1995. *A Dictionary of Modern Legal Usage*. 2nd edn. New York, Oxford: Oxford University Press.

———. 2001. *Legal Writing in Plain English*. Chicago and London: University of Chicago Press.

Jackson, B.S. 1999. 'Legislation in the Semiotics of Law'. In: Hanneke van Schooten ed. *Semiotics and Legislation*. Liverpool: Deborah Charles Publications, pp. 5–26.

Joseph, J.E. 1995. 'Indeterminacy, Translation and the Law'. In: M. Morris ed. *Translation and the Law, American Translators Association Series*, vol. VIII. Amsterdam, Philadelphia: John Benjamins Publishing Company, pp. 13–36.

Kimble, J. 2007. *Lifting the Fog of Legalese: Essays on Plain Language*. Durham, North Carolina: Carolina Academic Press.

Kischel, U. 2009. 'Legal Cultures – Legal Languages'. In: F. Olsen, A. Lorz and D. Stein eds. *Translation Issues in Language and Law*. Basinstoke: Palgrave Macmillan, pp. 7–17.

Lane-Mercier, G. 1997. 'Translating the Untranslatable: The Translator's Aesthetic, Ideological and Political Responsibility', *Target*, vol. 9(1), pp. 43–68.

Nord, C. 1991. *Text Analysis in Translation*. Amsterdam/Atlanta: Rodopi.

Phillips, A. 2003. *Lawyer's Language*. New York: Routledge.

Pym, A. 1996. 'Venuti's Visibility', *Target*, vol. 8(2), pp. 165–177.

Quirk, R., Greenbaum, S., Leech, G. and Svartvik, J. 1992. *A Comprehensive Grammar of the English Language*. London, New York: Longman.

Riches, S. and Allen, V. 2009. *Keenan & Riches' Business Law*. 9th edn. Pearson Education Ltd.

Šarčević, S. 2000. *New Approach to Legal Translation*. The Hague: Kluwer Law International.

Smyth, J.E., Soberman, D.A. and Eason, A.J. 2004. *The Law and Business Administration in Canada*. Pearson Education Canada.

Triebel, V. 2009. 'Pitfalls of English as a Contract Language'. In: F. Olsen, A. Lorz and D. Stein eds. *Translation Issues in Language and Law*. Basinstoke: Palgrave Macmillan, pp. 147–181.

Trosborg, A. 1997. *Rhetorical Strategies in Legal Language: Discourse Analysis of Statutes and Contracts*. Tubingen: Gunter Narr Verlag.

Van Laer, C.J.P. and Van Laer, T. 2007. 'The Shortage of Legal Dictionaries Translating European Languages', *Terminology*, vol. 13(1), pp. 85–92.

Venuti, L. [1995] 2008. *The Translator's Invisibility: A History of Translation*. London, New York: Routledge.

Warendorf, H., Thomas, R. and Curry-Sumner, I. 2009. *The Civil Code of the Netherlands*. Kluwer Law International.

Wagner, A. 2003. 'Translation of the Language of the Common Law into Legal French: Myth or Reality', International Journal for the Semiotics of Law, 16, pp. 177–193 (Kluwer Academic Publishers).

Zoulík, F. 1996. Průvodní zpráva k materiálu „Koncepce nového civilního kodexu" [An explanatory report on the document "The Conception of a new Civil Code"]. Právní praxe 8–9/1996, Vol. XLIV, 582–604 (Praha: Ministerstvo spravedlnosti ČR).

Dictionaries

Black's Law Dictionary. 2009. 9th ed., edited by Bryan Garner, Thomson Reuters.
Bouvier Law Dictionary. 2011. Compact Edition, edited by Stephen M. Sheppard, New York: Wolters Kluwer Law & Business.
Curzon, L.B. 2002. *Dictionary of Law*, 6th ed., Harlow: Pearson Education Limited.

Chapter 17
Multilevel Translation Analysis of a Key Legal Concept: *Persona Juris* and Legal Pluralism

Sandy Lamalle

'The problem of translation and translatability takes on the cosmic dimensions of all existential issues: it encompasses everything.'

(Flusser 2002: 194)

Optics is as much a science of measuring distances as an art of discerning scales. In both cases, it is about adjusting vision. Such is the dynamic of translation—a creative operation in language (Kemp 2008), which can be envisaged as a problem solving action, but also as a whole paradigm (Ost 2008). Through the lenses of legal linguistics, semiotics and theory, different ways of expressing concepts in various legal languages and systems can be focalized with a comparative and plurilinguistic approach to legal institutions (Mattila 2012: 477). Such lenses provide tools for the science and art of translating, allowing "multilevel translation analysis". As importing a new concept can alter or even transform the integrity of the original structure of language (Steiner 1998), it appears that changes occur on different levels. In order to identify the implications of translation at various scales, we need to use different lenses. At each scale, translation operates in a specific way. Fundamentally, the law refers not only to narratives, theories and practices but also, primarily, to representations (Rouland 1991: 182). As a first operation on language, it seems it all begins with the choice of a mode of representation for a legal technique. At that level of translation, a mode of representation is conveyed by a word, which is used as a legal concept. At the next level, the concept can be translated into another legal language or system—'horizontal translation'—, or from a certain field of knowledge to another (from theology to law, for instance)—'vertical translation' (Flusser 2002: 194). Such operations imply changes at different scales. At one level, the concept can be considered relatively to its 'family of operative notions' or 'performative structure' (Gémar 1995: 93), which situates it within a certain frame of logic and reasoning. At another level, the concept can be seen in the context of the legal theory from which it arose. This level of translation is concerned with the transplantation of a legal theory into a certain doctrine, in the same or another language or legal system. It requires the study of the general context containing the legal theory (MacCormick 1984: 131).

In the same way that a pattern of fractals at multiple scales may reveal a multidimensional picture, there is a key legal concept whose mode of representation and performative structure have shaped the landscape of modern western legal theory. Its original legal formulation was in Latin, designating a free citizen in Roman law. Its first denomination is *persona juris*—the conceptual ancestor of modern legal personality. According to Auerbach's modes of representing reality in western literature, its first translation as a legal tool combined two opposite modes of legal symbolization: the so-called Homeric style, defined as instrumental; and the biblical style, described as figurative (de Sousa Santos 2004: 256–257). Such a combination has major implications for translations operating on other levels. With a first set of lenses, we will investigate its vertical translation, including its conceptual genealogy and the alternative meanings and significations it gained during the process. And with a second set, we will explore the field of horizontal translation and its implications for various legal languages and systems, by examining ontological and epistemological structures, issues of compatibility and impacts on legal cultures. Such implications raise delicate issues going beyond a comparative approach (Gémar 1979: 44) and dealing with the expression of cultural diversity in transnational and international legal languages. The emergence of a global legal science clearly calls for a 'consciousness of diversity', and a 'pluralistic vision of legal theory which includes a variety of perspectives and a multiplicity of levels of generality' (Menski 2005: 7). To that end, the process of reflection starts with the recognition of the multifarious legal traditions in the world, and with a systematic rethinking of legal theory (Glenn 2000). In order to overcome «narrowly defined traditional methods», we need to use different and complementary instruments of analysis (Menski 2005: 6), notably comparative law, legal theory and legal linguistics, thus moving 'towards trans-systemism' (Kasirer, in Mattila 2012: IX). Considering the crucial role of the concept of *persona juris* in international legal reasoning, logic and language, we intend, in this chapter, to highlight its role and point out the limits of its multilevel translation from the perspective of a 'plurality-focused international legal science' (Menski 2005: 6).

1. Implications of Vertical Translation

The mobility of the term *persona* from one field of knowledge to another has a series of implications for its use and understanding in legal language. Through the process of vertical translation, it has acquired ontological and epistemological dimensions. Such a process has its source in the genealogy of the word *persona*. This genealogy sheds light on the term's general and legal polysemy, which explains the ambivalence of its mode of representation, which is instrumental yet figurative. *Persona,* in its common Latin usage, refers primarily to a real person but it can also refer to a character played by an actor, as well as by metonymy, to his theatrical mask (Trigeaud 1989: 108). Its use as a mode of representation in its translation into Roman legal language, as a concept designating a social role, refers to a legal status. In Roman law, it means the possession of certain attributes in the framework of the *libertatis, civitatis,* and *familiae.* In the legal logic of Roman law, *persona* belongs to an epistemological triad with *res* (goods) and *acta* (actions), into which reality is divided in the legal language.

The polysemy of the Latin word *persona* comes from its translation from the Etruscan word φersu ("phersu"), meaning "duality" and "character played", and from the Greek πρόσωπον ("prosopon") meaning "individual face" as well as "existence, substance, good" (Benveniste 1969: 301). This dual genealogy is found not only in the term's mode of representation but also in the legal concept itself—a technique designating a legal status and which is based on an ontological stance. The meaning of such an ontological content was first questioned in theology and philosophy, after which the term acquired new dimensions in the legal field. In the process, *persona* took on a specific ontological and epistemological meaning, as well as alternative significations in the context of its application to different realities in the legal field. The polysemic use of *persona,* as well as its development in other fields of knowledge, have contributed to transforming its legal meaning. During medieval scholastic tournaments, and through the combined study of the Justinian *Corpus* (*Corpus juris civilis*) and canon law (*Corpus juris canonici*) (Gaudemet 2005: 299), pragmatic elements of Roman law were analyzed in the light of philology, logics and theology (Mausen 2005: 1394).

Initially, theological reflections on the meaning of *persona* determined the ontological basis of the *persona juris*. These debates concerned the notion of person in relation to the Trinity ("hypostasis"), and led to the formulation of a definition: *Naturæ rationalis individua substantia*—an individual substance of a rational nature (Boethius 1342: LXIV). In this meaning, *Persona* refers to persons conceived as intellectual beings. This definition was specified by Aquinas: *Individua substantia* means "*substantia, completa, per se subsistens, separata ab aliia*"—a substance, complete, subsisting per se, existing apart from others (Gilson 1945: 420). Those elements of *persona* have been passed on to the legal field, notably through the comments of the glossators. Later, the use of *persona* in the debates of the neo-Thomists led to a controversy between East and West in the Christian realm, due to its genealogical derivation from "prosopon" and its correspondance as "hypostasis" of the Latin *substantia*. 'Three hypostases (. . .) appeared to conflict with the Nicaean doctrine of unity of substance in the Trinity. This difference was a main cause of the Antiochene schism of the fourth century (see Meletius of Antioch)' (Geddes 1911). In the West, it was decided that the equivalent of 'hypostasis' was not *substantia* but *subsistentia*, and in the East that "prosopon" could not be interpreted as *persona*, meaning individual. 'By the First Council of Constantinople, therefore, it was recognized that the words 'hypostasis', 'prosopon', and *persona* were equally applicable to the three Divine realities' (Geddes 1911). In that sense, the ontological qualities retained by *persona* are: that which perpetuates in time; and "hypostasis", that which stands before,—the designation. Nevertheless, it is Aquinas' definition, emphasising the notions of individuality and autonomy, which inspired the philosophical reflections of the humanists on *persona* and the notion of *subjectus* (Gilson 1945: 421).

The understanding and use of *subjectus*, in relation to *persona*, has notably been debated in the theological works of Dun Scotus and William of Occam (meaning as submitted to divine law with an autonomy); in the political works of Hobbes and Pufendorf (meaning as submitted to a sovereign autority); and in the works of the Enlightenment philosophers (meaning a free and rational person). The subject, drawing from those reflections and definitions, is equated to the individual, defined as *persona* or intellectual being. The notion of person, through the use of *persona*, is understood as a philosophical, political and legal subject. Contrary to its position in Roman law, the subject is the centre of legal reasoning and logic in modern law (Villey 1968: 663). The law becomes a quality of the person.[1] And *persona juris* is then defined as the quality of the legal subject (Grzegorczyk 1989: 23). Such equations associate exclusively *persona juris* to the human being, as the owner of rights and obligations (Villey 1968: 664). The construction of *persona juris* as designating the legal subject is thus characterized by the modern representation of a person as an independent, rational, free and capable being. Such an ontological founding of the legal subject has decisive implications on the structuring of legal thought and on correlated fields of knowledge, such as economics and political science. The process of vertical translation of *persona juris*, from Roman law, through canon law, theology and philosophy to Modern law, shaped its definition and use in the legal field.

The evolution of this concept led to an epistemological framing or "performative structure" of its legal usage, in stark contrast to the way it was used in the Roman and medieval legal practices. Indeed, *persona juris* was applied to different realities, notably to the *universitas* or groups forming a corpus (Lefebvre-Teilhard 2005: 1153). Such applications as *nomen juris* or legal designation were in continuity with their use in Roman law. Medieval legal language distinguished between the use of *persona juris* as applied to individuals, on the one hand and to groups, on the other, through the notion of temporality (Kantorowicz 1989: 220–222). In order to highlight the distinction between the legal language and the everyday use of *persona*, the concept gained a new representative or figurative epithet, thereby designating *universitas*

1 According to Grotius, '*Jus est qualitas moralis personae competens*' (*De jure belli ac pacis*, I, Ch.1 §4).

and other groups as *persona ficta* (Burns 1993: 520). In contemporary English, the epithet *ficta* is translated, either as juridical, juristic, artificial or fictitious, depending on the interpretation of the founding of the distinction between *persona juris* and *persona ficta*. During the development of legal language in the Middle Ages, philology and literary tools had a creative impact on legal notions and narrative. But with the correlated evolution of *persona*, exclusively understood as a human/rational being, and the use of other designations as *nomen juris* such as *persona ficta*, legal reasoning based its logic on personification in order to adapt to these changes. Such a figure of speech consists in attributing human properties to other entities by analogy. Its legal usage was much debated by the glossators in the context of the legal theorization of collective entities or groups (Burns 1993: 565). Those decisive discussions clearly sought to cope with the consequences of using such a figure of speech in legal language, as literary and linguistic tools have their own rules and logic. Personification involves the use of one of the following: metaphor (attribution of a personal nature or human characteristics), synecdoche (figure of speech in which the part designates the whole), or metonymy (ambivalent designation of the entity to all its elements). Their respective effects on legal reasoning are quite different. Inducing legal logic from these various figures of speech generated controversies over the legal status of entities, their constituents and the goods they contained: *Persona juris* designated the whole entity as an individual, or an abstract entity separate from the individuals in the group, or as the sum/succession of its constituents. In the 19th century, the controversy over the notions of juristic and moral persons in civil and administrative law,—together with the debates on the reality or fiction of legal personality—, had its origins in the use of personification in legal language. It was criticized in different branches of legal theory, notably by Brinz in German private law and Duguit in French public law. Contemporary legal theory still struggles with the consequences of personification, despite its becoming obsolescent as a mode of representation with the development of legal technique. The reflections of Jellinek in German political theory, Michoud in French legal theory, and Ferrara in Italian legal theory all managed to get beyond personification and acknowledged the concept of *persona juris* as a legal tool. At the beginning of the 20th century, the legal concept was definitively detached from its mode of representation in French legal theory. The concept's technical evolution, in private law notably, generated new distinctions apart from the personification's narrative (Gény 1921: 218). In spite of personification's lasting imprint on the logic underlying legal thought, such a development reaffirms the primary function of the concept as *nomen juris* or legal designation.

At the level of the translation of legal theory from one branch of law to another, or from one field to another, the importing doctrine has its own structure and reasoning. This usually implies the need for an adaptation of the imported legal theory. This task is all the more delicate when the imported legal theory is from another language and/or legal system. In that regard, *persona juris* and the legal theory explaining its functioning and logic take on different forms and pragmatic legal applications according to the language and legal system in question. Studying the history of legal discourse and identifying the introduction of new or imported theories can help us to understand the specific meaning of the concept in context. Studies on the importing and translation of legal theories related to the concept of *persona ficta* or juristic personality are particularly telling. Salient aspects of such translations include the varying effects of personification and the figure of speech used to structure the legal reasoning, as well as the major differences in the use of *persona* as a legal technique in, respectively, common law and civil law systems. Whereas the debate on personality as either reality or fiction was closed in the first part of the 20th century in French legal theory and most civil law systems, it is still active in English legal theory and common law systems—with a particular prominence and intensity in the United States. At the crossroads between vertical and horizontal translations, the level of legal theory is revealing of the various factors influencing the translation of a concept. Illustrating such crossroads, the study on the 'transplantation of the legal discourse on corporate personality theories' demonstrates how, following its codification in German law, the theory was imported into British doctrine and American legal theory (Harris 2006). The study sheds some light on why the debates over reality and fiction of personality developed differently in different places, and notably why the German theory in particular was imported. 'Just as Savigny and his German disciples had systematized Roman law . . . American and English scholars strove for a similar systematization of their own common law tradition' (Rabban 2003: 558–559). At the time, 'the discourse in Britain and the United States only began when the discourse in Germany neared its end' (Harris 2006: 1476).

Such a study of the transplantation of legal theories also underlines the specificity of the debates on legal personality: they have a 'transnational dimension' (Harris 2006: 1424). The imported theory on legal personality in Britain and North America seems to come from Gierke's critique on Savigny, taking into account German jurisprudential traditions, historical narratives and political context. 'The first theory to appear both in Germany and in the Anglo-American world was the state grant theory, also called the fictitious personality theory, the artificial personality theory, the concession theory or the hierarchical theory. (. . .) The second theory was the contract, aggregate, or partnership theory. Groups became legal entities by a voluntary and consensual undertaking of their members. (. . .) The third theory, whose formation in Germany and import into Britain and the United States initiated the discourse, is the real entity theory, also called the natural entity theory. This theory holds that the real and social existence of a group makes it a legal person' (Harris 2006: 1423). Those three theories derive from the different reasonings induced by the use of personification as their mode of representation.[2] They are shaped by the doctrine and structure of the legal system from which they originated. The real entity theory, 'in its abstract form', was imported 'without the full historical narration that legitimized it and without the direct policy conclusions that resulted from it in the German context' (Harris 2006: 1423). In the latter case, the political context highlights the choice of translation and understanding of the theory and concept. 'While in the context of trade unions the discourse was used in Germany to promote freedom of association, in Britain and the United States the discourse was applied in order to expose unions to tort liability in employers' suits' (Harris 2006: 1429). Consequently, it appears that we need multiple lenses to observe translation at the levels of legal theory, doctrine and general context. Where a case involves different legal systems and languages, it seems we have to deal with a 'complex linguistic transplant' (Crépeau 1995: 53). This also implies taking into account the different relationships between words and concepts in their respective languages, such as in German and English (Sacco 1987: 850). In that regard, the respective designations in Germany, Britain and the United States are *Juristische Persönlichkeit*, juristic personality and corporate personality. The notion of corporate personhood in the United States is understood as a metaphor for personification, implying that the corporation is treated as a person in legal reasoning. It is interesting to note that the word "corporation" has evolved differently in England and in the United States. 'Older English discussions use the word "corporation", but usage has changed, and present practice reserves this word for public (i.e. governmental) bodies, with the word 'company' being used as a general word for the (mainly) business mechanism. A further complication arises from the North American use of "corporation", widely recognized internationally, as the equivalent of the modern English "company"' (Foster 2000: 578). Such cases can be considered as 'system-bound terms': 'they designate concepts and institutions peculiar to the legal reality of a specific system or related systems' (Sarcevic 2000: 233). In

2 A certain indeterminacy of those theories was underlined (Dewey 1926: 655). It can be interpreted as an expression of the dependency of legal reasoning upon the mode of representation of the concept of *persona juris* and its legal narrative.

addition to the specific use of the word "corporation" in Britain and the United States, there are debates on the reality and fiction of legal personality in common law systems, presenting a conceptual and theoretical landscape contrasting with civil law systems. These considerations provide some insights into how we can combine different lenses for a multilevel analysis of the translation of a concept. 'The intellectual history of the transnational dimensions and multifaceted contexts of this discourse provides insight into the journeys of legal discourses, their transplantation, the formation of legal-historical narratives and the interplay between theory, doctrine and policy' (Harris 2006: 1477).

2. Implications of Horizontal Translation

We have experimented different lenses and emphasized some important aspects of vertical translation from one field of knowledge to another, as well as important factors in a combined analysis of vertical and horizontal translations. Continuing our investigation on *persona juris,* we now need to focus on the specific implications of horizontal translation into different languages and legal systems. The objective is to pinpoint the functions and limits of the translation of the concept with regard to a plurality-based approach to legal language. Comparative law proposes several classifications of legal systems on the basis of various criteria, such as language, structure of legal thought or cultural traditions (Sousa Santos 2004: 302). René David distinguishes between five main legal families: Western, Socialist, Islamic, Hindu, and Chinese. Considering legal thought or language, various systems are alternatively suggested: for instance, the French, Germanic, Scandinavian, English, Russian, Islamic, and Hindu systems (Arminjon, Nolde and Wolff). Another classification, based on legal style criteria — with the factors of genealogy and historical evolution, mode of legal thought, founding institutions, legal source and ideology — identify the Roman, Germanic, Nordic, Common law, Socialist, far East, Islamic, and Hindu families (Zweigert and Kötz 1997: 75). Such classifications leave other legal traditions unexplored, such as the chthonic systems, for instance African, Native American and Australian laws and traditions (Glenn 2004: 61). Studies in sociology and legal anthropology are particularly helpful when it comes to opening a window onto the diversity of legal landscapes. They allow the making of a distinction between legal system and legal tradition, the latter bridging legal system and legal culture. As our exploration of vertical translation emphasized the role of other fields of knowledge and practice in shaping a legal concept, knowledge of the cultural context and tradition is necessary in order to understand its meaning and pragmatic usage in a legal system. For instance, as a consequence of the mode of representation and philosophical construction of *persona juris,* the concept does not come alone but with a set or family of operative notions and concepts (such as will, consent, autonomy, independence, etc.): its "performative structure". This one concept designating the legal subject of rights and obligations simultaneously encompasses ontological, epistemological, logical, cultural, and linguistic elements. In this light, we propose to explore the landscape and a set of main directions, including Chinese, Indian, Hindu, Islamic legal systems and traditions, as well as chthonic systems.

Persona juris was forged in the European legal tradition. As Roman law—in particular through the Corpus juris civilis—has been the jus commune and Latin the legal lingua franca in Europe for centuries, a founding "system of concepts" is shared by the legal systems of European countries (Mattila 2012: 207–208). In all the civil law systems, one finds the same major divisions and branches of law, so that there is a common conceptual background to the translation of legal terms from Latin to, respectively, French, German, Spanish, Italian, Dutch, Greek, or Portuguese (David 1996: 64; Mattila 2012: 207–224). Persona juris translates into words and legal terms with the same etymology: "legal personality" in English; "personnalité juridique" in French; "personalità giuridica" in Italian; "personalidad jurídica" in Spanish; "personalidade jurídica" in Portuguese; "personalitate juridică" in Romanian; "Rechtspersönlischkeit" in German; "rechtspersoonlijkheid" in Dutch; "juridisk personlighed" in Danish; "νομική προσωπικότητα" (from "prosopon") in Greek. In Slavic languages, such as the Czech "právní subjektivita", the etymology comes from *subjectus*, and the term inherited the theological and philosophical connotations we outlined in our study on vertical translation. The Justinian Institutes, including the epistemic division into persona/res/acta, are spread out, not only in civil law systems, but also in the common law system, notably from their integration in the English legal system in the Middle Ages from Roman and French law (Mattila 2012: 405–406).

We underlined the difference, at the theoretical level, between the use and understanding of *persona ficta* in, respectively, Europe and North America. The debate over the fiction of *persona ficta* in North America is about the use of a mode of representation and a figure of speech such as personification, and their implications for legal reasoning and practice.[3] In that context, "piercing the corporate veil" refers to looking at the individual natural persons acting as agents involved in a corporate action or decision; this may result in a legal decision in which the rights or duties of a corporation are equated to the rights or liabilities of that corporation's shareholders or directors. There are implications on the legal reasoning, notably with such a literal interpretation of the word "person" in the Fourteenth Amendment, American courts have extended certain constitutional protections to corporations. Virulent opposition to corporate personhood has emerged due to the instrumentalization of their legal status and a lack of legal means to sanction them. The issues of a lack of liability of corporations and weak enforcement have also contributed to this movement. These matters are also the subjects of a lively debate in Canada, where since 1985 incorporation is defined in the Canada Business Corporations Act (CBCA). This can be done either at the federal or provincial level, where different procedures apply. But the case of Quebec stands apart because it developed a specific legal understanding of corporate personality—drawing on its civil law tradition and elaborating new approaches in order to fill gaps in the Napoleonic Code (Bouchard 1997: 57). The concepts of *persona ficta* and corporation result from a unique synchretism of legal theory and practice in Quebec, notably through case law construction.[4] It reconsiders the founding of classical personality theory and unity of holding, and calls into question the legal theories of fiction and reality of *persona ficta* (Bouchard 1997: 17–19).

Nevertheless, in Europe and North America, there are debates on the status and application of *persona ficta* not only to groups, but also to other entities, which have gained rights with the development of law and practice, such as non-governmental organizations. In the same line of reflection, there are debates over the Roman epistemic structure of *persona*, *res* and *acta* and its ability to deal effectively with the evolution of law and society, notably with regard to the legal status of various realities such as animals, forests or ecosystems (Le Moigne 2000: 416).

The concept of *persona juris* and the designation of a legal person as a legal subject is now central to Western law, but it is also found in all the other major legal systems, as well as in international law, due to historical and legal influences, and colonization and decolonization processes. The real challenge here is not so much in studying the translation of the concept into the major legal systems per se (as many adopted a certain structure inherited from a European

3 See notably a founding decision: in *Louisville, C. & C.R. Co. v. Letson*, 2 How. 497, 558, 11 L.Ed. 353 (1844), the US Supreme Court held that for the purposes of the case at hand, a corporation is 'capable of being treated as a citizen of [the State which created it], as much as a natural person.' These concepts have been codified by statute.

4 See, for instance, Cass.civ. 2, 28 janvier, 1954: JCP 1954, II, in which decision personality is not considered a creation of the law, but of every entity able to express itself to defend its interests.

legal tradition), but its translation and transplantation into various legal traditions (still present in the legal cultures even if not represented or expressed in the legal systems inherited from colonization). From that perspective, we propose to analyze the concept notably as a structure of thought and reasoning, and consider whether it allows the expression of diversity or rather prevents it.

At the junction of various major influences, the Chinese legal system is 'a complex amalgam of different systems' (Menski 2005: 22). It encompasses principles and concepts from civil law systems; procedures and theories from the common law system; principles and procedures from the socialist legal system (including reactions to those imports); as well as customary law and traditional Chinese cultural values (Piquet 2005: 245, 270). There are different analyses of Chinese law and of what can correctly be considered to be "legal". At first sight, it seems Chinese law gives less importance to custom than to the philosophical codes of Confucian ethics (Menski 2005: 494–495), generating a dynamic involving state law, social norms and value systems. Such synchretism is visible in Chinese contract law (Piquet 2005: 229), in which the transnational role of the concept of legal personality appears (Zhongfu 1989: 1). For instance, there are many examples of the explicit recognition of the legal status of state enterprises in Chinese civil law, notably in resolutions dating from the 1950s and in the Treaty Agreement on the Trade Relations between the United States and the People's Republic of China of 1979, which serves as an example of the recognition of legal person status in international treaties (Zhongfu 1989: 2). The General Principles of Civil Law of the People's Republic of China (1986) defines legal persons as 'organizations that have civil capacity, are competent to perform civil acts, and according to law independently enjoy civil rights and assume civil duties'. (Chapter 3, Article 36). Such a definition of legal persons as being the subject of civil rights is perfectly in line with *persona ficta* in civil law systems. Influences of different legal systems, notably the socialist one, can be seen in the division of categories of legal persons with different sets of rights, functions and organization. There are 'enterprise legal persons, government agencies legal persons, institution legal persons, and association legal persons' (Zhongfu 1989: 2–4). In addition, the use and understanding of *persona juris* is particularly interesting, as it highlights the specificities of Chinese legal tradition and culture. Indeed, the logic based on the legal status of agents rather than the applicable legal norm belongs to Confucianism (Piquet 2005: 52). The notion of "ren" or "human sense/approach" conveys to the designation of legal status a philosophical meaning from its vertical translation, which contrasts with the ontological founding of *persona juris* (Cheng 1997: 62). Instead of permanence and separation from others, the ontological stance is based on change and relationships. The concept of "guanxi", understood as the circle of relationships of a person, is crucial in that respect, as it constitutes a performative approach to legal status, notably considering the role of Li (rules of behaviour) in relation to state law (Wu 1968: 396). The concept of "guanxi" and the five founding relations delimit a circle of relationships and obligations of members. According to such an approach, drawing on both ontology and political philosophy, members of society were defined in the Imperial system as "social persons" (Piquet 2005: 42). This system had its philosophical roots in the ancient and complex notion of "Tao", referring to the notions of order (such as the Greek "cosmos", combined with a dynamic of change), totality, integrity, and responsibility (Escarra 1936: 13). The different factors shaping the understanding and use of *nomen juris* to define a legal status in China have an important impact on the translation of *persona juris.* They put an emphasis on the simple role of legal denomination of the concept, and at the same time, on the differences of its Chinese ontological and epistemological approach. They reveal the flexibility of the concept as *nomen juris* in the legal language up to the limits and boundaries of legal tradition, culture, and practice, as the induced reasoning is quite different (Fu 1993: 261–265, 293–297).

The Indian legal system is another direction we propose to explore. It is a 'complex mixture of various legal systems and traditions' and teaches us, with the Chinese system, 'to look out for the larger issues raised by governing multitudes of people' (Menski 2005: 203). Despite being often described as a common law system, it is "a plurality-focused construct", and as such is particularly interesting for our investigation on *persona juris* and legal pluralism. 'On its independence in 1947, India inherited an extremely complex legal system characterized by remarkable plurality of laws, while Anglo-Hindu law was turned into an official legal system based mainly on case law' (Menski 2005: 249). It also includes 'traditional personal law, with Hindu law, but also Muslim, Christian, Parsi and Jewish law as well as secular family law"' (Menski 2005: 250). In this context, traditional Indian and Hindu concepts of governance have an important influence on Indian constitutional law (Menski 2005: 259). Therefore, even if the concept of legal personality is present in the common law, conceptual elements and ontology of Hindu law give a specific framework to its use in the Indian legal system. One notable aspect is the 'anti-legal attitude from ancient times similar to the Chinese aversion to the "fa" as "state law"' (Menski 2005: 202). Another of its major aspects is the founding ontology of Hindu thought from the Vedas, and the notion of "rita" (and later "'dharma") as "cosmic interlinkedness". This refers to a social order, an 'order in which everything and everybody is interconnected and has a role to play' (Menski 2005: 214). This concept is notably integrated into modern Indian constitutional law within the definition of "public interest"' (Menski 2005: 204). In Hindu law, in which the notions of individuality and autonomy are important, 'any individual is thus, not alone in this world but is interlinked in many ways, to family, clan, village, society as a whole, ultimately the universe' (Menski 2005: 206). Evoking some aspects of the definition of the *subjectus* in the European philosophy of the 17th and 18th centuries, 'classical dharma (. . .) relies on the individual self-controlled ability to discern appropriate action' (Menski 2005: 217). In this sense, *persona juris* is transplanted into a complex and challenging context. First, it underlines the functional characteristics of the concept as *nomen juris* and allows its application to a range of legal subjects. Second, it puts an emphasis on individuality as well as interlinkedness. Third, it presents a political understanding as "self-controlled ordering", contrasting with the roots of *subjectus*. In the same way, the sophistication of the Indian legal system is envisaged 'as a key example of postmodern legal reconstruction' at the global level (Menski 2005: 277), its use and understanding of the concept provides food for thought for its application in international legal language.

The Indian Constitution states the personal status of Hindu legal subjects, but it has also applied Islamic law to Muslim legal subjects since the Muslim Personal Law Application Act of 1937. Islamic or Muslim law is considered to be a 'religion-based legal system', with a 'plurality of socio-cultural manifestations' (Menski 2005: 279). As such, it is a complex family of laws rather than a single legal system (Menski 2005: 281). In our investigation on the translation of *persona juris*, this family of laws acknowledges 'the presence and impact of concepts of religious natural law' (Menski 2005: 289). In this context, the question is rather: to what extent are the ontological and epistemological dimensions of *persona juris* compatible with a set of different ontological assumptions? Islamic jurisprudence ("fiqh") divides law into two main sets of rules: rules in relation to actions, and rules in relation to circumstances surrounding actions (Levy 1957: 150). In contrast to the modern development of the Justinian division, *acta* is central to its reasoning, rather than *persona*. It is notably under the category of "dealings and transactions with people" ("Mu'amalaat") that issues concerning *persona juris* and *persona ficta* appear (Levy 1957: 150–51). Some aspects of these concepts may prevent their usage and function as *nomen juris*. In Arabic, *persona* translates as شخصية ("shakhsiyah"). In Islamic law, the term "musyarakah" or "shirkah" is used to refer to business entities (Hassan, Ghadas and Rahman 2012: 191). "Shirkah", which can be considered as the functional equivalent of *persona ficta*, means literally "intermingle", in the sense that properties forming the capital cannot be differentiated from one another. The classification of business entities is different in common law and Islamic law. In common law, the legal regime applying to companies differs from the one applying to partnerships and these two types of entity are subject to different laws. In Islamic law, "shirkah" can refer to both company and partnership structures. The definition of the various types of "shirkah" includes their individual members. A "shirkah" is not considered to be a legal person (Hassan, Ghadas and Rahman 2012: 191–198). This concept, as used in Islamic law, does not use personification or a metaphor as a founding mode of representation. Rather, it refers to the unity of holdings. In that sense, and in contrast to the epistemic division used in Roman law, the prominent aspect in Islamic legal reasoning related to legal personality is *res* (goods). Further studies analyze the compatibility of "shirkah" with the theory of corporate personality, notably in the case of Malaysian law, which provides that 'a company shall be regarded as a body corporate, capable of exercising all the functions of an incorporated company' (Companies Act 1965 (Act 125), Section 16 (5)). In Islamic legal doctrine, there is a debate on corporate personality concerning the representation as an artificial person ("shakhsiyah i'itbariyah") (Hassan, Ghadas and Rahman 2012: 193). Some authors argue that the use of the concept dates from the early times of jurisprudence ("fiqh"), notably for the recognition of the mosque as an entity—which reminds us of the origin and use of *persona ficta* in respect of monasteries in Europe. It seems that the discussions concern the metaphoric and metonymic understandings of the entity as distinct and separate from its constituent parts, in the case of personification. There is strong opposition to the doctrine of corporate personality. The latter is considered to be 'untenable in Sharia' in relation to other Islamic concepts such as "waqf"; to jeopardise the whole legal structure; and to stand in opposition to principles of Islamic contract law (Hassan, Ghadas and Rahman 2012: 194). These debates have direct implications for legal practice, notably for the validity of Islamic corporations, which are formed under the Companies Act 1965 in Malaysia (Hassan, Ghadas and Rahman 2012: 195). Some conciliatory approaches suggest that the theory of corporate personality could be applied to 'Islamic companies indirectly, subject to certain conditions and with certain modifications' (Hassan, Ghadas and Rahman 2012: 197).

The last area we will explore is a desert landscape. In such lands, the concept of *persona juris* has not been translated due to historical factors of domination, and the absence of recognition of legal tradition or system. Most chthonic systems enter into that category, such as Native African, Australian, and American laws and customs. In this context, the question takes another form: can the concept of *persona juris* be translated into such systems, or how could it allow the expression of such laws and customs. In order to be able to ask such questions in the legal field, we need to push away some boundaries with the tools of socio-legal approaches, which define chthonic systems as 'a related family of laws composed of principles of moral philosophy and prescriptions of behaviours' (Okupa 1998: xiii). Key elements of those systems are orality and informality (Menski 2005: 394). This endeavour 'requires a plurality-conscious, multidisciplinary approach which must be at liberty to cross academic boundaries as and when required to follow the traces of oral traditions and local practices' (Menski 2005: 396). The logic and structures of such systems are completely different from those of positive modern law. They are based on an ontology of interconnectedness and constant change. The human being is not separated from its environment and other beings. 'The role of lineage or clan is the next largest unit in society, emphasising its socio-economic insurance functions, again matched with legal responsibilities' (Menski 2005: 426). For instance, the 'African conceptual equivalent to Hindu 'sadacara', Muslim 'shariat' and Chinese 'li' relates to the socio-political level as well as religious authority, and thus comprises all three elements of the conceptual triangle of law-making' (Menski 2005: 430). In that sense, the ontology founding the concept of *persona juris* and the performative structure operating on the legal reasoning might be fundamental obstacles to the translation of such a tool into the chthonic legal languages. But if we cannot envisage the translation of the concept into chthonic systems in its current form, its use as a legal designation without the current performative structure could be envisaged as a solution. The latter would constitute a bridge, a way of communicating, and therefore, beyond its use as a legal tool, form of recognition.

3. The International Legal Language

Our enquiry into the vertical and horizontal processes of translation of *persona juris* illustrates that legal translation operates across time and space, levels and disciplines. The "cultural turn" (Snell-Hornby 2006: 50) can contribute to the 'knowledge of similarities and differences between legal concepts of various countries (and) helps avoid misunderstandings in international cooperations' (Mattila 2006: 106). But with regard to the international domain, it points to the necessity of integrating such a consciousness into the international legal language. 'The challenge of the international discourse can be best met by proactive responses to problems emerging from the interface between local perceptions and the international discourse. This is then exactly where jurisprudence and anthropology meet' (Hinz 2003: 117). 'If legal theory is to engage seriously with globalization and its consequences a critical re-examination of its agenda, its heritage of ideas, and its conceptual tools is called for — harmonious diversity should be promoted on the global level' (Menski 2005: 16, 46). The translation of such diversity into the international legal language can be compared to a paradigmatic transition: 'not in order to create a separate and isolated form of superior knowledge, but becoming itself a new common sense liberating: as a rehabilitation of a common sense. It is practical and pragmatic' (de Sousa Santos 2004: 60, 121). Conceived as a 'process of communicability', the international language can become an 'instrument of the legal dynamic' (Gounelle 2005: 114). From that perspective, and invoking the concept of 'linguistic hospitality' (Ricoeur 2004: 174), the international language lacks interfaces, means of expression and approaches to the diversity of legal traditions. These observations coincide with attempts in legal theory to reestablish the bridge between law and society (Menski 2005: 47), taking into account sociological, anthropological and metaphysical considerations into the law but also into the legal language. The legal critique condemned the disappearance of ontological considerations in modern legal thought. And the postmodern critique shed light on the absence of a stable ontological basis for international law (Kennedy 1987). The crisis of the concept of *persona juris* in international law is a symptom but also a window of opportunity to address its ontological foundations and reconsider its role and functions in the context of global law.

In the vertical analysis of its translating process, we noted various understandings and uses of the concept in the different branches of law. These vary depending on whether the concept is applied to physical persons, civil society organizations or corporations. Seen from a broad perspective, one of the specificities of the use of *persona juris* in international law comes from its application to the level of societies, and to the level of societies of societies. At such levels, the concept has to be operative and able to address the diversity of legal systems and cultures. In that sense, it can be seen as a gate, rather than a box or label. The horizontal analysis underlined the use and functions of the concept in addressing plurality-focused legal systems. Further investigation in that in this field of study could provide clues as to how we could adapt *persona juris* in the context of the international legal language. In this connection, research in the fields of legal theory, semiotics and translation can help identify a mode of representation, narrative and theory (Berlioz and Nef 2005). This would allow the concept to operate as a gateway for the plurality of legal systems and traditions – based on an ontology allowing change and diversity. From this perspective, the international legal language appears as a "Third Space" of legal translatability, 'a space of possibilities, an autonomous realm of 'cross-cultural events' ', a space 'which enables other positions to emerge' (Wagner, Sin and Cheng 2014).

References

Badr, G.M. 1978. 'Islamic Law: Its Relation to Other Legal Systems', *The American Journal of Comparative Law*, vol. 26, pp. 187–198.

Benveniste, E. 1969. *Le vocabulaire des institutions indo-européennes*. Paris: Minuit.

Berlioz, D. and Nef, F. (eds). 2005. *Leibniz et les puissances du langage*. Coll. Bibliothèque d'histoire de la philosophie. Paris: Vrin.

Bleuchot, H. 2000. *Droit musulman*. Coll. Droit et Religions, T.1. Marseille: Presses Universitaires d'Aix-Marseille.

Boethius. 1342. *De Persona et Duabus Naturis*. P.L.: LXIV.

Bouchard, C. 1997. *La personnalité morale démythifiée – contribution à la définition de la nature juridique des sociétés de personnes québécoises*. Sainte-Foy: Presses de l'Université de Laval.

Brinz. A. 1873–1895. *Lehrbuch der Pandekten*. Erlangen: A. Diechert.

Burns, J.H. (ed.). 1988. *The Cambridge History of Medieval Political Thought c. 350 – c. 1450*. The Cambridge University Press. Version française: 1993. *Histoire de la pensée politique médiévale*. Paris: Presses Universitaires de France.

Cheng, A. 1997. *Histoire de la pensée chinoise*. Paris: Seuil.

Crépeau, P.-A. 1995. 'La transposition juridique'. In: Snow, G. et J. Vanderlinden dir. *Français juridique et science du droit*. Bruxelles: Bruylant.

David, R. 1996. *Les grands systèmes du droit contemporain*. Paris: Dalloz.

Dewey, J. 1926. 'The Historic Background of Corporate Legal Personality', *Yale L Journal*, vol. 35, pp. 655, 669.

Escarra, J. 1936. *Le droit chinois – Conception générale, aperçu historique*. Paris: Éditions Henri Vetch, Pékin Librairie du recueil, Sirey.

Flusser, V. 2002. *Writings*. In: A. Strohl ed., E. Eisel trans. University of Minnesota Press.

Fontanier, P. 1977. *Les figures du discours*. Paris: Flammarion.

Foucault, M. 1969. *L'archéologie du savoir*. Paris: Gallimard.

Fu, I. 1993. 'Legal Person in China: Essence and Limits', *AJCL*, vol.41(2), pp. 261–297.

Gaudemet, J. 2005. 'Corpus iuris civilis'. In: *Dictionnaire de la culture juridique*. Paris: Presses universitaires de France, pp. 1394–1398.

Gémar, J.C. 1979. 'La traduction juridique et son enseignement', *Meta*, 44.

———. 1995. *Traduire, ou, l'art d'interpréter: Langue, droit et société: éléments de jurilinguistique*. Tome 2. Presses de l'Université du Québec.

Geddes, L. 1911. 'Person'. In: *The Catholic Encyclopedia*, vol. 11. New York: Robert Appleton Company.

Gény, F. 1921. *Science et technique en droit privé positif*. Paris: Sirey.

Gessner, V. 1994. 'Global Legal Interaction and Legal Cultures', *Ratio Juris*, vol. 7(2), pp. 132–145.

Gilson, E. 1945. *Le thomisme*. Paris: Vrin.

Glenn, H.P. 2003. 'La tradition juridique nationale', *Revue internationale de droit compare*, vol. 2, pp. 276–278.

Gounelle, M. 2005. 'Communicabilité en droit international public'. In: M. Baudrez and T. di Manno eds. *Liber Amicorum Jean-Claude Escarras, La communicabilité entre les systèmes juridiques*. Bruxelles: Bruylant, p. 107.

Grewe, C. 2005. 'Entre la Tour de Babel et l'Espéranto: les problèmes du (des) langage(s) du droit comparé'. In: M. Baudrez and T. di Manno eds. *Liber Amicorum Jean-Claude Escarras, La communicabilité entre les systèmes juridiques*. Bruylant: Bruxelles, pp. 115–129.

Grzegorczyk, C. 1989. 'Le sujet de droit: trois hypostases'. In: *Archives de Philosophie du Droit*. Tome 34 (*Le sujet de droit*). Paris: Sirey, pp. 9–32.

Harris, R. 2006. 'The Transplantation of the Legal Discourse on Corporate Personality Theories: From German Codification to British Political Pluralism and American Big Business', *Washington Lee Law Review*, vol. 63.

Hart, H.L.A. 1953. *Definition and Theory in Jurisprudence*. Oxford: Clarendon Press.

Hassan, H., Abd Ghadas, Z.A. and Abdul Rahman, N. 2012. ''The Myth of Corporate Personality': A Comparative Legal Analysis of the Doctrine of Corporate Personality of Malaysian and Islamic Laws', *Australian Journal of Basic and Applied Sciences*, vol. 6(11), pp. 191–198.

Hinz, M.O. 2003. 'Jurisprudence and Anthropology' In: *Anthropology Southern Africa*, vol. 26(3&4), p. 114.

Kantorowicz, E. 1989. *Les deux corps du Roi, essai sur la théologie politique au Moyen Âge*. Paris: Gallimard.

Kemp, P. 2008. 'Rethinking Philosophy as Power of the Word' (Opening talk), *22ème Congrès Mondial de Philosophie: Rethinking Philosophy Today*. Séoul.

Kennedy, D. 1987. *International Legal Structures*. Baden-Baden: Nomos.

Lefebvre-Teillard, A. 2005. 'Personne'. In: *Dictionnaire de la culture juridique*. Paris: Presses universitaires de France, p. 1153.

Le Moigne, J.L. 2000. 'Sur quelques topiques de la complexité . . . des situations que peut connaître le juriste dans ses pratiques', *Droit et Société*, vol. 46, pp. 407–427.

Levy, R. 1957. *The Social Structure of Islam*. Cambridge: Cambridge University Press.

MacCormick, N. 1984. 'On Reasonableness'. In: C. Perelman dir. *Les notions à contenu variables en droit*. Bruxelles: Travaux du Centre national de recherches en logique.

Mattila, H.E.S. 2006. *Comparative Legal Linguistics*, trans. C. Goddard. Aldershot: Ashgate.

———. 2012. *Jurilinguistique comparée: Langages du droit, latin et langues modernes*. Texte français par J.-C. Gémar. Cowansville, QC: Yvon Blais.

Menski, W. 2005. *Comparative Law in a Global Context: The Legal Systems of Asia and Africa*. Cambridge University Press.

Ost, F. 2008. 'La septième cite: La traduction'. In: C. Eberhard dir. *Traduire nos responsabilités planétaires. Recomposer nos paysages juridiques*. Bruxelles: Bruylant.

Pigeon, L.P. 1982. 'La traduction juridique: l'équivalence fonctionnelle'. In: J.-C. Gémar ed. *Langage du droit et traduction: Essais de jurilinguistique*. Montréal: Linguatech Collection et Conseil de la langue française.

Piquet, H. 2005. *La Chine au carrefour des traditions juridiques*. Bruxelles: Bruylant.

Rabban, D.M. 2003. 'The Historiography of Late Nineteenth-CenturyAmerican Legal History', *Theoretical Inquiries in Law*, vol. 4, pp. 541–559.

Rials, S. (dir.). 1994. *Le droit des Modernes (XIV-XVIIIe siècles)*. Paris: Librairie générale de droit et jurisprudence.

Richard, P. 2005. La communicabilité ou l'interprétation de la différ(a)nce . . .' In: M. Baudrez and T. di Manno eds. *Liber Amicorum Jean-Claude Escarras, La communicabilité entre les systèmes juridiques*. Bruylant, Bruxelles, p. 167.

Ricoeur, P. 2004. 'Défi et bonheur de la traduction'. In: *Sur la traduction*. Paris: Bayard.

Sacco, R. 1987. 'La traduction juridique: un point de vue italien', *Les Cahiers du Droit*, vol. 28(4), pp. 845–859.

Sarčević, S. 2000. *New Approach to Legal Translation*. La Haye: Kluwer Law International.

Snell-Hornby, M. 2006. *The Turns of Translation Studies: New Paradigms or Shifting Viewpoints?* Amsterdam/Philadelphia: John Benjamins Publishing Company.
Sousa Santos, B. de. 2004. 'Vers un nouveau sens commun juridique – Droit, science et politique dans la transition paradigmatique'. In: N. Gonzales-Lajoie trad. *Droit & Société*, Série sociologie 39. Paris: Librairie générale de droit et jurisprudence.
Steiner, G. 1998. *After Babel: Aspects of Language and Translation*. Oxford University Press: Oxford.
Strangas, J. 1989. 'Les implications philosophiques de la notion de sujet de droit'. In: *Archives de Philosophie du Droit*. Tome 34 (*Le sujet de droit*). Paris: Sirey, pp. 123–157.
Tiphanus, C. 1634. *De hypostasi et persona.*
Villey, M. 1968. *La formation de la pensée juridique moderne*. Paris: Presses Universitaires de France.
Waël, H. de. 1989. *Le droit musulman, nature et evolution*. Paris: C.H.E.A.M.
Wagner, A., Sin, K.K. and Cheng, L. 2014. 'Legal Translatability Process as the 'Third Space' – Insights into Theory and Practice'. In: L. Cheng, K.K. Sin and A. Wagner eds. *The Ashgate Handbook of Legal Translation*. Law, Language and Communication Series. Aldershot: Ashgate.
Wu, H.C. 1968. 'The Status of the Individual in the Political and Legal Traditions of Old and New China'. In: C. Moore dir. *The Status of the Individual in East and West*. Honolulu: University of Hawaï Press.
Zhongfu, Z. 1989. 'Enterprise Legal Persons: Their Important Status in Chinese Civil Law', *Law and Contemporary Problems*, vol. 52(3).
Zweigert, K. and Kötz, H. 1987. *Introduction to Comparative Law*, 2 vols. Oxford: Clarendon Press.

Afterword: The Trials and Tribulations of Legal Translation

Deborah Cao

He stood, with a deadpan expression, just inches from President Barack Obama and other world leaders speaking at Nelson Mandela's memorial. Dressed in a dark suit, with a blue security lanyard bearing the words 'state funeral' draped around his neck, he flapped his arms and gesticulated in what was supposed to be sign language for the deaf (Eligon 2013). However, as *The New York Times* tells us, the man was a fraud, an impostor who pulled off a shocking stunt. His constant presence on the stage of the memorial of Nelson Mandela was watched not only by the audience in the 93,000-seat soccer stadium in Soweto but also by hundreds of millions on television around the world (Eligon 2013).

In 2012, it was reported, a murder trial in the UK was temporarily halted when the court realized the interpreter was leaving out key words and phrases in his translating. The interpreter turned out to be a fake. He confessed half an hour into evidence of a murder trial that he was not a qualified interpreter, and that he was just filling in for his busy wife who was the booked interpreter but could not be there (Clark 2012). In another 2012 UK case, a defendant's wife acted as the interpreter in court (Martin 2012).

For the purpose of our discussion of legal translation, the focus of this collection, one may wonder and legitimately ask: are there any fake legal translators, that is, unqualified persons translating texts used for judicial and other legal purposes? And how would anyone recognize a fake legal translator? Written translation is often a faceless and nameless task as opposed to interpretation, which usually requires the physical presence of the interpreter, such as in the case of court interpreters who are formal sworn in during court proceedings. Who are the invisible translators and, more importantly, who are the monitors of such translation, ensuring the quality and integrity of the tasks performed? And above all, who may be considered a qualified or competent legal translator?

There are two aspects I would like to mention in this short note in relation to legal translation. One is the ethics of legal translation in practice and the other is the discussion of legal translation ethics. Legal translation practice and theoretical exposition, the two components of this volume, are very much related. Together, they serve to keep the legal translation profession professional and legal translation studies viable.

In the academic discussions of legal translation and translation studies in general, ethics has not been a focus of a great deal of attention (Cao 2007); or, when ethics of translation is discussed, it is narrowly focused on fidelity and invisibility (Van Wyke 2014). The translator's competence and qualifications are central concerns, but ethics goes beyond whether a translation, oral or written, is a faithful or accurate rendering of the original. Even if the defendant's wife, cited earlier, had translated everything accurately, the issue of conflict of interest may have been a much more serious cause for concern. This is very different, for example, from the translation of a novel by the author's wife. In many ways, an author's wife may be a much better translator than any other translator unconnected with the author. Professional ethical issues do not arise. Indeed, the author can be the translator of his own fiction, as is sometimes the case in real life. However, for a legal document, such as a contract or evidentiary court document, the issue of conflict of interest and perception of bias would inevitably arise if the author of such documents acted as the translator. In such legal situations as cited above, as far as the translators or interpreters are concerned, what they did was not illegal and did not break any laws. However, we all know and should know that what they did was unethical, and such conduct would be unacceptable both in the interpreting and translation profession and in society at large.

In today's world, ethics is very much part of what we do in many spheres of life. For instance: the ethics of business dealings, the ethics of eating as regards the treatment of animals, the ethics of consumption, ethics in sports, in politics, in investment, and many other areas of our everyday life. In real life situations, in the everyday work of the professional legal translator and court interpreter, ethics figures much more prominently than in the rarefied atmosphere of academia. Ethics is integral to the job of the legal translator and interpreter, not infrequently confronting and challenging us as a moral person and as a professional, impacting on the quality of our work as well as our moral stance. A standardized code of ethical principles is a sign of the maturity and professionalism of a profession, and translation and interpreting is no exception Adhering to such a code of moral principles is required, although not legally, but ethically, of every practising translator and interpreter.

Interpreters and translators are human, and have failings, just as in any other profession. We sometimes make mistakes. However, in judicial settings, errors, big or small, can have far-reaching and serious consequences. A crucial interpreting or translation error in court proceedings, or even the use of words with unintended connotations, could produce an outcome that may mean the difference between a 'guilty' and 'not guilty' verdict, a difference between freedom and loss of liberty for a particular person. For this and other reasons, there are established legal frameworks and laws in some, although not all, countries and jurisdictions governing the provision of interpreters and translators. They aim to uphold the rights of the parties concerned when different languages are involved. Translators and interpreters working in a legal setting must act in accordance with the general principles of professional conduct; fulfil obligations in relation to the administration of justice; and supply services of the highest standard. I also propose that legal translators and interpreters have a duty to the law and a duty to the court. They must act with honesty, integrity, and candour, and must discharge duties owed to a court or tribunal, and also a duty to clients; that is, one must act with skill and diligence while maintaining a client's confidence and avoiding conflicts of interest. Such translators and interpreters also have secondary obligations to other practitioners, to third parties and wider society. These principles are irrespective of where the translating/interpreting takes place in different jurisdictions around the world, some which are discussed and detailed in this volume, and regardless of which theoretical stand one may take, as demonstrated in the in-depth discussion in this text.

In my discussion of legal translation research elsewhere (Cao 2014: 415–424), I have suggested that applied legal translation studies consist of legal translator and interpreter training, professional development and ethics, and legal translation quality testing and assessment, including court interpreter/translator accreditation, among others. I further suggest that these areas need to be further researched and warrant more discussion, especially on the ethics of legal translation.

Lastly, Justice Michael Kirby (2007: x), a retired justice of the highest court in Australia, once wrote that legal translation is a subtle and challenging job, and an area of great importance for the future of law and life on this planet. I respectfully and wholeheartedly concur.

References

Cao, D. 2007. *Translating Law*. Clevedon, UK: Multilingual Matters.

——— 2014. 'Legal Translation Studies'. In: C. Millan and F. Bartrina eds. *The Routledge Handbook of Translation Studies*. London and New York: Routledge, pp. 415–424.

Clark, E. 2012. 'Trial Stopped as Murder Case Translator was Only There Because His Wife, the Real Interpreter, was Too Busy to Show Up', *Daily Mail*, 21 July. Available at: http://www.dailymail.co.uk/news/article-2176840/Trial-stopped-murder-case-translator-wife--real-interpreter--busy-up.html#ixzz2tvFHxRep [Accessed 21 July 2012].

Eligon, J. 2013. 'Interpreter at Memorial Service Said to Have Been an Impostor', *The New York Times*, 12 December A14. Available at: http://www.nytimes.com/2013/12/12/world/africa/interpreter-at-mandela-service-said-to-be-an-imposter.html [Accessed 12 December 2013].

Kirby, M. 2007. 'Foreword'. In: D. Cao ed. *Translating Law*. Clevedon, UK: Multilingual Matters, pp. vii–x.

Martin, D. 2012. 'Trials Collapse'. *Daily Mail*, 24 November. Available at: http://www.dailymail.co.uk/news/article-2237656/Trials-collapse-interpreter-shortage-cripples-court--reliance-Google-Translate-putting-public-safety-risk.html#ixzz2tvUBR0u0 [Accessed 24 November 2012].

Van Wyke, B. 2014. 'Translation and Ethics'. In: C. Millan and F. Bartrina eds. *The Routledge Handbook of Translation Studies*. London and New York: Routledge, pp. 448–560.

Index

Note: page references to Figures are in **bold** text

For Product Safety Concerns and Information please contact our EU representative GPSR@taylorandfrancis.com
Taylor & Francis Verlag GmbH, Kaufingerstraße 24, 80331 München, Germany

www.ingramcontent.com/pod-product-compliance
Ingram Content Group UK Ltd.
Pitfield, Milton Keynes, MK11 3LW, UK
UKHW050051200926
475702UK00019B/2781
* 9 7 8 1 1 3 8 7 0 0 7 8 9 *